YELLOWSTONE:
A WILDERNESS BESIEGED

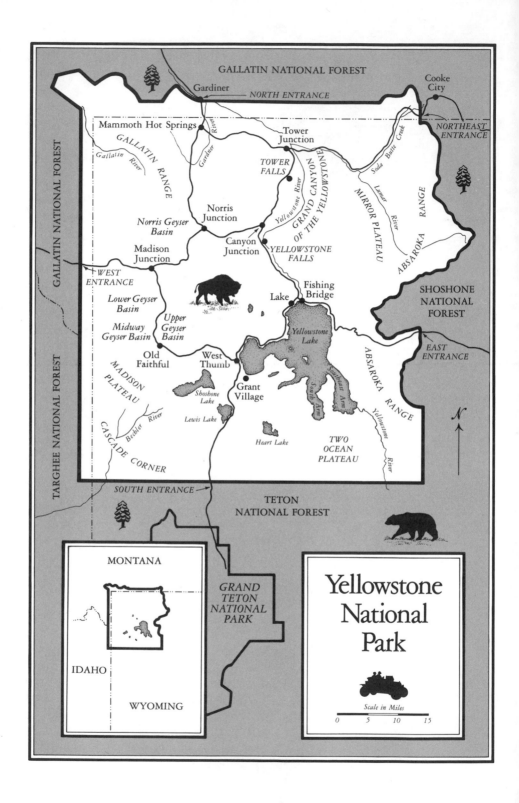

YELLOWSTONE
A Wilderness Besieged

Richard A. Bartlett

THE UNIVERSITY OF ARIZONA PRESS
TUCSON, ARIZONA

Second printing 1989

The University of Arizona Press

Copyright © 1985
The Arizona Board of Regents
All Rights Reserved

This book was set in Linotron Garamond #3 types.
Manufactured in the U.S.A.

Library of Congress Cataloging in Publication Data

Bartlett, Richard A.
    Yellowstone, a wilderness besieged.

    Bibliography: p.
    Includes index.
    1. Yellowstone National Park—History.   I. Title.
F722.B33   1985   978.7'52   85-988
ISBN 0-8165-1098-9

Contents

ILLUSTRATIONS

ABBREVIATIONS

The following abbreviations are used in the notes at the end of chapters:

ADLR	Letters Received
ADLS	Letters Sent
	Both from the National Archives, Record Group 48 (listed in Microcopy as No. 62): Records of the Office of the Secretary of Interior Regarding Yellowstone Park, Appointments Division
Hague Papers	National Archives, R.G. 57, Arnold Hague Papers
Inquiry	"Inquiry Into the Management and Control of the Yellowstone National Park," 53d Cong., 1st Sess. (1892 Serial No. 3051)
Norris Papers	Philetus Norris Papers, Huntington Library, San Marino, California
N.P. Papers	President's Subject File: Yellowstone, Northern Pacific Railroad Co. Records, Minnesota Historical Society, St. Paul
Peterson Collection	Northern Pacific Papers in Custody of Professor Robert Lewis Peterson, University of Montana, Missoula
PMLR	Letters Received
PMLS	Letters Sent
	Both from the National Archives, Record Group 48 (listed in Microcopy as No. 62): Records of the Office of the Secretary of Interior Regarding Yellowstone Park, Patents and Miscellaneous Division
Report	Duff, Anderson, and Clark, Industrial Investment and Financial Analysts, "Report: Yellowstone Park Company Proposed Transfer of Ownership to Wyoming Park Commission," August, 1955

R.G. 48 Central Classified File	National Archives, R.G. 48, Department of the Interior, Office of the Secretary, Central Classified File, "Yellowstone," with subheadings
R.G. 79	Records of the National Park Service, National Archives
R.G. 98	National Archives, R.G. 98, Records of U.S. Army Commands, Fort Yellowstone, Letters Sent, Letters Received, Orders, Circulars, Memoranda
Special Report	"Letter of W. H. Phillips on the Yellowstone National Park," 49th Cong., 1st. Sess., Sen. Executive Document No. 51 (Serial No. 2333).
Toole Collection	Professor K. Ross Toole's Collection, "Harry W. Child's Miscellaneous Files"
Y.A.	Yellowstone Archives

Preface

*I*n northwest Wyoming, spilling over slightly into Montana and Idaho, lies one of the world's geologic hot spots, a place where molten magma rises close to the earth's surface and heats water and chemicals which spew out of the earth as geysers and hot springs. Besides these unique attractions the region contains many lakes, one of them being among the largest high-altitude bodies of water in the world. Mountains, streams, and a magnificent grand canyon add to the beauties of the area, which is known everywhere as Yellowstone National Park.

The first people into the region were primitive ancients with spears and spear throwers. Centuries later Stone-age humans, called Sheepeaters by anthropologists, entered the area with travois, dogs, wickiups, and bows and arrows. Still later, they watched as white trappers came in with horses, guns, and beaver traps. At a later date erect equestrians dressed in the uniform of the United States Army policed the park. About the same time, stagecoaches and tally-hos frequented trails that were becoming roads. Then a squarish, awkward, noisy conveyance made its appearance; with the coming of the automobile Yellowstone was never to be quite like it had been before.

Yellowstone National Park: over one hundred and ten years ago a group of men brought about its creation. They wanted to keep it out of homestead entry until they, Northern Pacific Railroad executives, could take steps toward controlling the region for an anticipated lucrative tourist business. Yet the reality of what they accomplished represented a great step forward for mankind. Men had inadvertently defied the Judeo-Christian tradition of controlling and exploiting the earth and instead had taken measures to protect a vast region in its natural state "for all the people."

In creating Yellowstone National Park, the U.S. Congress, which was allowing itself to be lobbied into passing the "Act of Dedication" (March 1, 1872), was flying in the face of a human habit of spoliation more than two thousand years old. Congress was, indeed, legislating an experiment. This book is an attempt to show how the venture has fared during a century in which the nation's population has increased from about 40 million to 220 million; transportation has changed from steam locomotives chugging along at thirty-five miles an hour to passenger jetliners speeding across the country and the world at more than five hundred miles per hour; and communications have progressed from telegraph to telephone by satellite.

Mostly it is a story of people: the strong-willed men who desired to use and exploit the park for selfish purposes, and the strong-willed men of good will who fought to preserve this beautiful national experiment. It is also a narrative about a democratic government, busy with more pressing matters, that somehow, by some miracle, rose in the nick of time, again and again, to insure the park's preservation.

And it is history with a happy ending. Yellowstone is still very much a national park in 1983, and it is still beautiful, and because of the dedication of still more strong-willed men—and women—of good will, it will still be here as a national park a hundred and another hundred years hence, and be worth seeing, too.

ACKNOWLEDGMENTS

In the summer of 1963 I drove my "old stove bolts" (car lover's jargon for a used Chevrolet) from Tallahassee, Florida, to Yellowstone National Park. In the museum at Mammoth Hot Springs I spent several days investigating the research materials on Yellowstone's history that are stored there. The Park Service historian, Mr. Aubrey Haines, gave me a hint of the fascinating, complex story that I would be developing if I wrote a history of the park. Intrigued and challenged, I launched my project.

I have tried to place the history of this first great national park within the perspective of a rapidly changing nation. I realized that a city park was one thing; a national park as large as Rhode Island and Connecticut combined was something else. The hallowed Judeo-Christian concepts of using, abusing, changing and exploiting the land as befitted the pragmatic needs of the people—pure, nineteenth-century American dogma—had been, by act of Congress, suspended for this new national park. And what of the acquisitive

American frontier spirit, the spirit of laissez faire that dominated American business? How would entrepreneurs interested in profitable ventures within the national park react to government restrictions implied by the act of Congress? How would the American people greet such a new idea?

These were among the principal questions I kept in mind. It added up to a fascinating story, one that is continuing right now. That the Yellowstone National Park is into its second century proves that the decision to disregard the Judeo-Christian tradition vis-a-vis exploitation of the land was not entirely wrong. But the continuing threats to the Yellowstone wilderness by poachers, concessionaires, miners, irrigationists, railroad and automobile enthusiasts; visitors; technology, and scientists in search of new energy sources; politicians, and even by the bureaucracy responsible for its protection, lead to the conclusion that the battle between defenders and despoilers continues even as this is written. However, my conclusion is that a century from now Yellowstone National Park as a protected reservation will still exist, and still be a beautiful wilderness worth visiting.

A number of institutions aided my work. In 1979 and 1980 I was a Fellow at the Woodrow Wilson International Center for Scholars in Washington, D.C. This good fortune made possible my in-depth study of Yellowstone material at the National Archives.

During my many years of research I have also received aid from the Florida State University Research Council, the Henry E. Huntington Library, the American Philosophical Society; and once or twice in the early years, the Yellowstone Library and Museum Association.

I cannot possibly list all the people who have aided in my research over so long a period. In recent years I have been helped by Richard Crawford in the National Archives; Timothy R. Manns, North District Naturalist/Park Historian, Yellowstone National Park; Professor Alfred Runte, University of Washington; Miss Judith Austin, Idaho State Historical Society; John Albright, Project Manager, National Park Service, Denver; Dr. Gene Gressley, Director, American Heritage Center, University of Wyoming; Professor H. Duane Hampton, University of Montana; Professor Emmett Essin, East Tennessee State University; Robert Utley; Mrs. Valerie Black, Librarian, Yellowstone Research Library; the late Dr. Oliver Wendell Holmes; Dr. Michael J. Lacey, Woodrow Wilson Center; Professor Dwight Waldo; and Professor William H. Graves of the University of Northern Iowa. Since 1978 I have corresponded with more than fifty individuals who are authorities on some phase of Yellowstone history. Space forbids listing their names here, but their willingness to write lengthy, informative letters, or furnish illustrations, is greatly appreciated. (Many are cited in the notes or in photo credits.)

In earlier years I received aid from Park Historian Aubrey Haines, Mrs. Marion Drew and Mrs. Jean Newhouse of the Yellowstone Library, the late Miss Catherine Dempsey and Mrs. Harriett Meloy at the Montana Historical Society, Ed Carpenter at the Henry E. Huntington Library, Mrs. Alys Fries at the Western History Room of the Denver Public Library, and from Joe Evans, N. Orwin Rush, and the late Reno Bupp at the Robert Manning Strozier Library at Florida State University. In addition, information was provided by Professor K. Ross Toole, University of Montana, Edmund B. Rogers, Horace Albright, the late Ray Allen Billington, Professor W. Turrentine Jackson, the late Willard Fraser, Don Russell, Dr. Harry Kelsey, Mrs. Jane Reamer White, and above all, by Mrs. Bessie Haynes Arnold. There were others; their contributions are equally appreciated.

To my wife Marie and to Rich, Margaret, Mary, and Tom, all now grown, I extend my gratitude for their patience and forbearance.

This book is very much the product of my research, my writing, my judgments, and my errors for which, wherever they may be, I take full responsibility.

RICHARD A. BARTLETT

YELLOWSTONE:
A WILDERNESS BESIEGED

Prologue

*T*he winter of 1872 was not marred by natural cataclysms, unusual political scandals, or economic disturbances. It was quiet like the lull before the storm, for before the year was out an unusually vicious political campaign would place Ulysses S. Grant into the presidency for a second term and leave his defeated opponent, Horace Greeley, insane and then dead.

The most sensational event of the season was "Gentleman Jim" Fisk's murder. All the lurid details of Jim's life and loves were presented in that quaint Victorian style in which the reader understood all the sordid business by reading between the lines. Fisk's unexpected demise was hardly more interesting than the usual fare consumed by newspaper readers of the time. In Chicago they read of the seduction of a fair maiden by a minister, a "base and blackhearted knave" who had blighted a young life "as the tender rosebud by the early frost." There were also the usual lengthy reports on the execution of a condemned man, the clergyman and others shaking hands with him, and bidding him "a long farewell."

On a more serious side, occasional items appeared about the Alabama Claims negotiations, an attempt upon Queen Victoria's life, a little scandal being investigated by Congress on the legal aspects of an arms sale to the French, and controversy over railroad franchises. Mormons were reported as opposing the secret ballot. Texans were angered over depredations by Mexican armed raiders, and personnel of the new Japanese embassy reached Washington, D.C. In Chicago it was noted that "fifteen to twenty miles of buildings" were being constructed in that city, a response to the terrible fire of the previous October. [1]

Financially times were bullish, and advertisements urged investors to purchase railroad bonds paying "8 Per Cent. Gold." One of the heaviest of such advertisers was the Northern Pacific Railroad Company. Emphasizing that its tracks would reach the Missouri River during 1872, the promoters stated that this would give bondholders a lien "upon millions of acres of the finest land in the country." It was further stated that the bonds were "secured by a first and only mortgage on over two thousand miles of road . . . and on over *twenty-*

1

three thousand acres of land to every mile of finished road. . . . Fifty million acres . . . extending in a broad, fertile belt from Wisconsin through the richest portions of Minnesota, Dakota, Montana, Idaho, Oregon, and Washington, to Puget Sound." Prospective buyers could contact Jay Cooke & Co., New York, Philadelphia, and Washington.[2] In a little more than a year Jay Cooke and Company would fail, bringing on a serious depression that lasted more than five years.

It had been Northern Pacific officials, including Cooke, general passenger agent A. R. Nettleton, and William Darrah "Pig Iron" Kelley, a heavy investor in the N. P., who had greased congressional machinery and brought about passage of the Yellowstone Park bill during that winter of 1872.[3] The legislation had received minor notice in periodicals and newspapers, but the signing by President Grant of the "Act of Dedication" (as it is known) was not noted at all. The death of Jim Fisk, debate over arms sales, and the usual news of seductions, rapes, "horrible murders," and grisly executions all took precedence over the debate, passage through Congress, and final signing into law of a bill to create a new governmental obligation called Yellowstone National Park.[4]

The act ran to less than six hundred words. It defined the boundaries of the new park, reserved and withdrew its lands "from settlement, occupancy, or sale," and set it "apart as a public park or pleasuring ground for the benefit and enjoyment of the people." It placed jurisdiction under the secretary of interior, who was to promulgate rules and regulations which would "provide for the preservation from injury and spoliation of all timber, mineral deposits, natural curiosities, or wonders within said park, and their retention in their natural condition." He also was empowered to grant leases "on small parcels of land" for buildings; it was anticipated that revenues from these leases would provide funds for construction of roads and bridle paths. No funds were allotted to pay the salary of the superintendent, nor were penalties specified for violations of regulations.[5]

In essence, a Congress concerned with what was at the time considered more important business passed a very minor bill because the power structure wanted it passed and because the legislation had hardly any opposition. Northwest Wyoming Territory, wherein lay most of the park, was a long way out West. Only one transcontinental railroad was yet completed, and at the closest point, which was Corinne, Utah Territory, it was still hundreds of miles from the park. In terms of population the Territory of Montana had just over twenty thousand residents as of the 1870 census, Wyoming fewer than ten thousand, Idaho barely fifteen thousand. These regions were not yet secure from Indian depredations: Custer's fight on the Little Big Horn was more than four years away. The nation's population lay far to the east, but even so, fewer than forty million souls lived in the United States.

For those few Congressmen who put any thought to the park bill, surely the belief was that they had reserved an unusual area in the distant Northwest for the benefit of future generations. Therefore it should not concern Congress again until decades into the future. Even Northern Pacific officials knew that their railroad would not reach its closest point to the park for years—and as it turned out, for many more years than they anticipated in 1872.

But the park did not remain as a segregated, inviolable parcel of land, unoccupied and unexploited. Those many who believed it would remain so had failed to take into account the frenzied expansion, the dynamic drive, the productive energy of the American people after the Civil War. The mere existence of a park larger than and unlike any other in the world prompted the curious. Sportsmen wanted to go there to hunt and fish, scientists to investigate, the wealthy to "rest," and citizens of the towns and ranches surrounding the park to see the thermal phenomena, the lake, and the canyon. Others saw in the park the potential for business and high profits.

Even before businessmen and administrators arrived, the visitors were there. First they were a mere trickle of humanity. But each year there were more, barring occasional fluctuations due to economic conditions, until a hundred years later upwards of two million of them annually passed through one or another of the five major park entrances. They always came too fast and too many. Never could the government, represented by the Department of Interior directly, the army, or Interior's bureau, the National Park Service, quite keep up with the increasing hordes. Neither could the concessionaires supply the necessary services in a consistently satisfactory way. The visitors simply appeared; they were "the people" referred to in the enabling act, and they deserve our first attention.

From the beginning some visitors were exploiters and some were protectors. The men of the Cook-Folsom-Peterson expedition of 1869, the Washburn-Langford-Doane expedition of 1870, and the Hayden Survey of 1871 and 1872, had viewed the geysers, the canyon, the falls, and the lake, and were understandably impressed by the unusual, one-in-all-the-world beauties of the region. To them as a group, the segregation of such a region, thereby restraining America's territorial imperative, preventing exploitation for profit and the consequent, inevitable spoliation, constituted a patriotic act. In a republic (democracy not then being in use as a complimentary term) the preservation of the park "for all the people" seemed a logical growth of the great American idea.[6]

Between late 1871 when the campaign got under way to have Congress pass the enabling act and the turn of the century, visitors who loved Yellowstone offered still other arguments justifying the park's continued sanctity. A note of national pride was injected. Europe had her Greek and Roman ruins, her gloomy castles and gothic cathedrals, but Americans could boast of natural scenery that Europe could not duplicate. Here in remote American territory were geysers, hot springs, mud pots, incredibly awe-inspiring waterfalls, a variegated canyon painted by nature (read God) and a high-altitude lake to match the beauties of Switzerland's Lake Constance. Here, in a region sixty-two by fifty-two miles, was picturesque America, mountainous, unusual, and beautiful, concentrated and on display for all the world to see. So Yellowstone was a place in which every American could take pride. It should be preserved in its pristine condition, becoming America's first theme park—a sort of predecessor of Nashville's Opryland and California's Disneyland.[7]

Another incentive for creation and maintenance of the park, but more difficult to substantiate, was a religious one. While there has been some tendency through the ages to see Wilderness as a place for easy sinning (as demonstrated in Hawthorne's *The Scarlet Letter*), the trend in the nineteenth century was toward a concept of wilderness as a place for moral and spiritual rejuvenation. In Yellowstone people indeed felt close to God and sometimes even closer to Satan. Visitors read the majesty of His work in the falls and the canyon, while at other stops on the "grand rounds," as the tour around the park was often called, they smelled the rotten egg odor of sulphur that reminded them of Satan's home; in the mud pots and hot water geysers they imagined Hell as a very real place, somewhere just below their feet. "When Robert Ingersoll [the great nineteenth-century agnostic] died, all the geysers erupted in celebration," wrote one of his critics.[8]

Sportsmen likewise manifested interest in the park, an interest that grew as the nineteenth century drew to a close. For the first decade of the park's existence hunting was indulged in almost indiscriminately in Yellowstone. After it was forbidden, sportsmen were among the first to be aware of the park's value as a protective reservation where species such as deer, elk, bear, and buffalo could be protected and propagate. That a small strip south of the park and an area extending twenty-five miles east of it became a timber reserve is partly due to sportsmen's concern. Similarly, sportsmen working through the Boone and Crockett Club did watchdog duty over the park in the 1880s and 1890s.[9]

Upon such reasons did the visitor-protectors build their defense of Yellowstone. But the visitor-exploiters deserve some credit too, for not everything they advocated or accomplished was bad. They helped sell Yellowstone to an affluent clientele that rarely turned against the park after seeing it. Some of their improvements blended well with the rustic scenery. By controlling the movements of thousands of tourists through the park by stagecoach from one hostelry to another rampant spoliation was prevented.

Those promoters of the park with the most mercenary aims were, essentially, the railroad interests, more especially officers of the Northern Pacific Railroad. They hardly considered themselves exploiters, however. After all, their interests were consistent with the thinking of most railroad promoters of the time, who saw nothing wrong with using for profit whatever of value lay close to the line's right-of-way. This included scenery and curative waters.

Spas and watering places were the early nineteenth-century resorts for the few affluent Americans with the leisure to take extended periods of rest. There was a moral problem involved here. The Puritan ethic did not allow for holidays or vacations. Even for the wealthy, then, the rigid Calvinist code did not justify two to eight weeks or more every summer devoted to leisure. A good Calvinist would surely fall from grace if he took that much time away from the Lord's work! The nineteenth-century tycoon might be absent for a season in Europe "on business" or go there for his wife's health, or for his own. Or, he could justify a few weeks of rest on the grounds of health. But one did not go to a *resort* for one's health: one went to a spa, a watering place offering health-giving spring waters (as well as horse racing, fine food and drink, possibly card playing and flirtations on the extended piazzas). Saratoga Springs, New York, thus became a social resort, but its initial success was because of its hot springs and their supposed medicinal values. [10]

Increased affluence and proliferation of wealth after the Civil War created a need for more spas and watering places. At the same time the Puritan ethic was breaking down. More and more wealthy people were going to Europe for extended holidays. Newport and Long Branch began to compete with Saratoga, while southern spas such as the Greenbrier in West Virginia continued to flourish despite the region's poverty. Resort hotels began to appear without any therapeutic or medicinal connection. Still another phenomenon brought on change: the railroad. To the ritual of "taking the waters" or just vacationing was added the railroad trip to and from the hostelry.

By the 1870s a trip on a railroad was no more exciting, or unusual, or dangerous than a trip on a modern commercial airliner. The Pullman car came along in the 1860s, the dining car in the 1880s, and private cars for the very rich at about the same time. The super rich could rent a string of cars or a whole train, stopping off at sidings at a whim. Like a magic carpet, the railroad could whisk people across the continent in five days.

The West had always beckoned Americans. Since Jefferson's time it had resided in the national psyche as a place of romance, adventure, great untapped wealth, beauty, and new beginnings. Its picturesque scenery, awe-inspiring natural curiosities, and mild dangers such as a few wild Indians, uncontrolled (and fast disappearing) herds of buffalo, or gun-toting cowboys could be experienced from the comfort and safety of a Pullman car. The opening of the railroad West coincided, then, with the decline of the spa and the Puritan ethic and the proliferation of affluence. Almost simultaneously arose the resort hotels. They were huge, cavernous, luxurious wooden structures in sylvan settings where "the right people" might enjoy leisure amongst their own class. Many of these hostelries, such as the Del Monte at Monterey, California, the Antlers at Colorado Springs, and the Montezuma at Las Vegas, New Mexico, were built by railroad interests. The hardheaded businessmen of the time knew there were profits in transporting, feeding, and lodging the wealthy. [11]

Northern Pacific managers envisioned immense profits from thus serving Yellowstone-bound passengers and lodging and feeding them once they were in the park. This explains their interest in keeping the park free of entrepreneurs, especially innkeepers, until the Northern Pacific reached the region immediately north of the reservation. (In 1872 Jay Cooke and Company believed its line would reach there in two or three years. The depression and Northern Pacific's bankruptcy set back the clock: not until 1882 did the rails reach due north of the park.) If Yellowstone was segregated from the public domain as a national park, then, politics being what they were, N. P. officials did not doubt that they could prevent major construction of hotels in the park until they were ready to do the building themselves.

The promise of the park in 1872 was, then, that tourists would be of the wealthy class; they would be prideful Americans drinking in American rather than European scenery; they would be Christian Protestant, seeing God's sure hand in the beauties of the falls, the canyon, and the lake, and Satan's Hell in the smelly hot springs, the grunting mud pots, and even in the hot water geysers. Sportsmen would also visit the park, for it was already known as a feeding ground for animals, game birds, and fish. Among these sportsmen would be military men and Civil War veterans who loved the outdoors. America's poor were never considered as possible guests, as they are not considered today, since the park demands several "days off" and substantial expense to get to it. The rising middle class was ignored also, but long before the century was out that most prevalent of all American income groups had reached sufficient opulence to pay for a trip to "Wonderland," and its members were soon being catered to as well.

Finally, no one thought of the residents of surrounding territories as park visitors, but citizens of Montana, Idaho, and Wyoming, most especially of Montana, possessed a strong curiosity. After the harvest and before the snows, many of them trekked into the park "to see the elephant." There they did a bit of hunting, hacked off some of the sinter from the geyser cones, and stowed away some petrified wood to be used as a conversation starter on long winter's evenings.

So, even before there were park officials enforcing regulations and concessionaires operating inns, liveries, general stores, and stages, visitors were already taking the measure of Yellowstone's wonders. From the Cook-Folsom-Peterson expedition of 1869 until today, visitors have been of first importance in Yellowstone's history. It is, then, to their experiences, needs, and control that Part I is devoted.

NOTES TO PROLOGUE

1. *Chicago Tribune,* February 29, 1872.

2. *New York Times,* March 1, 1872; March 2, 1872.

3. See Richard A. Bartlett, *Nature's Yellowstone* (Albuquerque: University of New Mexico Press, 1974), 194–210.

4. For example, "The Proposed National Park in the Yellowstone Country," *Frank Leslie's Weekly,* Vol. 33, No. 85 (March 2, 1872), 398.

5. 17 *U. S. Statutes at Large,* 350.

6. Aubrey L. Haines, *The Valley of the Upper Yellowstone* (Norman: University of Oklahoma Press, 1965); Nathaniel Pitt Langford, *The Discovery of Yellowstone Park,* Foreword by Aubrey L. Haines (Lincoln: University of Nebraska Press, 1972); Aubrey L. Haines, *The Yellowstone Story,* two vols., Vol. 1 (Boulder: Colorado Associated University Press, 1977); and Bartlett, *Nature's Yellowstone.*

7. This matter of cultural nationalism is discussed in Alfred Runte, *National Parks: The American Experience* (Lincoln: University of Nebraska Press, 1980), 11–18 and, in a sense, throughout the book. See also Earl Pomeroy, *In Search of the Golden West* (New York: Alfred Knopf, 1956), 48. Roderick Nash, *Wilderness and the American Mind,* revised ed. (New Haven: Yale University Press, 1978) and Hans Huth, *Nature and the American* (Berkeley: University of California Press, 1957; Lincoln: University of Nebraska Press, 1972) both delve into American attitudes toward wilderness of which Yellowstone was a part.

8. Charles Francis Adams, *Jim Bridger and I Discover Yellowstone Park* (no place, no publisher, no date). This pamphlet appears to have been sent as a Christmas card by Adams; a copy is in the Newberry Library, Chicago.

9. See John F. Reiger, *American Sportsmen and Conservation* (New York: Winchester Publishing Co., 1975), especially chapters 5 and 6, pp. 93–152.

10. Edward C. Atwater, "The Lifelong Sickness of Francis Parkman," *Bulletin of the History of Medicine,* Vol. 41 (September-October, 1967), 413–39.

11. Although this subject has not been dealt with adequately, see Pomeroy, *In Search of the Golden West,* chapters 1 and 4; Richard Van Orman, *A Room for the Night: Hotels of the Old West* (Bloomington: University of Indiana Press, 1966), Sandra Dallas, *No More Than Five in a Bed* (Norman: University of Oklahoma Press, 1967), and Dixon Wecter, *The Saga of American Society* (New York: C. Scribner's Sons, 1937), 446–47.

THE VISITORS

CHAPTER ONE

Pioneer Tourists of the First Decade

*I*t should come as no surprise that the first visitors into Yellowstone were residents of nearby localities, most of them in Montana. That territory had several population centers near the park: Virginia City (first known as Alder Gulch) to the northwest, Bozeman to the north, and Helena (first known as Last Chance Gulch) north by northwest. Other mining camps were speckled throughout central and western Montana, while the Gallatin Valley to the north was already being taken up with farms and ranches.

The literacy of these pioneer people was high. They came from all over—Southerners who had fled the War Between the States or the sufferings of Reconstruction, Yankees who had left New England's austere land to make their fortunes elsewhere, and Midwesterners bent on establishing profitable farms and ranches or setting up businesses. It had been Montana residents who explored the upper Yellowstone in 1869 (the Cook-Folsom-Peterson expedition) and in 1870 (the Washburn-Langford-Doane expedition). It was Montanans who willingly enlisted in the crusade to have the Yellowstone region declared a national park. Some of the Yankee residents had organized the Montana Historical Society in 1865. Certainly the territory had its share of drifting, semiliterate frontier types (the notorious Plummer gang had carried on its activities from Virginia City) but vigilantes, representing a dominant, better element, had made short shrift of those desperadoes. Simply, the dominant society that was establishing the Montana Commonwealth was anything but illiterate and disreputable.[1]

Montanans were well informed about the nearby Yellowstone region. They also knew that the easiest routes into it were from Montana, rather than from Idaho and Wyoming. One way led up the Madison River from Virginia City via the Horseback Trail; a variation was to Henry's Lake in eastern Idaho, then over a plateau, "the Highlands," to the geyser basins. The other gateway was up the Yellowstone River to the Gardner River, which led the tourist to Mammoth Hot Springs (at the time called White Mountain Hot Springs). Bozeman would be the outfitting point for those going in by that route.

One well-organized group went in from Deer Lodge, Montana, a small community 150 miles northwest of the park, in the late summer of 1871. Their reactions reveal much about the ingrained human desire to exploit, the religious awe of the "infernal regions" (as their chronicler, C. C. Clawson, called the geyser basins), and the already established human occupation there. The party apparently numbered five men, including Rossiter W. Raymond, the United States Mining Commissioner and editor of the *Mining and Engineering Journal*. Nine horses, some used for pack purposes, and a tailless black dog named "Nig" rounded out the expedition.

From Virginia City the party headed up the Madison, following a well-used trail, to the graves of a murdered man and a child. There they crossed the river and headed for Henry's Lake, where lived a bachelor named Gilman Sawtelle. On the way they met a dozen soldiers and the artist Thomas Moran, all of whom had been with the Hayden Survey, bound by way of Virginia City for Fort Ellis, the army reservation just east of Bozeman.

The tourists camped at Sawtelle's house, which had "all the appearances of an old fashioned farm-house of the States." Then they went on toward those "infernal regions," passing in the Madison Basin the old Road Agent Trail, more commonly known as the Skull and Crossbones Trail, again clear enough to be defined.

As this early party gazed upon the hot springs, their narrator thought in mercenary terms. He suggested that whittled, wooden wheels with a hole in the center be thrown into the hot springs and, when heavily encrusted with sinter, be pulled out and used as grindstones. And why not embalm human beings in the waters? He even thought the paint-pot muds would make good ladies' cosmetics!

After experiencing some earth tremors and an Indian scare, the Montanans returned to Virginia City and Deer Lodge, unaware that they constituted the first group of sightseers, pure and simple (not counting earlier explorations), into Yellowstone.[2]

In 1872, with the park a reality, two more parties "did" the "grand rounds" of Yellowstone's wonders. The one we know most about was organized early in September at Virginia City. Consisting of perhaps seven persons, it included the editor of the *Deer Lodge New Northwest,* the owner of a local telegraph line, a physician, and the party's chronicler, Harry J. Norton. On a lovely autumn afternoon the group, mounted and with three pack animals in tow, left for the Madison divide and the geysers along the Firehole River. Already local citizens were profiting from Yellowstone: the tourists spent the first night at a hostelry known as English George's. Even though the facilities were crude, they were appreciated, for these were "city fellers" by Montana standards, saddle sore and uncomfortable. "Indeed," wrote Norton in the first of several letters published in the *Virginia City Montanian,* "it is presumed that the first night out for the entire human race is proverbially unhappy."

The next day they followed a narrow, zig-zagging bridle path through thick timber, guided along the way by blazes hacked out previously by Nathaniel Pitt Langford, Yellowstone's first superintendent. At the Lower Geyser Basin they encountered more "cultured" society in the presence of still other tourists out of Bozeman.

Norton's purple passages remind us of how primitive civilization was just over a century ago. In the absence of man-made miracles, nature's were subject to great study and wonderment. It is unlikely that one of today's tourists would describe how, at the Grand Prismatic Spring, one could "look an unknown depth into its fairy regions, discovering caves, bowers, castles, and grottoes painted in every color of brightest rainbow, and magically carved. . . . Standing on its margin [Norton continued] and gazing enraptured into its unfathomable depths, one becomes enchanted with this delightful realm, and calls to mind all that he had heard or read about the airy phantoms and ogling water-sprites of mythological tales."

Or would a geyser eruption cause a modern tourist to do as did the physician member? He sprang from the river bank, waded waist-deep to the other side, stood under the shower created by the Fan Geyser, waved his hat over his head and shouted "Hurrah!" until he was hoarse! It is unlikely that today's visitors, even if permitted, would brew tea, boil meat, and cook two quarts of navy beans in a dormant geyser, as the Norton party did.

The group crossed the mountains to the lake, then trekked down to the falls and canyon, Tower Creek and finally to Mammoth—still called White Mountain Hot Springs—where they found "fifteen or twenty persons . . . doing penance for past indiscretions by a glorious exile and hot-water baths three times a day."[3]

The second group of sightseers, known as the Bullock party from Bozeman, had met Norton's group in the Lower Geyser Basin. They too had a narrator who commented on the invalid colony at Mammoth. The waters were said to be especially good "for bachelor and rheumatic diseases." The region was also commended for religious revivals. "Hell," he wrote, "is sure close to the surface here."[4]

In view of the nineteenth-century emphasis on spas and places to "take the waters," it is not surprising that interest was manifested in Yellowstone's thousands of springs. One "authority," citing Hot Springs, Arkansas, as precedent, urged that "the therapeutic value of [Yellowstone's] countless waters" be advertised and that certain springs, among them those at Steamboat Point on the eastern shore of Yellowstone Lake, be set aside "for the health of . . . soldiers and sailors as do all the nations of Europe." He cited the waters as useful for "herpetic diathesis, catarrhs of the respiratory passage; common application for stimulation of the skin, thermality, chronic uretretics, catarrh of the urinary organs, surgical diseases and dyspepsia."[5]

Long before the Department of Interior had adopted rules and regulations providing for Yellowstone's protection, local businessmen were profiting from its proximity. Harry Norton's letters from the "Grand Rounds" (as he dubbed the park tour), along with tourist information, proved so popular that he soon published his *Wonder-Land Illustrated: or, Horseback Rides Through the Yellowstone National Park* (1873). This was the first of many such offerings. In a moment of capitalist inspiration he also accepted advertising.

That the text included a lot of practical advice about equipment which, it just happened, demanded outfitting by local merchants, was probably not a coincidence. Norton recommended warm substantial clothing, stout boots, and, for protection from the sun, a broad-brimmed hat. Ladies, he said, should select practical garments "rather than stylish ones; coarse shoes, mosquito-nets . . . and other creature comforts that good taste will suggest." One pack animal would do for two people, even with the sportsman's accoutrements of shotguns, rifles, and fishing tackle (for in 1873 hunting was still assumed as a Yellowstone sport). For the rich, he also recommended light canvas boats to be used "while exploring the islands [of Yellowstone Lake] or gunning for waterfowl. If you have a good retriever," Norton added, "he will be useful to bring in game, and a pack of deer [hounds] or bloodhounds will furnish the sportsman fine amusement among the bear, deer, and elk."

Of equal interest to Norton's suggestions are the advertisements in his *Guide*. At Virginia City tourists could put up at the Claseby House or the competitive Crescent Hotel, both claiming first class accommodations. Two local general stores, Patton and Lambrecht and Raymond Brothers, promoted outfitting supplies. Livery operator T. J. Farrell offered a "Coach to the Geysers" and E. H. Bartlett, the blacksmith, suggested that "Tourists call around and get their Luggage Animals heeled." A local barber invited Yellowstone Park tourists to drop by for a shave and a bath. Local saloons invited tourists' patronage ("12½ cents for drink or cigar. Call,") and already, in 1873, Tilton and Barber's Stationery Store offered National Park Stereoscopic Views.[6]

Author Norton and his advertisers clearly anticipated vigorous Yellowstone-oriented business from afar. They knew that Virginia City and Bozeman were assured a monopoly of the tourist trade for at least a decade. In 1873 the regions south and east of the park had not yet been adequately mapped and explored.

In the mid-1870s one could take the Northern Pacific to Bismarck, board a river steamboat and push up the Missouri to the junction of the state road to Bozeman. As of late 1873, the road was not yet finished. Or one could go from Bismarck up the Missouri to Fort Benton, thence via Gilmer and Salisbury's stage line to Helena, on by stage to Virginia City or Bozeman, and thence into the park. Either of these routes involved some small possibility of losing one's hair to a raiding Sioux or Blackfoot war party.

The safest and most comfortable route was via the Union Pacific west to Corinne, Utah, (or via the Central Pacific east from California) and then north by Gilmer and Salisbury's Overland Stage Line to Virginia City. A tourist could purchase through tickets from Omaha to Virginia City including first class railroad fare, for $116.75. The distance was 1,055 miles, the stage line accounting for the final 380 of them.

Eager for tourists and perhaps no more guilty of stretching the truth than most travel writers then or now, Norton described the stage ride from Corinne to Virginia City as being "over a splendid road, in fine, commodious four and six horse Concord coaches, which are run through from Corinne to Virginia City in three days."[7]

Travel reminiscences hardly confirmed this description. Carrie Adell Strahorn, the spirited young wife of a Union Pacific official, made the journey with "Pard," her husband, in 1878. After a night at Corinne's hotel, which turned out to be a "crude, crowded cabin" with no partitions either in the loft or on the ground floor, they boarded an old Concord so packed with mail bags that there was no way for passengers to stretch out, "or to do other than sit in a perfectly straight position day and night. . ."

The first night out the coach drew up to the stage station, a small cabin where dwelt a solitary stock tender. What most fascinated Mrs. Strahorn was the big sign over the door: "HOTEL de STARVATION, 1,000 miles from hay and grain, seventy miles from wood, fifteen miles from water, and only twelve inches from h--l."

Here they changed drivers—for the worse—and coaches, Mr. Norton's "comfortable Concord" being replaced by a smaller "'jerky' with sides and top of canvas and a boot fore and aft to resemble the regular coach in all but size and comfort." Norton's "splendid road" also left something to be desired. "We listened," said Mrs. Strahorn, "to the grinding of wheels in the deep sand, and watched the clouds of dust roll into the coach, enveloping us in gray cloaks until we looked like hooded monks. Our eyes and nostrils were full of the fine alkiline ash that cuts the tender skin like acid."[8]

Despite the hardships, some intrepid tourists did make the journey in those early years. As the narrow-gauge Utah Northern advanced from Corinne north into Idaho, visitors took passage to the railhead, thus avoiding some of the discomforts of coach travel. By 1878 the line had progressed 100 miles north of Corinne; by 1881 it had reached well into Montana. The departure point for Yellowstone from the railroad was a rustic little settlement called Beaver Canyon, Idaho.* Here, by the late 1870s, the six Bassett brothers dominated the Yellowstone outfitting business, furnishing tents, tools, horses, and guides. And, as Mrs. Mary B. Richards in the summer of 1882 discovered, it was at Beaver Canyon that camp life commenced.[9]

The Richards party, from Massachusetts, may be considered typical of Eastern tourists to Yellowstone in those early years. *Most* affluent people still sailed to Europe or headed for socially accepted watering places such as Saratoga or the Greenbrier. However, among these people was a growing number with a love of the outdoors and the willingness, even the desire, to "rough it." The first glimmerings of this are apparent in the extended vacations of such people as the Richards. They were not hunters or sports fishermen who for years had been making exclusively masculine expeditions into the wilderness. The Richards were typical of a new type of visitor party, the family group.[10]

Mrs. Richard's reminiscences are of particular interest for their picture of the camp organization of such a party, its day-by-day itinerary and, perhaps most important of all, the image conveyed of the almost unbelievable wilderness abundance—the wild animals, fish, birds, and the virgin flora.

Outfitters supplied the party with a wall tent, blankets, buffalo robes, axe, hatchet, ropes, hammer, and wheel grease. Food included flour, sugar, lard, ham, "eggs packed in oats," and canned goods. For cooking they were furnished a "long tailed frying pan," bake kettle, coffee pot, knives, spoons, tin plates and cups. The Bassetts also supplied a driver, a cook, "two large balky horses and lastly the all important spring wagon, canvas-covered, large, strong, rather stiff in the joints. . . ." The cost was $18.00 a day.[11]

From Beaver Canyon the party followed a well-defined route to the park. They made excellent time. At Camas Meadows, their first overnight, camp was prepared with a minimum of effort. Inside their tent the Richards shared a bed of blankets folded on a rubber sheet; a hamper served also as a table, a wagon seat for a sofa, and a candle set in a bottle for illumination. A tin wash basin was provided, and soap and towels were laid in a pile on the grass. The horses, kept healthy with oats brought along for their benefit, strayed little and, come morning, came in close to camp. On that first day, still many miles from the park, Mrs. Richards had already spied a herd of antelope and observed scores of sage and pine hens.

The first morning out they were brought to life by the aroma of breakfast coffee in the clear mountain air. It took just an hour "to strike a tent, clear table, feed and harness horses and to start." That day they forded the Snake River twice, made rapid progress when attacking horseflies spurred on their

*Beaver Canyon is the present Monida, Idaho, on Highway 91, close to Monida Pass.

stock, and by noon had reached a high ridge near the river where a cool breeze drove off the insects. Two elk, another herd of antelope, brant, wild geese, snipe, and pine hens were all in evidence. Past sunset Henry's Lake came into view, encircled by mountains and framed by forests of pine and aspen. Raynolds Pass over which they had come lay to the northwest.[12]

Henry's Lake, southwest of Yellowstone Park by just fifteen miles, was a natural camping place for tourists and a veritable Garden of Eden for hunters. Nearby marshes attracted bird life by the thousands while four-footed game had always frequented the area. The old mountaineer, Gilman Sawtelle, had lived there since 1866, earning his livelihood by selling fresh trout and game to dealers and restaurateurs at Virginia City. An annual catch of forty thousand trout, upwards of four hundred elk, deer, antelope, moose, and bear, and untold bags of mallards, teals, canvasbacks, and swans, pelicans, cranes, and cormorants, is difficult to believe, but the abundance of all forms of fish, fowl, and animals was such that the old man at least approached such catches annually.[13]

While encamped at Henry's Lake, Mrs. Richards and her party met another phenomenon of the Yellowstone country in these years, the drifting mountaineer. Several years earlier the Earl of Dunraven, an English nobleman who hunted in the West, met a number of these mountain men on the Black Tail Deer Plateau in Yellowstone. He described one patriarchal camp of two men, their Indian wives and several children, half a dozen dogs and about fifty horses. Such hunters, trappers, and stockmen aroused the earl's envy. They "looked very happy and comfortable," he wrote. But, he warned, be careful: "Encountering people in these solitudes is like meeting a suspicious sail at sea when your country is at war. . . ."[14]

Mrs. Richards first spied her "knight of the frontier" riding rapidly towards them across the prairie. "He was a fair specimen of Idaho frontiersman . . . of fine form and features; thin, agile, brown as a chestnut and with uncombed hair and beard," she reminisced. His worldly effects were his rifle, cartridge belt, "an awful looking knife at his side, a long barreled revolver stuck in the back of his pantaloons, [and] a pipe tied into a string around his hat." Mrs. Richards was certainly impressed. The guest slept outside their tent with his head on his saddle, his gun and pistol covered with Mrs. Richards's plaid shawl. When she awoke the next morning he was gone, her shawl folded smoothly, and a half dozen salmon trout on the grass.[15]

From 1873 until the coming of the army engineers and the application of civil engineering to Yellowstone's roads, the two routes into the park from the west, the National Park Free Wagon Road and the Horseback Trail, became better defined through use if not through improvements. From Henry's Lake tourists usually crossed Targhee Pass and then followed along a high plateau, with colorful fields of larkspur, monkshood, and gentian waving in the breeze, and antelope, deer, elk, badger, and bear livening up the journey. At the end of this drive the stage drew up at Riverside Station on the Madison River. From there tourists had a choice of roads into the park: one ran up the Madison Canyon and the other went over the ridges and down into the Lower Geyser Basin. The coach company, Marshall and Goff, chose the latter route for its Concords.

In October 1880, Carrie Strahorn and Pard had been guests at the still unfinished Marshall's Hotel in the Lower Geyser Basin, the first true hotel within Yellowstone's borders. Their quarters were partitioned from the rest of the log, story-and-a-half, unfinished lodge by a wagon cover. Mrs. Marshall was at the time of the visit big with child. Before spring she would give birth to a little girl, the first white child, so far as is known, born in the park: Rosa Park Marshall.[16]

Although the west entrances appear to have been most used in the early years, the north entrance out of Bozeman and Fort Ellis likewise saw a constant parade of Yellowstone-bound tourists. Probably most of these people had come up from Corinne (later from Franklin, Idaho), but had for various reasons decided to swing east and enter the park from the north. The presence of Fort Ellis, just east of Bozeman, had something to do with this. It was considered the most important military post in the territory, protecting both the Yellowstone and Gallatin valleys, although it was not an impressive installation.[17]

From Bozeman travelers to the park often chose Bottler's ranch as their midway stop. The food was excellent, the milk rich and fresh. The Bottler men were knowledgeable of the region, the park, and hunting and fishing prospects. S. Weir Mitchell, a well-known writer-physician in the 1880s, described the ranch with its rough corrals, wide fields, and abundance of irrigation facilities. One ditch behind the cabin carried so many trout that, when it sloshed into the fields, the fish went with the water, helping to fertilize the soil.[18]

During these years tourists coming up the Yellowstone River were almost certain to take "Yankee Jim's" toll road up Second or Middle Canyon, beginning at Donohue Creek, a few miles above Bottler's, and extending to Cinnabar Mountain. James George ("Yankee Jim") claimed to have spent $25,000 on the road, which was probably $23,500 more than he had ever seen in a calendar year. He had blasted portions of his high road out of solid rock, however, and his improvements did make it the only practical route up the Yellowstone for a wagon.[19]

Yellowstone's first roads, in contrast to trails, were hacked out of the wilderness by crews working for Philetus Norris, the park's second superintendent. By 1883 only about half of them were considered passable for carriages. For example, the road from Mammoth to Swan Lake Flats, only a mile or two, was so steep that one guidebook said that it would take a loaded wagon, drawn by four mules, a half day, "allowing proper time to breathe the animals on the successive terraces. . . ." Mrs. Strahorn despaired of describing accurately the "horrible roads," the "public highway that was cut through the timber over rolling ground, with the stumps left from two to twenty inches above ground, and instead of grading a hill it went straight up on one side and straight down on the other. . . ." Mrs. Richards described the road from Firehole Basin down to Mammoth as consisting of "stumps set singly or in clumps at every hitable [sic] position, steep pitches both short and long, terminating invariably in either bog holes or a yard of corduroy, and perpendicular or soft bottomless approaches to the frequent fords make the way," she wrote, "like Jordan's, a 'hard road to travel'."[20]

The vandalism practiced by early tourists is shocking to us now but probably did not register as a crime to more than a handful of the few souls who entered the park in those early days. S. Weir Mitchell described "a lean, sallow man in a linen duster and armed with an axe" who strode up to the terraces at Mammoth and started hacking away. The doctor lectured the culprit, persuading him that "it was hardly fair to other travelers to ruin these charming bits of Nature's handiwork. . . ." But this was just one culprit converted (if he *was* converted), while the destruction continued. "I saw over and over again rough men with axes engaged in this vandal work," said Mitchell, "and was made to feel as a man might feel who saw a mob engaged in destroying a reverently-builded stonework of some gray cathedral. In most cases we were utterly helpless to stop this destruction. . . ."[21]

The editor of one paper commented in May 1877 that vandalism had already done "irreparable damage, and it should be stopped and punished, if not, the cartage of specimens by wholesale to the four quarters of the globe will continue until digging them up be stopped by striking the infernal regions beneath."[22]

Their destructiveness was probably no worse than today's tourists who, if there were no regulations or rangers around to prevent them, might commit similar acts of vandalism. Yet there was a shade of difference. Nineteenth-century visitors, unlike today's, lived in a sparsely populated land in which many were still fighting a battle with the wilderness. To shoot birds and animals, catch more fish than they could eat or give away, start a forest fire through negligence, or hack away at the delicate rims of hot springs and geysers came as natural actions to these people. Government had not yet arrived; no rules or regulations were posted until 1877. Visitors did not feel themselves violators of the law. To them nature's abundance was so obvious, so overwhelming, that restrictions upon abuse of the natural order seemed ridiculous.

If their wilderness was wilder and more beautiful than it is today, the hardships suffered by early tourists will not arouse our envy. If we worry about automobile accident fatalities, we may be made to feel better about them from an understanding of the hazards of travel with beasts of burden. Until the early 1880s most park travel was on horseback; if it was by wagon, buggy, or carriage, then horses or mules provided the motive power.

A camping spot was chosen as much for good grazing as for the comfort of the riders. When morning came the horses were often nowhere to be seen and a worrisome day and a half could be lost before they were found. Even when hobbled, horses could put quite a distance between themselves and camp. (In one instance they hesitated crossing the hot Firehole River, thus being prevented from returning all the way from the geysers to their livery stable at Virginia City.) Superintendent Norris was severely injured when his horse tossed him off near Tower Falls; Supreme Court Justice Morris R. Waite suffered a similar accident in the park. It is a long way to the ground from the hurricane deck of a cayuse. The wonder is that more people were not injured by their mounts.

Wild animals do not appear to have frightened the early tourists. Extensive, unrestricted slaughter had driven the deer, elk, antelope, moose, bison, and bear into the high country or into secluded valleys. This irritated many visitors because they were armed and had intended to bag all the game they could get a bead on.

One visitor who expressed shock at nimrod callousness toward bird life was General William Tecumseh Sherman's son Tom, who accompanied his father to Yellowstone in 1877. The young man's tendency toward mysticism and religion is apparent in his letters from the park, especially in one describing a discovery he had made near their camp at the Yellowstone Lake. "Against a great tree," he wrote, "a huntsman had left proof of his marksmanship. A huge swan, delicate in plumage, hung with outstretched wings nailed to the rough bark. What a mass of down on its swelling breast, what power in those long, tapering wings, what a silky gloss on the neck, once proudly arched, now dropping like a bruised reed." Then he added bitterly, "God sends us a creature pure and white and spotless. Man welcomes it with a bullet and three nails."[23]

Early tourists found the park an angler's paradise. Secretary of War Belknap and his fellow dignitaries caught 489 trout running from two-and-a-half to four-and-a-half pounds during their brief sojourn on the reservation in 1875. General William Emerson Strong, the expedition's chronicler, estimated members of the army escort "undoubtedly caught, all told, three thousand large trout. . . ."[24]

Camping under the stars was not a matter of choice, it was a necessity. Until Marshall's rustic hotel in the Lower Geyser Basin opened in 1882 and the big hotels were built in the next few years, camping was the only way to live in the park. Wealthy parties, as would be expected, fared very well. They hired plenty of guides, packers, and cooks, so that just about all a gentleman and, rarely, his lady, had to do was hunt, fish and sightsee. Poorer visitors had to do the chores for themselves.

To take ill while on a park tour is the most miserable kind of bad luck, but it was not uncommon then, nor is it uncommon now. When people's daily routines are broken, when the water they drink and the food they eat is changed, upsets are inevitable. And the misery is acute, humiliating, and unpleasant, for then as now the most common ailments were centered in the digestive system. But if there was no modern plumbing back then, there were nearly two million fewer visitors per season, and plenty of brush and woods offered privacy.

General Randolph B. Marcy caught pneumonia while visiting Yellowstone as a member of Secretary Belknap's party in 1875. It was his own fault. He was having so much fun fishing that he refused to come into camp and change into dry clothes after falling into the Yellowstone River. Sure enough, his temperature rose and by the time the party reached the Upper Geyser Basin he was flat on his back and running a high fever. The group's doctor insisted that the general be brought back to the vicinity of the Mud Volcano where pure water was available. He was conveyed there on a litter carried by two mules, one in front and one in back. He made a rapid recovery.[25]

Horse thieves, highwaymen, and renegade Indians, while no longer prevalent in most parts of the nation, remained for a few years longer a source of apprehension in Yellowstone. Travelers in that lonely country always reached for their rifles when a strange horseman appeared on the crest of a ridge or down in a valley. One's flesh prickled when hoofprints were spotted, or a skulking dog, sure sign of Indians, was sighted off from the trail.

In 1877, 1878, and for brief periods in the following two decades, Indians frightened park visitors. The most tragic incident took place in 1877 when Joseph, Looking Glass, and White Bird, chiefs of the Nez Perce, led their warriors, their aged, their women and children on a 1,500-mile Anabasis. From ancestral lands in western Idaho and eastern Washington they sought safety in Canada via passage east across Yellowstone Park and the high plains of north-central Montana. They defied, outwitted, and outfought the United States Army when forced to do battle with it. Not until autumn did they surrender to Colonel Nelson Miles near the Bear Paw Mountains in north-central Montana.

The Nez Perce entered the park via Henry's Lake (where they destroyed some of Gilman Sawtelle's improvements) and Targhee Pass, and on August 22 were camped along Nez Perce Creek (as it has since been called) in the Lower Geyser Basin. By this time these six to eight hundred desperate people with all the belongings they could carry, and two to three thousand horses, had been on the trail for about five weeks. They had already engaged army units a half dozen times.[26]

The park, in August 1877, was occupied by a number of visitors. The most prominent of them was General William Tecumseh Sherman, commander in chief of the army. He was determined to see the park even though couriers brought him disconcerting news, not only of the Nez Perce, but of the serious railroad riots then taking place in the East. The general, however, possessed the complacency that accompanies age and experience. He kept right on, according to plan, spent about two weeks in Yellowstone, and never saw the Indians.[27]

From Helena, where he arrived on August 21 after his park tour, Sherman studied his maps and concluded that the renegades would probably be trapped just outside the park. One-armed General Oliver O. Howard was resting his troops at Henry's Lake while two of his scouts led about fifty Bannocks ahead into the park. Two of Howard's companies pushed around the north end of the reservation and bolstered the personnel at Fort Ellis, where plans were hastily drawn to enter the campaign. Lieutenant Gustavus Doane headed for Mammoth Hot Springs with a company of the 2d Cavalry, accompanied by Lieutenant Charles C. De Rudio with a company of the 7th Cavalry and a party of Crow Indian scouts. In an arc northeast to southeast of the park were various army contingents on the alert for the renegades while far out on the plains, at Fort Keogh (near present Miles City, Montana), Colonel Nelson Miles waited, watching developments closely, prepared to participate in the final action. Only the troops and scouts under General Howard and those under Lieutenants Doane and De Rudio would enter the park.[28]

Meanwhile the Indians had arrived in the vicinity of the Lower Geyser Basin and the Firehole River. There an elderly prospector, John Shivley, was captured. Because he cooperated with them fully, and convinced the Indians that he could guide them onto the plains, Shivley was forced to accompany the Indians as the ward of an English-speaking brave named Joe. For the next thirteen days the prospector remained with the Nez Perce while they traveled eastward. "As I could not help myself," Shivley later informed a reporter, "I promised all they asked, and kept my promise. . . . I always showed a willingness to get on or off a horse when they told me. . . and to this fact I am probably indebted for kind treatment." Finally, somewhere along a tributary of Clarks Fork, this sensible prisoner made good his escape.

Before his capture Shivley, who had lost his horses, had planned to join a tourist party out of the reservation. At the time of his capture they were sightseeing at the Lower Geyser Basin; camped close by them was another prospector, William H. Harmon, who also planned to accompany them out of the park. He too was subsequently captured but later escaped.[29]

Who were these people whom the prospectors had planned to join? They have been called the Radersburg tourists because most of them came from the mining village of that name, about thirty-five miles southeast of Helena. There were nine of them. They interest us not only because of their capture by the Nez Perce, but also because they left the best descriptions of what it was like in the 1870s for ordinary people, the "sagebrushers" in farm wagons, buggies, or on horseback, to visit Yellowstone. They were typical American pioneer stock. The impression they leave us with is that they had more fun than any twentieth-century tourist can hope for. They hunted and fished and observed and (for shame) vandalized geysers, and they sang and danced and staged high jinks and ate like wolves and loved every minute of their outing. They "had a ball"—until the Nez Perce intervened.

The idea of a trip to Wonderland originated with a young man named Frank Carpenter, at the time living in Helena; in due time two other Helena men, J. A. Oldham and A. J. Arnold, joined the party. By the time the group left Radersburg they had added six new members: Mr. and Mrs. George F. Cowan (Frank's sister Emma and his brother-in-law), and Frank and Emma's thirteen-year-old sister Ida; eighteen-year-old Henry Meyers who handled the wagon and team loaned by Frank's father; and, picked up somewhat along the way, Charles Mann and William Dingee.[30]

Frank and his sister with their family had crossed the plains from Wisconsin, settling first in Virginia City in 1864. Mrs. Cowan, whose portraits suggest beauty, sensitivity, and intelligence (as does the one of her younger sister Ida), had nothing but happy memories of that journey. "I enjoyed beyond measure the gypsy style of travel, journeying toward the setting sun," she reminisced. She savored the wildflowers, remembered the "great white-capped wagons," the "never-failing pleasure of appeasing prodigious appetites," the sight of Indians bartering for beads, and her first lessons in riding horseback on an Indian pony. Since their father had never had a fear of Indians, always laughing at Indian scares, the children harbored few apprehensions about them either.

While at Virginia City Mr. Carpenter had brought home an old man who lived at Henry's Lake and marketed fish at the diggings. He told amazing stories about Yellowstone, implanting in the little girl's mind a desire to visit it some day. (Probably the old man was Gilman Sawtelle.) In 1873 she had seen Mammoth Hot Springs, remembered how the road had been so bad in places that they had unhitched the horses and pulled the wagon along by hand. Obviously the Carpenters were a family of many interests and considerable vigor.

According to Frank Carpenter's diary, the nine tourists and a pregnant dog named Dido left Radersburg on Sunday, August 5. Their route lay up the Madison and overland to Henry's Lake, then via wagon road to the Lower Geyser Basin. It took them ten days to get there, but they suffered little boredom. They hunted antelope, occasionally bagging one, enriched their larder with fat mallards and succulent sage hens, but hardly expected to eat two bald eagles they had shot. They fished, with excellent luck. The women picked ripe raspberries, currants, and strawberries. They all ate well and felt well.

When they started up the Firehole River the whole party acted like children on Christmas morning. They ran from one strange phenomenon to another. Finally they pitched a home camp in the Lower Geyser Basin. This was the day that Meyers stepped into a hot spring, his agonizing cries bringing sympathizers who could do little to alleviate the pain. This did not dampen the good times had by everyone else.

Perhaps the worst recorded attempt at geyser jamming was done by the Radersburg tourists, and they did it to Old Faithful. "Wishing to experiment," Frank Carpenter wrote, "we collect an immense quantity of rubbish and drop it into the crater. We have filled it to the top with at least a thousand pounds of stones, trees, stumps, etc. . . ." Then they sat down to await developments. Old Faithful threw rocks, trees, and rubbish seventy-five feet into the air. They also threw their laundry into the orifice; it too came up "nice and clean as a Chinaman could wash it with a week's scrubbing," Frank wrote.

The known presence of several other groups in the park enhanced the Radersburg party's feeling of security, so that it was all good fun when some members decorated their horses with feathers and galloped into camp eliciting Indian war whoops. On their last night in the Lower Geyser Basin the tourists built a big fire and participated in nonsense and merriment, unaware that across the marsh Yellow Wolf and his braves watched.

Early the next morning the Indians appeared. Leaderless and unprepared for crisis, the tourists did not know what to do. Rapid events and instructions from the Indians dictated their movements. Inside the tents the women dressed and remained hidden as long as possible. The men gave out flour and sugar while the Indians wolfed down breakfast. Save for Mrs. Cowan's husband George, who acted with arrogance, threats, and rudeness, all of the party cooperated with their red captors. In due time, with an Indian guard surrounding them, they mounted and started across the marsh. From a rise in the ground they saw the hopelessness of their situation. The fleeing Indians were moving slowly up the east fork, ever since called Nez Perce Creek. "As far as we could see," Frank Carpenter later wrote, "up and down the river, they were moving abreast in an unbroken line ten or fifteen feet deep, driving ponies and constantly riding out and in the line. We could see about three miles of Indians, with 1000 to 1500 ponies, and looking off to the left we could see more Indians looking at the geysers in Fire Hole Basin."

Two miles up the Mary's Lake Trail (which led to Hayden Valley and the Yellowstone River) the buggy and wagon bogged down amid fallen timber. Here the Indians slashed the harnesses and destroyed the vehicles, ransacked the supplies, and even took the wheel spokes, which they used for whip handles. One young buck tied several yards of mosquito netting to his horse's tail and went dashing off with it waving in the air.

Before that longest day was over, their good mounts were "traded" for worn out Indian nags. Two of the men, Arnold and Dingee, escaped into the woods. Two men were shot: Oldham took a ball in his left cheek which cut a dab of his tongue and exited beneath his jaw on the right side; he hid, made his escape, and survived. At almost the same time grumpy George Cowan took a ball in his head from an enormous navy pistol. During this bloodletting two other Radersburg tourists, Meyers and Mann, made a successful dash for freedom. When order was restored, only three of the nine tourists remained with the Indians: Frank Carpenter and his two sisters.

As they plodded along with their Indian captors, they assumed that Emma's husband, George, was dead. Actually George's adventures had just begun. Because the powder charge had been light, the ball had simply flattened against his skull. He recovered consciousness with a headache and a burning thirst. As he grasped a pine branch to help himself up, an Indian shot him again, this time through the hip, the ball coming out through his abdomen. Down went George. When he again recovered consciousness he crawled to a nearby stream for water, in the process almost suffocating in the muddy embankment. Finally he reached the remains of the buggy and wagon where the pregnant Dido, somehow escaping an Indian's stew pot, joined him. Later his cooking fire, with which he was trying to brew some coffee from used grounds spilled by the Indians, got out of control and burned his hands and knees. Finally rescued, he and his wife Emma (by now freed from her Indian captors) left Bottler's ranch for Bozeman in a double-seated carriage. They expected an uneventful trip. However, about seven miles from their destination, where the road ran along a steep hillside, a pole strap broke. The carriage lunged into the horses and the buggy tongue fell to the ground, snapped, and lifted the carriage into the air, spilling out its occupants. The vehicle ended upside down in tree tops three hundred feet below. Emma was unhurt, but poor George! He was dumped out, his wounds broken open again. That night his hotel bed gave way and down he went once more. Wistfully, the suffering man looked up at his wife and friends and suggested that if they really wanted to kill him, please call out the artillery.

As for Frank and his sisters, they had remained with the Indians into a second day. That afternoon the Indians gave them bedding, clothing, bread, matches, and two worn-out horses, and let them go. They made contact with some soldiers and rode all night to Mammoth Hot Springs; subsequently Emma was reunited with her husband, and they all reached home safely.

All the Radersburg tourists survived. After a long winter of convalescence, George Cowan recovered. He lived to celebrate his golden wedding anniversary with his devoted Emma, who never let him forget that by his grumpiness and arrogance he had brought all his miseries on himself. Even Dido, in her interesting condition, returned and had her puppies. They were soon given away to people who linked them with the late Nez Perce unpleasantness.

The Radersburg tourists were representative of the "covered wagon" stage in park history. This period lasted until about 1915, during which thousands of "sagebrushers" explored the park. The logistics of horse-drawn travel precluded really long-distance travel. Most of them came from Montana, Idaho, or, on occasion, from as far away as Utah. That American pioneer stock manifested this desire to visit Yellowstone under circumstances entailing weeks of going and coming, chasing stray horses, fussing over loose rims or weak axles, and fretting over the health of the participants, speaks well of the pioneers' high level of intellectual curiosity, says something about their love of the outdoors, and of their enjoyment in doing things as a family. The modern American who stores the children in the camper, while he drives the pickup truck with his wife at his side, is truly a descendant of these adventurous people.

The other group that ran into trouble with the Nez Perce has been designated the Helena tourists, typical of a different kind of party that was prevalent in Yellowstone in the early years. These were informal groups of two or three to a dozen men (ten were in the Helena party). The mastic that joined them was companionship and the common goals of seeing the park and having a good time. In a West that had a shortage of women, such groups were common. The Helena tourists had an informally designated leader and a black man, Ben Stone, hired as "commissary," but it is clear that everyone did pretty much as he pleased.[31]

These vacationers from Helena chose to see the park via the north entrance and Mammoth Hot Springs. They set out in three units and became a single party at the springs.* On August 22 they marched to Tower Falls and on August 23, the day the Radersburg tourists were captured, skirted Mount Washburn and reached Yellowstone Falls. On the twenty-fifth, the day the Carpenters were freed, the Helena men headed upriver toward the Mud Volcano. A mile or so beyond Sulphur Mountain they spied the Indian camp across the river.

One member of the party panicked and galloped off. Another suggested that they all enter the Indian camp under a flag of truce. The consensus, however, was to backtrack a few miles and camp in a safe place. That safe place was found easily by Kenck, the panicky one, who trotted back into camp sheepishly. How had he found it? By the smoke of their fire, of course. So had the Indians, who attacked the next morning, killing Kenck and wounding another. The rest of the party disbursed, every man for himself. Each one experienced a series of hair-raising adventures before reaching safety.

Before the Nez Perce left the park a second man had been killed and two others (not all of them members of the Helena party) wounded. McCartney's hotel at Mammoth had been pillaged and Henderson's ranch down the Gardner River (but out of the park) had been burned. As the Indians left Yellowstone, they burned Baronett's bridge across the Yellowstone.

The Nez Perce, including the horse-stealing party that had attacked the Helena tourists, made their way up the Lamar and over an old Bannock Indian trail to Clarks Fork, which they followed out onto the high plains. They had spent fourteen or fifteen days in the park, from August 22 until September 5 or 6, while troops under General Howard plus contingents from Fort Ellis tried unsuccessfully to intercept them. Not until October 5, on the storm-swept plains of north-central Montana, did they surrender.[32]

In the summer of 1878 about one hundred Bannocks under Chief Buffalo Horn took to the warpath in Idaho and Oregon. By August the war had become a mopping up operation for the army, with splinter groups of renegades marauding all over the Northwest, including the Yellowstone country. Some of the hostiles dreamed of making their way via the Bannock Trail across the park, which their people had used for generations, to the buffalo plains where they anticipated linking up with Sitting Bull and his Sioux in Canada.[33]

At Henry's Lake this small Bannock war party struck at the camp of A. D. Wilson of the Hayden Survey, running off his stock and pilfering his

---

*Their names were Andrew Weikert, who kept a diary; John Stewart, who was wounded: Leslie Wilkie, August Follor, Joseph H. Roberts, Richard Dietrich and Charles Kenck, both murdered; Leonard Duncan, Frederic J. Pheister, and the black cook, Ben Stone.

provisions. Those Indians were attacked two days later in the same area by a military contingent from Fort Ellis. The soldiers captured fifty-six head of stock but the Indians escaped into the park. A horse-stealing party, probably the same band, appeared between Mammoth and Bottler's in the next week, making off with most of the stock in the area, including still more animals belonging to the Hayden Survey.[34]

Fortunately few tourists were in the park in 1878, probably due to fear aroused by the Nez Perce depredations of the year before. When Superintendent Philetus Norris heard of the Bannock presence he, with $10,000 that year for park improvements, ordered constructed "a route connecting the two entrances to the park for military as well as other purposes." By August his laborers had hacked a wagon swath—let us not compliment it by calling it a road—all the way from Mammoth to the Upper Geyser Basin. Eventually the Indian scare drove his force back to Mammoth, where he found Major James S. Brisbin with troops from Fort Ellis armed with a Gatling gun. Subsequently Norris and the major discovered that the Indians had crossed from west to east somewhere between them.[35]

The principal band of Bannock renegades was finally defeated as a result of a tourist party headed for Wonderland. Colonel Nelson Miles, commander at Fort Keogh, had received permission to lead a party of officers and their families to Yellowstone for a vacation. Accompanied by a detachment of soldiers and the 5th Infantry band, they headed for Yellowstone on August 15, nearly a hundred strong.[36]

When the party reached the Crow agency north and east and adjacent to the park, on August 29, Colonel Miles, learning of the renegades' proximity, at once took steps to intercept them. Part of his force under Lieutenant Clark of the 2d Cavalry encountered the hostiles first near Index Peak, inflicting some damage. Then, on the morning of September 4, it was Miles's turn. He surprised the Bannock camp, killing eleven and capturing thirty-one Indians with about two hundred horses and mules. In the skirmish Captain Bennett was killed as was a Crow Indian and an interpreter, and a soldier was wounded. Thus ended the Bannock problem.[37]

Visitors no longer had to fear Indians in Yellowstone, although until the mid-1890s small parties, mostly of Bannocks and Shoshones, continued to hunt in the south and southwest sections of the park. Superintendent Norris built his impractical headquarters fortress on top of Capitol Hill at Mammoth with Indian attacks in mind. Through 1881, when he left office, he conferred often with Indian agents and was successful in preventing serious trouble. In 1879 the army maintained a small summer camp at Henry's Lake as a deterrent. In 1895 a false rumor spread that ten Princeton men had been captured by hostiles, but the Indians by this time were cowed and restricted to their reservations. Yellowstone was off limits.[38]

When the park was created in 1872, much of its 3,000 square miles was still untraversed and unmapped; so too was a vast, mountainous region to the south, southeast, and east. Trappers and prospectors had without doubt covered much of the region, but expeditions by scientists and army personnel had hardly penetrated what are even today considered formidable mountain barriers. In the decade of the 1870s many park visitors were scientists.

First and foremost in carrying on scientific investigations was the U.S. Geological and Geographical Survey of the Territories, better known as the Hayden Survey. Hayden men had been in the park in 1871 and had played an important role in the park's creation. They were in Yellowstone again in 1872, 1877, and 1878, continuing to work there after the consolidation of the several surveys into the U.S. Geological Survey in 1879.[39]

The most ambitious of the Hayden expeditions into the Yellowstone country was that of 1872. With a $75,000 appropriation, its largest to date, Hayden had collected an impressive corps of scientists, camp men, and packers. Among the personnel were Henry Gannett, later one of the nation's leading geographers; William Henry Holmes, later head of the Bureau of American Ethnology and the National Collection of Fine Arts; C. Hart Merriam, who would become a world renowned zoologist, and John Merle Coulter, who became one of the world's great botanists. Along that season as a guest was William Blackmore, a British entrepreneur, and his nephew, the perspicacious young Sidford Hamp.[40]

In 1877, after five years in Colorado, the survey returned to Yellowstone and the surrounding territories. There its work continued until publication of an illustrated report in 1883. Volume 2, 503 pages long, deals exclusively with "Yellowstone National Park: Geology—Thermal Springs—Topography," and includes contributions by many experts. Facing page 62 is a spread of William Henry Holmes's panoramic views, a notable example of the man's remarkable artistry. Not until the work of Arnold Hague, published in 1912, and of Allen and Day in 1935, would so thorough an investigation be reported again. To science as well as to the tourist, then, Yellowstone by 1883 was no longer *tierra incógnita*.[41]

Most exploring expeditions approached the park from north or west. Yet today hundreds of thousands of tourists each year enter the park via Highways 14-16-20, west from Cody, Wyoming, up the Shoshone River Canyon; or via 26-287 over the Wind River Mountains at Togwotee Pass and on to the Jackson Hole village of Moran; or via 26-89-187 from Rock Springs to Moran, and then northwest by north on 89-287 which leads them into the park.

Or they enter on Highway 212 over the Beartooth Plateau from Red Lodge, Montana. Until 1873 none of these southern or eastern entrances was considered feasible; the Beartooth route was not yet explored and the road was not completed until 1935.

Consensus was that the park could be entered only from the north or west. Captain Raynolds in 1860 had failed to break through the snowfilled Absarokas; in 1871 Hayden had described the same range, as viewed from the Wind River, as presenting "a nearly vertical wall from 1,500 to 2,000 feet high, which has never been scaled by white man or Indian, but is covered with perpetual snows to a greater or lesser extent." And Nathaniel P. Langford wrote the following year (1872) that the park was impossible to enter from Wyoming.

The myth of inaccessibility was shattered in 1873 when Captain William A. Jones of the Corps of Engineers led a reconnaissance northward from Fort Bridger, in extreme southwest Wyoming. His specific assignment was to test the feasibility of a "wagon-road from the line of the Union Pacific Railroad in Wyoming Territory, to the Yellowstone National Park and Fort Ellis, Montana Territory."[42]

Jones assembled an impressive entourage. He had another captain and a lieutenant along, considerable enlisted personnel, about fifteen Shoshone braves, a well-known geologist, Theodore B. Comstock, and a noted botanist, Dr. C. C. Parry. Eight wagons and sixty-six pack and saddle mules carried personnel and equipment. With four months' provisions the expedition left Fort Bridger on June 12, 1873. By July 27 the party had struck the north fork of the Shoshone (then known also as the Stinking Water) and had started up the canyon. They had already noticed hot springs, both active and nascent, the reddish soil, and the weird formations, all of which suggested volcanic origin. "The conglomerate weathers into the most fantastic pinnacles, needles, and grotesque forms," the captain wrote, intrigued as are modern tourists on Highway 14-16-20 west of Cody.

On August 2 they crested the divide. Captain Jones could see Yellowstone Lake in the distance "embosomed in its surrounding plateau. . . ." They made their way to the lake outlet, on down the east side of the canyon, and eventually reached Mammoth Hot Springs where they met a pack train returning from Fort Ellis with supplies.

Not desiring to return exactly the way they had come, Jones placed the route in the hands of a Sheepeater Indian named Togwotee who led them up the Yellowstone River above the lake, over Two Ocean Pass, and then to a pass between the head of Wind River and a small tributary of the Snake. From a nearby height Captain Jones could make out far to the south, near which was Crow Heart Butte, Camp Brown (near present Lander, Wyoming). The Indian had been true to his word. In his honor the pass was given his name: Togwotee. Highway 26-287 runs through it today.

The expedition returned to Camp Stambaugh and disbanded. On the basis of Captain Jones's report, General Ord, commander of the military district of Missouri (which embraced the region), recommended an appropriation of $60,000 for construction of a wagon road, to which crusty, sensible General William Tecumseh Sherman replied: "I am not prepared to give even a shadow of support to anything so absurd as the military necessity for such a road."[43]

The present highway does not cross Two Ocean Pass. Instead it follows rather closely the old trail along the Lewis Fork of the Snake. It does, however, cross Togwotee Pass. Certainly the Jones expedition of 1873 is of significance, for from then on it was understood that trails, a wagon road, possibly even a railroad, could be built into the park from the Wyoming side. Montana's monopoly of Yellowstone entrances could last just a few more years.

Captain Jones's exploration exemplifies the army's continuing interest in the park. Rarely did a summer pass without someone military visiting Yellowstone. In 1875 it was a party of VIPs led by Secretary of War William Belknap. William Emerson Strong (a former Civil War general) narrated the trip, which impresses the reader as being a sumptuous frolic at taxpayers' expense. A more serious expedition that summer of 1875 was led by Captain William Ludlow, chief engineer of the Department of Dakota. He was ordered to make a "Reconnaissance from Carroll, Montana, on the Upper Missouri, to the Yellowstone National Park and Return." His party consisted at no time of more than twenty-two persons. These included young George Bird Grinnell, who became a park defender, and "Lonesome Charley" Reynolds, "the well-known frontiersman who was to act as guide and hunter for the expedition."[44]

Some of Captain Ludlow's descriptions indicate the beauty still remaining in the park in 1875. Here is his passage about Old Faithful's crater: "The lips are molded and rounded into many artistic forms, beaded and pearled with opal, while closely adjoining are little terraced pools of the clearest azure-hued water, with scalloped and highly ornamented borders. The wetter margins and floors of these pools are tinted with the most delicate shades of white, cream, brown, and gray, so soft and velvety it seemed as though a touch would soil them."

Yet civilization was intruding. Ludlow refers to "a whiskey trader snugly ensconsed beneath his 'paulin [tarpaulin]," and the presence in the Upper Basin, while he was there, of more than thirty people. "The visitors prowled about with shovel and axe, chopping and hacking and prying up great pieces of the most ornamental work they could find; women and men alike joining in the barbarous pastime."[45] By September 18, Captain Ludlow's party was back at Carroll.*

Late in 1876 a harebrained military expedition started out of Yellowstone Park. It is fortunate that it resulted in no casualties. The expedition was planned by Lieutenant Gustavus Doane of the 2nd Cavalry stationed at nearby Fort Ellis. Lieutenant Doane, a tall, straight-as-a-ramrod officer, had been with Langford in Yellowstone in 1870, with Hayden in 1871, was also in the park in 1874 and was a guide to Secretary Belknap's party in 1875. Thirty-six years old, Doane was still a first lieutenant in that period of maddeningly slow promotions. His sense of destiny demanded that he do something to further his career. He therefore proposed and was granted permission to float down the Snake River from Heart Lake, in southern Yellowstone Park, all the way to the confluence of the Snake with the Columbia, in *midwinter!* (One suspects the lieutenant conceived his expedition after noticing the notoriety received by John Wesley Powell by floating down the canyons of the Colorado River.)

With one noncommissioned officer and five enlisted men, pack animals, sixty days' rations, and a small boat which was packed in to Yellowstone Lake in pieces, Doane set out from Fort Ellis on October 11. At the lake they launched their boat, "a double-ender twenty-two feet long, forty-six inches beam and twenty-six inches deep," and were pleased with its behavior in the water. Then they placed poles under its hull to act as runners, and in bitter cold, dragged it over the divide to Heart Lake. Much of that body of water was frozen over, however, and the outlet, where Doane had planned to begin floating downriver, ran just six inches deep. This was not one-fourth what he had anticipated. Tenaciously and foolishly the lieutenant led his men on, dragging the boat out of the park and down to Jackson Lake, then down the Snake River, until by mid-December the party had to set out overland or else die of exposure and starvation. For the ambitious lieutenant the trip was in vain. He did not achieve national fame, nor did the army reward him with a promotion.[46]

By the early 1880s the Very Important People visiting the park had become so numerous that most of their experiences became commonplace. Their visiting does, however, remind us of the park presence in the national psyche. In 1880 Secretary of Interior Carl Schurz and Webb Hayes, the President's son, escorted by General Crook and fourteen mounted infantrymen, passed through. The secretary's displeasure with Philetus Norris's road building may have influenced his decision to replace him.[47]

---

*The site of Carroll is now inundated beneath the waters of Fort Peck Dam on the Missouri River.

Also in 1881, to mention just two of several military excursions into Yellowstone, Governor John W. Hoyt of Wyoming Territory with a military escort entered from the upper Yellowstone and left via Jones Pass, indicating interest in opening the park from the Wyoming side. General Phil Sheridan worked through the reservation from east to west. In 1882 Sheridan returned, coming in from the south with a dozen high army officers, Togwotee as a guide, and an entourage of 128 men and a squaw. At the Lewis River they met a party of engineers making a reconnaissance for a possible railroad into the reservation from the south.[48]

The Sheridan party of 1882 is important because of its route out of the park. The general planned to exit on the Clarks Fork Trail onto the eastern plains, but this route was barred by a forest fire. When a hunter named Geer described the trace across the Beartooth Plateau, Sheridan determined to try it. Under Geer's guidance they crossed the magnificent tableland, descended by a precipitous trail into the valley of Clarks Fork, followed the river until its debouchment with the Yellowstone, rode four more miles and struck the Northern Pacific tracks; there they entrained for Chicago.

Until the Sheridan trip, the Beartooth route had been considered impassable by anyone except prospectors. Now General Sheridan had negotiated it with a substantial party, thus proving that there was still another way to enter or leave Yellowstone: via the Beartooth Plateau. Today that is Highway 212 from Red Lodge, Montana, over the plateau and down to Cooke City and Silvergate, the northeast entrance to the park.

It is clear, from the number of army visitors to the park, that the military branch of the government had a distinct interest in Yellowstone. It began with Captain Raynolds in 1860, was continued with Lieutenant Doane, who accompanied the Washburn party in 1870, with Captains Barlow and Heap and Lieutenant Doane with Hayden in 1871; Captain Jones in 1873, the secretary of war in 1875 and Captain Ludlow the same year. In 1876 Lieutenant Doane led his ill-conceived expedition down the Snake River from Heart Lake. In 1877 General Howard, Lieutenant Doane, and others, were in the park on the trail of the Nez Perce, and General Sherman made a rapid sightseeing tour. In 1878 Colonel Nelson Miles led an excursion there; General Crook was in the park with Carl Schurz in 1880 and General Sheridan visited in 1881 and 1882. Several other parties of military men, or parties accompanied by a military contingent, were exploring the park in these years. Was there an ulterior motive behind all this activity?

No indication exists of a fixed aim, but the general army reaction to what its personnel witnessed in the park does indicate concern and consistency of thought. Secretary Belknap sounded the official alarm in his Annual Report for 1875, in which he expressed the wish of his department "to unite

with the Secretary of the Interior in doing what is possible . . . for the opening and surveying of this region, so appropriately called 'Wonder Land.'" He
then suggested that the engineer corps could build roads to the interior for a
"modest sum," adding that the park curiosities were being rapidly destroyed.
If authority were given, he wrote, the army could station one or two companies of troops in or near the park for the prevention of spoliation. "Surely,"
he said, "everything should be done that can be [done] to protect all that is
grand and beautiful in that remarkable region."[49]

In that same year Captain William Ludlow was appalled at what he saw.
In their natural state the geyser craters were beautiful. Yet, he wrote, this
work of centuries could be destroyed "in five minutes by a vandal with an
axe, and nearly all the craters show signs of the hopeless and unrestrained
barbarity of their visitors. . . . To procure a specimen of perhaps a pound
weight, a hundred pounds have been shattered and destroyed. . . ."

The captain also noted the wholesale destruction of game that was under
way in the mid-1870s. Between fifteen hundred and two thousand elk had
been slain during the winter of 1874–75 within a radius of fifteen miles of
Mammoth Hot Springs. These elk were skinned, for which the hunters received $2.50 to $3.00 each, and the carcasses were left in the snow "to feed
the wolves or to decay in the spring." Such butchery made extermination
inevitable, he emphasized, and this in a region where the animal should have
protection, "and where his frequent inoffensive presence would give the
greatest pleasure to the greatest number."

Ludlow's cure for these evils was specified: a strong mounted police in
the park. "In the absence of any legislative provision for this," he wrote,
"recourse can most readily be had to the already existing facilities afforded by
the presence of troops in the vicinity and the transfer of the park to the
control of the War Department."[50]

Since the War Department did receive the road-building assignment
beginning in 1882 and was charged with policing the park in 1886, it may
be assumed that there were elements who coveted such a turn of events.
These included the officers at the northwest posts, notably at Fort Ellis, who
knew the Indian menace was ended and were seeking new assignments.
However, as late as 1878 army policy had not solidified, for General Sherman, who in that year had endorsed correspondence from Fort Ellis officers
advocating army jurisdiction, added: "It is not the business of the Army to
protect or preserve the game or natural objects of the Yellowstone National
Park." And again, "The troops have enough to do without guarding it. The
public cannot carry away the geysers—the only real object of great National
Curiosity. New incrustations form each year and are of no real value."[51]

Sherman's fellow general, Phil Sheridan, felt differently. When he
reached the Northern Pacific tracks after his trip through the park in 1882,

he learned of the new franchise that had been let by the Department of Interior for park hotel and transportation facilities. He registered his strong dissent to the contract. Yellowstone, he said, is a national park, and it should be in the hands of an officer of the government who can make necessary improvements with small appropriations from Congress. He also regretted the destruction of game. He had heard that as many as four thousand elk had been killed by skin hunters in a single winter, "to say nothing of the great mountain sheep, antelope, deer and other game slaughtered in great numbers." Then he made the wisest suggestion of all:

> I would like to see the government extend the park to the east as far as a north and south line through Cedar Mountain; this would be due east about 40 miles, at the same time placing the southern boundary of the park at the 44th parallel of latitude, which would be due south 10 miles. This would increase the area of the park by 3,344 square miles, and would make a preserve for the large game of the West, now rapidly decreasing.

He added that this would take nothing away from the people of the territory, for it was rough, mountainous terrain, too high for cultivation and too cold for grazing cattle. Moreover, if the skin hunters were restrained, game animals would gravitate to the park. Sheridan then requested the support of sportsmen in prevailing upon Congress to make this change in the boundaries, and he offered to furnish troops from Forts Washakie on the south, Custer on the east, and Ellis on the north to keep out the skin hunters.[52] (Sheridan's excellent suggestions were ignored.)

How had Yellowstone fared vis-a-vis tourists in its first decade as a park? By today's numbers, of course, relatively few human beings had entered the park, probably less than ten thousand in all. Yet the region was already under siege. Hunters shot deer, elk, moose, and bison for skins and trophies. Birds, so prevalent on Yellowstone Lake, were killed indiscriminately with shotguns. Fish by the thousands were caught, most of them left to rot on the river banks or lake shores. Every tourist seemed to be a vandal throwing stones, sticks, branches, stumps, garbage, and clothing into the geysers and hot springs. Visitors tore at the delicate sinter with axes and removed it by the hundreds of pounds. Forest fires blazed out of control, often the result of campfires deserted while still burning. People rolled boulders down the precipitous walls of the Grand Canyon of the Yellowstone. Firewood was fetched wherever available and whenever needed.[53]

If a few visitors were doing untold damage, the portent for the future when thousands more would enter the park was frightening. A rapidly expanding railroad network offered an equally increasing population an easy way to reach Yellowstone. It was already a race between destroyers and preservers, a race which, even today, is not entirely decided.

Yet, by and large, as of 1882 the forces of recovery were able to keep pace with the forces of destruction. Then the stillness in the park from October through April was not broken by the clatter of snowmobiles. Given seven to nine months a year to recuperate, nature did the job very well. It was able to keep up.

In 1874 the Earl of Dunraven was still in Yellowstone as autumn closed down over the land. Everyone else had left the park; the sky had turned leaden and the breeze, so gentle and warm a few days before, had changed into a bitter cold wind. Old newspapers, tin cans, and the black coals of campfires long dead swirled through the gale which smoothed out the man-made irregularities on the land. Stable doors, not secured, flapped open and shut. Bears, fat rippling beneath glossy coats, cast about for hibernation lairs; and deer, elk, and moose took refuge on the south side of mountains, in canyons and deep woods. Geese in great Vs honked saucily on high, scudding southward with the wind.

The earl and his party arrived at Mammoth Hot Springs. His men were tired and out of sorts, their animals worn to a state of near uselessness, and the hunting had been poor. "How delicious it would be, we mutually speculated," he wrote, "to lie up to our chins for an hour in the warm, soft, invigorating water, calmly smoking the calumet of peace. Thoughts of supper too at the hotel reconciled us a little to our present discomforts."

They knocked at the door of McCartney's Hotel, but got no answer. "An ominous darkness enveloped the house; the door was fastened; we burst it in, but beat a hasty retreat from two or three skunks who appeared inclined to resent our intrusion." The tired sportsmen found the place otherwise uninhabited; not an article of food, drink, or utensils remained. "An owl . . . hooted dismally round the solitary shanty . . . a skunk walked disdainfully and slowly . . . out of the saloon; squirrels were the only visitors at the clubhouse. We had to camp as best we could," sighed Dunraven, "upon the bare, dirty floors, and well nigh supperless to bed."[54]

Soon the earl left, and before many days the cold wind would carry snow, and then the wind would die down, and a blanket of velvety white cover the ground, hiding the tourist's dead campfire, covering the old newspaper, the tin cans, the stones that traced the site of the tourist's tent. The few buildings would be frosted, their unpainted sides clashing with the white of roofs and surrounding land. The bears would sleep, the little rodents would go about their business beneath the safety of snow cover, the elk and deer and buffalo would drift down the valleys, paw away the snow and munch the dry grasses underneath.

And, months later, the land would look new again.

NOTES TO CHAPTER ONE

1. Montanans' interest in their history is reflected in a number of good state histories. Recent ones include Kenneth Ross Toole, *Montana: An Uncommon Land* (Norman: University of Oklahoma Press, 1959); Michael P. Malone and Richard B. Roeder, *Montana: A History of Two Centuries* (Seattle: University of Washington Press, 1976); and Clark C. Spence, *Montana: A Bicentennial History* [the States of the Nation Series] (New York: Norton, 1978).

2. C. C. Clawson, "Notes on the Way to Wonderland, or, A Ride to the Infernal Regions," in *The New Northwest* (Deer Lodge, Montana), Vol. 3, No. 10 (September 9, 1871); Vol. 3, No. 48 (June 1, 1872).

3. Henry J. Norton, *Wonder-Land Illustrated: or, Horseback Rides Through the Yellowstone National Park* (Virginia City: No publisher, 1873), 18, 14, 30, 46–49.

4. Seth Bullock, "Diary of a trip to the Yellowstone in 1872," in custody of the Montana Historical Society.

5. National Archives, Record Group 48, Records of the Office of the Secretary of the Interior, Patents and Miscellaneous Division, Letters Received, Charles L. Heizman to Major W. A. Jones, U.S. Engineers, February 15, 1883.

These records, which I have used extensively, were filed in the Patents and Miscellaneous Division or the Appointments Division. Hereafter for brevity reference to these sources will be as follows: Office of the Secretary of the Interior, PMLR (for Patents and Miscellaneous Letters Received); PMLS (for Patents and Miscellaneous Letters Sent); ADLR (Appointments Division Letters Received); or ADLS (Appointments Division Letters Sent), followed in all cases by name of sender, addressee, and date. Save for the abbreviations, this is in accord with National Archives suggested documentation.

6. These advertisements appear in a business directory at the end of Norton, *Wonder-Land Illustrated*.

7. Ibid., 52. A recent book about this "Montana Trail" from Corinne into Montana is Betty M. Madsen and Brigham D. Madsen, *North to Montana!* (Salt Lake City: University of Utah Press, 1980).

8. Carrie Adell Strahorn, *Fifteen Thousand Miles by Stage* (New York: G. P. Putnam's Sons, 1911), 77–81. Present Highway 91 closely follows this trail. Another travel reminiscence describing a group of VIPs over this route in 1875 is William Emerson Strong, *A Trip to the Yellowstone National Park in July, August, and September, 1875,* Introduction by Richard A. Bartlett (Norman: University of Oklahoma Press, 1968), 15–17.

9. Lawrence G. Lashbrook, "The Utah Northern Railroad, 1871–1878" in *The Golden Spike,* Edited by David E. Miller (Salt Lake City: University of Utah Press, 1973), 63–77; Mrs. Mary B. Richards, *Camping Out in the Yellowstone* (Salem, Massachusetts: Newcomb and Gauss, 1910), 3–22.

10. Pomeroy, *In Search of the Golden West,* 86.

11. Richards, *Camping Out,* 9.

12. Ibid., 10–15.

13. Norton, *Wonder-Land Illustrated,* 54.

14. Windham Thomas Windham-Quin, 4th Earl of Dunraven, *The Great Divide* (London: Chatto and Windus, 1876), 208–11.

15. Richards, *Camping Out,* 14–17.

16. Strahorn, *Fifteen Thousand Miles by Stage,* 258–59; Richards, *Camping Out,* 22–23. Marshall's Hotel was at the foot of a ridge due west of the present road through the Lower Geyser Basin. Nothing is left of it, the site having been cleared during the depression by the Civilian Conservation Corps. See also Lee H. Whittlesey, "Marshall's Hotel in Yellowstone Park," *Montana,* Vol. 30, No. 4 (October, 1980), 42–51.

17. Captain William Ludlow, *Report of a Reconnaissance from Carroll, Montana Territory, on the Upper Missouri, to the Yellowstone National Park and Return in the Summer of 1875* (Washington: Government Printing Office, 1876), 16. See also the Earl of Dunraven's description, *The Great Divide,* 55–56.

18. Mabel Cross Osmund, "Memoirs of a Trip Through the Yellowstone National Park in 1874," manuscript in custody of the Yellowstone Park Library; Strong, *A Trip to the Yellowstone Park,* 33; quotation from S. Weir Mitchell, M.D., "Through the Yellowstone Park to Fort Custer," *Lippincott's Magazine,* Vol. 25, No. 4 (June, 1880), 690. Fort Custer was established in 1877 on the Little Big Horn near the Custer Battlefield. See Mark H. Brown, *The Plainsmen of the Yellowstone* (Lincoln: University of Nebraska Press, 1969), 316.

19. Henry J. Winser, *The Yellowstone National Park: A Manual for Tourists* (New York: Putnam's, 1883), 13. This is another of the early park guides. That it was

issued by a New York publisher attests to the widespread interest in Yellowstone even at that early date.

20. Winser, *Yellowstone National Park*, 25; Strahorn, *Fifteen Thousand Miles by Stage*, 268; Richards, *Camping Out*, 32.

21. Mitchell, "Through the Yellowstone Park," 693.

22. M. A. Switzer, "1876 Trip to the Geysers Written as a Diary in a Book Dated 1874," original in custody of Montana State University Library, Bozeman, Montana; *Livingston Enterprise*, July 18, 1885; *Bozeman Avant Courier*, May 26, 1877.

23. General P. H. Sheridan and W. T. Sherman, *Reports of Inspection Made in the Summer of 1877 by General P. H. Sheridan and W. T. Sherman of Country North of the Union Pacific Railroad* (Washington: G.P.O., 1878), 30–33; Robert G. Athearn, *William Tecumseh Sherman and the Settlement of the West* (Norman: University of Oklahoma Press, 1956), 317–22; Joseph T. Durkin, *General Sherman's Son* (New York: Farrar, Strauss, and Cudahy, 1959), 46; Tom Sherman, "The National Park," in *The Woodstock Letters* (a periodical issued by the Jesuits at Woodstock College, Maryland), Vol. 2 (1882), 25–42. I have also examined the W. T. Sherman Papers in the Manuscripts Division, Library of Congress. Box No. 55 contains Sherman's letters from the park as well as a letter to Sherman from Justice Waite expressing satisfaction with his (the Justice's) recovery from a horseback accident there.

24. Strong, *A Trip to Yellowstone Park*, 165.

25. Ibid., 81–86.

26. The Nez Perce have been the subject of a number of excellent books. Although it is often confusing, Mark H. Brown, *The Flight of the Nez Perce* (New York: Putnam's, 1967) is the best of what Colonel Brown calls an "estimate of the situation." Chapter 20, "The Yellowstone Park Tourists," leaves little to be added. Also useful is Merrill D. Beal, *"I Will Fight No More Forever": Chief Joseph and the Nez Perce War* (Seattle: University of Washington Press, 1963).

27. Sheridan and Sherman, *Reports of Inspection Made in the Summer of 1877*, 30–33; Athearn, *William Tecumseh Sherman*, 317–22; Sherman Papers, Sherman to brother, August 23, 1877.

28. Beal, *"I Will Fight No More,"* 156–69. Actually the situation was more complex because the units were constantly moving. One might with justification use army jargon to describe it: "All fouled up," since the troops failed to catch their prey save Miles's men on the plains of north-central Montana. Brown, 298–354, details the confusion and shows why plans failed.

29. Beal, *"I Will Fight No More,"* 163–164; Brown, *Flight of the Nez Perce*, 314–16; Edwin J. Stanley, *Rambles in Wonderland, or, A Trip Through the Great Yellowstone Park*, 5th edition (Nashville: Publishing House of the Methodist Episcopal Church, South, 1898), 175–78. Shivley's narration appears in Frank D. Carpenter, *Adventures in Geyserland*, edited by Heister Dean Guie and Lucullus Virgil McWhorter (Cald-

well, Idaho: Caxton Printers, 1935), Appendix 2. This is a reprint of Frank D. Carpenter, *The Wonders of Geyser Land* (Black Earth, Wis.: Burnett, 1878). See also S. G. Fisher, "Journal of S. G. Fisher, Chief of Scouts to General O. O. Howard During the Campaign Against the Nez Perces Indians, 1877," *Contributions of the Historical Society of Montana*, Vol. 2 (1896), 272.

30. Sources for this narration are Carpenter, *Adventures in Geyserland*, and Mrs. George D. Cowan, "Reminiscences of a Pioneer Life," which appeared in a short-lived newspaper, *Wonderland* (Gardiner, Montana, March 12, 1904), copy in Yellowstone Park Library.

31. My narration of the Helena tourists' experiences is based upon the following sources: Andrew J. Weikert, "Journal of the Tour Through the Yellowstone National Park, in August and September, 1877," *Contributions of the Historical Society of Montana*, Vol. 3 (1900), 153–74; "Stewart's Story," *Bozeman Avant Courier*, September 27, 1877; "Ben Stone's Account," Ibid., September 6, 1877.

32. Fisher, "Journal," 175; Brown, *Flight of the Nez Perce*, 338–39. Merrill Beal gives a somewhat more intricate description of the Nez Perce's probable route (*I Will Fight No More Forever*, 189). For more about General Howard and Yellowstone, see John A. Carpenter, *Sword and Olive Branch: Oliver Otis Howard* (Pittsburgh: University of Pittsburgh Press, 1964), 260–78, and Whittlesey, "Marshall's Hotel in Yellowstone Park."

33. Wayne F. Replogle, *Yellowstone's Bannock Indian Trails* (Yellowstone Park, Wyo.: Yellowstone Library and Museum Association, 1956). For information on the Bannock War, I have used General John Gibbon, "Report of the Commanding General of the Department of Dakota, General Gibbon Commanding," *Annual Report of the Secretary of War*, 45th Cong., 3rd Sess., House Exec. Doc. No. 1, 1878, Vol. 1. See also George F. Brimlow, *The Bannock Indian Wars of 1878* (Caldwell, Idaho: The Caxton Printers, 1958), 202–30.

34. A. D. Wilson, "Report of A. D. Wilson, Chief Topographer," in F. V. Hayden, United States Geological and Geographical Survey of the Territories, *Eleventh Annual Report* (Washington: G.P.O., 1878), 649; 657–58; Brimlow, *Bannock Indian Wars*, 183.

35. Office of the Secretary of the Interior, PMLR, Norris to Schurz, August 4, 1878; Ibid., Norris, "Preliminary Report," November 10, 1878.

36. Mrs. Alice Blackwell Baldwin, *Memoirs of the Late Frank D. Baldwin, Major General, U.S.A.*, edited by Brigadier General W. C. Brown, Colonel C. C. Smith, and E. A. Brininstool (Los Angeles: Press of the Wetzel Publishing Company, 1929), 22. See also General Miles's letter to General Sherman from Fort Keogh in which Miles says, "As you will remember I anticipated the movements of the Bannocks and having taken one hundred old soldiers who had been in these Indian fights I was prepared to take them [the Indians] in. . . ." W. T. Sherman Papers, Box 48.

37. Gibbon, "Report," 67. Those Indians who escaped from Miles were captured

near the headwaters of Wind River on September 12 by Lieutenant Bishop of the 5th Cavalry. Ibid., Brimlow, *Bannock Indian Wars*, 186.

38. Disbursed throughout the park papers in the Yellowstone archives are a few references to rumors of Indians hunting in the southwest or southern part of the reservation.

39. For an overview of the Hayden Survey in Yellowstone see Richard A. Bartlett, *Great Surveys of the American West* (Norman; University of Oklahoma Press, 1962, 1980), 35–73; for a detailed essay on Hayden's explorations in 1871 and his part in the creation of the park, see Bartlett, *Nature's Yellowstone* (Albuquerque: University of New Mexico Press, 1974), 188–93. The report is listed as Ferdinand Vandiveer Hayden, United States Geological and Geographical Survey of the Territories, *Twelfth Annual Report*, two vols., Vol. 2 (Washington: G.P.O., 1883).

40. Sidford Hamp, "Exploring the Yellowstone with Hayden, 1872: Diary of Sidford Hamp," Edited by Herbert O. Brayer, *Annals of Wyoming*, Vol. 14 (October, 1942), 252–98.

41. Arnold Hague, *Geology of the Yellowstone Park*, U.S. Geological Survey Monograph No. 32, Part 2 (Hague never completed Part I), (Washington: G.P.O., 1899); E. T. Allen and Arthur L. Day, *Hot Springs of the Yellowstone National Park* (Washington: Carnegie Institution of Washington, 1935). A newer pamphlet that gives a glimpse of a massive study of Yellowstone's geology using modern research techniques is William R. Keefer, "The Geologic Story of Yellowstone National Park," U.S. Geological Survey Bulletin No. 1347 (Washington: G.P.O., 1972). The survey is supposed to produce a massive, modern survey of Yellowstone's geology, but it had not appeared as of 1984.

42. Quoted in Captain William A. Jones, *Report Upon the Reconnaissance of Northwestern Wyoming, Including Yellowstone National Park Made in the Summer of 1873*, 43rd Cong., 1st Sess., House Exec. Doc. 285, 1875, 44. Serial No. 1615. Portions of Jones's *Report* appear in Kenneth H. Baldwin, *Enchanted Enclosure: The Army Engineers and Yellowstone Park* (Washington: G.P.O., 1976), 45–63.

43. Jones, *Report*, 1–6; Theodore B. Comstock, "Geological Report," in Ibid., 85–191; "The Yellowstone National Park," *American Naturalist*, Vol. 8, No. 2 (February, 1874), 65–79 and No. 3 (March, 1874), 155–66; "Geology of Western Wyoming," *American Journal of Science and Arts*, Vol. 6, No. 36 (December, 1873), 426–32. Parry also wrote "Botanical Observations in Western Wyoming," *American Naturalist*, Vol. 8, No. 3 (March, 1874), 175–80. An interesting narration of the Jones expedition is Paul LeHardy, "Expedition into Yellowstone Plateau under Captain W. A. Jones in 1873," typescript in Yellowstone Library.

44. Strong, *A Trip to Yellowstone Park*, 34; Ludlow, *Report of a Reconnaissance;* Baldwin, *Enchanted Enclosure*, 67–83. An intriguing novella which has Captain Ludlow and his progeny as its characters is Jim Harrison, *Legends of the Fall* (New York: Delacorte Press/Seymour Lawrence, 1979).

45. Ludlow, *Report of a Reconnaissance,* 26;35.

46. Orrin H. and Lorraine G. Bonney, *Battle Drums and Geysers: Lieutenant Doane* (Chicago: The Swallow Press, 1970); Robert B. Betts, *Along the Ramparts of the Tetons* (Boulder: Colorado Associated University Press, 1979), 127–37. Doane's own narration is interesting reading; he wrote well. I have read a copy entitled "Exploration of Snake River from Yellowstone Lake to Columbia" in custody of the Yellowstone Park Library. In 1878 Doane applied unsuccessfully for the superintendency of the park. Office of the Secretary of the Interior, PMLR, Doane to Major Brisbin, Commanding Officer at Fort Ellis, July 21, 1878.

47. This expedition is described in George Crook, *General George Crook, His Autobiography* (Norman: University of Oklahoma Press, 1946, 1960), 235–37.

48. The brief narration of Sheridan's 1882 trip is taken from Lieutenant-Colonel James F. Gregory, "Report of Lieutenant-Colonel James F. Gregory" in "Report of Lieutenant General P. H. Sheridan. . . of his Expedition Through the Big Horn Mountains," (Washington: G.P.O., 1882), 19–35.

49. *Annual Report of the Secretary of War for 1875* (Washington: G.P.O., 1876), Vol. 1, 27–28.

50. Ludlow, *Report of a Reconnaissance,* 26; 36.

51. Office of the Secretary of the Interior, PMLR, summer of 1878.

52. "Report of General P. H. Sheridan . . . Through the Big Horn Mountains." See also Richard A. Bartlett, "The Army, Conservation, and Ecology: The National Park Assignment," in *The United States Army in Peacetime,* edited by Robin Higham and Carol Brandt (Manhattan, Kansas: Military Affairs/Aerospace Historian Publishing Co., 1975). 41–58.

53. Aubrey Haines, for many years Yellowstone Park historian, estimates the cumulative number of visitors to the park through 1882 at 8,330. *The Yellowstone Story* (Boulder: Colorado Associated University Press, 1977), two vols., Vol. 2, 478.

54. Earl of Dunraven, *The Great Divide,* 347–49.

CHAPTER TWO

The Railroad Age: 1883 to 1915

*I*n 1883 railroad and population expansion burst upon Yellowstone. It was the park's first vintage year. Afterwards, though some years were better than others, annual visitation steadily increased. For the affluent, Pullman-carriding tourist, Yellowstone offered unusual sights of geysers, wildlife, and a grand canyon, all of which were observed under circumstances of progressively better food, shelter, and transportation. The great middle class, Very Important People, and many of the super rich considered "doing Yellowstone" a part of life's adventure. They helped imprint the park in the national psyche: the national psyche in turn prompted still more visitation to Wonderland. Who these people were and what they experienced is our concern.

Just as in viniculture, so in the lives of people and institutions, there are good and bad years. Life may go along for an extended period on an even keel, but eventually momentous events take place, or business is unusually good, or catastrophically poor, and changes occur. Such a year in Yellowstone's history was 1883. What happened there was a microcosm of the state of the Union. The year was exceptionally prosperous, as had been the previous two years, and people were energetic, restless, politically conniving, and bullish. It was one of those years when the prevailing assumption was that this was the best of all possible worlds.

Prosperity was particularly apparent in the great Northwest. In 1883 railroad builder Henry Villard drove the final spike of the Northern Pacific just outside of the west Montana railroad town of Garrison. Simultaneously the N.P. was advertising the vast lands of the Northwest, selling those vacant prairies to colonizers for a pittance. Well was management aware that the railroad's continuing prosperity depended upon settlement and productive activity along its main line.

The boom towns of Bismarck, Mandan, Glendive, Richardson, Gladstone, Miles City, Big Horn, and Billings sprouted out of the windswept prairies like mushrooms after a rain. About fifty-six miles north of the Yellowstone boundary the railroad town of Livingston came into being.

Years before, the site had been nothing but a sagebrush flat along the Yellowstone River, but now, in 1883, it was a bustling rail and tourist center boasting a population of nearly two thousand. It was, said a visiting Englishman, "a village . . . rising, progressing, active, and pushing." Another writer described the growing settlement as "pulsating with all the vigor and virility of the West . . . ."[1]

Livingston citizens then as today profited from the park and took an active interest in it. During the railroad era supplies and tourists both had to be transferred from the Northern Pacific main line to the Park Branch Line which, again reflecting the bullish activity of the times, was constructed from survey to final spike in just six months. Even though a railroad can be built more rapidly and cheaply than an automobile highway, the Park Branch Line was quite an achievement. From Livingston, at 4,491 feet, the rails climbed to 5,174 at Cinnabar, "using easy curves and moderate grades" to "permit a safe speed of forty-five miles per hour."

A manifestation of the interest in Yellowstone and the Northwest was the composition of the first regular passenger train up the line. It included a luxurious Northern Pacific coach, the "Montana," bearing the chief engineers of the N.P. and the Branch Line. Also attached was a beautiful car belonging to the Louisville and Nashville Railroad, carrying that company's vacationing VIPs. The second train up, thereafter known as the afternoon train, had attached to it the "Railway Age," said to be the finest railroad car in the world.[2]

Local folk were delighted with the completion of the Park Branch. No one in the region believed that Cinnabar (a community downriver a few miles from Gardiner) would be the permanent end of the line. The town of Cinnabar had been platted by Northern Pacific surveyors when land litigation prevented the railroad from obtaining a right-of-way on to Gardiner, the acknowledged park gateway.

That setback did not deter Gardiner's boosters. They were making auspicious plans for their future. Early in June 1883, the town boasted a heterogeneous population of nearly two hundred souls, most of whom were living in tents. All this array was lined up, like soldiers at inspection, along the north side of the street that constituted the park boundary. A number of businesses were flourishing, including twenty-one saloons, six restaurants, and five general merchandise stores. "The town," commented a reporter for the *Livingston Enterprise,* "is fairly orderly, but its inhabitants are probably not conspicuous for religious tendencies as two dance halls and four houses of ill fame flourish in their midst." Late in July, gold was discovered within the town limits, a mining district was organized, and Gardiner experienced a brief flurry of placer mining.[3]

Still another center of activity was into the park, northeast to Lamar junction, up the Lamar Valley and Soda Butte Creek into the mountain bastions just outside the boundary to the tiny mining camp dubbed Cooke City. Its two hundred inhabitants thrived on dreams of future wealth. They lived for the present in dirt-covered log shacks along the narrow gulch that provided a main street with "barely enough room for two parallel buildings to occupy level ground." Proud Cooke City could boast of neither a hotel nor a regular eating house. Still, times were good in the camp; boosters insisted it was a "second Leadville." All they needed was cheap transportation.

Trouble was, the only practical route to the outside world was by way of the Lamar Valley in Yellowstone Park. This fact was to complicate park history for a full decade, into the mid-1890s. That the route was practical for a railroad from an engineering point of view greatly enhanced the threat to park integrity, for the demand came at the height of railroad construction throughout the nation. It was rumored that the Northern Pacific and/or Rufus Hatch, the entrepreneur involved with the railroad and the park hotels, would ask Congress for the privilege of laying rails into the park. Residents believed that a spur line would branch to the east from inside the reservation, running up the Lamar Valley to the mining community of Cooke City.[4]

The confidence of local inhabitants north of the park received encouragement not only from signs of railroad construction and town growth, but from the presence of notables visiting the park in the 1883 season. Several score of celebrities were, for the most part, attached to one of a half dozen groups: President Arthur's party, Hatch's "dudes and dudesses," Henry Villard's trainloads of excursionists celebrating completion of the Northern Pacific, the Associated Press editorial group, a United States Geological Survey field group, and numerous representatives of the great and near-great in the middle years of the Gilded Age. The *Enterprise* staff that summer was kept busy checking the arrival and departure of notables.[5]

Of all the parties to Wonderland in 1883, President Arthur's was the most publicized. Politics was a national pastime in those years; naturally the press refused to leave Arthur alone. His plight vis-a-vis the press was not unlike that of his successors a century later. As a result, that portion of America that read newspapers—and that included just about everyone who was literate—learned more about Yellowstone National Park than it had in all the years before.

Arthur, just fifty-two, had suffered a chill on the night of the nineteenth of April. Although the public, aware that there was no vice-president to succeed him should he die, was assured of the president's recovery, his aides were aware of his failing health. Arthur stood six feet two inches tall and, like so many Gilded Age politicians and robber barons, had grown corpulent. When a lightened work schedule did not help, a summer trip was organized to Yellowstone National Park. Possibly this would restore his vigor.[6]

In the politically charged atmosphere of 1883, someone immediately raised the cry that the public was going to pay for this junket which, it was said, would include the erection of a telegraph line and the hire of 180 horses. The official reply was that it was "not a pleasure party for the benefit of the President, but an official exploration party" with the president along as the guest of General Sheridan, who had invited him months ago and would accompany him.[7] This was the nineteenth-century counterpart of the politician using an Air Force plane which "had to make the journey anyway." Substitute horses for airplanes and the situation remains the same.

By July 12 General Oliver O. Howard, who had traveled West to make preparations for the trip, was back in Omaha and the president's route was announced. He would ride the Union Pacific to Rawlins, Wyoming Territory, then by wagon or army ambulance to Fort Washakie, (near present Lander), thence "by the route followed by General Sheridan last year." Supply depots were to be established, and relay stations and soldier couriers provided for above the Fort, which was the terminus of the telegraph. It was arranged that the party would travel by horses or mules from Washakie on.[8]

Among those with the president as he waited on an early August sabbath at Green River were Secretary of War Robert Lincoln; Senator George Graham Vest and his son, George Jr.; General Philip Sheridan and his brother, Colonel Michael Sheridan; General Anson Stager of Chicago; Governor Schuyler Crosby of Montana; and Major James Forwood, a surgeon. Several guides had reported for duty, most important of whom was Yellowstone resident Jack Baronett, and the military escort was waiting. F. Jay Haynes, the Yellowstone photographer, was along to record the journey on film.[9]

As planned, the president and his guests rode wagons to Fort Washakie and horses thereafter. By August 23 they were encamped at the northeast end of Lewis Lake in the park. General Sheridan had forbidden hunting, though deer, antelope, elk, Richardson grouse, and ducks were prevalent. But the fishing was unrestricted and superb.[10]

Many an American fisherman must have developed a hankering to go to Yellowstone after reading about the president's piscatorial success. He definitely enjoyed good fishing. Although one newspaper quipped that his first trout was to be embalmed and forwarded to the Smithsonian, even the critics had to accept reports of his fishing prowess. Actually it is more a commentary on the natural, undisturbed richness of the trout streams in that part of

the country in 1883, than a testament to the president's abilities with a fly
rod. At one cast he caught three fish weighing four and a quarter pounds in
the aggregate. Senator Vest took the most fish, but the president's weighed
the most, totaling 105 pounds.[11]

After more than three weeks in the field, the party arrived at Mammoth
Hot Springs where they encamped in the superintendent's yard. Some of the
vacationers were hinting that the "roughing it" had lasted a bit too long.
Physically they were suffering from sunburn and mosquito bites; financially
some were hurting thanks to Governor Crosby's consistent winnings at the
nightly poker party. Moreover, the president's aides sensed that he did not
feel his best. Arthur had exchanged his horse for the comforts of an army
ambulance during some of his time in Yellowstone. "The President is by no
means indisposed," wrote Colonel Sheridan, "but, though his cheeks are
bronzed and healthy looking, he looks old and worn and stoops as he rides.
The long journey has evidently been too fatiguing."[12]

During his afternoon at Mammoth Hot Springs Arthur chatted with all
comers around a big campfire. These included some Englishmen who could
not believe that the man with the sunburned nose and shabby clothes was
President of the United States. That evening, dressed a little more formally,
the president "held court" at the hotel. Then he boarded the train from
Cinnabar for Washington. The next year (1884) he was repudiated by his
own party, retired to private life, and died of Bright's disease in November
1886.

President Chester Arthur's junket surely gave Yellowstone the widest
publicity it had yet received. Articles about the chief executive in the park
appeared daily in the press for at least three weeks, sufficiently long to fix
Wonderland in the national psyche. Many thousands who had not given
Yellowstone more than a passing thought now cherished a desire to visit the
fabulous land. They were also an electorate that was likely to want the park
protected.

However, the eighties were still an era of class. After all, who, save the rich
or distinctly upper middle class, could afford the cost of a train trip to the
park? Who else could take the time? Yellowstone entrepreneurs were certainly aware of the financial status of their clientele. The principal investor,
Wall Street tycoon Rufus Hatch, set out to popularize the park both as a
place to visit and a place in which to invest. Only one giant hotel had been
built (and it was not yet completed); he would need much more money in
order to build the others he had planned. What better way to raise money

and advertise the park than by giving a trainload of European investors a free park visit? Moreover, such a flock of dignitaries would prompt other wealthy tourists from across the seas to visit Wonderland.

Such were the thoughts behind "Uncle Rufus's" trainload of English and European entrepreneurs, aristocrats, and newspapermen who visited Yellowstone in the summer of 1883. "His collection of celebrities is simply wonderful," commented one reporter. "Barnum never succeeded in bringing together, even in wax, so many illustrious personages."[13]

All told, Hatch recruited more than fifty men, women, and young adults. A few were Americans, including correspondents for the *New York Times*, the *New York World*, the *New York Tribune*, and the owner of the *Chicago Tribune*, Joseph Medill. From overseas came John LeSage, editor of the *London Telegraph;* William Hardman of the *London Morning Post;* Baron Albert Salvador of Paris, the diplomatic writer of *Figaro;* and Dr. Oskar Bergruen of Vienna, an economist who wrote for both the *Imperial Gazette* and Munich's *Algemeine Zeitung*. The remaining forty or more guests were people of wealth, including wives and relatives.[14]

The guests had to pay for their ocean passage, but from Hoboken, where they debarked and boarded Hatch's special train, until their return to port weeks later, they were the guests of "Uncle Rufus." With its baggage car, Pullmans, dining car and observation car, wrote the *London Times* correspondent, it was truly "American yachting on wheels." Finally the train, five days out of St. Paul, entered the mountains; before sundown it pulled into the Livingston station.[15]

The long boredom that characterized the trip across the northern prairies gave way to anticipation with the knowledge that they would be in Wonderland the next day. Just at sunrise their train pulled out of Livingston and began the long climb up the valley on the Park Branch Line. As the train passed the Gate of the Mountains, the sun disappeared again behind the great north-south-running mountain bastion on their left. An hour lapsed before it rose again above the peaks to flood the valley in which their train, like a centipede in that gargantuan land, chugged southward.[16]

Three hours out of Livingston the engine and cars screeched to a halt. The end of the tracks consisted of a few planks alongside the rails, with some benches occupied by "rough-looking men"; nearby was a canvas "drinking saloon," its bartender prepared to soothe dry thoats with American whiskey—for a price. One suspects that the timid dudes huddled together, eyeing the locals with a combination of curiosity and fear, as the lounging, unshaven frontiersmen appraised them with a combination of curiosity and contempt.[17]

While waiting for the park conveyances to arrive, Hatch's dudes and dudesses, who numbered seventy-five with additions along the way, had their attention diverted to two professional hunters and a third man sitting dejectedly on a mound. The dejected one was described to the tourists as a murderer, though he looked as "docile as a lamb, and the least formidable of the three." They were told that in Gardiner this "mad Dutchman" (as he was known) had killed a man in front of Charlie's Beer Hall, the result of a fracas involving four dollars. His captors, Bill Germayne and George W. Grow, from the Little Missouri country, had come to see the park "and follow their avocation if good opportunity offered." Learning of the murder and suspecting the pedestrian they had met earlier in the day, they had crept upon his camp and wakened him at midnight with pistols aimed at his head. Meekly, the "mad Dutchman" had surrendered.[18]

Finally the rolling stock arrived. Most of the vehicles were the typical American buckboard, a wagon with seats bolted to the floorboards which in turn were attached directly to the axles. They sported canvas tops, but the sides were open to the elements. Most wagons carried eight passengers two abreast, with luggage underneath the seats. Riders held on for dear life as the wagons clattered through dust raised by the caravan "like an army train." They suffered still more discomfort because the luggage kept sliding backwards and forwards.

Once they halted for refreshments at a tent saloon whose prices, one correspondent wrote, like the hills, were high. Commenting that the half dollar was almost the smallest coin thereabouts, it was predicted by one of the shorn lambs that the proprietor hoped soon to return East a millionaire.[19]

By noon the party had arrived "at the rough wooden steps of a huge wooden structure," the Mammoth Hot Springs Hotel, "as yet incomplete," wrote the *Times* man, "like everything else in this country of magnificent scenery and inflated prices." It seemed impossible that so imposing, so modern, so plush a hotel could have been erected in such a wilderness. "It was simply the most remarkable product of civilization in my experience," Hardman of the *London Morning Post* said, adding that none of the party appreciated its true value until they had quitted it. Electric lights, two billiard tables, and a huge Steinway piano amazed them most.[20]

"Hunters, drivers, settlers, and 'cowboys' [were] . . . congregated in the great hall of the hotel until it resembled a stage fixed for the 'supers' in 'Fra Diavolo,'" Hardman noted. "Sombrero hats, high leather boots and leggings, belts of cartridges, and revolvers abounded, especially at night." It rather alarmed the ladies, but in due time they got accustomed to it.[21]

After crawling over the Hot Springs terraces and hanging up "horseshoes, bottles, jugs, cups and other articles to be coated and carried off as curiosities," the Hatch party slept that night at the hotel and headed out the next day in their improvised wagons for the Norris Geyser Basin. Forest fires had swept over most of the region they were to see, making it a desolate, dusty journey. Finally they arrived at Hatch's "canvastown" hotel in a meadow close to the Norris Geyser Basin, twenty-five miles deeper inside the park.

Indeed, "Uncle Rufus's" hotels, save for the one at Mammoth, had not advanced beyond the tent stage in 1883. The Norris hostelry boasted all of six tents in a row, "the most surprising sort of inns that ever attracted a traveler," complained the *London Times* reporter. "They charge a sovereign a day, like the most sumptuous hotels in America, and the guests have to behave very well indeed to get any accommodations."*

Arriving at Norris tired, hungry, and dusty, he found a single bench with two wash basins for the entire company, provided they brought the water up from the river themselves. The landlady insisted that "one towel was enough for any two men in the outfit." Looking glasses were noticeable by their absence and the only chairs were in the dining area. Four beds filled each tent. Two persons were to sleep in a bed with overflow sleeping on the dining tent floor. A single candle stuck in an empty bottle provided light. "The pillows," Hardman complained, were "the thinnest ever seen in this free country, with not a sheet or pillow-case in the entire 'hotel'."

Meals, though good, were served only at regular hours, with too few chairs at the table. "The free-born citizens of the Great Republic who 'run' this establishment are independent enough, too, to brook neither criticism nor complaint," Hardman added. "With nothing to eat, and not a house or shed within twenty miles, you are at their mercy, and they know it."

The weary tourists retired early, but the beds were very hard. "You were ready to rise very early in the morning," Hardman added, "to shiver in the cold wind outside the tent while you wait for your turn at the two wash basins provided for the forty or fifty people who usually huddle overnight."[22]

In the evening they found the Norris Basin especially eerie, fires having decimated the woods, leaving many a gaunt stump that took on ominous contours in the night shadows. Other visitors' campfires flamed merrily here and there. The odor of sulphur, and the persistent new springs appearing even in the roadway, created an uneasy feeling of instability. "Some of the visitors carried off bushels of specimens of the geyserite incrustations," one dude commented, while Hardman described the unsuccessful attempts of his party to make the Monarch geyser erupt. "We did our best to provoke it," he said, "by pitching great lumps of rocks down his throat so as to destroy the equilibrium below." But nothing happened save a little grumbling from the geyser.[23]

---

*Twenty shillings equalled a sovereign or a pound. Hatch was charging at least $5.00 for a bed in his tent "hotels."

The second day's trip, from Norris to the Upper Geyser Basin, was worse than the first: the "road" filled with stumps, occasional bogs, one or two sections running right up the river bed, and at one place leaning toward the Gibbon chasm, the passengers "holding on by their eyelids." Just at sunset the guide announced that he had "brought them to the front door of Hell." They had arrived at another canvastown, the Firehole Hotel. It consisted of about twenty tents formed in a semicircle. As at Norris, smoke emitted from a forest fire in the woods nearby. Again the tourists suffered inconveniences, but Old Faithful and other geysers made even the grime, the dust, and the poor accommodations endurable.[24]

The next day Hatch's guests went over Mary Mountain to Yellowstone's Grand Canyon. The canvastown there was arranged "prettily" on two sides of a street with the large dining tent at the central point. It was, said the *London Times* reporter, "the best kept of all these stopping places, and is the most comfortably appointed for the 'roughing' process that the park tour requires." From Yellowstone Falls most of the party retraced their trail, although the *Times* man and a few others pushed on over Mount Washburn to Tower Falls, and on to Mammoth. Over a period of several days the several sections of the Hatch entourage straggled in. A number of them were ill, or had suffered slight accidents, had tales to tell of bad water and worse food, but quickly renewed their spirits at the big Mammoth Hotel.[25]

After meeting President Arthur, the Hatch visitors left the park. The sky was incredibly blue, the atmosphere amazingly clear, and a cool breeze caressed their cheeks. They discovered that in the ten days or so they had been in the park the railroad had advanced seven miles to Cinnabar. Feeling like explorers returning to civilization, they entered the cars, met with their black porters, and rejoined the mainstream of civilization.[26]

Rufus Hatch later boasted of this great promotional scheme. He said it cost him $40,000. "It is worth millions to the Northwest," he said. "Foreign capitalists will bring $100,000,000 into the country to invest this year." Yet by late autumn Hatch was in serious financial difficulties, and by winter his Yellowstone Park Improvement Company was bankrupt. So too did the Northern Pacific pass through difficult times. Henry Villard, the flamboyant German immigrant who had pushed the line to completion, was out, replaced early in 1884 by Frederick Billings.

As autumn came on, the people of the park and the upper Yellowstone Valley could look back upon the most active, exciting, and varied season in the park's history. Some old-timers later insisted that never since has the park been such an exciting topic of conversation. It had welcomed European nobility, people of wealth, a president of the United States, many a politician, Supreme Court justices, government geologists, journalists, a murderer, railroad surveyors, and army brass. Superintendent Pat Conger estimated that

20,000* people had visited the park during the season, about a fourth of them coming by rail and stage, and the remainder by private conveyances.[27]

How did Yellowstone fare from all this activity? From the 1883 season on, the park was a fixture of the American scene, a national treasure well known and cherished by the American people. No longer was Yellowstone National Park considered as inaccessible to ordinary people as were the Swiss Alps or Asia's Himalayas. If a president could visit it, so could any other American. The Northern Pacific, now a transcontinental railroad, was already advertising the park widely, if prematurely (since facilities were still hopelessly inadequate for heavy visitation). And Hatch's entourage had expanded knowledge of Wonderland into England and the continent.

But in terms of its wildlife, thermal wonders, and forests, the park had suffered more in 1883 than in any previous season. Though vigorously denying its guilt, all evidence indicates that the new hotel company had contracted for elk meat obtained in the park and had been indiscriminate in cutting timber for its hotels and adjoining buildings. For these actions the company could be blamed, but vandalism to geysers and the firing of woods were actions of which company personnel were probably innocent. The habit of conservation, the implied, subconscious understanding on the part of tourists as to how they should and should not behave toward the park, its flora and fauna and thermal wonders, had not yet crystallized in the visitor's mind. The tourist-in-general had wreaked substantial damage. Soldiers escorting VIP groups from the president down had added to the destruction. They did start fires, shoot game, and harm the geysers and hot springs. The greatest damage of the season was attributed to President Arthur's escorts. "One soldier," so it was reported, "took a long pole and pried off a piece from the mouth of 'Old Faithful' geyser, that weighed over 150 pounds," for which the culprit received two days in the guardhouse. The authenticity of this incident is subject to question, but the vandalism was in keeping with crimes committed against the formations.[28]

Fortunate is Yellowstone to have seasons. Autumn arrived. The park was vacated of humanity save for a few caretakers, the superintendent and his small force, a few poachers, and possibly a party or two of horse thieves herding their booty across the Skull and Crossbones Trail. A soft blue haze covered the mountains; aspens flared in yellow and red and gold. In the freezing temperatures of night and the coolness of the days incipient forest fires, which tended to "boil up" at midday in summertime, finally died out. The land and the forest and the animals were exhausted after a long season's run. On October 1 the first heavy snowstorm struck.

---

*Aubrey Haines estimates the 1883 visitation at 5,000 and he is certainly closer to the reality. *Yellowstone Story* 2, 478.

The hamlets of Gardiner and Livingston settled down for the long winter. Perhaps for lack of other news the perceptive editor of the *Enterprise* asked the why of the "glorious sunsets" his readers had noticed recently— "brilliant crimson coloring the sky at and long after sunset." On December 12 people observed an even more gorgeous display. "The light, filmy waves of clouds were dyed a blood red color along the whole northwest horizon, and remained so after 6 o'clock, or fully two hours after the sun had sunk behind the mountain horizon," observed the editor. Some thought it was due to a conflagration to the west, others that the earth was passing through a meteor shower. Whatever the cause, the editor commented, "these sunset splendors are something out of the ordinary."[29]

Indeed they were out of the ordinary. In December 1883, they *were* blood red and gorgeous and indeed it *was* a rare phenomenon. Nearly five months before, on August 17 and 18, while VIPs were marveling at Yellowstone's thermal phenomena, a result of vulcanism, the great volcano of Krakatau in the Sundra Strait between Java and Sumatra had blown its top in the greatest eruption of recorded time. An estimated cubic mile of rock was blasted into the atmosphere as volcanic dust. Now the resultant cloud had circled the world, giving birth to the blood-red, glowing sunsets, so noticeable in the Yellowstone country, at the end of the park's first vintage year: 1883.

From the vintage year until 1915, a generation, Yellowstone experienced relative tranquility. Visitors arrived by train, not just on the Northern Pacific, but after 1901 via the Burlington to Cody, and after 1908 via the Union Pacific to West Yellowstone; they then rode stagecoaches into the park. Canvastowns gave way to cavernous wooden structures such as Old Faithful Inn, Lake Hotel, and Canyon Hotel. Roads improved, but dust remained exasperating. After 1886 the army policed the park in a military way, "persuading" many a tourist to respect the woods and flowers, animals and thermal springs. There were ups and down in annual visitation, but on a graph the general trend was up, and markedly so.*

During this period the government, represented by the Department of Interior, which administered Yellowstone, and the army, which secured it, worked out a modus operandi. Visitation under the army's watchful eyes was still sufficiently low for flora and fauna to snap back every spring with little sign of permanent harm.

*Haines specifies 1897 as the first year with over 10,000 visitors; the number rises gradually to 51,895 in 1915. *The Yellowstone Story,* 2, 478.

It was a happy time in Yellowstone history. The park enjoyed worldwide prestige. Not only did Americans, tastemakers of the time, add glitter by vacationing there, but thousands of upper class foreigners joined them in marveling at nature's wonders.

In Yellowstone history this is also the era of "sagebrushers" and "couponers." "Sagebrushers" was the derisive name applied by hotel and transportation company employees to those independent people who visited the park on their own. They brought with them their food, bedding, and transportation, and shunned company facilities. These people, who earlier had been pretty much restricted to Montana and Idaho residents, now often came from farther away. A lucrative outfitting business arose from Livingston all the way up the Yellowstone Valley to the park as well as to the region beyond its western boundary. Well-to-do visitors of adventurous inclination also took advantage of the opportunity to rough it; sometimes they hired guides, cooks, and packers to make "roughing it" considerably smoother.

The couponers were affluent people who desired to "do" the park but without too much loss of comfort. They purchased package tours which included the five-day trip around the park in a horse-drawn coach and food and lodging at the big hotels. The name came naturally from the coupons they were issued for each segment of the excursion.

In the 1890s another class of couponers appeared. These were people of less means such as school teachers who had time for a Yellowstone outing but, then as now, had to do their vacationing on restricted funds. For them came into existence the camps: the Wylie Way, Shaw and Powell, and others that lasted just a season or two. Instead of overnights at the hotels, these people put up in tent camps.

The typical sleeping "tent" was floored and had wooden sides about halfway up; then canvas took over. Central facilities were provided for human ablutions and dining halls for food. The convivality around an evening campfire was considered by many to exceed anything the hotels offered to the uppity people. As for transportation, there was no difference in the quality of nags, coaches, and drivers.

Still other visitors made Yellowstone their vacation home for the season. Well-to-do and with plenty of time, they spent several weeks at one hotel and then transferred to another. This was an overfed era as well as a slower-paced one. Sitting for hours a day on a shaded veranda was not considered dull or unusual. Occasionally these patrons bestirred themselves to hire a horse to ride, or a hack or surrey to drive to places of interest. Vehicles were drawn by two or four horses; single animals pulling a vehicle stumbled over the stones and stumps in the middle of the two-tracked roads.

A sampling of the experience of sagebrushers, couponers, and a few notables adds up to an impression of enjoyment at a more leisurely pace then we experience today, and perhaps creates within us a yearning for life in a less hectic era.

In 1898 a party of twelve, mostly from Iowa, made a wagon excursion into the park from Kemmerer, Wyoming, 300 miles south of the reservation. They rode in a horse-drawn "light canvas-covered spring-wagon" and for their equipment employed a heavy emigrant wagon. They took along an extra team for use in an emergency and two good saddle ponies, "Dutch" and "Gootch," for themselves.

When they arrived at the Snake River Station, about five miles south of the park boundary, they endured a required ritual. The soldiers took their firearms and tied "the lock of the gun securely with a piece of 'red tape' and seal[ed] the knot with wax, on which [was] stamped the great seal of the United States." At one point on their journey they met a dejected party under military escort on its way to Mammoth to face Judge Meldrum, the United States commissioner in the park, for breaking the seal on their guns and killing game. The writer was thankful that his party had honored the regulations.[30]

Twelve or so years later a group of young women rode to the park on horseback by way of Lander and Dubois, Wyoming. At the check station a "cultured young foreigner . . . in command over six boys of Troop E" supplied chairs for the ladies and played a phonograph while their gun was sealed. The girls camped nearby and made fudge for the soldiers. These young women, like most visitors, had a good time in the park. Most young people were friendly, although the guests in company coaches, dressed in "white dusters and panama hats, and ladies heavily veiled to protect their complexions," were most likely to ignore the sagebrushers or glance down upon them with an air of disdain.

Most shocking to these young ladies was the failure of the Yellowstone soldiers and concessionaire employees to observe the Sabbath. "Mother mine," wrote Miss Elliott indignantly, "isn't it a sad state of affairs in a camp where there are 200 young men with souls?"[31]

One of the most charming sagebrush narratives is George W. Wingate's *Through the Yellowstone Park on Horseback*. This easterner brought his wife and seventeen-year-old daughter to Yellowstone in June 1885. At Bozeman he hired a camp crew, a four-horse wagon and three riding horses, all for eighteen dollars a day. "All the men were the best type of Western frontiersman," Wingate related, "quiet, self respecting, obliging and always respectful. . . . While they expected to be treated as equals and were so treated, there was no attempt at undue familiarity." These capable men quickly established a routine. They slept under stars with a heavy revolver handy. "They slept very lightly, and at short intervals one or the other would sit up and peer around to see if the horses were all right." Wingate wrote. "The least sort of uneasiness on the part of the latter, a snort or stamp would bring all the men to their feet like lightning."

On the road from Mammoth to Norris the Wingates "were astonished at encountering that product of Eastern civilization, a tramp." He was "blear-eyed and dirty, clothed in a patchwork of rags, with a smoky tin pot at his side." Another time they heard singing behind them. It turned out to be "a four-horse stage laden with a full cargo of clerical gentlemen . . . who . . . were making the woods fairly rattle with Sunday-school hymns." Later they met a leaderless outfit of forty tourists "with stages, baggage wagons, tents, horses, and attendants, resembling a traveling circus," all of the men quarreling among themselves.

Wingate estimated that in the twenty-six days from the railroad and return his party rode more than 460 miles until they "were brown as Indians and able to spend eight hours a day in the saddle without excessive fatigue."[32]

Some Montana folks took a trip through the park in 1885. The title of their reminiscences is one of the most amusing in the Yellowstone collection: *The National Park from the Hurricane Deck of a Cayuse, or the Leiderkrantz Expedition to Geyserland.* The book is dedicated to members of the Leiderkrantz Society of Butte, Montana, whose common love was music. It consisted of several German families with members ranging in age from four months to sixty years; they numbered thirty people in all.

These energetic, pleasure-loving people set out in mid-August by way of Anaconda, Deer Lodge, Helena, and Bozeman; in each town they presented concerts or held a ball. For transportation they used heavy covered wagons, while five of the men, including Dudley, the narrator, rode horseback. The party carried supplies enough for a five-week tour.

Dudley made comments that shed much knowledge on the Yellowstone tourist of that bygone era—and possibly on today's visitors as well. Here are his comments about the typical tourist at a hot spring: "The first thing he does is to put both hands in his pockets, straighten himself up and gaze at the spring and the geyserite formation surrounding it. He then takes his right hand out of his pocket and puts it into the spring. . . . If it is only lukewarm, or moderately hot, he takes it out slowly, wipes it off on his handkerchief and proceeds to interview another spring; but [if] it should happen to be at the boiling point, he removes his hand with alacrity and immediately says, 'whew, that's hot'—he's made a discovery, you see. . . . No matter how often he gets burned, he goes directly to another spring and repeats the operation."[33]

In 1889 a young Englishman entered the park. He came via the Northern Pacific not from the East, but from Tacoma, Victoria, Portland, and San Francisco, Japan and India. He had formed already a rather dim view of

Americans from experiences with them aboard ship, with American customs officers, and with the citizenry of San Francisco. His name was Rudyard Kipling.

Gradually his scorn and criticism changed. He fished the waters of the Yellowstone somewhere between Livingston and the park and found the river an angler's paradise. "I simply dare not give my bag," he wrote. "At the fortieth trout I gave up counting, and I had reached the fortieth in less than two hours." A young ranch wife cooked his fish. She did not wear stays, he observed, but "was beautiful by any standard of beauty." (Kipling was just twenty-three and had an eye for pretty women.)

Finally he wrote: "Today I am in the Yellowstone Park, and I wish I were dead." He had detrained at Cinnabar with a Raymond excursion group, a party of Cook's tourists in Paris being, by contrast, "angels of light."* Then, too, it was the Fourth of July, the horses were bedecked with American flags in their headstalls, and some of the women waved flags and patriotic hand-kerchiefs. Kipling described the Mammoth Hotel as "a huge yellow barn" and the park as "just a howling wilderness of three thousand square miles." He had to listen to an Independence Day oration and then watch as the vacationers shot off firecrackers on the veranda. And he noted how the ground on the hotel plateau "rings hollow as a kerosene-tin," and predicted that someday "the Mammoth Hotel, guests and all, will sink into the caverns below and be turned into a stalactite." And, one suspects, he ardently hoped so.

He was happily surprised to discover one of the soldiers guarding a hot spring formation to be "a spectacled Scot" who "had served the Queen in the Marines and a Line regiment," and who was soon joined by "the 'Henglish-man',," a Cockney who had served her Majesty in Egypt. Later a young troop-er informed him that "just now it seems the English supply all the men to the American army." Meanwhile the young writer and his round-the-park companions, an elderly Chicago couple, were viewing the thermal phe-nomena, she exclaiming "Good Lord!" every thirty seconds, her husband lamenting the waste of steam power.

Surely the good fishing, the attractive ranch wife, and his discovery that so much of the United States Cavalry was foreign born, and not a small percentage of it native to the British Empire, contributed to Kipling becom-ing more tolerant and considerably more enthusiastic about the people and the park. Or were his taunts delivered with tongue in cheek? For by the time he and the Chicago couple, and a New Hampshire man, wife, and lovely

---

*In 1881 the Boston firm of Raymond and Whitcomb had commenced guided tours into the American West. See Earl Pomeroy, *In Search of the Golden West* (New York: Alfred Knopf, 1957), 13–16.

young daughter, had gone through the silly exercise of washing their pocket handkerchiefs in a hot spring near Larry's lunch station at Norris, Kipling was captivated. The pool "turned the linen white as driven snow in five minutes," he recalled. Then he and the lovely girl "lay on the grass and laughed with sheer bliss of being alive. This I have known once in Japan, once on the banks of the Columbia . . . and once again in the Yellowstone by the light of the eyes of the maiden from New Hampshire."[34]

Kipling was just one minor figure among the stream of dignitaries into the park. Senators, representatives, governors, Supreme Court justices, cabinet officers, business tycoons, opera stars, literary figures, scientists, and their foreign counterparts visited Yellowstone in droves. (Wingate in 1885 had commented on the prevalence of foreigners, adding that Americans forsook their native land to travel in Europe. There is still validity to his comment; this explains in part the "See America First" campaigns of later years.)[35]

Henry Adams camped for five weeks in Yellowstone and the Tetons in 1894. He went there following a hectic year in which a financial panic had threatened his family's fortune. Accompanying Adams was his close friend John Hay; Hay's son, Del; geologist Joseph Paxton Iddings; W. Hallett Phillips, a Washington, D. C. lawyer and acknowledged expedition leader; and Yellowstone guide, Billy Hofer. They traveled three or four hundred miles on horseback, much of the time camping in the Two Ocean Pass area. They fished and (south of the park boundary, we presume) hunted. Neither Hay nor Adams particularly liked roughing it. "Never," wrote Adams in his *Education,* "did a band less bloody or bloodthirsty wander over the roof of the continent . . . . Compared with the Rockies in 1871," he added (when he had also been West), "the sense of wildness had vanished; one saw no possible adventures except to break one's neck as in chasing an aniseed fox." He finally ordered Billy Hofer to head for the settlement. "I am bored," Henry Adams announced.[36]

At Livingston this little man of giant intellect but small physical stature (scarlet fever was probably responsible for stunting his growth to five feet three inches), so alienated from the world in which he lived, learned of the death of his brother John Quincy. What to do? Why go home if a brother is already dead and buried? Hay and the rest of the party had already entrained for the East. "I am alone, and as I have a month to spare, I turn westward again. . . ." he wrote. "No one wants me, but by October 1 I shall probably appear at the Knickerbocker Club."[37]

Yellowstone denied to Henry Adams the will-o'-the-wisp he pursued so assiduously. From Cuba to Tahiti, from Massachusetts to Alaska to Japan to Italy to France to England and back again to Massachusetts and down to Washington, D.C., this most remarkable personage quested for—what? In Yellowstone in 1894 he "found there little to study." Whatever was Adams's quest, it was not located in Yellowstone Park.

Five years after Dr. S. Weir Mitchell had visited the reservation, he gave some professional advice to his nephew: go to Wyoming and stay on a ranch. If Dr. Mitchell had not toured Yellowstone and developed a love for the West, would he have prescribed such therapy for his nephew, Philadelphia-born Owen Wister?[38]

Young Wister followed his uncle's advice and recovered his health. He returned West in 1887 and this time entered the park. His party of four whites (two of them hired hands) and a Shoshone named Tighee entered from the Snake River Soldier Station. Ever the romantic, Wister noted the muffled thumps as the horses wound through the silent jack pine forest. "Mud pots of old hue and consistency were passed; one's horse went down into them deep and suddenly; once through the trees we saw a little pond steaming; stealthy, unusual smells prowled among the pines . . . ."

He had harsh words for the tourists who engraved their names with hairpins, pencils, and sharp-pointed sticks on the sides and bottoms of hot springs and geysers. "I hope they'll have to write their names in Hell with a red-hot pen holder," he commented. After several weeks in the park his party left from Gardiner for the East and the world of obligations.[39]

Wister was back in 1896. This time he met "Uncle John" Yancey, the grizzled character who had run a hostelry at Pleasant Valley, near Lamar Junction, for many years. This "goat-bearded, shrewd-eyed, lank Uncle Sam type" who never wore blue jeans "because they reminded him of the Union Army," obtained a guide for Wister's party. They were led to the Hoodoos, "pillored erosions of sandstone . . . like a church organ that has met with a railroad accident." On returning, Wister was given some of Uncle John's fermented orange and whiskey. The old gentleman even lent him a hundred dollars.[40]

With a bit of the snob showing through, the young writer described the sagebrushers, who by the 1890s were coming into the park in droves. He saw the "park as an immense thing for the American bourgeoisie. Popper takes mommer and the children in a big wagon with two mules and their kitchen and beds, and forth they march hundreds of miles and summer in the park." By 1911 the democratic influences of the times must have leveled Wister, for in that year *he* took *his* wife and four oldest children into the park with two teams, a buckboard, and a wagon. He also employed two drivers and a cook: the family was still traveling a cut above the American bourgeoisie.[41]

In 1902 Wister published his great cowboy novel, *The Virginian*. In it he mentioned Yellowstone Park twice, but neither time was it germane to the plot. It has been said that his prototype of the Virginian was one Edward Trafton, who was convicted of a 1914 Yellowstone stage holdup. However, we know that there were several "Virginians": a Philadelphia policeman named Skirdin whom Wister had known and various ranchmen and other westerners with such names as John Hicks, Frank Canton, Guy Waring,

William Hines, and Charles B. Fall. Who was the Virginian? Wister asked himself this question in the Preface to his collected writings. "The answer," he wrote, "is—metabolism. Most characters in fiction are the product of impressions, somewhat as flesh and blood are the products of daily diet; they're seldom unassimilated reality."[42]

Henry Adams, John Hay, Joseph Paxton Iddings, W. Hallett Phillips, Billy Hofer, Rudyard Kipling, and Owen Wister all knew personally or had friends who knew the most bombastic and energetic of American presidents, Theodore Roosevelt. TR first saw Yellowstone on an early autumn hunt in 1891. He was roughing it, as became a wealthy Easterner, with two hunter-guides, a packer-cook, and a boy to herd the fourteen pack horses, six saddle horses, and three spares. Though he and his ranching partner tramped hundreds of miles in snow, wind, and cold autumn rain, when the day's hunt was over there was always a cheerful fire to return to, good food, and a dry, warm bed.

Although Roosevelt entered the park from Gardiner, the party's destination was the Absaroka-Shoshone country southeast of the park. The real ordeal began at Heart Lake, whence they headed southeast through the broken pines, swamps and meadows south of Yellowstone Lake and among the streams that headed up the Snake River. "We went over mountain passes, with ranges of scalped peaks on either hand; we skirted the edges of lovely lakes, and of streams with boulder-strewn beds; we plunged into depths of sombre woodland, broken by wet prairies," Roosevelt narrated.

Three days out of Heart Lake a storm blew in but the party kept on, emerging onto a "bleak and windswept" tableland, past alpine lakes, while "a cutting wind blew the icy rain" in their faces. And then, he continued, "as we neared the edge the storm lulled, and pale, watery sunshine gleamed through the rifts in the low scudding clouds. At last our horses stood on the brink of a bold cliff. Deep down beneath our feet lay the wild and lonely valley of Two-Ocean Pass, walled in on either hand by rugged mountain chains. . . ." For nearly two weeks they camped in that vicinity; then Roosevelt and guide Billy Hofer pushed northward across the park to Gardiner, where TR boarded a train for the East.[43]

Even as his career led him inexorably to the White House, Roosevelt continued to love the outdoors. He tried to get away into the wilderness at least once a year. In April 1903 he and naturalist John Burroughs visited the park. After dedicating the Roosevelt Memorial Arch at the north entrance, they continued into the reservation, a runaway team of horses adding a bit of excitement. The president enjoyed a lunch within fifty yards of several hundred elk. At his Tower Falls camp he emerged from his tent half shaved, one side clean and the other lathered, because he wanted to watch some mountain sheep coming down the cliffs. "By Jove," he said, "I must see that. The shaving can wait, and the sheep won't."[44]

Roosevelt's interest in Yellowstone never lagged. In 1908, when he heard that the army had erected at Mammoth headquarters a fountain sporting a bronze cherub, he promptly wrote to General Young, the superintendent. "A more ridiculous and incongruous thing cannot be imagined," the president wrote. "Will you have it removed forthwith?"[45]

Interesting yet "ordinary" people also visited Yellowstone in the period 1883 to 1915. Sometimes they were what sagebrusher Wingate called "professional emigrants," people "possessed with a desire to roam," who never settled, but wandered "from East to West, and then back to the States as their inclinations led them." Wingate hastily added that they were "not tramps or anything like it. On the contrary," he insisted, "they are self-supporting and marvelously independent."[46]

Sometimes they were loners. The Leiderkrantzers found worth noting their encounter at the lake with seventeen-year-old James Nesbit, who, with pack horse and camping supplies, was doing the park. He was known throughout the reservation that summer as "the kid tourist."[47]

The first visitor to walk around the belt roads* and write about it was an Englishman, C. Hanford Henderson, who accomplished the feat in August 1898. He detrained at Cinnabar prepared for his long walk with light clothes, light shoes, and, he said, "an umbrella (to kill rattlesnakes and frighten off bears) and a modest little paper bundle, in my pocket a package of soda crackers, in my heart many things." Soon he was at the Mammoth Hot Springs Hotel, of which he commented, "The first effect is disappointing. In truth, so is the last."

Henderson set out the next morning while the coaches were driving up to the veranda to take on passengers. By noon he was at the Norris lunch station, twenty-two miles from Mammoth; five hours later he had arrived at the Fountain Hotel. "The last stretch of road seemed interminable," he wrote, the road being "half prairie and half marsh." He described it in a word as "hydropathic."

The walker's second night was spent with a corporal at the Thumb Soldier Station. The next day he hiked six hours from Thumb to Lake, and six hours down to the Canyon Hotel, a total of thirty-six miles. On his fourth day out, he hiked over Mount Washburn and down to Yancey's; by noon the next day he "was sitting on the porch of the [Mammoth] hotel waiting for the stage to carry . . . [him] back to Cinnabar."[48]

---

* "The belt roads" was the phrase describing the park's basic road system.

Besides horses and horse-drawn conveyances, and walking, there had appeared upon the American land in the 1880s a new vehicular device, the bicycle. Although its developers were Europeans, in the 1880s it took America by storm; the 1890s were the golden age of "wheeling" in the United States.

By then the high-wheeled "doctor's friend" had given way to the "safety bicycle" with its two wheels of equal size and other accoutrements of the basic vehicle still used today. It was then, and remains, the fastest practical device with which humans with their own physical power can propel themselves across land. For Americans it was a boon. Horses were expensive to buy and care for, while a "wheel," at about one hundred dollars—admittedly a respectable sum in 1890—was still within reason in relation to average income.

The fad extended from sea to sea. "We have some capital cycling here in Montana," reported a correspondent to the cyclist's publication, *Outing,* in 1884. "Indeed, some of the Eastern riders, who have penetrated our region, seem surprised at the number of our riders." Helena had a cycling club boasting eighteen members; the author had "made a run of eighty-five miles" through the Montana countryside. [49]

With this much interest in bicycling in 1884, surely it would not be long before someone took his wheel through Yellowstone Park. Probably such a tour was accomplished several times by wheelmen who never thought of the honor of being first; but the *claim* to making the first park bicycle tour belongs to three members of the Laramie Bicycle Club. Their names were C. S. Greenbaum, W. K. Sinclair, and W. O. Owen, the latter being the group's chronicler. This is an interesting point, because he is probably the same W. O. Owen who disputed the Langford-Stevenson ascent of the Grand Teton in 1872, insisting that he and Bishop Franklin Spalding were the first ones to attain the summit, in 1898. [50]

Whether their bicycle tour of Yellowstone in 1890 was or was not a first, as Owen claimed, it was a rather interesting trip. They detrained at Beaver Canyon, Idaho, where they rented supplies and a wagon (and presumably a wagoner) to follow them. Often they walked their vehicles uphill and coasted down; Owen described part of the journey as "wheeling and walking over the vilest of roads. . . ." The wheelmen stayed at Marshall's old hotel at the Lower Geyser Basin, rode to the falls and back, then down to Mammoth and return, finally exiting as they had entered via the west entrance and Beaver Canyon. Owen not only claimed a first for seeing the park on bicycles, but asserted that his group was also the first "to cross the Continental Divide awheel." [51]

Two years later, in 1892, a brave, lone bicyclist named Frank S. Lenz arrived at Mammoth. He had pedaled there from New York state on his proposed world tour, financed by Victor bicycles and *Outing*, to which he submitted an article each month. Lenz paused at Mammoth only briefly, then biked to Norris; the next day he forded the Firehole River and bicycled into the Upper Geyser Basin. There he met a fellow wheelman, sick from the water, heading home to Bozeman. Lenz continued on, crossing the divide, cycling along the shores of Shoshone Lake, finally reaching the Thumb. Four hours later he was at the Lake Hotel. On his way down to the falls he wheeled through rain, snow, and hail. Persistently he pedaled on to Norris, where the sun came out; twenty more brisk miles returned him to Mammoth. "My cyclometer," he announced, "showed just 139 miles around the park. . . . To all wheelmen in search of a holiday amid the fairest and most wonderful of nature's handiwork, I say, Take your pneumatic and see the Yellowstone Park awheel as I did."

Alas for poor Lenz! The January 1897 issue of *Outing* carried an asterisk at the head of his monthly report. A footnote stated that this would be Lenz's last article. While bicycling between Tabriz and Erzerum in eastern Turkey, five hundred miles west of the Caspian Sea, he had been shot and murdered by brigands.[52]

By the mid-1890s cyclists in the park were not unusual. Yet the horse was still king, and at least half of all visitors enjoyed park wonders in transportation company coaches. The whole excursion was reduced to a businesslike routine; for the folk who could afford it, the six-day (later five-day) trip through the park was a never-to-be-forgotten experience.

The period 1883 to 1915 experienced a marked improvement in roads, lunch stations, and hotels. Not for many more years did women visitors have to tolerate conditions such as those experienced in 1886 by an English lady at Cinnabar's only hotel. She was given the only jug and basin available, and probably the cleanest bedroom. "There was no door," she related, "but she [the landlady] nailed a sheet over the doorway and unnailed it in the morning." The lady found the Mammoth Hotel not much of an improvement with its "unfinished bare walls, unplastered ceiling. . . as to cookery and attendance, the less said the better." The road into the upper park she described as "execrable"; the Firehole Hotel was "an unfinished log hut, the daylight peering through every plank." Her room was about six feet square, the bed the sole piece of furniture and the door would not shut. "The walls were stretched over with canvas . . . and every snore was audible."[53]

Until 1901 when the Burlington Railroad reached Cody, or 1908 when the Union Pacific chugged into West Yellowstone, the Northern Pacific carried most of the nonsagebrushers to near the park gates. At Cinnabar (Gardiner after 1903) the couponers transferred to a thirty-six-passenger tally-ho. "When you clamber to the top seat of one of them and look down, you wonder if you are back in New York on top of the Flatiron building," commented a Gotham visitor. As soon as the passengers had boarded, the driver in his campaign hat, linen duster, and Berlin whip gloves lashed the horses into action and the coach headed for the Mammoth Hotel. Those unfortunate tourists in the last six or eight vehicles were enveloped in dust; some tied handkerchiefs over nose and mouth. By about noon the visitors were checked in to the hotel. Before long the trunk wagon, specially designed for carrying the heavy, deep luggage so common then, came clattering up and unloaded, the trunks to be checked and to remain at the hotel during the tour.[54]

At Mammoth the visitors spent the afternoon touring the springs, the Devil's Kitchen, no longer marked, and McCartney's Cave, no longer open. Later they heard the boom of the army sunset gun from its position on Capitol Hill; taps sounded and all was right with the world. Later there was a dance: uniformed, handsome officers swung sweet young things around the floor while mothers kept a sharp eye on their daughters. Husbands smoked cigars and talked business and politics. Many, however, passed up the festivities and retired, for it had been a fatiguing day.

The next morning they assembled on the veranda, awaiting arrival of the coaches. These were Yellowstone Concords, built by Abbot and Downing of Concord, New Hampshire, to transportation company specifications. The vehicles were open at the sides, painted green and yellow (though a few were funereal black), had three seats, were horsehair-upholstered (not for comfort, obviously, but to keep out vermin) and, in later years, had lap robes. The Haynes's Yellowstone and Monida coaches, which used the west entrance, were painted red.

In time the vehicles themselves were advertised as an attraction. "The stage coach . . . the rocking cradle vehicle that served so well when civilization was beating its way westward . . . holds the first right of way through the park," boasted a Union Pacific-Oregon Short Line folder. Seven to eleven passengers, many of them strangers, entered their designated coach. For the next several days the coach, horses, driver, and other passengers became more than passing acquaintances. "Something in the air, in the scenery, in the novelty of the thing, soon breaks down all constraint," one couponer said, "and you will find yourself talking more nonsense in the next few days than you ever thought possible."[55]

Prior to the opening of Old Faithful Inn in 1903, the couponers went the first day to the Fountain Hotel in the Lower Geyser Basin, to the Upper Basin and return the second, then back to the Upper Basin and over the divide to the Thumb and down to the Lake the third, to Canyon on the fourth, on the fifth back to Fountain, and to Mammoth via Norris on the sixth day. After Old Faithful Inn opened, they generally stayed at Fountain the first night out of Mammoth, at Old Faithful Inn the second, at Lake the third, at Canyon the fourth, and on the fifth day returned to Mammoth either by way of Norris or Mount Washburn, Tower Falls, and Yancey's. Similar patterns of four-, five-, and six-day tours were run out of Cody, Beaver Canyon (later Monida), and after 1908 out of West Yellowstone.[56]

Indeed there is something intriguing to us, with our five-hundred-mile-a-day, three-day park tour, about a leisurely visit in a horse-drawn coach. However, one traveler's description of such a trip hardly encourages us to yearn for "the good old days": A person, he wrote, was expected "to squeeze in among men in yellow dusters and women in gray dusters and red Shaker bonnets, and drive along . . . in a chaos of alkili dust . . . until the fifth day brings him back to his starting point a wiser and dustier man."[57]

How did these tourists behave? In many ways they were mere counterparts of today's visitors. They were busy snapping pictures; they waxed enthusiastic over hot springs and geysers. Unlike today's tourists, however, they filled small bottles with thermal water, or "little boxes with pink mud," according to Ray Stannard Baker, "all very jolly, all expecting to be astonished, and all realizing their expectations." Yet many of them, as he pointed out, were as blasé as today's sophisticates. "Most of the tourists remain pretty snugly in their coachseats or near the hotels," Baker said. "One meets them in great loads, some wrapped in long linen coats, some wearing black glasses, some, broad, green-brimmed hats. . . . Usually they come in trains, a dozen or twenty or even forty great coaches one after another, and when they have passed one sees no more of them until another day."[58]

On five occasions Yellowstone stages were held up in the traditional Wild West style. To the drifting laborers who worked in the park the temptation must have been strong. Guns were sealed at park entrances and the 400 soldiers were widely dispersed. Tourists were known to carry fairly large sums of money in those days before credit cards. Stagecoaches clattering along the lonely park roads were fair game indeed.

Of the five incidents, the third one, which took place on the morning of August 24, 1908, on the old road between Old Faithful and the Thumb, was by far the most daring. One man held up seventeen coaches, surreys, and spring wagons, taking $1,365.95 in cash and $730.25 in watches and jewelry. He was able to accomplish this because the vehicles were spaced about a hundred yards apart. An angle of the road separated each other's view. Authorities believed they knew his name—William Binkley—but Mr. Binkley never came forward to verify his guilt.[59]

In general the trip around the park was so tame as to become boring. The driver's repertoire of tall stories grew stale. Bear-feeding at the hotels constituted the most exciting event, especially after a few geysers and hot springs had been observed. And one's fellow passengers were not always congenial.

Every year some runaways, stagecoach accidents, and drownings occurred; sometimes they were tragic. Mrs. Bessie Haynes Arnold's diary records a dreadful stagecoach accident three miles west of Dwelles, a hostelry just beyond the west entrance. On a dark, stormy night the top of a stagecoach was sheared off, possibly by a stroke of lightning, "one lady was thrown against a tree and an arm broken off and her neck broken so she died instantly. One man had seventeen stitches taken in his scalp and another his hip dislocated. Awful. Eight injured." Thus did nineteen-year-old Miss Haynes record the event, August 28, 1897. In that same month other entries mention a student badly burned at the Castle Geyser and a young "savage" from Fountain Hotel drowned at Bath Lake.

All the while the coupons were clipped, souvenir stores counted their profits, and the hotel and transportation companies flourished. The clientele was so *nice:* well-to-do, genteel, white Anglo-Saxon Protestant people who appreciated linen tablecloths in the dining rooms and fresh cut flowers in their bedrooms. The army had few problems to upset its routine. Yellowstone remained safe, controlled, adequately managed, and beautiful.

This is not to say that all visitors were satisfied with the treatment they received. As always, even in the best of times and best of worlds, some complained of prices and services, and without doubt, often with good reason. A resort functioning just three months of the year in a remote wilderness rarely operates smoothly. True, the concessionaires in time adhered to an annual schedule, or routine, designed to assure smooth operations despite the seasonal aspects of their businesses. But, being profit-and-loss oriented, they usually planned conservatively and when a season was abnormally busy their facilities and services proved inadequate.

But generally things went well during the railroad age, 1883 to 1915. Visitors were not yet destructive through sheer numbers, the wilderness absorbed what few depredations occurred, and firewood was available without noticeable harm to the forest. Sanitary facilities, while crude, did not overwhelm the waters or the land. Trails were not so overused as to deteriorate the terrain or the flora. Garbage was considered as being disposed of satisfactorily. We might say with justification that Yellowstone was in balance with civilization.

Yet events far away, technological advances, the increase of the nation's population, rising affluence, and changes in governmental policy merged from 1915 to 1920 to put an end to Yellowstone's happy stagecoach and hotel era.

NOTES TO CHAPTER TWO

1. William Hardman, *A Trip to America* (London: T. V. Wood, 1884), 138; *Livingston Daily Enterprise,* August 27, 1883 (quoting from an article by Charles E. Nixon, reporter for the *Chicago Inter-Ocean*); see also *Enterprise,* July 18, 1883; December 12, 1885.

2. *Enterprise,* September 3, September 4, 1883. *Railway Age* was also the name of the industry's weekly illustrated journal. I have examined the publication in the Library of Congress for several years in the 1880s but found it nearly devoid of information on Yellowstone.

3. *Enterprise,* June 6, July 31, and August 22, 1883.

4. Ibid , October 17, November 28, 1883.

5. The issue of December 22, 1883, gives a listing of Very Important People who passed through the town on their way to the park.

6. George Frederick Howe, *Chester A. Arthur: A Quarter Century of Machine Politics* (New York: Dodd, Mead and Company, 1934), 246–47; Thomas C. Reeves, *Gentleman Boss: The Life of Chester Alan Arthur* (New York: Random House, 1975), 318–24.

7. *Omaha Daily Bee,* June 19, 1883.

8. Carpenter, *Sword and Olive Branch,* 277–78.

9. *Enterprise,* July 12, 1883. See also Jack Ellis Haynes, "The Expedition of President Chester A. Arthur to Yellowstone National Park in 1883," *Annals of Wyoming,* Vol. 14, No. 1 (January, 1942), 31–38. Facing page 35 is a copy of Haynes's map, marking each camping spot.

10. I have used news items covering the trip from the *Enterprise, Omaha Daily Bee, St. Louis Post-Dispatch,* and *New York Times.* An official record of the trip was published by the Government Printing Office in 1883. Entitled *Journey Through the Yellowstone National Park and North-Western Wyoming, 1883, Photographs of Party and Scenery Along the Route Traveled, and Copies of the Associated Press Dispatches Sent Whilst En Route,* just twelve copies were made; I have used the one in custody of the De-Golyer Library at Southern Methodist University, Dallas, Texas. I have also examined the portions of F. Jay Hayne's diary, which he kept while with the party. It is in the custody of his daughter, Mrs. Bessie Haynes Arnold, of Tucson, Arizona, whom I interviewed on October 7, 8, and 9, 1970.

11. *Omaha Daily Bee,* August 13, 16, 17, and 20, 1883; *St. Louis Post-Dispatch,* August 11, 27, 1883.

12. *Enterprise,* August 30, 1883.

13. Ibid., August 17, 1883 (quoted from the *New York Journal*).

14. The complete list may be found in the *New York Times,* August 11, 1883, and the *Enterprise,* August 22, 1883.

15. *London Times,* "An American Tour," September 5, 10, 1883; Hardman, *Trip to America,* 137–38.

16. *Enterprise,* August 23, 1883.

17. Ibid.; Hardman, *Trip to America,* 143.

18. *Enterprise,* August 24, September 4, 1883; Hardman, *Trip to America,* 141.

19. *London Times,* September 15, 1883.

20. Ibid.; Hardman, *Trip to America,* 143, 144.

21. Hardman, *Trip to America,* 144–49.

22. *London Times,* September 19, 20, 1883; Hardman, *Trip to America,* 159–60.

23. Hardman, *Trip to America,* 159–60.

24. Ibid.

25. *London Times,* September 8, 1883; Hardman, *Trip to America,* 169–70; *Enterprise,* September 4, 1883.

26. *London Times,* September 25, 1883; Hardman, *Trip to America,* 176–77.

27. *Enterprise,* August 28, October 11, 1883.

28. Ibid., September 25, 1883, "quoting a dispatch from Ogden."

29. Ibid., December 13, 1883.

30. Gardner Wilson Turrill, *A Tale of Yellowstone* (Jefferson, Iowa: The G. S. Turrill Publishing Co., 1901), 56.

31. L. Louise Elliott, *Six Weeks on Horseback Through Yellowstone Park* (Rapid City, South Dakota: *The Rapid City Journal,* 1913), 102; 115–16; 141–43, quotation on p. 143. This narration is in the form of letters home; it is in the custody of the Newberry Library, Chicago.

32. George W. Wingate, *Through the Yellowstone Park on Horseback* (New York: O. Judd Co., 1886), 10; 17, 20–22; 34; 50–51; 83; 94; 127.

33. William Henry Dudley, *The National Park from the Hurricane Deck of a Cayuse, or the Leiderkrantz Expedition to Geyserland* (Butte City, Montana: F. Loeber, 1886), 1–16; 18; 52–53; 116.

34. Rudyard Kipling, *From Sea to Sea, and Other Sketches; Letters of Travel* (London: Macmillan, 1904), two vols., Vol. 1, 473; Vol. 2, 68; 78–79; 96–97; 109. Reprinted as *American Notes: Rudyard Kipling's West*, edited and with an introduction by Arrell Morgan Gibson (Norman: University of Oklahoma Press, 1981). See also Pamela Herr (Introduction), "Kipling Among the Geysers," *The American West*, Vol. 15, No. 4 (July-August, 1978), 24–27; 59–61.

35. Wingate, *Through the Yellowstone on Horseback*, 30.

36. Henry Adams, *The Education of Henry Adams* (New York: The Modern Library, 1931), 350; Elizabeth Stevenson, *Henry Adams: A Biography* (New York: Macmillan, 1955), 255–56.

37. Harold Dean Cater, *Henry Adams and His Friends* (Boston: Houghton Mifflin Co., 1947), 326–27. Additional information on Adams in Yellowstone is in Henry Adams, *Letters of Henry Adams*, edited by Worthington Chauncey Ford (Boston; Houghton Mifflin Co., 1938), two vols., Vol. 2, 53–55. A photograph of Hay and Adams in camp is in William Roscoe Thayer, *The Life and Letters of John Hay* (Boston; Houghton Mifflin Co., 1920), two vols., Vol. 2 fronting p. 116. John Hay, *Letters and Diaries of John Hay*, edited by Clara S. Hay (Washington: Printed but not published, 1908) three vols., Vol. 2, 303–35 contains Hay's letter home in which he describes their trip including a cruise on the Yellowstone passenger vessel, the "Zillah."

38. S. Weir Mitchell, M. D., "Through the Yellowstone Park to Fort Custer," *Lippincott's Magazine*, Vol. 25, No. 41 (June, 1880), 688–704; Vol. 26, No. 1 (July, 1880), 29–41; Owen Wister, *Owen Wister Out West: His Journals and Letters*, edited by Fanny Kemble Wister (Chicago: University of Chicago Press, 1958), "Introduction," x.

39. Fanny Kemble Wister, *Owen Wister Out West*, xv; 66–71; Owen Wister, "Old Yellowstone Days," *Harper's*, Vol. 172, No. 4 (March, 1936), 471–76.

40 Wister, "Old Yellowstone Days," 478–80.

41. Fanny Kemble Wister, *Owen Wister Out West*, xv, Wister, "Old Yellowstone Days," 478–80.

42. Owen Wister, *The Virginian* (New York: Macmillan, 1902), 87; 192; Mrs. E. A. Stone, *Uinta County, Wyoming: Its Place in History* (Laramie: Laramie Printing Co., 1924), 296; Orin H. and Lorraine G. Bonney, *Guide to the Wyoming Mountains and Wilderness Areas* (Denver: Sage Books, 1960). 53; N. Orwin Rush, "Fifty Years of the Virginian, 1902–1952," *The Papers of the Bibliographical Society of America*, Vol. 47 (Second Quarter, 1952), 99–120; Owen Wister, *The Writings of Owen Wister* (New York: Macmillan, 1928), eleven vols., Vol. 4, *The Virginian*, Preface, xiii.

43. Theodore Roosevelt, *The Wilderness Hunter* (Upper Saddle River, New Jersey: Literature House, 1970. Reprint of the 1900 edition), 203–4; 207; 222.

44. John Burroughs, *Tramping and Camping with Roosevelt* (Boston: Houghton Mifflin Co., 1907), 23–25; 47–49; 51.

45. Theodore Roosevelt, *Theodore Roosevelt's Letters,* edited by Elting E. Morison (Cambridge: Harvard University Press, 1951–1954), eight vols., Vol. 3, 1232; 1290–91.

46. Wingate, *Through the Yellowstone on Horseback,* 144.

47. Dudley, *National Park from the Hurricane Deck,* 113.

48. C. Hanford Henderson, "Through the Yellowstone on Foot," *Outing,* Vol. 34, No. 2 (May, 1899), 161–67.

49. (No author), "Bicycling in Montana," *Outing and the Wheelman,* Vol. 5, No. 3 (December, 1884), 216.

50. For more on Owen's fixation, see Orin H. and Lorraine G. Bonney, *Bonney's Guide: Grand Teton National Park and Jackson Hole* (Houston, Texas: Published by the authors, 1972), 80.

51. W. O. Owen, "The First Bicycle Tour of the Yellowstone National Park," *Outing,* Vol. 18, No. 3 (June, 1891), 191–95. The periodical changed its name to *Outing* with Volume 6.

52. Frank Lenz, "Lenz's World Tour Awheel: Yellowstone Park," *Outing,* Vol. 22, No. 2 (February, 1893), 378–83; Vol. 30, No. 1 (January, 1897).
Lenz's reference to "cycling along the shores of Shoshone Lake" is puzzling. He either followed a trail, or loosely described a view from the road as the equivalent to "cycling along the shores."

53. C. S. T. Drake, "A Lady's Trip to the Yellowstone Park," *Every Girl's Annual,* 346–49. Copy in Yellowstone Library.

54. Edward J. Wheeler, "A Trip Through Yellowstone Park," *The Literary Digest,* Vol. 28, No. 11 (March 12, 1904), 383–85; interview with Mrs. Bessie Haynes Arnold, October 7, 8, and 9, 1970.

55. Henry D. Sedgwick, Jr., "On Horseback Through Yellowstone Park," *World's Work,* Vol. 6, No. 2 (June, 1903), 3,572; Edward F. Colburn, *To Geyserland* (No place: Oregon Short Line Railroad, 1913), 10–11; Wheeler, "A Trip Through Yellowstone Park," 383.

56. Some of my information is culled from conversations with Mrs. Arnold; Aubrey Haines, for many years a Yellowstone Park ranger and later park historian; former superintendent Horace Albright; and from the annual reports of the secretary of interior for these early years. See also C. Van Tassell, *Truthful Lies of Yellowstone Park* (Bozeman: Published by the author, 1932); Department of the Interior, *General Information Regarding Yellowstone National Park, Season of 1912* (Washington, D. C.: G.P.O., 1912).

57. Sedgwick, "On Horseback Through Yellowstone Park," 35.

58. Ray Stannard Baker, "A Place Of Marvels: Yellowstone Park as It Now Is," *Century Magazine,* Vol. 66, No. 4 (August, 1903), 484; 491.

59. Yellowstone Archives, (hereafter Y. A.), Letters Sent, Vol. 19, Superintendent S. B. M. Young to Secretary of the Interior, September 9, 1908; Jack Ellis Haynes, "Yellowstone Stage Holdups," *Denver Westerners Brand Book* (Denver: Denver Corral of the Westerners, 1952), 85–98.

CHAPTER THREE

Auto Tourism Conquers Yellowstone

*M*ajor political upheavals swept the American governmental arena during the years in which the army maintained security in Yellowstone. While the agrarian movement known as Populism had no effect upon the park, the Progressive Era that followed had a concomitant activity known as conservation, whose proponents would shape resource philosophy to the present day. The woodsman best known in the field was Gifford Pinchot, a crusading, well-trained forester with a massive ego and narrow perspectives. Pinchot believed a forest should be used; the Forest Service's multiple use policies flow directly from his scriptures. Beauty and aesthetics held no place in Pinchot's galaxy of forest values. Neither did preservation of habitats as breeding areas (gene preserves) for wilderness animals. [1]

However, even Pinchot saw nothing wrong with Yellowstone Park, "not, however," he wrote in his autobiography, "as a forest for the production of timber, but as a park in which cutting, and therefore Forestry, were forbidden." Because of its thermal phenomena and grand canyon—exotic, one-of-a-kind attractions—he justified the preservation of Yellowstone as a park. But that was about all: he was never its champion. [2]

Pinchot's ideas gained wide acceptance; yet, even as he was succeeding, opposition forces were gathering. Some of his fellow conservationists were evolving a different philosophy. They emphasized preservation of natural places for their beauty alone rather than because of their usefulness as timber farms, grazing areas, or water supplies. Adherents of this view were supporters of the national park movement. Railroad advertising, which from 1906 to 1910 began a "See America First" theme with emphasis on America's national parks, inadvertently brought onto the side of these preservationists thousands of park visitors who became champions of the parks' integrity. When the First World War began, preventing thousands more from sailing to Europe, they "discovered" instead their own country, including its parks, thus adding still more defenders of the park idea.

Although Pinchot's policies remained dominant, one of the pragmatists' victories resulted in a reaction that greatly strengthened the national park—

73

preservationist cause. This was the Hetch Hetchy controversy in which a valley over the ridge from Yosemite, and a part of that park, was given to San Francisco to be dammed and used as a reservoir. National park defenders vowed never again to allow a national park's integrity to be compromised. Gradually these wilderness advocates evolved arguments justifying their point of view and, as elaborated by forester-naturalist Aldo Leopold, gave it a scientific basis. A sign of their growing power was the creation of the National Park Service in 1916, an event of considerable importance in Yellowstone history.[3]

National park enthusiasts, in their drive for protection of the park from railroad, timber, grazing, and water interests, saw in the visitors an especially forceful ally. True, tourists had to be controlled so that park attractions were not harmed. However, once this was accomplished, officials realized, tourists could be turned into ardent park defenders. Even their complaints, such as those over Yellowstone's poor roads, could be turned into arguments for more substantial appropriations.

Aside from food and lodging, which involved the concessionaires, those who managed Yellowstone heard most complaints about the reservation's road system. By common agreement roads were the government's responsibility. If a stagecoach bogged down on a rotting corduroy road, or was engulfed in suffocating dust, Congress heard about it and something was done.

Long before automobiles clattered through the park, a well-planned road system had been surveyed. Then as now funds were insufficient to maintain the highways adequately, but dedicated park personnel achieved a remarkable maintenance record with skimpy appropriations.

Since it was primarily visitors who demanded better roads—or concessionaires who wanted more visitors—and since roads had to exist before coaches and carriages, then automobiles, could traverse the park, the time has come to trace briefly the history of Yellowstone's highway system.

For anyone who had been to Yellowstone a logical road system appeared almost naturally. The park had two principal entrances. One was via Bozeman or (after 1882) Livingston up the Yellowstone River Valley to the north entrance, and then to Mammoth Hot Springs. The other, the west entrance, was up the Madison River to Virginia City and across the park boundary to the forks where the Gibbon and Firehole rivers merge. Tourists, regardless of their point of entrance, would want to see Mammoth Hot Springs, Norris and Lower, Midway, and Upper geyser basins, Yellowstone Lake, the Grand Canyon and Yellowstone Falls, Mount Washburn, and Tower Falls. Because of mining activity, some kind of wagon road must run up the Lamar Valley and Soda Butte Creek to Cooke City. Park geography suggested a linkup of the north entrance road with the highway from Virginia City, possibly at Madison Junction; a drive from there would lead on up to the Upper Geyser Basin from which, sometime, a road should lead over the continental divide to Yellowstone Lake. (In early days such a route was only contemplated, so steep and tortuous was the terrain.) Instead, a route east from the Lower Geyser Basin over Mary Mountain to the Mud Volcano would do; from its terminus roads could lead up the lakeshore or down the Yellowstone River to the falls and the Grand Canyon. Construct a highway from the canyon over one of Mount Washburn's ridges to Tower Falls and build a final span northwest from Tower Falls back to Mammoth and the park would have a Grand Loop, the name actually given to this 140-mile circle.[4]

For several years no government funds were expended for park roads. However, explorers had made a few recommendations and Nathaniel P. Langford, the first superintendent, had even suggested the basic loop road system. As of 1877, however, what traces existed in the reservation, as well as those leading to them, were the results of private effort, or were tracks worn from repeated usage. Some had been opened by General Howard during his pursuit of the Nez Perce in 1877.[5]

Then quixotic Superintendent Philetus W. Norris arrived. During his five-year stint (1877–1882) he spent nearly $70,000 in government funds for improvements, most of it on roads. He built over two-thirds of the basic Grand Loop (104 of 140 miles).[6]

Norris believed in making funds go as far as possible. He cut scars through the wilderness, over a mountain here, through a swamp there, then along the edge of a cliff. Tourists rose up in righteous wrath at his dusty, muddy, boggy, steep, stump-strewn, crooked thoroughfares. He replied that he had forged crude, two-track wagon lanes to most of the scenic attractions. This was more than had been done before, and, in his view, it represented money well spent.

Gradually, in the slow manner of Congressional action, something was done. The Sundry Civil Bill of 1883 provided that road and bridge construction be implemented "under the supervision and direction of an engineer officer detailed by the Secretary of War for that purpose." Under this provision the engineers began a thirty-three-year assignment in Yellowstone. Two early officers in charge, Dan C. Kingman and Hiram Martin Chittenden, manifested interest beyond the call of duty. Kingman's concept of a wilderness policy, and its rationale, were similar to later National Park Service theory.[7]

Kingman was first on the scene. Thirty-one years old in 1883, he had graduated second in the West Point class of 1875 and was assigned to the army engineers. In the eight years between graduation and his Yellowstone appointment he successfully carried out increasingly responsible tasks. Afterwards his career continued its upward spiral until by 1913, when he was a brigadier general, he was appointed chief of engineers.

Dan Kingman was an ardent outdoorsman, a true wilderness lover, an excellent civil engineer, a leader of men, and an extremely likable man. He received $29,000 of the $40,000 park appropriation in 1883, leaving Superintendent Conger with no funds for anything beyond salaries. Yet the hard-pressed Conger was "much pleased with the gentleman personally, and there can be no doubt," Conger wrote, "of his eminent fitness for the duties to which he has been assigned."[8]

The young engineer arrived at Mammoth on August 13 of that "vintage year," and immediately appraised his task. He found about 160 miles in the reservation "over which one could pass with a wagon with more or less difficulty," and many more miles of blazed trails passable on horseback. But it was the condition of the roads that was shocking. They were, he reported, "barely passable even in good weather." Without mentioning Superintendent Norris by name he suggested that "the lack of means and the desire to accomplish a great deal had apparently led those . . . in charge to be guided in their location [of roads] mainly by the question of first cost." Roads were just wide enough for passage of a single wagon, with stumps left standing high above the ground. So few turnouts existed that an outrider was a necessity for every wagon train. Bridge beds were made of small poles. There were long stretches of corduroy "to weary and vex people who were obliged to travel over them." Since little or no attention had been paid to drainage, water often found its easiest exit down the middle of the track.[9]

Road work in those days was a fairly simple task, although sound engineering was still essential. Even good roads were narrower and the tonnage of vehicles passing over them less than today; the speed of trotting horses was not over eight miles per hour, of a Yellowstone Concord not more than six, and of a freight wagon four at most. The horse-drawn scrapers and plows as well as the manpower—men with axes, picks, shovels, and wheelbarrows—were uniquely capable of constructing the kind of roads and bridges that animal-drawn vehicles demanded. Primitive by modern standards, the road equipment was adequate then.

Kingman soon had several work parties in the field. Despite the park's remoteness he found no lack of laborers who were "of more than ordinary intelligence, but somewhat fickle and restless." Cost of a day's work averaged out to $2.45 plus an additional ten percent for supervision, while a span of horses or mules, harness, wagon and driver came to $125.00 a month with the driver receiving board; the teams were foraged at the owner's expense.

To obtain timbers for bridges and culverts Kingman set up a portable sawmill at Mammoth. With a crew supervised by a Swede named E. Lamartine he cut three-inch planking from the nearby burn of 1882 at Bunsen

Peak. Another Swede supervisor, Oscar Swanson, accomplished with his crew most of the hardrock work and blasting. Before mid-October snows halted operations, the forty-mile span from Mammoth to Madison Junction had been greatly improved. [10]

By season's end Kingman had acquired a firm grasp of the park terrain and the transportation needs of the reservation. He declared that Yellowstone presented "almost every obstacle that nature ever offered to the construction and maintenance of roads." These included "a moist climate and heavy snows, besides the peculiar hot springs formations which are," he said, "very extensive and afford the worst road material ever met with. . . . I would earnestly recommend," he added, "that . . . hereafter they [the roads] have something of the solid, durable and substantial quality that usually characterizes the works constructed by the national government." [11]

Then he established some standards. Roads were to be "at least 18 feet wide and well rounded in the center, and [be] provided with suitable side ditches and cross culverts"; all trees were to be removed for a width of thirty feet, and the fill from sidehill cuttings was to be retained by a dry stone wall. An "ample ditch" was to be placed on the uphill side at least a rod [16½ feet] from the road to catch snow water and convey it to its natural water courses. In marshes and meadows the corduroy was to be replaced with a plank road. Culverts were to be of stone or three-inch plank and all bridges of sawed lumber. [12]

Some stretches of road were so poorly located that he recommended their abandonment. One of these was the way to Swan Lake Flats. Norris had cut an incredibly steep road behind the hotel and the hot springs terraces past the Orange geyser and through Hell Gate (Snow Pass) onto the flats. This was a 1,200-foot rise in about two miles, not by a uniform grade, Kingman explained, "but by a series of inclines so steep as to be almost impassable for a loaded wagon when the ground was wet, and dangerous to descend at all times." Fidgety passengers often got out and walked; so did humane tourists who felt sorry for the toiling horses. Such an intolerable road had to be abandoned for something better.

The route Kingman wanted was up the West Fork of the Gardner River, uniting with the old road near Swan Lake. He saw no serious obstacle until the head of the canyon was reached. Here (as everyone who has passed through the Golden Gate and parked to observe Rustic Falls is aware), the canyon narrows and the rock walls are nearly vertical. How to build a passage there? Noting that the stone was of columnar structure with a narrow bench at just about the right height for the road, Kingman decided to make that the route. Soon he had Oscar Swanson and his Swedes "making a highway into Wonderland that will surpass the famous Appian Way." Meanwhile, having submitted an estimate of $210,000 to put the roads in shape or build essential new ones, Kingman headed East. [13]

In 1884 appropriations were less than ten percent of what he requested, but with his $24,000, not released until August, Kingman launched or continued four projects. One consisted of bridge and road work near Yellowstone Falls and a second consisted of sidehill cutting in Gibbon Canyon where the roadway had been forced into the stream. The third project was a new Gardiner–Mammoth Hot Springs road. Kingman disliked the old route which ran along the slopes of the mountains parallel but far above the Gardner River. At its best it was narrow, steep, and slippery in bad weather. "But," Kingman emphasized, "its most serious defects are manifest in winter." Snow settled deep, resulting in snowslides, one of which killed a man in the winter of 1884. In spring the snow melt made the route soft and muddy. "Travel is delayed and freighters were sometimes obligated to camp twice in this short distance of about four miles," the lieutenant added. Therefore he ordered a road built up the Gardner Canyon floor and then up to the hotel terrace—essentially today's route. [14]

Work was also continued on the new route up the West Gardner to Swan Lake Flats. Where the canyon walls are nearly three hundred feet high and in places nearly vertical, Kingman ordered timber trestles installed, anchored deeply into the rock: these trestles supported the roadbed which jutted into space from the canyon wall. In June 1885 the West Gardner road was completed; it cut the time from Mammoth to the geyser basins from nearly six hours to four. [15]

Lieutenant Kingman considered this "the most important improvement yet undertaken in the park." Indeed, the Golden Gate and Kingman Pass became popular postcard views, one of the few man-made improvements in the park to add to the spectacular scenery already there. And it was a boon to beasts of burden. "When a team can haul a ton easier by the Golden Gate than it can haul an empty wagon the other way, there can be no doubt which road will attract even sinners who are not also fools," quipped the *Enterprise*. [16]

The lieutenant was involved in just one controversy: the "Four Inch Tire Order" of 1886. It was even mentioned in Congress. He simply wanted every freight wagon in the park equipped with metal tires at least four inches wide. As he explained it, the trachyte used for gravel in the park contained a high percentage of soft feldspar which park freight wagons, equipped with one and three-quarter inch tires, bearing loads up to 4,500 pounds, simply ground to a fine powder. The narrow wheels cut clear through the surface, forming deep ruts which, when filled with rainwater, made the roads nearly impassable.

The secretary of interior approved Kingman's suggestion and issued the order, but Yellowstone draymen, supported by the concessionaires, refused to obey. Eventually the regulation was rescinded. Kingman fumed. "It is re-

gretfully submitted that it is not right to permit a few men for their temporary advantage and profit to injure and destroy the public property," he protested. "It would be cheaper for the government to buy these lessees all the
wide-tired wagons they want . . . than it will be to go on repairing the
injuries they do under the present system. . . ."[17]

In sum Kingman's accomplishments were substantial although he never
had more than $25,000 to work with, far less than was at the disposal of his
successors. He supervised construction of thirty and a half miles of new road
and by the end of the 1886 season considered another thirty miles to be in
first class condition, or nearly so. Above all, Kingman loved the wilderness.
Speaking *ex cathedra,* he said that if the park should "become the resort of
fashion, if its forests are stripped to rear smooth hotels; if the race course, the
drinking saloon, and the gambling-table invade it; if its valleys are scarred
by railroads and its hills pierced by tunnels . . . if, in short, a sort of Coney
Island is established there, then it will cease to belong to the whole people
and will be unworthy [of] the care and protection of the National government." In 1886 he was reassigned along with a deserved promotion to the
rank of captain.[18]

Kingman's road plan as well as his concepts of proper park usage were
heartily embraced by succeeding engineer officers. They always requested of
the government a hundred thousand dollars or more, in 1889 submitting an
estimate for turning 225 miles of park roads into first-class condition for
$444,779; Congress gave them a pittance of that. Yet in the fiscal year end-
ing June 30, 1890, that august body upped the ante to $50,000 and in 1891
raised it to $75,000. Pressure on Congress was having an effect. Gradually an
annual road building and maintenance program developed for Yellowstone.

The slow but steady improvement of park roads can be traced through
the annual reports of the chief of engineers. The first formally built bridle
path, one from near the bridge over Cascade Creek to the crest of the Lower
Falls of the Yellowstone, was built in 1888. Specifications for roads became
more stringent. Engineers began to widen them; they began surfacing roads
to a depth of six inches with macadam (loose gravel) and commenced building parapets along the outer edges of precipitous mountain segments. Major
William A. Jones in 1890 suggested that sprinklers be used to keep down
the dust, a plan that materialized into an annual $50,000 anti-dust appropri-
ation.[19]

Increased road appropriations reflected not only increased national interest in Yellowstone but also lobbying by concessionaires. Park Company
President Charles Gibson in 1888 called for completion of the Loop Road.
He pointed out that Yellowstone Lake, Shoshone Lake, Mount Washburn,
and Tower Falls were "still approachable only to hardy mountaineers." Until
the Loop was finished, Gibson well knew, tourists were denied views of some

spectacular scenery. Visitors traveled from Mammoth the fifty-eight miles to the Upper Geyser Basin, returned to Norris, struck off at right angles for the Grand Canyon over a new road begun by Lieutenant Kingman, returned again to Norris over the same road and then retraced their route back to Mammoth. This, Gibson stressed, made "seventy miles of staging on the backtrack." Moreover, even the roads in existence needed repairs. "When one stands before the majesty of nature in the park, and then sees the roads, he feels like the peacock when he looks down upon his feet." Gibson taunted. "When he is being jostled over the stumps, gullies, and rocks of the trails in the park his spread-eagle Americanism droops in shame. . . . If these roads are never to be built," he asked, "why was the park established? And if they are to be made, why not make them now?"[20]

Gibson was not going to see any "instant highways" in Yellowstone, but progress was being made. Engineer officer William E. Craighill first made a reconnaissance for a route from the Upper Geyser Basin to the Thumb; subsequently he ordered the road built with crews working from both ends. It is incomprehensible, yet a fact, that the engineers did not know precisely where the route would go—they only knew its two ends. The terrain was (and is) a maze of canyons and mountains; the continental divide twists like a snake through the area. The lieutenant, however, left for another assignment before the road was finished.[21]

His successor was Captain Hiram Martin Chittenden, a slim West Pointer who was plagued with illness. He arrived in the park still recovering from a bout with typhoid fever. He did his best engineering work in the park, using political sagacity to gain continuing appropriations that were so necessary if the Loop Road project, brilliantly planned by Dan Kingman, was to be completed. During his two tours of the park (1891–1892 and 1898–1906) Chittenden fell in love with Yellowstone. He wrote its first history.[22]

One of his first efforts was to complete the link from the Upper Geyser Basin to the Thumb. With a hand level and a five-foot-long stick he headed out from Yellowstone Lake, crossed the divide, and finally came upon the work accomplished by the crew working east from the geysers. Then he returned, discovering on the way Isa Lake and a canyon that crossed the divide. In this manner, crude even for 1891, Chittenden determined the final route. It is essentially today's road, failing in one of Captain Kingman's recommendations in that it does not touch Shoshone Lake.[23]

Chittenden saw the Loop roads completed, made improvements on Kingman's Golden Gate Road (but in his reports said nothing of his predecessor's accomplishment there), and completed the east entrance road from Sylvan Pass and the south entrance route from the Snake River. The west entrance road was greatly improved. He constructed the road up Mount Washburn, a project that would be considered environmentally unsound today, and built the useless Roosevelt Memorial Arch at the north entrance.

Visitors in the late 1800s were allowed to examine geysers such as the "Spoon" up close. The elderly man is George Henderson, one of Yellowstone's first interpreters. *G.R. Hebard Collection No. 8, courtesy Archives-American Heritage Center, University of Wyoming.*

Train at Cinnabar, Montana, September 1896.
F. Jay Haynes photograph, courtesy Timothy Manns, Yellowstone National Park; Haynes Foundation Collection, Montana Historical Society.

Yellowstone's most distinguished visitor in the early years was President Chester Alan Arthur, shown here, seated in chair, at lunch with fellow campers. *From Journey Through Yellowstone, Government Printing Office, 1883, courtesy The DeGolyer Library, Southern Methodist University, Dallas.*

Among those who fell in love
with Yellowstone was Owen Wister,
author of the great cowboy novel,
The Virginian. Here he is wearing
his jauntily positioned hat, cigar
in mouth, landscape camera in hand.
*Owen Wister Collection, courtesy
Archives-American Heritage Center,
University of Wyoming.*

Theodore Roosevelt visited Yellowstone several times and was a staunch
park defender. Here he is, right, with guns and an unidentified hunting partner.
Date unknown.
Courtesy The DeGolyer Library, Southern Methodist University, Dallas.

Not everyone rode coaches, wagons, or horses in Yellowstone.
This is an artist's rendition of round-the-world bicyclist Frank G. Lenz, pedaling
along Yellowstone's Grand Canyon. From *Outing*, February 1893.
Courtesy Iowa State University Library.

One can only hope that this overloaded coach in Gardner River Canyon
arrived safely with its cargo at the Mammoth Hotel.
William H. Jackson photograph, courtesy Colorado Historical Society.

Captain Dan Kingman, who laid out the park road system, rose to the rank of Brigadier General, Chief of the Army Corps of Engineers.
Courtesy U.S. Army Corps of Engineers Museum.

Many visitors entered from Cody and the Sylvan Pass Road.
One of its attractions was the "Loop the Loop," shown here in a 1905 picture,
being crossed by Yellowstone-bound coaches.
*Mr. and Mrs. Frank E. Gilmore Collection, courtesy Archives-American Heritage Center,
University of Wyoming.*

Dr. and Mrs. Kingman R. Seiler in their Model "T" Ford Runabout at the start of
their trip to Yellowstone. Theirs was the first tourist car officially admitted
through the north entrance, 7:00 P.M., July 31, 1915.
Courtesy Mrs. Maude S. Bull

Western Writer Emerson Hough is at the wheel of this automobile
on Dunraven Pass.
*Replogle-Hough Collection, courtesy Archives-American Heritage Center,
University of Wyoming.*

Captain Chittenden understood public relations and politics. He took credit for persuading the Honorable Joe Cannon ("Uncle Joe" Cannon, the dictatorial Speaker of the House of Representatives from 1903 to 1911, and before that a powerful committee chairman) "to guarantee a continuing appropriation of $750,000. This," he added, "enabled me to lay out the whole system, build it in quite thorough shape and place it in a condition which it has never surpassed since."[24]

There is no question of the major's hard work, dedication, and ultimate success. Yet is is impossible to study Kingman's and Chittenden's accomplishments in the park without concluding that the wrong man received most of the credit. Kingman laid out the basic road plans, reconstructed the most glaring weak spots such as the Gardiner-Mammoth road and the Golden Gate, and squeezed every last drop of good out of the limited funds at his disposal. His superiors recognized his abilities and promoted him while sending him to what they considered more challenging assignments. Chittenden had to make his name in Yellowstone. Determined to succeed, fighting ill health all the way, he must have been a rather humorless, intense man. "I don't think I ever saw Major Chittenden smile," recollected Mrs. Bessie Haynes Arnold, who had known him in the park. He never rose above the rank of major.[25]

Mention of the south and east entrance highways demands some explanation. The incentive for an artery from the south originated with Wyoming's Senator Francis E. Warren. He introduced a bill in Congress in 1891 calling for such a road to connect Forts Washakie and Yellowstone. "Thousands of tourists," he said, ". . . want to go in with wagons, horseback, stages, etc., over this wild region." Such a road would pass "through the haunts of the notorious horse thieves of the Wind River Mountains and would have, as one of its results, the breaking up of the mischievous robber band." The park section of the proposal began with a Congressional appropriation in 1892 for construction from the Thumb to the Snake River entrance. This was completed in 1895 while the military road from Fort Washakie into Jackson Hole had also been completed by that time.[26]

The east entrance highway was constructed as a result of the interests of William F. "Buffalo Bill" Cody and the Burlington Railroad. The town of Cody was founded in 1896 by "Buffalo Bill" and his business friends who contemplated damming the Shoshone River nearby for an irrigation project. (The dam was completed with federal funds in 1910.) Next, Cody persuaded Burlington officials to build a spur from Toluca, Montana, south of Billings, 131 miles to Cody. Next, Buffalo Bill and the Burlington interests prevailed upon the federal government to fund the Cody, or Sylvan Pass, or east entrance highway. The first authorization came in 1900; the road was completed in 1909. By 1901 the railroad had reached its destination and "Buffalo Bill," despite serious financial reverses, ordered construction of the lavish

Irma Hotel. Considering that the town boasted just eighty-nine inhabitants when the hostelry was opened, one must grant the famed scout great optimism about the region's future. He was right, although he did not live long enough to prosper from its growth or enjoy its beautiful Buffalo Bill Museum and Whitney Art Gallery.[27]

The Cody Road passed through fifty miles of what in the early 1900s was virgin wilderness. Great trees still stood along the way, for the whine of the traveling sawmill had not yet been heard there. Fishing along the river was superb. "So alive is the stream with trout," one enthusiast wrote, "that the number of fish caught at one cast is only limited to the number of flies on the fisherman's leader." The route follows a narrow trail that had been used by Indians and trappers on the way to and from Yellowstone Park.[28]

With an acceptable macadamized road system through the park and similar arteries feeding into it, Yellowstone by 1909 possessed an adequate transportation system for horse-drawn conveyances. Stagecoaches, hotels and camps catering to tourists resulted in a controlled, manageable humanity that did little harm to the flora, fauna, and thermal wonders. As for the visitors, they appreciated the gentility that characterized their transportation, food, and shelter, and enjoyed the summer season acquaintances they made on the tour.

Then came the automobile. As early as the spring of 1902 the question of allowing those rattling, backfiring denizens of internal combustion into the park was called to the attention of Major John Pitcher, acting superintendent, by Secretary of Interior Ethan Allen Hitchcock. "The department," began the letter, "has been unofficially advised that there is a likelihood of persons making a tour of the park during the coming season, using therein, for transportation purposes, automobiles." The secretary requested Major Pitcher to "look into this matter carefully" and advise as to whether "it would be practicable or desirable to permit conveyances of the character indicated to be used in the reservation under your supervision."[29]

Automobiles in Yellowstone? Actually Major Pitcher had contemplated buying one for himself but had refrained because he was "confident that its use in the park during the tourist season would result in serious disaster to someone else." His good judgment extended to the secretary's general question. The major rejected the idea but added that "at some time in the future the automobile [would] be the best and most suitable means of transportation in the park. . . ." On May 12, 1902, the secretary authorized the prohibition of automobiles in Yellowstone "until further orders."[30]

Inadvertently Major Pitcher had revealed the problem of technological advance and its reception in Yellowstone and, indeed, in all national parks. Mankind loves technology. People purchase the new "toy" whatever it may be—an automobile, motorboat, trailbike, snowmobile, camera, walkie-talkie, recreational vehicle, television dish antenna—and promptly use it for purposes good or bad. National park management exists confronted with the dilemma of technological innovations.

The "further orders" were long in coming and even longer in being carried out. A stubborn resistance developed, shared by the army, the Interior Department, and the concessionaires. The new vehicles created the economic problem of disposing of the hayburning equipment. They also presented the very real danger of frightened horses, runaways, and resultant injuries and lawsuits. Possibly a thousand rigs ranging from the big tally-hos down to two-horse surreys, and as many as two thousand horses, were in use at the top of the seasons from 1890 until 1915. Only the despised sage-brushers, who had their own horses and mules, or an occasional brave walker or bicyclist, could do the park without renting a horse or rig or purchasing a ticket on a company coach.

So if automobiles did enter Yellowstone during these years, and there is evidence that some did, their movements along the quiet roadways were a sub rosa affair, the sort of thing administrators did not discuss or write about, save in hushed tones and blind letters. As an example, one story relates how, after the close of the 1897 season, one James T. Turner of Butte, Montana, chauffered a "Thomas Flyer" through the park. The car was owned by Augustus Heinze, the copper tycoon. The trouble is, the Thomas Flyer was not manufactured until 1899. It seems probable that Turner did drive a car into the park, with special dispensation from the authorities, but in relating an experience of more than six decades ago, Mr. Turner got his dates mixed. Nor does he state whether "Gus" Heinze was or was not a passenger. Rumors are rife of other auto forays into Yellowstone in these years, but proof is lacking.[31]

In 1908 Representative Franklin W. Mondell of Wyoming transmitted two petitions to the secretary of interior. One was signed by residents of Cody, Wyoming, and vicinity; the other by the flamboyant Buffalo Bill. Both petitions requested permission to run motorcars up the Cody road, through Sylvan Pass to at least as far as the Lake Hotel.[32]

At that time the army superintendent was Colonel S. B. M. Young, who clearly liked things the way they were. He replied that while perhaps some people wanted to see the park from automobiles, "they [were] few in comparison to the number who prefer traveling otherwise." And he stated further "that many horses which will not frighten at passing automobiles in a city, *will* frighten when meeting them on a country road. . . . I therefore recommend that the present rule prohibiting automobiles from entering the park be continued in force."[33]

But the army men and the concessionaires saw that the change was coming. They were aware that in 1908 the secretary of interior had allowed automobiles into Mount Rainier, that in 1910 they were admitted to General Grant, in 1911 to Crater Lake, in 1912 to Glacier, in 1913 to Yosemite and Sequoia, and in 1914 to Mesa Verde. Dreading the inevitable, Yellowstone's officials adopted delaying tactics. They insisted that the roads were not in satisfactory condition for automobile traffic. Congress accepted the challenge. On April 2, 1912, the Senate demanded of the secretary of interior a cost estimate of such satisfactory new roads in the park.[34]

Captain C. H. Knight of the army engineers suggested, in the subsequent report, that separate roads for automobiles be constructed. Conceding that cost made his proposal prohibitive, the captain submitted an alternate solution: improving the present roads at a cost of $2,000,000 or $10,000 a mile, simply astronomical for those times. He added that the reconstruction would take four or five seasons and that during that time the horsepower (literally) owned by the transportation companies could be dispensed with and plans made for motorization.[35]

F. Jay Haynes, whose Monida Transportation Company owned hundreds of vehicles, gave Captain Knight strong support. "It would be out of the question for any driver . . . to be able to handle his team on any portion of the roads in the park when meeting or passing an automobile or motorcycle," he stated, going on to complain that insurance was already hard to obtain, present policies being with a foreign company, no American company showing interest.[36]

The excessive road cost ploy did not deter Congress for long. In August 1912 that body appropriated funds to reconstruct the Cody-Sylvan Pass-Lake Hotel, West Yellowstone-Madison Junction, and West Thumb-South Entrance roads, making them acceptable for automobile use. But the park bureaucracy, with encouragement from the concessionaires, dragged their feet. The highways were not in condition for automobiles in either 1913 or 1914.[37]

Meanwhile Senator James J. Brady of Idaho and Representative Franklin W. Mondell of Wyoming kept up the pressure. On June 20, 1913, Senator Brady announced that Colonel Lloyd Brett would allow a trial run of automobiles from West Yellowstone to the West Thumb. At about the same time a high Interior Department official wrote the colonel, who was a spit-and-polish officer of the 1st Cavalry, "I am hopeful that you may see your way to cooperate with him [Senator Brady] in this matter . . . unless you feel . . . that such an experiment would be premature and ill-advised."[38]

Colonel Brett grabbed at that last phrase like a drowning man grasping a straw. He conceded that automobiles could travel that stretch of road without accident, "provided troops clear the road of all horse-drawn vehicles during the specified hours, . . ." But, he reminded the official, "the horses drawing the coaches . . . are range horses. They are driven from the ranges to the park, work three months, and [are] then returned to their pasturage, so it is a question if they would ever become accustomed to machines."

Moreover, since motorists were suggesting that automobiles could use the roads during the night and early morning hours when stages were not in use, the colonel countered that stages were in use from early morning to nightfall. "The automobile travelers would not long be satisfied to remain within even generous restricted hours," he continued. Finally, he defended the concessionaires: "The transportation companies, which own thousands of horses are entitled to consideration. . . ." He blamed the agitation on local inhabitants. "They see the business possibilities in this wonderland," he said, "and, if they are permitted to have their way, will, in years, turn this park into a place of entertainment that will make Coney Island look like a dime museum."39

Nevertheless signs of the coming automobile age began to affect the thinking of the army and the concessionaires. Harry Child, the park hotel and transportation tycoon, now owned a White motorcar. It was a bit of a nuisance having it loaded on a horse-drawn wagon to be hauled up to his Mammoth shops for painting, and returned to Gardiner the same way! Even the army engineers requested permission to use a motor truck for freight hauling during the 1915 season. Request refused.40

The concessionaires saw the light and, so to speak, pulled out the plugs. In 1915 the Panama-Pacific Exhibition would be held in San Francisco, bringing increased visitation to Yellowstone. F. Jay Haynes did some figuring. He concluded that with motor buses he could increase the number of tourists handled on one tour from 180 per day to 225, and on another, from 128 per day to 225, an increase in the latter case of 40.6 percent.41

During these years, so goes one story, the western manager of the American Automobile Association, Mr. A. L. Westgard, made an annual pilgrimage to one of the park entrances, climbed out of his car and shook his fist at the soldiers on duty there, climbed aboard and drove away until another year rolled by.42

Finally Secretary of Interior Franklin K. Lane had his assistant, Stephen T. Mather, appoint a committee to determine the feasibility of automobile travel in the park. It included A. K. Batchelder, president of the A.A.A.; Colonel Brett, acting superintendent; and a man named Marshall of the U.S. Geological Survey. It reported in favor of automobiles. Acting on the committee's recommendations, the secretary of interior on April 21, 1915, announced that commencing August 1, 1915, privately owned automobiles would be allowed in Yellowstone National Park.

This order, with its air of finality, prompted a wave of activity in Yellowstone. In June Colonel Brett and several dignitaries made an automobile trip around the park and concluded—surprise!—that automobiles could indeed make the tour. Concessionaires stocked gas and oil and made plans for disposing of their horses and horse-drawn equipment. (However, concessionaire Child did not have buses until 1917 and continued using the hayburning equipment until then.)

Intricate regulations were established. All traffic was one way. Cars could leave designated check points one-half hour before horse-drawn stages. Speeds were limited to twelve miles per hour ascending and ten miles per hour descending steep grades, to eight miles per hour approaching sharp curves, and to twenty miles per hour on the level if no teams were within two hundred yards. When beasts of burden approached, automobiles were to take to the outer edge of the highway regardless of the direction in which they might be headed. Teams had the right of way.[43]

August 1 approached. On July 29 Colonel Brett, fidgety about congestion at Gardiner where all thirty-five vehicles were lined up and waiting, requested authority to open the park to them on the evening of July 31; permission was granted. For the other two entrances also opening, however, August 1 remained the day. Jacob Schwoob, a Cody businessman, led a small caravan of automobiles out of Cody toward the Sylvan Pass entrance, while the largest number of cars entered from the west entrance. All told, fifty automobiles with 171 passengers entered the park on August 1; in the first three days 104 automobiles clattered in, forty-nine via the west entrance, thirty-two over Sylvan Pass, and twenty-four through the north entrance at Gardiner. (The colonel had overestimated the number of cars by eleven.)[44]

The first car through the north entrance with official permission on the evening of July 31, 1915, was owned by Mr. K. R. Seiler of Red Wing, Minnesota. It bore state license Minnesota 60236, and its serial number was 23863. At 7:00 P.M. it carried the gentleman and his wife into the park. Where the vehicle should have had a gearshift, it had a third pedal; it had no battery, just a magneto, and it bore the name of its manufacturer and the letter of that series: FORD, MODEL "T" Runabout.[45]

It was symbolic that it was a Ford, the car for the millions that put middle America on the road. Like it or not, the reality was that the teeming millions were going to come. Concessionaires and administrators did not like it: they desired neither the cars nor their tin-can tourist occupants. But an America whose citizens were achieving the greatest mobility ever enjoyed by a people forced the entrances. The lesson was that technological advance has to be accepted; to fight it is not unlike sweeping the tide back into the sea. The challenge lies not in combating such change, but in learning to regulate it so that the environment suffers the least possible damage. Understanding the nature of the problem has come hard to park administrators, again and again and again.

Between 1916 and 1929 America had a Mexican adventure, fought in a world war, suffered reaction from wartime idealism, legislated public morality with prohibition, and gave women a measure of liberation with the nineteenth amendment and acceptance of their smoking cigarettes or drinking with men in speak-easies. In these same years the common man or woman purchased his or her first motorcar and first radio.*

If the trend of the times was not toward egalitarianism, then it represented something nearly as good, or at least constituted a step in the right direction—an upgrading of the material well-being of white Americans. Fifty years later American democracy would manifest an equal concern for Blacks, Chicanos, and Native Americans. Still, in terms of the slow, agonizing progress of human kind, who can deny that the attainment of mobility and of material things by a greater number was not significant and good?

Yellowstone entered the automobile age just when the National Park Service became operational (1916), bringing to park administration new enthusiasm and new ideas. Director Stephen Tyng Mather harbored little or no hostility to motor cars. One of his major aims was to persuade Americans to visit the national parks—the "See America First" movement. His publicity man, Robert Sterling Yard, heartily agreed with this promotional policy, while Horace Albright, Mather's protégé, enthusiastically encouraged auto tourists into Yellowstone. Yet the new management team still cooperated with the concessionaires, who held on tenaciously to a genteel but diminishing clientele of railroad tourists, and lagged—without strong Park Service protest—at building facilities catering to the automobilists.[46]

Mather's, Albright's, and Yard's promotional activities found a receptive audience, for automobiles and affluence made possible the fulfillment of Americans' lust for travel. Millions used their new machines to roam to places about which they had previously fantasized. Touring was the ultimate joy to be derived from the new toy. Parker Brothers, the parlor game people,

*In 1910 just 181,000 passenger cars were built in the United States; by 1920 the annual number had jumped to 1,196,000 and by 1930 to 2,787,000. *Statistical Abstract of the United States, 1974*, 556

profited from the new national pastime with a best-selling game appropriately called TOURING. Flat tires, burned-out bearings, thrown rods, detours, storms and other calamities stood in the way of reaching the destination and thus winning the game. A favorite comic strip of the times was "Gasoline Alley." Today its original theme is forgotten, but in the early 1920s the neighborly alley where the neighbors fussed over their beloved automobiles carried all the identification with real life necessary to make the comic strip a success.

Indeed, touring in the teens and twenties *was* an adventure. Whereas today pliers, a screwdriver, lug wrench and a jack are the only tools carried, the passenger car of sixty years ago was equipped with a metal toolbox filled with open-end wrenches, a monkey wrench, Stillson wrench, and spark plug socket wrench; pliers and chain-repair pliers; hammer; large and small screwdrivers; a spool of soft iron wire; assorted nuts, bolts, and cotterkeys; extra tire valves, tire pump, pressure gauge; extra spark plugs and rim lugs; some cable; a grease gun; an extra fan belt; cork for making gaskets; a box of talcum powder; and shellac. (The last two were for cementing tires and tubes to rims.) It was recommended that the tourist carry two spare tires and three spare inner tubes along with a box of tube patching and a blow-out tire patch. The cautious traveler was sure to have packed for quick access a collapsible bucket, tire chains, and towrope.

In the 1920s highways acquired names, and distinctive markers were erected along the way: the Geysers to Glaciers Trail, Regina-Yellowstone Trail, Theodore Roosevelt International Highway, National Park to Park Highways, and the Yellowstone Trail. Yet few highways were paved, detours were common, and getting stuck in the mud in rainy weather was to be expected.[47]

The newly mobile people fascinated Emerson Hough, author of *The Covered Wagon,* a best-selling western novel later made into an epic motion picture. Hough was also an active participant in Park Service activities. In Yellowstone he strolled through the auto camps, sat around campfires with people whose only link with home was the black, open touring Ford. (More than half the cars in the park in those early automobile years were Model Ts.) Then Hough thought about the phenomenon and wrote an article about it: "Maw's Vacation."

Even the title bespeaks of rural and small-town America, the love implied in "Maw" something different, more as if she was the executive officer of a ship battling a storm, than the softer "Mom" of the 1940s, or the "Mother" of today. Father was "Pa," and he loved Maw very much, as did her sons and daughters. Maw complained very little, though she worked very hard; Maw gave out much free advice which usually sounded more like orders to be obeyed. Maw kept the family ship on an even keel. Pa bought a tent and camp stove from Sears, Roebuck and the family headed for a *vacation*, first ever, and where spend it but in Yellowstone National Park? Hough suggested that 60,000 Maws were having the first vacation of their lives there. Vacations? Yes, though the Maws still did all the cooking and still had daughters and sons and a husband and a dog to look after.

"I know Maw loves it all," Hough wrote with warmth, "because she never has told me so. She is very shy about her new world in this new day. She wouldn't like to talk about it. We never do like to talk about it, once we really have looked out across our valley of dreams." You could not help seeing them, "Paw and Maw and Cynthy in her pants and Hattie and Roweny in overalls and puttees." They were, Hough suggested, "the new people of America who never have been out like this before. . . . So they have swung out from the lane at last, after forty years of work, and on to the roads that lead to the transcontinental highway . . . and so they have at last arrived among the great mountains of which Maw had dreamed [during] all her life of cooking and washing and ironing."[48]

Superintendent Albright's positive response to the influx of auto tourists fitted the temper of the early 1920s. He visited them in their camps and lectured to them by evening campfires. Always the optimist, he promised better things in Yellowstone and did his best to improve conditions. He admitted that campgrounds, sanitary facilities, roads, and other services never caught up with demand. However, the lag in improvements vis-a-vis visitors never reached catastrophic proportions during his superintendency (1919–1929).

In the 1920s the most persistent complaints by visitors involved roads, both the access roads to the park and the Loop system roads within. Automobile engineering and metallurgical developments were at a rudimentary stage. Spring leaves broke easily, brakes failed, starters balked, rods were thrown, bearings burned out, gears were stripped, and tires failed with maddening frequency. Concomitant with the existence of such undependable equipment were dirt roads that would put even a modern vehicle to the test. Auto touring as an adventure was fine in the abstract, or as tales told after the fact, but a broken spring leaf or a bent wheel caused by an unexpected pothole twenty miles out from Fishing Bridge was not a pleasant happening. People commiserated at campgrounds about vehicle problems and the virtues and drawbacks of various makes of automobiles; about their roads, they wrote their Congressmen.

Even with federal appropriations for road improvements, park officials were beset with serious problems. Park road construction had been by the army engineers, but just when automobiles began swarming in, making road improvements and maintenance essential, the engineers were busy with the First World War. Yet, despite constant personnel changes and lagging service, the engineers held on to their park assignment. Horace Albright began a campaign to get rid of them. "The Engineers," he wrote Secretary of Interior Franklin K. Lane, "never let go of anything if they can help it. . . . We need trained road builders in the parks, not inexperienced West Point graduates who go there [to Yellowstone] to learn this branch of engineering . . . . The Yellowstone has the worst roads of any national park. . . ." Albright and Lane won out. The engineers left for good on July 1, 1918. After that the National Park Service's own engineers drew up road plans while, after the mid-1920s, the Bureau of Public Roads actually built them.[49]

As early as 1920 plans were underway for paving the Loop roads. Secretary Lane in that year approved $100,000 for that purpose, hoping it would improve the ten worst miles. So rapidly were cars coming into the park— 5,703 in 1917 increasing to 10,737 in 1919—that he feared the whole system might disintegrate. Each year since has seen planned road improvements or new construction.[50]

Automobilists soon discovered that reaching the park was also a problem. Congressmen heard their complaints and soon the Park Service was drawn into discussions over what should be done about the poor access roads. National grants to states for road construction had begun in 1916 with passage of the Federal Highway Act, and Wyoming, Idaho, and Montana interests were quick to manifest their desire to obtain federal funds to improve their highways or build new ones leading to Yellowstone.

Wyoming's principal concern was the Cody Road leading to the east entrance. From its opening in 1909 it was popular, even though its narrow, precipitous right-of-way seemed especially hazardous for motor cars. Interior Secretary John Barton Payne was told that "sometimes women came in [to Cody] in automobiles from the park weeping because of the very great danger. . . ." He noted that of 79,777 tourists into the park that summer (1920), 19,871 had entered or departed via the Cody Road, "and to my mind it is really remarkable that some serious accidents did not occur."[51]

While Wyoming's citizens reaped profits from Yellowstone tourism, they were reluctant to spend state funds on their access roads, sure that federal funds would be forthcoming. They were. As Horace Albright reminded them, the Cody Road was built "almost entirely" with federal funds; moreover, the Park Service was still maintaining twenty-eight miles of the road outside the park in Wyoming's jurisdiction. The service had also constructed the highway south in Wyoming from the Snake River entrance to the settlement of Moose, in Jackson Hole, and was still maintaining it. By contrast, not one cent of Park Service money had been spent on Montana's approach roads.[52]

Idaho's interest in an access road involved a route along the Bechler River into the southwest corner of the reservation. When an irrigation project fell through that would have cut off from the park this "Cascade Corner," the road plans likewise failed to materialize.

Montana's interest lay in a highway from Red Lodge, southwest of Billings, over the scenic Beartooth Plateau to the northeast entrance of the park at Silver Gate. The recent part of the story begins in 1925 when Montana's senators, Thomas Walsh and Burton K. Wheeler, wrote Interior Secretary Hubert Work about the merits of such a highway. Their primary interest, however, was neither in scenery nor in a new entrance to Yellowstone, but rather in construction of a nonpark outlet for the Cooke City mines. They saw nothing wrong, however, in enlisting Park Service aid in obtaining funding. Secretary Work replied that the service was indeed favorable and would "help obtain its construction in any way possible."[53]

From then on, pressure for construction of the Red Lodge-Cooke City road (as it was known locally) never let up. Finally Congress in 1931 passed the Leavitt Act which, among other things, provided for "national park approach roads." Interior Secretary Ray Lyman Wilbur pushed for construction of the Beartooth Highway under the act's provisions and met with success. The highway was completed in 1935; during this same period the Cody Road and the Moran-Yellowstone Road were improved with these "approach road" funds. By the mid-1930s visitors to Yellowstone had little to complain about with regard to roads, although maintenance in high altitudes is a ceaseless struggle.[54]

Not everyone desired to see Yellowstone by public conveyance, whether by stagecoach prior to 1916 or motor bus after, or by private car. Affluent visitors since 1883 had followed one of the original dude ranchers, a big, husky outdoorsman named Howard Eaton, on bridle paths around the park. Because they catered to the wealthy, many of whom were both young and celebrities, Howard and his brothers, Aldon and Willis, became well known. Howard, however, was the predominant figure, warm-hearted, jovial, and competent.

Although Eaton led his first pack trip into Yellowstone in 1883, his big, annual, three-week excursions into the park did not begin until 1898, in 1902 the first women went along. By the 1920s, when dude ranching crested, so many ranchers took their guests on pack trips into the reservation that one authority stated that "dude ranchers and their guests were probably the prime users of Yellowstone Park at this time"—hardly likely with annual visitation ranging from 79,000 to 260,000 in the 1920s decade! Yet dude ranching activities in and about the park were significant in these years. Perhaps the largest single pack trip taken by dudes through Yellowstone was led by Dick Randall, whose ranch was north of the park. In 1926 he led 368 members of the Sierra Club of San Francisco through the park on a single pack trip.[55]

Meanwhile a New York woman, Mrs. Robert C. Morris, rode the bridle trails of Yellowstone's backcountry and presented Park Service officials with two maps and a report that suggested linking the segments into a single artery. Ultimately this was done. When Howard Eaton died in 1922, Superintendent Albright received permission to name the bridle path that follows the Loop Road the Howard Eaton Trail. It was 157 miles long at its inception, bringing to seven hundred the number of miles the park offered equestrians.[56]

New gadgetry of the twenties decade confronted the Park Service with the need for new regulations. Hard to believe, but from 1920 until 1926 permission was required to use a motion picture camera! Traveler's checks were not accepted as payment for entrance fees until 1929. Even before Lindbergh's transatlantic flight in 1927, applications for air service into the park were being received—and rejected. Hertz was denied the privilege of renting cars at the gateways for use in the park, primarily because concessionaires protested and an Interior Department solicitor submitted a negative opinion.[57]

In spite of rapid changes taking place in America in the 1920s, Yellowstone Park operated to the apparent satisfaction of most visitors. On one hand, the care and treatment of couponers was handled with éclat just as the whole system was about to become obsolete. On the other hand, growing numbers of automobilists, often subjected to poor service and inconveniences, seem to have accepted the hardships as a part of the great western adventure.

Not until the late 1920s—possibly not even until the depression of the 1930s—was railroad management willing to forfeit to motor vehicles the transportation of people. Towards the Yellowstone business, the railroads throughout most of the 1920s acted as if passenger service would continue into the foreseeable future; any decline in sales and revenues was viewed as a temporary aberration.

The Union Pacific continued to promote its service to West Yellowstone, which was just thirty miles from Old Faithful. Although business lagged badly after the Second World War, the company held on to its line until the Hebgen earthquake of 1959. The Burlington ran its first train into Cody on November 12, 1901. In 1924 the railroad expanded its Cody facility to include the eighty-room Burlington Inn. Business slackened after World War II and the inn was eventually leased, ignominiously, to an adjunct of the automobile industry, the Husky Oil Company.[58]

Old Codyites swear that on occasion cowboys rode their horses into the Burlington Inn dining room, poked six-shooters into sugar bowls, blowing them to bits, then, whooping and hollering, galloped out and back to downtown Cody. The guests were delightfully terrified. One suspects the Codyites exchanged knowing winks.[59]

All the while the Northern Pacific continued bringing passengers up the Park Line to Gardiner. One company to expand its tourist business despite passenger decline was the Chicago, Milwaukee, and St. Paul. It built forty miles of track through Gallatin River Canyon, and, at the terminal built an inn which the company claimed cost one million dollars. In tabulating its Yellowstone business for 1927, the first full season its Gallatin Gateway facility was operative, the Milwaukee railroad boasted that 5,200 passengers had used it.[60]

Even the Chicago and Northwestern Railroad, which served Lander, Wyoming, nearly 150 miles southeast of the park, made arrangements with the "Lander-Yellowstone Autobus Line" to convey passengers to the Tetons and Yellowstone. During the twenties their service was considered equal to that of any of the other railroads.[61]

Treatment of railroad-traveling clientele had changed little since stage-coach days. The basic park tour, cut to four-and-a-half days with the advent of motor buses, in 1925 cost $54.00 for transportation, food, and hotel lodging; if the guest chose to stay at the "permanent camps" (in 1927 the name was changed to "lodges"), the cost was $45.00. The greatest change for railroad-transported visitors was the substitution of motorized equipment for horse-drawn coaches. When the horses and tack and running gear left, so too did the personnel who serviced or used it, and so ended a colorful chapter in Yellowstone's history. Whereas "gearjammers," the name given bus drivers, tended to be one-season-only college students, many coachmen had been perennials. They had added color and interest to the grand rounds: "This is Alum Creek [in Hayden Valley]," announced the coachman. "Be very careful. Woman wearing size 8 shoes stepped in yesterday and when she came out they were size 1!"[62]

With a $500,000 loan Harry Child was a prime client for bus and automobile salesmen. A Mr. Kelly, representing the White Motor Corporation of Cleveland, Ohio, had the inside track. Child already owned a White passenger car. The automobile used for Colonel Brett's trial run in August 1915, had been a White "4-45." Big White automobiles and ten- and twelve-passenger buses were already in use in several national parks. White landed the contract.[63]

From an initial 125 vehicles (106 of which were three-quarter-ton, four-seated buses, the rest passenger cars) the number of "Yellowjackets," so named for their yellow color, increased until by 1927 more than three hundred White buses, touring cars, and trucks graced Child's Yellowstone fleet.

The old Whites were soundly engineered, state-of-the-art vehicles. The four cylinder engines started by cranking, but a "compression release" ended much of the muscle power that would otherwise have been expended. The engine had a $5'' \times 3\frac{3}{4}''$ bore, giving the motor very low torque. A four-speed, non-syncromesh transmission included an extra low gear. The combination was well balanced: engines ran cool even at Yellowstone's altitude and over its mountains. The 35″-×-5″ demountable rim wheels were something else! Changing them—and flats and blowouts were part of a gearjammer's day—was an exasperating task. Nor did these open touring vehicles have a horn; instead, they sported an "exhaust whistle" that commanded authority when blown. With carbide lamps and two-wheel brakes, without shock absorbers or windshield wipers, those old buses were dependable and, in those slow-moving days when the White's top speed was fifty miles an hour on the level ground, they served Yellowstone well.[64]

More Whites, bigger, improved, and enclosed, were acquired through the years until 1937 when White ceased bus manufacture. In 1923 two twenty-five passenger enclosed vehicles, a door for each seat, were added; in the early 1930s a newer model was introduced with a tarpaulin roof that could be unrolled, exposing passengers to sky and scenery. Old-timers speak nostalgically about those old people carriers, which they often called "box cars."

Only occasionally do the files reveal official dissatisfaction with bus and hotel services. When a woman took ill on a bus, requiring special transportation to a lower altitude in accordance with doctor's orders, Assistant Interior Secretary Finney expressed official shock at the amount the company charged. "It does seem to me," he wrote Acting Park Service Director Arno Cammerer, "that the transportation company for the sake of its own reputation should have been willing to have transported this sick woman and her husband either for nothing or at the exact cost of the trip. In other words, they should not take advantage of the necessities of their own passengers in order to wring out $50 for a trip of this kind."[65]

In a long memorandum from Superintendent Albright to Washington headquarters on the subject of "How to Improve Tourist Facilities," Albright's principal suggestions were to improve dining room bill of fare, obtain better orchestras for the evening dance, have a better host and hostess service to deal with the public, and maintain generally closer supervision of operations. Such suggestions hardly implied any serious deficiencies.[66]

Adding to the general satisfaction with the railroad-transportation-hotel system during the 1920s was its profitability. Harry Child and his son-in-law, Billie Nichols, and their park companies made substantial if not excessive profits during the twenties decade. The reduction in railroad passenger traffic was not evident in the number of visitors arriving by rail, as is seen from the statistics: from 1924 through 1928, ridership stayed at about 41,000 people, reaching a high of 44,786 in 1925.

During the period 1924 to 1928 the transportation company earned per rail visitor a net profit of $8.89. In 1929, although rail passenger visitation declined to 38,979, net profit per visitor was the highest ever at $9.58; the average rate of return on vested capital of the transportation company over the five years was 22.41 percent. Figuring the company's "return on invested capital, after elimination of assets not used in the business (excessive cash balances and intercompany accounts), for the years 1924–1928," the average was 51.37 percent; the "net profit derived from each dollar of revenue for the years 1924 to 1928, inclusive," was 33.2 cents.[67]

Since Child's hotel and transportation companies for certain accounting and tax purposes were allowed to combine their credits and debits, we know that between 1922 and 1929 net profits of the two companies combined were $4,290,892. Depreciation expense was $2,431,687, or a total of $6,722,579. The net profit and depreciation expense of the two companies exceeded expenditures for new assets and dividends by $1,885,309. Even considering professional accounting legerdemain, it is clear that the twenties decade was immensely profitable for Harry Child's two companies.[68]

While rail visitor figures remained fairly stable during the decade, they fell precipitously in terms of percentages of total visitation. Whereas in 1924 forty-one thousand of a total of one hundred forty-four thousand reached the park by rail, a little over 35 percent, in 1929 just under thirty-nine thousand of two hundred sixty thousand arrived that way, or about 6.7 percent.[69]

Everyone else came by private conveyance, the ubiquitous automobile. By no criteria were the new visitors rich or, for the most part, upper middle class; yet they were far from poor. They had money to spend.

Superintendent Albright's welcome to these people was far more genuine than the greetings extended by personnel of the hotel and transportation companies. To them these newcomers flooding the roads, stores, and campgrounds were hoi polloi spoiling the nice, contained, and profitable railroad-bus-hotel business. The concessionaires made money from these newcomers, however, and learned to cater to them even as the auto tourists became Yellowstone's dominant clientele.

Truth was, each group had to learn about the other. For example, the concessionaires soon learned that auto tourists, even if they could afford the tariff, shied away from the hotels. Whether they were big or small, prestigious or sleazy, the hotels made middle-class travelers feel awkward and ill at ease. In addition, motoring in the early years in open touring cars was a dusty business. Respectable people did not feel comfortable entering a lobby in dirty touring clothes.[70]

Where, then, did the auto tourists reside while in the park? Many put up at public campgrounds which Superintendent Albright expanded in size and number as funding permitted. Others headed for the "permanent camps," those crude facilities of half-cabin-half-tent construction that had been erected in earlier years by Wylie Way, Shaw and Powell, and other entrepreneurs licensed to cater to the lesser middle class. Included with them were the rustic, inferior hostelries known as Lake Lodge, Old Faithful Lodge, and Roosevelt Lodge. (The "camps" and lodges were all grouped as "lodges" after 1927, and all were under Child's monopolistic control after 1924.)

In early 1927 Albright sent a long memorandum to Washington in which he recommended certain improvements for Harry Child's camp company. He preceded his list by advocating no change in rates ($4.50 a night), providing the company carried out his suggestions. Since the camp company earnings in 1925 were in excess of 26 percent on invested capital, and remained good throughout the decade, the superintendent's requests seem mild. Albright wanted erected more than one hundred cabins dispersed as needed at the various camps. As soon as a cabin was built, a "temporary" tent dwelling was to come down. He wanted to supplant single beds for double beds and replace comforters and quilts with good blankets. He requested more bathing facilities, new employee dormitories, an upgrading of the lodges as "secondary hotels," construction of a recreation building or two, and additional cafeteria facilities; these were to serve more fresh vegetables, berries, and fruits. An Interior Department inspector agreed with the superintendent's suggestions.[71]

Today it is doubtful if even the most placid visitors would tolerate the facilities offered auto tourists in the 1920s. Some of the cabins, though no longer in use, were still standing at Fishing Bridge in 1981. One would think the Park Service would destroy them out of shame. There they were, down narrow little streets dusty in dry weather and muddy in wet, interspersed occasionally with an ugly bathhouse and here and there an outside water hydrant. They are now, and were when they were built, as ugly, cheap, and unaesthetic as miner's cabins in a nineteenth-century gold camp. No soiled dove on maiden lane would have tolerated such housing. Yet, with incredible lack of taste, the Park Service allowed a company earning more than one-quarter of its invested capital every year to build these cheapest of cheap hovels, charge for occupancy at $4.50 a night per person, and *continue using them well into the 1970s!*[72]

As for the half-cabin-half-tent installations, known as "canvas and frame cabins," they too experienced longevity. Even though Albright did not like them, insisting they were just tents, they were moved to auto camps where they rented for as little as $1.50 a night.[73]

But tourists tended to forget the hardships when the vaction ended. They remembered instead the evening campfire lectures by friendly park rangers, the bear-feeding at Canyon (ended after the 1941 season); casual conversations with friendly strangers about sightings of buffalo, elk, or moose, or serious discussions about radiators boiling at Dunraven Pass; rumors of this or that geyser about to erupt; hair-raising tales about bears mauling tourists—all this, and much more, constituted the life experience labeled Yellowstone.[74]

When Very Important Persons arrive in Yellowstone, the National Park Service, as befits any well-run organization, tries to be aware of their presence and makes plans accordingly. Congressmen, governors, cabinet officers, the powerful and friends of the powerful are given special treatment if the service knows of their coming. Their arrival is noted in a weekly bulletin; concessionaires, acutely aware of the politics involved in their franchises, also use common sense and give such guests special attention.

During the twenties Superintendent Albright hosted several very special guests. The first of them was President Harding's Interior Secretary, Albert B. Fall. As secretary, Fall was in a strategic position to aid or harm the Park Service and the whole national park movement. Fortunately the "Duke of Yellowstone" (Albright) did his job well. Fall did not meddle in Yellowstone Park matters.[75]

President and Mrs. Harding visited the park for two days in 1923. Again, it was important that Albright impress the chief executive because the Park Service was a new agency, attempts by irrigationists to wrest control of parts of the reservation and build dams and tunnels inside its boundaries were multiplying, and bitter controversy had been engendered over a proposal to extend park boundaries southward to include Jackson Hole. If Harding was to speak out in favor of such annexation, it would help the cause. Both he and Mrs. Harding had been in Yellowstone before, Mrs. Harding twice, once with a party on horseback with her husband.

This time they cavorted for photographers with a couple of bears. Mrs. Harding fed Max, a pet cub, a bowl of molasses. More to the president's nature was his offer to autograph a menu for each of the young waitresses at the Old Faithful dining room. The president publicly announced that he favored boundary extension southward to include the Tetons. His party entrained for Seattle; less than a month later he was dead.[76]

For Albright, President Calvin Coolidge's arrival in the summer of 1927 was the most memorable guest visit of all. Interior Secretary Hubert Work had urged the Coolidges, the president, his wife, and his son, at their vacation lodge in South Dakota's Black Hills, to take the trip to Yellowstone. Coolidge was proud of his piscatorial prowess, having made good catches of fat, sluggish trout, fed on ground liver and horse meat, that had been stocked in the Black Hills stream unbeknownst to him. Surely he would want to try his luck in Yellowstone Park![77]

Colonel Edmund W. Starling, head of the White House Secret Service detachment, impressed upon the hosts, "Don't tell him what to do!" This posed a problem, for Coolidge fished with worms, and worm fishermen did not have much luck in Yellowstone's waters. Rangers escorted the president to the Lamar Valley where fish were plentiful, hoping the trout would take the worm. They did not; Coolidge's mood that first evening was more sour than usual. The next expedition was to Yellowstone Lake. Albright decided that he *must* tell Cal what to do. He got him started on a shiny Colorado spinner, whereupon the president caught seventeen fine trout. Cal's Vermont granite countenance softened a bit. The next day Mrs. Coolidge went fishing and caught eight; she then quit because, she confided, she did not want to outfish her husband.[78]

In other matters with Coolidge, Albright was less successful. The president embarrassed the superintendent by walking out on members of the Wyoming Press Association who were meeting in the park; he refused to be driven south to the Tetons (although Mrs. Coolidge went), and it required the planning of a revolutionist pulling a coup to persuade Coolidge to leave via Sylvan Pass instead of retracing his route back through the North Entrance.[79]

One family that visited the park first in 1924, and appreciated Albright's hospitality, reciprocated generously. It traveled under the pseudonym of Davison, but the real name was Rockefeller—John D., Jr., his three sons and, on some trips, his wife. Shocked at the brush, stones, and other debris left by road crews, Rockefeller over the next several years contributed substantial sums for park cleanup, museum development, and other purposes.[80]

With the national park idea accepted by the people and Yellowstone's integrity assured, with the administration functioning smoothly, the concessionaires well established, and visitation under control, the future of Yellowstone National Park by 1930 bore promise of dull routine and little more history.

To a degree the promise was fulfilled. Yet whatever affects the nation is reflected in what happens in Yellowstone. A depression reduces tourism; a war virtually places the park in suspension and nature gains a respite; and the energy, technological developments, and mobility of the American people have an enormous influence upon the park. Other factors affecting the park are population growth and the increasing affluence of other peoples of the world, who then become tourists to the United States, certain to want to see Yellowstone.

The Great Depression curtailed visitation, though perhaps not as much as the economic severity of the times would suggest. In prosperous 1929 an estimated 260,697 tourists entered the park; visitation then fell to a low in 1932 of 157,624, but in 1934 the 1929 number was surpassed (260,775). Gains were steady and rapid after 1934. In 1940 the number reached the half million mark (526,437).[81]

In the worst year, 1932, only 8,575 tourists arrived at Yellowstone's gateways by train—just 19 percent of the number taking that mode of travel in 1925. The loss of railroad passengers was reflected in the nearly empty hotels and to some degree in the lodges, where a few rail tourists of lesser means stayed. The hotel company suffered a decrease in 1930 of 35 percent over its business of the previous year (1929), with a net loss of $77,621.[82]

During the twenties concessionaires had blinded themselves to the reality that auto tourists preferred the lodges, which included the tent cabins, to the hotels. Now the fact was brought home to them, for while Lake Hotel was closed and Mammoth's services were curtailed, Canyon and Old Faithful Inn still failed to register enough guests to pay expenses. To reverse the trend the company equalized tariffs, a three-and-a-half-day package tour costing $39.50 for housing at the lodges and just two dollars more, $41.50, for the hotels. But it made little difference. Concessionaires had to face the facts: hotels were obsolete, at least for the depression years.[83]

By 1934, with visitation back to past levels and growing steadily, park company managers realized that profits lay not in their hotels and transportation facilities, but elsewhere in their wide-ranging monopoly. Yet they were still reluctant to rearrange priorities, to concentrate on developing realistic facilities for the new clientele, so entrenched were their prejudices against the automobile tourists. They willingly took their captive customers' money but gave minimally in return. From 1930 through 1933 the Yellowstone Park Lodge and Camps Company earned a yearly average net return of 6.03 percent and in its worst year, 1933, it earned just 1.8 percent. By 1934 it was earning a 12.9 percent rate of return and in 1935, hardly a prosperous year in American history, it earned 26.17 percent on its net worth of $652,009. In deflated depression currency that came to $179,658.[84]

Hamilton Stores and Haynes Picture Shops, the other principal park businesses, continued to serve the public, charging the same or a little more than the going rate on like commodities outside the reservation. Groceries, for example, cost about the same as at Hall's Store at Gardiner, and liquor prices were those set by the state of Montana for its state liquor stores.[85]

Rates for goods and services have always struck many tourists as being excessive. "Dear Sir," began a postcard addressed to Interior Secretary Ickes, "If you would pay more attention to the running of the national parks (Yellowstone) where the charges remind the public of the war debt, and paid less attention to throwing mud, the whole country would appreciate it and the attendance at the above park would be much larger."[86]

Yet such indications of dissatisfaction rarely appear in the files. Through the years visitor complaints seldom have advanced beyond protests to clerks, hotel managers, and storekeepers. Protests against park personnel appear at a minimum. The scantiness of written complaints has been used by Park Service and concessionaires alike as an indication of visitor satisfaction. At the end of the 1949 season Superintendent Rogers submitted to Washington a tabulation of the season's written compliments and complaints. "When it is considered that 1,133,516 persons visited Yellowstone during the travel year," Rogers wrote, "the number of both compliments and complaints is extremely small. . . ." He was proud that of 115 letters, seventy-seven were complimentary and only thirty-eight critical. Of the latter, twenty-eight were in three categories: eleven protesting "efficiency and courtesy of concessioner personnel," nine unhappy over "service at hotels and lodges," and eight grumbling about "transportation services."[87]

But do this: ask anyone who visited Yellowstone prior to 1981 for his or her treatment by concessionaires—quality of food and housing, treatment by personnel, and prices—and the chances are very high that a strong, negative reply will be forthcoming. How, then, do we account for the paucity of complaints in the files?

A common-sense understanding of the life styles of middle-class Americans explains it. Park tourists are vacationing from the pressurized pace of modern life. For every mile they put between Yellowstone and home the unpleasant incident, whatever it was, in some measure is forgotten while memories of the happy experiences are retained.

Then the family arrives home. The car has to be unpacked, the neighbors drop over to welcome them back. The telephone rings: it is the boss who wants to see Dad about a pressing problem, first thing in the morning. Susie's orthodontist expects her in his office tomorrow at 9:00 a.m. In the stack of accumulated mail are bills to be paid and a certified letter, which should not have been delivered but was, ordering Mom to report for jury duty on a date already passed: "Fail You Not." Within minutes of their homecoming the family has been engulfed in the complexities of everyday life. The complaint letter is never written.

As few criticisms appear in Park Service or Interior files, so were few charges aired in the press. When, in September 1929, the mayor of Lynn, Massachusetts, Ralph S. Bauer, fired off a broadside accusing Yellowstone Park of being operated "as a shakedown for concessioners who are said to be making millions by bleeding the people of the last dollar possible," the *New York Times* editorialized that "so much has been said in praise of the national parks that it is a novelty to learn that someone feels that they could and should be improved."[88]

VIP treatment remained during the depression, as in all other times, excellent. To end the busy season of 1937 Superintendent Rogers was informed that President and Mrs. Franklin D. Roosevelt, their son-in-law John Boettiger, his wife Anna, her two children, and the whole entourage of Secret Service men and journalists would visit on the 25 and 26 of September.[89]

By the fourth week in September in Yellowstone the thermometer drops below freezing every night, the equinoctial sun shines over the land from a lowering angle and for shorter periods every day, patches of snow mottle the mountainsides and blanket the forest floor. It was the troublesome depression era at home, while problems of totalitarianism were rising abroad. A presidential visit in autumn seemed appropriate.

Several Montana officials met the president at Livingston and rode up to Gardiner with him. There he was met by Superintendent Rogers, who accompanied the party to Canyon Hotel. Clad in a tweed sport coat, wearing a light topcoat and over it (for President and Mrs. Roosevelt rode in an open car) a heavy navy cape with a velvet collar, the harassed president gave every evidence of enjoying the outing. Several times the car was stopped so he could observe the sleek, fat, black and cinnamon bears. "The bears looked at him, too," commented a correspondent. (Indeed, they do stare back, and one wonders what thoughts are passing through their brutish minds.) At the Dragon's Mouth Spring Mrs. Roosevelt, clad in fur coat and hiking shoes, got out and took a good look. She said she was looking for her uncle Teddy's laundry, he having lost it in a Yellowstone hot spring during one of his visits.[90]

Lunch was at the Fishing Bridge cafeteria where the waitresses, crisply attired in green and white uniforms, snapped their pictures. On the return trip to Mammoth they passed several Civilian Conservation Corps camps where the youths stood at attention. The Roosevelts spent the night at Nichols's cottage, proving that Harry Child's son-in-law was carrying on a family tradition of always catering to whoever occupied the White House, regardless of political party.[91]

Under instructions from the director, Superintendent Rogers used the president's visit to speak to Roosevelt about Park Service opposition to irrigation proposals still being pushed to dam Yellowstone Lake or divert its waters to the Snake River. After viewing that beautiful body of water for some time, "The President turned to me," Rogers reported, "and said, 'You do not need to worry, Mr. Rogers, no one will ever be permitted to touch that lake.'"[92]

Following the night at Mammoth the party viewed the geysers and entrained at West Yellowstone. Before leaving that tiny community the president addressed a small crowd. "Our chief problem of the future will be in taking care of people," he said, "because people are going to come whether we like it or not and it is up to us to look after them."[93]

Roosevelt's speech made sense: each year park visitation increased and each year the service and the concessionaires were more hard pressed to serve them. In its slow, bureaucratic way the service was grappling with the resultant problems when the United States entered World War II. Tourism plummeted: in 1943, the year of least patronage, just 64,144 people entered Yellowstone; the total for the war years 1942 through 1945 reached only 519,617—less than in the single prewar year 1941.

Yellowstone emerged from the Second World War unscathed and even refreshed. But when the great resurgence of visitors hit, neither the service nor the concessionaires was ready. Protests against poor housing, poor food, and inadequate service were heard in Congress.

It is not fair to blame entirely the Park Service for its failure to be ready when the nation was once again at peace, when gas, oil, and automobiles were once more available at reasonable prices, and middle America renewed its love of mobility. Even if planning for the postwar boom had taken place—and some had—pent-up postwar demands for everything-at-once precluded any quick, satisfactory solution to the problems brought on by the tidal wave of visitation that flowed into all of the nation's parks, Yellowstone included.

And indeed, a tidal wave it was. Even in 1945, the last war year, 178,296 tourists witnessed Yellowstone's beauties; in 1946 the number shot up to 814,907, and it topped a million for the first time in 1948. With only an occasional year of slight decline, visitation has continued rising until the Park Service now has to be prepared for more than two and a half million visitors into Yellowstone every year![94]

It is all well and good to lament the fecundity of the American people and the population explosion that followed the war, but it is a sterile exercise, unproductive of solutions. The real problems are in meeting the challenge of people handling, of preserving a wilderness in the face of overwhelming numbers of human beings. Planning helps some, trial and error perhaps even more, while solutions to other problems still defy the experts. They must be lived with since there is no other choice.

NOTES TO CHAPTER THREE

1. See Samuel P. Hays, *Conservation and the Gospel of Efficiency* (Cambridge: Harvard University Press, 1959), Chapter 3, "Woodsman, Spare that Tree," for an elaboration of Pinchot's arguments.

2. Gifford Pinchot, *Breaking New Ground* (New York: Harcourt, Brace, and Company, 1947), 26. I have examined the checklist of the Gifford Pinchot papers in the Manuscripts Division of the Library of Congress, but found nothing of importance in the two or three Yellowstone items listed.

3. The literature of Hetch Hetchy, of Progressivism, and the conservation movement is voluminous. A thoroughly researched article on Hetch Hetchy is Kendrick A. Clements, "Engineers and Conservationists in the Progressive Era," *California History*, Vol. 58 (Winter, 1980), 282–303. On the nature ethic see Aldo Leopold, *Sand County Almanac* (New York: Oxford University Press, 1949). The growing national park idea is discussed in Runte, *National Parks*.

4. The Grand Loop today consists of the following segments: Mammoth Hot Springs Junction to Norris Junction (20.6 miles); Norris Junction to Madison Junction (13.7 miles); Madison Junction to Old Faithful, in the Upper Geyser Basin (16.2 miles); Old Faithful to West Thumb Junction (16.9 miles); West Thumb to Lake Junction (20.4 miles); Lake Junction to Canyon Junction (15.4 miles); Canyon Junction to Tower Junction (19.2 miles); Tower Junction to Mammoth Junction (18.1 miles). Add the entrance roads, the road from Norris to Canyon, and the primary first class road total is 319.7 miles. United States Department of the Interior, National Park Service, "Roads List," 1–2.
This is quoted in Dr. Robert R. O'Brien, "The Yellowstone National Park Road System: Past, Present, and Future" (Ph.D. dissertation, University of Washington, 1964). I hereby acknowledge my indebtedness to Dr. O'Brien, who is a geographer.

5. Road suggestions of R. Hering and Henry Gannett are in F. V. Hayden, *Sixth Annual Report of the United States Geological and Geographical Survey of the Territories* (Washington: G.P.O., 1872), 92–95: 802–7. Langford's statement is in his *Report of the Superintendent of Yellowstone National Park for the Year 1872*, 2. See also General O. O. Howard's letter to Lieutenant Dan Kingman in Kingman's Report of 1883, National Archives R.G. 79, PMLR, Chief of Engineers to Secretary of the Interior Teller, January 10, 1884.

6. O'Brien, "Yellowstone Road System," 56.

7. 22 *U.S. Statutes at Large*, 626.

8. *The National Cyclopedia of Biography*, Vol. 28, 265; *Enterprise*, October 5, 1883; R.G. 79, PMLR, Conger to Teller, August 18, 1883. The sum was later reduced to $24,000. PMLS, Conger to Kingman, October 27, 1883.

9. Kingman's reports of his Yellowstone operations do not appear in the *Annual Report of the Chief of Engineers* for 1883 through 1886. I have used copies in the PMLR files. The *Annual Report of the Chief of Engineers for 1887*, Vol. 4, Appendix AAA, 3133–38, quotes extensively from Kingman's reports.

10. Ibid.; *Enterprise*, November 21, 1883.

11. Kingman, "Report for 1883."

12. Ibid.

13. *Enterprise*, November 21, 1883.

14. Kingman, "Report for 1884."

15. Kingman, "Report for 1885." The present road was built by his successor, Hiram Martin Chittenden; it was widened in 1934. See Bruce LeRoy, *Hiram Martin Chittenden, A Western Epic* (Tacoma, Washington: Washington State Historical Society, 1961), 22.

16. *Enterprise*, January 12, 1884.

17. Kingman, "Report for 1886"; PMLR, Kingman to Interior Secretary, September, 1886, PMLS, Assistant Secretary Muldrow to Superintendent Wear, May 25, 1886; PMLR, Captain Moses Harris to Interior Secretary, September 12, 1886; Kingman to Secretary, September, 1886. The tire order was mentioned in Congress—*Congressional Record*, 49th Cong., 1st Sess. (August, 1886), 7865. Whether the order had anything to do with Kingman's being transferred is conjectural, but transfers do result from such quarrels. Arnold Hague stated that Kingman was transferred because the engineers considered him "underused." R.G. 57, Hague Papers, Hague to Captain Harris, March 25, 1889.

18. Kingman, "Report for 1886."

19. *Annual Report of the Chief of Engineers* for 1889, 1890, and 1891.

20. Y.A., File No. 3, Charles Gibson "To the Committee on Appropriations of the House of Representatives, May 1888."

21. Lieutenant Craighill, "Report for 1891."

22. A good biography is Gordon B. Dodds, *Hiram Martin Chittenden* (Lexington: University of Kentucky Press, 1973); see also Le Roy, *Chittenden,* and my review of the Dodds book in *Pacific Historical Review,* Vol. 43, No. 3 (August 1974), 423–24.
Chittenden's *The Yellowstone National Park* first appeared in 1895 and went through many editions. A reprint is available, edited by Richard A. Bartlett (Norman: University of Oklahoma Press, 1964).

23. Craighill, "Report for 1891."

24. Le Roy, *Chittenden,* 22.

25. Interview of author with Mrs. Arnold, October 4–6, 1970.

26. *Congressional Record,* 51st Cong., 2d Sess. (February 9, 1891), 2373; W. A. Jones, in *Annual Report of the Chief of Engineers for 1893,* Appendix EEE, 4392.

27. Richard C. Overton, *Burlington Route: A History of the Burlington Lines* (New York: Alfred Knopf, 1965), 233; Don Russell, *The Lives and Legends of Buffalo Bill* (Norman: University of Oklahoma Press, 1960), 426–28. The spur also gave business to the railroad in the Big Horn Valley.

28. *Indianapolis News,* May 18, 1910.

29. Y.A., Box No. 21, Interior Secretary Hitchcock to Major Pitcher, April 16, 1902. See also my essay, "Those Infernal Machines in Yellowstone," *Montana: The Magazine of Western History,* Vol. 20, No. 3 (July, 1970), 16–29.

30. Y.A., Letters Sent, Vol. 11, p. 316, Major Pitcher to Interior Secretary, April 23, 1902; Y.A., Box No. 21, Secretary to Pitcher, May 12, 1902.

31. "First Car to Venture in Yellowstone Park," *Montana Motorist* (September, 1962), 5. See C. B. Glasscock, *The Gasoline Age: The Story of the Men Who Made It* (New York: The Bobbs Merrill Co., 1937), 88

32. Y.A., Box No. 29, Petitions Sent by Representative Franklin W. Mondell to the Secretary of the Interior dated January 17, 1908; see also Y.A., Letters Received, Vol. 7, 160.

33. Y.A., Box No. 29 and Letters Sent, Vol. 18, 233, Colonel S. B. M. Young to the Interior Secretary, January 25, 1908.

34. John Ise, *Our National Park Policy* (Baltimore: Johns Hopkins University Press, 1960), 202.

35. Y.A., Box No. 43, copy of report of Captain C. H. Knight, Corps of Engineers, to Colonel Lloyd M. Brett, Acting Superintendent, April 8, 1912.

36. Ibid., copy of letter from F. Jay Haynes to Captain Knight, April 16, 1912.

37. Ibid., copy of letter from Louis C. Laylin, Assistant Secretary of War, to a Mr. S. A. Hutchinson of Chicago. This letter was included as an enclosure in Hayne's letter to Captain Knight, cited above.
Hardly worth mentioning was the opening of a miserable stretch of road in the extreme northwest corner of the park in 1913. Not until 1914 did two automobiles and a motorcycle dare its dangers. Ibid., Colonel Brett to Mr. A. W. Hjorth of Casper, Wyoming, July 4, 1913; Box 118, Weekly Outpost Report, Gallatin Station, August 12, 1914.

38. Y.A., Box No. 43, newsclipping from an unidentified Idaho newspaper; letter from Adolph Miller, Assistant Interior Secretary, to Colonel Brett, July 3, 1913.

39. Ibid., Colonel Brett to Miller, July 9, 1913.

40. Ibid., correspondence of Colonel Brett, June-November, 1914.

41. Ibid., copy of letter from F. Jay Haynes to the Assistant Interior Secretary, May 16, 1914.

42. Related by Horace Albright to author, April 16, 1970.

43. Y.A., Box No. 44, copy of regulations for the season of 1915.

44. Y.A., Box No. 43, telegram. Colonel Brett to Secretary of the Interior, July 29, 1919; Secretary to Brett, July 31; Colonel Brett to editor, *Motor Age,* August 3, 1915.

45. Ibid., Colonel Brett to Frank M. Thomas, President, American "Ford" Owners Association, Inc., Albany, New York, September 3, 1915.

46. Robert Shankland, *Steve Mather of the National Parks,* 3rd ed. (New York: Alfred Knopf, 1970); and Donald C. Swain, *Wilderness Defender* (Chicago: University of Chicago Press, 1970); Horace Marden Albright and Frank J. Taylor, *"Oh, Ranger!" A Book About the National Parks,* rev. ed. (New York: Dodd, Mead, and Co., 1934); Runte, *National Parks.* Policies of the superintendents are discussed in greater detail in Part III here, "The Superintendents."

47. There is as yet no satisfactory social history of the automobile in America. I have used Rand McNally's Golden Anniversary Celebration, Facsimile Edition (1926) *Auto Road Atlas of the United States* (Chicago: 1974), and Warren James Belasco, *Americans on the Road* (Cambridge, Mass.: The Massachusetts Institute of Technology Press, 1979).

48. Emerson Hough, "Maw's Vacation: The Story of a Human Being in Yellowstone," *Saturday Evening Post,* Vol. 197 (October 16, 1920), 14–15; also published as a pamphlet by J. E. Haynes, St. Paul, 1921.

49. R.G. 48, Department of the Interior, Office of the Secretary, Central Classified File, 1907–1936, File No. 12-12 (Part 1), "Parks, Preservations, and Antiquities, Yellowstone National Park," Roads, December 21, 1917–August 6, 1928. Horace Albright to Interior Secretary Franklin K. Lane, December 21, 1917. (Hereafter, citations will read "R.G. 48, Central Classified File.")

50. Ibid., Roads, Franklin K. Lane to Senator Francis E. Warren, January 20, 1920.

51. Ibid., Secretary John Barton Payne to Mr. Eustis of the Burlington Railroad, August 20, 1920; Payne to unknown recipient, November 21, 1920.

52. Ibid., Albright to P. Beall, Chairman of the Special Committee, the Cody Club, March 24, 1931.
I have found considerable animosity among Yellowstone personnel towards the state of Wyoming which, they feel, always takes from the park but gives nothing in return. The Wyoming sales tax, collected in the park since 1941, is a good example of Wyoming's "take," they say.

53. Ibid., Secretary Hubert Work to Senator Walsh, January 29, 1927.

54. Ibid.; 46 *U.S. Statutes at Large,* 1053; R.G. 48, Central Classified File, Secretary Ray Lyman Wilbur to Commerce Secretary Robert P. Lamont, April 1, 1931; Walter B. Sheppard of Denver to Interior Secretary Harold L. Ickes, April 10, 1933.

55. Lawrence R. Borne, *Dude Ranching: A Complete History* (Albuquerque: University of New Mexico Press, 1984), 21, quotation on 49.

56. *New York Times,* Magazine Section (February 10, 1918), 7; R.G. 48, Central Classified File, Albright to Director, June 30, 1932.

57. R.G. 48, Central Classified File, "Rules and Regulations," File No. 1; Ibid., "Privileges," Arlo Cammerer, Acting Director, to Interior Secretary Work, March 5, 1927; Ibid., Memorandum from Stephen Mather to Work, June 9, 1927. Harry Child, who possessed considerable political acumen, was afraid that General Motors' political power was behind the Hertz request. Northern Pacific Archives, Office of the President, Box No. 81, Item 210I-A, June, 1926. In custody of the Minnesota State Historical Society, Minneapolis.

58. "The Dowager Queen's Demise," *Inside Husky* (house organ of the Husky Oil Company) No. 2 (March-April, 1981) 1, 5, 8.

59. Ibid., 3. Dick Frost, curator of the Buffalo Bill Museum, claims this event happened several times. Dick Frost to author, 1982. The inn was torn down in 1980.

60. R.G. 48, Central Classified File, Chicago, Milwaukee, and St. Paul news release dated September 23, 1927, and sent to Secretary Work.

61. Y.A., Department of the Interior, "Manual for Railroad Visitors; Time Tables Yellowstone Park Tours: 1925."

62. Ibid.; R.G. 48, Central Classified File, "Privileges," Memorandum from Horace Albright to Stephen Mather, November 17, 1927. Such tall tales as the Alum Creek story are common banter in the Yellowstone region.

63. Yellowstone Park Transportation Company ledger, 174. This is in Professor K. Ross Toole's microfilm collection of Yellowstone materials, reel no. 15. Hereafter cited as Toole Collection. See also Northern Pacific Archives, Box 81, item 210-I, Burlington Vice-President to Harry Child, September 16, 1916. This letter adds that while Stephen Mather wants the park motorized next season (1917), and desires that there be just one transportation company in the park, Mather "will fully protect the interests of the hotel company." A narration of Colonel Brett's trip around the park is in *The Albatross* (White Company house organ), No. 32 (August, 1915), 5– 9.

64. Diane Thomas, "White Bus is Veteran of Yellowstone Scene," *Old Cars,* no volume or number (August 1–15, 1973), 20–23; *The Albatross,* No. 87 (no date), 22.

65. R.G. 48, Central Classified File, "Privileges," September 27, 1926.

66. Ibid., "Administration," February 3, 1927.

67. Ibid., "Privileges," Memo of W. A. Blossom, Park Service Auditor, to Director, February 5, 1930; Ibid., Memo of Charles L. Gable, Chief Auditor, Park Operators' Accounts, to Director, January 6, 1930. These concern a Park Service suggestion that the transportation company reduce its rates. It was pointed out that at the close of 1928 the transportation company had on hand and in the bank $1,606,052, "being an increase in that year alone of almost a half million dollars over the previous year" (Blossom memo). Billie Nichols was protesting the recommendation.

68. Ibid., Blossom memo.

69. Haines, *Yellowstone Story,* 2, 479.

70. Belasco, *Americans on the Road,* 41–61.

71. R.G. 48, Central Classified File, "Complaints," Letter from Director Cammerer to Secretary Wilbur, December 4, 1926; Secretary Wilbur to Director Albright, October 21, 1929; Ibid., "Administration," Memo from Albright to Assistant Secretary Edwards, February 3, 1927.

72. When I lunched with a personnel director for General Host, which ran park facilities in the mid-1970s, and inquired about those horrible cabins, his reply was "What's the matter with 'em? We fill 'em up every night, and a conglomerate likes that!"

73. R.G. 48, Central Classified File, "Privileges," Memorandum to Interior Secretary from Acting Director of the Park Service, January 13, 1927.

74. Ibid., "Animals," Assistant Interior Secretary Chapman to Senator James E. Murray, August 31, 1944. Albright, always the public relations person, protested this decision and even had Bert Griffin, secretary of the Bozeman Chamber of Commerce, file a protest. Ibid., Memorandum, Director Newton B. Drury to Assistant Secretary Oscar Chapman, September 15, 1944.

75. Swain, *Wilderness Defender,* 144–45; interview of author with Albright, April 16, 1970.

76. *Enterprise,* July 24, 1923; Horace Albright, "Harding, Coolidge, and the Lady Who Lost Her Dress," *The American West,* Vol. 6, No. 5 (September, 1969), 25–32; Swain, *Wilderness Defender,* 152; 173–75.
Although much of Albright's time in the 1920s was taken up with the Teton matter, I have avoided discussion of it here since it does not directly concern Yellowstone. A superb analysis of the controversy is Robert W. Righter, *Crucible for Conservation* (Boulder: Colorado Associated University Press, 1982).

77. R.G. 48, Central Classified File, "Privileges," Secretary Work to Harry Child, September 3, 1927. In this letter Work thanks Child for the excellent service

he gave to the president's party. For Coolidge's Black Hills vacation, see W. J. Bulow, "When Cal Coolidge Came to Visit Us," *Saturday Evening Post,* Vol. 219, No. 27 (January 4, 1957), 65, and Edmund W. Starling (as told to Thomas Sugrue), *Starling of the White House* (New York: Simon and Schuster, 1946), 246–60.

78. Interview with Albright; Starling tells another story about Coolidge and trout fishing. Starling, *Starling of the White House,* 254–55.

79. Ibid. Albright is a magnificent raconteur; a couple of his yarns about Coolidge are hilarious, but space prevents including them here.

80. Swain, *Wilderness Defender,* 154–55. Examples of the gifts are in R.G. 48, Central Classified File, "Donations," Arthur E. Murray of the Park Service to Interior Secretary, $5,000 from John D. Rockefeller, Jr., "for roadside cleanup in Yellowstone National Park," September 13, 1929; Superintendent Roger W. Toll to Director, funds for museum development through a "Committee on Outdoor Education," $5,050, May 23, 1930.

81. Haines, *The Yellowstone Story,* 2, 479.

82. R.G. 48, Central Classified File, "General," Superintendent Roger W. Toll to Director, September 23, 1932.

83. Ibid., "Privileges," Superintendent Albright to Secretary Wilbur, February 14, 1931; Ibid., May 11, 1932; Ibid., Director Cammerer to Assistant Superintendent, granting permission to close Lake Hotel and Lodge, July 5, 1932; Ibid., Cammerer to Assistant Interior Secretary, February 5, 1936.

84. Ibid., Memorandum from Director Albright to Interior Secretary, February 6, 1931. Albright adds that the average annual rate of return 1924–30 was 27.36 percent.

85. Ibid., "Privileges," Hamilton Stores, schedule of basic rates for 1936 season.

86. Ibid., "Complaints," postcard from Harry L. Jones, Baltimore, to Secretary Ickes, June 16, 1936.

87. Ibid., "Administration," Letter included in memo from Director Drury to Interior Secretary, September 30, 1949.

88. *New York Times,* September 3, 1929, 2; September 4, 1929, 28. Later the paper reported the Park Service denial, that the mayor "must be generalizing from some personal experience which should have been reported to the local superintendent." *Times,* September 5, 1929, 18.

89. R.G. 48, Central Classified File, "Administration," Memo from Director Cammerer to Secretary Ickes, September 17, 1937.

90. *New York Times,* September 26, 1937, 1, 39.

91. Ibid.

92. R. G. 48, Central Classified File, "Administrative," Rogers to Director, October 5, 1937.

93. Ibid. It was good that Superintendent Rogers spoke to the president against the irrigation plans since Idaho's Senator James Pope, a sponsor of the plan, boarded the train at West Yellowstone.

94. Haines, *Yellowstone Story,* 2, 479.

THE CONCESSIONAIRES &
THEIR PERSONNEL

CHAPTER FOUR

Early Yellowstone Enterprises

*T*he first facilities for tourists in Yellowstone were built around the use of Mammoth Hot Springs' therapeutic mineral waters. Even if the water was nothing but pure H_2O, it was guaranteed by the spring owner to help cure many ills.

Indeed, "taking the waters" was the principal form of vacation in America during most of the nineteenth century. However, just about the time Congress created Yellowstone National Park in 1872, changes in the American mode of leisure were beginning to take place. These alterations had an impact upon the development of visitor facilities in Wonderland, and so they warrant our attention.*

Holidays, vacations, and leisure were anathema to most Americans at the time. It was suggested by a writer in the 1850s that his generation was dedicated "not to enjoy life, but to prepare it for the enjoyment of those who are to come after. . . . We are," he wrote, "a race of pioneers whose object is to clear the land, and not to reap its fruits. . . ." Certainly the challenge of conquering this last great temperate zone wilderness left little time for leisure. Fortunately the challenge was met by a people fortified with a Calvinist Protestantism that stressed hard work. Toiling long hours six days a week was part of the creed. There was, then, something irreligious and dangerous to one's immortal soul about taking time off unless for good and substantial reason. So the Protestant vacation had to be called by another name, and it must be in the guise of something that represented a useful spending of time. Restoring one's health might do. So people "took the waters."[1]

Indeed, "taking the waters" was the great vacation ploy. The eastern United States proliferated with such resorts. New York had Saratoga with

*By a vacation I mean a sustained period of two weeks or so to an entire season. This differentiates it from the American meaning of "holiday" which is usually considered a day set aside for leisure or recreation, whereas to the British and Europeans, "holiday" is synonymous with the American vacation.

such great hotels as the United States, the Congress, and the Grand Union; elsewhere in the Northeast were the Catskill Mountain House, the Round Hill Water Cure Retreat, the Brattleboro (Vermont) Hydropathic Establishment, and many others. In the South, Virginia and (after 1863) West Virginia dominated the scene with the Greenbrier at White Sulphur Springs and many other spas. Along the Northern Pacific Railroad into the Pacific Northwest were Broadwater Hot Springs, Bozeman Hot Springs, Chico, Corwin, and Hunter's. Some had plunges under glass domes while others advertised the healing qualities of their mud and mineral baths. Actually no part of the nation was lacking in these thinly veiled pleasure emporiums.

Such sanitariums, spas, water retreats, springs, baths, or by whatever name they were called, were socially acceptable, desirable because expensive, and morally satisfactory because one's leisure could pass as a quest for health. It was, writes one authority, "an admirable application of the Puritan ethic regarding cleanliness and godliness, to say nothing of temperance." Certainly it was better than the purge with calomel and the phlebotomy then so much in vogue.

The hypocrisy of it all was rather transparent. The father of the family was prone to imbibe more in bourbon than in the healing waters, and discover the gaming table before he visited the baths. Ninepins on the green and quoits, later croquet and tennis, were the usual sports. Often an in-house orchestra provided music for dancing. Flirtation was another diversion. Wooded paths bore such names as Lover's Walk or Courtship Maze; at Saratoga one spa even had a "proposal sofa" while another boasted a "Billing, Wooing, and Cooing Society."[2]

In the last third of the nineteenth century these watering places went into decline. Improvements in medical knowledge with a resultant loss of faith in waters as a cure had something to do with it. A weakening of the Protestant ethic, especially its harsh Calvinist concepts, encouraged open acceptance of the vacation as a time of leisure. Finally, the increasing mobility that railroads afforded encouraged time spent in travel to faraway places, like Yellowstone. Why go to the same old nearby retreat when it was within one's budget to visit the great, romantic, Golden West?

Railroad officials noticed this growing broad-mindedness. They undertook to build resort hotels along their rights-of-way. They needed the business, for they faced stiff competition. By 1883 the Northern Pacific, Union Pacific, Santa Fe, and Southern Pacific were operational transcontinental lines; in 1893 the Great Northern joined them. Steadily lowering passenger tariffs, culminating in a rate war in 1886 and 1887, further enticed vacationing Americans and produced a demand for exclusive hotels.

The railroads, along with a few independent entrepreneurs, built enormous luxury hotels. the Southern Pacific built the Del Monte at Monterey, opened in 1887; the Santa Fe the Montezuma at Las Vegas, New Mexico in

1882 (hot springs determined the location); Henry Flagler in Florida built the Ponce de Leon at St. Augustine in 1885; General W. A. J. Palmer of the Denver and Rio Grande Railroad opened the Antlers at Colorado Springs in 1883 and the Broadmoor a few years later. Nonrailroaders financed the Hotel Raymond at Pasadena and the Palace at San Francisco. By the 1890s scenic points such as the Grand Canyon of the Colorado, Yosemite, and, of course, Yellowstone entered heavily into railroad plans. In 1883 interests close to Northern Pacific management opened the big hotel at Mammoth Hot Springs. Travel agencies, such as Raymond and Whitcomb of Boston, chartered tours to these places. In short, a grand trip West became a part of the upper middle class scenario. At least one historian has suggested that this change to long-distance vacations represents "a minor social revolution." Earl Pomeroy states that by the early 1880s "family groups of tourists (with women uniformly exceeding men) were dominating whole trains to Florida and California, and whole steamers to Europe."[3]

Still another development in the uses of leisure had its effect upon Yellowstone, though it was a serendipitous one. This was the rise of that class of vacationers calling themselves sportsmen, hunters and fishermen. According to historian John Reiger: "Before the Civil War most Americans viewed these activities as acceptable only when necessary or helpful to the maintenance of a livelihood. . . . As the editor of one of the later outdoor journals put it, 'a man who went "gunnin or fishin" lost caste among respected people just about in the same way that one did who got drunk.'"[4]

By the 1870s and 1880s a change had taken place in this American outlook. Perhaps increasing numbers of wealthy sportsmen gave respectability to these diversions; possibly the hundreds of thousands of Civil War veterans who cherished the manly sports of hunting and fishing made them acceptable. American nimrods and piscators emulated the British image of the gentleman sportsman. The image took root quickly on American soil partly because of several new periodicals that propagandized high sporting principles: *The American Sportsman* (1871), *Forest and Stream* (1873), *Field and Stream* (1874), and *The American Angler* (1881). So rapidly did these sports grow that by 1874–75 "nearly 100 sportsman's associations were organized all over the country, ten or twelve state associations and one national association." By 1878 at least 308 such organizations were functioning. It was such sportsman-advocates as Theodore Roosevelt, George Bird Grinnell, and W. Hallett Phillips, aided by the impressive membership of the Boone and Crockett Club, who led the nation's sportsmen in a campaign for Yellowstone's inviolability. They helped save the park from undue exploitation and even dismemberment.[5]

Yellowstone's visitor facilities reflected national trends. In 1872, with the park still at least six hundred miles from the Northern Pacific's railhead in Dakota, several entrepreneurs had already staked out claims and opened for business. Most of their properties were in the vicinity of Mammoth Hot Springs where the alleged therapeutic qualities of the waters provided the attraction.

There were three such resort owners: James C. McCartney, Henry R. Horr, and Matthew McGuirck. They were without doubt among the persons Superintendent Langford referred to in his annual report when he said that "a few months before the Act of March 1, 1872. . . several persons had located on land. . . with a view to establish a squatter's right of preemption."[6]

In a sworn statement James McCartney said that he had located in June 1871, at Mammoth Hot Springs, where he had "erected two houses at said springs for the accommodation of visitors and travelers"; in 1872 he had added a storehouse, and the next year "another dwelling house and a stable 50 by 16 feet."[7]

Adjoining the claim or possibly at one time sharing it with McCartney, was Henry Horr's homestead. At almost the same time down on the Boiling River (where the waters from Mammoth Hot Springs surge out of an embankment into the Gardner River) Matthew McGuirck built a hostelry. He hoped, as did the others, for eventual ownership through the right of preemption.

By the summer of 1872 these crude installations were catering to tourists and invalids. "We found houses and men and women and children in adundance, which were great curiosities," seventeen-year-old Sidford Hamp, with the Hayden Survey, wrote to his mother in England in 1872. "We bought some butter and fruit which were equal curiosities and very good." All that summer there was quite a camp at Mammoth, with Montanans predominating, the visitors including a "goodly number of Eve's fair daughters."[8]

When the preemptioners heard that the park was a legal reality they applied for the usual 160-acre quarter sections, including within their claims all improvements. Everything was denied them on the grounds that only Congress could adjudicate such claims; but they were allowed to remain on their "claims" temporarily.[9]

All three men stayed for years in the Yellowstone vicinity, although McGuirck and Horr eventually obeyed mandates to leave the park. Horr later stated that "Mammoth Hot Springs [was] the name given by me to my former home." In 1880 he circulated a petition advocating his appointment as park superintendent. A friend of Norris's, in relating this knowledge, described Horr as "a drunken worthless sort of man with no ability or qualification for the position he seeks. . . ."[10]

The most stubborn squatter was James C. McCartney. Claiming that he had constructed some of his improvements prior to the enabling act, he steadfastly refused to abandon his land and buildings at the entrance to Clematis Gulch. When Norris assumed the superintendency, he referred to

McCartney as "the pioneer proprietor of the Mammoth Hot Springs Hotel." In the absence of a thorough knowledge of conditions, Norris even appointed him "Resident Assistant" of the park. [11]

McCartney, meanwhile, tenaciously held on, a prime believer in the adage that possession is nine-tenths of the law. He hired lawyers, wrote letters, enlisted political influence, and ignored the United States Supreme Court. This involved a decision of December 1872, in the "Yosemite Case" (*Hutchings* vs. *Low*), in which that tribunal had established "that mere settlement on the public lands does not, previously to proving up and payment, vest the settler with such an interest in the premises as to deprive Congress of the power to divert it by otherwise disposing of it." [12]

McCartney stayed on. In 1878 Norris tried in vain to evict him by occupying McCartney's main building; in Norris's absence McCartney returned and locked *him* out. At last the superintendent gave up. The squatter had too many friends in high places, he explained, as well as "the armed sympathy of the Military at Fort Ellis . . . the active sympathy of the Delegate {to Congress} from Montana and also the drunken and debased portion of the Mountaineers." [13]

Norris, a teetotaler, was most exasperated by McCartney's liquor business. On the Fourth of July 1879, a blowup occurred. "J. C. McCartney," Norris wrote Secretary Schurz, "has slyly sold intoxicating liquors, . . . resulting in a quarrel, fist fight, and shooting affair." A "stalwart mountain desperado named McCarley" was bested in an altercation with one of Norris's men, made threats, and ambushed four of the superintendent's followers, firing two shots at them at short range. Whereupon a Norris employee rushed up, dashed the gun aside and struck McCarley senseless "with fist blows which would have killed a mule. . . ." Norris and some of his men then marched to McCartney's grog shop, halted the sale of whiskey, cared for the whipped McCarley, and the next day escorted him under guard to Bozeman. [14]

McCartney held out until the late 1880s. When the superintendents were in residence he usually moved "down from Mammoth," though never abandoning his claim. "Down from Mammoth" meant that he settled on land in the "Montana Strip," that two-mile width within the park north of the 45th parallel and therefore outside of Wyoming's jurisdiction. He carefully fenced about eighty acres and constructed a saloon, stable, and other buildings within a disputed north-south span of seventy-five feet that remained in legal limbo. (The dispute arose over the question of what constituted the mouth of the Gardner River, which was the specified park boundary in the enabling act.) Here this frontier Raynard continued his activities. [15]

Two other innkeepers appeared in the early years and held onto leases under park regulations dated May 4, 1881. The first of these individuals was George W. Marshall, who in 1879 held a mail contract from Virginia City to

Mammoth Hot Springs. When this route was discontinued, Marshall established a crude inn at a site he had spotted in the Lower Geyser Basin, Marshall's Hotel. On January 30, 1881, the Marshalls had a baby girl, the first white person born in the park. According to Marshall in an interview many years later, Governor John W. Hoyt of Wyoming, upon seeing the little girl, "named her Rose Park, 'Rose' because roses were scarce in the park, and 'park' because she was born in the same." Marshall's was later replaced by the Fountain Hotel.[16]

The other squatter made honest with a lease was John F. Yancey. "Uncle John" was related to the southern fire-eater William Lowndes Yancey. He had built a small hostel to serve the Cooke City trade. A log structure 50 by 30 feet with beds in the upper half-story, it was located at Pleasant Valley not far from Roosevelt Lodge. On April 1, 1884, he was granted a formal lease. Yancey's letterhead for his Pleasant Valley Hotel emphasized a "Saloon in Connection." He imported an orange concentrate from California which, added to his forty-rod whiskey, made it somewhat more palatable. He charged a dollar a shot, serving the liquor in one dirty glass which he boasted had never been touched by water. His dogs ran wild and he was convicted of killing an elk in 1902. "Uncle John" died in 1903; his hotel burned to the ground in 1906.[17]

One early occupant of the park, Collins J. ("Yellowstone Jack") Baronett, chose to earn his living by owning a toll bridge across the Yellowstone River near Lamar Junction. In 1870 this intelligent Scotsman, a soldier of fortune with complex past and uncertain future, discovered the one place along the Yellowstone between the Nez Perce ford (between the falls and the lake) and the mouth of the Gardner River where the stream could be crossed. There "Yellowstone Jack" hewed a trail down one embankment and up the other, and then, according to Philetus Norris, built "a timber pier . . . upon a huge boulder amidst the roaring torrent and covering it with huge cross timbers formed a good foot bridge for men and mules. . . ." On a bench of land on the east side, a hundred feet above the junction of the Lamar and the Yellowstone, he built his cabin. If Norris is to be believed, Baronett also maintained a veritable arsenal in a cave in the cliffs overlooking the bridge.[18]

The charge was one dollar per man or mule. He collected his fee under the threat of a steady arm, a good eye, and a Winchester rifle. The bridge was used mostly by miners going to and from the New World Mining District centered at Cooke City. In 1877 the Nez Perce burned the span. When General Howard, in hot but tardy pursuit, found his passage blocked by the mass of burned timbers, he ordered some of Baronett's buildings cannibalized for a temporary bridge. Baronett reconstructed it, but insisted that after 1877 he did not charge tolls. Not until the mid-1880s was the bridge finally sold to the government.[19]

"Yellowstone Jack" was an important participant in Yellowstone events into the 1880s. General William Emerson Strong described him as "of medium stature, broad shouldered, very straight, and built like Longfellow's ship, for 'strength and speed'; eyes black as a panther's and as keen and sharp; complexion quite dark, with hair and whiskers almost black. . . ."[20]

In 1877 Baronett left his Yellowstone quarters for a brief fling at gold mining in the Black Hills of Dakota. While there he was the winner in a typical western-style shootout; his adversary was killed. Superintendent Norris clipped the newspaper story of the affair, adding, "As well might the eastern miners walk with their shotguns into a gulch lair of Hogback Grizzlies as to arouse Baronett . . . and other comrades from the upper Yellowstone. . . ."[21]

"Yellowstone Jack" returned to the park from the Black Hills, remaining at his bridge for several more years, serving as a guide and sometimes as a game warden. Then one day he announced that he was leaving the Yellowstone country. One authority says he went to Alaska, lost his savings, and was last heard of in 1901 as an indigent in Tacoma, Washington.[22]

For years McGuirck's, McCartney's, and Baronett's claims lingered between lawyers' offices, the Interior's solicitor's office, and the halls of Congress. In 1899 Congress finally got around to settling these annoyances by appropriating small sums in final settlement: McGuirck received $1,000, McCartney $3,000, and Baronett $5,000. "Uncle John" Yancey's nephew, Dan Yancey, filed a claim with the government in 1935, which Congress honored in 1940 with an appropriation of $1,000.[23]

These individuals, plus George Marshall, were the prominent, most visible and stable entrepreneurs inside the park in the early days. However, any impression should be crushed that they were the only ones preying on, or serving, tourists. "Let the tourist beware," warned the Earl of Dunraven, an English nobleman who spent much time in the West, and indeed, there were people to serve or fleece visitors inside the park and for a hundred miles outside it. Some hired out as guides, some grazed horses and rented them within the park without government permission, and some hoped to earn their keep in less honest ways. "You can hardly realize the number there is of all grades of vagabonds and tramps that under various pretenses are trying to obtain some sort of a foothold or settlement in the park," Superintendent Conger wrote his superiors in 1884.[24]

Some squatted, built "improvements," and gave every indication of remaining. Superintendent Carpenter in 1884 set out to eject a few settlers who could not resist the lure of the hayfields and grazing lands in the Lamar and Soda Butte valleys. His targets were the ranch houses of Tate and Scott, and Jackson and "Buckskin Jim" Cutler. Captured, the four were sent in an open wagon several hundred miles south to the jail at Evanston, Wyoming.

They were brought before a judge, but no indictments were handed down.[25]

The formal granting of leases, begun in the early 1880s, and the harsh measures taken to evict squatters were harbingers of an increased interest and concern over the park's security. By the early 1880s the Northern Pacific Railroad was approaching completion as a transcontinental artery. New investors sensing great profits from tourism appeared on the scene. They were backed by eastern capital. Major changes were about to take place in Yellowstone.

Although American railroad mileage did not crest until 1911, the industry was vigorous and expansionist in the 1880s. Nowhere was this more apparent than in the West where, in 1883, the Atchison, Topeka, and Santa Fe and the Northern Pacific both achieved transcontinental status. Now there were four transcontinentals (the Union Pacific and Southern Pacific being the other two) vying for business, each one trying to make high profits.

Of the four, it is the Northern Pacific that most interests railroad historians. The road was rarely well surveyed, soundly constructed, honestly financed, or well run, all of which makes its history a fascinating study of Gilded Age big business. Due partly to the unstable nature of its management, the line was more subject than most railroads to the boom and bust, roller coaster Gilded Age economy. And since the N.P. became closely involved with park concessions, this instability extended to Yellowstone and affected its visitor facilities.

The N.P.'s beginnings started with an impractical Yankee visionary who nonetheless had made two fortunes. His name was Josiah Perham. On March 30, 1860, his company received a charter from the state of Maine. Perham then journeyed to Washington to lobby for his enterprise but lost out to the Union Pacific-Central Pacific crowd. No matter: he simply rerouted his railroad from the central route, preempted by the U.P.-C.P., to a more northerly one. Thaddeus Stevens, the powerful Republican Congressman, liked the idea; with Stevens's aid the Northern Pacific charter passed Congress and was signed by President Lincoln July 2, 1864.[26]

In 1868 Perham died in poverty, having lost control over the railroad. Jay Cooke, a financier of the Civil War, grabbed control and by September 1873, his road had reached the Missouri River. A town had been platted and named Bismarck in the futile hope that such an honor to the Iron Chancellor would bring in German investors. It did not. Construction halted and Jay Cooke and Company collapsed. By that time in 1873, however, survey crews working under protection of the U.S. Cavalry, including Custer's 7th had worked up the long, southwest-running valley of the Yellowstone. Management, foreseeing tourist profits from the Yellowstone region, had helped bring about passage of the Yellowstone Enabling Act in 1872.

After the crash, the N.P. stagnated. Some said the railroad went from "Nowhere, through No-Man's-Land, to No Place." Yet always there were optimists who predicted an end to the depression, revival of business, and renewal of railroad construction. They never ceased activity. While in the mid-1870s the nation's economy stagnated, the Sioux were rounded up and life on the northern plains became safe from Indian depredations. As early as 1868 cattlemen had invaded Wyoming, while Montana's Beaverhead Basin had grazed cattle since as early as 1850; by 1880 nearly a million beeves grazed on the plains of Wyoming and Montana.[27]

By the late 1870s the depression was clearly on the wane. It was apparent that European emigrants as well as restless Americans were once more suffering from the western itch. A capitalist named Frederick Billings brought about the refinancing of the Northern Pacific. Track laying was renewed; by 1880 the N.P. had just about a thousand miles left to go before its east- and west-running rails would meet.[28]

In the Northwest, German-born Henry Villard in 1882 succeeded Frederick Billings as president of Northern Pacific. With Teutonic vigor he pushed track laying until on September 8, 1883, at Gold Creek in western Montana, the last spike was pounded. Meanwhile the firm's house organ, a flamboyant booster-type paper called the *New North West,* scattered propaganda far and wide about this "land of the future"; included in almost every issue was information on Wonder Land—Yellowstone National Park.[29]

Knowledge that now the West was safe spread across the eastern United States like a gentle zephyr. Suddenly Americans clamored to go West, and they wanted to include Yellowstone in their itinerary. Only the Northern Pacific could take them there. Trouble was, Yellowstone in 1882 was lacking in adequate facilities. The few locally owned establishments were limited in space and were disgustingly crude. Massive, expensive hotel construction was necessary if the anticipated flood of visitors-via-railroad was to be accommodated.

But the Department of Interior had no plans for meeting this inevitable flood of visitors. After all, no true bureaucracy existed in the early 1880s; not until 1883 was there a Civil Service, and for years it embraced only a small percentage of federal employees. The "Great Miscellany," as Interior was known, simply accumulated more agencies to administer because no one else wanted them. The department was also the great agency for patronage jobs. Generally the unstable politics of the era resulted in change not only of the secretaries and their assistants every four to eight years but also of many if not a majority of the clerks. Continuity in the Interior Department seems to have rested primarily in the person of the chief clerks, one of whom was Edward M. Dawson, who figures in the Yellowstone story. No blue-ribbon committees or high-cost consulting firms existed to advise the secretary. The department lived from day to day transacting what business came across the desks. Tomorrow had to take care of itself.[30]

Interior Department files for the years 1872 through 1882 are crammed with queries, proposals, and applications for concessions in Yellowstone. They range from practical requests for hotel, lunch room, livery, stagecoach, and boating franchises to ludicrous proposals such as a "landscape gardening plan" for the park; establishing a town at the south end of Yellowstone Lake; a museum of natural history; a saloon; an assay office; a lime kiln; a menagerie; and "a race course and observation grounds," including tablets upon which were to be inscribed the world's history, with some allegories from the Bible and the pyramid of Gisah worked in.[31]

What these requests lack in common is indication of fiscal backing—to say nothing of brain power—to carry out the proposals. Only occasionally does a solid businessman come forth with a proposal, but even then are missing the follow-up letters, recommendations from powerful people, and requests from Congressmen for special attention to sincere, determined applicants. Clearly, in the first decade of the park's history such entrepreneurs showed little inclination to invest in the park.

Insofar as park superintendents were concerned, they had relatively little to say about concessionaire policy. Langford, who never resided in the park, suggested in 1873 that he be appropriated $15,000 for constructing wagon roads, "and when this is done, private enterprise will provide commodious public houses and other necessary comforts for tourists." He suggested that "the rental value of leased premises . . . will be sufficient to defray all expenses necessary for keeping the improvements made, in proper place." A year later he wrote that he had received applications for leases but had "not deemed it advisable to grant them, until proper police regulations are established." Langford also advocated changing the lease period from ten to twenty years, believing, correctly, that a longer period would meet with favor from investors.[32]

Superintendent Philetus Norris, who had made himself financially comfortable through real estate promotions, would be expected to show a businessman's interest in concessionaire policy. Norris's only interest, however, as revealed by his official correspondence, was in bringing under control or expelling those businesses that were already there. After Norris came Conger, Carpenter, and Wear in rapid succession. As a threesome they covered the feverishly active period of 1880 to 1886.

Conger did examine several requests. Beginning with his tour of duty there was an upsurge in the number of queries and some improvement in their quality. Yet the same problems remained, as Conger informed Secretary Teller upon his (Conger's) rejection of a hotel application from W. H. Thurston of Bismarck, Dakota. The applicant had failed to follow up on the initial query. "I am forced to the conclusion," Conger wrote the secretary, "that Mr. Thurston like so many of your petitioners for favors in the park have not duly considered the undertakings which they propose and would not be likely in many cases to fulfill on their part should you decide to grant their prayers."[33]

At this time (1881 to 1883) the center of policy moved east to Washington. Until March 4, 1881, the secretary of interior was Carl Schurz, an honest, plodding, hard-working German emigrant who had achieved high status in the Republican party. Schurz possesseed keen foresight; he was aware of the embracing tentacles of the octopus called monopoly. This is evident from his rejection letter to Messrs. J. B. and A. W. Hall of Fargo, Dakota Territory, who had applied for monopoly hotel privileges in Yellowstone. "I have to state that the Department must decline to grant to any person or firm, exclusive privileges in the matter referred to," Schurz stated forthwith.[34]

When Schurz penned his rejection he was a lame duck secretary with just six weeks left in office. He must have been aware that Yellowstone Park would soon lose its isolation. The Northern Pacific was already publicizing Wonderland. Certainly the secretary knew that park facilities were woefully inadequate to meet a tourist influx. He was also realistic enough to know that the problem was not to be his, but his successor's. Nothing indicates, however, that any committee, or even a permanent employee, was charged with studying the problem and coming up with solutions.

Instead, the Department of Interior was plunged into a period of turmoil. Garfield's appointee, Samuel J. Kirkwood, assumed the office of secretary. But President Garfield was shot and died just over six months after taking the oath of office. Chester Arthur became president; Secretary Kirkwood was replaced in 1882 by Henry M. Teller of Colorado who remained in office until the end of Arthur's term in March 1885. Instability in the patronage-filled department must have been acute. If a nascent park concessionaire policy had existed, as Schurz's statements against monopoly concessions implied, that policy was lost in the chaos. Under such unstable conditions a strong vested interest with political sagacity would be able to shape policy in its own interests. This is exactly what happened with regard to concessions for Yellowstone Park.

While the federal government muddled through an assassination crisis, the Northern Pacific went right on building. Interior's obligation as Yellowstone Park administrator demanded that facilities be there as needed. If suitable roads, rest rooms, hotels, lunch stations, liveries, and stagecoaches were not available and serving the public adequately, then criticism would be leveled at the administration. By 1882 the condition was present and worsening, for already park tourism was on the rise. What should be done?

At this juncture certain private interests offered a solution. As Yellowstone's potential as a resort became closer to reality, more hardheaded businessmen turned their attention to it. Early in 1882 an application arrived in the secretary's office from ten men of the Northwest, most of whom had been in the park and one of whom, George Marshall, ran a decrepit hotel there. They applied for a park hotel monopoly.

Interior policy had always been to forward applications to the park superintendent for his comments, and this was done with Teller requesting Pat Conger to "enquire into the responsibility of the applicants named." Moreover, it was Conger's responsibility to inform the applicants of departmental regulations: leases for just ten years, nontransferable except with consent of the secretary, and to be cancelled if no improvements were made within the first eighteen months after signing. No leases were to be granted "that will in any way prevent free access to . . . curiosities or springs." This, Teller added in his covering letter, was "to prevent monopoly." Furthermore, since the law authorized leases "on small parcels of ground," no application would be entertained for "more than twenty acres in one tract. . . ." Selection of building sites was left to the superintendent, though the secretary retained final power of approval.[35]

This application constituted a master plan for construction of permanent facilities on a scale designed to meet anticipated business. Secretary Teller's letter conveyed every indication of a sincere intention to process the proposed lease in an honest and businesslike manner. Yet nothing more was heard of this application; it was pigeonholed in deference to another monopoly proposal.

First wind of the new plan appeared in the January 16, 1882, issue of the *New York Times*. Under a St. Paul dateline, the article stated that a syndicate had been formed "of wealthy gentlemen, more or less intimately connected with the Northern Pacific to build a branch tourist's line . . . to the heart of the Yellowstone National Park, and erect there a large hotel for the accommodation of visitors." Listed as interested members were Senator William Windom of Minnesota, Superintendent Carroll Hobart of the Northern Pacific, and other prominent men of the Minnesota-Dakota country. The syndicate would enjoy "exclusive hotel privileges in the park," and would invest $150,000 for a 500-room hotel. Although filled with discrepancies, the article was basically accurate.

Here the story gets murky—hard evidence is lacking—but it is obvious that political pressure was brought to bear upon Interior Department officials to issue to a single company a contract granting ownership, control, or both of just about every park visitor facility. Sheer political pressure plus the urgency of the situation seem to explain what was later called "the park steal." It appears to have been a pragmatic action with little underlying thought being involved in the decision.

The ramifications of this granting of monopoly privileges in the park are nevertheless of extreme importance in national park history because the monopoly lease established a policy maintained for nearly a century. Given the urgent situation in Yellowstone and the political climate of the time, what were the secretary's alternatives? We have already observed that investing in the park in this early period was risky business. Yellowstone was still far removed from population centers. Shipping costs were high. The season was short. Leases were for just ten years and, politics being as they were, the risk was very real that a concessionaire could lose his franchise and be left with nothing but debts. No wonder there were few solid businessmen applying.

In the absence of viable applicants, the only practical alternative Interior could employ was to grant leases to small business people such as those already doing business in the park, men such as Yancey, Marshall, McCartney, and Baronett. This posed a problem of trying to establish and maintain standards from entrepreneurs of very limited means who probably lacked the vision to contemplate, let alone serve, the hordes of tourists who would soon be entering the reservation.

Should Interior run the facilities? In the political climate of the 1880s this was out of the question. A somewhat more conservative solution—for Interior to build and maintain facilities and lease them to private parties on a season-by-season basis—did not appear at the time as an alternative or even a thought. An urgent need combined with scarce options was aided by a period of instability in the department and pressure by a powerful outside interest to bring about Yellowstone's first monopoly lease.

Not until July did the group mentioned in the *Times* approach Secretary Teller officially through Carroll T. Hobart, one of the men specified in the report. Shortly thereafter an application for an *agreement* to *grant leases* reached Teller's office. The request was signed by Hobart and Henry M. Douglas; it had been transmitted from Senator William Windom's office. Windom was no run-of-the-mill senator. He had been secretary of the treasury in Garfield's brief administration; his continued prestige is verified by his appointment as treasury secretary by President Benjamin Harrison in 1889. "I am personally acquainted with both the signers of the application," Windom stated in his covering letter, "and I have no doubt of their ability to carry out their proposition to the entire satisfaction of the Department. Will take occasion to see you in regard to this matter in a day or two."[36]

Initially the application was treated like all others. It was handed over to Teller's assistant secretary assigned to Yellowstone affairs, Merritt Joslyn. In accordance with established procedures he sent a copy of the proposal to Superintendent Conger in Yellowstone. "Will thank you to report as early as practicable, your views as to propriety of granting to said parties the privileges asked," Joslyn concluded.[37]

When Conger read the application he saw the proposal for what it was, a masterpiece of Gilded Age monopolism. He readily perceived that the grant would allow the company to control every exotic view in the park. And so did he express his reaction: "Notwithstanding the high endorsement the gentlemen have received from Senator Windom, and their undoubted respectability and financial ability, yet it is my judgement that they ask to cover too much ground. . . . I believe the public would be restive were all of these privileges granted to a single party or corporation," Conger reported to the Washington office.[38]

Indeed, the "steal" was very clearly worded. Conger's condemnation was mild. Article I was "open sesame" to monopoly: the government "agrees to lease unto the said parties of the second part, such parcels of land within the said park as may be selected by the said parties of the second part necessary to fully carry out the objects and purposes hereafter mentioned. . . ." This materialized into 4,400 acres which, at seven sites, averaged 628.57 acres per unit, or nearly a square mile. These huge lots could be shaped as the company saw fit. Annual rental was not to exceed two dollars per acre.

A key phrase in Article II gave to the company "so much of the timber, coal and other material within the said park as may be required . . . ." Tracts were to be available for raising fruits and vegetables. Park waters were free for the hotels "and other buildings (including bathhouses) . . . and for the use of power. . . ." The company was to construct all buildings necessary and provide stages, telegraph lines, and delivery services from railway stations to the park. On the lakes it was to provide "yachts and other sailboats and rowboats." Minuscule government control was indicated by the company's obligation to submit to the secretary, for his approval, a complete tariff on rates. Should Interior fail to renew the leases, the property would revert to the government "subject to such compensation therefor as may be granted by Congress."

Article XIV specified monopoly control: "The party of the first part hereby agrees that the parties of the second part shall have and enjoy the privileges herein and hereby conferred, and granted to the exclusion of any person or persons for the term of ten years commencing from the date of the first lease hereinafter to be granted. . . ." The final article (XIX) also proved important: "And it is further agreed by and between the parties hereto that this agreement may, by mutual consent, be changed, altered, modified, or abrogated in whole or in part."[39]

Yancey's, Marshall's, and McCartney's small hotels, Baronett's toll bridge (although he claimed that he ceased charging in 1877), a minor lease dated July 17, 1882, to Major James S. Brisbin to run a steamboat on Yellowstone Lake—a lease he subsequently relinquished—and F. Jay Haynes's photographic studio at Mammoth still remained operational. But they were small installations compared with the huge plans being made by the newcomers.[40]

Political pressure for the sellout must have been intense. On August 24 Joslyn received a telegram from Senator Windom: "Hobart and associates propose reaching Washington next Thursday morning. Can contract for park privileges be prepared and executed by that time answer." No reply has been found, but on September 1, before Conger's critique from his Yellowstone headquarters could have arrived in Washington, Assistant Secretary Joslyn, in Teller's absence, signed the agreement on behalf of the Department of the Interior. It was a very formal document running more than twenty-five hundred words. From a legalistic point of view it is important to keep in mind that it was a contract or an agreement providing for the granting in the near future of formal leases on sites not yet specified or surveyed.* The "parties of the second part for themselves, their heirs, executors, and assigns, and such other parties as may hereafter be associated with them" proved to be Carroll T. Hobart of Fargo and Henry F. Douglas of Fort Yates, both in Dakota Territory.

From Secretary Carl Schurz's antimonopoly statement of January 1881, the Department of Interior had done a complete reversal. Though details of the agreement remain obscure, it is clear that pressure came from Northern Pacific interests. It is probable also that the lobbyists and their political allies found Henry Teller and his aides unexpectedly receptive. This was because Yellowstone Park, with the railroad approaching, was of great concern to them, and here was a quick, convenient way out of the impending visitor facilities problem.

In view of nearly a century of concessionaire relations based upon monopoly or near monopoly privileges, it is worth noting the advantages Teller must have considered. The monopoly gave strongest indication of having the financial resources to accomplish what needed to be done. Its presence dimin-

---

*Shortly thereafter the sites were surveyed, though so poorly that conflict arose over specific metes and bounds, at Mammoth, Lower, Midway, and Upper geyser basins, West Thumb, Lake, and Canyon. It has been said that Teller absented himself from his office in order to avoid signing the agreement. This could have been, but I have found no evidence corroborating this statement.

ished rivalries by reducing the number of establishments; it simultaneously reduced the number of people with whom park authorities, in their capacity as regulators and protectors, had to deal. In many ways monopoly rights seemed to offer then—and to some groups today—the greatest assurance of good service to visitors and harmonious relations with the government.

Obviously the Interior Department found many facets of the concession monopoly system to its liking, for it has retained the policy, with some restrictions, to the present. The concessionaires were assumed to be people of integrity; they were to be treated by the government as any other public utility. And so Interior has stuck with the system through years of mismanagement, insufficient financing, economic recessions, bankruptcy of the Northern Pacific, and strong opposition from elements both within and without the government. By about 1900 a modicum of stability, a modus operandi, had evolved in Yellowstone which had as its anchor one powerful company. In addition, as noted above, a few small businesses were allowed to continue such operations as bathhouses or photo shops. In time, in Yellowstone, the entrepreneurs constituted sort of a Yellowstone peerage with their own pecking order of power and privilege. But the company was always king.

The real story begins, however, with creation of the Yellowstone National Park Improvement Company, and that brings us back to the year 1882 and Carroll T. Hobart and Henry F. Douglas. Hobart had been a section superintendent on the N.P.; Douglas had been sutler at Fort Yates, the military post that secured the Standing Rock Agency.[41]

Hobart appears to have been the chief architect of the plan although it is possible, perhaps probable, that Northern Pacific executives, already planning the Park Branch Line to Yellowstone's boundary, were the instigators. Possibly, for reasons known only to them, they approached Hobart with the idea, or it could have been the other way around.

Hobart and Douglas had signed the agreement as "the party of the second part," but their troubles were far from over, for the two men had little money. Therefore, a third person was involved as part of the "party of the second part." This was Rufus Hatch, a shrewd Wall Street financier, who by age fifty (in 1882) had already made and lost two fortunes. "Uncle Rufus" as he was known on Wall Street, was supposed to provide the money.*

One source of Hatch's unsavory reputation was his control of the Cattle Ranche and Land Company, a corporation which he founded in London. It claimed to hold "range rights" in the Texas Panhandle, rights also claimed by

---

*Wall Street so dubbed him because he was free with his advice, beginning his counsel by saying, "Now, you listen to your Uncle Rufus. . . ." *New York Times,* February 24, 1893, Section, I, p. 1.

the United States government and the states of Texas, Kansas, and Colorado. By 1884 this company had experienced disaster as had Hatch, who, as we will see, had lost heavily in the Northern Pacific Railroad and his Yellowstone National Park Improvement Company.[42]

Hatch had become well known to N.P. financiers. "In 1882," he later wrote Superintendent Wear, "I took a trip West, at the invitation of Mr. Billings and other officers of the Northern Pacific Road. . . ." He went on to explain that at Fargo he "was met by Mr. C. T. Hobart who presented me with an introduction from Mr. Oakes [a high N.P. official] setting forth the fact that Mr. Hobart had a contract with the government for developing the wonders of the park, and asking that I take hold of the affair with Hobart, and try to make it a national undertaking." He further elaborated that Hobart and Douglas assigned him 35 percent interest in the project, and that "upon that basis" he formed a company "with the best men I could think of as Directors, trying to secure an equal number of Democrats and Republicans, Eastern and Western men."[43]

Hatch's contract with Hobart and Douglas appears to have been signed September 19, 1882; on January 18, 1883, Hatch and his friends, among whom was New York politician Roscoe Conkling, organized the Yellowstone National Park Improvement Company under the laws of New Jersey, and the Hobart-Douglas agreement with the Interior Department was "duly assigned to the Company." Hobart was appointed vice-president and general manager to supervise activities in the park, while Hatch and his friends supplied the money. According to Hatch, the initial investment came to $112,000 "hard cash," with "guaranteed $30,000 additional, to build the hotel at Mammoth Hot Springs, and to erect temporary structures at other points in the park."[44]

Certainly the company meant business. Early in the fall of 1882 Hobart arrived in Yellowstone and made preparations for hasty construction of the big hotel at Mammoth and other improvements throughout the park. In due time he had chosen a hotel site northeast of the hot springs and the Liberty Cap. Times were propitious for luxury resort developments, and "Uncle Rufus" and his Northern Pacific friends were not going to be caught waiting on the siding.

Hobart erected sawmills, hired a substantial crew, and by the time snow fell was diligently at work on the foundations of the proposed 250-room hotel. Plans were ambitious, time was short, and at this stage money was no problem. Hobart proceeded to cut all the wood he wanted wherever he found it in the park. He contracted with local hunters to furnish his men with meat, especially elk meat illegally killed on the reservation. Machinery and supplies had to be hauled by teams from the end of the N.P. In Hatch's first annual report to the secretary of interior he stated that over 1,686,000 feet of timber had been cut in the twelve months beginning September 1, 1882.

Annual reports omit the ten thousand and one problems, annoyances, crises, vexations, and irritants that occur when too much construction is demanded too quickly. One night some employees obtained whiskey and got drunk, with the result that one man shot and seriously wounded another. In June 1883, when the company was working desperately to get the hotel into usable condition, the carpenters struck for better food and pay. Only when they received the promise of better food and a fifty-cents-a-day increase in wages did they go back to work. On June 30 two workmen fell fifty-four feet from a scaffolding. There was no telephone; the injured men waited hours in agony while someone rode to Livingston, obtained a doctor, and brought him back to the hotel. One poor fellow died after ten days, but the other recovered and was described later as being "about ready to resume work."[45]

Meanwhile other necessities were taken care of. A brook had to be dammed and pipe laid for the hotel water supply. Electrical equipment was installed by the same New York company that had lighted the Brooklyn Bridge. (Only corridors and piazzas were lighted, but it was still a marvel to the natives in 1883.)[46]

St. Paul merchants were awarded most of the furniture, carpeting, and plumbing contracts. Captain John Smith, a well-known Montana saloonkeeper, was awarded bar privileges. A Mrs. McGowan was hired to handle the "ladies department of the hotels and tents"—whatever that position entailed. Two French chefs, a German baker, and two cooks were brought in. Noticed by a reporter at the railhead where it awaited drayage to Mammoth was an enormous stove, twenty-two feet long and nearly six feet wide. Somehow a Steinway grand piano was freighted in.[47]

Small wonder the local inhabitants were impressed! When A. I. Hatch, Rufus's brother, appeared from the East in charge of a large supply of elegant silverware, the *Enterprise* editorialized that the park hotel was to be "furnished and managed in . . . style second to nothing at the various pleasure resorts of the world. . . . The Improvement Company," it added, "expect that the Yellowstone Park will always be visited by a large representation of the wealth and fashion of America and Europe, and propose to furnish accommodations suited to the taste even of children of luxury."[48]

The rising hotel building was evidence of the way Rufus Hatch did things. Plans were drawn by architect Leroy S. Buffington of St. Paul, the distinguished designer of a number of St. Paul mansions and "father of the skyscraper." The structure was to be 414 feet long, fifty-four feet deep, and four stories high. As it stood in the late summer of 1883, it had 141 "commodious" rooms and, wrote Hatch, was "substantially built," which rather stretched the truth since only the great central section had been completed. "There has never been a building of the magnitude of this one constructed in

such a wilderness," Hatch boasted, insisting that the hotel had already cost
$140,000. Moreover, in the first year at Mammoth the company had built a
two-story warehouse, a large stable, and four smaller buildings for such uses
as dairying and laundering.[49]

In addition the company established tent camps at Norris, the Upper
Geyser Basin, and at the Great Falls of the Yellowstone. "These," Hatch
wrote, "were all equipped with substantial wall tents, carpeted and furnished
with bedsteads, spring mattresses, chairs and other conveniences, and the
kitchen tents provided with large hotel cooking ranges." All of this required
drayage of an additional twenty-seven to eighty-five miles over horrible
roads. Finally, telegraph poles had been erected from Cinnabar to Mammoth,
seven and a half miles, and the wire would be strung in the spring of 1884.

Transportation was handled by contracting with Wakefield and Hoffman, Montana stage line operators, even though their coaches that first year
were mere spring wagons. Then, working through Secretary Teller and/or
Assistant Secretary Joslyn, company officials were instrumental in having
Superintendent Conger deny livery and stage privileges to anyone else inside
the reservation. Conger posted notices around the park forbidding anyone
from hiring teams or conveyances of any kind within the park boundaries,
except those of Wakefield and Hoffman.[50]

One entrepreneur whom Hatch, Hobart, Douglas, and company did not
touch, although he was running a photographic studio within easy walking
distance of the hotel, was F. Jay Haynes. He had come out from St. Paul in
1881 and at once became a Yellowstone devotee. Of all the lessees and franchised operators in Yellowstone's history, no one came within shouting distance of the Haynes family for business ethics. They conducted business with
integrity, cooperated with park officials, and expressed a concern over the
park's destiny that was lacking from all other concessionaires. F. Jay Haynes
was succeeded in 1916 by his son Jack Ellis Haynes, who lived seventy-five of
his seventy-seven years in Yellowstone; upon his death his wife assumed management of the firm and only disposed of the holdings in 1968.[51]

As the season of 1883 approached, activity increased at Mammoth and
along the miserable roads that led to interior points of interest as well as
down the Yellowstone Valley to Livingston. No one knows the number of
visitors that year—Conger estimated five thousand—but we do know that
among the number were many wealthy and distinguished persons, led by
President Chester Arthur.[52]

The progression from concessionaire-squatters such as Baronett and Mc-
Cartney to a monopoly primed with large sums of eastern capital and influential political power was complete in 1883. The few small concessionaires
were to be small satellites in the presence of Yellowstone National Park Im-

provement Company. But if officials in the Interior Department felt they had settled the thorny problems of concessions for years to come, they were badly mistaken. Trouble was brewing before the foundations had been laid for the great hotel at Mammoth. To understand what happened it is necessary to return to the autumn of 1882.

NOTES TO CHAPTER FOUR

1. "Are We a Happy People?" *Harper's New Monthly Magazine,* Vol. 14, No. 80 (January, 1857), 207.

2. Sources include Harrison Rhoades, "American Holidays: Springs and Mountains," *Harper's Magazine,* Vol. 129, No. 720 (July, 1914), 211–21; William Frederick Dix, "American Summer Resorts in the Seventies," *The Independent,* Vol. 70, No. 3261 (New York: June 1, 1911), 1211–15; Edward C. Atwater, "The Lifelong Sickness of Francis Parkman (1823–93)," *Bulletin of the History of Medicine,* Vol. 41, No. 5 (September-October, 1967), 413–39. The listing of spas along the Northern Pacific is from Chet Huntley, *The Generous Years* (New York: Random House, 1968), 152. See also Billy M. Jones, *Health-Seekers in the Southwest, 1817–1900* (Norman: University of Oklahoma Press, 1967).

3. Pomeroy, *In Search of the Golden West,* 5–6.

4. Reiger, *American Sportsmen,* 25.

5. Ibid., 39–40.

6. Langford's Report is in the *Annual Report of the Secretary of the Interior for 1872* (Washington: G.P.O., 1873), 4.

7. Y.A., Box No. 1, Item No. 1, "Affidavit of James C. McCartney." The dwelling, which he shared occasionally with Henry P. Horr, was hidden among tall pines in Clematis Gulch. *Bozeman Avant Courier,* November 2, 1871. One report states that McCartney and Horr fenced some two to three hundred acres near Clematis Gulch. Ray Mattison, "Report on Historical Structures at Yellowstone National Park" (Washington: Mimeographed National Park Service document, 1960).

8. Sidford Hamp, "With Hayden in the Yellowstone," edited by Herbert O. Brayer, in Denver Posse of the Westerners, *1948 Brand Book: Twelve Original Papers Pertaining to the History of the West,* edited by Dabney Otis Collins (Denver: Artcraft Printers, 1949), 253; *Avant Courier,* July 11, 1872.

9. PMLS, Acting Secretary to Langford, October 28, 1872; Ibid., Secretary Columbus Delano to Horr, May 9, 1873; Ibid., Delano to Langford, June 3, 1873.

10. PMLR and PMLS, Horr to Langford and reply, dated February 5, 1873, although Langford's letter was written earlier. McQuirck filed on March 9, 1872, for 160 acres three miles south of Gardiner; when this failed he petitioned the secretary for a deed to "McGuirck's Medical Springs," but the petition was rejected. Mattison, "Report on the Historical Structures" 24. ADLR, George W. Monroe to Norris, April 1, 1881. As an example of how rumors carried in frontier Montana, Horr heard of these accusations and requested from the secretary the names of his "detractors" while at the same time maligning several of his enemies, Norris in particular. ADLR, Horr to Secretary, Aguust, 3, 1881.

11. Philetus W. Norris, "Annual Report for 1877," 1; PMLR, Norris to McCartney, April 17, 1877.

12. Y.A., Box No. 1, Joslyn to Conger, November 13, 1882.

13. PMLR, Norris to Schurz, August 1, 1878; September 4, 1878.

14. PMLR, Norris to Schurz, July 5, 1879.

15. PMLR, Carpenter to Secretary Teller, October 22; November 14 and 24, 1884.

16. Interview with G. W. Marshall in custody of the Bancroft Library, copied by Olaf T. Hagen for the National Park Service on January 25, 1938, in the information files of the National Park Service Historian's office, 1100 L Street, N.W., Washington, D.C., as of March 28, 1980.

17. *Enterprise,* January 1, 1884; PMLS, Secretary Teller to John G. Carlisle, Speaker of the House, April 17, 1884; Mattison, "Report," 17.

18. PMLR, Baronett to Kirkwood, October 6, 1881; Philetus W. Norris, Letter No. 21, Norris Papers, Huntington Library, San Marino, California. These letters were printed in the *Norris Suburban* and are in the form of newspaper clippings.

19. Norris Papers, handwritten, 97. Where possible, I will cite a page number, but much of the material is jumbled and cannot be readily located. See also PMLR, Baronett to Kirkwood, October 6, 1881.

20. Strong, *A Trip to Yellowstone National Park,* 47–58.

21. Norris Papers, 33. Norris republished the clippings from an unidentified newspaper in the *Suburban* in the later winter of 1877.

22. Norris Papers, Letter No. 7, handwritten from Bottler's ranch, August 5, 1877. Aubrey Haines, *The Yellowstone Story,* 2, 442–43. Unfortunately the statement is not documented.

23. 30 *U.S. Statutes at Large,* 918.

24. PMLR, Conger to Teller, June 23, 1884.

25. First correspondence with regard to removal of the squatters is in PMLR, Carpenter to Teller, November 13, 1884. More information is in PMLR, Carpenter to Teller, December 16, 1884, and the *Enterprise,* December 13 and 16, 1884; Weekly *Enterprise,* April 4 and 18, 1885; ADLR, Carpenter to Lamar, April 17, 1885; PMLR, George Jackson, from Cooke, Montana, submits statement relative to actions of Conger, December, 1885.

26. Eugene V. Smalley, *History of the Northern Pacific Railroad* (New York: G. P. Putnam's Sons, 1883), 99–118, quotation p. 103.

27. Ibid., 204; Edward Everett Dale, *The Range Cattle Industry* (Norman: University of Oklahoma Press, 1930) and Ernest S. Osgood, *The Day of the Cattlemen* (Minneapolis: University of Minnesota Press, 1929) are both good on this phase of the industry.

28. According to the 10th Census (1880), Wyoming had 20,789 residents as compared with 9,118 in 1870, while Uintah County, which borders the park, had risen in population to 1,729 souls compared with 489 a decade before. Montana Territory nearly doubled its population in the same period, rising from 20,595 in 1870 to 39,159. *Compendium of the Tenth Census,* Vol. 1, 431, 451.

29. Michael P. Malone and Richard B. Roeder, *Montana: A History of Two Centuries,* Chapter 8, is particularly good on the early history of railroads in Montana.

30. A source for the administrative history of the federal government in these years is Leonard D. White, *The Republican Era* (New York: The Macmillan Co., 1958; Free Press paperback edition, 1965), Chapter 9, "The Department of the Interior," 175–195.

31. PMLR, correspondence 1872–84. The "Landscape Gardening Plan" was the brainchild of S. J. Hoyt (letter to Secretary Schurz, 1879) and the "Race Course and Observation Grounds" of F. Hess to Congressman C. C. Carpenter, forwarded to Teller, February, 1883.

32. R. G. 79, Langford to Secretary Delano, February, 3, 1873. This sum was requested. See House Exec. Doc. No. 241, 42nd Cong., 3rd Sess. (1873); R. G. 79, Langford to Delano, February 6, 1874; House Exec. Doc. 147, 43rd Cong., 1st Sess.

33. R. G. 79, Conger to Teller, September 18, 1882.

34. PMLS, Schurz to J. B. and A. W. Hall, January 13, 1881. That the applicants were from Fargo, Dakota Territory, on the Northern Pacific, is a striking coincidence, but I have found nothing supporting such a connection.

35. PMLS, February 17, 1882.

36. PMLR, Windom to Teller, July 31, 1882.

37. PMLS, Joslyn to Conger, August 10, 1882.

38. PMLR, Conger to Joslyn, September 20, 1882; also in Y. A., Box No. 1, Item No. 96.

39. PMLR, Carroll T. Hobart to Henry F. Douglas to Teller, July 28, 1882.

40. The Brisbin lease is discussed in PMLS and PMLR correspondence; it is also mentioned in a letter from Teller to the President of the Senate, December 11, 1882.

41. Officials of the North Dakota Historical Society have found nothing additional on either Hobart or Douglas.

42. Quoted by W. Turrentine Jackson, "British Interests in the Range Cattle Industry," in Maurice Frink, W. T. Jackson, and Agnes Wright Spring, *When Grass Was King: Contributions to the Western Range Cattle Industry Study* (Boulder: University of Colorado Press, 1956), 210–12.

43. PMLR, Hatch to Wear, October 31, 1885.

44. PMLR, Hatch to Assistant Secretary Muldrow, November 30, 1885.

45. *Enterprise*, May 15, June 30, and July 10, 1883.

46. Ibid., July 17 and 30, 1883.

47. Ibid., June 16, 1883; "Information Received from Mrs. Julia S. Brackett, November 9, 1950," Manuscript in Y.A.

48. *Enterprise*, July 20, 1883.

49. Buffington is said to have designed forty-four hotels, of which the National Hotel at Mammoth was an early example. *Cyclopedia of American Biography*, Vol. 22, 364; *New York Times*, February 17, 1931.

50. *Enterprise*, August 17, 1883; Leslie W. Randall, *Footprints Along the Yellowstone* (San Antonio: The Naylor Company, 1961), 46.

51. Freeman Tilden, *Following the Frontier with F. Jay Haynes, Pioneer Photographer of the Old West* (New York: Alfred Knopf, 1946). A complete listing of the Haynes photographs is now available from the Montana Historical Society.

52. Richard A. Bartlett, "Will Anyone Come Here for Pleasure?" in *The American West*, Vol. 4, No. 5 (September, 1969), 10–16.

CHAPTER FIVE

Enter Silas Huntley and Harry Child

With money no problem and with an agreement granting virtual monopoly rights to the company, Carroll T. Hobart prepared to push construction of facilities in time for the 1883 season. It would seem that "Uncle Rufus" Hatch, Hobart, Douglas, and the Yellowstone National Park Improvement Company (YNPIC) had a clear track to good business and high profits. Probably Secretary of Interior Teller thought so too. Yet the company was earning a bad reputation in the park almost from the moment Carroll Hobart arrived in the autumn of 1882. Before the year ended, Congress had gotten wind of the "park steal." Within two years the great monopoly that was supposed to serve visitors in Yellowstone was bankrupt. What went wrong?[1]

Haste and greed on the company's part, an almost unbelievable insensitivity to people of the Yellowstone region, and arrogance, the basis of which was a conviction that the monopoly was invulnerable, contributed to its troubles. In addition, the enterprise suffered because a United States senator got wind of the "steal" and did something about it.

At Yellowstone Superintendent Conger was shocked at the way Hobart allowed company employees to cut timber, abuse hot springs, and obtain whatever they wished, including deer and elk meat furnished by local hunters under contract. Poor old Pat Conger poured out his troubles vis-a-vis the company in a letter to Teller early in November 1882:

> In the first place I have never been informed what privileges has [sic] been granted this company in the park. I only know that they help themselves indiscriminately to whatever they want . . . without reference to any other interest than their own. They have cut . . . nearly all of the timber available for building purposes. . . . They have over-run the park with their herds of horses and cattle. Have wilfully and purposely broken down and destroyed the fences around the Government pastures which I have taken great pains to repair. . . . Mr. Hobart has been heard to say that he would tear down the fences as often as I put them up, that he would show me that he had a right to do as he pleased here. The pastures as a

consequence are eaten entirely bare of everything that an animal can subsist upon. . . . They monopolize all the hay within twenty miles of here. . . . Hobart has boasted in my hearing of his influence with you and he told one of my Assistants that you had promised him that I should not visit Washington this winter and he also said that the reason you would not write me was, that you was [sic] not going to have my letters paraded before Congress. . . .[2]

One of Conger's friends in the area, writing in his defense, quoted a Yellowstone resident as saying of the company, "By G-d, they're fixing that thing so that if you want to take a whiff of a park breeze, you will have to pay for the privilege of turning your nose in that direction." He hated to see the company "Niagarizing" the park, and wanted to see the "gigantic scheme for stealing the park . . . sat down on."[3]

The company had alienated Superintendent Conger, the few small concessionaires in the park, and most of the nearby Montana citizenry that occasionally earned cash by maintaining livery and guide services for park visitors. Carroll Hobart was a man singularly incapable of understanding the virtues of good public relations. When opposition surfaced, his reaction was simply to complete the facilities as soon as possible.

In July 1883, the schedule of rates was approved and published by the Interior Department. So much has the dollar deteriorated since 1883 that it is difficult to appreciate the high prices, but $6.00 a day for "A" tents was roundly criticized as being exorbitant although some of the other rates, such as $5.00 per day for a single room at the hotel and $3.50 per day for rental of a horse, appeared reasonable, at least to the *Enterprise* editor. George Bird Grinnell's *Forest and Stream* took a different view. "Those who propose to visit the park this summer should count the cost," it warned. "It will only cost those who desire to dwell in tents about the same price they would have to pay at a first-class hotel in a big city. . . . These charges are monstrous, and are in almost all cases double what they should be. . . . There is no reason under Heaven why such rates should be fixed, except the uncompromising greed for profits of this insatiable company." *Forest and Stream* was especially critical of the "A" tent charge since the tents cost just $12 to $18 new.[4]

With the 1883 season in full swing, YNPIC was already in serious trouble; it needed all the money it could make. Its difficulties, which had begun in the autumn of 1882, affected the permanence of the company's franchise; this in turn affected its owners' ability to raise money. Without capital the monopoly was unable to carry out satisfactorily its obligations to the visiting public. The story also raises an unanswerable question: If the monopoly had proceeded as planned, would the situation in Yellowstone have been satisfactory?

If none but the politically weak residents of the upper Yellowstone Valley had known of the monopoly's actions, doubtless little would have happened. But a United States senator raised questions. He soon discovered that he had allies both in and out of Congress. In a short time there came into existence a coterie of national park protectors whose activities helped preserve the park from spoliators both within and without the reservation.

The senator who heard about the park steal was George Graham Vest of Missouri. From 1882 until the end of his public career in 1903, he was the Senate's self-appointed protector of Yellowstone National Park. He battled concessionaires, railroads, and most of all, Congressional complacency toward Wonderland. George Graham Vest may have been an ordinary politician in other matters, but toward Yellowstone he was a statesman manifesting concern for preservation of the park for people of his and future generations.

He was small of stature, but with his silver hair and moustache, his southern mannerisms as befitted a son of old Kentucky, his black string tie, gold watch and chain, and black suit, there was about the senator from Missouri (where he had established his law practice) an air of dignity, honor, integrity, and courage.[5]

As a young man Vest had sided with the Confederacy, representing southern Missouri in the Confederate House of Representatives during the Civil War. Then he returned to Missouri and resumed his law practice. In 1870 his southern oratory reached its greatest heights in his now famous eulogy to the dog. "A dog," George Vest stated eloquently, "is the only friend a friendless man ever has that does not care to inquire into his family pedigree or look into his pocketbook or question his politics." George Vest won that case.[6]

When it came to Yellowstone National Park, Senator Vest rarely indulged in oratory. He was too concerned and considered the business too grave for such theatrics. The debates on Yellowstone, says a Vest authority, "represent an important contrast between what we might term political debate designed for impressing the general public on major issues, and true legislative debate intended to influence other Senators. Vest's speeches on the Park were in completely different form and style from his political addresses."[7]

The story of how the senator heard of the park steal cannot be corroborated, but it has the ring of authenticity. It is known that he was a member of an Indian commission that traveled extensively in the West, so there is justification for his being at some small town with its station, rustic hotel, and restaurant along the tracks of the Northern Pacific one cold, blustery evening in the early autumn of 1882. Unobtrusively he entered the restaurant and, as befitted a lone traveler small in stature, Senator Vest sought a dark corner where he could dine without attracting attention.

Had the participants in the boisterous party that sat at a nearby table bothered to take notice of this stranger, they might have curtailed their discussion or carried their celebration to a more private place. One quick appraisal of this man would have told them that he was no drummer selling buttons and bows to general stores along the N.P.

As he dined, he overheard the boasts of the celebrants. They appeared to be businessmen returning from Yellowstone Park. The wonders they had witnessed convinced them of the profitable scheme they had engineered, for through shrewd, Gilded Age politics, they had persuaded the Department of Interior to promise them a lease of virtually all hotel privileges, as well as other prerogatives, in the new Yellowstone Park. A large acreage was to be at their disposal, and Interior had been so generous that the land could be divided by the hotel men in any way they wished. They could have claimed a strip of land a hundred feet wide down the brink of each side of Yellowstone's Grand Canyon, or around every important geyser and mud pot. It was, simply, a land grab, a steal. Furthermore, Yellowstone being so far away, and Congress being always busy, who would ever discover this ploy before it was an accomplished fact?[8]

They did not reckon with the quiet little man dining in the corner. The senator returned to the East and immediately began investigating the history and present state of Yellowstone. And on December 7, 1882, Senator Vest began his long campaign to protect the park. He introduced the following resolution, which was agreed to:

> Resolved: That the Secretary of the Interior be directed to transmit to the Senate copies of any contracts entered into by the Interior Department in regard to leasing the Yellowstone National Park, or any part of said park, to any person or company, with the privilege of erecting hotels, constructing telegraph lines, and running stages therein, together with such other information as to the condition and management of said park as he may think important.[9]

By this time Senator Vest already knew that he had the backing of a few friends of the park, both in and out of Congress. Indeed, a great change of heart was becoming discernible in the nation toward the exploitation of natural resources. That both Republicans and Democrats were becoming aware of the threat to America's natural heritage was indeed a good sign, for it meant that the impetus came from an approving electorate. Another good omen was the appearance of a number of associations dedicated to conservation. These included the Appalachian Mountain Club (1876), the Sierra Club (1892), the National Geographic Society (1888), and the Boone and Crockett Club (1887). Such organizations were but leaders among many sportsmen's groups that emphasized conservation. Similarly, sportsmen's periodicals began to appear and they editoralized strongly in favor of conservation. Grinnell's *Forest and Stream* kept up a drumbeat of opposition to park "raids" and would not be suppressed. In addition the popular press of this period such as the *Nation, Harper's Weekly,* and *Century Magazine* began running articles on conservation, the nation's dwindling forests, and the beauties of Yellowstone, Yosemite, and the Grand Canyon of the Colorado. Already apparent was the conservationist position of the *New York Times,* while a popular weekly Sunday supplement, the *New York Graphic,* ran many articles on the park. Congress began to feel the pressure. [10]

Among colleagues sharing Vest's concern were such power brokers as Senators John A. Logan of Illinois and Henry L. Dawes of Massachusetts; Senator Charles F. Manderson of Nebraska was likewise a concerned and influential solon. In the House of Representatives Vest also found some park defenders: Mark H. Dunnell of Minnesota, David B. Henderson of Iowa (who was at one time Speaker of the House and whose brother George lived in the park); and John F. Lacey of the same state. [11]

Of these individuals Congressman Lacey deserves special attention. After valiant service in the war, Lacey returned to Iowa and was admitted to the bar. A Republican, he was elected to Congress in 1870, 1889, 1893 and thereafter until March 4, 1907. Lacey was an archconservative in the Gilded Age Republican tradition, save that he had a prophet's concept of the tragic despoilment of the country's flora and fauna. In this one respect he stood far above his colleagues. He is honored by having his name given to the act of May 7, 1894, for the protection of birds and animals in Yellowstone, an act which also provided penalties for crimes committed within the reservation. [12]

Chief executives and cabinet members were consistently interested in Yellowstone. No president has ever criticized the park and many have supported it actively. James A. Garfield and Chester Arthur had visited there, as had presidents-to-be (as of 1883) Harrison and Theodore Roosevelt; it hardly needs to be said that TR was to be the most ardent champion of park integrity. Most secretaries of interior in these turn-of-the-century years were likewise friendly, although they did not concentrate on problems of park policy. Lucius Q. C. Lamar for Cleveland and John W. Noble for Harrison as well as Ethan Allen Hitchcock during McKinley's and Theodore Roosevelt's administrations were friendly. The weakest secretary from the park's interests was Henry Teller in Arthur's administration.

Outside the political arena were several individuals who actively defended Yellowstone. Among them none stands in greater importance than George Bird Grinnell. This Yale-bred Easterner first saw the West in 1871 with a fossil-collecting expedition led by Yale paleontologist Othniel Charles Marsh. For Grinnell it was a case of love at first sight for the West; he was back again in 1874. This time he accompanied Custer on an expedition into the Black Hills. The next year Grinnell was with Captain Ludlow into the park, fell in love with it, and expressed shock at the destruction of the forests, game, and thermal phenomena. [13]

In 1876 Grinnell became natural history editor of *Forest and Stream,* operating from his position at the Peabody Museum at New Haven. Upon receiving his Ph.D. from Yale in 1880 he became editor-in-chief and president of the publishing company, a position he retained until the journal was sold in 1911. During those thirty-five years Grinnell used *Forest and Stream* as a sounding board for conservationists. He defended Yellowstone in his editorials and was a watchdog over its integrity. Long after he had left the journal, he continued to defend the park. Yet his greater contributions are usually considered in the realm of Indian affairs. He defended the Cheyenne and Blackfeet and wrote significant books about them; he also played a major role in the creation of Glacier National Park. [14]

Still another park defender was United States Geological Survey scientist Arnold Hague. He was a respected member of a small coterie of highly trained, imaginative, and brilliant geologists of the generation that reached maturity about the time of the Civil War. Along with his brother and a close friend, Samuel Franklin Emmons, Hague joined Clarence King's 40th Parallel Survey. Later he worked in Guatemala and China; in 1880 he accepted a position with the new U.S. Geological Survey. In 1883 he was assigned as geologist in charge of the survey of Yellowstone National Park. He spent the remainder of his career in this pursuit, in the course of which he became an ardent conservationist, especially of the Yellowstone region which was, he emphasized over and over again, the source of the Missouri and Columbia river systems. [15]

Hague was a most sensitive man, appreciating the grandeur of mountains, colors of a sunset, the change of seasons, and the charm of wild animals. When he was voted honorary membership in the Boone and Crockett Club, he wrote Theodore Roosevelt thanking him, but adding, "I fear . . . that . . . I am ineligible, as I have never killed any large game. To me personally it is unpleasant to kill game and I have never done so and have sworn never to kill any wild animal. . . ." [16]

He particularly liked the elk. "In an unexplored country," he once wrote, "elk trails afford the best means of travel. . . . Moreover, if there are any outlooks . . . the trails will pretty surely take over. I am indebted to the elk for fine points of observation. From long observation I believe they have an appreciation of the picturesque and grand . . . ." Hague noted that an old Scottish friend had spent two weeks in the park playing bagpipes, trying to reproduce the elk's "whistle." The elk reportedly left the area, with Hague's full sympathy. [17]

Hague stressed the retention of natural beauty, urging that the hotels, army installations, and even Yellowstone's roads be hidden from the natural scene, or at least designed to blend aesthetically with it. His official papers are filled with Yellowstone business. He knew the park better than any of its other defenders, usually led the offensive for corrective legislation and— unusual for a scientist—shrewdly diagnosed the political climate. He knew that sentimentalism over beautiful scenery would never convince a callous, mercenary Congress to pass protective legislation. His argument was as cold and pointed as a geologist's pick. If the forest cover is destroyed, he warned, then destructive floods and drought will result. Commenting upon Senator Vest's park protection bill, he wrote to an interested correspondent, "It would seem that there would be but little opposition . . . but all matters of legislation which carry no politics and no whiskey have to depend largely on friends of the measure. . . ."[18]

Least known of the park defenders was a prominent Washington lawyer named William Hallett Phillips. By the 1880s he was known affectionately as "Judge" to such notables as Henry and Charles Francis Adams, Theodore Roosevelt, George Bird Grinnell, L. Q. C. Lamar, John W. Noble, Arnold Hague, members of the Supreme Court, and many Congressmen including Senator Vest. Phillips practiced law before the U.S. Supreme Court and issued a new edition of his father's well-known *Phillips' United States Supreme Court Manual*. At the time of his tragic death at age forty-five in a boating accident, May 9, 1897, he was busy revising Wharton's *Digest of International Law* for the State Department.

Phillips was an ardent fly fisherman. Possibly it was from a Yellowstone fishing trip that he became interested in the park. At least twice he traveled there as confidential agent for the secretary of interior. One of his reports was published as a government document. More important than this, however, was his dedication to the proposition that the park must be made safe from poachers, aggressive concessionaires, and encroaching railroads.

As Hague was the field representative for the Yellowstone defenders, Phillips was the unappointed and unofficial Washington agent for the loosely structured cabal that was determined to save the reservation. He kept them informed of legislation, activity in the Interior Department, and whatever gossip he heard concerning the park. Grinnell consulted him before running items in *Forest and Stream*. Phillips also corresponded extensively with Superintendent Wear and acting superintendents, Captains Harris and Boutelle. It is significant that all three were pushed out of their positions by concessionaires. The "Judge" could not help them much, but he did speak up for Captain Harris, trying to keep his removal from damaging his military career.[19]

Phillips, possibly as a result of Hague's missionary work, was concerned also with preservation of timber stands. Strong evidence exists that the all-important Timber Reserves Act of 1891, an act which was a rider to a longer bill, got there because of his influence with Secretary of Interior John Noble. It was Phillips's nature to let the secretary take full credit for the rider. [20]

Passage of the Lacey Act, which provided penalties for violation of park regulations, was enacted due more to his efforts than to anyone else's. Grinnell's *Forest and Stream* editorialized that it was regretful that the public did not know to whom they were indebted for such service. Phillips, who elected to remain anonymous, had "labored heart and soul for the best interests of the National Park. . . ." [21]

Phillips's tragic death was a loss to the park and to the forces of preservation. "His whole mental attitude," ran one of the obituaries, "was one of good natured hostility to the restraints of civilization." [22]

Fortunately at this juncture in history, roughly 1880 to 1900, Washington, D.C., was a focal point of concerned individuals who were determined to prevent irreparable harm from being done not only to Yellowstone but also to much of America's environment. They developed a conscious, viable modus operandi based upon common concerns and a sense of noblesse oblige. The Cosmos Club, founded in 1878 by John Wesley Powell, was often their meeting place. From Senator Vest's resolution in late 1882 until the late 1890s, these and other dedicated men watched over Yellowstone. [23]

Senator Vest's resolution nipped the park steal in the bud. Secretary Henry M. Teller had no choice in the matter; he had to submit a copy of the agreement made with the park monopolists. This he did on December 11; Senator Vest had it printed and issued as a executive document. [24]

It materialized that there had been two parts to the negotiations. The first document had been approved, as an agreement to let a contract, by Assistant Secretary Merritt L. Joslyn on September 1. On December 6 the second document came to light. In this statement Hobart and Douglas revealed that Rufus Hatch had joined the enterprise. Moreover, they specified the seven points in the park at which they proposed to build hotels. This document, when signed, would have constituted a legal contract. [25]

The nature of the monopolists' aims is best demonstrated by their description of the 640 acres, one square mile, that they wanted at the Upper Geyser Basin. It started as follows: "Beginning at the center of 'Old Faithful' . . . ." The plat of their Grand Canyon location began "at the head of canyon or Great Falls" and the one at Lake commenced at the outlet. Much of the land they specified would have so embraced the views that tourists would have had to pay the company for the privilege of looking.[26]

The story got around Washington that Secretary Teller had planned to sign the formal lease—the one including mention of Rufus Hatch—on the very day that Senator Vest introduced his resolution. The secretary did not sign, however, clearly because of Vest's action. Nevertheless, Teller defended Joslyn's original agreement on the grounds that he (Teller) was obliged to honor the actions of his subordinates when they acted in his capacity.[27]

These revelations, which Senator Vest impressed upon his until then disinterested fellow lawmakers, not only stymied the park company's plans but also spurred Vest to introduce corrective legislation providing funds and methods of law enforcement for the park. The bill engendered considerable debate. Senator Harrison of Indiana (the future president) amended one clause so as to prevent any one party (individual or corporation) from holding more than ten acres in the park. This passed, with the additional provision inserted by the Missourian that in no case should a lease "include any ground within one-quarter of a mile of any of the geysers or of the Yellowstone Falls. . . ."[28]

An example of the climate of opinion these protectors of the park, and of the environment in general, were going to have to overcome was the comment of Senator John James Ingalls of Kansas who professed disgust with the debate. "The best thing that the government could do with the Yellowstone National Park," he grumbled, "is to survey it and sell it as other public lands are sold."

Senator Vest replied with a bit of Old South oratory, ending with a defiant statement of his own position: "I am not ashamed to say that I shall vote to perpetuate this park for the American people. I am not ashamed to say that I think its existence answers a great purpose in our national life. . . ."[29]

When the 47th Congress adjourned on March 4, 1883, the legislators were more aware of Yellowstone National Park than at any time since its creation in 1872. Thanks to the energies of one man, the monopolists and their Interior Department cohorts had been checked, the annual appropriation for the park had been nearly tripled (to $40,000), a provision had been made for assistants to aid the superintendent, the size of leases had been restricted to ten acres, and none of the land leased was to come within a quarter mile of a geyser or Yellowstone Falls.[30]

Senator Vest undoubtedly packed his bags for Missouri content in the knowledge that his legislation had stymied the park monopolists. He was not concerned over the future of the Yellowstone National Park Improvement Company. Neither, so far as is known, was he aware of the predicament into which he had placed Secretary Teller and the Interior Department. Yet both the company and Interior were left with serious problems.

Hatch, Hobart, and Douglas, and investors in the YNPIC, were left with a truncated franchise. Their lands had decreased from 4,400 acres to ten. Yet, with the arrival of the railroad, they were expected to furnish food, shelter, and transportation to an anticipated swarm of visitors exceeding by four or five times the number visiting the reservation in any previous season. Moreover, the company had already invested thousands of dollars in secondary structures; the foundations were laid for the hotel at Mammoth although construction had been halted until the leases, placed in jeopardy by the Vest resolution, were once more legally secure. More money would be needed but who wanted to invest in a company not holding secure leases?

Their solution was carried out in defiance of the "sense of Congress." The ten-acre restriction was so interpreted that the company was allowed to divide the ten acres into seven parts. Construction of the great hotel at Mammoth proceeded at all possible speed, the hotels and lunch stations were made ready for the impending season, and when July 1883 arrived, a semblance of refined hosting was offered to the genteel clientele. When autumn came, the small business people of the park and of Livingston, Bozeman, and Gardiner counted their cash and pronounced it a profitable season. But this was not so for the great, all-embracing Yellowstone National Park Improvement Company. It was flat broke.[31]

Rumors that the company was in financial straits were wafted about because a number of Livingston merchants had not been paid for goods sold to YNPIC. At the company's December stockholders' meeting in New York City two Livingston businessmen were placed on the board of directors and the executive committee. However, the debts owed them remained unpaid. Not only did the company owe money at Gardiner and Livingston, but it owed large sums to St. Paul merchants for furniture, mattresses, iron pipe, crockery, glassware, and lamps. All told, Rufus Hatch estimated that the company owed more than $85,000.[32]

Late in January George Carver of Livingston, one of the new directors, ignored the obvious intent of his appointment and took action. He attached the company's sawmill at Cinnabar, 180 head of cattle, and thirty of its horses. He hoped, however, that at a director's meeting on January 26 in New York the necessary money would be raised. It was not forthcoming, however, and Carver, though he was only a small-town merchant, would not be intimidated. He well understood that his directorship was "a sop intended to appease him temporarily from the non-payment of the bill of $8,000 to $9,000 due him from the Company."[33]

Then something even more serious than unpaid creditors began to plague the company. Thirty-five to forty artisans at the hotel at Mammoth had not been paid since July. When, late in February, they learned that the company had taken no direct action to solve its indebtedness, they staged one of the first sit-down strikes in American history. They asserted the right of possession "on the ground that the work was incomplete and had never been turned over to the company." The men were desperate, prepared to retain occupancy with rifles and shotguns if necessary until the $7,000 to $10,000 due them was forthcoming.[34]

Along with these problems, and undoubtedly the source of many of the company's troubles, was infighting among its administrators, Hatch, Hobart, and Douglas. Rufus Hatch, no "lamb on Wall Street" (though he coined the phrase), planned strategy from his New York office overlooking the Hudson River Narrows. "Uncle Rufus" moved first and shrewdly. Since the YNPIC was chartered in New Jersey he applied to the Federal District Court at Trenton for a receiver in bankruptcy. The court not only was amenable to Hatch's request but went along with his choice of receiver, A. L. Love, a Livingston banker.

On or about March 10, 1884, Mr. Love was in control of the company holdings and was expecting to run the facilities during the coming season for the benefit of the creditors. The local people were delighted with this turn of events. They had been worried because the legal brambles involving bankruptcy of YNPIC posed, for small creditors at least, the threat of total loss. Now, with a respected local banker running the company, everyone felt that the bills would be paid.[35]

When Hobart and Douglas heard of Hatch's coup they were furious, charging Hatch with violating his agreement with them. "Uncle Rufus" replied that he had given Douglas plenty of time to raise the necessary money, but Douglas had failed. "If Douglas or anybody else can make a proposition satisfactory to me and the creditors, the company becomes solvent, and the court will at once dissolve the receivership on proper application," Hatch announced. "I have no hesitation in saying that I would consider a proposition from Senator Vest, General Sheridan, any officer of the Northern Pacific Railroad Company, William Endicott, Jr., of Boston, or even an honest cowboy."[36]

In a number of ways Hobart and Douglas, especially Hobart, who was at the scene, interfered with Love's duties. Probably with good reason they suspected Love of being favorable to Hatch's interests, which they considered inimical to their own. Hobart, who was on speaking terms with the hotel strikers (he had advanced them $200 for necessary clothing), advised Love not to go near there or he would certainly get a bullet through him. Mr. Love took the advice, and instead, talked with a striker's delegation at a private residence at Mammoth.[37]

However, since Love could make no commitments that the strikers considered sufficiently binding, they remained within their Mammoth Hotel stronghold. One way or another the men received fresh elk meat and firewood. They presented their case in letters to the secretary of interior and the president of the United States. "There are none of us that have got any money at all," one poor artisan explained, "and no place to get work." The president simply routed the letter to the Interior Department. Secretary Teller informed the strikers that the department "cannot afford you any relief in the matter nor advise you as to the proper course to pursue in order to secure payment."[38]

Spring dragged on, another tourist season impended, and the laborers still held the hotel. During these months Hobart and Douglas enlisted legal aid to protest appointment of a receiver from a federal district court in New Jersey. The company property, they pleaded, was in Wyoming; it did not even maintain an office in New Jersey. In addition, the request for receivership had not come from a creditor but from the company treasurer. The case was sufficiently cogent to sway another judge to appoint a second receiver so that for several weeks in May and June 1884, the YNPIC had two of them.

Hobart's and Douglas's choice was George B. Hulme; he was appointed by the Federal District Court of Wyoming Territory, sitting at Cheyenne. While the dispute over receivers was being settled between the two district courts, Hulme having applied to the New Jersey court for an order nullifying Love's appointment, the new receiver (Hulme) went about his job with the confidence of a man who was certain of ultimate success. He examined the company's records. "Upon a cursory view," he informed a reporter, "the books and accounts of the company are about as intelligible as Runic script would be to a cowboy." He concluded that the company was only in debt about $38,000, not $220,000 as stated at one time by Hatch. He further predicted that he would soon make a settlement with the unpaid workers. Then, when he was in full legal possession of company facilities, he would pay the creditors and the hotel could be opened by June 15 "at the latest."[39]

It was Rufus Hatch the financial wizard against a couple of mercenary partners in the field. In getting Love appointed receiver, Hatch had committed a stock jobber's trick, hoping to wrest all control from Hobart and Douglas. Hatch claimed to have invested $106,000 in the company while Hobart and Douglas together had advanced only $6,000. The implication was that obviously he, Hatch, had the greater rights.

Hatch gave four explanations for the company's sad plight. One was Hobart's incompetence. A second was the depression of 1883 and 1884 which frightened away would-be investors. A third was the bankruptcy of Henry Villard of the Northern Pacific, for Hatch and a number of other YNPIC investors lost heavily when Villard went under. And the fourth reason was the senate investigation and the forceful reduction of the company's lease of 4,400 acres to ten acres distributed in seven places.[40]

The enmity between Hobart and Douglas on the one hand and Hatch on the other was compounded in the late spring by the failure of either party to notify Northern Pacific officials that park facilities were not yet operational. Tourists began arriving with N.P. tickets granting them hotel and transportation privileges. Secretary Teller warned both Hatch in New York and Hobart in Yellowstone "that unless the hotel is duly opened and provision made for the comfort of visitors according to the terms of your agreement with this Department, the lease will be declared at an end as therein provided." Hobart replied that he had arranged to have three sleeping cars and a "hotel car" (a diner) placed at Cinnabar. Furthermore, temporary arrangements to handle guests had been made at Norris and the Upper Geyser Basin.[41]

One all-important fact had emerged by this time: Although the company was in a financial mess, all three partners, Hobart, Douglas, and Hatch, were most apprehensive about losing the lease. They considered it valuable, the company's bankruptcy notwithstanding. Hatch had paid when due the annual rental of twenty dollars (two dollars per acre), and in an effort to ward off cancellation, described the legal and fiscal difficulties which would confront Interior in such an event. He declared that it would cost a minimum of $30,000 to pay off the striking laborers, stock the hotel and have it ready for summer. "A serious question arises whether parties can be found who, on short notice, would be ready to put up that sum of money," he added.

Hatch's attorney brought the conflict over receivers to the attention of the attorney general of the United States, who by June 10 had ruled that the Hobart-Douglas man, George B. Hulme, was the legitimate receiver; Love then withdrew. Hatch had received a setback. Late in June Hulme was able to settle with the workmen. On the evening of July 3 he took possession of the Mammoth Hotel and by July 4, 1884, it was once more open for guests.[43]

For the next two years (1884–1885) the YNPIC functioned in the park under the nominal direction of receiver Hulme. However, he was far away and busy with other affairs. Carroll T. Hobart, a man who was there at the right time, was forthwith hired as manager, leasing company property at a rental of one dollar per annum.[44]

Service that season of 1884 was poor, but Hobart somehow offered a semblance of hotel and restaurant facilities sufficient to prevent a public protest. Late in November when he and Douglas went over the books with receiver Hulme, the records showed a season's loss of $4,587. They predicted that the next year, if facilities could be opened earlier, the company would end up in the black. Furthermore, since their arrangement with Hatch had been that he was to have 35 percent of the stock in return for raising all capital needed, and since he had failed to fulfill his part of the bargain, his claims, they insisted, were no longer recognized by the original stockholders.[45]

In spite of Hobart's apparent pleasure with the arrangement, receiverships cannot go on forever; in spring 1885 rumors flew that there would be a sale, that a new company would take over. It was hinted that Hobart would retire. "He is affable, courteous, an undeniable rustler," commented the *Enterprise,* "but he seems to have remarkable luck in throwing a shadow over whatever he puts a hand to." Yet in June he was back again with his family. This time his backers were said to include officials of the Northern Pacific Railroad. This was probably correct. The previous year the N.P. had loaned receiver Hulme $20,000 as working capital, to secure which, receiver's certificates were issued by the Improvement Company. It must always be kept in mind that the Northern Pacific envisioned good profits from Yellowstone traffic.[46]

The hub of the Improvement Company's activities was, of course, the half-completed but functioning hotel at Mammoth. The company had been granted two acres in the Mammoth area but the hotel was not constructed on that land. An eyesore of a bathhouse plus several other company-owned buildings were scattered over forty acres. As for the hotel, it was a health hazard in 1884 and 1885, with an extinct hot springs hole being used as a sink for refuse. In August 1885 a physician visiting the park grew curious about the source of the diarrhea that was afflicting so many guests.

"The atmosphere of the hotel was often loaded with offensive odors," he wrote in a letter appended to Special Agent Phillips's report, "that, followed up, would unmistakably lead a novice even to the water closets and privys. . . . The privy bowls were more or less filled with human excrement; some even overflowing upon the surrounding floor. . . ." The doctor was informed that the "closet for females" was in equally filthy condition. Going outside to the back of the hotel, he discovered sewage flowing over the surface of the ground.[47]

Elsewhere in the park Hobart supervised facilities far more rustic than the Mammoth Hotel. At Norris tourists put up in tents although plans called for a permanent lodge. The tents were not on land specified in the lease. At Lower Geyser Basin the company had expended $450 to erect a small building of undressed pine slabs. Phillips described it as "hardly more than a shanty."[48]

At the Upper Geyser Basin in 1885 the company offered the public half-completed housing that was contracted for at a cost of $3,000. Of rough pine boards and consisting of just three bedrooms, it was likewise built on land not specified in the lease; Haynes, the photographer, claimed it was built on land allotted to him. It also fell within a quarter mile of the geysers. At Canyon the company had erected tents containing all of twenty-one beds, but claimed accommodations for forty-two people. Again, in violation of regulations and stipulations of its lease, the company's tent hotel was situated too close to the Grand Canyon: the "hotel" spoiled the view.[49]

Phillips submitted his report to the secretary on September 12, 1885, and from then on Hobart's days as manager were numbered. Now his old partner and present adversary Rufus Hatch went after him anew, petitioning the court that Hobart's service was "entirely unsatisfactory to the majority of stockholders," that his invested interest was limited to $16,000, most of which was his own estimate of services rendered. Hatch was concerned also over rumors about a pending sale of Improvement Company facilities.[50]

The rumors were well founded. The first notice of a change in ownership appeared in mid-October when an accurate listing of investors in the new organization appeared in the press. The leading figure involved was Charles Gibson, a wealthy St. Louis lawyer. He was also a philanthropist whose particular interest was public parks. So prominent was he in the development of St. Louis's parks that a monument has been erected in his memory. In 1885 Gibson was sixty years old.[51]

When he visited Yellowstone in the summer of 1885, he had been shocked at the poor security and miserable visitor facilities. "There is not a large city in the country," he wrote the secretary, "that does not spend annually on its park more than the nation does on this park, which is worth all the city parks put together." The hotels, he said, charged four or five dollars a day, and yet the walls of the rooms "consist of one plank, in some papered and in some others bare." The meats were "so tough and mean as to be unpalatable and indigestible and there was available only condensed milk and rancid butter. . . . In several places the ladies had to sleep all in one room and the gentlemen all in another room."[52]

On October 3 he and Frederick Billings, John D. Perry, T. B. Casey, M. D. Carrington, C. B. Wright, and John C. Bullitt formally requested a lease in the park of ten acres covering six sites. On November 2 these several gentlemen accepted Interior's terms. "We will state now," they said, "that we have no ulterior collateral or speculative designs, and that our sole object is to provide proper accommodations for visitors and sojourners in the park. . . ."[53]

Between November 2 and March 20, 1886, (actually April 5, due to a technicality), when Gibson signed for the leases, there was much maneuvering. A sign of some maturity at the Department of Interior was the careful preparation of plats of sites at Mammoth, Norris, Upper Geyser Basin, and the Grand Canyon of the Yellowstone. Not until these were in the secretary's hands were the leases signed.

Rufus Hatch vigorously protested this change of ownership, but to no avail. There was some validity in his defense, that he had come out to remote, windswept Fargo at the behest of D. C. Oakes of the N.P., and had then spent much time and money to launch the big hotel company. Now that it had fallen on hard times, it seemed rather callous of the Northern Pacific people to abandon him. Yet this was exactly what they did; despite their protestations of "no ulterior . . . designs," most of the new company's investors, including Frederick Billings, were directly involved with the Northern Pacific, or were among its heavy investors.[54]

And so it happened that in 1886 a new company assumed responsibility for serving Yellowstone's visitors. Towards the end of that season the United States Army assumed policing of the park. For more than a year (since March 4, 1885) the secretary of interior had been L. Q. C. Lamar, one of the better ones. Yet, as we shall see, there was little sign of improvement in overall policy towards the Yellowstone concessionaires.

While the complex affairs of the big concession, whoever owned it, controlled it, and ran it, were in turmoil, a number of lesser concessionaires plied their trade in the park. In at least one instance, that of photographer F. Jay Haynes, some stability was achieved. Truth was, so weak was the controlling arm of government that many businesses operated illegally on a fly-by-night basis, often out of tents.

Even Carroll Hobart protested the presence of such flotsam. At Mammoth in 1884, he wrote, there were three livery stables, two stores, two game hunter camps, a "house of doubtful character," and aside from these, "tents on every part of the ground surrounding the hotel property. . . . These camps," Hobart continued, "are filled with the very worst element found in the country. They have no visible means of support; in fact, they are a thorough type of Eastern tramp, only more desperate." More than twenty permanent residents were squatting around Mammoth, he reported, building houses, barns, and other facilities.[55]

In June 1885, the *Enterprise* described Mammoth as assuming the aspects of a city. Among those there, wrote Special Investigator Phillips, were "hordes of worthless fellows . . . who frequently succeed in palming themselves off as guides." No regulations existed requiring the licensing of such individuals. Rules against the sale of intoxicating liquors within the park were flagrantly violated. "At the geyser basins there are saloons of the lowest character separate from and adjoining the hotels, and in full view of everyone entering the hotels," he wrote.[56]

A year later the situation was as bad, or was even deteriorating. "It was the rendezvous of all sorts of bad characters," Charles Gibson recalled. "No pure woman would go there unless well protected. Men had to go armed to protect themselves."[57]

The drifting humanity included Chinese who, now that most of the railroads were built, were all over the West, and again, this included Yellowstone. There was a "Chinaman's garden" (so-called) tolerated inside the park south of Gardiner. Not far from Old Faithful is the Chinaman's Spring over which an enterprising son of the Middle Kingdom pitched his tent and took in laundry. Once, inadvertently, a box of soap fell in and the spring became a geyser—with disastrous results!

Operating with a legitimate franchise was F. Jay Haynes and his successors, his son and his son's widow, who operated photo shops in Yellowstone from 1881 until 1968—eighty-seven years. The Haynes photographs, of which there must be millions of copies buried in old trunks and in library and museum collections, are lackluster. The Haynes were not photographic artists, they were business people; they all made money. Their steady annual profits raise questions about the validity of the continual complaints of park concessionaires that their seasonal operations rarely break even.

F. Jay Haynes was born in Saline, Michigan, in 1853 of good American stock. The family soon moved to Detroit, where F. Jay, tiring of school by the fifth or sixth grade, ran away from home. Already the lad had been attracted to the odor of hyposulfite, to big black cameras on heavy tripods, to breakable glass negatives, and completed prints. All of these he had observed at the photographic studio of a Miss Gillette in Detroit.[58]

In due time the boy made his way to Ripon, Wisconsin, where a photographer named Lockwood took him in as an apprentice. As he grew to manhood, F. Jay began doing outside assignments, photographing buildings, farms, and so forth, while his employer concentrated on portrait work. This arrangement was to F. Jay's liking, for he grew to love landscape photography but never did enjoy portrait work.

While working in Ripon he made the acquaintance of Lily Snyder, a lovely, artistically inclined girl who did touch-up work for Lockwood. When Haynes set up his own shop at Moorhead, Minnesota, he continued corresponding with Lily. Those letters, still preserved, narrate F. Jay's journeys West. They contain vivid descriptions of such landmarks as the Mullan Tunnel on the Northern Pacific and the frontier towns of Bismarck and Deadwood, and they trace the progress of a cordial friendship into the life-long love of the young photographer for his "Darling Lily." On October 9, 1875, he contracted with the Northern Pacific to make stereopticon pictures of "all important points from Duluth to Bismarck 450 miles." Thus began F. Jay's relationship with the railroad, an arrangement that eventually took him across the Northwest and, in 1881, into Yellowstone Park.

When he was debt-free and had $600 in the bank, F. Jay married Lily. This was in January 1878; in 1888 they moved their studio from Fargo to St. Paul. During these years F. Jay also ran a photographic car along the Northern Pacific and, after 1881, spent a part of each year in the park. He wanted the Department of Interior to grant him a lease and bestow upon him the prestigious title of "official photographer."[59]

Secretary of Interior Samuel J. Kirkwood offered Haynes a lease but no appointment as "official" photographer; in time, however, that honor would befall him in an unofficial way. When F. Jay returned to St. Paul in the fall of 1881, he had assembled a catalog of 120 Yellowstone views, many of them stereopticons. He sent a set to Secretary Kirkwood, reminding the secretary of his offer of a lease; by 1884 Haynes held two leases of four acres each at Upper Geyser Basin and Mammoth.[60]

From 1881 on, Haynes spent at least part of each year in the park. In mid-April 1885, he arrived at Livingston with a partly assembled building, an 1885-vintage prefab, which he then freighted to Mammoth. At the foot of the Terraces and at approximately right angles, south and west of the Mammoth Hotel, he erected a two-story house with a veranda; it served as studio and residence. In due time he had the lot green with grass, protected by a fence of elk horns (which his children greased with Vaseline every autumn since F. Jay thought this would preserve them). The structure was in the style of the time, but was hideously out of harmony with the surroundings; it was dismantled in 1928.[61]

In his first years in Yellowstone Haynes was involved in several incidents which, taken together, helped link his name forever with the park. In 1883 he served as official photographer for President Arthur's Yellowstone vacation. In the winter of 1887 he agreed to accompany Lieutenant Frederick Schwatka, who had gained some renown as an Alaskan explorer, on a winter's journey through Yellowstone sponsored by the *New York World*. The expedition was a fiasco, but Haynes emerged from the park interior with a set of beautiful winter scenes. He was also involved in the campaign to control poachers, being present along with western story writer Emerson Hough when scout Felix Burgess captured buffalo hunter Ed Howell. Hough furnished the dramatic narration of the capture while Haynes photographed the slain buffalo and the poacher, under guard, hauling his trophies into headquarters on a toboggan.[62]

Throughout his thirty-six years in the park Haynes steadily expanded his business. In 1890 he published the first of many editions of *Haynes Guide*, factual, accurate, and uninspired. In 1886 he branched out into the lucrative transportation field. He was first affiliated with stage operator George Wakefield, but this was of short duration; in 1898 Haynes and a man named Humphrey formed the Monida and Yellowstone Stage Line which carried passengers into the park from the Utah Northern (later the Oregon Short Line) west of the reservation. He later bought out Humphreys and still later added to his holdings the Cody–Sylvan Pass Stage Line. When he sold out in 1916 his lines bore the name Yellowstone and Western. In contrast to the yellow coaches of the Park Company, Haynes's Concords were painted red. The Haynes Picture Shops continued under Haynes management until the firm's sale in 1968, profitably run and ever sensitive to raids by other concessionaires into their merchandise territory.[63]

A number of other valid leases existed in the park in 1886, but none of them would last as well as the Haynes concession. George L. Henderson, whose brother was a Congressman, lived with his family on ten acres which overlapped YNPIC's hotel land. He owned or controlled at least seven buildings of one kind or another, most of them unsightly. His son Walter and Walter's wife Helen in 1885 and 1886 were busy building the Cottage Hotel at Mammoth. A livery owner, J. A. Clark, had erected a stable, blacksmith shop, dwelling house, and bathhouse on the Mammoth plateau and was contemplating building his own hotel to appeal to the less affluent. Half of his four acres conflicted with F. Jay Haynes's declared acreage. Taking the park as a whole, in 1886 there was a mish-mash of conflicting land claims by several small concessionaires. George Marshall, for example, sold out to one of the Hendersons, who then sold it to Henry Klamer who at one time ran a slaughterhouse on Indian River Creek for the hotel company.[64]

We must now return to Mr. Gibson and his Yellowstone Park Association (as it was called). The Gibson–Northern Pacific interests with the old Improvement Company facilities at their disposal, plus additional sites granted them by Interior, tried very hard to offer good services and turn a profit. Times were good, Yellowstone's security was greatly improved with the coming of the army in 1886, and visitation reached five thousand annually.

The Park Association's new sites were at Mammoth (but did not include the hotel, although the association purchased it and ran it under a decree from the Federal District Court of Wyoming), Norris, Grand Canyon, and Yellowstone Lake. By the terms of its contract it could also run steam launches on the lake, erect telephone lines between the hotels which should be free for government use, use dead and fallen timber, and graze livestock for food. The lessee was not to mar or deface the park, or mine coal or metals, and the association was responsible for employee obedience of park regulations. The park superintendent was granted police powers to enforce the terms; all buildings were to be open for inspection at all times.

Because of the adverse experience with the old Improvement Company, Interior Department lawyers placed in the new contract a stipulation for fulfillment of the firm's obligations. Article II stated that buildings at Upper Geyser Basin and at Canyon were to be completed by October 1, 1886, and that telephone service was to be operational a month earlier. As it turned out, this was too stringent; the association was unable to complete these obligations even though it may have acted in the best of faith.[65]

On the part of both parties, the association and Interior, there were between-the-lines indications of misunderstandings at best, of purposeful chicanery at worst. None of the new Park Association's leases covered the land that was shortly occupied by its improvements. It ran the Mammoth Hotel, not on its land; it occupied and managed the old Improvement Company hotel at the Upper Geyser Basin, which was not only not on its lease but was within one-quarter mile of Old Faithful and therefore illegal under any circumstances. Neither was its temporary hotel at Canyon erected within the metes and bounds of the leases; in addition, the association failed to dismantle the hotel at the end of the season, as required.[66]

Despite these aberrations, Gibson and his associates went at their task with energy and apparent good intent, and by the season of 1886 they were able to give a modicum of service to tourists. Their letterhead read: "Yellowstone Park Association's Hotels: The Mammoth Springs Hotel, Norris Geyser Hotel, Upper Geyser Hotel, Lower Geyser Hotel, and Grand Canyon Hotel." (Several of these installations were leased from the old YNPIC.)[67]

During the next six years the association made good progress. It improved some facilities and built new ones, such as respectable hotels at Lake and Norris. In 1892 Gibson stated that the firm had invested $500,000 in the park, paid no dividends, nor had its managers, Gibson and Theodore B. Casey, received any salary.

Their principal difficulty with Interior officials was over the leases. The association had used, as we have noted, old Improvement Company facilities while its own leases, the surveying of which turned out to be faulty, went unused. Interior needled company officials about this but was singularly adamant about a settlement. "On the one hand the Superintendent berates us for not erecting a better hotel," Gibson complained, "and on the other the department declines to relocate the lease to cover the building, and has a rule forbidding any hotels to build until a lease is made for the ground it covers."[68]

There *was* something sinister about Interior's foot-dragging. Much suspicion focused on Carroll T. Hobart, who during these years was moving about in park circles and even running the Upper Geyser Basin Hotel for the association. He also maintained close connections with Interior officials. Somehow he held onto the old Improvement Company leases at Norris and Canyon. Surreptitiously Gibson had been informed that Interior would not hand association officials new leases until they settled with Carroll T. Hobart. At one point in 1886, Interior had held up signing of the new leases for a month due to efforts of YNPIC lawyers; at another time, Gibson testified to a Congressional committee, he was approached by "a gentleman from New Jersey" who said that if the new men would pay the old YNPIC $120,000, they would get the lease, "and not otherwise." "I told him," Gibson said, "I would not pay 120 cents." But Gibson did obtain the lease. Another time, after the company had spent $50,000 on a hotel at Norris, Hobart sent his representative, a Mr. Thorne, to Gibson with a bombshell. Hobart, it seemed, possessed a lease on that very land: Another settlement with the old YNPIC had to be made.[69]

Legally the association was involved in still another technicality. This concerned the stagecoach firm of Wakefield and Hoffman, which had sub-contracted with the Park Association to furnish public transportation through the reservation. Very little is known about Hoffman—he appears to have furnished the capital—but George Wakefield was one of those colorful figures of the Old West who knew his men and his horses equally well, and was an excellent judge of both. His service was the best of any kind offered in the park. "The coaches were kept clean; a good many of them new," G. L. Henderson, who lived at Mammoth, testified. "The harness was clean, and the horses were safe and good. [Wakefield] had no plunging, kicking, rearing horses."[70]

Interior had been uncertain about the legality of its right to issue franchises exclusively for transportation, and so had rejected Wakefield's and Hoffman's application. The workable solution had been for Wakefield and Hoffman to link with the hotel company in a subcontract, with the hotel firm assuming enforcement of reasonable tariffs, good service, and good behavior of personnel. Neither the association nor Wakefield and Hoffman were at ease with this situation, and ultimately it became the cause of a Congressional investigation. This happened even though Wakefield (for Hoffman's name was left out in common parlance) eventually formed, along with Gibson, Casey, and Oakes, the Northern Pacific Transportation Company in hopes that it would meet with Interior Department approval.[71]

In 1890 the Yellowstone Park Association and Wakefield learned just how precarious their position was. They ran afoul of politics, and in the 1890s as today, politics can be very foul indeed. Trouble began in the form of complaints that barely transcended routine. Late in the 1890 season a misinterpretation of instructions resulted in nearly one hundred guests being crowded into the small hotel at the Lower Geyser Basin. Among those discombobulated were a prominent Chicagoan, Judge Lambert Tree, and the Postmaster General of the United States, John Wanamaker. Somewhat earlier in the season an ex-Congressman, seventy-six-year-old Guy Ray Pelton of New York, had died of a heart attack while walking up Mary Mountain. He and the other passengers had chosen to walk so that the tired horses could have an easier pull.[72]

Neither the jam at the Lower Basin Hotel nor the Mary Mountain incident was of a nature so unusual as to have prompted more than the ordinary number of complaints. Yet in August Wakefield received a disturbing letter from Secretary John W. Noble. It stated that "the complaints were coming in so rapid[ly] that I thought I must be neglecting my business," Wakefield testified before a Congressional committee. Even more disconcerting were rumors that began to circulate in and around the park that the government was going to cancel the transportation company's franchise, and that a Montana Republican, Silas S. Huntley, would get the contract.[73]

Something was in the air. Montana at that time had some powerful Republicans among its politicians. President Benjamin Harrison's son Russell was an investor in various promotions there. Thomas Henry Carter, former delegate to Congress, then representative, in 1891 commissioner of the General Land Office, and future Republican senator from Montana, was a power in national as well as in state circles. Such men were not above making deals and grabs and power plays.

In October 1890, the blow fell. Secretary Noble informed Wakefield that he must cease his agreement with the Park Association and sign a contract or lease with the government. A month earlier, in September, Silas S. Huntley had applied for such a lease granting him monopolistic transportation rights in the park, with no provision requiring him to carry on hotel operations also. In February 1891, Wakefield, Casey, and Gibson, apprehensive of the situation, went to Washington to confer with the secretary. He seemed to assure them that they were in no danger of losing the transportation business.[74]

But on March 30, 1891, Secretary Noble arbitrarily and without prior warning gave the transportation franchise to Silas S. Huntley. It was incredibly lenient. Huntley was given until June of 1892—fourteen months—to begin business. He was guaranteed "the right to be heard in defense of any charge, to be apprised of the nature of a complaint or charge, and to be given reasonable time to furnish explanations, etc., before any forfeiture." He was also "guaranteed charges sufficient to earn a profit," Charles Gibson added bitterly. And, as things materialized, Huntley was even allowed to commence his business without posting the usual $10,000 bond. Four days later on April 3, 1891, Noble

> . . . declared a forfeiture of the right of transportation of the Association without notice, without trial, or any statement of any complaints for nonuse or misuse of the right, and at the same time provided that the forfeiture should not take effect until the first of November thereafter, thus in effect requiring the Association to do the business for 1891 at the same time that he had forfeited the right because of the manner in which it had or had not been done for the previous years.[75]

Politics had won a big one here. Huntley had to raise about $70,000, the sum he virtually dictated to Wakefield and the association as the price he would pay for their livestock, tack, and stages. Its probable value was about $125,000 but in remote Montana, in 1891, there was no market. Huntley was unable to raise the $70,000, and several deadlines passed. Finally, T. B. Casey and T. F. Oakes of the association settled with Huntley's backer, who was also his brother-in-law; his name was Harry Child. On April 17, 1892, the purchase was concluded.[76]

Gibson, Wakefield, and their associates raised enough comment to bring about a Congressional investigation. It linked President Harrison's son Russell with Carroll T. Hobart and a Park Association employee who was to cause trouble for years to come, Eli C. Waters. It focused on Hobart's links into the Department of the Interior and made crystal clear why Gibson had been unable to obtain a settlement of the lease problem. When Mr. Thorne, Hobart's aide, informed Gibson that Hobart and he (Thorne) "have our friend in the Department and we can get anything first before anybody else knows about it," he was being truthful. The Congressional investigation, if it accomplished nothing else, exposed the spy in the department who for years had given inside intelligence to Hobart. He was Edward M. Dawson who had been chief clerk of the Patents and Miscellaneous Division and, later, chief clerk of the Interior Department.

The man who exposed Dawson was George L. Henderson, the gadfly, who as patriarch of a family that had been running small businesses in the park for several years, probably knew as much about Yellowstone affairs as anyone alive at the time. Although Henderson had fought Gibson and the Park Association, Dawson's forty-page brief denouncing the big concessionaires was too much for Henderson to swallow. Where, he asked, was Dawson, the great park protector, when he let Hatch, Hobart, and Douglas have their leases at two dollars an acre? Said Henderson:

> I know that Honorable Chief Clerk Edward M. Dawson then and ever since has been the personal friend of C. T. Hobart, the general manager of the Park Improvement Company's hotels. I know, too, that they corresponded together unofficially on matters relating to the interest of the Yellowstone Park Improvement Company. Hobart told me himself that Mr. Dawson was his friend and adviser, and that through him he could procure the dismissal of any superintendent who might antagonize his (Hobart's) interests. Hobart repeatedly asserted this in my presence, and did not seem to care about keeping the matter a secret. It is my candid opinion based upon these facts, that this Mr. Dawson has had more baleful influence in the misdirection of Secretaries of the Interior than all other influences combined.[77]

The committee majority, Democratic in that 52nd Congress and therefore hostile to the Republican Harrison administration, filed a scathing report. The exercise of the right of forfeiture, it said, "for the purpose of taking away the private right of one man in order to give it to another for any other motive or object than to protect the public or promote and preserve the public service is gross abuse of power." It chastised Russell B. Harrison and said his use of position as the president's son "stands out for legislative condemnation." It also criticized Eli C. Waters whom the association had permitted to come to Washington to defend himself against charges levied by Superintendent Boutelle. "He was not turned out by the Secretary," the report noted. "On the contrary, Captain Boutelle was relieved. . . ."[78]

The actions of one man, Secretary John W. Noble, remain still to be examined. At the hearings he insisted that what he had approved of was for the good of the park and finally, in a moment of irritation because his weakness and lack of integrity were being exposed, he blurted out that he was leaving the government service soon anyway, as indeed he was, for this was late in the spring of 1892 and the Harrison administration would be out of office the following March.[79]

Noble's public record was spotty. As secretary of interior he settled thousands of timber claims in such a liberal manner that many a fraudulent claim gained validity. On the other hand he showed statesmanship in supporting the forest reserve rider in the Land Laws revision of 1891, although he probably was not the originator of the legislation nor was he responsible for its passage. All things considered, Secretary of Interior John W. Noble was not so noble.[80]

Silas Huntley and his brother-in-law, Harry Child, now had the transportation concession in the park. They had obtained it in a time-honored fashion, combining shrewd planning and political influence to wrest a lucrative franchise from businessmen whose only faults were being of the opposite political party and too preoccupied with honorably handling their franchise.

Examples of such influence peddling show up in the national tapestry like tufts of cloth. Manasseh Cutler in 1787 used influence with the president of the Confederation Congress, Arthur St. Clair, to obtain lands for the Ohio Company. In the 1980s oil companies gain "assurances" of government acquiescence before they swallow up their competitors. Seamy politics are endemic in our national life and even worse in other governments both to the political left and political right of ours. It is part of the human condition.

What is peculiar to America is our persistent refusal to condone these practices. Politics as represented by Senator Vest exposed the park "steal," and politics brought about the hearings on the transportation company's forfeiture of franchise. But the exposés are not as common as the manipulations. Not a single year has passed in the history of Yellowstone Park concessions in which something less than the conditions intended by Congress has existed. But Congress has been busy with other matters. So too has the

Department of Interior and, since 1916, its concerned bureau, the National Park Service. And so conditions far from the ideal continue to be the norm.

Silas Huntley and Harry Child probably looked upon their success in winning the transportation concession as the reward of good business tactics. After all, what they had done was not unusual in terms of the business ethics of the 1890s—or of the 1980s. Now the question was, could they make a success of their opportunity? A morality play would condemn their enterprise to failure, but morality plays and good business do not mix. Having acquired the transportation concession, Huntley and Child proved themselves good businessmen. They ran their stages well and made money. In time they came to own the great hotels. They borrowed so much money from the railroads that the railroads dared never desert them, or call in the loans. And Huntley's and Child's siblings, and even their descendants, continued to run the transportation system, the great hotels, the tent camps, and shared in the profits from the service stations until 1967 —three-quarters of a century! This is "passing strange" in a national park, where concessions are supposed to be granted in a democratic and periodic way. How it happened and how well the concessionaires served the public is the subject next at hand.

NOTES TO CHAPTER FIVE

1. The only biography of Teller is Elmer Ellis, *Henry Moore Teller: Defender of the West* (Caldwell, Idaho. The Caxton Printers, 1941) Yellowstone Park is not mentioned. Teller was of the robber baron mentality, in his three and a half years as secretary giving away to private interests vast acreages of the public domain. His cooperation with the YNPIC fits his political and economic orientation.

2. PMLR, Conger to Secretary Teller, November 6, 1882.

3. PMLR, L. B. Cary, a rancher living in Paradise Valley north of the park, to Frank Hattan, Esq., February 2, 1884. The letter somehow reached the secretary of interior.

4. *Forest and Stream,* Vol. 21, No. 1 (August 2, 1883), 1.

5. Manuel Irwin Kuhr, "How George Vest Came to Missouri," *Missouri Historical Review,* Vol. 59, No. 4 (July, 1965), 424–427.

6. Vest's "Eulogy to the Dog" may be found in *The World's Great Speeches*, edited by Lewis Copeland and Lawrence Lamm (New York: Dover Books, 1958), 677–82.

7. Correspondence with Manuel Irwin Kuhr, Professor, Speech Department, Slippery Rock State College, January 26, 1966.

8. Sources for this story may be found in Walter Williams and Floyd Calvin Shoemaker, *Missouri: Mother of the West* (New York: American Historical Society, 1930), Vol. 2, 310; Senator Vest's own reference to the incident, or at least his trip to Dakota and its relevance to his interest in Yellowstone, is in *Congressional Record*, 47th Cong., 2d Sess., Senate, 3269. It is worth noting, however, that Vest had corresponded with Sam Hauser, a member of the Washburn-Langford-Doane party that went into the Upper Yellowstone in 1870, and Vest's concern could have stemmed from Hauser's information. See *Progressive Men of Montana* (Chicago: A. W. Bowen and Co., 1902), 203. A distillation of the story as I interpret it is in Richard A. Bartlett, "The Senator Who Saved Yellowstone Park," *The Westerners New York Posse Brand Book*, Vol. 16, No. 3 (1969), 49–52; 66.

9. *Congressional Record*, 47th Cong., 2d Sess., Senate, 71.

10. Reiger, *American Sportsmen*, elaborates upon the contribution of sportsmen to the conservation movement, while Runte, *National Parks*, elevates the discussion to a synthesis of ideas that were "in the air" at the time.

11. A listing of "Congressional Friends of Yellowstone" is in Louis C. Cramton, *Early History of Yellowstone National Park and Its Relation to National Park Policies* (Washington: G.P.O., 1932), 52–60.

12. *Major John F. Lacey Memorial Volume*, edited by L. H. Pammel (Cedar Rapids, Iowa: The Torch Press, 1915, for the Iowa Park and Forestry Association of Ames, Iowa) is the best source on Congressman Lacey. Senator Vest had worked hardest and longest for this legislation, but, being a Democrat, was not honored with the bill's name. The first Migratory Bird Act (1907) was also passed through Lacey's endeavors.

13. Ludlow, *Report of a Reconnaissance*, 61. No satisfactory biography exists of Grinnell. A good short sketch is that by Albert Kennick Fisher, "George Bird Grinnell," *The Auk*, Vol. 56, No. 1 (January, 1939), 1–12. See also *The Passing of the Great West: Selected Papers of George Bird Grinnell*, edited by John F. Reiger (New York: Winchester Press, 1972).

14. Ibid., See also "Through Two-Ocean Pass," in Grinnell Papers, Southwest Museum, Los Angeles, Item 300.

15. Joseph P. Iddings, "Memorial to Arnold Hague," *Bulletin Geological Society of America*, Vol. 29 (March, 1918), 35–48; "Arnold Hague," *Dictionary of American Biography*, Vol. 3, 85–86.

16. Iddings, "*Memorial to Hague*," R. G. 57, Records of the U.S. Geological Survey, Arnold Hague Papers, Hague to Theodore Roosevelt, February 20, 1888. (Hague's membership was retained.) For more on Hague, see Thomas G. Manning,

Government in Science: The U.S. Geological Survey, 1867–1894 (Lexington: University of Kentucky Press, 1967), 151–167.

17. R. G. 57, Hague Papers, Letter Press Books, Series No. 1, "The Yellowstone Park as a Game Reservation."

18. R.G. 57, Hague Papers, Hague to Moses Harris, January 6, 1888 (this bill never passed); Ibid, Hague to Professor J. A. Jones, University of North Carolina, January 24, 1888. For Hague's stand on timber cover for water conservation, see Hague to Senator Charles Manderson, February 4, 1886. "In my opinion," begins Hague's argument, "the object of first importance in maintaining the Yellowstone Park is the preservation of the forests. . . ."

19. My two sources for information on Phillips are the Phillips-Myers Papers in custody of the Southern History Collection at the University of North Carolina, and Harold Dean Cater, *Henry Adams and His Friends* (Boston: Houghton Mifflin Co., 1947), lxxi–lxxiii.

20. So far no one knows for sure who inserted the clause. See Hague Papers, Hague to Secretary of the Interior, March 25, 1891, and Hague to Charles D. Borgwart, April 7, 1891, for positive confirmation of Hague's responsibility, at the very least, for the initial Yellowstone Forest Preserve, about 15,000 square miles extending eight miles south of the park boundary and twenty-four miles east of it. See also the chapter on Hague's interest in the park in Manning, *Government in Science,* 151–67.

21. *Forest and Stream,* May, 1894, quoted from obituary notice in Phillips-Myers Papers, Vol. 10 (Selected).

22. Phillips-Myers Papers, obituary notice from *New York Tribune,* May 9, 1897.

23. The intellectual ferment of the 1880s and 1890s in Washington, D.C., has been the subject of an excellent study: Michael James Lacey, "The Mysteries of Earth-Making Dissolve: A Study of Washington's Intellectual Community and the Origins of American Environmentalism in the Late Nineteenth Century," Doctoral Dissertation, George Washington University, 1979.

24. Senate Executive Document No. 10, 47th Cong., 2d Sess. (Serial No. 2073).

25. Ibid.

26. Ibid.

27. *Congressional Record,* 47th Cong., 2d Sess., Senate 3270.

28. Ibid., 3488.

29. Ibid.

30. The debates are in *Congressional Record,* 47th Cong., 2d Sess., February 26, 1883, 3268 ff. and March 1, 1883 3482–88.

31. Ibid., 48th Cong., 1st Sess., Senate, 4548, and correspondence for the year 1883 in PMLR and PMLS. See also *Congressional Record,* 49th Cong., 1st Sess.,

House, August 2, 1886, 7845. See also Bartlett, "The Senator Who Saved Yellowstone Park."

32. *Enterprise,* December 14, 1883; February 4, 1884; PMLR, Creditors to Secretary Lamar, May 1, 1885, via Senator G. L. McMillan; Ibid, Hatch to Teller, May 29, 1884.

33. *Enterprise,* January 29, February 4, 1884.

34. Ibid., February 25, March 11, March 29, April 14, April 15, 1884.

35. Ibid., March 21,. 1884. This article states that W. R. Stebbins, Mund, and Company, and the Bank of Livingston, "were the principal instigators of the movement for a receivership." But the sure hand of a Wall Street tycoon is too present to be discounted. See also Ibid., quoting from the *New York Times,* (May 12, 1884), "An Interview With Hatch." In this article Hatch takes full credit for bringing about the receivership. Yet Mr. Love said that the order was made by action brought by one C. E. Quincy, "a stockholder and creditor." PMLR, Love to Secretary Teller, April 27, 1884.

36. *Enterprise,* March 26, 1884. William Endicott, Jr., of Boston, was a judge of the Massachusetts Supreme Court and Secretary of War, 1885–89.

37. Ibid., March 21, March 26, 1884. It was G. L. Henderson's residence.

38. Ibid., March 29, 1884; PMLR, E. D. Kelly on behalf of employees, to Teller, March 25, 1884; Ibid., W. H. Briggle to President of the United States, April 5, 1884; PMLS, Teller to Briggle, April 10, 1884.

39. *Enterprise,* May 8, 1884, quoting from the *Pioneer Press,* Minneapolis.

40. *Enterprise,* February 5, 1884; PMLR, Hobart to Muldrow, no date but obviously 1885; Ibid., Hatch to Teller, May 19, 1884.

41. PMLS, Teller to Hobart, May 27, 1884; PMLR, Hobart to Teller, June 25, 1884.

42. PMLS, Teller to General James A. Williamson, acknowledging payment of rent, March 6, 1884; PMLR, Hatch to Teller, May 19, 1884; Ibid., Hobart to Teller, June 25, 1884.

43. PMLR, E. John Ellis to Secretary Lamar, April 3, 1886, implies that the matter of who was the legitimate receiver was never settled. See also *Enterprise,* June 19, June 26, and June 28, 1884.

44. PMLR, Hatch to Third Judicial District of Wyoming, October 13, 1885 (copy).

45. *Enterprise,* December 6, 1884.

46. Ibid., May 23, June 6, 1885. See also W. Hallett Phillips's Special Report to the Secretary dated September 12, 1885. This was published as "Letter of W. H. Phillips on the Yellowstone Park," 49th Cong., 1st Sess., Senate Exec. Doc. No. 51 (Serial No. 2333).

47. Letter of Dr. B. P. Lincoln, M.D., Appendix "G" of Phillips's Special Report, 28–29.

48. Ibid., 12.

49. Ibid., 13.

50. PMLR, copy of petition from Hatch, sent by investors Allen Moon and Company, to Third Judicial District Court, Territory of Wyoming, October 13, 1885; Ibid., letter from attorneys Johns and Newborn representing Rufus Hatch, November 20, 1885.

51. *Enterprise*, October 17, 1885; *The National Cyclopedia of American Biography*, Vol. 5, 114–115.

52. Gibson to Secretary, August 24, 1885, included in testimony of Chief Clerk of the Department, Edward M. Dawson, in Committee on Public Lands, "Inquiry Into the Management and Control of the Yellowstone National Park," 52nd Cong., 1st Sess. (1892) (Serial No. 3051), 241–42. Hereinafter cited as Inquiry. See also Richard A. Bartlett, "The Concessionaires of Yellowstone National Park: Genesis of a Policy, 1882–1892," *Pacific Northwest Quarterly* Vol. 74, No. 1 (January, 1983), 2–10.

53. Inquiry, 243; 246.

54. PMLR, copy of petition from Hatch to Third Judicial District Court, October 13, 1885; Inquiry, 253.

55. Inquiry, 241–42.

56. *Enterprise*, June 12, 1885; Phillips's "Report."

57. Inquiry, 19.

58. Freeman Tilden, *Following the Frontier with F. Jay Haynes*, devotes some eighty five pages to Haynes's Yellowstone activities; interview with Mrs. Bessie Haynes Arnold, October 7, 8, and 9, 1970. Mrs. Arnold also made available to me her collection of family letters, diaries, and photographs. These include Haynes's letters to his fiancée, Lily Snyder.

59. PMLR, W. C. Butler of Winnepeg, Canada, to Secretary Kirkwood, July 3, 1881; Ibid., no date save 1881.

60. Ibid., Haynes to Kirkwood, August 29, 1881; Tilden, *Following the Frontier*, 376–78. Tilden writes that Teller hedged on the lease but that Senator Vest intervened in Haynes's behalf. See also PMLR, Haynes to Kirkwood, December 30, 1881; PMLS, Assistant Secretary Joslyn to Haynes, October 7, 1884, and August 6, 1886. Haynes had some difficulties with his lease locations.

61. *Enterprise*, July 27, 1883.

62. The most recent article on the Schwatka expedition is William L. Lang, "At the Greatest Personal Peril to the Photographer," *Montana: The Magazine of Western History*, Vol. 33, No. 1 (Winter, 1983), 14–29. Other sources include the Arnold

Hague Papers, Hague to Grinnell, December 29, 1886; to Elwood Hofer, February 23, 1887, and to F. Jay Haynes, February 25, 1887. Hague wrote to Haynes that, "From all accounts published here [in Washington] Schwatka made an entire failure of his trip. He must have been very drunk from the time he first entered the park. People here are laughing a great deal at the story of his exploration of this well-known country." Another source is G. L. Henderson, "Haynes Winter Expedition" in Ash Scrapbook, Y.A., which appears to be clipped from the *Helena Independent*, February 6, 1887. Tilden, *Following the Frontier*, discusses the trip on pp. 339–56. See also Jack Ellis Haynes "The First Winter Trip Through the Yellowstone National Park," *Annals of Wyoming*, Vol. 14, No. 2 (April 1, 1942) 89–97.

The Howell buffalo poaching incident is described by Emerson Hough in *Forest and Stream*, Vol. 42, No. 18 (1894). It is mentioned in Ralph Pierson, "The Czar of Wonderland," Denver Westerners *Brand Book*, Vol. 11 (1955), 376–86. See also James B. Trefethan, *An American Crusade for Wildlife* (New York: The Winchester Press and Boone and Crockett Club, 1975), 86–88.

63. The correct citation to the first *Guide* is A. B. Guptill, Practical Guide to Yellowstone National Park (St. Paul: F. Jay Haynes and Bro., 1890). Information about the Haynes's coach business is from Mrs. Arnold.

64. Phillips, Special Report, 12 20; PMLS, Muldrow to Superintendent, April 3, 1885; Interview with Mrs. Arnold; PMLR, Wear to Muldrow, April 17, 1886; Ibid., "Declaration of Trust of H. C. Davis."

65. PMLS, Muldrow to Wear, April 6, 1886, copy of lease enclosed.

66. Y.A., File No. 1, Gibson to Muldrow, July 18, 1887.

67. PMLR, Gibson to Secretary Lamar, June 19, 1886.

68. Inquiry, 21.

69. Ibid., Gibson's statement, 247.

70. Ibid., 220.

71. Ibid., 78 ff., iii; Northern Pacific Papers in custody of the Minnesota Historical Society, Office of the President, Box No. 27, T. F. Oakes to Peace, Treasurer of the Yellowstone Park Association, September 4, 1890.

72. Inquiry, 29; *Biographical Directory of the American Congress, 1774–1971*, 1526.

73. Inquiry, 206.

74. Ibid., vi.

75. Ibid., ix.

76. Ibid., x; 75.

77. Ibid., 280–83. During my research it became clear that someone in the Interior Department was informing Hobart and his cohorts about Interior's interests

in Yellowstone, someone who was able to bend policy in the YNPIC's favor. Ex-superintendent Edmund G. Rogers related an incident that confirmed the existence of such a spy. While Rogers and Billie Nichols, the Park Company president, disposed of old papers found in the attic of the old Mammoth hotel when it was being dismantled, they came across a crumpled telegram, apparently addressed to Hobart, informing him that Pat Conger was fired, but would not hear of it until the dismissal notice arrived by mail in ten days. Rogers and Nichols, lacking the historian's sense of preservation, destroyed the telegram. Interview with Mr. Rogers, October, 1970.

78. Inquiry, xiii.

79. Ibid. A minority report was filed briefly by Republican Congressmen Pickler and Townsend. It is brief, thoroughly partisan, and no impartial reader can consider it anything but political hyperbole.

80. *Dictionary of American Biography,* Vol. 13, 539–40.

CHAPTER SIX

The Golden Age of Park Concessionaires, 1892 to 1929

Due west of the old Haynes Picture Shop at Mammoth Hot Springs are several attractive residences surrounded by carefully manicured lawns. By their architecture these houses are clearly not of government issue. Yet few people ever ask about their ownership, although some visitors to the park may have a fleeting moment of curiosity. Who lives there?

These are the homes of the park nobility. One of them belonged until 1968 to the Haynes family, which for eighty-seven years enjoyed the photographic concession in Yellowstone. Until 1967 the most pretentious of the dwellings belonged to Mrs. William M. Nichols, an aristocratic heiress to the Yellowstone Park Company. Even as an octogenarian she enjoyed the status in the park as "the Duchess of Yellowstone." For seventy-five years, beginning in 1892, she or her progenitors—families named Huntley and Child—had dominated park concessions. Smaller entrepreneurs orbited around the Haynes and Huntley-Child-Nichols families, and were occasionally absorbed by them.

The occupants of those houses could have been equally well ensconced in granite castles protected by moats and portcullises. Such structures would not have been out of keeping with the power held by the concessionaire families, a peerage that held onto its fiefdoms in the face of changing political parties, evolution of Interior Department regulatory structure, the coming of the automobile, depressions and prosperity. Whatever else might be said about them, no one can question their tenacity. [1]

By 1892 the Haynes family was firmly established in the park while Silas Huntley and his wife's brother-in-law (his wife's sister's husband, Harry Child) were busily entrenching themselves in the park's transportation business and eyeing other potential sources of profit. Above those entrepreneurs, most especially overseeing the transportation and hotel operations, were the managers of the Northern Pacific Railroad Company (or, after a second bankruptcy and reorganization, the Northern Pacific Railway Company), sort of a corporate king overlooking its vassals.

Little evidence exists that the railroad made any determined attempt to keep secret either its interest in park concessions or its role as a silent partner. Certainly its cooperation with the big park concessionaires was widely known. It was also resented. "The betrayal of the park into the hands of the Northern Pacific Railroad began with Secretary Teller," G. L. Henderson informed Acting Superintendent Captain Moses Harris in 1888. Henderson then related the demise of the old YNPIC, "killed," he said, "by its own incapacity." Then Gibson came in, and his gang was even worse. "Gibson and Waters [the general manager] have given me fair notice that they will either buy, scare, or drive us out," he cried, and went on to elaborate how the Park Association and the railroad connived to squeeze out the independent concessionaires, of whom Henderson was one.[2]

Such opposition never appears to have bothered Northern Pacific interests. Passenger traffic was coveted then, and the attraction of Wonderland offered the possibility of enormous profits. Therefore the Northern Pacific helped plan and subsidize the large park and transportation concessions. As N.P. President C. S. Mellen wrote in 1897 to Colonel D. C. Lamont, a vice-president of the Park Association (who was also affiliated with the N.P.), "The amount we have heretofore lost in connection with the Park, charged out as a commission on the business of the Road is not in my judgement an unreasonable sum to pay to procure such business."[3]

Equally significant was the interest in park affairs of N.P. executives who had invested heavily in the park hotels or the transportation system. It follows that their interests swayed N.P. decisions involving the reservation. Finally, perhaps in spite of itself, the railroad became involved financially in the park to the extent of around a million dollars. By then N.P. officials were understandably meddlesome because they needed to protect the corporation's large investment. By way of example, note President Howard Elliott's letter to John H. Carroll, a legal and public relations consultant in Washington D.C.:

March 15, 1912—Private
My Dear Mr. Carroll,
Please see Senate Resolution Number 246, introduced by Senator Warren, about automobiles in the Yellowstone National Park.
It is very important to our interests that no steps be taken that lead to the introduction of automobiles in that Park. Mr. Child's companies owe us $700,000 secured on the notes and securities of the Yellowstone Park Company. Should automobiles be permitted in the Park . . . it would cause a very large pecuniary loss to Mr. Child and the Northern Pacific.

Howard Elliott[4]

This much is clear: the Northern Pacific was involved with the big park companies (the hotel and the biggest transportation company) into the World War II period. Its history down to the end of the army period in the park (1916–1918) is one of ever deepening involvement at the very same time that it was trying to get out. The story is filled with the legerdemain of high finance but with embarrassing gaps, missing details of events that obviously happened but with neither the date or the details of the transaction or the reasons being chronicled. Such is the nature of much business history. An example is the report of "E. Askevold, Auditor, Jersey City, New Jersey, January 30, 1917," which purported to give the financial history of the park companies. It is filled with such statements as the following:

> Just when the old R.R. Co. found it necessary to acquire sole ownership of the Association is not stated in any of the files. . . .

> The Nor. Pac. Ry. Co. acquired the Association stock from the old R.R. Co. presumably as of September 1, 1896. . . .

> The correspondence does not show when or why Mr. Child was elected President of the Association. . . .

> I found nothing in the files I went through, which showed the date when the names of the two companies were changed to "Yellowstone Park Hotel Co." and "Yellowstone Park Transportation Co." It must have taken place in August, 1910, because we begin in that month to take joint notes of the new companies to cover advances. . . .[5]

In admitting to gaps in the record the auditor was essentially correct, although some of them can be filled. The Yellowstone Park Association stockholders split into two factions, a St. Louis group headed by Gibson and not directly associated with the railroad, and a faction cemented by common financial interests in the Northern Pacific. The St. Louis group managed the Park Association while the railroad faction manifested little interest in it. The association, without financial backing from the N.P., not only began to lose money but had no funds for essential maintenance. Irate members of the St. Louis faction proved, to their satisfaction at least, that the railroad was making a profit from carrying freight and personel bound for association facilities in the park, yet was not helping the association financially. They complained, further, that the railroad people had insisted on the opening and closing of the hotels earlier and later in the season than was profitable, and in 1896 had even insisted on the association charging a dollar less per room than Interior would allow.[6]

For the concerned minority, the St. Louis group, the way out of the dilemma was to suggest to the minority stockholders, who held 2,125 shares (while the railroad faction held 3,088 shares of the total of 5,213—shares taken as collateral on loans to the Park Association) that they sell at thirty dollars a share to a broker, Mr. E. D. Adams, at 35 Wall Street, New York City. In turn it was hoped that the Northern Pacific, "being the only company or individual that can reasonably expect to make any money from the operation of hotels in the Park, should, in our judgement, be willing to buy out the minority stockholders of the Association at a figure that will be equitable to others and profitable to itself."[7]

Ultimately this suggestion was carried out. In June 1898, all 5,213 shares were sold by the Northern Pacific Railway to a Northwest Improvement Company, at thirty dollars a share, or $156,390. Within the Improvement Company the Yellowstone Park Association retained its identity. By this time the condition of the association's properties was causing great concern. Including the construction of new hotels demanded by Interior and repairs on old ones (Mammoth, for example, leaned with the wind "which [was] very disagreeable to the occupants") the estimate for putting the physical properties in shape was $302,510. New hotels were contemplated at Tower Falls and Upper Geyser Basin. The former was never to have a hotel, but the pressure from Interior was intense for a hostelry at the Upper Basin. Tourists, read an Interior Department letter to the Park Association, "are now subjected to the delay, inconvenience and fatigue of being hauled three times over the same ten miles of road [between Fountain Hotel and the Upper Basin] because there is no hotel at the Upper Basin." The letter added that while other parties were interested in building such a hotel, the Park Association would have first chance.[8]

With such a plethora of difficulties as the end of century approached, the Park Association needed vigorous management, but such was not forthcoming. Charles Gibson was an old man. On May 31, 1898, he settled with Northern Pacific interests for $36,150. At that time the general manager of the hotels was J. H. Dean, who had succeeded Eli Waters upon that individual's removal; this had taken place at least by May 1892. A significant note from Dean to W. G. Pearce, treasurer of the Park Association, stated that he had met both Huntley and Child.[9]

Regardless of the unscrupulous way in which those two had wrested the park transportation monopoly from Wakefield and the Northern Pacific interests, Huntley and his source of financing, Child, proceeded to run the business as if they were in the park to stay. Huntley came to be well liked by the park people. During the nineties the two concentrated on their transit business. By 1898 Child, as vice-president and a rising power in the Yellowstone National Park Transportation Company, was signing that company's leases with the Interior Department. The two men had their hands full, for they faced some competition: F. Jay Haynes and a partner, William H. Humphrey, on June 1, 1891, had signed with Interior for the Monida and Yellowstone Transportation Company. It would enter the park exclusively from the west entrance. Haynes also threatened to build the hotel at the Upper Basin, thus forcing the Park Association's hand, although it was not inclined to sink large sums of money into the park.[10]

Park Association managers (who were also executives of the railroad) had always known that the real profits in the park lay in transportation, not in hotels. In February 1898 they had requested a ten-year extension of their lease even though the present one still had seven years to run; *plus* the right to transport parties through the park "by land and water." A year later association attorneys were reminding Interior that the hotels were never presumed to be "a very remunerative investment," but with the revenues from transportation a fair profit could be earned. The secretary was reminded that the transportation franchise had been denied the association. At least partly as a result, the company, its attorneys claimed, was losing about $25,000 per annum.[11]

Meanwhile Huntley and Child were consolidating their interest and maintaining political ties. As early as December 31, 1897, Senator Thomas Carter of Montana had broached Huntley about getting together and bringing about "harmonious action" in the park.[12]

Frustrated in its efforts to improve its profits (or cut its losses), the Northern Pacific was by the turn of the century intent upon ending its park activities as then structured. Eli C. Waters, who by then had the boat concession on Yellowstone Lake, negotiated for purchase of the hotel facilities, but N.P. President Mellen cancelled discussions and had the papers returned to St. Paul. Eighteen months later N.P. Vice-President Lamont recommended selling the association "to Child and Bach" (Child's brother-in-law). The advice was followed.[13]

In essence, Northern Pacific management's financial adventures into park concessions by way of Hatch's YNPIC, Gibson's Yellowstone Park Association, and possession of that association within N.P.'s subsidiary, the Northwest Improvement Company, all aimed at maintaining Yellowstone concessions at a quality conducive to the railroad's tourist business, had not worked out satisfactorily. N.P. President C. S. Mellen and Vice-President D. C. Lamont searched for a workable solution. They wanted an arrangement whereby the railroad would still have a heavy financial investment while an outsider established stability and adequate management of the concessions. Perhaps Harry Child was their man.

As of April 1, 1901, Harry Child had acquired a one-third interest in the Yellowstone Park Association. Actually, because of marriage connections, he had more power than the one-third implies, for Child had 1,737 2/3, Silas Huntley had 1,727 2/3, and Edmund W. Bach had 1,727 2/3. A few remaining shares were held by an N.P. official (a Mr. Bunn) "in order to qualify him as Director" and thus maintain a Northern Pacific interest. Shortly after the April 1 transaction, Child was elected president of the Yellowstone Park Association. Later in that same year, while most of the army and concessionaire "establishment" were in Swan Lake Flats celebrating the dedication of a new water supply system, news came that Silas Huntley had died. Now Harry Child was well on his way toward dominating Yellowstone's major concessions. Who was this man?[14]

This lord of the Yellowstone nobility stood small and tubby at five feet five inches. Born in 1857 in California, Child, with his family, rounded the Horn in a move to New England, where Harry received his education. As a young man he went to Montana and became involved in mining and smelting enterprises. Then he became agent for the capably managed Gilmer and Salisbury Stage Lines that ran down to Corinne, Utah. Child was a successful businessman before he became involved in the park.[15]

He was a large landowner in Montana's Gallatin Valley. From Bozeman he managed the "Flying D" Ranch where he and C. L. Anceney headquartered their land and cattle operations. Together they controlled 500,000 acres and grazed 15,000 to 20,000 cattle. He was a heavy investor in Helena, Montana, real estate. He had stock in a La Jolla, California, bank and a Scratch Gravel Company. He understood the magic of a good accountant and hired one of Montana's best, Hugh Galusha. Child appears to have been worth about four million dollars in 1911. In 1921 he gave five dollars to the Community Chest, ten dollars in 1922, and in 1930 gave it a hundred dollars—and the Red Cross a dollar. Yet not all went Harry Child's way. He was diabetic but was saved from an early death by the discovery of insulin in 1921, just in the nick of time. He died in 1931 at the age of seventy-four.[16]

One thing is clear. Harry Child wanted to own every hotel, lodge, tent camp, camping outfit, stagecoach line, bus line, livery, grocery, curio store, photo shop, garage and gas station in the park. As Howard Elliott, a president of the N.P., said, Child was afraid of competition in spite of his influence at the White House. When Haynes talked of building a hotel at West Yellowstone, Child not only fought him but made reference to "how many kinds of damn liar Haynes is. . . ." In 1926 Child referred to the Hertz Drive-Ur-Self Company as "a bunch of bandits"; his real worry was that they would succeed in getting into the park because General Motors was backing Hertz, and G.M. just might have more influence in Washington than he did.[17]

Although he was a Republican in a Republican age, and was on excellent terms with Senator Carter, Harry Child made it a policy to *always* be on good terms with whoever was in the White House, regardless of party. His power in Washington crops up again and again in Northern Pacific files. "Billie [his son-in-law] just wires me that Secretary [Director] Mather announced yesterday that transportation companies would use horses next year, same as this," Child wired an N.P. official in 1915. "The old man won out again. Congratulate me." He was far more prepared for motor vehicles when they finally did arrive, in 1917.[18]

"He was a typical robber baron," recalled former Superintendent Edmund G. Rogers, who considered Child as unscrupulous as any of the operators mentioned in Matthew Josephson's *The Robber Barons;* but Child operated in the sparsely-settled Northwest, so that his dealings were not on so grand a scale as those of the eastern nabobs. "He was," Rogers added, "utterly ruthless."[19]

"His motto was never to be in debt to a railroad for less than a million dollars," says Horace Albright, who had to deal with him.[20]

"If Harry Child died and appeared at the Pearly Gates, and St. Peter suggested they flip a coin to see if he would enter Heaven or Hell," said Jack Ellis Haynes, "Harry would have agreed. Then he would have caught the coin in mid-air and run away with it."[21]

His sister-in-law, Silas Huntley's widow, married Acting Superintendent S. B. M. Young. One of the Child's daughters married handsome young Lieutenant William Nichols; better known as Billie, he later became president of the company. When the government was reluctant to allow Child to run the stores in Yellowstone, he subsidized an employee of his, Charles Ashworth Hamilton; thus Hamilton Stores came into existence. (Hamilton's daughter married Trevor Povah, who controls both the Hamilton Stores and the Haynes Picture Shops today.) Together Child and Hamilton managed and profited immensely from the gasoline stations on the reservation. F. Jay and his son Jack Ellis were never sure what Harry might do next, and they knew he coveted their business. So chronic a complainer was he that he was widely dubbed "Harry Hard-up."[22]

The intricacies of his relations with the railroads (plural because in time other lines besides the Northern Pacific were involved) form a study in themselves; only the highlights can be mentioned here. In 1905 a major shift in power and ownership took place. It involved not only the hotel company of which Child was president, but also the transportation company whose ownership changed with Huntley's death. In 1903 the Northern Pacific had acquired some transportation company stock "to protect the interests of the Northwest Improvement Company [its subsidiary] as the result of the death of S. S. Huntley, the conduct of Mr. E. W. Bach, and the political complications of Mr. T. H. Carter." To quote from the auditor's report, "as of February 1, 1905 . . . Mr. Child became one-half owner of both the [Yellowstone Park] Association and the Transportation Company, he giving his note for $82,150.25." The N.P. (or its affiliate, the Northwest Improvement Company), made Child agree "that the Improvement Company should have full jurisdiction over records pertaining to finances and accounts . . . [and could] if it so desired, control the companies in a stockholders' or directors' meeting."[23]

Matters did not remain at this stage for long. The eyes of the public were fixed upon the Northern Pacific in 1901 and for several years thereafter. During this period it was one of three railroads, the other two being the Great Northern and the Chicago, Burlington, and Quincy, which after a massive battle on the New York Stock Exchange, were brought under unified control in the Northern Securities Company. It was this trust that President Theodore Roosevelt chose in a test of the validity of the Sherman Antitrust Act. In 1904 the government won its case and the Northern Securities Company was ordered disbanded. Northern Pacific management, once burnt, was now twice shy of the accusation of monopoly. When Eli C. Waters began stirring up rumors about the railroad monopolizing business in Yellowstone Park, the decision was made to have all Northern Pacific companies (such as their Northwest Improvement Company) dispose of all their stock. In accordance with this policy, in January 1907, the firm's Washington counsel, John Carroll, advised N.P. President Elliott to sell to Child. What with Progressive Senator LaFollette in the neighborhood, Elliott agreed, and steps were taken to dispose of park interests before trouble arose.[24]

Therefore the Northern Pacific "sold all Improvement Company holdings to Mr. Child for $268,195.00, taking as part payment his note dated March 1, 1907, for $225,000 with the stock purchased as collateral thereunder." As President Elliott explained, "this proposition practically puts us in the position of changing our stock ownership into notes due to Mr. Child. . . . I believe we would be better off for Mr. Child to owe us money." He also predicted that Congress would be far more amenable to such an arrangement. Then he added what was indeed a prophetic statement of policy: "The Northern Pacific, on account of having started in on the Park business, will always have to take a large interest in it, and will always have to help Mr. Child in such ways as it can by advancing him money from time to time and

Howard Eaton was the leading dude rancher in the nineteen twenties.
He is astride his horse "Danger" in Yellowstone.
*Eaton Brothers Ranch Collection, courtesy Archive-American Heritage Center,
University of Wyoming.*

In 1926 all 321 buses and trucks of Harry Child's fleet were lined up outside the company shops south of Gardiner.
Courtesy Motor Bus Society Library.

In 1931 the transportation company updated its Yellowstone fleet with new White 614s, with doors for each row of seats and a removable canvas top.
Courtesy White Motor Corporation.

Marshall's Hotel in the Lower Geyser Basin was expanded with two,
eight room cottages in 1887. This was the North Cottage.
F. Jay Haynes photograph, courtesy Bessie Haynes Arnold.

One did not need much capital to set up business in early Yellowstone.
This was Bozeman photographer H.B. Calfee's "store"
in the Upper Geyser Basin in 1880.
Courtesy Montana Historical Society.

F. Jay Haynes's Mammoth Hot Springs home was of strictly Victorian design, but elk grazing in the front yard and a fence of 400 elk horns gave it a Yellowstone touch. Photograph taken in 1898.

Courtesy of Bessie Haynes Arnold.

F. Jay Haynes on "Rock" with "Rye's" legs and neck in the background.
"Rye" always followed like a colt.
Courtesy of Bessie Haynes Arnold.

W. Hallett Phillips, a young
Washington, D.C., lawyer,
surveyed conditions in
Yellowstone as a secret agent
for the Department of Interior.
*Courtesy Southern Historical
Collection, Library of the University
of North Carolina at Chapel Hill.*

Robert Reamer, brilliant architect
of the Canyon Hotel, Old Faithful In
and other structures in the park,
was one of the outstanding architects
of the Pacific Northwest.
Courtesy Mrs. Jane Reamer White.

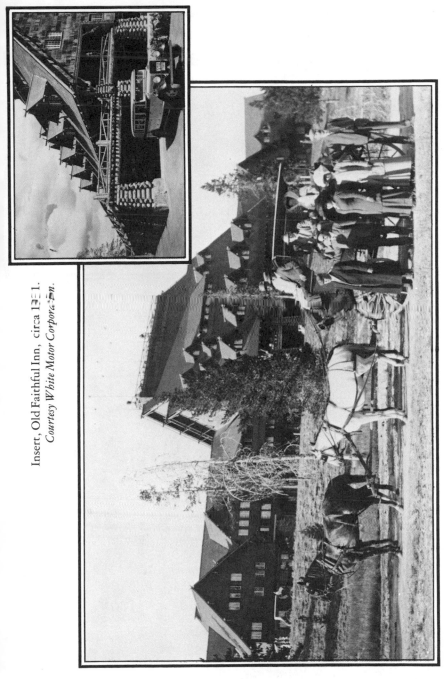

Insert, Old Faithful Inn, circa 1921.
Courtesy White Motor Corporation.

"Cal Bill' (Elmer A. Douglas) with his horses, Sweetheart, Fox, Smoky, and Johnny, pose with tourists in 1909 in front of Old Faithful Inn.
Courtesy Henry H. Douglas.

Something of the immensity of the old Canyon Hotel can be estimated
by this photograph, taken in the nineteen twenties.
Courtesy Montana Historical Society.

Still functioning is the beautiful but architecturally misplaced Lake Hotel.
Photographed in 1905 by William Henry Jackson,
courtesy Colorado Historical Society.

standing back of him, but that is a little different from being an actual owner in the property."[25]

Just two months later (March 8, 1907) President Elliott informed Child that the Northern Pacific "will be disposed to make temporary advances rather than to force you to go elsewhere for the needed funds." Yet the railroad considered itself clear. If anyone asks you, Elliott wrote the company counsel in Washington, you should say that the Northern Pacific "has no stock ownership, directly or indirectly, and that it has sold all its holdings in the Park companies."[26]

Sometime prior to 1919 Harry Child changed the names of his properties to the Yellowstone Park Hotel Company and the Yellowstone Park Transportation Company. In that year the Northwest Improvement Company began taking notes on the two companies to cover advances. By 1916 a million dollars had been advanced and only $150,000 repaid. Although the auditor could not account for the uses put to $435,000 of the sum advanced, surely the money figured into the additions to the Lake and Canyon hotels and the total construction of Old Faithful Inn. Some of it could have been involved easily in the acquisition of the Yellowstone Lake Boat Company. A statement in Elliott's files, written by A. H. Foss (not otherwise identified) and dated December 7, 1912, says the average profit each year from 1905 through 1912 was $202,261 on hotels, telegraph, garden, store, and transportation company, with an estimated value of $2,952,444.39—a little less than 8 percent.[27]

Indeed Child did pay off many of his debts and he appears to have made his interest payments promptly. N.P. President Elliott was informed in 1912 that Child owed the Improvement Company "something over $500,000 for monies we have advanced him from time to time to help him keep the hotels in good condition. This loan is well secured and he pays the interest promptly and has just paid off $100,000 of the principle." Unquestionably Northern Pacific officials backed Child consistently and considered him a good businessman. In 1905 Elliott had assured Child of this confidence. "There is no disposition on the part of . . . The Northern Pacific Railroad . . . to have you give up the business of managing and developing the Park so long as you handle it in the present efficient manner," he wrote, and this appears to have been the railroad's policy as long as Child was active. Officials panicked when in 1912 Child, using an old ploy, hinted at selling out for $3,000,000 to a combine believed to consist of the Union Pacific and/or the Chicago, Milwaukee, St. Paul and Pacific. Nothing came of it.[28]

In 1916 Child needed a large sum of money to finance the purchase of a fleet of automobiles and buses, for even he could not stave off their adoption any longer. Steve Mather indicated that the Park Service would like just one transportation company in the park and that the service would be protective of the Child interests. The Burlington Railroad, which wanted bus service from its terminus at Cody to Sylvan Pass and around to Lake, and the Northwest Improvement Company appear to have lent Child the necessary $470,000 for motorization. Representatives of the White Motor Car Company likewise politicked for it. Some $500,300 was listed in 1917 under "equipment" for the transit company, of which $458,739 went for the 125 White buses which became a company symbol throughout the 1920s. It was at this time that Haynes's "Yellowstone and Western" (the old Monida) and his "Cody and Sylvan Pass" lines were consolidated with the Child system. Haynes was now out of transportation and exclusively in the picture shop business. Child must have liked that.[29]

In the mid-1950s Child's heirs sought professional help in disposing of their park interests. The appraisal firm predicated its analysis by making this statement: "It is quite evident to us during our survey that the members of both the Child and Nichols families have devoted their lives to the business and have a sincere interest in the welfare of the Yellowstone National Park and the proper conduct of the concessions."[30]

There is very little evidence that the Child-Nichols interests ever manifested much concern over the park proper. Harry Child did, however, exhibit interest and pride in two of his many Yellowstone concessions: the transportation company and his hotels. He was proud of his fleet of White "Yellowjackets" and of his inns at Lake, Old Faithful, and Canyon.

Perhaps, being wealthy himself, he believed in the permanence of an Edwardian or McKinleyesque world in which a distinct upper class lived by rights on a higher scale of gentility than the hard-working lower and middle classes. Maybe Harry Child thought that world would go on forever. Sad to say, the age of elegance was on the wane by the time the great Yellowstone hotels were ready for guests, but never mind: he maintained them in the face of a changing clientele. Rustic lodges and crude, ugly cabins and tent camps not fit for a migrant worker were later erected nearby but discretely obscured from the beautiful inns. These catered to middle-class automobilists. For management, however, they were simply a way of making money, a necessary nuisance. Harry Child's heart lay in the great hotels.

When he assumed possession, most of the facilities were in poor condition. Mammoth Hotel was compared to a barn, too high for its width; expensive bracing had to be installed to make it safe. Foundations of both the early Canyon and first Lake hotel were so poorly laid that in 1889 expensive repairs had to be made to prevent them from falling down. In 1890 T. B.

Oakes of the Northern Pacific approved construction of the 143-room Fountain Hotel in Lower Geyser Basin. It was a cut above the others, at least when it was new. It had baths using hot springs water and was so positioned that the rooms across its wide front overlooked the geysers. However, even in 1892, and rustic as they were, Mammoth, Fountain, Lake and Canyon hotels had electricity.[31]

When Child assumed the presidency of the Yellowstone Park Association, the new Lake Hotel was still under construction, Canyon was much too small, Mammoth was in constant need of repair, Fountain was quite new and in relatively good condition, and luncheon facilities at Norris, the Upper Basin, and the Thumb needed constant attention. Moreover, since the opening of the road from the Upper Basin to the Thumb in 1891, the Department of Interior had been pressuring concessionaires to build a facility at the Upper Basin. Clearly bold and competent management, capable of acquiring loans for use in the unstable resort business, was called for. Harry Child supplied the energy and management; the railroad furnished the money.

He was aided by several Congressional actions. First of these was the Hayes Act, passed in 1894, which granted concessionaires up to ten acres at a single site and up to twenty acres total. This was far more realistic than the limit of ten acres for everything, especially if the government favored monopolistic conditions. An act of 1906 granted up to twenty acres at a single site and included the franchiser's right to mortgage his rights, contracts, and property. An amendment in 1907 extended franchises to twenty years, which greatly aided the concessionaires in raising money.[32]

It was under Child's management that the canary-yellow-walled, white-pillared Lake Colonial Hotel, so out of place in its wilderness setting, was completed. Its reception room (lobby) was finished in California redwood. "Steam heat, baths, and the usual accessories of modern hotels are of course to be found," read a Northern Pacific travel folder, "and the room furnishings are all that could be desired."[33]

It was with regard to enlargement of the Canyon Hotel and construction of Old Faithful Inn that Child's latent aesthetic tastes were manifested. Both of these magnificent structures did justice to their surroundings. Canyon no longer exists, being replaced by Canyon Village, but Old Faithful Inn, bless its pine-knotted walls, still stands; it is Park Service property. To dismantle it would be an act of barbarism equal to clogging up Old Faithful geyser.

Who was Harry Child's architect for these two buildings? Whoever he was, he possessed the elements of genius. He stressed dignity with simplicity and believed a building should be keyed to its environment. That today's life style has outmoded some of the societal customs for which he designed his buildings does not deter from the brilliant concepts which he so faithfully carried out in their construction. The same man also remodeled much of

Lake, built additions to it and to Mammoth, designed the Norris Ranger Station, the Northern Pacific Station at Gardiner, the Park Company transportation buildings, and Harry Child's home at Mammoth. He drew the specifications for the Roosevelt Memorial Arch at the north entrance and designed many structures—hotels and movie houses especially—outside Yellowstone. The architect's name was Robert C. Reamer.

He was born September 12, 1873, in Oberlin, Ohio, where he attended public schools until age twelve. At thirteen Robert went to Detroit to visit relatives. A short time after his arrival his parents heard that he was working in an architect's office. Presumably he remained several years with the firm, learning much about the profession. From there Reamer's trail leads, dimly, to Chicago, where he again took employment with an architect. We do not know how many years he spent there, but it is certain that he emerged into manhood as a self-made architect. By the later 1890s he was practicing the profession in San Diego as one-half of the architectural firm of Zimmer and Reamer. It was probably while there, his daughter surmises, that Reamer met Harry Child, for Child wintered in California. "What does seem certain," says his daughter, Mrs. Jane Reamer White, "is that Mr. and Mrs. Child took quite a personal interest in my father, right from the start. For extended periods during construction in the Park, he resided in their home. To them he was 'Robert'."[34]

This was the architect who designed and supervised the construction of Old Faithful Inn in 1903 and 1904, with wings added in 1913 and 1928. In 1909, with the new Canyon Hotel addition in prospect, he accompanied the Childs to Europe. "This," writes his daughter, "was the most enjoyable and educational experience for him, affording opportunity to observe many of the famous architectural achievements abroad. It was his way to be eternally searching out new ideas for his own work. I'm sure he found much to inspire him for the construction the following winter."[35]

By this time he had met Miss Louise Chase of New York while she was visiting her uncle, United States Commissioner to Yellowstone John W. Meldrum; Reamer and Miss Chase were married in Chicago in October 1911. During the First World War, after being rejected by the army, he took work in the shipyards at Bremerton, Washington. He liked the Pacific Northwest and joined the Metropolitan Building Company in Seattle after one of its executives had been favorably impressed with his work in Yellowstone.[36]

Reamer's design for Seattle's Olympic Hotel was accepted by the company, which then waged a campaign to raise building funds. Harry Child heard of the situation and wrote a supporting letter to the Seattle Chamber of Commerce. "In my opinion and in the opinion of thousands upon thousands of people who have visited Yellowstone Park, [he] is one of the most noted architects in the country today, notwithstanding his youth," Child wrote. "There is only one trouble with him—he is too modest to submit his ideas to enquiring people and some person who knows his ability has to talk to him."[37]

Child saw Reamer's genius in the design of the Olympic Hotel. It, like Canyon and Old Faithful Inn, had plans for an impressive lounge and dining room. If he was allowed to execute his plans, Child added, "it [the Olympic Hotel] will be written up all over the world in every language the same as Old Faithful Inn and the Grand Canyon Hotel. . . ." Unfortunately Reamer did not get the contract.[38]

His greatest triumph outside Yellowstone was the Edmund S. Meany Hotel in Seattle, still functioning in the 1980s as the University Tower. It boasted of "every room a corner room," and in 1938 was chosen by the American Institute of Architects as one of the one hundred most distinguished buildings constructed since 1918. Reamer died less than a month before that selection.

What kind of man was Robert Reamer? A Seattle business publication mentioned his quiet manner and his ability as a good listener. "His friends know he appears to be looking down, while he builds looking up. Some might think him odd. If they have a chance to be with him, they are astonished and impressed with the depths of a gracious and understanding individual. The effort to impress is not his. He is too busy looking down . . . creating."[39]

Reamer's Yellowstone activity began in 1903 and 1904 when Child had him design and then supervise construction of Old Faithful Inn. He was just thirty years old in 1903, which may explain why Child referred to him as a "kid." Perhaps the entrusting of a $200,000 project at the value of 1903 dollars focused comment on the architect's age, which seemed rather young for so much responsibility. Whatever the circumstances, Harry Child certainly had faith in "the kid," and Harry Child was never a squanderer. He appears to have given Reamer a free hand. The result was a unique hotel building.

It was to be built on the north side of the Upper Geyser Basin overlooking Old Faithful. At times, as Reamer envisioned his structure, guests from the front windows would observe spouting geysers from Old Faithful at one end of the geyser basin to the Castle at the other. Just a little east of the proposed site was the big pine tree under which President Arthur camped in 1883. For the imaginative young architect the site was very near ideal. In his mind's eye a magnificent turn-of-the-century luxury resort hotel arose, clear and precise, as if it already existed.

"They say," wrote Charles Francis Adams, who was a guest at Old Faithful in its early years, "the architect forgot to shave, forgot to undress at night, or breakfast in the morning, he was so engrossed in his work." An old-timer said workmen compared Reamer with Charley Russell, the great cowboy artist and sculptor, who knew in his mind, precisely, everything he wanted in his painting down to the most minute detail. In Old Faithful Inn Reamer supervised nearly everything that was done, and designed nearly everything that was used. The wrought iron hardware and the huge clock were of his design, and much of the iron work was hammered out on the site.[40]

Gradually the log hotel took form. Rising high for its width to blend with the mountain landscape, Old Faithful Inn was topped with an observation platform thirteen feet wide and seventy-two feet long. Above the platform rose six flagpoles, each eighteen feet high, each topped with a copper ball twelve inches in diameter. In the peak of the highest was a crow's-nest.[41]

Reamer planned Old Faithful Inn to be rustic throughout. From the stately porte-cochere and the massive log exterior walls, through the two-inch-thick-slab lobby doors, and upwards to the observation platform, logs, wood slabs, and semifinished planks met the eye. To blend with the rustic lumber, guests admired on the entrance doors the specially designed wrought iron lock, the locking bar, the grilled peephole, and the heavy iron studs. The theme carried to the clerk's counter which rested on natural volcanic stone quarried just five miles away. The counter was a single piece of oak with an eight inch wide, half-inch thick wrought iron band around the front of it. The main stairway had steps seven feet six inches across; each step was half of a twelve-inch thick log, and the hardware holding it was of rustic wrought iron. The ceiling was of six-inch slabs with a natural finish, nailed to the rafters.[42]

The huge lobby extended to the roof eighty-five feet above, with balconies surrounding it at each floor. The lobby's focal point was the fourteen-foot square fireplace. It had four large hearths, one on each side, and a smaller hearth in each corner, thus totalling eight fireplaces in one. Volcanic stone for the fireplace weighed five hundred tons. A huge corn popper hung against one of the walls; close by was a hollowed-out pine knot with a hinged door where the muncher could obtain salt. On the most exposed side of the fireplace was the wrought iron clock with its skeletal frame, a dial sixty inches in diameter, numerals eighteen inches high, and a long pendulum with a copper disk at the bottom; altogether the clock from top to bottom was twenty feet long.[43]

The inn also boasted a massive, half-octagon-shaped dining room sixty-two feet across. It too had a huge fireplace; through plate glass windows diners could watch geysers spout. On the upper floors were 120 guest rooms. Patrons who had never slept in rustic surroundings were charmed by bedrooms with walls of logs adzed on just two sides, so that rough bark remained. Bedroom doors were all of oiled rough-sawn pine, with a heavy, hand forged wrought iron latch, three common hinges, and one mortised lock.[44]

When Old Faithful Inn was well underway, the furnishings were chosen. According to Bessie Haynes Arnold, the guiding hand for interior decoration was Mrs. Child. Reamer's collaboration with her seems evident, since they were the best of friends and corresponded regularly. Everywhere an arts and crafts motif was carried out. Candles were really electric lights. Indian rugs lay on the gleaming maple floors. A grand piano graced the lobby. Conveniently placed were heavy oak tables with square legs and leather-covered tops, oak davenports, armchairs, settees, and arm rockers; there was a log cabin mail box, a rustic pine shoeshine stand, and forty or fifty simple hickory chairs with split seat and back. A bubbler (drinking fountain) was made of the volcanic stone.[45]

Old Faithful Inn was completed in time for the 1904 season. To its guests during those early years the hotel was as memorable an experience as the sight of the geyser of the same name, or the first glimpse of the Falls and the Grand Canyon. There are many of the usual "oooooh" and "ahhhhhhhh" descriptions of that remarkable building, but Charles Francis Adams, who could turn a neat phrase, expressed a guest's feelings best of all: "There is," he wrote, "one-man-made structure in the Park that looks as though it grew there . . . and that is 'Old Faithful Inn.'. . . All I can say is that the greatest travelers in the world say, 'There is nothing in the world like it or to compare with Old Faithful Inn.'"[46]

While the building impressed Adams, he was utterly bored by the "beautiful people" who lounged on the veranda. From the nearby tent camp which lodged lower middle-class tourists came sounds of singing and laughter, and the fragrance of popcorn popped over an open campfire. Why, Adams protested, should *they* have all the fun? Why should *he* be denied it? And so, he wrote (with tongue in cheek?—for really, now, would an Adams from Quincy, Mass., do this?) he climbed to Old Faithful Inn's observation platform, struck up an acquaintance with the man in charge of the big navy searchlight that cast its powerful beam on Old Faithful Geyser every evening, and persuaded him to turn the beam into the nearby woods. They discovered two "rotten loggers" and held the light on them until they fled! ("Rotten loggers" was the terminology of Yellowstone's college-age employees for petters, neckers, or, in today's terminology, those "making out.")[47]

In 1913 and again in 1928 wings were added to the inn, but neither carried out the original motif beyond having a rustic trim. In addition, men's and women's employees dormitories, and powerhouse and laundry, an engineer's cottage, a fire pumphouse, a girl's laundry, two bunkhouses, tailor, carpenter, and plumbing shops; a greenhouse, chicken house, and hose house; five utility tunnels, several bridges, fences, and walks; a wood lot, stable, water supply and sewage system also must be included in any inventory of Old Faithful Inn. Such a listing helps explain the heavy overhead involved in maintaining and operating the facility. Subsequently a more moderately priced Old Faithful Lodge was built nearby. *

So impressed was Harry Child with Old Faithful Inn and its architect that he had Reamer draw up plans for an addition to the Canyon Hotel. It tripled the number of rooms and was in many ways a greater architectural triumph than was Old Faithful Inn. In the six years that elapsed since completing that structure, Reamer had visited Europe and acquired greater understanding of the intricacies of depths and angles and perspectives, and people's psychological yearnings that could be fulfilled with good architectural design. Now, on a barren hillside overlooking the Grand Canyon of the Yellowstone, he had his opportunity.

The Canyon Hotel, with Reamer's additions, was so massive as to be unbelievable in its remote setting. Its cement foundations were said to measure a full mile. The wooded structure was 629 feet long and at one point 415 feet wide, five stories high and with a basement, with a total floor space of 171,151 square feet; it had 430 rooms and 1,205 windows. [49]

One observer called it "an oddly splendid structure." He said that "without yielding anything of its own well-contained individuality, its surrender to the vast nobility of the scene in which it is placed, is complete, natural, and captivating. . . . [It] is an architectural triumph of singular and striking symmetry with its natural environs." The foundations seemed to cling to the contour of the mountain slopes "in lines of uneven and yet beautiful accord which suggest that the architect esteemed obedience to and sympathy with the master landscape gardening of Nature herself." [50]

---

*Everyone who has been around Yellowstone Park has heard the story about Harry Child wanting Robert Reamer to design a hotel for the Upper Geyser Basin. He found Reamer in a San Francisco (or Los Angeles) hotel in advanced state of delirium tremens. He "dried him out" and put him on a train bound for Livingston, Montana. When Reamer arrived there he had sketched out the plans for Old Faithful Inn.

This is a canard, a grave injustice to one of the outstanding architects of the twentieth century. The story can be neither proved nor disproved, but the implication—that Old Faithful Inn was designed by a drunk—is an outrage. It took thousands of hours of Reamer's time at his cold sober best to design and supervise construction of Old Faithful Inn. If he had a drinking problem, what of it? He surmounted it sufficiently to have a long, distinguished architectural career.

In recreation areas such stories with a kernel of truth become tall-tale yarns when narrated by bellhops, park rangers, and, yes, even superintendents. Wide-eyed, questioning tourists expect to be entertained with amusing answers. After a few tellings even the kernel of truth is lost and only a humorous or shocking anecdote remains. So is it with Old Faithful Inn's architect's canard. Most of those telling the story never even heard of Robert Reamer!

As a writer of bunkhouse doggerel, Dan W. (alias "Red") Gibson wrote:

There is endless variation
There are walls that twist about
As though more or less in doubt
    As to destination
While the kitchen wing strikes out
Like a long tea-kettle snout!
There are hip-roofs, there are gables;
There are roofs as flat as tables;
Dormer windows by the score. . . .[51]

Entrance was through a regal porte-cochere from which guests set foot into a lobby and lounge of gigantic proportions. A graceful spiral staircase said to be copied from the one in the Paris Opera House led to the second floor. Reamer was quoted as saying that Americans did not want large apartments in their hotels as did Europeans, desiring instead "great lobbies where to see and be seen, to witness the joyful pageantry of the guests in promenade to study character and apparel, to gossip and to listen to the music seemed the sum and crown of the desires of the pleasure-loving guests. . . ."[52]

And so the lounge-lobby was the salient feature of the Canyon Hotel. It was 200 feet long and 100 feet wide, with a floor of polished oak and walls and ceiling of finely finished red birch. Save for alternating pillars that sustained the high roof, the walls were almost wholly of French plate glass. "It extends lengthwise from the south front of the hotel building," one admirer wrote, "and from its middle at either side, facing east and west, are two spacious, pillared porches, opening through wide doors and French windows onto the main level of the floor of the interior. The north end of the lounge contains the stage or platform for the orchestra, flanked by wide, grand staircases which lead back of the stage through a broad open space, into the spacious lobby of the hotel proper."[53]

In the park environs construction of the Canyon Hotel was a great event, the topic of conversation for years to come. Child wanted the facility ready for the 1911 season. To accomplish the building of so massive a structure at over 7,000 feet altitude in the midst of winter, forty miles from the railhead at Gardiner, the company hired fifty teamsters with 200 horses. They were supplied with low-pitched, cumbrous sled wagons pulled by six horses; each day the sleds carried a railroad freight car load to the building site. The carpenters at Canyon, more than a hundred of them, lived in bunkhouses in much the same way as lumberjacks, and they worked seven days a week. Reamer, often dressed in a woolen tweed suit, pants legs stuffed into high boots, got around on skis and, one suspects, was as constant and diligent in his supervision as he had been seven years before at Old Faithful Inn.[54]

The goal was met: by the beginning of the 1911 tourist season even the barren piles of earth had been smoothed, landscaped as planned, and sodded. Again, Mrs. Child chose the furnishings. Wherever possible a motif consisting of a pine tree branch was followed. It was apparent in the pillars, transoms, chairs, linens, and even in the fringes of the rugs throughout the hotel.[55] Dan Gibson, again, expressed himself in verse:

> Can you not in fancy see
> All the place agog, alive?—
> Coaches whirling up the drive
> And into the depot swinging,
> Dudes—and dudesses—a-bringing
> Can't you hear the laughter ringing
> Through the lambent evening air
> As they are dismounting there?[56]

For nearly fifty years (until 1960) Canyon Lodge basked in the dimming afterglow of the genteel tradition, while Old Faithful Inn continues to charm visitors to this day. But the horse-drawn coaches were replaced in a few years by motorbuses and Fords and Buicks and Dodges and Studebakers driven by middle-class Americans. These people possessed neither the financial means nor the inclination to stay at the great hotels. The golden age was not to last much longer.

Regardless of his favoritism to "the right people" and the cultured world of linen tablecloths, gleaming silver and flashing crystal, Harry Child was keenly aware of new sources of profit even if they were marketplace mundane. He was also aware of a new type of competition within the park: the permanent camps, best known of which was the Wylie Way. Others, such as Shaw and Powell, the R. C. Bryant Company, and the Old Faithful Camps, operated under yearly licenses. They flourished during the army period and were finally denied the right to operate, or were sold to others which retained the privilege, including Child, in the period 1916 to 1921.

Their development followed the normal progression from simple to complex. Many a rancher and a few businessmen, even a schoolteacher, earned additional income by guiding and supervising parties through the park. At first their operations were simple affairs—a wagon, tents, saddle and pack horses, leader-guide and a camp helper or two. Soon a few individuals were making a season-long business of this work, earning most of their annual income from it. They were soon building an inventory of equipment and supplies.

The Interior Department instructed the army to issue annual permits to these people; duplicates of forty or more permits per year can be found in the Yellowstone archives. These authorizations gave the guides a measure of legitimacy. They could advertise themselves as licensed escorts and, of course, it gave the army a measure of control. By natural selection, in due time three or four companies dominated the field. Without doubt the most important of them was the firm headed by William W. Wylie of Bozeman.

As early as 1880, or so he claimed, Wylie, a schoolteacher, was guiding tourists through Yellowstone. Year by year his business grew larger. At one time he and a man named Wilson teamed up and used for their business a "McMaster Camping Car." This was a horse-drawn wagon home similar to a gypsy's cart and an identifiable ancestor of the modern recreational vehicle. In 1897 Wylie was permitted to establish semipermanent camps—meaning they remained through a season—at strategic points around the reservation. Now his patrons could make the five- or six-day tour and still sup in dining rooms and sleep on beds, just as did the coach and hotel people. Eventually Wylie had "permanent camps" at Swan Lake Flats, Riverside, Upper Geyser Basin, Yellowstone Lake Outlet (Fishing Bridge), Grand Canyon, one near Sylvan Pass and one in the vicinity of Tower Falls. His facilities were available from the north, east, and west entrances. At first he was granted an annual contract but eventually obtained a ten-year franchise. Yet neither the army nor Interior liked the Wylie Camps (later known as the Wylie Permanent Camps) even though the facilities filled an obvious need for less expensive food and housing. Wylie was also very careful, initially at least, about absolute obedience to park rules and regulations. He knew he was disliked.[57]

In time the facilities of these permanent camps became loosely standardized. Their tent cottages had wooden floors and sides four to six feet high; from there on up the sides and roof were of canvas, often livened with red and white or blue and white stripes. A Wylie Camp had rows upon rows of these tent cottages served by strategically located dining halls, rest rooms and bathing facilities. The owner's emphasis on leisure and gaiety is somewhat demonstrated by street names at the Upper Geyser Basin Wylie facility: "Pleasant Way, Rough Way, No Way, Tough Way, Simple Way, Narrow Way, Wrong Way, Right Way, Forbidden Way"—or the names of the tent cottages assigned to the young women "heavers" (waitresses): "Do Drop In, Sneak In, Rough House Inn, Paradise Inn." A Wylie trip around the park in 1912 cost $35.00 compared with a minimum of $55.00 with the hotel company.[58]

The camps were, in fact, increasingly prosperous; they gained in popularity in spite of the army, Interior, the hotel and transportation company and the railroads. "If you are under fifty," wrote Charles Francis Adams, "and can get in front of a Wylie camp fire on a stump or fallen log, smoke and discuss things that count RIGHT THERE, get in on the Wylie cheers, Wylie songs, enjoy a Wylie laugh, or whirl in the open-air dance, possibly go rotten-logging—well, you will have to take your choice—just satisfy yourself."[59]

Truth was the Wylie Way, Shaw and Powell, and other camping companies catered to the American class whose affluence and mobility was rapidly rising. In the Wylie concept was a recognition of the nearly ceaseless movement, the abounding energy that characterize middle-class Americans. The permanent camp companies gave their guests an activity-filled, never-a-dull-moment regimen. Sitting by the hour on a veranda or in a luxurious lobby had little attraction for people who spent most of their lives working long hours fifty weeks a year.

Northern Pacific management was increasingly alarmed at their popularity. "It seems to me a word from you might be of some service with the Department as to curtailment of Wylie's privileges," wrote N.P. President Mellen to his vice-president, Lamont. "He will in a short time run the first class business away from the Park with the mobs he is taking in and the class of facilities people are putting up with. It exercises a deterring influence," he added, ". . . upon the class of business which ordinarily seeks the hotels. . . . I think he should be confined hereafter to such personally conducted parties as he may secure for his trip." President Mellen further predicted that if Interior gave Wylie a ten-year lease (which it did), it "would operate, in the end, to practically close the hotels in the Park." This was in 1899, many years prior to the coming of the automobile.[60]

The railroad and Child did more than just worry about Wylie and the other camping companies. They lowered the cost of their package tours in order to make them competitive. Moreover, the railroad's subsidiary, the Yellowstone Park Association, forbade nonaffiliated companies such as Wylie from soliciting patronage along the railroad, at its stations, or on hotel property.

Wylie complained, enlisting the aid of Shaw and Powell as interveners. Their lawyers suggested that this constituted unfair discrimination. In a decision dated June 23, 1905, the Interstate Commerce Commission agreed, finding the railroad and the park companies in violation of certain statutes relating to making traffic agreements.[61]

Wylie and his permanent camp allies continued catering to school teachers, ministers, and other genteel visitors of modest means. Harry Child growled and followed the aphorism, if you can't beat 'em, join 'em. He purchased stock in Wylie's company. By 1911 he owned 666 2/3 shares with an estimated value of $150,000.[62]

The period 1916–1920 in concessionaire history is confusing. At one stage Steve Mather rescinded Child's franchise. Child's son, Huntley, who had been running the concessions during his father's illness, had alienated Mather. Albright suggested that Child get out of his sick bed and see Mather, and, writes his grandson, Huntley Child, Jr., "after a few days Mather gave him back his concessions but with the stipulation that Huntley Child could not return to the park." The camp companies (Wylie Way, Shaw and Powell, and others) were consolidated into the Yellowstone Park Camps Company. It was run by Howard Hays, who had been an executive with both the Union Pacific and Chicago and Northwestern railroads, and had held high office during the World War in the Railroad Administration. Interior Secretary Franklin Lane praised Hays's "program of development of the camping system. . . . You entertain the same ideals," he added, "regarding the public use of the parks that guide our administration of the National Park Service. . . ." As of 1924, when Hays became ill and Harry Child stepped in, Child had an absolute monopoly on the hotel, transportation, and hotel facilities in Yellowstone Park.[63]

Again, it must be emphasized that Harry Child was heavily indebted to railroad creditors. An example of the complications of the financial arrangements may be surmised, if not known in detail, by a memorandum of October 20, 1928, from Park Service Director Arthur Demaray to an assistant secretary in which Demaray states that company mortgages of September 29, 1917, September 10, 1921, November 21, 1922, and May 1, 1925, have been paid in full and a new mortgage issued to the Yellowstone Park Hotel Company, the Yellowstone Park Transportation Company, and the Yellowstone Park Camps Company, by the Northwest Improvement Company (the N.P.'s subsidiary), the Union Pacific Railroad Company, the Chicago, Burlington, and Quincy Railroad, and the Chicago, Milwaukee, St. Paul and Pacific Railway, dated July 26, 1928. Thus the railroads involved in the Yellowstone business were acting in concert to subsidize by mortgage the concessions which Child was operating, apparently to their satisfaction.[64]

Still another concession became a part of the Child enterprises during the period 1910 to 1924. This was the Yellowstone Lake Boat Company, a minor star in the galaxy of concession enterprises that nevertheless promised small but steady profits. Its history involved probably the most difficult concessionaire who ever operated in Yellowstone Park, Eli C. Waters.

In the Yellowstone Archives there is a bulging dossier on him. Waters was selfmade as were so many men in those days. He had served in the Civil

War, at age fourteen; he was mustered out of service on July 26, 1865. Twenty-two years later he was in Montana, deeply involved in politics, had been a member of the territorial legislature, and in 1887 was departmental commander of the territorial G.A.R. He was, wrote Captain Boutelle, known as "one of the followers of Russell Harrison, son of the President, who went to Montana hoping to become a United States Senator when the territory was admitted to statehood. It was always understood that Waters was under presidential protection." [65]

Exactly when he became associated with the muddy mixture of park concessions and politics is not known. It may have been as early as 1883 with the Hatch-Hobart-Douglas crowd; he was certainly there by 1886. As early as 1889 a Park Association comptroller who was protesting his living quarters on the third floor of the Mammoth Hotel included manager E. C. Waters among his grievances. "The moral status of the upper stories is not of a very high order," he wrote. "The management, or rather mismanagement here is a disgrace to the Association. . . . What Mr. Waters's hold in the Association is I know not—and care less— . . . . the management has a very unsavory reputation and from what has come under my personal notice I think it is deserved."[66]

Eighteen years later, in a letter to Major Pitcher, Captain Boutelle also mentioned the man's depravity. "Aside from the [his] bad business practises," Boutelle recalled, "the man was morally rotten. It was a commmon practise for him to leave the Mammoth Hot Springs hotel at sundown, en route to one of the hotels, with some poor girl, employed for service, and spend most of the night on the road between the starting point and Norris."[67]

It is known that Waters had stock in Wakefield's transportation company and that he was known to all the concessionaires and Northern Pacific people. From the first he was not liked. During the 1892 Congressional hearings involving the transportation company, Waters tarnished his already unsavory reputation. Such was his political clout, however, that his archenemy Captain Boutelle was transferred out of the park while Waters enhanced his position as president of the Yellowstone Boat Company by obtaining a lease for additional land along the lake shore.[68]

From Yellowstone's creation as a park, people had inquired about a boating concession on the lake; the number of queries on the subject is remarkable. The possibility of a lucrative run between Thumb and Lake Hotel, and rowboat rentals, seemed to insure good profits. Yet until about 1890 only one concession had been granted, to Major Brisbin of Fort Ellis, and he dispensed with it almost immediately.

Charles Gibson of the Park Association finally possessed the means and inclination to bring this concession into being. He purchased a steam launch that had been operating on Lake Minnetonka, in eastern Minnesota, had it dismantled and transported to Gardiner by rail, and by wagon to the lake. Presumably it was operational by the 1890 season.[69]

Arrangements for its management were tenuous and, from the point of view of Gibson's Park Association, unwise, although the association's lease granted it the right to run a boat on the lake. "It belongs to another concern but it is governed and is to be run under the Association, the same as the stages of the transportation company," Gibson explained to Captain Boutelle, who had requested clarification of the matter. "The entire arrangement was discussed and agreed to by the Secretary of the Interior, Mr. Waters and myself last winter, and was satisfactory to the Department, and I hope it will be with you." Waters did not own the boat or the boat company at this time, but clearly he was running the operation under Park Association auspices.[70]

Whatever the arrangement had been for the 1890 season, on October 11, 1890, Secretary Noble informed the superintendent that he had "this day entered into a preliminary contract with the Yellowstone Lake Boat Company, whereby E. C. Waters is President," and that certain parcels of land were to be leased to him, as well as his having the right to run the steamboat on the lake.[71]

By 1897 Waters was owner of the boat company, having somehow raised sufficient funds to purchase it from the Gibson interests. In that year he obtained a ten-year lease. In the following decade ending in 1907, Harry Child's hotel and transportation business flourished and F. Jay Haynes operated lucrative picture shops and ran the Yellowstone and Monida coaches. Money was being made in the park. At or near the end of the list of profitable enterprises was the Yellowstone Lake Boat Company. Under Eli Waters's management, it gave evidence of sinking. Always an obnoxious character, Waters became impossible to deal with as his business declined.

In desperation he resorted to additional measures to enhance his profits. He maintained a small menagerie consisting of some buffalo and elk on Dot Island in Yellowstone Lake, using these poor creatures as incentives for his boat ride. T. S. Palmer, a vacationing Department of Agriculture employee, protested the filthy conditions he witnessed on the island: "Soon after the passengers landed, several large tubs of garbage were brought ashore and dumped in troughs in the elk enclosure. The hungry animals eagerly picked out potato peelings, pieces of vegetables, and even bits of meat. . . . The sight of elk fed like hogs on stale garbage disgusted several of the passengers and caused considerable unfavorable comment." Another writer added that "the buffalo confined there are in almost as bad shape [as the elk]." Early in the fall of 1907 the department ordered the animals released, and Waters adhered to the mandate.[7]

Waters thought he saw a sinister plan in Captain Chittenden's construction of a section of road from Thumb to Lake. The boat company president wrote at length to Senator Allison of Iowa suggesting that the new road would ruin his business, that the Northern Pacific, Child, and Chittenden were building the road at public expense with funds allocated for repairs, all for the one purpose of forcing him (Waters) out of business. This letter made the rounds from Allison to Interior to the army. Major Pitcher's endorsement stated that the transportation company coaches would continue to stop at the Thumb lunch station where Waters picked up his passengers (Waters had stated that the coaches would not stop there), and Pitcher added that Waters's charges against Chittenden were "absolutely false and that Mr. Waters knew they were false when he made them." In a fourth endorsement, dated October 5, 1904, Pitcher added about Waters, "his rambling communications referring to many subjects, are a nuisance to everyone, and confirm the suggestion made some time since that he is mentally disordered."[73]

Indeed, this minor concessionaire became so desperate for business that visitors protested his sales tactics. In 1902 one angry tourist wrote that "the man in custody of this boat, and I presume the owner . . . is perhaps the most unmitigated nuisance that I ever encountered and inflicts himself on all travelers in an odious and unpleasant fashion in obtaining customers for his boat. . . . If this man Waters if not a rogue and a fraud, then the Lord does not write a legible hand, because he has a most detestable, dishonest face." Another prospective passenger was appalled when he saw Waters's boat, the "Zillah," moored at the wharf. "It was such an old rattletrap that I would not risk passage on it," he wrote.[74]

On January 6, 1905, at the family home in Fond du Lac, Wisconsin, Waters's attractive eighteen-year-old daughter Anna committed suicide with chloroform followed by a dose of carbolic acid; Waters at the time was in Red Lodge, Montana. "To those of our friends who have expressed a wish to know what prompted this desperate action on the part of our beloved daughter, I wish to say:" began a form letter Waters sent to sympathizers, "that we believe it was fear of financial ruin, despondency and humiliation over our business troubles, caused by the indignities, falsehoods and vituperation heaped upon our business in the Yellowstone National Park by one H. W. Child, . . . F. Jay Haynes, . . . Major John Pitcher, . . . the Northern Pacific Railway, and others."[75]

Waters continued in business for another two years. Then he in some way alienated Representative W. Bourke Cockran of New York who was so incensed that he protested to President Roosevelt. On June 6, 1907, Roosevelt replied. "I know but little of Waters and I am sorry to say that little is to his discredit, . . . I have . . . sent your letter and papers to General Sam Young, now Superintendent of the Park. You know the General, don't you? He is a man of rugged independence and he can be depended upon to do absolutely what he thinks is right without regard to any other consideration."[76]

The result of Roosevelt's interest was apparent success in ridding the park of E. C. Waters, for a park bulletin dated October 16, 1907, read as follows:

NOTICE!

E. C. Waters, President of the Yellowstone Lake Boat Company, having rendered himself obnoxious during the season of 1907, is, under the provisions of paragraph 11, Rules and Regulations of the Yellowstone National Park, debarred from the Park and will not be allowed to return without permission in writing from the Secretary of the Interior or the Superintendent of the Park.

YOUNG

However, a handwritten notation at the bottom of the notice raises some doubts as to the permanence of the banishment: "Removed June 21, 1909, by Secretary of the Interior."[77]

For Eli C. Waters had obtained legal aid and headed for Washington, D.C., where he proceeded to stir up trouble for the Northern Pacific. He might well have been back in business had not a respected scout and animal hunter for the Smithsonian, T. E. Hofer, started the T. E. Hofer Boat Company with the backing of eastern sportsmen. On July 1, 1910, Waters sold out to Hofer, and by October of that year the difficult Mr. Waters had removed from the park everything that belonged to him that had not been sold to Hofer save two, old, domestic sheep that had become rather wild. After nearly a quarter century in the park, Eli C. Waters had finally departed.[78]

Hofer was an excellent scout and hunter but a poor businessman. In a complicated series of financial deals involving Hofer, his creditors, Waters, Child, and the Northwest Improvement Company, Harry Child emerged as the man in charge. As of May 27, 1911, the Yellowstone Park Boat Company was incorporated at Helena, Montana. Total capitalization was fixed at $200,000. Both the T. E. Hofer Boat Company and the Yellowstone Lake Boat Company (Waters's old company) were merged to form it. As of 1917 Harry Child was in debt for most of the boat company purchase, but "Harry Hard Up" had a monopoly on the lake, which after all, was what he wanted.[79]

It soon became clear that boat company profits lay in boat rentals and fishing tackle. By 1930 the company's investment was estimated at only $28,617 and its return for that year—which was a good year, the Great Depression just getting under way—was $2,022 or 7.06 percent.

Places selling groceries, sundries, camping supplies, satin pillows picturing Old Faithful, and Hong Kong—made back scratchers imprinted with "Souvenir of Yellowstone Park" have a fairly simple history. When Henry Klamer died in 1912, George Ashworth Hamilton, who was Harry Child's secretary, with Child's help bought the store at Old Faithful; in 1953 he acquired stores at Canyon and Mammoth that had been run, first by George Whittaker and then by Mrs. Anna K. Prior and her maiden sister, Elizabeth Trischman.

Hamilton's daughter Eleanor had married Trevor Povah, who gradually took over management of operations. When Hamilton in 1948 expressed the desire to assign his contract with the Park Service to Mr. and Mrs. Povah, C. Girard Davidson, the assistant secretary assigned to Park Service matters, shot a memo of protest to Director Newton B. Drury. "I cannot agree that we would further an anti-monopoly policy, either in fact or from a public relations point of view," he wrote, "by permitting Mr. Hamilton to divest himself of part of his operations in favor of his children. In fact, the only practical effect of the assignment would be to confer on Mr. and Mrs. Povah whatever preference accrues to present concessioners in the consideration of new contract proposals."[80]

But C. Girard Davidson was, after all, just an assistant secretary. The Povah's were allowed to assume management (Hamilton had incorporated in 1930). It was an increasingly lucrative concession, expanding from the single Upper Geyser Basin (Old Faithful) store to several units, operation and profits of the automobile service stations split on a fifty-fifty basis with Child, and, after 1930, management of curio shops and fountain services at the lodges (not at the hotels). Povah assumed the Henry Brothers' plunge and bathhouse franchise. In 1968 the Hamilton Stores purchased the Haynes Photo Shops. The firm, with daughter and son-in-law Povah as inheritors, was, therefore, a prominent member of the Yellowstone peerage. The links among these concessionaires were many. Hugh Galusha, Child's chief auditor, was also Hamilton's. Of the Child-Nichols, Haynes and Hamilton concessions, only Hamilton's remains today.[81]

We may assume that profits of these retail concessions were good in the 1920s, ranging from 8 to 20 percent with the estimate being, if anything, short on the plus side. Pryor and Trischman's profits for the depression decade are available. For the eleven years 1930 to 1940 their average rate of return was 11.51 percent. In 1931 and 1932 they operated in the red (minus 1.94 percent and minus 16.13 percent) but in 1933 they turned a profit of 0.88 percent. Then things improved rapidly: in 1934 they earned 15.05

percent, the next year, 19.84 percent, and in 1936 realized a profit of 32.63 percent on capital and surplus (net worth) of $79,715. Income in that year was $176,859, expenses $150,844, and the profit came to $26,015. This was their best of eleven years but their rate of return continued in double digits save for 1939 when, on a net worth of $120,840, they realized an 8.27 percent rate of return. (In terms of 1984 dollars, multiply these figures by five to ten times. Compare Pryor and Trischman's 1941 coffee shop prices with today's: ice cream soda, fifteen cents, sundae with ground nuts, twenty-five cents, chocolate malted milk, twenty cents, and twenty cents for a bottle of "eastern" beer such as Budweiser or Pabst Blue Ribbon. Their best dinner was a large, thick T-bone steak with salad, vegetable, potatoes, rolls, butter; pie, ice cream, or cake; and tea, coffee, milk or iced tea—$1.00.)[82]

Hamilton's profit and loss history is available for the nine years 1931 through 1939. The firm's average capital and surplus of $218,107 was much larger than Pryor and Trischman's; Hamilton's was a much larger operation. He conducted it at a loss only in 1932 and 1933 (0.005 percent and 0.96 percent) and barely broke even in 1931 (.56 percent) and 1934 (1.32 percent). But in 1935 the rate of return was 12.53 percent, and in 1937 profits were the highest for the nine-year period at 25.32 percent or $62,852 on a net worth for the year of $248,259; in 1937 profits were 20.78 percent and in 1939 a comfortable 19.69 percent.[83]

F. Jay Haynes and his son Jack Ellis, who succeeded his father in the business, were satisfied in running photo shops save for the early years of the century when they were involved in operations of the Yellowstone and Monida and Yellowstone and Western stages. Surprisingly, the files do not contain annual fiscal statements of their photo business (although they undoubtedly exist somewhere among the massive Park Service archives), but enough materials exist to draw some conclusions. The Haynes were good business people. Except for the depression years, they made steady, modest profits in some contrast with the occasionally glamorous earnings of their fellow concessionaires. In 1920 Haynes grossed $70,000, netted a 6 percent profit and invested $10,000 into his business. In applying for a new contract he noticed that the Park Service had fixed the top percentage of gross receipts due the government from the other concessionaires at 4 percent. Haynes's percentage had been fixed at 5 percent of net profit. He asked that it be reduced to 4 percent and it was.[84]

In cheerfully complying with his request Mather also gave Haynes permission to establish a shop at Tower Falls on the grounds that his stores had to compete with competitor's units at Mammoth, Upper Geyser Basin, Yellowstone Lake, and Grand Canyon. "Mr. Haynes," Mather wrote, "is very progressive and is constantly enlarging and improving his shops along lines approved by the Government. . . . [He] is one of the best operators that we have in the national park system today in that he is always ready and willing to cooperate in any project that will benefit Yellowstone Park or the national park system as a whole. . . . [The Haynes's] interests have not been wholly financial nor have they subordinated the larger question of public service to the commerical features of their operations."[85]

That the family loved Yellowstone and gave pictures free for promotional uses to the government and the railroads was well known. (In the 1921 contract one item stipulated that Haynes should furnish the government with pictures valued at up to $200 a year, gratis.) That the family was not getting rich was also clear: the average capital and surplus of their facilities, 1926–1935, was fixed at $99,713.78, and the average rate of return was a mere 2.62 percent or $2,617.26. Haynes appears to have lost money from 1932 through 1934.[86]

Perhaps this explains an agreement reached by the Yellowstone operators in 1930 "for the purpose," as Albright described it, "of adjusting the store and photographic activities in the park." Hamilton's new contract reflected the agreement, excepting Hamilton from the sale of photographs, photographic equipment and supplies. This clause insured Haynes a park monopoly in the all-important photography business and certainly helped him earn a larger profit. Whatever the conditions under which he carried on his business, over the years the Haynes family clearly made money.[87]

Among Park Service old-timers "Old Faithful Bathhouse" is surely a phrase not to be used in polite company. This may seem strange, for the idea of bathhouses where invalids could take the therapeutic waters (as they were believed to be) and even swim, were from earliest times considered a logical business for Yellowstone. Even today many a vacationing pater familias and his tired wife, tempers frazzled after a long day's drive with scrapping siblings in the back seat, have yearned for lodging with a swimming pool in which their children's exuberance could be exhausted. Alas! Such a facility no longer exists in Yellowstone.

It was not always so. Primitive tent bathhouses were enticing health seekers at Mammoth Hot Springs prior to the park's creation. It would be impossible to trace with accuracy the come-and-go installations of this kind that may have existed in the 1880s and 1890s. As government increased its authority, however, the squatting businessmen folded their tents and left. Interior finally granted a franchise for a bathhouse to Henry P. Brothers of Salt Lake City, who by July 1, 1914, had a facility functioning near Old

Faithful in the Upper Geyser Basin. In 1924 his contract was renewed for ten years; it granted him additional land for improvements subject to the super-intendent's approval and "upon the recommendation of the Landscape Engineer of the National Park Service."[88]

By 1928 Brothers's improvements included a swimming pool although his rates listed only "Bath in Large Pool including Bathing Suits: fifty cents." He also offered "Bath in Private Pool: $1.00" and tub baths for fifty cents; children were charged twenty-five cents. In time Brothers had baths with laundry and ironing facilities (but not swimming pools) at some of the auto-mobile campgrounds. In 1930 he was granted a twenty-year contract along with permission to establish a bathhouse with tubs, showers, laundry and irons at Fishing Bridge.[89]

From 1930 through 1933 Brothers's capital and surplus (net worth) aver-aged only $34,167, and his average profit per year was a mere $554, a rate of return of just 1.22 percent. In 1930 he went in the red $127.29. Perhaps this explains his desire to sell. In June 1933, Director Albright telegraphed Hamilton with permission to purchase Brothers's Yellowstone facilities "*sub-ject to removal of the Old Faithful Bathhouse within a year to another location.*" (Italics mine)[90]

The service had good reason to require removal. Although policy evolves slowly in a bureaucracy, by 1933 N.P.S. had a well-planned program de-signed to remove "artificial intrusions" that impaired the attractiveness of natural features. Previous lack of planning had resulted in a particularly bad situation at Old Faithful. The bathhouse and swimming pool, a Haynes photo shop, a Hamilton store and service station, the government's sewage disposal plant, and even the highway were too close to the geysers; plans were made for their removal. As Assistant Interior Secretary Abe Fortas ex-plained in 1945, "visitors to Yellowstone National Park approaching Old Faithful from the north frequently get their first view of the eruption of Old Faithful over the roof of Mr. Hamilton's bathhouse and swimming pool."[91]

Within two or three years Haynes had complied with the removal order and Hamilton had moved his store and service station, while the govern-ment, at considerable expense, had removed its sewage disposal plant and routed the road back from the geyser formations. The view had been greatly improved. Only one artificial impediment remained: the bathhouse/swim-ming pool.[92]

Even a Philadelphia lawyer would find it difficult to ferret out ambiguity in Albright's telegram of June 1933: "subject to removal of the Old Faithful Bathhouse within a year to a new location." Yet for reasons obscure and now impossible to explain, the bathhouse/swimming pool purchased by Hamil-ton was neither destroyed nor removed. In spite of Albright's telegram, Hamilton obtained permission to cut some two hundred trees. These, as an assistant secretary explained to a senator, were "to be used in repair work and in improving the appearance of the bathhouse until such time as it was moved. Mr. Hamilton was also given permission to cover the pool with glass. . . . He stated that . . . the glass could be removed when the building was constructed elsewhere . . . . and when the superintendent returned to the park it was a fait accompli."[93]

This was in 1934 or 1935. The superintendent was Roger W. Toll and indeed he could have been absent from the park at the time; even so, the excuse was flimsy. Whatever the facts (for both Park Service Director Cammerer and Toll died in the mid-1930s), the de facto remodeling became a prime argument for retaining the bathhouse/pool at its original location.[94]

And so the bathhouse/swimming pool remained. In its remodeled appearance, at least in the mind of one United States senator, it was "a beautiful building and not an eyesore. . . . In my opinion as a layman," he continued, "it adds to rather than detracts from the beauty of the Upper Geyser Basin."[95]

In June 1944, Director Newton Drury reminded Hamilton that the contract for the bathhouse/swimming pool had expired, that it had required that the facility was to be removed and Hamilton had not carried out this provision. "After further careful consideration," Drury wrote, "it has been decided there shall be no further extension of the concession privilege, that the swimming pool is not to be operated again, and that it must be removed." Because there was a war on and labor was scarce, the mandate did not have to be carried out until up to six months after the end of the war.[96]

But Mr. Hamilton did not want to abide by the removal clause in the contract. Through politics he obtained delays: Congressman Homer D. Angell of Oregon, Senators John Chandler Gurney of South Dakota and Burton K. Wheeler of Montana; and Treasury Secretary Fred Vinson through his secretary, Mr. Ferrell, all sent strong letters protesting the order to the assistant secretary in charge of Park Service matters. Assistant Secretary Abe Fortas, in replying to one of them, insisted that "the decision to clear the downstream approach to the Old Faithful area was made after many years of study and planning and not, as you [Mr. Ferrell] suggest, as the result of 'the destructive program by some local park commissioner, who dislikes it because it was not authorized by him personally or some other wild-eyed thought." Fortas further pointed out that "the Department did not serve notice for its [the swimming pool's] removal on Mr. Hamilton until the seventh year of his contract and then he was given until the expiration of his contract—a period of nearly three years—in which to remove it."[97]

The Park Service had indeed tilted in favor of Mr. Hamilton. It allowed him to amortize his investment, from 1933 through 1943, at $54,874, not at the 3.2 percent depreciation he had begun with but, after 1938, at 10 percent; it was pointed out that he had withdrawn $40,688, leaving a value of $15,281 of net fixed assets; his profits during the ten-year period had been $16,390.[98]

The season of 1946 approached—thirteen years since Albright's telegram. Director Drury sent a memo to the interior secretary stating that he had received numerous letters protesting the order to remove the pool. The hard-pressed director, facing still another difficult season in the immediate postwar years, recommended that Hamilton be allowed to operate his pool through the 1949 season providing he would promise removal and restoration at another site after season's end. These terms were embodied in the new three-year contract.[99]

Missing from the files is a communication from Interior Secretary Julius A. Krug to Director Drury, whose reply indicates that Krug had been informed of the pending destruction of Hamilton's pool. "We have tolerated this unauthorized building for fourteen years . . . merely to give the concessioner an opportunity to remove it without hardship," Drury replied. "The removal of structures from the geyser area is desired in order to clear the down-valley view. . . . I hope that you approve the principle that we should not permanently sanction a structure of this type in the foreground of Old Faithful, one of the wonders of the world." To which Krug scribbled on Drury's memo, "I would not like to see the pool demolished until you can provide another in the same general area."[100]

In September 1949, the Park Service, in accord with Secretary Krug's request, chose an alternate pool site and Hamilton was amenable to the move. At this point the situation became a bureaucratic fiasco. Hamilton wrote Drury in June 1950 explaining that on June 23, 1949, he had brought in contractors to give estimates on dismantling the pool; that then Park Service Acting Regional Director Howard W. Baker wired him stating that the pool was to remain, and then he was informed on April 21, 1950, that he was to have it demolished. How, he asked, does one act in good faith under such circumstances? Finally the U.S. Public Health Service closed the pool for the 1950 season because the water in it was not completely changed twice every twenty-four hours.[101]

Meanwhile the Park Service had offered Hamilton a five-year contract for a pool if he would spend $30,000 to $35,000 to bring it up to Public Health Service standards (but it is not clear whether this entailed a new location or reconstruction at the old one). All the while Hamilton was using political friends to help him retain his franchise. Defending Park Service policy, Acting Secretary Dale Doty wrote explanatory letters to Senators Taft of Ohio, Dworshak of Idaho, and Mansfield of Montana.[102]

The pool was dismantled in 1957, twenty-four years after Albright's telegram calling for "removal of the Old Faithful Bathhouse within a year to another location." Some way other than frolicking in a swimming pool must be found to tire out the children.

The golden age of park concessions ended like a western sunset—gradually. They flourished from about 1900 until 1929 and then slowly declined. Some lost money during two or three of the worst depression years, but all subsequently experienced a steady improvement in earnings down to the outbreak of the Second World War. They were difficult businesses demanding full attention by the operators for many weeks prior to the opening of the short season. Estimates had to be made on merchandise needs, orders filed and goods delivered on time. Personnel had to be recruited—neither too few nor too many—and trained. The physical plant had to be made ready. Start-up funds had to be available. Even in a good year a concessionaire might not show a cent of profit until the second or third week of August. Always there was the stressful realization that a depression, a railroad strike, an earthquake, or a war could ruin a season. And above all there was the unpredictable government. Was the Park Service going to force a change of location or a new facility that could deprive an operator of profits, on paper at least, for several years? Could the contract be renegotiated? What was the new superintendent like? Troubles and more troubles: from the concessionaires' view, profits were hard earned.

The operators, being human, wanted sympathy, but in the category of government interference, at least, their problems during the golden age were not severe. Indeed, Interior regulations enforced first by the army and then by the Park Service were lax. Child, Haynes, and Hamilton were old hands at the Yellowstone business, knowing service personnel on a first-name basis. Most of the time the concessionaires knew what they could and could not do without incurring official disapproval. Government officials possessed only a superficial knowledge of the investments, expenditures, and profit and loss of the park businesses. If these public utilities (as the Park Service likes to designate them) did not harm the natural scene, and providing there were few complaints from the public, the concessionaires were nearly as free to operate their businesses as were their counterparts outside the reservation. When they were forced to adhere to costly regulations or abide by government decisions, the trade-off in being a government-protected monopoly compensated quite well.

In December 1937, an Interior Department special agent was sent to Helena, Montana, to audit the books of the Yellowstone Park Hotel Company. When he arrived, the company auditor, Hugh Galusha, informed him that the books were located at various points in the park, and, it being winter, they were inaccessible. Interior's frustrated acting director of investigations suggested that "the concessioners should be required to remove their books and records from the park at the close of each season to some point where they will be available during the winter." Only gradually, it seems clear, was the service tightening its controls over the operators. Hamilton was not ordered to install a cost accounting system showing correctly revenue, expense, and net profit for his various enterprises until 1939.[103]

Only rarely did someone in high office question concessionaire profits. Memos exchanged between directors and assistant secretaries in 1939 indicate some concern with Hamilton's earnings which were 15.96 percent of invested capital in 1936, jumped to 25.32 percent in 1937, and fell slightly to 20.78 percent in 1938. His average profit on net worth from 1931 through 1938 was 10.21 percent, unexceptionally good for the depression decade. "The Service has noted with growing concern the increase of the rate of return of this park operator," one memo reads, "and we feel that his profits should be reflected in lower prices to the public." Nothing came of this concern, however, prior to the post–World War II period.[104]

In 1930 the service tried to deal firmly with Child, urging him to charge just 15.5 cents per mile for local transportation rather than the 18.5 cents he was asking. Since the per mile cost of the Loop trip was just 11.58 cents, and since Child's company paid out in dividends $666,195 early in 1929 followed with another $450,000 at season's end, Park Service auditor W. A. Blossom considered all of Child's arguments against the reduction absurd. Child's loss in revenue would have been infinitesimal—$2,000 to $3,000 a year—but remember that "Harry Hard Up" hated to lose a cent! He countered that if he was allowed to retain the 18.5 cents charge he would launch a five-year plan calling for the expenditure of $1,568,250. He would purchase 225 new buses and make other improvements. Albright implied that the proposition should be accepted. The depression intervened, however, and apparently Child retained the 18.5-cents charge; if he did not, it was the economic situation and not the Park Service that led him to make a reduction.[105]

One interesting aspect of Interior Department concessionaire relations in the first forty years of this century was the continual request by concessionaires for early contract renewals. Usually these legal agreements were for twenty years but it was not unusual for a concessionaire to request a renewal before even five years of a current one had elapsed. Sometimes the request was honored, sometimes not. Child's twenty-year franchise signed in 1917 was canceled six years later, in 1923, and a new one granted, "in order," Albright explained, "that a little more protection, by virtue of the extension of the term of the franchise, might be given." Again in 1927 Child requested renewal, although the present contract had another fifteen years of validity. This time his request was peremptorily rejected by Interior Secretary Hubert Work. [106]

In 1921 Haynes's 1917 contract was canceled and a fifteen-year one issued in its place. This was canceled in just five years; in 1926 Haynes received a new twenty-year contract. In 1930 Hamilton, whose contract had two years to run, requested renewal; given it, he then floated a $100,000 bond issue to raise funds to improve his facilities. [107]

The reasons for these requests are apparent to any business-oriented person. It was easier to obtain loans, and when obtained, at lower interest, the longer the contract had to run. Moreover, both the Park Service and concessionaires became dissatisfied with contract provisions as times changed. Haynes felt he had a right to earn more money, while the service on occasion wanted to charge a greater percentage of gross revenues from certain concessionaires. Even so, the litany of continual cancellation and renegotiation implies a lack of research and planning by both sides prior to the signing of contracts and too little respect by both parties for the sanctity of the contractual term.

Again and again incidents appear indicating Park Service cooperation with the concessionaires that seems to place consideration for these businesses above the public welfare. Admittedly some of it was simply mild regulations, laxly enforced. For example, not until 1928 did the Interior Department solicitor emphatically rule that local beef being brought into the park for public consumption must be inspected, even though such a regulation would add ten cents a pound to the 35,000 pounds being imported each year. [108]

In 1933 concessionaires were exempted from compliance with codes of the National Industrial Recovery Administration, granted with the understanding that the operators would be "completely regulated in all matters by [the Interior] Department under the contracts they hold." [109]

Such was the relationship of concessionaires with the Interior Department and its agents. Excluding until a later chapter the question, "Was the public well served," it must be concluded that it was a workable relationship that functioned quite smoothly. It was highly profitable for the operators. It did not cause the Interior Department much trouble. And it was at least sufficiently within reason of costs and services in the America of 1900 to 1940 to cause little complaint from the visiting public.

The real difficulties came in the post–World War II period. That is the subject of a later chapter.

NOTES TO CHAPTER SIX

1. These paragraphs are smiliar to the first three in Bartlett, "The Concessionaires of Yellowstone National Park," 2–10.

2. Y.A., File No. 5, G. L. Henderson to Captain Moses Harris, February 27, 1888. Note, however, that Henderson testified in favor of Gibson at the Congressional hearing in 1892, and later lobbied for the Northern Pacific.

3. Northern Pacific Papers, President's File, Box No. 79, November 29, 1897. Hereafter cited as N.P. Papers.

4. N.P. Papers, Box No. 80, File 210-A, Part 2.

5. I have in my custody "copies of copies" of documents culled from the N.P. Papers by Professor Robert Lewis Peterson of the University of Montana, Missoula. Citations to Professor Peterson's collection are cited as Peterson Collection. The document herein cited bears the title, "Report on Yellowstone Park Association and Yellowstone Park Transportation Company and Their Successors Yellowstone Park Hotel Company and Yellowstone Park Transportation Company." It consists of seven typewritten pages.

6. Peterson Collection, "Minority Report," of Park Association Stockholders, St. Louis, December 17, 1896; printed letter to minority stockholders, January 2, 1897.

7. Ibid.

8. N.P. Papers, President's File, Report of E. Askevold, Auditor; Peterson Collection, Statement of Board of Directors of the Yellowstone Park Association, December 6, 1897; Interior Department letter to Yellowstone Park Association, March 25, 1898.

9. N.P. Papers, Box No. 80, File 210-I; Ibid., Box No. 27, Dean to Pearce, May 12, 1892. Harry Child first appears in Y.A. (File No. 4) in a letter of June 6, 1893, from the Norris Geyser Basin. He is protesting to Captain Anderson the deplorable lack of rest room facilities. "There are twenty ladies here hunting the woods," he wrote. "Can you get a club and swing it a few times?"

10. N.P. Papers, Box No. 27, May 12, 1892; Ibid., Box No. 80, File 210-A, Part 2, Notification of March 1 and July 11, 1898; Ibid., Box No. 81, J. H. Dean to N. P. President Mellen, July 25, 1900.

11. Yellowstone material in custody of Montana State University Library, Bozeman. Yellowstone Park Association to Acting Interior Secretary Thomas Ryan, February 15, 1898; Ibid., Association attorneys to Secretary Ethan Allen Hitchcock, March 1, 1899.

12. Ibid., Carter to N.P. Vice-President Lamont, December 31, 1897, in which Carter states that he has approved Huntley.

13. N.P. Papers, Box No. 79, President Mellen to Lamont, July 15, 1899; Lamont to Mellen, December 31, 1900.

14. Peterson Collection, N.P. Papers, Box No. 79, R. W. Reef, Assistant Secretary of the Northern Pacific to President Mellen, April 4, 1901; interview of author with Mrs. Bessie Haynes Arnold, October 4, 1970. That Huntley had finished off a meal with a dish of fresh pineapple in cream was considered a contributing factor in his demise.

15. "Montana News Association Inserts," May 3, 1920.

16. Ibid.; see also C. L. Anceney in Who's Who in America, 1928 edition, 169. I have also used Professor K. Ross Toole's microfilmed "Harry W. Child's Miscellaneous Files."

17. N.P. Papers, Box No. 79, Howard Elliott to James N. Hill, Vice-President of the N.P., January 16, 1907; Ibid., Stock Ownership File, Part 3, Child to George H. Lamar (not otherwise identified), December 23, 1911; Ibid., Child to Charles Donnelly, President of the N.P., June 11, 1926; see also letters on the Hertz question in Box No. 81, File 210-J.

18. N.P. Papers, Box No. 80, Child to J. M. Hannaford of the N.P., September 10, 1915.

19. Author's interview with former Superintendent Edmund G. Rogers, October, 1967.

20. Author's interview with Horace Albright, April, 1970.

21. Author's interview with Bessie Haynes Arnold, October, 1970.

22. "Montana News Association Inserts"; K. Ross Toole's Child collection, and interviews with Mr. Rogers and Mrs. Arnold.

23. N.P. Papers, Box No. 79, Stockholders' Meeting of September 5, 1903; Peterson Collection, "Report of E. Askevold, Auditor."

24. Ibid., John Carroll to President Elliott, January 26, 1907; Elliott to Vice-President Hill, February 1, 1907.

25. Peterson Collection, "Report of E. Askevold, Auditor"; N.P. Files, Box No. 79, Elliott to Hill, February 1, 1907.

26. Ibid., Elliott to Child, March 8, 1907; Ibid., Elliott to J. H. Carroll, February 26, 1907.

27. Peterson Collection, "Report of E. Askevold, Auditor"; N.P. Papers, Box No. 79, A. H. Foss to President, December 7, 1912.

28. N.P. Papers, W. P. Clough to Elliott, November 2, 1912; Ibid., Elliott to Child, January 12, 1905; Ibid., Clough to Elliott, November 2, 1912.

29. Ibid., Box No. 81, Burlington Vice-President to Harry Child, September 16, 1916; K. Ross Toole's Child Collection, Reel No. 15, "Yellowstone Park Transportation Company Journal, May, 1910-June, 1923," p. 169.

30. "Report of Duff, Anderson, and Clark, Industrial Investment and Financial Analysts," (1956), 4. This document is in custody of the Western Heritage Center, University of Wyoming, Laramie.

31. Peterson Collection, Report of J. H. Dean, President, Yellowstone Park Association, to the Directors, December 6, 1897, 2; N.P. Papers, Box No. 27, E. D. Buchanan, Comptroller, to W. Y. Pearce of the Yellowstone Park Company, November 12, 1889; Ibid., Telegram, Oakes to Pearce, August 13, 1890; Ibid., Pearce to Western Electric Company, August 18, 1892.

32. 28 U. S. Statutes at Large, 222–23; 34 U. S. Statutes at Large 208; 1219.

33. "Land of the Geysers," an N.P. promotional booklet in custody of the Denver Public Library Western History Room. The pamphlet is undated but since it describes the Fountain Hotel, closed in 1917, and the stagecoaches, it was issued prior to that date. The Lake Hotel is said to resemble a resort structure in Maine.

Appearing too late for inclusion of their information in my text is Barbara H. Ditti and Joanne Mallman, "Plain and Fancy: The Lake Hotel, 1889–1929," *Montana: The Magazine of Western History,* Vol. 34, No. 2 (Spring, 1984), pp. 32–45. They stress Robert Reamer's role in remodeling the structure.

34. Most of my information on Robert Reamer is based upon correspondence with his daughter, Mrs. Jane Reamer White, of Tryon, North Carolina, during the summer and fall of 1970, and an interview with her at Tryon in the summer of 1971. Her letter dated August 31, 1970, is particularly informational.
In 1897 Reamer was listed in the San Diego Directory with the architectural firm of "Zimmer and Reamer" and in 1899 and 1901 by his name only. "It appears he was here only a short while, and apparently did not leave his mark architecturally," writes Sylvia Arden, Head Librarian, San Diego Historical Society. Letter to author dated August 8, 1978.

35. Correspondence with Mrs. Jane Reamer White.

36. Reamer appeared in the Cleveland Directory in 1915 and 1916. Correspondence with James B. Casey, Head Librarian, Western Reserve Historical Society, August 9, 1978.

37. Enclosure with Mrs. White's correspondence. Mrs. White adds, concerning her father's reticence, that "this was not the case except, perhaps, during his younger years."

38. Ibid.

39. Ibid.

40. Charles Francis Adams, *What Jim Bridger and I Saw in Yellowstone Park* (no place, no date, but clearly 1912–1914), 12–18. This pamphlet, which was probably

Adams's "Christmas card," is in custody of the Ayer Collection, Newberry Library, Chicago. Interview with Mr. Ragsdale, rancher and long-time resident of Emigrant, Montana, October 15, 1970; Northern Pacific Railroad Company, "Land of the Geysers" (no place, no date), custody of Denver Public Library Western History Room.

41. K. Ross Toole Collection, Microfilm Roll No. 11, "Appraisal Inventory of Yellowstone Park Hotel Company, September 30, 1929: Old Faithful Group."

42. Ibid.: Adams, *Jim Bridger and I.*

43. Ibid.

44. Ibid.

45. Author's interview with Bessie Haynes Arnold and correspondence with Mrs. Jane Reamer White dated August 31, 1970.

46. Adams, *Jim Bridger and I.*

47. Ibid.

48. K. Ross Toole Collection.

49. John H. Raftery, *The Story of Yellowstone* (Butte, Montana: McKee Publishing Co., 1912), 103–5; ———, "A Miracle in Hotel Building; Being the Story of the Building of the New Canyon Hotel in Yellowstone Park" (no place, no publisher, 1911?), 15.

50. Raftery, *The Story of Yellowstone.*

51. Dan W. Gibson, "Souvenir of Construction of the New Canyon Hotel, Yellowstone National Park, 1910–1911" (no place, no publisher, 1911?). Courtesy Mrs. Jane Reamer White.

52. Raftery, *The Story of Yellowstone,* 106–7.

53. Ibid.

54. Ibid.

55. Ibid.

56. Gibson, "Souvenir of Construction."

57. Wylie Company pamphlets in Y.A.

58. U.S. Department of the Interior, "General Information Regarding Yellowstone National Park for the Season of 1912" (Washington: G.P.O., 1912), 3–10.

59. Adams, *Jim Bridger and I.*

60. Peterson Collection, Mellen to Lamont, December 29, 1899.

61. Ibid., "Before the Interstate Commerce Commission, No. 800, William W. Wylie *vs.* Northern Pacific Railway Company, Yellowstone National Park Transportation Company and Yellowstone National Park Association. Decided June 23, 1905: Report and Opinion of Commission."

62. K. Ross Toole Collection, Reel No. 1, 115.

63. Letter from Huntley Child, Jr., September 18, 1985. N.A., Central Classified File, "Privileges," Lane to Hays, April 19, 1919.

64. Ibid., Demaray to Secretary.

65. Y.A., File No. 33, "Case of E.C. Waters": Adjutant General to Superintendent Young, June 15, 1907; Ibid., Major Pitcher to Mr. Frank Sterling, Helena, Montana, G.A.R. Post, June 11, 1907; Captain Boutelle to Major Pitcher, June 15, 1907.

66. N.P. Papers, Box No. 27, E. C. Buchanan (Comptroller), to Pearce, Treasurer, Yellowstone Park Association, June 23, 1889.

67. Y.A., File No. 33, Boutelle to Pitcher, June 15, 1907.

68. Ibid., Secretary Noble to Captain Anderson, June 20, 1892. See also Arnold Hague Papers, Hague to Captain Moses Harris, January 17, 1889; Hague to Weed (geologist), September 10, 1890; Boutelle to Hague, April 26, 1891, for negative observations about Waters.

69. *Enterprise,* July 20, 1889.
An inspector's report in 1905 described the vessel, dubbed the "Zillah," as having been built in Dubuque, Iowa, in 1884. It had a steel hull, was of forty gross tons displacement, had staterooms and berths, could carry up to 120 passengers, and was required to carry a full complement of six or seven officers and crew. It was powered by one steam engine and one boiler "made of lawful steel, in the year 1890, . . ." Y.A., File No. 26, Certificate of Inspection of the Zillah, from the firm of Douglas and Douglas, September 5, 1906.

70. Y.A., File No. 33, Gibson to Boutelle, January 6, 1890.

71. Ibid., Copy of statement, Noble to Boutelle, October 11, 1890; File No. 2, Noble to Anderson, June 20, 1892 (with contract leasing certain land to Waters).

72. Ibid., T. Gilbert Pearson to Young, August 15, 1907; W. F. Scott to Young, August 24, 1907; Young to Interior Secretary, October 15, 1907.

73. Ibid., "Exhibit 'I'," Copy of Waters's letter to Senator William B. Allison of Iowa, dated July 22, 1907, with Endorsements.

74. Ibid., "Exhibit 'J'," W. J. Rossington to Secretary, July 26, 1902; William Thomas to Superintendent Young, July 2, 1907.

75. Ibid., A. J. Simmons, General Eastern passenger agent of the Northern Pacific, to Child, June 7, 1907, containing a news item of the young woman's death;

unaddressed form letter from Waters dated Fond du Lac, Wisconsin, January 18, 1905.

76. Ibid., File No. 33; also, "Special Letter Press Book" on correspondence in regard to E. C. Waters.

77. Ibid., "Special Letter Press Book."

78. Ibid., Major Lloyd Brett, Acting Superintendent, to Secretary, October 12, 1912, and other correspondence in File No. 33 dossier; Peterson Collection, E. Askevold, Auditor, "Report on Investment in Yellowstone Park Boat Company," January 30, 1917.

79. Peterson Collection, E. Askevold, Auditor. He states that in 1908 Child bought out Waters for $50,000, but a letter from Waters to Hofer dated December 21, 1908, raises doubts about the validity of this statement. Letter in Y.A., File No. 33.

In 1902 Waters brought into the park from Tacoma, Washington, and floated in time for the 1903 season, a larger vessel dubbed the "Eli C. Waters." It was, if a newspaper article can be accepted as accurate, 140 feet long and 30 feet wide and could carry 600 passengers. Trouble was, the authorities refused to allow him to place it in service on the grounds that it was unsafe. Waters eventually sailed it to Dot Island where he moored it; it became an ugly hulk and was finally burned. *Montana Standard* (Butte, Montana).

80. N.A., Central Classified File, "Privileges," Davidson to Drury, August 26, 1928.

81. Ibid., Memo, Superintendent Albright to Assistant Secretary, December 12, 1930, and scattered references throughout the "Privileges" file.

82. Ibid., Memo, Director Demaray to Secretary, no date but clearly 1941; Ibid., memo of prices, Pryor and Trischman, for season 1941.

83. Ibid., Director Cammerer to Assistant Secretary, February 3, 1940. It is not stated if these figures represent also Hamilton's percentage from the automobile service stations but I presume so, since his investment in 1930 is given by Albright as $437,909.01. Ibid., Albright to Assistant Secretary, December, 1930.

84. Ibid., Memo, Assistant Secretary Vogelsang to Secretary, January 12, 1921.

85. Ibid., Mather to Interior Secretary, February 18, 1921.

86. Ibid., Cammerer to Assistant Secretary, April 7, 1936; Demaray to Assistant Secretary, May 11, 1935.

87. Ibid., Albright to Assistant Secretary, December 12, 1930.

88. Ibid., Privileges, Acting Director to Acting Secretary, November 4, 1924.

89. Ibid., Privileges, list of prices for Brothers's bathhouse for 1928 season; Memo, Acting Director Demaray to Secretary, September 2 , 1930.

90. Ibid., Privileges, "General," Director Albright to Superintendent, telegram of June 16, 1933; Albright to Secretary, January 26, 1932.

91. Ibid., Privileges, "Hamilton," Assistant Secretary Oscar Chapman to Congressman Homer D. Angell, February 1, 1945; Abe Fortas to Mr. Ferrell, secretary to Treasury Secretary Fred Vinson, November 15, 1945. These were influential people who came to Hamilton's defense.

92. Ibid., Assistant Secretary Michael W. Strauss to Senator John Chandler Gurney, February 7, 1945.

93. Ibid.

94. Ibid., Fortas to Ferrell, November 15, 1945.

95. Ibid., Senator Gurney to Assistant Secretary Chapman, January 18, 1945.

96. Ibid., Drury to Hamilton, June 1, 1944.

97. Ibid., Fortas to Ferrell; see also the above citations referring to this matter, plus a memo from Demaray to Chapman, August 7, 1945.

98. Ibid., Assistant Secretary Strauss to Senator Gurney, February 7, 1945.

99. Ibid., Drury to Secretary, June 7, 1946. The memo was after the fact.

100. Ibid., Drury to Secretary Krug, January 6, 1948.

101. Ibid., Conrad Wirth to Secretary, September 20, 1949; Hamilton to Drury, June 2, 1950.

102. Ibid., Secretary Chapman to Senator Gurney, July 10, 1950; Doty to senators, August 27, 1950.

103. Ibid., D. H. Rosier, Jr., to Assistant Secretary, August 18, 1938; Demaray to Assistant Secretary, April 12, 1939.

104. Ibid., Demaray to Assistant Secretary, April 12, 1939.

105. Ibid., Memo from Blossom to Director, February 5, 1930; Charles L. Gable, Chief Auditor, Park Operator's Accounts, to Director, January 6, 1930; Albright to Director, March 28, 1930.

106. Ibid., Memo, Albright to Secretary, February 10, 1923; Work to Child, April 14, 1928.

107. Ibid., Alexander Vogelsang to Haynes, February 18, 1921; Mather to Assistant Secretary, January 21, 1926; Albright to Assistant Secretary, December 12, 1930 and January 2, 1931.

108. Ibid., "Administration," Solicitor to Secretary, January 13, 1928.

109. Ibid., Material concerning N.R.A. scattered in "Administration" file.

THE SUPERINTENDENTS

CHAPTER SEVEN

"National Park" Langford and "The Man for the Mountains," Philetus Norris

*H*owever minor the Congressmen may have considered the legislation that created Yellowstone National Park during the second session of the 42nd Congress, the park from the very first enjoyed "a good press." One way or another, Americans were made aware of Yellowstone's existence. In April 1872, artist Thomas Moran displayed his massive landscape of the Grand Canyon of the Yellowstone, which Congress purchased for $10,000. Thousands of William Henry Jackson's photographs were sold, as were his stereopticon slides, which soon graced many a marble-topped parlor table. The *American Journal of Science and Arts* carried more than a score of scientific articles about the park from 1872 to 1886. Articles also appeared in the *American Naturalist* and the British publication, *Nature*. In 1876 the Earl of Dunraven published his popular travel book, *The Great Divide*, in which he related his Yellowstone experiences. [1]

Even the lad secreting forbidden but voraciously read dime novels knew of the park. The publishing house of Beadle and Adams offered stories with such tantalizing titles as *Yellowstone Jack, Yellowstone Trapper,* and *The Yellowstone Trail;* nearly a dozen novels had as their locale the upper Yellowstone River.

When Diamond Dirk entered Yellowstone and discovered a man giant residing in a hillside cave above a ring of hot springs, the impressionable lads of the 1880s were impressed! With such prose, who would not be:

The trail led him directly toward a boiling spring.

The roar of the falling waters was beneath him, and as he drew nearer the ground trembled beneath his feet. . . . The mists boiled up in the air in volumes, and the hiss of the seething caldron was distinctly heard, while the moonlight fell upon all, and brought to his mind the thought that he seemed indeed to be approaching a very hell on earth. . . . Feeling before him, with a stick he had picked up in the timber, he went forward to the very brink of the boiling lake. . . . [2]

Even poets wrote of Yellowstone. California bard Joaquin Miller wrote of the park, though not very successfully:

> . . . .
> O yellow-hued world on top of the world!
>   O walls where rainbows hang pendant in stone!
> O world where mountains on mountains are hurled
> And mother earth rocks and makes piteous moan.!
> . . . .[3]

And Walt Whitman mentioned it:

> . . . With presentment of Yellowstone's scenes, or Yosemite,
> And murmuring under, pervading all, I'd bring
>   the resulting sea-sound,
> That endlessly sounds from the two Great Seas of the world.[4]

Congressmen may not have been aware of what they had wrought in creating a national park, but the nation was aware, and it was now the duty of the federal government to administer it.

Until about two hundred years ago governments were concerned exclusively with four categories of activity: military security; taxation; law; and an infrastructure that built, maintained, and managed such necessities as roads, waterworks, and a postal system. Then, with the rise of democracies, the Industrial Revolution, the population explosion, and increasing technology, governments expanded with explosive rapidity. Yet many authorities still insist that government functions best within those original four categories. Such extraneous areas of government activity as health, welfare, and housing clearly have not been handled as successfully. And the success in administering a public domain that includes parks, forests, deserts, and prairies is still in question.

The creation of Yellowstone National Park was an experiment in government; administering such a region hardly fell within the four basic categories. What was entailed in administering a national park? In 1872 no one knew. Since the land it embraced was now segregated and closed to preemption or homesteading, it would seem that some policing was necessary. With no experience to fall back on, the first administrators had no profound underlying philosophy to guide them.

Nor did the machinery exist to develop a philosophy of administration, for, strictly speaking, Washington (meaning the federal government) did not in 1872 have a bureaucracy. It was a government run by politically appointed clerks; there was no formal Civil Service. Consultants, blue ribbon committees, administrative aides, and "think tanks" were nonexistent. No institutional machinery was in place to be charged with evolving policy, with look-ing into the future and projecting needs and pitfalls of a later time. Govern-ment functioned on a day-by-day, problem-by-problem, crisis-by-crisis basis.[5]

It was logical for the Department of Interior to be assigned the task. That executive agency had existed since 1849 and was already serving as a catch-all for bureaus ranging from the Office of Indian Affairs to the Colum-bia Hospital for Women and Lying In Asylum. Main offices of the depart-ment were in the ugly, cavernous Patent Office Building on F Street, but even in 1872 about a third of the 1,100 employees were toiling in suites situated in Washington, the result of bureaucratic proliferaton.

The department throughout its existence has not enjoyed a very high caliber of men as secretaries. Of the six who served during the years 1872 to 1886, when Interior had absolute control over the park, only two, Carl Schurz under Hayes and L.Q.C. Lamar under Cleveland, were above average. Both of these men manifested some concern over Yellowstone. Of the other secretaries, Columbus Delano and Zachariah Chandler under Grant, and Samuel J. Kirkwood briefly under Garfield and Arthur, displayed little in-terest. Finally, Henry M. Teller, secretary under Arthur from April 1882 until March 1885, was clearly a negative force.

Under these executives were five Yellowstone superintendents: Nathaniel Pitt Langford (1872–77), Philetus W. Norris (1877–82), Patrick W. Conger (1882–84), Robert E. Carpenter (1884–85), and David W. Wear (1885–86). Whatever their capabilities, and these ranged from excellent to incom-petent, all had to work within the parameters of Interior Department politics in a period of loose public morality.

For the most part the Interior secretaries simply assigned one of their assistants to handle park matters; only occasionally did a situation arise in which basic policy had to be determined from the top. Secretary Columbus Delano did not even mention Yellowstone in his *Annual Report of the Secretary for 1872.*

Such desultory treatment, such neglect, was harmful to the park. Its remoteness did not protect it from shrewd entrepreneurs or restive sightseers. All at once tourists, scientists, army expeditions and VIP groups entered the reservation, while local frontiersmen were in and out of it constantly. These people (with apologies to modern park alarmists) threw more stones, tree trunks, soap, and clothing into Old Faithful and other geysers and hot springs than ten thousand times their number do today. Indeed, Old Faithful has a cast iron stomach and her persistent regularity, at least until 1984, is nothing short of miraculous.

Thus, when Nathaniel P. Langford assumed the superintendency on May 10, 1872, conditions there were dynamic rather than static. Tough federal policy was needed, backed with adequate policing and provisions for punishment of violations. Yellowstone did not receive such guidance until 1894.

A distinguished, even an arrogant-looking man, Langford was forty years old in 1872 and had already made his mark in Montana politics. He was one of the Masons who in the 1860s took the law into their own hands as Montana's vigilantes. He also had been one of the leaders of the Langford-Washburn-Doane expedition into the Upper Yellowstone in 1870. He had lectured widely on the region, at first independently and later in the employ of the Northern Pacific. In 1904 he published a book about the 1870 expedition, in which he proudly boasted of his own participation and noted that correspondence often reached him addressed to "National Park" Langford.[6]

Since the position of superintendent carried with it no stipend, and Langford was not financially independent, he accepted the assignment with the knowledge that he must earn his living elsewhere. In fact, no franchises were issued during his five-year regime, though there were many applicants, and revenue from leases was his only source of income as superintendent; he had other financial resources in Montana.[7]

The new superintendent's letter of appointment spelled out his duties with remarkable clarity, but left their implementation, and especially suggestions for development of policy, up to him. He was "to carry out the Act of Congress under such instructions" as he may receive from the department. He was "to preserve from injury or spoliation the timber, mineral deposits, and various curiosities of that region so far as possible in their natural conditions. . . . [and was to] forward also . . . reports of the condition of the Park, and such suggestions relative to its management and care as . . . [his] experience may dictate."[8]

Even within these limited parameters Langford did little for Yellowstone. He had to make a living and did so as a bank examiner; he never tried to create revenue to pay him a salary (unless he received a retainer from the N.P.), nor did he try to expel squatters from the reservation. There is no question of his love for Yellowstone, but as superintendent he spent little time there.

Langford was most active in 1872 when he accompanied into the park a division of the Hayden Survey; he also submitted an annual report for that year, the only one of his tenure. Possibly he was in the park briefly in 1874, but there is no evidence of his being there at all in 1873, 1875, 1876, or 1877. His minor contributions can be encapsulated briefly. From his experience with Hayden, Langford was able to round out the geographical knowledge of the southern, southwestern, and western portions of the park and its environs. He also envisioned much of the park's present highway system. In 1873, backed by Montana Delegate William H. Clagett, he pleaded for a $15,000 appropriation for development of the northern and western entrance roads; these would, he argued, entice investment capital and produce lucrative lease income. On several occasions he argued that lessees could also do guard duty.[9]

It is to Langford's credit that he was concerned over spoliation. He advocated the prohibition of all fishing and hunting "except for purposes of recreation by visitors and tourists, or for use by actual residents of the Park." He wanted laws prohibiting the cutting of timber, and severe penalties for leaving campfires unattended. He also recommended that the park be placed under the legal jurisdiction of Gallatin County, Montana, which at that time adjoined it to the north. Late in 1873 Langford wrote from Helena that his assistant superintendent, D.C. Folsom (one of the three men into Yellowstone in 1869), reported serious depredations. "The parapets of sinter surrounding the 'Castle' and 'Old Faithful'," he said, "and the symmetrical cone of the 'Bee Hive,' have been much defaced by visitors to the Park."[10]

Truth was, even though the park was only two years old in 1874, the emergence in rapidly populating Montana Territory of concerned citizens was already leading to a concerted movement for change and improvement. In 1874 a bill was introduced into the U.S. Congress, backed by the secretary, governors of Montana and Wyoming territories, Langford, Hayden, and certain Montana petitioners. It requested funds for a resident superintendent, for twenty-year leases rather than the ten years provided for in the Act of Dedication, and for legal procedures and punishments for offenders of park rules. A hundred thousand dollars was sought. The bill never passed.[11]

As for Superintendent Nathaniel Pitt Langford, he practically drops out of Yellowstone after 1874. However, he held onto his position until Hayes became president and the competent Carl Schurz became secretary of interior. On April 1, 1877, Langford's appointment was revoked. The department proposed to "avail itself of the gratuities of a gentleman, as Superintendent, who visits the park in the interests of science." This was "the man for the mountains," Philetus W. Norris.[12]

By 1877 it was clear that Yellowstone needed a superintendent residing in the park at least during the summer months. The government may have been indifferent and neglectful, but the park was already gaining a place in the galaxy of American treasures. More tourists were coming in every year. Squatting entrepreneurs in the park offered, for a price, shelter, food, whiskey, guides, beasts of burden, and even a bridge across the Yellowstone River.

Philetus Norris was a reversal of his predecessor, remaining within the park boundaries for long seasons, constantly on the move, and prone to write his superiors at length on park matters. His immediate successors were political hacks, followed by army officers. Not until the hyperactive Horace Albright came on the scene in the 1920s was there a comparable figure. Both men were competent and imaginative; both earned small fortunes, Norris before and Albright after connections with the park. But here the comparison should stop. Both men were strong personalities. After each was born the mold was broken.

Philetus W. Norris was born on August 17, 1821, at Palmyra, New York, of pioneer New England stock. He grew up in the wilder sections of the state and by age ten was earning dimes by guiding tourists to the Great Falls of the Genessee. A little later the family moved to new lands in Michigan Territory where Norris's father took ill. Forced to help provide the family income, Norris learned the fur trade and at seventeen was working for the Hudson's Bay Company in Manitoba. Shortly thereafter he purchased lands in the extreme northwest corner of Ohio. He set out to educate himself and by the Civil War was working as a surveyor.

During the war he served with a battalion of West Virginia mountain scouts and was seriously injured in a guerrilla engagement. He then resigned to serve a term in the Ohio Senate. He purchased swampy land in Hamtramck Township, north of Detroit, developed it as the town of Norris, and prospered as his lands were sold. He also established a newspaper, the *Norris Suburban*, which he used as a publicity organ for his own achievements. His letters home appeared in it under the heading of "The Great West." He also envisioned himself as a poet, writing some of the worst published verses ever to emerge from the American West. [13]

This skimpy biography fails to convey Norris's personality. Colonel Norris (as he was best known) is interesting not for his vocation but for his avocations. By his own abilities he became economically capable of indulging his interests, and they were many: exploration, technology, archaeology, natural science, hunting, fishing, camping, carpentry, road building, writing and poetry. He was of average height, well built, with gray hair, flowing beard, regular features, and an aristocratic, outdoorsman's air about him. He loved to think of himself as a frontiersman. Of the two paintings of him that still exist, the one showing him in buckskin with a rifle would certainly have been his first choice.

A young couple in Yellowstone who found him a part of their camp entourage hardly showered him with compliments. It was autumn, and cold, when they saw "what seemed to be a flying centaur coming rapidly toward [them], but it proved to be the wings of Col. Norris's great coat flying in the wind as he rode madly down the trail." The young folks found him a bit on the talkative side. "We were lulled to sleep by the deep, sonorous voice of Col Norris who forgot to stop talking when he went to sleep, and he was still talking right along when we woke up at midnight," Mrs. Carrie Adell Stahorn recalled.[14]

Early Yellowstone historian, Hiram Martin Chittenden, scoffed at the colonel's achievements. "Colonel Norris," he wrote, "had a large admixture of Quixotism in his nature, and the park was just the place to draw it all out. He saw everything there through a magnifying glass; and, like Don Quixote, beheld in what he saw the embodiment of all his overwrought fancy had led him to expect. . . . ."[15]

Norris first attempted to enter the Upper Yellowstone region in 1870, but failed. In the summer of 1875 he headed for the region once again. Saying that he "needed the relaxing influence of travel" and yearned for the sight of his "old border haunts," he packed his outfit, including "a repeating Winchester rifle, belt, pistol, ammunition, knife and fishing tackle, . . ." and entrained for Franklin, Idaho. There his itinerary called for stagecoach conveyance to Helena. He was bucked off one day's trip because of Secretary of War Belknap's party of four, but in due time he arrived in Yellowstone.[16]

One stormy night he was encamped at Jack Baronett's cabin near Lamar Junction. Assembled there, taking refuge from the storm, were "full bleeds, half breeds, and mountaineers of every age, nationality, dress and arms." One of them was a man in his early thirties, "Lonesome Charley" Reynolds, a handsome, quiet person. Norris and Lonesome Charley became fast friends, talking late into the night. Only the noxious sulfurous fumes from thermal activity, that wafted down the canyon, bothered them.[17]

Yellowstone was the perfect setting for Norris's quixotic, imaginative mind. That summer he visited Specimen Ridge "with their [sic]ancient crests covered like Pompeii and Herculaneum with ashes, mud, and lava." This indefatigable man of fifty-four also descended to the canyon floor, barely scaling the "crumbling walls of the terrific chasm and staggering from the effects of sulphur gas and exhaustion" before he attained the plateau above. On his way home, staying a few days at Bottler's ranch just north of the park, he reported that the brothers alone in the spring of 1875 had packed more than two thousand elk skins from Lamar Junction. "As the only parts of the carcass of them saved was the tongue and hide," Norris wrote, "an opinion can be formed of the wanton, unwise, unlawful slaughter of beautiful and valuable animals. . . ." They would become extinct, he warned, "unless protected by a determined resident superintendent and police."[18]

He headed home via the Missouri River, arriving at Carroll, Montana Territory, by stage. There he met Lonesome Charley again, just arrived on a bull boat down the Judith River. As the two floated down the Missouri, they paused to visit the ruins of old Fort Union and the Fort Buford cemetery. There, "with a last lingering look at the turfy tomb of slaughtered friends," Charley turned to Norris and said, "Comrade, I am dreaming where a year hence will find us." They continued on downriver until Norris bade adieu to Lonesome Charley at Fort Abraham Lincoln.[19]

Nearly two years passed. Lonesome Charley met his fate with Custer at the Little Big Horn while Norris busied himself in Michigan. When the time arrived for him to assume his superintendent's duties in Yellowstone, he chose to travel a northern route by way of the Custer Battlefield. With him was Jack Baronett. With a "rough but accurate map made by Reno's scout Gerard, who saw Charley fall," Norris and Baronett set out to recover Lonesome Charley's remains. All they could find, Norris wrote sadly, "were a few small fragments of his hat and clothing, a few tufts of his well-known auburn hair from the back of his head which clung to the earth after wolf or ghoul had removed the skull."[20]

These remains were "gathered into a large handkerchief [and] were brought carefully away for decent burial in a Christian land," wrote Norris in a long letter home. When he camped that summer in Yellowstone, he used his saddle for a pillow, with the bundle of Charley's bones attached to it. And he wrote two poems in memory of his dead comrade: "Gallant Charley Reynolds" and "Reynolds's Dirge." One of the better verses is the fifth one of the former:

> Stricken in thy youth and beauty,
>   Sadly stricken ere thy prime;
> Fallen at the ford of duty,
>   Lo! An honored name is thine!
> Charley! May the foe who slew thee
>   Ever bear a tainted name!
> Reynolds! all the friends who knew thee
>   Shall award thee lofty fame![21]

At first thought such a romantically inclined person seems a poor choice for the Yellowstone superintendency, but remember that Norris had made himself financially independent. People have their idiosyncracies. Norris's was an unrestrained romanticism. Possibly even this worked for the good, for in an age of nascent conservationists whose ideas had not yet crystallized, he saw Yellowstone as a magical wilderness and, for that reason alone, wanted to keep it that way. With unusual vigor he set out to know the country, to grasp its problems and apply solutions. When he was removed in 1882 much progress had been made, and Yellowstone would never be quite the same again.

Norris's 1877 peregrinations took him from the Custer Battlefield up the Yellowstone River to Bottler's and Mammoth Hot Springs. In the next few weeks, using the knowledge of a local guide named Adam Miller, he explored much of the rugged country along the north and east boundaries. He then joined General Sheridan's party, but near Tower Falls was injured when his horse spooked and threw him. He returned to the states on a mackinaw boat down the Yellowstone, and steamboats and railroads thereafter.[22]

In his first report Norris revealed an excellent grasp of park problems. He pointed out that in this year of the Nez Perce difficulties he could have done little to control the Indians or to protect visitors since he had no park policy to follow, no escort, and no salary. He predicted friction between park authorities and the Clarks Fork miners, and between government and the few squatters within the park. He decried the unrestrained spoliation. Fires, he said, were destroying "vast groves of timber." Thousands of deer, elk, moose, and bison had been slaughtered since 1872, he reported, many of them "run down on snow-shoes and tomahawked when their carcasses were least valuable, and merely strychnine-poisoned for wolf or wolverine bait. . . ." He also called for considerable road building, stressing that if all his suggestions were adopted the principal showplaces would be accessible to tourists.[23]

Norris's suggestions did not go unnoticed by Interior Secretary Carl Schurz. Even so, Congress pretty well ignored Schurz's estimate of needs for Yellowstone but at least gave lip service to the concept of protection: it appropriated all of $10,000 "to protect, preserve, and improve the Yellowstone National Park." Even in 1878 this was a small sum, but it does mark the beginning of monetary aid, establishing a precedent broken just once since then.[24]

Arriving in the park late in July 1878, fortified by Schurz's support and with $10,000 at his disposal, Norris pitched into his task energetically and methodically. For public relations he made speeches to citizen groups in Bozeman and Virginia City, imploring them not to despoil the park, fire its forests, or kill its wildlife. He drew up rules and regulations, had them published in local newspapers and made 300 copies of them on weather-resistant muslin that he tacked on trees or buildings at frequented park sites.

Norris also entered the field of what the Park Service now calls "interpretation," erecting instructional signs and markers, informational guide boards and mileposts. The next year he had to report that most of the signs had been pilfered, washed away, or oxidized by chemicals around the thermal formations.[25]

And from 1878 until 1881, Norris's last year (though he remained in office until March, 1882), this energetic superintendent continued to wrestle with park problems. In doing so he aroused considerable opposition from local interests. Yet he persevered; he was the kind of person who works best under adversity. And, it must be added, occasionally his romanticism exceeded his common sense.

The superintendent needed a new home and headquarters building. In 1879, following Custer's defeat in 1876, Nez Perce depredations in the park in 1877, and a Bannock Indian scare in 1878, Norris determined to make his headquarters also a fortress. He chose as the site the crest of Capitol Hill, a 150-foot-high mound due east of the Mammoth Terraces. "It fully commands the valley, and terrace, within range of rifle or field artillery, and a fair view of the entire balance of the valley and all its approaches," he said.

During July of 1879 the blockhouse headquarters became a reality. No medieval robber baron was more securely entrenched, nor more uncomfortable during a blizzard. The building had two stories with balconies, surmounted by "an octagonal turret or gunroom, nine feet in diameter and ten feet high, well looploped for rifles, and all surmounted by a national flag fifty-three feet from the ground. . . ."[26]

In time Norris had also fenced a large, sheltered pasture. Concerned over the condition of that ugly thermal remnant, the Liberty Cap at Mammoth Hot Springs, he erected rough braces under a shoulder of the endangered side. He constructed bridges, barns, a blacksmith shop, and other service buildings; erected a crude bathhouse at the Queen's Laundry, a hot spring at the Lower Geyser Basin; and at the Upper Basin built a fortified house with adjoining stable and corral. At the mouth of Soda Butte Creek he built another cabin, later occupied by Yellowstone's first game keeper, Harry Yount. Between Mammoth and Gardiner he even planted a vegetable garden.[27]

The superintendent now began employing a staff. As assistants he hired men of his acquaintance from the East, his son, A. F. Norris, and local hunters. He also hired up to thirty laborers. Of all his activities, Norris's road building was the most important.[28]

Although it would have been better had Norris been a civil engineer, in those days such qualifications were not necessary. Horses can follow trails while coaches and wagons were narrow by present standards. True, there did exist a science of road building but, in a pinch, a road builder in the wilderness could dispense with such expertise. Norris posed just three questions: Where do I want to start? Where do I want to go? What is the shortest route between the two points? Then he armed his crew with shovels, axes, and saws, a few horse-drawn plows and scrapers, and started them in the right direction. In due time a swath six or eight feet wide was cut through the forest, straight over mountains, across streams at fords (bridges mostly came later), through bogs, and over prairie country. Twenty or thirty hefty laborers thus equipped could build miles and miles of such traces within a few months.

Hike the steep trail behind Mammoth Hot Springs to Snow Pass and envision two or three teams pulling a heavy Yellowstone Concord loaded with well-fed passengers—and pity the horses! Follow an old trail through a bog and contemplate how it was, with the corduroy timbers rotting and the coach wheels up to their axles in muck; drive along a clearing, and picture the road in gravel, fifty coaches loping along, and taste the dust. All of this was a concomitant of Mr. Norris's roads. *But,* he did get them built, ninety miles in 1879 and 234 miles of trails, many of which, to be entirely correct, already existed.

From the summit of Sepulchre Mountain on the park's northern fringe, he had scanned the terrain through field glasses. Carefully he traced in his mind's eye his route of 1875 when he had come north in snow to Mammoth from the geyser basins. From his vantage point Norris fixed "the most direct and practical [route] for a wagon road across the park." Then he set to work.

In a short time the colonel had a roadway three miles long behind and above the Mammoth terraces, through Snow Pass and into the West Gardner Valley, today known as Swan Lake Flats. Onward he pushed the crew, here building a bridge, there fording a stream, across the shore of Beaver Lake with a causeway, to Obsidian Cliff.

Today's Yellowstone tourists see in Obsidian Cliff just another rugged mountain spur across which a straight road has been cut. To earlier generations, however, it was a thing of wonder, as close as anything in nature to Jim Bridger's mountain of glass,* though anyone prone to take literally stories about the mountain is in for a disappointment. The dark, white- and black-flecked obsidian is shiny and glossy, but it is mixed with volcanic pumice.

Colonel Norris was no one to play down the mountain of glass. He wrote how huge masses of it had "fallen from this utterly impassable mountain into the hissing hot spring margin of an equally impassable lake. . . ." How, then, could his laborers cut through it? The solution lay in the colonel's knowledge of expansion and contraction of rocks by heat and cold. "We . . . with huge fires, heated and expanded, and then, men well screened by blankets held by others, by dashing cold water, suddenly cooled and fractured the large masses," Norris explained. "Then, with huge levers, steel bars, sledges, picks, and shovels, . . . we rolled, slid, crushed and shoveled one-fourth of a mile of good wagon-road midway along the slope. . . ."[28]

*Bridger said he had seen an elk, shot at it, and nothing happened: advanced upon it, shot at it again, and still no response; shot at it a third time and a fourth with no result; he finally ran toward the elk to club it with his rifle stock, only to run smack into a wall of glass. Not only that, the glass was magnified; the elk he saw on the other side was really twenty-five miles away. See J. Cecil Alter, *James Bridger,* p. 384.

Onward Norris pushed his men. They passed through a geyser basin which now bears his name, conquered Gibbon Canyon and Falls, crossed the road from Henry's Lake and pushed on fifteen miles into the Upper Geyser Basin. Their supply wagon, Norris boasted, was "the first to make a track along the Upper Fire Hole River." The superintendent accomplished all this in the short season of 1878. By autumn it was possible—not easy, but possible—with a stout wagon, strong teams, and an experienced teamster with a good command of obscenities, for a wagon to go from Mammoth Hot Springs to Old Faithful.

In 1879 Norris, again with a shortened season, set out along his "road" of the previous year, clearing it of downed timber, widening it, and making it more traversable. Next he built a road from the Upper Geyser Basin to Yellowstone Lake. He knew the region west and southwest of the lake was a confusing mass of timber, ridges, streams, lakes, and bogs. He was aware also that in the area the continental divide twisted like a snake, with some waters heading for the Columbia and the Pacific via the Snake River, while some flowed into Yellowstone Lake with the Gulf of Mexico their ultimate destination. The colonel traced a chain of meadows and lakelets and a narrow pass that brought him to West Thumb. He then hacked out a trail ten miles from the Upper Geyser Basin to Shoshone Lake and twelve more to West Thumb. Then he opened another trail through fallen timber some twenty-six miles down the west side of the lake to the outlet and improved the remaining sixty miles of trail to the Canyon, around the Mount Washburn to Tower Falls, and finally back to Mammoth.

Norris's roads were steep, narrow, swampy, full of stumps and downed timber. In his defense are his accomplishments: well over 150 miles of "roads" and over 250 miles of trails and bridle paths. Add to this the hundreds of signs and posted rules and regulations he put up, and a picture emerges of a man with a growing concept of his park responsibilities, of the park's uses, what visitors should and should not do, and of government's obligations.

Bad as it was, Norris's road system was an improvement over what had existed before. His roads and trails touched the primary scenic spots, geyser basins, Yellowstone Lake, Falls, and Canyon; Mount Washburn, Tower Falls, and Mammoth Hot Springs. The system linked with the north and west entrances. By its existence the road and trail network encouraged the systematic park tour, helped determine points for hotels and lunch stops, and created an aura of civilization that tourists found comforting amidst the wilderness.

Very little is left of Norris's roads today, for the activities of the army engineers and, after 1917, the Bureau of Public Roads and the Park Service have pretty well obliterated those crude beginnings. Occasionally, of course, a highway might for a short distance follow exactly where a Norris road stretched along a meadow or a mountainside. When a road has been abandoned in Yellowstone, park policy has been to plow back and forth over the road, loosening the hard top and inviting the growth of native flora. Within a few years what was a barren highway has become a grassy sward; within a few additional years, trees and bushes have sprouted, a few boulders will have rolled down the hillside onto the abandoned thoroughfare, a few old trees will have fallen across it, the embankments will have grown over with grass and wildflowers. It will be on the way toward a total return to nature. As for Norris's trails, again, some are essentially those he built, or old ones he improved upon, but the great majority are of later vintage.

Combined with Norris's road building were his activities as explorer and scientist. The man's curiosity was insatiable. He searched out new routes from place to place. In 1880, at the behest of O. J. Salisbury, a stagecoach entrepreneur, Norris, with a guide named James Goodwin, found "a route . . . so unexpectedly favorable that its adoption and opening were immediately determined upon." It is essentially today's west entrance road. Salisbury was so enthusiastic that he had a crew build a mail station at Riverside, near the present west entrance; he then went East in pursuit of contracts.

In that same year Norris explored Yellowstone Lake in an unwieldy boat, the "Explorer." He was prone to spice his reports with intelligence of his latest sufferings. "After encountering several heavy gales, one severe snowstorm, and a shipwreck," he reported, "I ascended Mount Chittenden* and other peaks of the Range. . . ." He also opened a new trail to the top of Mount Washburn and forged one to the foot of the Grand Canyon of the Yellowstone.

Eventually he reached the Hoodoo region on the east-central boundary, climbing several peaks south of Pilot Knobs on the way. The Hoodoos, fanciful rock formations, led Norris, with his romantic flair and rather childish imagination, to run amok with purple phraseology: "Few white people have visited it, and fewer still have ventured there and returned," he wrote sinisterly. "These monuments are from fifty to two or three hundred feet in height, with narrow, tortuous passages between them, which sometimes are tunnels through permanent snow or ice fields where the bighorn sheep hide in safety; while the ceaseless but ever-changing moans of the wild winds seem to chant fitting requiems to those gnome-like monuments of the legendary Indian gods."

From such a description one would expect the next paragraph to record the discovery of an ancient city like Petra. The *Haynes Guide* states that the

---

*Named for George B. Chittenden of the Hayden Survey, not Hiram Martin Chittenden.

Hoodoo region "consists of an area of tall, massed eroded rock pinnacles, which reveal to those who let loose their imaginations a large variety of forms of humans and beasts."[29]

In 1881, his last year in Yellowstone, Norris pursued his activities with vigor unusual in a man fifty-eight years old. He explored the eastern boundary and discovered what is, essentially, the Sylvan Pass route into Yellowstone, although the present highway hugs the northern shores of the lake instead of following Clear Creek, which Norris recommended.

He also pleaded for a careful survey of the park boundaries. Hayden's peremptory decision to make the northern line east and west from the mouth of the Gardner was most unwise. It is not always clear what constitutes the mouth of a stream. More seriously, Hayden ignored, or was ignorant of, Crow Indian Reservation boundaries established by the Treaty of Fort Laramie, May 7, 1868, which carried Crow country to the Yellowstone River as far south as the 45th parallel, then due east across the mountains. This meant that all the mines at Emigrant and up Bear and Crevice gulches, north of the park, were within Crow domains, as was Cooke City and the Clarks Fork mines. However, the Crows never molested the miners (unless it was a Crow party that attacked Adam Miller's party in 1870), probably because the whites were a buffer between the Crows and their enemies, the Sioux and Blackfeet.[30]

When Yellowstone Park was created in 1872, however, the Crow Treaty was ignored. *Did* park boundaries encroach upon the Crow Reservation? Norris got the backing of the commissioner of the General Land Office and of the Office of Indian Affairs, and of Carl Schurz; thus armed, he wrested from Congress a small appropriation to run a survey to find out. This was carried out in 1879 by R. J. Reeves, who proved the existence of the park's "Montana Strip." It extends two and one-half miles north of the Montana-Wyoming boundary, which is the 45th parallel. Yellowstone's west boundary, he discovered, lies three miles inside Montana and Idaho. Norris asked that these boundaries be changed to coincide with Wyoming's, but this was never done.[31]

The surveyor and his military escort foundered along the southern boundary. It took Norris's woodsmanship and several scouts to find them wallowing in the jack straw, lodgepole pine forest and swamps southwest of the lake. As a result of his own explorations Norris recommended that the eastern boundaries of the park be extended to embrace additional land, "a region," he pointed out, "ever useless for other purposes, while exceedingly interesting and valuable for the park." Eventually the boundaries were changed and did embrace some of this region.[32]

Norris the scientist was also kept busy. On July 29, 1879, he and his assistants took observations of an eclipse of the sun. He kept weather statistics and collected scientific specimens. He watched the eruption of the "great pool" in Midway Basin that spouted four to eight times a day. Named the Sheridan by Baronett and the Excelsior by Norris, this geyser nearly blew itself out in 1888, erupting since, as far as reported, less than a score of times. The superintendent discovered sites of Sheepeater Indian habitation. Near the Upper Falls he found the oldest marker in the park: "breast-high upon a pine-tree about 20 inches in diameter and still legible upon the bark 'J. O. R., Aug. 29, 1819'." His reports are full of such discoveries of the unusual.[33]

Nothing escaped his attention. To cut down on the killing of wild life he suggested hiring a game keeper to be stationed close to the mouth of Soda Butte Creek near the big meadows where they grazed. Harry Yount's employ as game keeper corresponded somewhat to Norris's suggestions. Yount expressed concern over the fate of the three park buffalo herds. And Norris killed what were then considered varmints: one mountain lion measured nearly nine feet from lip whiskers to tail, while of six grizzlies he bagged in 1879, one was eight and three-fourths feet from snout to roots of tail.[34]

Yet, for all his interests, Norris never became possessive, as some officials do, of the facility he administered. He welcomed Hayden and his scientists, as well as Senators John Sherman and Benjamin Harrison, Supreme Court Justice William Waite, Generals William T. Sherman and Nelson Miles, and the governors of Montana and Wyoming Territories. He welcomed sage-brushers and ordinary businessmen and their families on vacation as well, giving them advice (and perhaps talking them to drowsiness) and projecting plans for their comfort and convenience. He cooperated with railroad survey-ing parties. Possibly Norris was unaware that he was treading on thin ice in aiding Union Pacific and Utah Northern officials, for the Northern Pacific people coveted a monopoly on Yellowstone trade when their railroad was completed.

Superintendent Norris must have viewed the 1880 presidential election ap-prehensively, for in those years politics determined the duration of a govern-ment employee's job. The superintendency, now that appropriations were assured, had become a choice plum. Could this "Don Quixote of the Moun-tains" retain his position under a new president, even one of his own party?

Carl Schurz came through the park in the summer of 1880. He was short of patience for reasons best known to himself. Apparently he complained about the roads, for in a letter of September 20 Norris assured the secretary that he had kept the men "as you directed improving the road to the gey-sers." In October Norris indicated that criticism was coming from other,

more sinister quarters. "I refuse," he wrote, "to become a member of a syndicate for absorption of the best hotel sites within the park. . . ." And his
friend, Truman C. Everts, notified him in February 1881 that Schurz, "after
coming out of the park had made some remarks, as if he was not satisfied
with what had been done."[35]

Of all the opposition that surfaces more than a hundred years after the
fact, Norris's comment about "a syndicate" is most intriguing. It is an obvious reference to Northern Pacific interests, the first concrete indication in
the records of Northern Pacific concern in Yellowstone since the road went
into bankruptcy in 1873.

Garfield won the election of 1880. Although he was a Republican succeeding a Republican, he appointed a new Interior Secretary, Samuel J. Kirkwood of Iowa, who proceeded to make appointments in the accepted manner
of the time. Norris, who wanted to stay on, mounted a letter-writing campaign in his own behalf. One supporter wrote, "I wish to urge upon you
[Norris] the necessity of your return here, to finish up the great national
work you have so bravely begun." Another wrote, "We have got up a petition
for your benefit . . . and got 75 signatures all ready." Senator Henry Dawes
of Massachusetts, who had shown initial interest in the park, recommended
Norris's retention, as did ex-governor Dennison of Ohio.[36]

Whether it was Schurz's dissatisfaction with the way the park was run,
the machinations of an embryonic Northern Pacific syndicate coveting anticipated Yellowstone business, or simply the spoils system at work, Norris was
abruptly succeeded on April 1, 1882, by an Iowa politician's brother, Patrick
H. Conger. Less than three years later, on January 14, 1885, Norris died
suddenly while on a business trip to Rocky Hill in Warren Country, Kentucky. The *Enterprise* published a brief, much belated, garbled notice of his
demise, but it was correct when it said, "He was the pioneer pathfinder and
explorer of the park and enthusiast over everything pertaining to it."[37]

This was mild praise. Norris built the first roads, hired the first game
warden, disposed of the first federal appropriations, conducted the first public relations, and erected the first informational signs as well as the rules and
regulations. He welcomed tourists whether they were rich or poor, dignitaries or nobodies. He was ethnologist, zoologist, archaeologist, and geologist to the park. He was energetic to a fault, a jack-of-all-trades who with
ease could build a headquarters blockhouse or a bridge, shoot a bear, or write
a descriptive letter. He was a frontiersman when necessary, and by avocation;
but he was also a successful businessman, administrator, supervisor, and
planner by vocation. Even much of his flamboyant writing is attuned to the
times. When set alongside the insipid fiction and nonfiction of the era, it
appears no worse than much of it; even his poetry, bad as it was, is hardly
more hideous than much of that produced by his contemporaries.

In the four and one-half years after he left office (from March 31, 1882 until August 17, 1886, when the army assumed the policing of the park), there were three superintendents. This alone indicates some kind of breakdown in good management. In these same years the problems multiplied. If Norris had not begun the road building, tightened the regulations and tried to enforce them, attempted to protect wildlife and prevented the spoliation of the thermal areas, then Yellowstone might have reverted to the public domain, and fallen into the hands of exploiters. It almost suffered that fate anyway.

NOTES TO CHAPTER SEVEN

1. Earl of Dunraven, *The Great Divide.*

2. Albert Johannsen, *The House of Beadle and Adams* (Norman: University of Oklahoma Press, 1950), three vols., Vol. 2, 413,430. Johannsen lists fifteen stories which have as their locale either Yellowstone Park or the Upper Yellowstone country. The quotation is from Joseph E. Badger, Jr., *Diamond Dirk, or, The Mystery of the Yellowstone.* It is No. 13 in Beadle's Pocket Library.

3. Joaquin Miller, "In the Yellowstone Park," *The Youth's Companion,* November, 1910.

4 Walt Whitman, *Leaves of Grass,* "Thou Mother With Thy Equal Brood," (1881 Edition).

5. Interview with Professor Dwight Waldo, a leading authority on public administration, Woodrow Wilson International Center for Scholars, February 19, 1980. See also Leonard D. White, *The Republican Era, 1869–1901; A Study in Administrative History* (New York: Macmillan, 1958).

6. In 1890 Langford published a narration of this episode in Montana history in a book entitled *Vigilante Days and Ways* (Chicago: A. C. McClurg & Co., 1912).

7. Letter to author from Mr. Robert Budd, who at the time (November 20, 1969) was working on a biography of Langford.

8. R. G. 48, ADLS, Cowan, Acting Secretary, to Langford, May 10, 1872.

9. "Nathaniel Pitt Langford," *Dictionary of American Biography,* Vol. 10, 592–93: "During this period he protected the Park from numerous attempts at unscrupulous

exploitation, and he was thus largely responsible for what it is today." The record simply does not substantiate this statement. For letters see R. G. 48, PMLR, Langford to Secretary Columbus Delano, May 20, 1872; PMLS, Cowan to Langford, May 25, 1872. Langford claimed to have made four "extended explorations of the Park" while he was superintendent. PMLR, Langford to Senator Vest, January 15, 1883.

10. Bartlett, *Great Surveys of the American West,* 64–69. Langford's recommendations are in R. G. 48, PMLR, Langford to Secretary Delano, February 3, 1873; Delegate Clagett to Delano, November 7, 1873; and in Langford's *Annual Report for 1872.* His mention of Folsom is in PMLS, Langford to Delano, November 7, 1873.

11. House Exec. Doc. No. 147, 43d Cong., 1st Sess. (1874), and HR 2177, 43rd Cong., 1st Sess., in PMLS, 1874.

12. PMLS, Secretary Schurz to Langford, April 1, 1877.

13. *American Biographical History of Eminent and Self Made Men . . . Michigan Volume* (Cincinnati: Western Biographical Publishing Co., 1878) Part I, 106–8. See also John S. Gray, "Last Rites for Lonesome Charley Reynolds," *Montana: The Magazine of Western History,* Vol. 13, No. 3 (Summer, 1963), 40–51, and "P. W. Norris and Yellowstone," *Montana* Vol. 22, No. 3 (July, 1872), 54–63. I have consulted the Norris papers in the Henry E. Huntington Library, San Marino, California. Norris's poetry appears in Philetus Norris, *The Calumet of the Coteau* (Philadelphia: J. B. Lippincott & Co., 1883). Hard to believe, but it went into a second edition!

14. Strahorn, *Fifteen Thousand Miles By Stage,* 275–78.

15. Quoted in J. V. Brower, *The Missouri River and Its Utmost Source* (Minneapolis: Harrison and Smith, 1893), 22.

16. Norris tells of his failure to enter the park with Federick Bottler in 1870 in *The Calumet of the Coteau,* 237. See also Letter No. 18, Norris Papers, Huntington Library. The Norris Papers consist of tattered scrapbooks and clippings of his many letters bearing the title, "The Great West." Some pages are numbered; many are not. Sometimes the best identification is the number given by Norris to each of his letters. Yet even this breaks down occasionally because a letter will be unnumbered.

17. See Gray, "Last Rites," and Norris Papers, 63–65.

18. Norris Papers, Letters 21 and 22.

19. Norris, *Calumet of the Coteau,* p. 189; Gray, "Last Rites," 47.

20. Norris Papers, unnumbered; *Calumet of the Coteau,* 188.

21. Norris Papers, 50–52; *Calumet of the Coteau,* 61.

22. Norris Papers; Norris, "Annual Report . . . for 1877," in *Annual Report of the Secretary of the Interior for 1877* (Washington: G. P. O., 1878), 839–40.

23. "Annual Report . . . for 1877," 843.

24. Joseph Schafer, *Carl Schurz, Militant Liberal* (Evansville, Wis.: Antes Press, 1930), 215. The legislative history of the park in these years is condensed in Louis C. Cramton, *Early History of the Yellowstone National Park and Its Relation to National Park Policies* (Washington: G. P. O., 1932), 37–51. Schurz's estimate of needs for 1878 is found in House Exec. Doc. No. 75, 45th Cong. 2d Sess. It included a resolution passed by the American Association for the Advancement of Science as well as a statement from Dr. F. V. Hayden, in which he said that at the time of the passage of the original park bill he had to promise not to request money for the park for a number of years. The statement is puzzling: no explanation for it has appeared in any of the papers I have examined.

25. PMLR, Preliminary Report, Norris to Secretary Schurz, November 10, 1878; Norris, "Annual Report . . . for 1879."

26. Ibid.

27. See Norris's Reports for 1878, 1879, and 1880.

28. Unless otherwise indicated, the remaining material on Norris is from his Annual Reports for 1878, 1879, and 1880.

29. *Haynes Guide,* 62d Edition (1962), 154.

30. See Bartlett, *Nature's Yellowstone,* 132–36.

31. For the Crow Treaty see Charles J. Kappler, *Indian Affairs: Laws and Treaties* (Washington: G. P. O., 1903–1929), four vols., Vol. 2, "Treaties," 1008.

32. PMLR, "Preliminary Report for 1880."

33. PMLR, "Preliminary Report for 1881."

34. In addition to Norris's Annual Reports, see PMLR, "Preliminary Reports" for 1878 and 1881.

35. PMLR, Norris to Schurz, June 9, 1880; Ibid., Norris to Assistant Secretary Bell, July 12, August 26, 1880; Ibid., Norris to Schurz, September 20, 1880; Ibid., Norris to Bell, October 13, 1880; Ibid., Norris to Schurz, October 20, 1880, ADLR, Everts to Norris, February 2, 1881.

36. ADLR, Colin Campbell to Norris, February 20, 1881; H. B. Calfee (a Bozeman photographer) to Norris, March 1, 1881; Senator Dawes to Secretary Kirkwood, March 31, 1881; Governor Dennison to Kirkwood, March 29, 1881.

37. *Enterprise,* September 19, 1885.

CHAPTER EIGHT

Conger, Carpenter, and Wear

*O*n April 1, 1882, when Pat Conger succeeded Philetus Norris as superintendent, Yellowstone was just a decade and a month old. Considering its remoteness, the severe economic depression that slowed progress from 1873 until 1878, and the haphazard way in which the central government dealt with it, the first national park had advanced steadily from an intriguing place to read about to a locality visited more and more by the rich, the powerful, and even the common people.

Then, as can happen with people, the park encountered a short period of drastic change. The years 1882 to 1886 were such a time for Yellowstone and its environs. Some of the changes were good and some bad; many were permanent. Yellowstone as a place to visit would never be quite the same.

When Conger took over, the depressed years of the 1870s had passed and the nation's economy was booming. Although in July 1882 the Northern Pacific was still a hundred miles from what would be its nearest point to the park, its farsighted executives had already platted a townsite east of Bozeman on the banks of the Yellowstone River. The community, named Livingston after a railroad official, was an immediate success. By New Year's day, 1883, it was a permanent community of hard-working citizens. By June the population had reached 2,000.

With an eye on Yellowstone park as a source of profit, hardly had the Northern Pacific reached Livingston before officials ordered construction of a branch line to the park boundary. The Park Branch Line took as its insignia the Chinese monad, a perfect example of which found in nature is the meandering Trout Creek in Yellowstone's Hayden Valley.

All this activity prompted certain wide-awake Montanans to search out a site near the park boundary, claim the land, and lay out town lots. Soon the frontier community of Gardiner sprouted along the banks of the upper Yellowstone. Later survey was to reveal its main street to be the northern boundary of the park. By June 1883, it boasted 200 citizens. Everyone expected Gardiner to be the terminus of the Park Branch Line.

Then trouble arose. A local character named "Buckskin Jim" Cutler insisted he had a claim on lands across the railroad's right-of-way. While litigation dragged on, and old Buckskin remained adamant as a Rocky Mountain jackass, the railroad gave up on Gardiner and platted Cinnabar three miles downstream as the Park Branch terminus. Not until June 1902 did the rails finally reach Gardiner; somehow during the intervening years the town maintained its existence.

In the early eighties Cooke City citizens had great hopes also. When Jay Cooke, Jr. visited the district one winter, local boosters shoveled away eight to ten feet of snow in order to display the rich ore veins. It was this enthusiasm that spurred demands for a railroad through the park to the New World Mining District, of which Cooke City was a part.[1]

Even Virginia City on the west, with its era of mining glory at an end, boasted a population of hundreds, including energetic, straw-hatted Chinese who were busily processing the stream gravels to cull the last tiny flakes of gold from the already heavily worked gulches. An increasing percentage of park tourists was coming in by way of Virginia City.

Only on the Wyoming sides of the park was there continued isolation, and yet even from these directions and east one heard of ambitious plans for railroad construction into the park. Moreover, the Wyoming territorial legislature was keenly aware of the potential value of the reservation.[2]

Such increased activity in the park area meant more action in Yellowstone. Railroad and mining interests commenced lobbying for rights to invade the park. In 1882 the big hotel syndicate entered into park affairs. Tourists did not wait for an ideal time but flocked in before adequate facilities existed to take care of them. Vandalism was rampant. Killing of animals for profit, especially elk and buffalo, continued.

Strong administration was essential if the park was to withstand this abundance of problems, but Congress revealed only a half-hearted awareness of need. It belatedly provided the superintendents with ten assistants. An army engineer was assigned the task of constructing a road system which in its routing is almost identical to that which exists today. The Wyoming territorial legislature, for judicial purposes, embraced the park into Uinta County, placing two constables and two justices of the peace there and providing a schedule of fines for violations. Haphazardly, improvements and changes were being made in Yellowstone.

In Washington corruption was flagrant. Interior, always a bureau heavily tainted with politics, did not improve at all. Secretary Samuel J. Kirkwood was replaced by Henry M. Teller whose ambition seemed to be to give away all of the West that remained in the public domain. Both appointed park superintendents on the basis of politics; so too did Lucius Q. C. Lamar under President Cleveland, although his choices were somewhat better. The secretaries were empowered to choose the assistant superintendents, as sorry a bunch of incompetents as could be displayed to demonstrate what was wrong with the spoils system. In addition, there was talk of a corrupt ring operating in the department. Such a group was said to be dominated by Northern Pacific interests and their hotel monopoly cohorts. Although most of its influence had been in the General Land Office, the railroad's hotel interests were involved in Yellowstone business.[3]

Such a condition in Washington, just when the railroad was approaching the reservation and visitation was accelerating, hardly bode well for the park. Neither was it a favorable situation for the superintendents. True, they were politically chosen and theoretically in harmony with policies set in Washington; yet they emphatically were not always a part of departmental corruption. Even though politically appointed, some of them expected to administer their charge with integrity and dedication. Some, of course, were simply incompetent. Their story, and that of the assistants, is sometimes tragic, occasionally amusing, but rarely were their actions beneficial to the park. It is also a commentary on why a civil service was becoming necessary. Political influence might still be sufficient to obtain employment, but it no longer was adequate to handle the position once it was gained.

So restricted were superintendents by the limited powers granted them, so poorly were they supported by Washington, and so overwhelming were their problems that only men of unusual managerial abilities could have coped successfully with the situation. Anyone with lesser capabilities was foredoomed to failure. Patrick H. Conger (April 1, 1882–September 9, 1884), and Robert E. Carpenter (September 10, 1884–June 30, 1885) were most ordinary mortals; the third, David M. Wear (July 1, 1885–August 20, 1886), gave indications of administrative ability but was yanked out of his job before he could prove himself.

Patrick Henry Conger was sixty-two years old when he received his appointment as Yellowstone superintendent. He was a native of Vermont, but had gone West and settled in Dubuque, Iowa. He served six months in the Civil War and was for four years the agent at the Yankton Indian Agency, where he was known as "Major" Conger. From there he went to Yellowstone as superintendent.[4]

Pat's brother was Edwin Hurd Conger, a prominent Iowa Republican, a Congressman, and later a diplomat of some note, who certainly helped him into his job. Incidentally, another Iowa Congressman, David B. Henderson, had a brother in Yellowstone busily staking out a small empire. Secretary

Kirkwood was also an Iowan. So too was Senator William B. Allison who wrote President Arthur in Conger's behalf. "He [Conger] is eminently qualified for the place," said Allison, "and there are reasons personal to ourselves which make it important to us that this appointment should be made and we will thank you to consider it favorably." On February 3 Conger was telegraphed of his appointment at a salary of $1,500 a year.[5]

Just exactly what Conger accomplished in 1882 is a mystery. Surely he got the lay of the land. Six months after he assumed office a forest fire raged out of control between Swan Lake and Mammoth Hot Springs. Before the inferno burned itself out, the dense evergreen forests of Snow Pass, Limestone Cliffs, and Sheepeater Mountain were reduced to "a black and charred desert."

Protests against park management began to surface toward the end of the summer. On a grand tour through the park in 1882, General Sheridan was appalled at the spoliation of the thermal areas, the campfires left unextinguished, the litter, and the destruction of game animals by skin hunters. *The Nation* took cognizance of his complaint, suggesting that "all things considered, it would probably be best to put the park under the supervision of the War Department. . . ."[6]

In addition to grappling with an inadequate policing situation, the hard-pressed superintendent had to deal with the hotel monopoly that was constructing the big building at Mammoth Hot Springs. He had recommended against granting the contract, but his views had been ignored. Now the company was there. The arrogance of its agents as they violated rules and rushed construction of the hotel left little doubt in Conger's mind that they felt safe from rebuke in Washington. The aging superintendent was in a dilemma: if he adhered to high principles of public service he would antagonize his superiors in Interior; if he cooperated with the company, he was betraying his nation and compromising his own integrity.[7]

All was not lost, however, for Yellowstone's guardians in Congress, led by Senator George Graham Vest, exposed the hotel "steal." The senator also obtained a $40,000 appropriation for the fiscal year 1883, including a raise in the superintendent's salary to $2,000 and provision for ten assistant superintendents to be paid $900 a year. These aides were to preside year round in Yellowstone and "protect the game, timber, and objects of interest therein." Those chosen were to be "inured to that climate, mountaineers and trappers who are used to that northwest country." Finally, Senator Vest added a provision to the bill that if in need, the secretary of interior could request aid from the secretary of war to secure the park.[8]

Hardly had the bill passed before Interior's Applications Division was flooded with requests for the assistant superintendent positions. These ranged from the pitiful plea of a preacher for a son in advanced stages of tuberculosis to unemployed Civil War veterans who fought on the "right" side. "Sir," began a typical letter, "I wish to address you in behalf of an old soldier and comrade of the late war who bears the marks of an honorable war record upon his person in the loss of one eye, and other wounds of his body. . . ."

It will be recalled that Senator Vest had spoken of these employees being mountaineers and trappers used to the country, but such was the cupidity and political orientation of Secretary Teller that not a single one of the first eight assistants came from the Northwest. One observer described them as "weather-beaten politicians . . . the abomination of the natives for they wore 'boiled shirts and frills.' Evidently," he added, "they were sent there to die but I believe even the bears wouldn't have them probably because they did not like whiskey cured bacon."[9]

Secretary Teller appointed William C. Cannon, nephew of "Uncle Joe" Cannon who was a power in the House, and Samuel S. Erret, a relative of influential Senator Logan of Illinois. He chose G. L. Henderson, already the postmaster at Mammoth and brother of Representative David B. Henderson of Iowa. Political connections of the others are not so clear, but politics obviously guided all choices. Samuel D. Leech, the minister's son, was suffering from advanced stages of consumption. Three others initially hired were William Chambers, Jr., James H. Dean, and Edmund Isaac Fish. Of these seven only G. L. Henderson was competent by experience and location; a year or two earlier he had moved to Yellowstone from Iowa. His park business interests often conflicted with regulations, his large family included young adults seeking ways to make a living, and his quarrels with Conger reduced his value. An eighth choice was a good one. This was D. E. Sawyer, a Minnesota merchant suffering from tuberculosis. His health improved in Yellowstone and he proved himself a man of dedication and competence. From 1883 to 1886 assistants were hired upon the resignation or discharge of others, and an effort was made to keep the force at the allotted ten.[10]

Superintendent Conger was not consulted on the selections (save to rubber stamp Henderson's appointment), nor were the assistants held subordinate to him. They considered themselves responsible for their actions only to the secretary. In June poor Conger wrote Teller: "Having learned by the papers that you have made the appointments . . . I venture to ask you to define specifically their duties and powers." Was he expected to furnish subsistence and quarters? If so, Conger suggested that this be in the form of a cash allowance to each man. And to serve well, that man would need mounts. Was there provision for the purchase of horses? The men should be stationed at different points in the park, he added, but at present there were no quarters available.[11]

Congress had failed to provide funds for housing, clothing, or a way for the assistants to get around the park. Not until the end of the summer, when it was clear that the army engineers would not use their share of the $40,000 for roads, did Teller instruct the superintendent to purchase horses and build cabins for the assistants. In the meantime Conger housed some in the blacksmith shop at Mammoth and others in "an old shanty" in the Upper Firehole Basin. For a time he housed Sawyer in his own residence. For provisions the assistants used their own funds and until September, if an assistant had a horse, he had rented or purchased it with his own money. [12]

It is hard to believe that such haphazard beginnings evolved into the sound, workable concept of a ranger force. While most assistants were incompetent, two or three understood the task and by trial and error fashioned a routine of policing the park. This step forward came hesitantly and slowly but progress was made; the methodology was improved upon, first by the army and then by the Park Service. Here are some fragmentary career histories of a few assistants, mostly bad but occasionally good:

William Cannon was arrogant and insubordinate. At Yellowstone he took to a kind of life that included cards and whiskey. He caused trouble for three superintendents—Conger, Carpenter, and Wear. With the intervention of his "Uncle Joe," Cannon was, however, retained in office until April 18, 1886. [13]

William Chambers did not last long. He was probably the assistant who would not allow a Gardiner citizen to collect dead firewood in the park unless the wood gatherer gave him every fourth load. In December Conger requested Teller to dismiss him. He was "not attentive to his duties," he brought "reproach upon the Service by his vicious habits and disreputable associations," and he "drinks and gambles wherever there is opportunity to do so. . . ." The man pleaded for his job, but Teller fired him. [14]

Samuel S. Erret, Senator Logan's nephew, was another dismal failure although he was not discharged until the summer of 1886. As early as February 1884, he was charged with having accepted elk meat plus five dollars to keep silent about a poacher's activities. Conger, aware of Erret's connection in Washington, wrote his uncle: "I am very sorry to say to you that I think Mr. Erret to be a very worthless and bad man. He is guilty of the gross neglect of every official duty and of every act of insubordination and disrespect for his Superior officers that his small mind can conceive." The principal trouble involved a woman, which was doubly bad since Erret was married and the father of a baby girl. Erret denied having relations with this "woman of ill repute," and then accused Conger of allowing seven livery stables to operate illegally in the park, as well as "a fancy house near the Improvement [Company] Ice House." [15]

Samuel D. Leech, the consumptive son of a minister, penned his resignation on September 29, 1883. His father had written from Albany, New York, anticipating the young man's move and requesting Secretary Teller to refuse the relinquishment. Meanwhile the sick fledgling, who had suffered several hemorrhages, had left the park. "I have no knowledge of his whereabouts," Conger wrote Teller, adding that the young man was unfit for the task due to his health and immaturity.[16]

Among the assistants were gradations leading toward competence. Edmund Isaac Fish, along with another assistant, J. W. Weimer, was housed for a time in a deserted squatter's cabin in Lamar Valley. Most of Fish's correspondence concerns poaching, flagrant violations of regulations, and his chagrin at the lack of penalties or provisions for strong enforcement. He wrote that he could do nothing at the time about a particularly bold poacher, "but," he added irritably, "if we could be empowered to enforce the laws I should dearly love to snatch the son of a *Bitch* bald headed."[17] (italics Fish's)

James H. Dean of Maryland remained on the job until June 30, 1885. His reports reveal a good understanding of his duties and a conscientious effort to carry them out. From his headquarters at Norris Basin he described a typical day. "Each morning I look over the geyser basins, observe the actions of tourists, remove all debris that may be thrown in, . . . I then proceed to Gibbon Meadows . . . giving my attention to campfires that may have been left burning . . . returning to my quarters about noon." His morning tour was eleven miles, his afternoon patrol ten miles, "making in all twenty-one miles each day."

Dean found timbers and stones wedged so tightly into the geysers and springs that he had to enlist the aid of others to remove them. "In every possible instance," Dean reported, "I warned visitors not to leave their campfires burning, with some this warning had effect, with many it had none, judging from the large number I extinguished." And there were other troubles. "The shooting of game, rather than the shooting at it, by tourists, is their delight," he observed. At Mammoth he found cattle owned by the hotel company running all over the formations. This hard-working assistant ended one of his letters with a prophetic suggestion: "Let the military have charge of the park."[18]

He realized that the crying deficiency was the lack of jurisdiction to levy penalties save confiscating the offender's outfit. Although the rules and regulations were now handed out in pamphlet form, and the muslin signs that Norris initiated were tacked at busy places all over the park, the populace had to learn the meaning of "don't touch," a discipline that was slow to form. A continuing educational crusade was necessary.

Another above-average assistant was Josiah Washington Weimer, a college graduate who had served as state representative in the Kansas legislature. While in Yellowstone he usually patrolled the Upper Basin where he found the tourists' desire to abuse the geysers a "temptation unabating and determined." Still a young man, he commented cryptically upon his bachelor's life in the park. "Stagnated celibacy is yet too prevalent," he wrote. "Men make their own hell and Jackasses are plenty in the dude season."[19]

The best of the assistants was D. E. Sawyer. It was he who found fish killed by explosives in the Lamar River and traced the culprits to the hotel company; he also knew that at one time more than a ton of elk meat was in the company's ice house. However, since hotel officials boasted of a permit from Secretary Teller and since there was no law whereby Sawyer could make arrests for the killing of game, he had to let them go. When Sawyer was dismissed in July 1885, special investigator W. Hallett Phillips telegraphed Secretary Lamar that this man was the "most efficient of all assistants . . . invaluable for work in the park." Even the *Enterprise* said that Sawyer "deserved to be excepted" from the criticism leveled at most of them.[20]

One assistant was in a class by himself. George L. Henderson had already resided at Mammoth Hot Springs one or two years with his substantial family, including four grown daughters and a son. When he gave up his postmastership, a position he held thanks to his politician brother, that post was assumed by daughter Lillie while George became one of the assistants. From the very first Conger and Henderson disliked each other. That Henderson had occupied the headquarters building and was assuming Conger's powers did not endear him to the newly arrived superintendent.[21]

The Conger-Henderson feud lasted until Conger was removed, though within a year Henderson lost his assistantship also. Although it is hard to read the accusations and counteraccusations without disliking Henderson, the man is of historical significance in Yellowstone's development. He was, perhaps, Yellowstone's first "interpreter," or surely its second after Norris. Henderson explained, described, visualized, and gave names to things. He made Mammoth Hot Springs a lot more interesting. He understood the psyche of the increasing number of tourists coming in by rail. He knew they had come to "see the elephant," and G. L. Henderson prettied up Jumbo and gave him a name.

He approached Yellowstone's wonders like a child lying on a windswept hill, imagining figures in the cumulus clouds above. He installed progressive trails leading from one wonder to another, with explanatory signs along the way. At Mammoth, for example, he and Samuel Erret placed a ladder into Mammoth Cave "making it accessible to all who wish to explore this beautiful and unique formation which resembles a gigantic shell with white, flinty walls inhabited by thousands of bats. . . . We also put guide boards indicating the direction and distance to White Sulphur Spring Valley. A similar guide board was put up at the entrance of the White Elephant's body which we found to be nearly 200 yards in length and 400 yards from the forehead to the Mammoth Cave which is at the extreme north end of the trunk." He and Erret also explored some caverns, including a few located up

Sulphur Spring Valley, one of which had an "arched roof" covered with a magnesium crust "as white as snow." In another, there was a pool of water, with scum that was "brilliant crimson." The figures and the names were all of Henderson's imagination.[22]

Practical, crotchety Pat Conger believed such activities the work of a lunatic. In a letter requesting Henderson's removal, he included the man's report containing some of his purple descriptions. The superintendent suggested that when read, they would give "some idea of the man. Seven pages of stuff and not one word of information of any pertinence or importance."[23]

But it was Conger who was wrong. People love fantasy. They accepted the nomenclature of formations to whet the imagination. Only with the coming of the motorcar and the hurried three-day park tour did much of the fantasy disappear and the nomenclature fall into disuse. Yet today if one visits a theme park and observes apparently adult humans standing patiently in line in 95-degree heat and 95 percent humidity to visit a haunted house or a pirate land, one is reminded that the indulgence of fantasy is restricted to no era and no age.

When he was dismissed, Henderson expressed his feeling to such in, L. Q. C. Lamar: "If I am succeeded," he concluded, "by one who will do more to comprehend the marvels and interpret them to the thousands who annually visit these sacred precincts I shall rejoice and will avail myself of his labors and if possible secure his friendship." The *Enterprise* dubbed him the godfather of the park. "He has affixed characteristics and lasting names to every feature of interest in the park and has done more than any one person to inform the world of its peculiarly wonderful and beautiful features," the paper commented.[24]

Henderson was also beyond his time in comprehending the necessity of people control. He advocated the widest use of printed circulars and guideposts. When nearly three years elapsed before the Teller regime sent out new circulars, Henderson gritted his teeth and did his best with what he had. He endeavored to meet all parties coming in, informing them fully of rules and regulations. He interviewed the leaders or guide to each party, and "especially sought to impress upon them the importance of extinguishing campfires each night, and before leaving camp." He expressed in writing his approval of such competent guides as Elwood Hofer and a man named Crowel from Bozeman. And he understood the need for good statistics: "Since Saturday, June 28, 1884, twenty-nine parties of tourists have visited the park. . . . The whole not including guides was seventy. . . ." He also reported on park conditions, especially on the roads.[25]

From 1883 until the army took over in 1886 there were other assistants, for as a group they were an unstable lot, with resignations and dismissals common. Notably absent from their ranks were knowledgeable mountain men, although Superintendent Wear managed to hire Jack Baronett despite the man's lack of American citizenship. Henry Klamer, another mountain man who subsequently became a concessionaire, applied in 1884 but was passed over. Even "Uncle John" Yancey, who ran the hostelry at Pleasant Valley, was attracted to the $900 a year and the small bit of authority. "I resid here in the Park and no the trails and passes that hunter come in and go out I am wel satisfied I can be grait help in saving gaim," he wrote in a tortuous punishment of English. "This is the first time I ever ast for a Federal offic I have all my lifetime been a Democrat I suppose you wil no that when you see my name."[26]

Although they varied from dishonest sots to mature innnovators, in the balance most of the assistants were failures. "Quite a number are boys under age and a prairie wolf would frighten them out of their boots," one man wrote. One of Conger's defenders described them as "a lot of poor relations and hangers-on of officials. . . .These employees are . . . utterly incompetent . . . a couple of cowboys could put the whole brigade to flight with blank cartridges." The *Enterprise,* sizing them up after nearly two years, agreed that "there were some good men among them but as a whole they have proven very unsatisfactory."[27]

Yet the assistants, sorry as they were, made a distinct contribution. The concept of some kind of security force working in the park, making accustomed rounds and keeping track of tourists took root. The idea was followed by the army and adapted immediately upon the transfer of park security to the National Park Service. As noted above, Assistant G. L. Henderson made his own distinct contributions in the realm of interpretation and people management.

Pat Conger simply had the cards stacked against him. Senator Vest, George Bird Grinnell, and Arnold Hague were watching park developments and were ever alert for signs of favoritism, incompetence, and maladministration; the railroad was bringing in tourists, with the greatest assortment of Very Important Persons in park history appearing there in 1883; an arrogant gang of monopolists was attempting to preempt all powers, with plans under way for a road building program administered by the army engineers; and no penalties were levied for infractions save the confiscation of equipment. After his ouster, Conger lamented that "an order from the Secretary or the Superintendent [in the park] . . . is just about as effective as the Pope's bull to the comet."[28]

His greatest problem, one he may never have understood fully, was the ambivalent attitude of his superiors, Secretary Teller, Assistant Secretary Joslyn, and Edmund Dawson, chief clerk of the Interior Department. Intentionally or not, these three had led the Northern Pacific and hotel monopolists to believe that they had carte blanche to do whatever they wished to get their monopoly in Yellowstone functioning profitably.

The monopolists became reckless and desperate after their "park grab" was exposed. Conger tried to enforce the rules; the hotel men defied him, while high officials in Interior played politics, vacillating according to the winds of criticism and pressure. One of Conger's few defenders wrote of how "the gang of sharks who have already their clutches on the park . . . [want him] . . . replaced by one who will more pliantly bend to their will. . . ." The *Enterprise* said that "He interfered with the monopolizing power over the park they assumed to possess. He was a restraining influence which they could not control, and therefore they sought to get rid of him, and spared no effort, however low and despicable, to compass that end." On July 12, 1884, Teller requested Conger's resignation "in view of the unsatisfactory condition of affairs in the park and the improbability of improvement under present conditions . . . ."[29]

His resignation took effect on the arrival of his successor, who appeared on September 9 or 10, 1884. Even as he packed, however, Major Conger could take some solace in his accomplishments. He had completed a building for the superintendents at Mammoth—Norris's bastion being considered uninhabitable—and another at Norris, and had built some stables. He ended his final report with bitterness: "I have been maliciously, unjustly, and falsely assailed by my enemies here, who are the enemies of this park and for the sole and only reason that I sought to protect the interests of the government and the people that I was sworn faithfully to serve." Both Senators Wilson and Allison of Iowa were notified of Conger's dismissal nearly a fortnight before the superintendent knew of it (and there was indication that Hobart, of the Park Company, knew of the dismissal ten days before Conger did.)[30]

The sad state of affairs in Yellowstone Park now got worse. On July 3, 1884, the two senators from Iowa nominated for superintendent Robert E. Carpenter, brother of Cyrus Clay Carpenter, a former Iowa governor and Republican representative to Congress from 1879 until 1883. By September 10 Carpenter was on duty in the park.[31]

Within the month he was quarreling with the assistants and was himself the object of criticism. On the positive side he destroyed several squatter's quarters in the Lamar Valley and some poachers' cabins found nestled in the wilderness. Whatever his character, however true or false the charges brought against him may have been, Robert Carpenter's days were numbered. He was a

Republican and the Democrats won the national election in 1884; hardly had Cleveland settled in the White House before the Democrats were beating the drums for Carpenter's dismissal. "He is an unscrupulous politician," protested a loyal party man, "spending his whole time in packing political conventions and stumping for the Republican ticket. His specialties are his brother . . . and Senator Allison." Moreover, he had stumped Iowa's 10th Congressional ticket "and his main hobby was 'Maria Halpine,' ridiculing [Cleveland's] personal appearance, in a manner that was revolting to civilization."[32]

During the winter of 1884–85 Carpenter left Yellowstone for the comforts of Washington, D. C. There he was in constant communication with Carroll T. Hobart of the hotel company, living in the same house with him and dining with him. The inevitable inference was that he was connected with the park company. It was said that he had sent the government horses out of the park for the winter, thus making it impossible for the assistants to protect the game. It was rumored that he had pecuniary interests in the park and favored the railroad scheme to segregate the northeast part of the reservation.[33]

Senator Vest, a good Democrat as well as the park's principal defender in the Senate, penned a strong letter to Secretary Lamar. "I have received information recently which satisfies me that unless some change is made in its management, this park will become absolutely worthless for the purposes intended by Congress. . . . During this last winter the game was slaughtered by skin hunters. . . . I beg that in any event some one may be put in the place of Carpenter. His retention in office is equivalent to the destruction of the park."[34]

Carpenter was removed as of May 29, 1885; his successor, chosen by Senator Vest, was Colonel David W. Wear of Missouri. At the time a member of the state senate, Wear was described by his sponsor as a former colonel of a federal regiment, in the prime of life, an outdoor sportsman, "a thoroughly honest man" who would "make an active and intelligent superintendent." Vest said he was willing to be responsible for him.[35]

By no stretch of the imagination had Colonel Wear been offered a political plum, for Yellowstone had become a national subject. Before entraining for his post, Wear was called to Washington for consultation with Secretary Lamar and President Cleveland. "If you don't take care of the park," said Cleveland, "I shall have to turn you out." At least this was how the press reported it, giving the impression that the new administration was desirous of preserving Yellowstone Park.[36]

Wear appears to have received excellent indoctrination in Washington. At St. Paul he was joined by Arnold Hague, who no doubt furnished him with still more information during the long hours en route. On July 1, 1885, Wear arrived and took control; on July 2 he wrote his first letter to

Secretary Lamar. The assistants, he told him, were "old, worn out, and utterly unfit . . . a change of the entire force would be beneficial." And Wear did dismiss a number of them. He wanted his new men to be from the West—"sober men—truthful, brave, and well versed in woods or mountain craft. . . ," and he hired several such persons, including Jack Baronett.[37]

By August the change in park security was already apparent. The *Enterprise* reported that he was "making a determined effort to re-instate law and order. . . ." but followed with an ominous comment: "Colonel Wear . . . has therefore invited wholesale criticism." The hotel company, led by Hobart, fought him tooth and nail while the citizenry outside the park resented his clamp-down on poaching, timber-cutting, and other freedoms they were accustomed to exercising within the reservation.[38]

Then "help" came from an unexpected source. Wyoming's territorial legislature took upon itself the responsibility for park law enforcement. After soliciting advice from Secretary Teller, the legislators on March 6, 1884, passed a law providing for protection of the park by the Territory of Wyoming.[39]

Briefly, the act empowered the governor to appoint two justices of the peace and two constables "for the said precinct of the Yellowstone National Park in said county of Uinta. . . ." Each j.p. was to receive $300 a year and each constable $400, plus all fees. As the system evolved, the constable and j.p. split the fines fifty-fifty.[40]

Interior Department investigator W. Hallett Phillips found some provisions in the legislation commendable; unfortunately other sections conflicted with Interior Department regulations while other parts were "highly ridiculous." Section 7 of the Wyoming act, for example, made it unlawful for any person to remove any part, portion or particle of the natural curiosities or objects of interest, or anything whatever, and imposed a fine of $100 or imprisonment in the county jail for up to six months for violations thereof.[41]

Regardless of its doubtful legality (for here was a territory making and enforcing its own laws on a federal reservation), the new statute became operational. The governor appointed two constables and two j.p.s, one each for Mammoth Hot Springs and the Lower Geyser Basin. When Wear took over in July 1885, the assistant prosecuting attorney for Uinta County wrote him that the men offered their services "as a prompt legal engine to . . . aid you in your arduous and at times, rather unpleasant duty in protection of the Park from the encroachment of settlers and the ambition of some tourists and others to kill buffalo or elk." It should be added that Wear's federally paid assistants could also participate in Wyoming's brand of law enforcement.[42]

Colonel Wear saw that all were kept busy. His mountaineer assistant, Ed Wilson, arrested George Reader and John Ferguson at the Falls. They had in their possession four hindquarters of elk and eight beaver skins. Ferguson paid a seventy-five-dollar fine and costs and Reader paid $100 and spent six months in the Uinta County jail at Evanston. Stephen Alpin of the U.S. Geological Survey was charged with killing one of the largest bison in the park, for which he was fined fifty dollars plus costs. The *Enterprise* commented that the arrests had had a salutary effect. "During our recent trip we had the frequent privileges of seeing large flocks of ducks and geese remain fearlessly in the streams and ponds while their human enemies passed close beside them. A litter of otters exhibited the same carelessness at our approach and did not cease their gambols. Fresh signs of elk and antelope were often seen. . . ."[43]

The constables were also strict in enforcing regulations against fires. Assistant Godfrey arrested two prominent Bozeman citizens who were fined in spite of Arnold Hague and lawyer Phillips acting as character witnesses. The authorities were also guilty of enforcing too strictly Section 7, which Phillips labeled "Draconian" legislation. They arrested some prominent Philadelphians for picking up obsidian chips along the public road. Fine: five dollars. Other visitors "of the highest respectability, ladies and gentlemen, were arrested for picking up small pieces of the formation of the Hot Springs, and were likewise fined."[44]

It was inevitable that the park's zealous protectors were going to arrest the wrong party; the day was August 17, 1885. Judge Lewis E. Payson, an Illinois Congressman, was charged with leaving his campfire unextinguished. He was one of a party of eleven which included Joseph Medill, editor of the powerful *Chicago Tribune*. Although they were sure they had doused their fire, an assistant named Joe Keeney reported to "Judge" Hall, justice of the peace at the geyser basins, that a fire was still blazing at the Payson campground. Hall issued a warrant for the culprits' arrest. Warrant in hand, Keeney galloped after the party, bringing them to justice, Yellowstone style.

Everyone except the assistant testified in Judge Payson's defense while tempers frazzled. Payson asked "Judge" Hall where he got his authority, and then, where did the Territory of Wyoming get *its* authority, since Yellowstone was a national park under federal jurisdiction? Hall, possibly flustered, adjourned court for thirty minutes to confer with assistant Keeney. His decision: sixty dollars "for the ember that was found," and $12.80 costs.

Judge Payson refused to pay a cent. He denounced the decision as outrageous and ridiculous and insisted on paying bond and appealing the case. After more discussion, the fine was reduced from sixty to ten dollars and the costs from $12.80 to four dollars. Again Judge Payson refused to pay. To which Hall replied, "Judge Payson. . . you pay me $1 for the fine and whatever you consider right, for the costs." And Judge Payson countered, "Not one cent for a fine, but I am willing to pay for the trouble that the alleged constable has been put to." This was done, and the party turned homeward. "Judge" Hall and the assistant assumed the matter to be settled.

However, Joseph Medill, a man of words, delivered a biting denunciation of "Judge" Hall who, he said, was a former woodcutter. He called that "most wise and upright judge" a "damned old Dogberry." Not knowing the word, "Judge" Hall demanded a dictionary,* "doubtless," speculated a reporter for the *Enterprise,* "with the intention of fastening a charge of malicious slander or abusive language on Mr. Medill." The reporter chortled over "Judge" Hall's ignorance. "If Mr. Hall," he wrote, "has not yet laid the foundation of his case we commend him to a story called 'Much Ado About Nothing' by a writer of some repute named William Shakespeare, since deceased, for an explanation of the offensive epithet as well as for a very faithful mirror of the administration of justice at Norris Basin."[45]

At Mammoth, Colonel Wear fired Joe Keeney "and said that Justice Hall would receive the same medicine." But in his annual report the following December, Wear noted that the only protection he had been able to give the park had been through the territorial laws of Wyoming which, he added, were of questionable validity; he suggested that Congress furnish the legal machinery for the park.[46]

Certainly visitors were learning that laws were in force and penalities for violation would be levied. "The arrests made," commented the *Enterprise,* "have had a salutary effect. To extinguish his fire is now the aim of the most careless camper in the park." Even so the lesson came slowly. Wear stated in his annual report that his men had doused more than sixty fires.[47]

Political reverberations from the Payson incident were devastating. In a staunchly partisan era in which Republicans were "out" for the first time in twenty-four years, and Judge Payson and editor Medill were Republicans while Wear and Lamar were Democrats, incidents such as this one created waves all the way to Washington.[48]

In still another situation politics and the park emerged: assistants Erret and Cannon, nephews of Senator Logan and "Uncle Joe" Cannon respectively, still hung on even though their benefactors were Republicans. Logan and Joe Cannon were so powerful that Secretary Lamar urged Colonel Wear to toler-

*To save readers of our less educated generation a trip to Webster's Unabridged, Dogberry is an ignorant, foolish constable in Shakespeare's *Much Ado About Nothing.* It is a commentary upon our times and theirs that Joseph Medill should have known the character sufficiently well to apply the name to the ignorant constable who was fining him, and for the editor of the frontier *Enterprise* to also know the meaning.

ate them if at all possible. Wear understood and continued them on the payroll, saying that assistant Cannon had reformed but that he could "never trust Erret." He was, however, allowed to dismiss G. L. Henderson, whom he described as a "notorious character." Henderson's family by now ran a store, the post office, and was building the Cottage Hotel at Mammoth. Halfway through construction they changed the building material from boards, specified in the contract, to logs; Wear thereupon halted construction. The Hendersons seethed. So bad did relations become that Wear asked that his mail be delivered to Gardiner, since he suspected his adversaries of opening his correspondence at the Mammoth post office.[49]

Indeed, the sands of time were running out for David W. Wear's superintendency. National politics over which he had no control constituted a part of his troubles, while the Judge Payson incident reflected upon park administration and indirectly upon him. G. L. Henderson's Congressman brother did whatever harm he could do. The hotel monopolists and railroad promoters detested Wear, and some elements in the surrounding population had turned against him. Yet when the blow came, the form in which it appeared was a surprise to all of Yellowstone's defenders.

In 1883 Senator Vest had inserted a clause in the Sundry Civil Appropriations Bill which had read:

> The Secretary of War, upon the request of the Secretary of the Interior, is hereby authorized and directed to make necessary details of troops to prevent trespassers or intruders from entering the park for the purposes of destroying the game or objects of curiosity therein, for any other purpose prohibited by law, and to remove such persons from the park if found therein.[50]

Until 1886 this statement, like so many in legislation, remained unused, merely written into the law. But in 1886, when Senator Vest examined the appropriations bill for that year, he was shocked to discover that the only clause in it relating to Yellowstone Park provided for $20,000 for road construction under the supervision of an engineering officer; there was no provision for paying the superintendent and his assistants.[51]

Vest immediately moved to add $20,000 for their pay. He explained that three years before he had inserted the provision for troops "in the event that his assistant superintendents were not able to expel from the park the gangs of 'skin hunters' as they were termed, who would go in upon snowshoes and kill two or three hundred elk at once and skin them and leave their carcasses there." He added that he had no doubt that, if the army took over, "it is virtually an end of the Yellowstone National Park."[52]

The senator's Missouri colleague in the House, Representative Joseph O'Neill, carried the fight for the additional appropriation to the floor, defending Wear and his mountaineer assistants. Then G. L. Henderson's brother rose to attack, ridiculing the "mountaineers' from . . . every part of the country (except mountains), many of whom would not know a bear from a jackal or a jack-rabbit from a jackass. [Laughter.] These are the kind of 'mountaineers' that Mr. Wear, the superintendent, is putting in the park." In his tirade he failed to mention that he had a brother plus adult nieces and nephews making a living in the park. Clearly, Representative Henderson won the day, successfully arguing against the amendment granting $20,000 for the continued employment of the superintendent and his assistants.[53]

In the Senate there was also opposition. Senator Preston Plumb of Kansas suggested that the superintendents, so far away from the watchful eye of Congress, "were all tarred with the same stick" of despotism. "It all ought to be lopped off," he suggested of the park, "it ought to be put temporarily in the hands of the War Department . . . until we can devise some plan whereby we can save the curiosities . . . and turn the balance over to the public as a portion of the public domain."[54]

However, the Senate did vote to insist upon the insertion of the $20,000 provision for the superintendent and his staff, but the representatives in conference committee were adamant, the session was drawing to a close, Congress wanted to go home, and the House version prevailed. There was no provision to pay a red cent to the superintendent or his assistants.

When W. Hallett Phillips heard the news, he wrote Lamar urging him to request army aid immediately. "Should the civil force leave, the park will be at the mercy of the vandals of the surrounding country. . . ," he wrote.[55]

Phillips need not have worried, for already Secretary Lamar had contacted William C. Endicott, the secretary of war, quoted to him the pertinent statute, and requested "that a Captain, two Lieutenants and twenty selected mounted men from the Army be detailed for service in the park. . . . I have to request action be taken in the matter at the earliest practical date."[56]

Lamar's request for rapid action was not the reaction of an alarmist. In a telegram dated August 13 Wear reported upon his decline in authority. "Since action of Congress lawlessness in park has rapidly increased on part of lessees and others," he reported, and on August 17 he wired, "THREE LARGE FIRES RAGING IN PARK BEYOND MY CONTROL."[57]

On that very day Captain Moses Harris marched into the reservation with Company "M" of the 1st Cavalry stomping along behind him, unmounted, as their horses had not yet arrived. He led his troops to a point slightly southwest of Capitol Hill and there pitched Camp Sheridan. The army had taken over.

Colonel Wear returned East and into oblivion. However, his brief superintendency (July 1, 1885–August 20, 1886) leads us to believe that Interior, if allowed to continue along the path he was pursuing, could have managed Yellowstone satisfactorily; the thirty-year policing by the United States Army was not necessary. W. Hallett Phillips, in an extensive report, said that "never in the history of the reservation had it been so fully guarded. . . . Colonel Wear proved himself to be an able and energetic officer. . . . Honest, sober, scrupulously conscientious. . . he has done more for the park than all those who preceded him." Arnold Hague also supported Wear.[58]

The superintendent had recruited such a fine group of assistants that one of Captain Harris's first acts was to request authority to hire a number of them as scouts and to teach his soldiers knowledge of the country. With the aid of Wyoming law, Wear had struck fear into the hearts of would-be poachers and spoliators, and it had produced salutary effects.

Conger, Carpenter, and Wear: three superintendents in less than four years added up to administrative failure for the Department of Interior. Perhaps the times had some influence on these developments. Had the hotel monopolists and the railroad interests made their moves a decade earlier, they might have carried their designs and gained control of the park. But by the early 1880s the country was becoming acutely aware of trusts and monopolies, of "the money power." The year following the army assignment in Yellowstone, the act creating the Interstate Commerce Commission was passed (1887); three years later the Sherman Antitrust Act became law. The pressure was on to keep Yellowstone inviolate; it was a small manifestation of a national concern. However, Interior secretaries such as Samuel Kirkwood and Henry Teller were incapable of flowing with the stream of public opinion and instead cooperated with the vested interests. By the administration of Lucius Q. C. Lamar, however, and Colonel Wear's superintendency, the national desire to control monopolies and end government conniving had reached the halls of Congress. The solons saw a quick solution to the Yellowstone mess: call in the army. This they did.

Among some Yellowstone authorities the statement is made that "the army saved the park." To agree with this is to assume that the Interior Department would have plunged from the integrity that characterized L. Q. C. Lamar's administration into a morass of political favoritism and collusion with concessionaire monopolists. Yes, but only to a degree. Most secretaries of interior, while notably lacking in statesmanship and intellectual superiority when measured against other cabinet secretaryships, have been men at least equal to them in integrity. Some have been conservationists surrounded by profiteers. The policies that were pursued by Colonel Wear, with the department supporting him, indicate that Interior would have brought Yellowstone out of its quagmire had not Congress denied it the necessary appropriations. So the army, since it *was* there, receives the credit.

On the other hand, Senator Vest's foreboding predictions that army control would mean an end to the park, that soldiers could never police it, were erroneous. Not only did the military quickly master the geography of the reservation, it also evolved a system of patrol and check stations that gave the park unprecedented protection. Furthermore, Congressman Henderson and the shadowy figures of the hotel monopoly soon discovered that they had exchanged a known assemblage of devils (Wear and his assistants), for an unknown quantity that proved even more difficult to control. The "army way" involved regulations, good, bad, and stupid, and by the Eternal, they were to be enforced, as we shall see.

NOTES TO CHAPTER EIGHT

1. *An Illustrated History of the Yellowstone Valley, Montana.* No author or editor identified. (Spokane: Western Historical Publishing Co., 1908), 149–52, 161–65.

2. According to the 10th Decennial Census (1880), Wyoming Territory had 20,789 residents, while Uinta County, which bordered the park, had risen in population to 1,749 souls in 1880. Montana Territory had 39,159 residents. *Compendium of the Tenth Census,* Vol. 1, 432, 451.

3. Evidence of a "ring" is apparent in a letter from Secretary Kirkwood to an unidentified "Sir." PMLS, August 21, 1881.

4. Isaiah Van Merie, Editor, *History of Black Hawk County, Iowa, and Representative Citizens* (Chicago: Biographical Publishing Co., 1904), 381–82. This is an unreliable sketch but the only one found so far.

5. ADLR, Allison to President Arthur, February 1, 1882; Ibid., Kirkwood to Conger, February 3, 1882.

6. Quoted in *Congressional Record,* 47th Cong., 2d Sess., House, February 23, 1883, 3193. The general made this report to the adjutant general. *The Nation,* Vol. 35, No. 904 (October 26, 1882), 343–44.

7. Conger had opposed the contract. See *Congressional Record,* 47th Cong., 2d Sess., Senate (1883), 3482–88.

8. *Congressional Record,* 47th Cong., 2d Sess., House, February 23, 1883, 3192–94; Ibid., Senate, March 1, 1883, 3482–88.

9. ADLR, R. A. Chandler to Hon. E. N. Morrill, a representative from Kansas, who forwarded the letter to the Interior Department; ADLR, William H. Wiley (the New York publisher) to J. J. Cox, Assistant to Interior Secretary Lamar.

10. ADLR, List of Applications, 1883; ADLR, W. Hallett Phillips to Lamar, telegram of July 27, 1885.

11. *Bozeman Avant Courier,* March 22, 1883; PMLR, Conger to Teller, June 22, 1883; Ibid., July 5, 1884.

12. PMLR, Conger to Teller, June 22, 1883; July 5, 1884; PMLS, Teller to Conger, September 18, 1883.

13. ADLR, Cannon to Assistant Secretary Joslyn, August 1, 1884; Ibid., Cannon to Secretary Lamar, June 5, 1885; Ibid., Wear to Assistant Secretary Muldrow, April 20, 1886.

14. *Enterprise,* December 1, 1883. This could have been an assistant named Terry. Y. A., Item 1570, Terry to Conger, December 11, 1883; Ibid., Item 1566, Terry to Conger, April 19, 1884; ADLR, Conger to Teller, December 13, 1883; ADLS, Teller to Chambers, December 16, 1883. See also Y. A. Item 1346, Chambers to Conger, November 14, 1883, in regard to Conger's charge of gambling.

15. ADLR, J. A. Clark, Deputy U.S. Marshall, to Teller, February 8, 1884; PMLR, George Rice (the alleged poacher and keeper of a house of ill fame in Gardiner) to Teller, no date; PMLR, Conger to Senator Logan, 1884; PMLR, Erret to Joslyn, August 12, 1884. The birth of Erret's daughter is noted in the *Enterprise,* March 29, 1884.

16. ADLR, Leech to Teller, September 29, 1883; Ibid., S. V. Leech (the youth's father) to Teller, September 27, 1883; ADLR, Conger to Teller, November 3, 1883. See also PMLR, Conger to Reverend Leech, July 30, 1883.

17. *Enterprise,* December 1, 1883; Y. A., Item 1420, Fish to Conger, May 12, 1884.

18. Y. A., Item 1356, Dean to Conger, August 4, 1884; Item 1367, Dean to Conger, August 31, 1883; Item 1368, Dean to Conger, July 31, 1883; Item 1354, Dean to Conger, September 3, 1884; Item 1355, Dean to Conger, August 26, 1884.

19. Ibid., Item 1586, Weimer to Conger, August 10, 1884; Item 1587, Weimer to Conger, August 2, 1884; ADLR, Weimer to Alexander Hunter, January 24, 1884.

20. PMLR, Sawyer to Conger, August 5, 1883; Ibid., Sawyer to H. B. Serait, December 23, 1883; Y. A., Item 1553, Sawyer to Conger, September 26, 1883;

Item 1554, Sawyer to Conger, September 12, 1883; ADLR, W. Hallett Phillips to Teller, July 27, 1885; Weekly *Enterprise,* September 25, 1885.

21. *Enterprise,* January 15, 1884. Sale of specimens is mentioned in a letter of B. P. Van Horne to the Interior Secretary, PMLR, February 24, 1884.

22. PMLR, Henderson to Conger, June 16, 1884. All of these places were at Mammoth Hot Springs, but for the most part they have been forgotten. There was also a Cupid's Cave, Devil's Frying Pan, and Sulphur Pit.

23. PMLR, Conger to Teller, July 15, 1884.

24. ADLR, Henderson to Lamar, June 11, 1885; *Enterprise,* June 20, 1885; Henderson subsequently lobbied for the Northern Pacific Railroad.

25. PMLR, Conger to Teller, June 27, 1883; PMLS, Joslyn to Conger, August 3, 1883; Y. A., Item 1453, Henderson to Conger, June 17, 1884; PMLR, Henderson to Conger, January 26, 1884; Y. A., Item 1449, Henderson to Conger, August 2, 1884; Item 1452, Henderson to Conger, July 5, 1884.

26. ADLR, Klamer to Teller, September 4, 1884; Yancey to Lamar, April 4, 1885.

27. PMLR, B. P. Van Horne to Teller, February 24, 1884; Ibid., L. B. Cary, a rancher in Paradise Valley north of the park, to Assistant P. M. General Frank Hattan, February 2, 1884; W. Scott Smith, Special Agent, General Land Office, to Teller, October 15, 1883; *Enterprise,* February 4, 1884.

28. PMLR, Conger to Teller, June 23, 1884; Ibid., Report of Erret to Conger, included in a letter of Erret to Joslyn, August 12, 1884; Conger to Teller, November 27, 1883.

29. PMLR, L. B. Cary to Frank Hattan, February 4, 1884; ADLS, Teller to Conger, July 12, 1884.

30. PMLR, Conger to Teller, September 10, 1884; ADLR, Senators Wilson and Allison to Teller, July 3, 1884.

31. ADLR, Senators Wilson and Allison to Teller, July 3, 1884; ADLS, Joslyn to Carpenter, August 5, 1884; PMLR, Carpenter to Teller, September 18, 1884.

32. PMLR, Carpenter to Teller, October 7, 1884; ADLR, Olaf Anderson to Teller, December 30, 1884; Ibid., Weimer to Teller, January 15, 1885; ADLR, William Thompson of Humboldt, Iowa, to Lamar, March 26, 1885.

33. *Enterprise,* March 28; April 18, 1885. Carpenter remained in the park, becoming involved in the hotel system. Ibid., June 20, 1885. Arnold Hague also disliked Carpenter. R. G. 57, Arnold Hague Papers, Hague to George Bird Grinnell, April 1, 1885.

34. ADLR, Vest to Lamar, April 14, 1885.

35. ADLR, Vest to Muldrow, April 19, 1885. Wear had been lieutenant colonel of the 45th Missouri Volunteer Infantry. ADLR, Wear to Muldrow, May 13, 1886.

36. Weekly *Enterprise,* June 6, 1885.

37. Ibid.; ADLR, Wear to Lamar, July 2; September 7, 1885; PMLR, Wear to Vest (forwarded to Lamar), July 15, 1885; ADLR, Wear to Lamar, September 7, 1885.

38. Weekly *Enterprise,* August 15; September 19, 1885.

39. *Laws of Wyoming,* 177–83. Chapter 103, Yellowstone National Park, approved March 6, 1884. A copy of the law is in PMLR for 1884.

40. PMLR, Conger to Teller, April 10, 1884.

41. PMLR, Phillips to Lamar, September 12, 1885. This report is published: 49th Cong., 1st. Sess., Sen. Exec. Doc. No. 51 (1885).

42. Y. A., (no number), Box No. 4, D. H. Budlong to Wear, July 2, 1885.

43. Weekly *Enterprise,* August 15, 1885; PMLR, Wear to Lamar, August 12, 1885.

44. PMLR, Phillips to Lamar, September 12, 1885; Weekly *Enterprise,* August 15, 1885; PMLR, "Memorandum Prepared by the First Assistant Secretary Relating to the National Park," October 13, 1885.

45. The affair is discussed adequately in the Weekly *Enterprise,* August 29, 1885; PMLR, Phillips to Lamar, September 12, 1885, and in Appendix "A" of Phillips's Report.

46. Weekly *Enterprise,* September 19, 1885; Annual Report quoted in the *Enterprise,* December 19, 1885.

47. *Enterprise,* August 29, 1885.

48. Ibid.

49. ADLR, Wear to Muldrow, December 20, 1885; January 28 and April 21, 1886; PMLR, Wear to Muldrow, August 12, 1886; PMLR, Spangler, Special Agent to the Post Office Department, to the Postal Inspector, August 31, 1886. The inspector did not find sufficient evidence to charge the Hendersons with violations of postal regulations.

50. 22 *U.S. Statutes at Large,* 627.

51. 24 *U.S. Statutes at Large,* 240.

52. *Congressional Record,* 49th Cong., 1st. Sess., 7841.

53. Ibid., 7864–65.

54. Ibid., 7841.

55. PMLR, Phillips to Lamar, August 7, 1886.

56. PMLS, Lamar to Endicott, Secretary of War, August 6, 1886.

57. PMLR, Wear to Muldrow, August 13; August 17, 1886.

58. PMLR, Phillips to Lamar, October 4, 1886; August 7, 1886; Arnold Hague Papers, Hague to Captain Kingman, January 19, 1886.

CHAPTER NINE

The Army Regime

*F*or a generation the United States Army policed Yellowstone National Park. For those thirty-two crucial years, from 1886 to 1918, the steady, methodical routine that characterizes peacetime service life guided the reservation through the most massive changes of its official existence. When the army bowed out and the newly created National Park Service took over, the park was more secure than it had ever been before. In short, the army did a good job.

Elements of the army had long coveted the Yellowstone assignment. As the frontier drew to a close and Indian wars became incidents of the past, it was only natural for military men to look for new tasks. From Captain Raynolds's expedition (1859–60) through the explorations of Lieutenant Doane and Captains Barlow, Heap, and Ludlow, army personnel had manifested both interest and concern in Yellowstone. In 1875 Secretary of War Belknap had led some Very Important Persons into the park. In his annual report following the trip he had suggested stationing troops at strategic points there to curtail spoliation. Generals Sherman, Sheridan, Miles, and Howard, to name a few, had camped in the park and grown attached to it. And since 1883 Lieutenant Dan C. Kingman of the army engineers had been developing the park road system. Some civilian elements even mentioned the existence of an "army ring" that kept up the pressure for Congress to assign Yellowstone to the military since, supporters of this view maintained, Interior was unable to do the job. In contrast one writer feared not only monopolists but an "epauletted" park aristocracy that would limit people's enjoyment and use of Yellowstone.[1]

Now the army had its opportunity. If it carried out its tasks well, total control of the park system might become a permanent peacetime activity. Even if this was not uppermost in the minds of the army superintendents, their natural esprit, their desire to do the best job possible "for the good of the Service," demanded that the task, however long it lasted, be well done.

The man in Yellowstone most affected by the transfer was the last to hear about it. In a telegram of August 14 Superintendent Wear was informed officially and instructed to turn over to Captain Harris "all property and records taking his receipt thereof." On the seventeenth Captain Moses Harris arrived with fifty men, having come down in two days from Fort Custer; however, the captain, cavalryman that he was, refused to accept his new responsibilities until the horses arrived. It was at least two more weeks before he received detailed instructions from the Interior Department.

"M" Troop pitched its tents somewhat west of the road south out of Mammoth, opposite Jupiter Terrace, and dubbed the site Camp Sheridan. Three thousand dollars was allotted for buildings. After strong suggestions from Arnold Hague, in the park at the time, Captain Harris carefully chose a spot for wooden structures. It was about a half mile from the hotel, on the west side of the road, and about two hundred yards south of the house previously occupied by the superintendent. "Conformation of the ground is such," he assured Assistant Interior Secretary Muldrow, "that the buildings are not visible from any portion of the 'hotel terrace' nor do they obstruct either the view or approaches to the Hot Springs formation." The army was not blind to aesthetics after all.

Once his men had their horses and he had his orders, Captain Harris moved rapidly. Clearly, the system of having assistants stationed at strategic points of the park, as assigned by Superintendent Wear, had been a wise policy. Harris therefore replaced those vacated spots with military detachments. This was accomplished by September 1; by the end of October the entire Yellowstone operation was in the hands of the military. Five years later, on May 27, 1891, Camp Sheridan ceased to exist and was replaced with Fort Yellowstone on the eastern edge of the Mammoth Hot Springs plain.[2]

Thus began the army era in Yellowstone Park. In the thirty years and two months of army policing, at least twelve military officers assumed the tasks of acting superintendent. Of those twelve, three held the position for more than five years each. These officers were Captain George S. Anderson of the 6th Cavalry (February 1891–June 1897), Captain John Pitcher of the 1st Cavalry (May 1901–June 1907), and Colonel L. M. Brett of the 1st Cavalry (October 1910–October 1916). Next in length of duty was Captain Moses Harris (August 1886–May 1889). One officer served twice. As colonel in the 3rd Cavalry, S. B. M. Young was superintendent for five months in 1897; as a retired general he held the same office from June to November 1908. Three other officers were there for about two years each. These were Captain Frazier A. Boutelle, 1st Cavalry (June 1889–February 1891), Captain James B. Erwin of the 4th Cavalry (November 1897–March 1899), and Major H. C. Benson of the 5th Cavalry (November 1908–September 1910). The others were there hardly long enough to learn the ropes.*

*Other officers were Captain W. E. Wilder, 4th Cavalry (March-June 1899), Captain Oscar J. Brown, 1st Cavalry (June 1899-July 1900), Captain George W. Goode, 1st Cavalry (July 1900-May 1901), and Major Henry Tureman Allen, 2nd Cavalry (February-June 1908).

An army contingent remained in the park until October 1, 1918, when Captain Myer S. Silver, 11th Cavalry, issued "General Orders No. 2. The undersigned hereby relinquishes command of Fort Yellowstone, Wyoming." Since Captain Silver had assumed command just three weeks before, it is clear that there were a number of changes in personnel during the years 1916 to 1918, when the army was closing down Fort Yellowstone. After a generation of occupancy the inventories and other red tape aspects of the operation were undoubtedly large. Captain Frederick T. Arnold, according to his widow, did the final honors in turning over the park to the Interior Department.[3]

The quality of the army commanders at Fort Yellowstone appears to have been consistently good. Captain Moses Harris, the first military superintendent—actually, he was "acting superintendent" as were all the military men—had survived several Indian campaigns, was awarded the Medal of Honor in the Civil War, and "was tough, as only a frontier cavalryman knew how to be tough." Senator Vest described him as being "singularly adapted to the duties of his position, and   [he] is a gentleman of intelligence and justice and high character." Harris's fellow officer, Captain George S. Anderson, said of him that he was an "ideal selection . . . austere, correct, unyielding, he was a terror to evil doers . . . always *sure* he was right before he acted, and then no fear of consequences deterred him."[4]

When the army assumed control in 1886 the park was indeed in a chaotic state. Tourists were more prevalent than ever, drifters located their tents or lean-tos wherever their inclinations directed, and there was no satisfactory enforcement of regulations, though Superintendent Wear had done his best. In short order Captain Harris had his men "roaming the back trails and canyons, flushing out hunters, woodcutters, and souvenir collectors."[5]

In May 1889 Captain Harris was removed from the Yellowstone command. He loved the park and a letter to his successor, Captain Frazier Boutelle, raises questions about the details of his removal but does not answer them. Ultimately Captain Harris drew recruiting duty in Milwaukee, an assignment he had requested, but we do not know if it was prior to his transfer from Yellowstone. He later became an associate member of the Boone and Crockett Club and remained an ardent Yellowstone supporter.[6]

Frazier Boutelle also loved the park. He was instrumental in planting game fish in reservation lakes and streams, and his letters to his wife state repeatedly how busy he was at his Yellowstone assignment. In the spring of 1890 he was on official business in Washington; while there he worked actively to popularize the park, encouraging the secretaries of interior and war and other important persons to visit Yellowstone. "I am delivering lectures to everybody whose buttonhole I can get hold of," he wrote his young son.

He also appears to have been the one superintendent who favored segregation of the northeast section so that a railroad could be built to Cooke City.

"It will add considerably to my labors but these people are certainly entitled to some relief," he wrote his wife. He said he had the secretaries of interior and war, the head of the Bureau of Fisheries, and the Smithsonian Institution all on his side. "Now that I know that no one can injure me in the Interior Department and have silenced the *Forest and Stream,* I think I can go about with a good deal of confidence," he wrote his wife. He also appears to have taken steps to purchase some Cooke City property. Again, from New York where he went "on business connected with park legislation," he wrote that if he succeeded in what he was after, he would be "a big Indian with the lobby."[7]

Whatever were Captain Boutelle's motives—for these letters indicate sub rosa activities of a business nature antithetical to his official duties—as superintendent he alienated powerful elements over the probable poaching activities of Eli C. Waters. The captain was abruptly transferred out of the park. "Don't be alarmed at what you may see in the papers," Boutelle wrote his wife on December 17, 1890. "I am ordered to Keogh for garrison duty. . . .I am going with more compliments than ever a fellow ever left a post with. . . .Don't expect to suffer any hardship." But from frigid Fort Keogh [near present Miles City, Montana] he wrote her in a different vein. He wished he was "twenty years younger," he said. "I am afraid of breaking down with rheumatism and having to retire. . . .I want to hold on until he [Harry, his son] has an appointment to the Academy."[8]

For what it was worth, the Interior Secretary dashed off a letter to Captain Boutelle January 30, 1891, in which he stated in part, "General Miles made the order sending you to the field without my knowledge or consent, and as I understood, without the knowledge of the Secretary of War." He added that it gave him "great pleasure" to acknowledge Boutelle's "very efficient services. . . .You did your duty faithfully and well, and I thank you for it."[9]

His successor was the most successful of the army superintendents. This was Captain George S. Anderson, who retained the position for more than six years, from February 1891 to June 1897. He stood well over six feet tall and was well proportioned. A seasoned frontiersman, he had been assigned to Fort Lyon on the Arkansas in southeastern Colorado in 1871. By the 1890s this intelligent, authoritative captain had witnessed destruction of the buffalo and segregation of Indians on reservations. A sportsman and a lover of the outdoors, Captain Anderson was fitted for his Yellowstone assignment by temperament, experience, sympathy with the protective policies, and a tough old cavalry officer's attitude toward violators of regulations.[10]

It was said that he was the most hated man in the park, for he was stringent in his enforcement. He was also a lover of the good life. Judge Robert Meldrum, the United States commissioner to the park, first met

Anderson at the Fountain Hotel on a dusty, mosquito-plagued day in July 1894. A man in civilian clothes climbed down from the coach. He was travel-worn, "and," the judge reminisced more than forty years later, "he had a little old gray hat about as big as a tea-cup on his head. . . .I went up to him and introduced myself. He said right off the bat: 'Good to see you, let's have a drink!' So, we went in and had a drink. Every hotel had a barroom in those days."[11]

Commissioner Meldrum's first office, while his own quarters were being built, was at the Mammoth Hotel in a ground floor room with a big bay window fronting the porch. On the other side of the hall from his office was the barroom. "There was music every night until midnight in that barroom," the Judge recalled. "The chief trumpeter in there would always be Captain Anderson." He also liked to sing.[12]

Mrs. Bessie Haynes Arnold remembered the captain as a perfect host who always rode down to the hotel and met the coaches. His bachelor quarters were kept clean by his maiden sister, who lived with him. Quite a man was Captain George S. Anderson.[13]

Of the acting superintendents, only S. B. M. Young, who held the position twice, Moses Harris, and Frazier A. Boutelle were not West Point graduates. General Young, who dressed down a young volunteer colonel named Theodore Roosevelt during the Spanish-American War, had perhaps the most successful military career of the officers who were assigned to Yellowstone. Young's long and distinguished service included a term as chief of staff during Theodore Roosevelt's administration in 1903. The general also made a propitious marriage to Harry Child's sister-in-law (who was also Silas Huntley's widow).[14]

For about five months in 1908, from February 15 until the opening of the tourist season, Major H. T. Allen was superintendent during General Young's absence. Allen had met his wife in the park many years before when he and several other young officers stationed there had been ordered to "beau" some young ladies through the reservation. General Allen, who was considered (but not chosen) as vice-presidential candidate for the Democratic party in 1924, cherished one particular incident of his short tour of duty in Yellowstone.

His immediate previous assignment had been to form the Philippine Constabulary while William Howard Taft was high commissioner. Now, rather unhappy over his new assignment, Allen heard that Taft was coming to the park. It was imperative for his career, Allen thought, to make a good impression. Taft liked to eat, but even the officer's food in Yellowstone was none too good.

So the story goes, he had a Chinese cook "shanghaied" from San Francisco to park headquarters. His first night there the cook walked out of the kitchen with garbage and found himself face-to-face with a great big bear. This was enough to send the cook packing.

This would never do! Various methods were applied to keep him there. Finally Taft arrived and the Chinese cook outdid himself in his culinary abilities. He topped off the scrumptious dinner by entering the dining room bearing a beautiful, freshly baked cake. Carefully he set it down in the center of the table, then beat a hasty retreat. Hosts and guests noted the words spelled out in white frosting: GOOD BYE COLONEL ALLEN. The cook was never heard from again. [15]

Yellowstone was an expensive assignment for a commanding officer. Letters of introduction were "sent to him by the hundreds, and the smallest measure of hospitality requires the expenditure of his entire pay in very meagre entertaining," or at least, so reported the secretary of interior in recommending that Captain Anderson be compensated for this expense. [16]

A number of captains and first and second lieutenants were stationed in the park also. Captain Hugh Lenox Scott later became chief of staff of the United States Army. Second Lieutenant Jonathon Wainwright, the hero of Corregidor in World War II, served a tour in the park from 1910 until 1912. A young lieutenant who was allowed to resign his commission on September 1, 1905, was William M. Nichols of the 3rd Cavalry. As soon as Nichols resumed civilian status, Harry Child gave parental approval for him to marry his daughter. In time "Billie" Nichols became czar of the Yellowstone Park concessions. Lieutenant Frederick T. Arnold married Bessie Haynes, F. Jay's oldest daughter.

Within the framework of United States Army protocol, the officers appear to have been brusque, spit-and-polish men who went by the book and yet possessed the intelligence to recognize that the command was handling a peacetime policing action, not a military operation against an enemy. The commanding officer occasionally had to assure headquarters that the men were taught to ride and shoot well and that they were familiar with camp duties and "the army way." But, as Major Pitcher reminded his superiors, "as the object for which troops are here is to guard the Park, it is necessary to use them more as mounted police than as soldiers, and if they perform their duties properly in this connection, they will have about all they can attend to." [17]

Mrs. Arnold remembered a number of army superintendents well. She described Major Pitcher as a typical military man whose heart was not really in his work. He could not be drunk down. Captain Erwin was a southern gentleman. His family, which included two tennis-playing daughters, was well liked. As for Colonel Brett, he was "rather stiff and efficacious, and some liked him, some did not." General Young was known as "Czar" Young and was not too well liked. [18]

After 1908, upon being assigned duty at a park station, enlisted men were required to pass an examination on park rules and regulations; a small, printed regulations book was placed in the hands of every man on duty.[19]

The army made a conscious effort to reduce law enforcement from the harsh, strict discipline that characterizes a military base (at least in the layman's mind) to a milder form. In enforcing the rules, Major Pitcher instructed his command in 1902, it was the desire of the acting superintendent that the soldiers avoid if at all possible arresting anyone for trivial offenses. "Attention is invited to the fact," he said, "that a majority of the people who visit the Park during the summer are law-abiding citizens and as a rule it will be quite sufficient to courteously call their attention to the Rules and Regulations of which they may be ignorant, in order to have them enforced." In an order of June 1, 1916, Colonel Brett reiterated the same thought: "Tourists," he said "will be cautioned of dangerous places on the formations by the guards. If tourists ignore the caution they do so at their own peril. The guard will not try to restrain them."[20]

In every sense, then, policing was by the army, and Fort Yellowstone was emphatically an army base. There was, however, the hindrance of split control, for Interior was charged by Congressional act with policy. By assigning a permanent Interior Department clerk at the fort, this system was made workable, although it was always difficult. In policy matters the commanding officer and acting superintendent (one and the same) received orders from the interior secretary and filed annual reports with him; he also filed the usual reports with the commanding general of the department in which Yellowstone was located. One can imagine the reaction of a hard-bitten cavalry officer when he received such a telegram as Captain Anderson did from Interior Secretary John W. Noble. The message ended as follows: "You are transcending your authority so far as the records in this office show and such action will not be tolerated."[21]

In the thirty odd years of army security in the park the number of enlisted men fluctuated both seasonally and annually. During the busy summer the average was four troops, a troop being anywhere from forty-five to sixty-two men, depending upon vacancies in the ranks (rarely was a troop at full strength); it also included three or four officers and a hospital corpsman. Captain Harris began with one troop, which was there year-round, with a second troop in the park for the summer. In addition there evolved a clerical, noncommissioned headquarters staff, a detachment of hospital corpsmen, a signal corps detachment which maintained the telephone lines, and always there were the road builders—the army engineers. When the tourist season ended, two, and on occasion as many as three, troops were ordered elsewhere. In the early years of this century they often headed for duty in the Philippines.[22]

To house these men, temporary structures were first used, but when the army's assignment began to look permanent, steps were taken to build more substantial quarters. The army spelled out its desire for some twenty-two and a half acres at the east side of the plateau at Mammoth Hot Springs. This was to be the permanent site of Fort Yellowstone. Those buildings, still there in the 1980s, were all constructed under army supervision and arranged according to military plan. They were built over the period of a decade and a half, each year's progress depending upon Congressional appropriations. The stone came from a quarry just below Gardiner.[23]

In time Fort Yellowstone possessed all the accouterments of the typical army base. The headquarters building and the married officer's housing ran along the north-south street that today leads past the museum, the park superintendent's offices, and park personnel housing. Few take much notice of these structures, nor observe from the overlook at the hot springs terraces the layout of the installation. Those long stone buildings behind headquarters and officer's housing, which now serve so well as maintenance shops and garages, were once stables for the fine, well-groomed horses of the United States Cavalry. Other structures, most of which are still standing, housed everything from the post exchange to an auditorium of sorts for plays and, at least in the fall and winter of 1892–93, a lyceum. After 1902 the fort was electrically lighted.[24]

After passage of the Lacey Act in 1894, $5,000 was appropriated for construction of the commissioner's residence—not military, but certainly a federal building. This solidly built home and office was erected southwest of the present Hamilton Store at Mammoth. The tourist will notice it today: if he is a law-abiding citizen he should have no reason to visit it. And in 1904 the U.S. Weather Bureau established a station at Mammoth. It was the wooden house to the north and a little west, across the street from the post office. The old office of the commandant is the squarish stone structure across the street and north-northwest of the museum. It is now the park security headquarters. All of these structures were designed by the army and built to its specifications, but the actual construction, including the marvelous stonemasonry, was done by labor from the surrounding region. Those stout buildings housed personnel and horses at Fort Yellowstone very well. In fact, they have withstood the Hebgen earthquake, many a milder tremor, and nearly three generations of federal occupation. The army built as if it was to stay.[25]

No cavalry could ever function without a parade ground. The army commandeered the middle of the flat terrace in front of the officer's quarters and south of the Mammoth Hot Springs hotel. It was convenient; it also gave the cavalry a splendid opportunity to parade before the eyes of the beautiful people staying at the hostelry. To the clarion calls of the bugle the well-trained troops could—and did—display their equestrian and military expertise. In the Kiplingesque mood of the period, it was all very fine; beautiful people, a massive luxury hotel, splendidly uniformed soldiers, fine horses, and Old Glory being lowered to the booming of a cannon at sundown.

However, there was cause for concern over the hollow sounds as the troops paraded over parts of the terrace. The inspector general reported in 1902 the appearance of holes, "revealing deep, unexplored caverns beneath." Some predicted that the area was "a mere shell that may cave in any day. . . ."[26]

Arnold Hague of the Geological Survey seconded the inspector general's suggestion that the parade ground be closed. "In time," he predicted, "it may yield. It has, however, stood the strain without accident, and I see no reason why it may not continue to bear the necessary weight." Apparently the army chose to live dangerously, for it never ceased using the parade ground. In winter a part of it was flooded, electric lights were strung, and thus was created an excellent skating rink.[27]

The park could hardly be secured by soldiers snugly stationed in the garrison at Fort Yellowstone. Substations, sometimes called "outpost stations" or "soldier stations," were established at strategic points throughout the park. At least from Captain Anderson's time on, four or more of these installations remained in use throughout the year. These were the ones at Norris, Riverside, Snake River, and Soda Butte. A noncommissioned officer and three enlisted men were assigned to each place. By 1908 there were twelve of them; by 1916, fifteen. Some of them, those at Sylvan Pass, Thumb, and Soda Butte, for example, which were built by Major Chittenden, were described as being "very neat and comfortable."[28]

In addition a small, detached guest house was constructed close to some of these substations. Such houses were just large enough to hold a stove and a couple of bunks, but they made it possible for both visiting personnel and soldiers stationed there to have beds to sleep on. Stables were built also; horses were kept year-round save at the Snake River Station. Men were under strict orders not to let their mounts get run down.[29]

In summer at these outposts the men were kept busy with such tasks as registering all parties, securing their firearms by wrapping red tape around the trigger area and sealing the knot with wax, and, if a dog was along, issuing a permit and making sure Fido was on a leash. On their mounts the men made the rounds of the nearby attractions. Tourists were not to catch more than twenty fish; all campfires were to be extinguished. Soldiers were reminded that they were serving the public. "People come here for pleasure," read one set of orders to station commanders. "It is our duty to treat them politely and give them all information possible when requested. Don't forget that the National Parks belong to the people. Never lose your temper." Men on summer duty wore garrison uniforms consisting of a blue forage cap, blue blouse, blue trousers and black shoes. Mrs. Arnold could not recall ever seeing a soldier with a yellow handkerchief.[30]

The boredom of routine was often broken by the presence of female admirers who were attracted by men in their prime, in uniform, and having some authority. One writer dubbed the enlisted man "Tommy Atkins. . . . He it is that jumped into a boiling hot springs to save the life of the daughter of a private citizen—a deed for which the citizen, who was a rich man, proffered the astounding sum of $5, and the government the gold medal of honor."[31]

The soldiers made a campaign of keeping people from writing their names on the hot springs and geysers. "A very picturesque figure," said Captain Anderson, "is a sentimental youth at twilight as he transmits his name to fame by writing on the 'formations'—the hot springs deposits. A much more interesting figure is this same youth at sunrise the next morning, when, followed by a mounted soldier, he proceeds, scrub-brush and soap in hand, to the same spot and removes the perishable evidence, of his late presence."[32]

Winter duty at the substations was lonely. The isolation is demonstrated by the manner in which personnel traveled from Fort Yellowstone to some of the outposts. To reach the Bechler River Station in the southwestern corner, where poaching was a serious problem, the men traveled by rail from Gardiner to Ashton, Idaho, where horses were waiting to carry them in. To reach the Gallatin Station they first went to Eldridge, Montana. To go to Sylvan Pass they went by train from Gardiner to Cody, and then by wagon to the station.[33]

Winter life at these stations was considered so rigorous that the men were issued Alaskan rations. Supplies were delivered in autumn before the snows had set in. On occasion a shortage of pack mules was such that hunting hounds, used for running down predators, were drafted as dog teams to help deliver supplies. Captain Anderson even suggested that reindeer be imported for such uses.[34]

Despite these hardships, most of the men liked these assignments. (There were exceptions: it is believed that some cabins were fired on purpose so the lonely men could come in to headquarters.) Many of the soldiers, however, volunteered for this detached service. "There is little of the 'pomp and vanity' in this soldiering," wrote artist Frederick Remington, "and it shows good spirit on the part of the enlisted men. They are dressed in fur caps, California blankets, leggings, and moccasins—a strange uniform for a cavalryman. . . ."[35]

Duty during winter included making fixed rounds and keeping a weather eye out for poachers. Patrols, or civilian scouts on their assigned rounds, soon found that the distance a man could cover on snowshoes in a day was much less than he could traverse walking, or on horseback in summer. To solve the problem of shelter for these men, secreted throughout the park were "snowshoe cabins." Ordinarily they were about ten miles from the outlying posts—a "fair day's travel," wrote Major Benson, "for the men on snowshoes through the mountains." Moreover, just getting around in the snow made it difficult for the soldiers and scouts to carry substantial provisions on their backs. Therefore Interior allotted funds annually to stock these cabins. Described by Captain Anderson as "small huts, with fireplaces," they were in use shortly after the army came into the park. Captain Boutelle, as early as 1890, received authorization to build six of them at a cost of $100 each. By 1915 they numbered seventeen.[36]

Each month in the winter men on "Norwegian skis"* covered from two hundred to five hundred miles. Because there was always the possibility of personnel doing a little hunting on their own, they were held responsible for every bullet that was fired. At one time they were issued ten rounds of the revolver and, if also armed with rifles, twenty rounds of cartridges. Returning to the station the ammunition was verified and turned in, "and any shortage at once investigated and reported to the troop commander."[37]

From early in the first decade of this century telephone communication was maintained with headquarters. Time and experience brought about smooth liaison: five rings on the park phone line meant an emergency. In winter one station notified the station to which a man was going; when the soldier arrived, the first one was notified of his arrival.[38]

In March 1894, a private of "D" Troop, 6th Cavalry, left Riverside Station to pick up the mail at the Lower Basin. The sergeant in charge accompanied him halfway; with less than eight miles to go, the private disappeared. A year and a half later his remains were found, ten miles from where he was last seen, entirely away from the direction in which he should have been traveling.[39]

In February 1904 a corporal named Christ H. Martin, Troop "C," 3rd Cavalry, was buried alive in a snowslide at the Gallatin Station. To have gone there directly from Fort Yellowstone meant a thirty-five-mile ski journey in bad weather. Instead, help came from Bozeman into the station by sleigh; with the aid of five civilians, his body was recovered. In March 1918 a fire occurred at Gallatin Station, but no one was injured. Cold, getting lost, and, as Captain Anderson commented about the lost trooper from Riverside, the

---

*In correspondence "skis" and "snowshoes" appear to have been used interchangeably, but the phrase "Norwegian skis" certainly indicates skis.

possibility of foul play from poachers were all dangers faced by the men on winter duty.[40]

In addition, a conscious effort was made to appear unexpectedly at hard-to-get-at, out-of-the-way places. The soldiers, said Remington, "are instructed not to follow the regular trails, but to go to the most unfrequented places, so that they may at any time happen upon a malicious person, and perhaps be able to do as one scout did—photograph the miscreant with his own camera." Most of the time, however, it was work that was unexciting, routine, monotonous, and toilsome. But the usefulness of such *chevauchée*, as the artist explained, was "that it leaves the track of the cavalry horseshoe in the most remote parts of the preserve, where the poacher or interloper can see it, and become apprehensive in consequence of the dangers which attend his operations."[41]

Occasionally men were sent on special, serious assignments. Soldiers were often dispatched in the off-seasons to distant park boundaries to checkmate poaching activities. In January 1896 Captain Scott and Lieutenant Lindsley were ordered to Market Lake, Idaho, "thence through the southwest corner of the Park, [to] . . . carry out the verbal instructions received concerning poaching in the vicinity." According to the lieutenant, in the south and west corners of the park "lives a gang of mountain pirates who make a scanty living by hunting, trapping, and fishing. . . . Natural poachers, they are banded together and work in concert."[42]

The horses were in their stalls, the enlisted men on KP going about their chores lackadaisically, the buglers sounded the many calls, office work went on routinely, and Old Glory waved in the clear, light blue sky over Fort Yellowstone. For a generation all was right with the world.

From the commanding officer down to the lowest buck private it was considered a good assignment—active duty serving the public, shepherding tourists in summer and policing the big reservation. Some of the drill and dull routine that characterizes life at an ordinary military post was suspended; yet much of what constitutes army life still remained.

Officers never allowed the remoteness of their command to sever their old school ties. A Signal Corps telegram in the Fort Yellowstone archives dated November, 1911, carries this "tragic" message:

Army   0
Navy   3

And scribbled beneath in lead pencil: "Put on your old black bonnet with the crepe strings upon it." For that officer it was a bad day.

The few officers, especially during the off-season, found themselves delegated with many onerous duties. One was in charge of the PX, another was superintendent of schools (for there were always plenty of army brats), a range officer looked after both the indoor and outdoor target ranges. A topographical officer bore the innocuous additional assignment, "Officer in Charge of Post Gardens." (These were both vegetable and ornamental: the vegetable garden was between Mammoth and Gardiner and the flower garden at the north entrance.) On their arrival young officers attended a scheduled class with final examinations. And there were the usual inspections of the hotels and permanent civilian camps, and assignments to work on the telephone lines.[43]

The social life one expects at a military post prevailed at Fort Yellowstone. Concessionaire families were also active participants in this exclusive society. Siblings of the two elite groups played together, but both officers' and concessionaires' children were forbidden to mingle in areas where the enlisted men congregated. When they reached their teens they participated in card parties, skating, horseback riding, hiking, berrying, and dancing.

They were all equestrians in those days. "Got horses and saw inspection," reads Mrs. Arnold's diary for September 22, 1894, when she was not quite seventeen years old. "Ate lunch at hotel with Major General Swan, Captain Scott, Lieutenant Forsyth, and Bess. Lord Swansea sat at the table with us." Mrs. Arnold's diary notes such events as an officer's farewell dance and a Christmas vacation from school in Minnesota spent at Mammoth with Captain Scott's daughter. Even at age ninety-two she recalled the gloom, sorrow, and heartache when young Lieutenant Joseph McDonald was killed in a snowslide near Kingman Pass on January 9, 1916.[44]

In the days of Fort Yellowstone every unit did its own recruiting. Personnel were ordered to Bozeman, Livingston, Helena, Butte, and other relatively nearby towns for two or three weeks in hopes of enlisting a potential soldier or two. Though rarely very successful, one way or another a troop acquired two or three recruits. If four troops were stationed in the park, this meant a class of twelve or fifteen green ex-civilians. Since army "boot camps" had not yet been instituted, it was each troop's responsibility to turn the civilian into a competent soldier. In December 1910 such an assignment evolved upon Second Lieutenant Jonathon Wainwright. "The recruit instruction," his orders read, "will be progressive and will embrace the School of the Soldier and Trooper; the horse and his care; stable duty; manual of the saber and saber exercise; courtesies; the proper care of clothing, arms, accouterments, and horse equipment, and general duty."[45]

Soldiers were also assigned to train new horses, work up interest in sports, and accompany the post football and baseball teams, which played the pride of various Montana communities as well as other post teams. Competition was also engendered between the Swaddies (soldiers) and the Savages (civilian employees of the hotels and restaurants). Civilian scouts and soldier patrols likewise lost little love between each other.

Jack Ellis Haynes recalled with gusto the concessionaire-army baseball game one Fourth of July in the early 1900s. All went well until the fourth inning, when "an altercation developed in the vicinity of second base." Haynes went on to describe what happened. "Our second baseman, a drummer in the Mammoth Hotel orchestra, was involved. Three soldier players in succession set upon him with dire results, we having thoughtlessly neglected to tell our opponents that this gentleman was a professional prize-fighter from Chicago." The commanding officer halted the game, but "small-group battles" continued for the rest of the day. "The commandant, who dined at our house that evening, remarked that the guardhouse wasn't big enough to hold a fraction of the civilians—to say nothing of the soldiers—who should have been arrested."[46]

Even with these activities, time must have hung heavily on many a day, as it does at any peacetime military post. In early years commanding officers were prone to call "Boards of Survey" to investigate the picayune. For example, one "board" was called consisting of a captain and a first and second lieutenant, "to convene at this post tomorrow to examine into, report upon, and fix the responsibility for the loss by freezing of twenty bottles of blue-black ink, the property of the United States, and for which Captain Robert R. Stevens, Assistant Quartermaster, is accountable." Other boards of survey were called "to inspect and recommend the disposition of one public horse," or "to fix the responsibility for the unserviceable condition of one Sugar Bowl issued to Troop "H," Fourth Cavalry, as part of table ware equipment."[47]

And there were the constant problems of discipline. Peacetime army personnel have never been particularly good quality, especially in pre-World War II days, and the number of desertions and cases of inebriation and insubordination was substantial. Usually the culprits were "busted" in rank and fined a sum of money to be taken from their pay and/or sentenced to confinement for a short period. Only rarely was the convicted soldier sent to a disciplinary barracks; usually he served out his sentence at Fort Yellowstone. The records do not indicate any unusually severe sentences. If the prisoner accepted well his confinement in the guardhouse, as reflected by his good behavior, he was likely to be released to his unit before serving half his sentence.

Perhaps the paternal "live and let live" attitude that made life bearable at Fort Yellowstone is best reflected in Major Pitcher's explanation for the reduction of a sergeant to private: "The Sergeant is a good honest old soldier, but will occasionally get on a spree." There was the case of the young recruit who had shot a deer—he drew a bead on the animal and (he didn't know quite why) pulled the trigger! And the youngster who deserted after six weeks. The commanding officer reduced the court martial sentence in each case to almost nothing, for in each incident the thoughtlessness of youth had entered in, and both guilty ones had behaved well since their arrests.[48]

Less pleasant were the problems of venereal disease and alcholism. As would be expected, Gardiner became the place with the bright lights, the painted ladies, the saloons with beer and whiskey consumed to the strains of a cheap piano or turn-of-the-century Wurlitzer. On payday the whores of the region descended upon that western hamlet, adding the odor of cheap perfume and the attractiveness of soft flesh to the more constant lure of John Barleycorn. (After the soldiers had exhausted themselves and their pay and had returned to Fort Yellowstone, the "soiled doves" entrained for other places—Butte, for example, or Livingston at the time the railroaders were paid. They followed a scarlet route.)[49]

So Fort Yellowstone had severe VD problems, requiring men returning from such revelry to call at the dispensary to be administered prophylaxis. That they often did not bother to do this is apparent from the records, a case in point being the following notation concerning a private who "was discharged without honor at this post, April 4, 1906, on Certificate of Disability on account of chronic gonorrhea, gonorrheal cystalis and secondary syphilis, incapacitating by cachexis, inability to retain urine and danger of infecting others, due to soldier's own misconduct."[50]

Alcoholism was also a serious and continuing problem. Soldiers obtained liquor at Gardiner, and then the troubles began, for not only was Gardiner a whoop-up town for the army, it was also a gold and coal miners' mecca as well. Noncoms with "mounted passes" were required to leave "public horses" at the soldier station at the park boundary, walking on in to town. Most soldiers, however, walked the five miles from Fort Yellowstone to Gardiner's single row of false front saloons, parlor houses, and cribs. There they engaged in ruckuses. Even if they did manage to stay out of trouble, they were likely to carry a bottle back to the fort for future use. It was a hot climb back up to the Mammoth plateau. At about the halfway point they discovered a spring of crystal clear, cold water. They dubbed this "whiskey spring," some say because they hid their liquor there, others that it was a godsend to men with an agonizing thirst following a night of revelry and heavy drinking.[51]

Among the records are general orders informing the personnel that "the bringing of intoxicating liquors of any kind onto the military reservation of Fort Yellowstone, Wyoming, is prohibited under penalty of law," and special orders to commanding officers to the effect that "any case of drunkenness at this post will deprive that organization of passes to Gardiner for a period of thirty days." S. B. M. Young complained to the interior secretary that of the two troops stationed at Yellowstone for the winter, one was "undisciplined, with a large percentage of drunkards in its ranks."[52]

Despite problems of alcohol, sex, desertion, and insubordination, army discipline prevailed. Soldiers obeyed orders. Enlisted men were warned not to speak to strangers, especially to ladies, unless spoken to, and, when mounted, to move no faster than an eight-mile-an-hour trot. They were forbidden to use the stage road to Gardiner or the road immediately in front of the Mammoth Hotel and were prohibited from entering the hotels "except, on duty, or invitation of the managers." Nor could they loiter about the verandas or entrances. If they did attend dances, regulations called for "blue uniform (dress) with black shoes, white collars, and gloves."[53]

To young Rudyard Kipling the soldiers he met in Yellowstone were something less than spit-and-polish, their mounts of poor quality, their dress shabby, their discipline laggard. At first he resented their presence patrolling the Mammoth terraces "with loaded six-shooters . . . cavalry in a very slovenly uniform." Kipling sidled up to several of them. "By the mercy of Allah I opened conversation with a bespectacled Scot," he exclaimed. The man had "served the Queen in the Marines and a Line regiment, and the 'go-fever' being in his bones, had drifted to America, there to serve under Uncle Sam." " 'And how do things go?' " Kipling asked him.

To which the soldier replied that there was not half the discipline nor half the work as in the Queen's service. He pointed to a sergeant with a black eye that one of the men had given him. "They won't say anything about that, of course." The Scot was wearing a "made tie and a breastpin under his blouse," for, he explained, " 'I can wear anything I darn please.' " He was proud to be an American soldier. " 'But don't you forget, Sir, that it's taught me how to trust myself, and my shooting irons. I don't want fifty orders to move me across the Park, and catch a poacher. . . . This service isn't a patch on the Old Country's service; but you look, if it was worked up it would be just a Hell of a service.' "

Kipling was as nonplused by the mounts as he was by the soldiers. At Norris he met a young trooper, formerly of the Cape Mounted Rifles. The trooper boasted to Kipling that " 'As a matter of fact I suppose we're only mounted infantry, but remember we're the best mounted infantry in the world.' And the horse danced a fandango in proof."

" 'My faith!' said I, looking at the dusty blouse, grey hat, soiled leather accoutrements, and whale-bone poise of the wearer, 'If they are all like that, you are.' "[54]

Fort Yellowstone was a community unto itself. Civic tasks had to be carried out consistently and regulations were to be enforced. In winter the commanding officer forbade sledding on the Gardiner road. Skis were to be given special care. The quartermaster harvested ice for use during the summer. Sports tournaments were scheduled at the gymnasium where, by 1916, roller skating was also allowed. Fire regulations were intricate; they were

This is the "Zillah," Eli Waters's first passenger boat on Yellowstone Lake. *William H. Jackson photograph, ca. 1904, courtesy Colorado Historical Society.*

Philetus W. Norris in buckskins.
Photograph by Haynes Inc., courtesy Yellowstone National Park.

RULES AND REGULATIONS
OF THE
Yellowstone National Park.

DEPARTMENT OF THE INTERIOR,

WASHINGTON, D. C., May 4, 1881

1. The cutting or spoliation of timber within the Park is strictly forbidden by law. Also the removing of mineral deposits, natural curiosities or wonders, or the displacement of the same from their natural condition.

2. Permission to use the necessary timber for purposes of fuel and such temporary buildings as may be required for shelter and like uses, and for the collection of such specimens of natural curiosities as can be removed without injury to the natural features or beauty of the grounds, must be obtained from the Superintendent; and must be subject at all times to his supervision and control.

3. Fires shall only be kindled when actually necessary, and shall be immediately extinguished when no longer required. Under no circumstances must they be left burning when the place where they have been kindled shall be vacated by the party requiring their use.

4. Hunting, trapping and fishing, except for purposes of procuring food for visitors or actual residents, are prohibited by law; and no sales of game or fish taken inside the Park shall be made for purposes of profit within its boundaries or elsewhere.

5. No person will be permitted to reside permanently within the Park without permission from the Department of the Interior; and any person residing therein, except under lease, as provided in Section 2475 of the Revised Statutes, shall vacate the premises within thirty days after being notified in writing so to do by the person in charge; notice to be served upon him in person or left at his place of residence.

6. *THE SALE OF INTOXICATING LIQUORS IS STRICTLY PROHIBITED.*

7. All persons trespassing within the domain of said Park, or violating any of the foregoing rules, will be summarily removed therefrom by the Superintendent and his authorized employes, who are, by direction of the Secretary of the Interior, specially designated to carry into effect all necessary regulations for the protection and preservation of the Park, as required by the statute; which expressly provides that the same "shall be under the exclusive control of the Secretary of the Interior, whose duty it shall be to make and publish such rules and regulations as he shall deem necessary or proper;" and who, "generally, shall be authorized to take all such measures as shall be necessary or proper to fully carry out the object and purposes of this act."

Resistance to the authority of the Superintendent, or repetition of any offense against the foregoing regulations, shall subject the outfits of such offenders and all prohibited articles to seizure, at the discretion of the Superintendent or his assistant in charge.

APPROVED:

P. W. NORRIS,
SUPERINTENDENT.

S. J. KIRKWOOD,
SECRETARY.

Philetus Norris tacked onto trees hundreds of these muslin signs, the first posting of park rules and regulations. This one, still in remarkable condition, is among the Norris Papers.
Courtesy of The Huntington Library, San Marino, California.

From Jupiter Terrace at Mammoth Hot Springs visitors could view the unoccupied fortress-headquarters built by Philetus Norris.

William H. Jackson photograph, courtesy Colorado Historical Society

The army could take pride in Fort Yellowstone, which was laid out and maintained
in quintessential fashion. This is how it looked in 1902.
William H. Jackson photograph, courtesy Colorado Historical Society.

Soldiers did lonely duty at outposts such as this at Upper Geyser Basin,
close to the Giantess group of geysers, ca. 1902.
William H. Jackson photograph, courtesy Colorado Historical Society.

Three top military men in Yellowstone were, from left, Lieutenant W.W. Forsyth, Captain George Scott, and Lieutenant Elmer Lindsley.
Courtesy Bessie Haynes Arnold.

Superintendent Horace Albright, left, and Steve Mather, director of the National Park Service, right, pose in 1923 with C.W. Cook, who entered Yellowstone in 1869.
Courtesy National Park Service.

Army doctor Charles Gandy, Lieutenant John T. Nancy, Captain George Scott, and Lieutenant W. W. Forsyth (left to right) pose with buffalo heads confiscated from poacher Edgar Howell.
Photograph is credited to Dr. Gandy, courtesy Bessie Haynes Arnold.

Elk have been a Yellowstone problem for more than a hundred years. In this undated photograph they are being fed almost "out of hand."
Courtesy Archives-American Heritage Center, University of Wyoming.

"*Try and get it*"

Bears have been an attraction and a problem in Yellowstone from early days until
the present. Photographs such as this did not help at all.
Lawrence Baker Collection, courtesy Archives-American Heritage Center,
University of Wyoming.

ordered to be read periodically. Buildings were to be kept "neat and painted." Sick horses had to be cared for.[55]

A market wagon made daily trips to Gardiner, even in winter, and twice-a-day train service was maintained to Livingston. Personnel could look forward to leaves and occasional traveling assignments. They were issued rations for sustenance while on official business, or else were given funds for purchase of meals, plus spending money quaintly referred to as "funds for the purchase of liquid coffee."

Sanitation was a constant struggle. In our internal combustion age with its smog pollution, we tend to forget, or we are ignorant of, the unpleasantness of a more primitive time. Outdoor privies and the barnyard filth from large animals, the odors and the flies, are subjects more enjoyable read about than experienced. In the days before indoor plumbing and automobiles and insecticides the maintenance of good sanitary conditions was difficult in the extreme. In a mountainous location such as Fort Yellowstone diligent, constant vigilance was necessary to insure that the manure was removed from stables and deposited where it would not constitute a nuisance. Latrines had to be serviced adequately and often, and men were reminded of such simple measures as taking their drinking water from the stream *above* the latrines.[56]

Fort Yellowstone had its share of illnesses. On occasion the post surgeon required that all water for drinking and cooking purposes be "filtered through a cloth and boiled for at least five minutes before use." Hall's Store in Gardiner, where much Yellowstone shopping was conducted, was placed under quarantine for two weeks because the clerks had been exposed to smallpox. Fort personnel received typhoid inoculations. When a family came down with measles their home was placed under strict quarantine.[57]

Some deaths occurred. On the left side of the present road leading south past the Hot Springs, unbeknownst to all but a few park employees, is the neglected military graveyard. Its tombstones fail to reveal the act of cruelty brought about by army regulations. In a sense, the inscriptions are only half true, for the remains of all military personnel were disinterred and transferred to the military graveyard at the Custer Battlefield, leaving the interred spouses and children alone at the Fort Yellowstone cemetery. The number of infants buried there, as in all pioneer cemeteries, is shocking to us in this day of low infant mortality. One gravestone bears an especially poignant inscription: "Unknown Child."

Somewhere between a dozen and a score of servicemen were buried there, along with civilian saddlers, scouts, and teamsters, plus wives and children. They account for perhaps half the deaths at Fort Yellowstone: the other half was interred elsewhere at the request of survivors. When the army did bury one of its own at the fort, it handled the obsequies with eclat. Even the funeral of a lowly private included a procession involving a corporal and eight privates, pallbearers wearing dress uniforms and white gloves, the preacher or priest, firing of guns, taps, flag hung at half mast, and work canceled for the remainder of the day.[58]

The busy season was, of course, summertime. Then it was that the United States Cavalry presented itself best, and "secured the park." All the buglers were assembled to sound the notes for Reveille, Retreat, and To the Standard. Mounted Parade was designated for three days a week, with the bugle call for Boots and Saddles at 6:20 A.M., Assembly at 6:30 P.M., and Adjutant's Call at 6:35 P.M. "All men," read the order, "except guard, cooks, post bakers, sick, and men in confinement will attend." At Retreat roll call, out of barracks, on pass, and at all "formation dances at the hotel," enlisted men were to wear dress uniform; officers were under like orders save that on proper, unofficial occasions civilian evening dress could be worn. And, with the tourist season upon them the order went out that "all bathers in Bath Lake must have some sort of bathing costume."[59]

From the long veranda of the Mammoth Hotel the cavalry parades were observed by the beautiful people; the sweet, clarion notes of the bugle filled the clear, rarified atmosphere as Old Glory was lowered at sunset, and a cannon fired from Capitol Hill, marking the end of the day. Surely—surely all was well with the world, in those simple, slowpaced years, 1886 to 1918.

What was the public reception to military control of the park? Probably most visitors believed the army did a good job of protecting the reservation. Soldiers checked on sagebrushers, observing their campfires, making sure they did not destroy live trees for firewood, keeping tabs on the number of fish caught, checking the sealed firearms, and making sure dogs were leashed. Many tourists undoubtedly resented being stopped at entrance stations and questioned by armed soldiers. "We experienced a great relief on being at last out of the park," one citizen said. "It depresses one to be constantly under the watchful eye of the soldiers. They always treat you courteously enough, but for all that, offenders against the Park rules can expect little mercy from these vigilant guardians."[60]

The army also committed its usual sin of catering to the wealthy and powerful. Military officials saw eye-to-eye with the concessionaires in the belief that the park was primarily for those affluent enough to buy their way around the reservation in a company coach and stay at company hotels. Nowhere does it appear in the records, but Horace Albright says the army maintained an excellent VIP camp on the Lamar River where generals, Congressmen, Cabinet officers, and wealthy industrialists could "rough it" in the luxury of a camp policed by soldiers who cut the wood, built the fires, did the cooking, and cleaned up afterward.[61]

But let us give the army its due. With its tradition of order, its well-trained, obedient personnel, and its systematic enforcement of regulations, it secured Yellowstone during a critical era. Not until the aesthetic branch of conservationists brought about passage of the act creating the National Park Service was there a uniformed civilian force capable of doing the job as well. With the creation of the N.P.S. in 1916, the army left the park.

NOTES TO CHAPTER NINE

1. *Avant Courier,* February 22, 1883; *New York Times,* February 24, 1883, PMLR, Secretary of War to Secretary of Interior, March 17, 1883; *Enterprise,* September 18, 1883.

2. PMLS, Muldrow to Wear, August 14, 1886; PMLR, Wear to Muldrow, telegrams of August 19 and 22, 1886; Ibid., Captain Harris to Muldrow, September 1, 1886. According to the N.A., R.G. 98, Records of the U.S. Army Commands, Fort Yellowstone, Letters Sent, Annual Report [of acting superintendent] for 1915, "The barracks and stables originally known as Camp Sheridan located close to the road and opposite Jupiter Terrace," were torn down by the army in 1915.

3. R. G. 98, Fort Yellowstone Post General and Special Orders, October 1, 1918; author's interview with Bessie Haynes Arnold, October 1970.

4. James B. Trefethen, *Crusade for Wildlife: Highlights in Conservation Progress,* A Boone and Crockett Club Book (Harrisburg, Pa.: Stackpole, 1961); *Congressional Record,* 50th Cong., 1st Sess. (April 10, 1888), 2825; George S. Anderson, "Protection of the Yellowstone National Park" in *Hunting in Many Lands: The Book of the Boone and Crockett Club,* edited by Theodore Roosevelt and George Bird Grinnell (New York: Forest and Stream Publishing Co., 1895), 387.

5. Trefethen, *Crusade for Wildlife* 33.

6. F. A. Boutelle Papers, Special Collections, University of Oregon, Captain Harris to Boutelle, December 1, 1889.

7. Ibid., Boutelle to Harry Boutelle, March 26, 1890; Ibid., Boutelle to wife, April 6, 11, and 16, 1890.

8. Ibid. See also "Yellowstone National Park Investigation," 52d Cong., 1st Sess., Report No. 1956 (Serial No. 3051, Vol. 10), 164. In the "Testimony of E. C. Waters" contained therein, that individual said of Boutelle, "Last winter, while in Washington, the Captain favored cutting off a portion of the park rather than grant a railroad right of way through it. Three days after, he was at the opposite pole and lent his influence to the other party."

9. Boutelle Papers, Secretary Noble to Boutelle, January 31, 1891. In a letter to Arnold Hague, Boutelle blamed his removal on his defense of the stagecoachman Wakefield, and the intervention of the "crown prince"—President Harrison's son— on Silas Huntley's behalf. Hague Papers, Letters Received, Box III-B, April 26, 1891.

10. Ralph Pierson, "The Czar of Wonderland," The *Denver Westerners Brand Book,* Vol. 11 (1955), 375–86; George S. Anderson, "A Buffalo Story," in *American Big Game Hunting: The Book of the Boone and Crockett Club* (New York: Forest and Stream Publishing Co., 1901), 19–25.

11. Joseph Joffe, "John W. Meldrum," *Annals of Wyoming,* Vol. 13, No. 2 (April, 1941), Part 2, 109–10.

12. Pierson, "The Czar of Wonderland."

13. Author's interview with Mrs. Arnold, October 7, 8, and 9, 1970.

14. *Who Was Who in America,* Vol 1, 1392.

15. Author's interview with Lt. Colonel Heath Twitchell, May 12, 1971. Colonel Twitchell has since published his biography of General Allen, *Allen: The Biography of an Army Officer, 1859–1930* (New Brunswick, N.J.: Rutgers University Press, 1974).

16. *Annual Report of the Secretary of the Interior for 1896,* civ.

17. R. G. 98, Fort Yellowstone, Letters Sent, Major Pitcher to Military Secretary, Department of Dakota, February 18, 1906.

18. Author's interview with Mrs. Arnold.

19. R. G. 98, Circular, March 6, 1908. I have examined one of these books of Rules and Regulations in custody of the Western History Room at the Denver Public Library.

20. R. G. 98, General Orders No. 10, May 31, 1902; Ibid., Park Orders No. 6, June 2, 1916.

21. Y. A., File No. 2, Item 216, Noble to Anderson, August 24, 1891.

22. R. G. 98, Major Pitcher to Adjutant General, May 10, 1904; Ibid., Pitcher to Paymaster, Washington, D.C., June 1904. As an example of a typical troop transfer, in August 1905 Troops "C" and "D" of the 3rd Cavalry were ordered to San

Francisco and then to the Philippines. R. G. 98, Major Pitcher to the Military Secretary of Dakota, August 19, 1905.

23. Y. A., File No. 2, Item 217. Interior Secretary to Boutelle, October 23, 1890; Ibid., Item 301, statement of General Thomas H. Ruger, Headquarters, Department of Dakota, January 16, 1891. Arnold Hague had much to do with the site selection. See Hague Papers. For typical correspondence relating to construction of Fort Yellowstone, see R. G. 98, Pitcher to Adjutant General, Department of Dakota, November 3, 1904. See also David G. Battle and Erwin N. Thompson, *Fort Yellowstone Historic Structure Report* (Denver: U.S. Department of Interior, National Park Service, 1972).

24. R. G. 98, General Orders and Circulars.

25. Y. A., File No. 8, contains a series of letters between the Interior Department and the acting superintendent concerning the commissioner's building. For information on the Weather Bureau building, see R. G. 98, Pitcher to Chief Signal Officer Department of Dakota, St. Paul.

26. Y. A., File No. 21, copy of report of Inspector General's report, February 1, 1902; the inspection was made June 10, 1901

27. Ibid. Hague's Report, dated February 12, 1902, is filed with the Inspector General's. R. G. 98, Circular, January 16, 1905, states that lights will be turned off at 10:30 P.M. Mrs. Arnold did not recall an ice skating rink, but did remember roller skating. Author's interview.

28. Captain George S. Anderson, "Protection of the Yellowstone National Park," 7; R. G. 98, Park Orders No. 1, June 2, 1916, "By Order of Colonel Brett," gives a listing of stations then being manned; Ibid., Major Pitcher to Adjutant General, Department of Dakota, November 3, 16, 1904.

29. R. G. 98, Major Pitcher to Adjutant General, November 16, 1904.

30. Anderson, "Protection of the Yellowstone National Park," 7; Park Orders No. 4, June 30, 1917, Ibid., General Orders No. 7, May 29, 1904, author's interview with Mrs Arnold.

31. Lieutenant Alvin H. Sydenham, U.S.A., "Tommy Atkins in the American Army," *Harper's Weekly,* August 13, 1892, 780–81.

32. Captain Anderson, "Protection of the Park," 8–10.

33. R. G. 98, Special Orders No. 5, January 14, 1911; Special Orders No. 4, January 6, 1908.

34. Ibid., Major Pitcher to Adjutant General, Department of Dakota, November 3, 1904.

35. Frederick Remington, "Policing the Yellowstone," *Harper's Weekly,* Vol. 39, No. 1986 (January 12, 1895), 36.

36. Y. A., File No. 29, Major H. C. Benson to Interior Secretary, December 14, 1908; Ibid., File No. 2, Noble to Captain Boutelle, September 25, 1890; Anderson, "Protection of the Park," 8–9; R. G. 98, "Annual Report of the Superintendent, Yellowstone National Park, 1915," 30.

37. R. G. 98, General Order No. 7, May 29, 1904; Park Orders No. 7, June 2, 1916; Circular, June 22, 1908.

38. Ibid., Park Orders No. 16, June 2, 1916; General Orders No. 27, December 27, 1907.

39. Anderson, "Protecting the Park," 10.

40. R. G. 98, Special Order No. 142, December 15, 1902; Telegram, Captain Frank Barton, 3rd Cavalry, to Adjutant General, Department of Dakota, February 21, 1904; Ibid., March 12, 1918; Anderson, "Protecting the Park," 10.

41. Remington, "Policing the Yellowstone," 36–37.

42. R. G. 98, Special Orders No. 9, March 4, 1896; General Orders No. 80, December 2, 1891; Special Orders No. 2, January 20, 1896; Lieutenant Elmer Lindsey, "Winter Trip Through the Yellowstone," Harper's Weekly, Vol. 42, No. 2145 (January 19, 1898), 106–10.

43. See, for example, R. G. 98, Special Orders No. 8, February 28, 1898.

44. Author's interview with Mrs. Arnold.

45. R. G. 98, Memorandum, December 4, 1910; Pitcher to Adjutant General, Department of Dakota, December 11, 1904; April 27, 1904.

46. Jack Ellis Haynes, "Yellowstone Stage Holdups," The Denver Westerners Brand Book (Denver: Denver Corral of the Westerners, 1952), 86.

47. R. G. 98, Special Orders No. 10, March 5, 1896; Special Orders No. 12, March 23, 1896; Special Orders No. 139, January 5, 1899.

48. Ibid., Pitcher to Adjutant General, Department of Dakota, January 24, 1905; Ibid., Pitcher to Secretary, Department of Dakota, May 6, 1905.

49. Leslie W. (Gay) Randall, Footprints Along the Yellowstone (San Antonio: The Naylor Company, 1961), 84–85.

50. R. G. 98, Pitcher to surgeon, April 7, 1906.

51. Ibid., Circular, October 22, 1907; information from Aubrey Haines, former official Yellowstone Park historian.

52. R. G. 98, General Orders No. 6, March 27, 1905; Special Order No. 48, April 25, 1918; Ibid., S. B. M. Young to Interior Secretary, November 20, 1907.

53. Ibid., Park Order No. 2, June 16, 1908; Memorandum, June 2, 1916; Park Order No. 12, June 3, 1916.

54. Rudyard Kipling, *From Sea to Sea and Other Sketches: Letters of Travel* (London: The Macmillan Co., 1904), two Vols., Vol 2, 80–82; 87–88.

55. R. G. 98, Circular, February 14, 1908; Memorandum, January 23, 1915, and various orders and memos among the post records.

56. Ibid., Pitcher to Secretary, Department of Dakota, September 17, 1905, stating that the criticisms lodged by the Inspector General had been corrected.

57. Ibid., Circular No. 6 (no date); Memorandum, July 29, 1911; Special Orders No. 77, July 23, 1899.

58. Ibid., Circular, October 18, 1908. There was also a civilian cemetery on top of the hill behind the Mammoth Hotel.

59. Ibid., Circular, June 5, 1908; General Order No. 6, May 18, 1902; Circular No. 1, July 7, 1908; Circular, June 1, 1908.

60. Gardner Stilson Turrill, *A Tale of Yellowstone or, In a Wagon Through Western Wyoming and Wonderland* (Jefferson, Iowa: G. S. Turrill Publishing Co., 1901), 98–99.

61. Author's interview with Horace Albright, April 1970.

CHAPTER TEN

The National Park Service Takes Over

It would have been nice if the army could have left Yellowstone in a prideful display of the military at its best; however, "old army" departed in October 1916, then returned, and finally left for good in 1918.

The military had experienced a change of heart about the park assignment. In the 1870s and 1880s, with the Indian menace ending, it had wanted the job, but with America's rise to a world power, the army found itself increasingly hard-pressed to meet its global obligations. In 1916 troops commanded by General John J. Pershing chased Pancho Villa across northern Mexico. Add to this the buildup concomitant with the outbreak of the First World War, and the army's desire to be relieved of its policing obligations in the national parks becomes readily understandable.

When the army's orders to leave came through on August 26, 1916, it was generally understood that the War Department had been trying to extricate itself from the task for at least two years. In 1913 it had been removed from the California national parks. Citizens of Yellowstone's neighboring towns, especially Livingston, lamented the anticipated end of prosperity for the bars, bordellos, and poker dens frequented by the soldiers. The park concessionaires were apprehensive of the change. They knew, as anyone who has been part of the military is well aware, that despite the infinitude of regulations, an underlying cushion of "live and let live" makes life bearable under military control. They and the army were linked by a number of marriages. General S. B. M. Young had married Harry Child's sister-in-law, Huntley's widow.

Others were elated that the War and Interior departments had agreed to the removal. Happiest of all was a coterie of new administrators in a new branch of the Department of Interior, the National Park Service. It had been created by a briefly worded act of Congress on April 25, 1916. The service was "to promote and regulate" parks, monuments, and reservations in such a way as to "conserve the scenery and the natural and historic objects and the wildlife therein...for the enjoyment of the same in such manner and by such means as will leave them unimpaired for the enjoyment of future generations."[2]

American historians have given due credit to Gifford Pinchot, the great forest conservator, and to Theodore Roosevelt, who supported him with the prestige and power of the presidency in the crusade for forest conservation. The movement was successful. Pinchot, a champion of the "multiple use" idea under which the Forest Service functions, scattered his opposition and imposed his concepts not only upon key government personnel, but also upon the public mind. Nor did historians avoid the contagious philosophy. Forest conservation, Pinchot, and Roosevelt are the keys to the story as it is presented in nearly all American history textbooks.

Left out of the story is another facet of the movement: aesthetic conservation. As of January 1915, there were thirteen national parks and eighteen national monuments. The monuments were set aside under provisions of Congressman John F. Lacey's "Act for the Preservation of American Antiquities," passed in 1906. All of the parks and most of the monuments were under Interior's jurisdiction, the exceptions being assigned to the Department of Agriculture or the War Department. No overall policy existed for their administration. Congress was very busy, and if anyone had an interest in a park or monument, he was more likely to be a villain out to despoil rather than a knight seeking to protect.

Gradually a number of individuals demanded that some order be brought out of the chaos. At the Conservation Conference of Governors in 1908 Charles Evans Hughes of New York and J. Horace McFarland, president of the American Civic Association, spoke up for preservation of lands in the name of beauty. The first national parks conference, held at Yellowstone in September 1911, was supported by a powerful ally, the railroads, which still anticipated profits from passenger traffic. Supporters began arguing that men worked better after renewing their bodies and souls amidst the beauties of nature. They deplored the lost half billion dollars that Americans spent annually sightseeing overseas. Meanwhile the loss of the Hetch Hetchy Valley to San Francisco in 1913 alerted members of the Sierra Club, the Appalachian Mountain Club, and other organizations to the many threats to the national parks. Although Pinchot and his crew would have nothing of this, the concept of aesthetic conservation was born; it provided a viable though embryonic philosophy for justification of national parks and monuments and for their absolute inviolability.

Not until the Wilson administration and the appointment of Franklin K. Lane as interior secretary was any real progress toward centralized administration made. Because Congress hated to think of the creation of a new "bureau," the suggestion was made that a "service" be created. "As distinct from the word 'bureau,'" writes Professor Runte, "'service' implied that the new agency would not have as much political power." Now Lane, a Californian, brought in a Berkeley economics professor named Adolph C. Miller to lay the groundwork for such a "service." Miller, a man of some means financially, brought to Washington with him a young student of his, twenty-three-year-old Horace M. Albright.[3]

Miller, a top administrator, was making progress but proved too useful for so menial a task as creating a Park Service. President Wilson appointed him to the Federal Reserve Board. At this juncture a remarkable though somewhat tragic figure stepped onto the scene. This was Stephen Tyng Mather. Assigned as his aide was young Albright; it was January 1915. As Professor Swain says, neither the national parks nor Albright were ever the same again.[4]

Mather was a handsome, California-raised Yankee whose last name identified him, correctly, with the Puritan Mathers. In college he had been dubbed "the Eternal Freshman" because of his exuberance and enthusiasm for causes. After graduating from the University of California he worked briefly for the New York Sun and then took employment with a wealthy skinflint dubbed "Borax" Smith; Mather advanced rapidly as a promoter and advertising man. "Twenty Mule Team Borax" as a trade name was Mather's idea. Not until his thirty-sixth year did he leave Smith. Within little more than a decade thereafter he had made himself a millionaire in the borax business, and at age forty-seven this hyperactive man was seeking causes to espouse.

He had been shocked at conditions in Sequoia and Yosemite when he camped there in 1914 and had written Secretary Lane protesting the situation. Lane's reaction was to offer Mather the task vacated by Miller. That is why Mather was in Washington, D.C., in January 1915, taking control of the as yet unborn bureau, or service, or whatever it would be named, providing Congress passed a bill to bring it into being.

What set Mather apart from the run-of-the-mill huckster was his intellect. He chose his causes carefully, supported them with Calvinistic fervor, and promoted his ideas so energetically that they were crowned with success. He was a natural aristocrat instinctively accepted by the power elite. He was an outdoorsman who loved wilderness. He was a good aesthetic conservationist although his was not a contemplative nature. Inspiration Point would have held his attention for less than five minutes. Steve Mather was, in fact, too intense, too hard driving. He suffered nervous breakdowns which resulted in humiliating, embarrassing incidents of abnormal behavior.

Why was it necessary for the interior secretary to bring in wealthy men from outside the government to construct a new "service"? For not only were Miller and Mather well-to-do; they brought in wealthy men or subsidized good men of moderate means in order to keep them. In his will Mather left

$25,000 to both Albright and Arno B. Cammerer hoping to keep them in the government service. Both became National Park Service directors.[5]

Save for a few really outstanding civil servants, Interior's employees were not outstanding and in any event were not considered policy-makers or managers. Secretary Lane therefore searched elsewhere. He liked Californians because they shared with him a common heritage; besides, he knew a good many of his choices personally. Thus Steve Mather was asked to commit for his country an act of noblesse oblige. He did it admirably. And because of the way he did it, the National Park Service had an early growth unlike that of any other government agency.

Mather carried out his task in a most unorthodox fashion. By the time he arrived in Washington many aesthetic conservationists had decided their cause needed publicity. Mather determined to "sell" the park idea, not only to Congress but to the American public as well. He employed Robert Sterling Yard, a competent journalist, at $5,000 a year of Mather's own money, to help along the crusade. Some have called it the "See America First" campaign. Under Yard's direction a flood of news items, magazine articles, photographs and expensive books appeared to promote the national parks. Many were of Yard's own authorship. He also enlisted a number of contemporary literary figures in his campaign: Emerson Hough, whose best-known novel, *The Covered Wagon* was written in Yellowstone; mystery writer Mary Roberts Rinehart; a now forgotten western writer, Hal G. Everts; George Horace Lorimer, editor of the powerful *Saturday Evening Post;* and the editor of the *Brooklyn Eagle,* H.V. Kaltenborn. Mather's biographer states that between 1915 and 1919 some 1,050 magazine articles were published pertaining to national parks.[6]

It is hard to imagine a civil servant implementing such a publicity campaign, but Mather held a caveat from the head office warning old civil servants to let him operate as he wished. The result was that aesthetic conservationists for a few years surpassed in power and influence the multiple use foresters. The National Park Service became almost as well known as the Post Office, the park rangers in their green uniforms and broad-rimmed hats as readily identifiable as blue-uniformed mail carriers.

For a while in the public mind the service could do no wrong. Pride in this star in the Interior Department's galaxy of bureaus, departments—and services—was manifested in a warm welcoming statement Franklin K. Lane made to visitors to Yellowstone. It appeared in a pamphlet issued by the United States Railroad Administration (a wartime agency, 1918–21). One impressed reader was prompted to write the secretary as follows:

> 'Uncle Sam asks you to be his guest,' you say. There you have it! We are apt to think of the Government as taking from us in taxes, blood, in many, many ways, and returning us only certain invisible rather vague benefits.

You picture Uncle Sam as the genial host who has gone very much out of what we think of as his way to do a very happy, gracious, and tangible thing for the enjoyment of the people. . . .If all the people could be made to see this really beneficent and truly fatherly Uncle Sam, there would be no danger of Bolshevism in our country. . . .[7]

Floating through the period 1916 to 1945 on this wave of euphoria were the dedicated personnel of the new National Park Service. True, Mather's followers constituted a personality cult, but so strong were their ideals, and such fine men were they, that after a time the service advanced on its own momentum. Mather died in 1930, but Horace Albright, Roger W. Toll, Edmund G. Rogers, Arno B. Cammerer, and many other disciples carried on. The momentum began to fade in the 1930s, but not until the end of the Second World War did a new guard take over; then Mather and his followers, as well as much of their idealism, became passé.

The years 1916 to 1921 constituted another one of those brief periods in American history when much was happening and a greater-than-usual instability crept into the federal government. The First World War ended and a citizen military force was disbanded; a president became ill and his cause was lost; a sharp depression ensued, and the Republican party came into power. Franklin K. Lane resigned as interior secretary on February 8, 1920; John Barton Payne stepped in briefly (March 1, 1920–March 4, 1921); he was followed by Albert B. Fall, who resigned in disgrace in early 1923.

Lane is a problem for conservationists and park enthusiasts. Seven national parks and the service itself were created while he was secretary. He brought in Steve Mather. Yet he played a major role in the loss of California's Hetch Hetchy Valley and favored an irrigation plan that would have destroyed Yellowstone's integrity. Payne and Fall held office only briefly, yet Payne reversed Lane's position on Yellowstone's southwest, or Cascade Corner.[8]

Getting the army out of Yellowstone was a portent of what Park Service personnel were going to have to recognize—that politics is a continuing, insidious influence over the parks. In Livingston the chamber of commerce sent a local booster, Judge James F. O'Connor, to Chicago to confer with Senator Thomas J. Walsh "relative to keeping the soldiers in Yellowstone Park." The judge was successful. Secretary of War Newton D. Baker directed a stay in the orders for their removal "until he personally investigated the matter." Eventually Congressman John J. Fitzgerald, the negativistic chairman of the House Appropriations Committee, canceled funds in the Sundry

Civil Appropriations Bill providing for Yellowstone's protection and thus forced retention of the army in the park. The linkage is quite clear from the businessmen of Livingston to Judge O'Connor to Senator Walsh to Secretary Baker to Congressman Fitzgerald.[9]

So the troops marched out—and marched back again. They were absent during the winter of 1916–17, however, during which about forty civilian scouts, many of whom were soldiers allowed to resign to fill the positions, policed the park. Their supervisor and acting superintendent was Chester A. Lindsley who for many years had been the Interior Department clerk at Fort Yellowstone. In June 1917 Lindsley announced the return of the troops. The local newspaper chortled that the Park County Chamber of Commerce "was instrumental" in this action, adding that the troops gave "to Wonderland a distinctive, picturesque touch, which is attractive to the tourists."[10]

Although the army was back, Yellowstone's concessionaires and people in the park environs dealing with them or with the government were quickly aware that things were no longer the same. The active, guiding presence of Steve Mather, Horace Albright, and the new National Park Service which were now making policy was apparent. Motorized vehicles replaced horse-drawn ones, ending the nearby hay ranchers' lucrative market. A chaotic situation involving several permanent camping companies with agents hawking their services at Gardiner and West Yellowstone eased as Mather pushed a monopoly policy. People in the region came to accept as inevitable the removal of troops and the permanent presence of a completely civilian administration of Yellowstone.

The removal was not long in coming. Horace Albright quickly mastered the intricacies of Washington lobbying. He made friends on Capitol Hill, and when Congressman Fitzgerald failed to run for reelection the way was cleared to get those troops out of Yellowstone. The Sundry Civil Bill of July 1, 1918 (Public Law 81, 65th Congress), included, as Assistant Secretary Alexander Vogelsang reminded the Secretary of War, "funds for the establishment of a civilian ranger force, thus making the abandonment of Fort Yellowstone possible and granting authority for the Interior Department to assume control of the improvement of the park." On September 18 Troop G of the 11th Cavalry, the last unit to be stationed in the park, excepting some army engineers, were ordered out. Getting rid of the engineers took a bit longer. "I hope," said Albright, "that I may never run across another body of men that I dislike as much as the Engineer Corps of the Army."[11]

Not until July 1919, did Horace Albright, not yet thirty years old, assume the superintendency of Yellowstone National Park. Authority was no longer split, for the army was gone. The new National Park Service gave the park administrators a better home office than had ever before existed; no longer would an assistant secretary be delegated willy-nilly to handle park affairs in Washington. Albright had the backing of Steve Mather. To aid in the young superintendent's success was the impetus of park visitation inspired by the "See America First" movement. America was park conscious as never before; it was also more mobile and thus more prone to wander to places of beauty. Albright's very position made him an American celebrity: The Duke of Yellowstone.

He was born and raised in Bishop, California, in the northern reaches of the Owens Valley. By the time he graduated from high school Albright was already an inveterate joiner, gregarious, cheerful, and bright. After receiving his bachelor's degree from the University of California in 1912, he worked toward a law degree, earning his keep as general assistant to his economics professor, Adolph C. Miller; it was he whom Albright accompanied to Washington. When Miller moved on to the Federal Reserve Board, young Albright went with Miller's successor, Steve Mather. When his boss became ill, Albright stepped into the breach with equal enthusiasm but much more balance. By the fall of 1918, when Mather had recovered from one of his breakdowns, Horace—although he desired to leave the service—was pressured into remaining. When he was offered the superintendency of Yellowstone National Park, he accepted, and stayed on.[12]

The man possessed incredible confidence and was an excellent executive. He arrived in the park with hard-set notions of his role. He was to run Yellowstone as smoothly as possible "for the people," protect it from damage, keep its land, waters, animals and thermal phenomena absolutely inviolate, and be a public relations man enhancing at every opportunity the park's world wide reputation. He fought for park extension into the Tetons; faced angry Wyoming, Montana, and Idaho irrigation, ranching, and hunting interests; and stuck by his beliefs.

When he issued orders, his subordinates knew they must be carried out: the duke could hire and fire, and he did. He was quick to praise when praise was due. In August 1919 he released a news item commending chief of scouts Jimmy McBride and announcing that the scouts (rangers) had done a better job at policing the park than the soldiers had ever accomplished. He gave short shrift to the Ku Klux Klan that was powerful in those years in the upper Yellowstone Valley. He refused to join, warned his personnel to avoid them, and defended Roman Catholics in his employ when the Klan wanted them fired. (But he did not interfere when the Klan coerced neighboring bootleggers. Some of the gulches north of the park were as full of stills as a West Virginia "holler," and one large family of bootleggers was from the Mountain State.)[13]

Albright's relations with concessionaires are puzzling. His biographer, Professor Donald Swain, describes a tug-of-war with Harry Child which ended in an Albright victory, or at least in a workable understanding. By 1924, according to Swain, Child had decided that Albright was better as a known devil than some unknown who might replace him. This was in spite of the fact that Albright insisted that Park Service personnel be allowed in the hotels (enlisted soldiers had been denied this privilege). He made the big company cease the misuse of park resources. And he insisted that Child upgrade his services. Park buses were to obey speed laws. When the drivers hung black crepe on their vehicles and purposely made their guests late for dinner, blaming it on the superintendent, Albright stuck to his guns. The following season from opening day on he stomped down hard on violators and pretty well won the battle. [14]

But did Albright, and the Park Service, apply sufficient pressure to the concessionaires for improvements in facilities and services? In 1924 Child gained control of the permanent camps, thus becoming the park transportation, hotel, and camps monopolist. One of Child's former employees, Charles Hamilton, ran the retail stores. "Service improved consistently through the twenties, as Child and Albright worked together, hammering out the final guidelines of a policy of 'regulated monopoly' in Yellowstone," writes Swain, adding that "Mather and Albright always operated on the theory that since Congress refused to appropriate enough money to develop the parks the only alternative was to turn to private capital, making each park a well-regulated business preserve for a single franchise holder." [15]

Unquestionably the regulated monopoly—which park personnel increasingly called "public utilities"—became stronger and more powerful than ever. A question does arise, however, about whether service improved through the twenties. In each successive year more visitors had to be serviced, but improvements came slowly: many would insist that facilities and services did not keep up with increased visitation. Another question is, whom did the service defend when complaints were lodged against the concessionaires? Once the Child forces and Albright had settled upon a working relationship, the record shows that the young superintendent appears to have become the concessionaires' most ardent defender. As early as 1919 he was defending the hotel company against a complainant. "It would have been impossible to have satisfied him at the Waldorf-Astoria," Albright wrote to a superior in Washington. [16]

An acting director (not otherwise identified), replying in 1926 to a query by Gray Line Motor Tours as to the possibility of running its tour buses across Yellowstone from the west to the east entrances, peremptorily refused permission. The letter includes a peculiar, illogical denial of monopoly: "There are no monopolies within the Yellowstone National Park, nor within any other national parks," it reads. "There are hotel companies, camp companies, and transportation companies that operate within Yellowstone National Park under contracts authorized by statute over such periods of time as

make possible investments of sufficient size to secure for the public the necessities and conveniences that could not be secured without such contracts."
The letter further stated that "if the park were thrown open to any or all
individuals, corporations, or organizations," they would stay while money
was to be made and leave when profits dried up "as has been borne out by
experience in the past." Thus ran the Park Service's stubborn defense of its
concession policy, a defense often reflecting bureaucratic paranoia with arguments that defied logic. [17]

Even after Albright had left Yellowstone for the Park Service directorship, he continued his defense of the concessionaires. He informed Secretary Ickes in 1933 that their profits "were not excessive even during the
period of heavy travel prior to 1930." While it is true that a few growth
industries such as automobiles and radio, and some highly speculative areas
of investment such as electric utilities, earned enormous profits on invested
income in the 1920s, most corporations during the era were pleased to earn 8
or 10 percent; anything over that was considered corporate fantasizing. By
this average most concessionaires' profits *were* excessive during the era
Child's Lodge and Camps Company, for example, averaged a net profit of
27.36 percent per year from 1924 to 1930. His transportation company
averaged a rate of return of 22.41 percent from 1924 to 1929. The rate of
return on the hotels is not available, but net profits for the two companies
(hotel and transportation) from 1922 to 1929 were $4,290,892. Even the
little Yellowstone Boat Company, another Child operation, earned in excess
of 7 percent in these years. [18]

As director, Albright carried his defense of concessionaires further than
simple statements to the secretary of interior. In April of the depression year
1933 he wrote Yellowstone's Superintendent Roger W. Toll that he had "not
forgotten that signs point to one of the poorest years in the history of our
public utility operators and I am overlooking no possibilities of assisting
them in carrying on during the present adverse conditions." He then informed the superintendent that a contract would be let for transporting the
Civilian Conservation Corps to their work places and back to their camps.
Albright suggested that the concessionaires "with large fleets of idol [sic]
buses will find it a good business proposition to make a very low rate for the
service. . . . If the rate quoted by the park operators is satisfactory the Secretary can authorize such a special rate and a contract can be let at once without
the delay incident to advertising and letting to the lowest bidder." He ordered Toll to "discuss this at once with the park operator, [and] work out
such a schedule rate which you feel will be satisfactory, and submit to me as
soon as possible for consideration." [19]

After 1924 Albright was involved in very few controversies with concessionaires. Haynes, Hamilton, Pryor and Trischman, and above all Child, got

along well with the garrulous superintendent. There was continuous, though mild, policing of the concessionaires. Their accounts were now audited and they paid the Park Service a graduated percentage of gross profits, never over 4 percent. "Bring us no trouble and we will cause you no trouble" seemed to be the understanding. If profits were excessive, that was not the concern of the National Park Service.[20]

Occasionally the interior secretary did have conditions called to his attention that seemed wrong—conditions the Park Service should have been aware of and rectified—and nudged the service into taking action. The department still assigned an assistant secretary to oversee park affairs, and often it was through this individual that faults were revealed. It was Assistant Secretary E.C. Finney, for example, who, after a Yellowstone trip, noted that the concessionaires were charging forty-five cents a gallon for gasoline in the park and forty cents near the railroad terminus, while local dealers in Gardiner were charging just thirty-one and thirty-three cents. The government, he discovered, was being charged twenty-one cents a gallon wholesale at the Gardiner entrance. "Apparently, therefore," he reported to the secretary, "the profits of the concessioners on gasoline in the park were about 100%." The result, on orders emanating from the secretary's office, was a five-cent cut. It was also Finney who wrote transportation company officials informing them in no uncertain terms what he thought of their charging an ill passenger fifty dollars to be driven to a lower altitude.[21]

That Interior officials outside the Park Service were uncertain of the soundness of the service's regulated monopoly policy, at least as it was being administered, is evident in a letter from Secretary Ray Lyman Wilbur to Superintendent Albright. "I recognize that there are very important advantages in authorizing one company to furnish a particular service or group of services to the public in a national park," he wrote, "but a company having such authority and a preferential right franchise must at all times be mindful of its obligations to give the best possible service within all the lines of activities assigned to it. . . . .I think the large profits these companies are making and the accumulation of a large surplus is worthy of careful review. . . ."[22]

Horace Albright does not seem to have been bothered one whit by those excessive profits. He was Steve Mather's protégé; Mather had promoted the policy, was a millionaire and thought like one. It was a Republican era. What was wrong with fortunes being made in the park? And always Albright had to be aware that, by a conservative estimate, half of his predecessors had been removed—fired, transferred, or "kicked upstairs"—because they had clashed with the powerful concessionaires. Young Horace Albright liked his job. Finally, by maintaining smooth relations with Child, Haynes, and Hamilton, the three most powerful, he had time to devote his excessive energy to other activities. There were a number of them, they were important, and he had his hands full.

When he arrived in Yellowstone Albright was shocked at the accumulation of refuse and junk. Old army had never been a very good housekeeper. Abandoned sites of some of the camping companies lay in decrepitude. As for the army engineers, they may have been very good at building roads (though Albright would dispute that), but they left massive piles of timber and brush along the roadsides. With minimal funds Albright did what he could, but it was not until he hosted the Davison family—née Rockefeller—that he gained private funding to have the job well done.[23]

At public relations Albright sometimes acted like a combination of P. T. Barnum and Flo Ziegfield. Effervescent, talkative, and gregarious, the Duke of Yellowstone was always ready to entertain visitors. He cared not whether they were Europeans born to the purple, presidents of the United States, or three farm families from outside Coffeeville, Kansas, camping together at Indian Creek, their Model Ts parked crank handle to crank handle like three docile mules standing head to head. He introduced himself, sat down on a log by the fire, accepted a cup of coffee and chatted on and on. They loved him for it. Of average height, slim, healthy and photogenic, he was always amenable for photographs. Once, however, his good judgment let him down. It resulted in a journalistic brouhaha that harmed his good name—not much, but a little. It happened this way:

In 1924 Famous Players-Lasky Corporation (which used the name and logo of Paramount Pictures) began filming Zane Grey's novel, *The Thundering Herd*. The script called for a buffalo stampede of epic proportions, the biggest ever. But as the producers soon discovered, there were in the United States only about a dozen herds in private hands, and only two of them approached as many as five hundred head. Director William K. Howard wanted more rampaging beasts than that.

Then someone became aware of the estimated two thousand buffalo that grazed in Yellowstone National Park. According to the *New York Times,* Colonel Tim McCoy, formerly adjutant general of Wyoming and later a western film star, interceded in behalf of the film company to gain Superintendent Albright's permission to film the Yellowstone herd. Subsequently for several weeks "eighteen expert rangers" under supervision of the reservation gamekeeper, Bob LaComb, busied themselves in the frustrating, difficult, and dangerous task of rounding up the herd. The time for filming arrived.

Cameramen risked their lives as their protective battlements were unexpectedly nearly surmounted by the stampeding beasts. Mounted actors, by the script spurring their horses just ahead of the rampaging herd, were terrified at discovering the buffalo gaining on them. Despite a few narrow escapes, no one was hurt; the photographers did their work well and the stampede was one of the film's highlights. [24]

For reasons unrecorded but not difficult to surmise, Albright had a note appended to the movie's end. In it he stated categorically that there had not been a single instance of animal cruelty in the filming. Unfortunately for the young superintendent, *The Thundering Herd* was replete with scenes in which horses fell, ran at high speed into the sides of covered wagons, slipped on ice, and were otherwise, in the film at least, subjected to excessive cruelty. [25]

Hardly had *The Thundering Herd* had its premier showing before R. Lee Ste. Fleure, District Marshal of the Santa Barbara, California, Humane District, was firing off protest letters. "We are respectfully requesting that the Secretary of the Interior . . . cause an investigation to be made as to why the buffalo in Yellowstone National Park were used in this evidently brutal way. . . ." read one letter. To Will Hays of the Motion Picture Producers and Distributors of America Ste. Fleure added: "if you want to see . . . the enlightening sight of the wounded buffalo squirming in agony on the ground despite the very evident erroneous statement made by the Superintendent of Yellowstone National Park appended to the end of the picture stating that there was no cruelty attached to any of the thrilling episodes of the pictures . . . [then see *The Thundering Herd*]." [26]

Mather defended Albright, saying that the use of buffalo "was authorized under permit from the National Park Service," that "the filming was done under the personal supervision of Superintendent Albright and park rangers, so there would be no mistreatment of buffalo. Only one buffalo was roped, thrown and photographed to present the killing that nearly exterminated the buffalo in this country. The particular buffalo was none the worse for the experience." Mather also reminded the Interior secretary that the horse scenes in which excessive cruelty was so evident were not shot in the park. Albright expressed the wish that he had stated in his end-of-picture disclaimer that "there was no cruelty practised on the *buffalo* in securing any of the thrilling effects in the picture." (Italics his.) This should have ended the controversy. [27]

But the rumors refused to die. In August 1925 during a Senate committee hearing at Gardiner charges were made that while the motion picture company was on location in the park the herd was stampeded not once but eight or nine times a day, many animals were killed, the picture crew feasted on buffalo steaks and took buffalo hides with them when they departed!

Apparently none of these allegations was true, but such is the power of malicious gossip that they are still heard in the Yellowstone region.[28]

Although Albright became widely known in the northern Rockies, he was not widely loved by the residents. Some disliked him because he was a tough law enforcer. Nearby inhabitants were disciplined for bootlegging, exceeding speed limits, hunting inside the fringes of the reservation, and for a variety of other violations. In the summer of 1925 these malefactors were given an opportunity to vent their anger and they made the most of it. Their forum was the Senate Committee on Public Lands which in the 1920s was the handmaiden of irrigation, lumber, and grazing interests. Chairing the group was Arizona's Senator Ralph Henry Cameron. He hated Steve Mather and was determined to destroy him and the National Park Service. He and his packed subcommittee set out on a "fact-finding" junket through the West.[29]

Cameron was teamed with a fellow Republican, Senator Robert Nelson Stanfield of Oregon, a cattleman harboring a personal grievance against the Forest Service. Senator Tasker Oddie of Nevada was the third Republican on the subcommittee. The Democratic members, Senators Clarence C. Dill of Washington, John B. Kendrick of Wyoming, and Frank R. Gooding of Idaho, appear not to have relished the hearings the group held in a number of western cities; by the time the subcommittee reached Yellowstone, they had departed.[30]

The general passenger agent of the Union Pacific Railroad informed Albright that the subcommittee was bound for Yellowstone via the west entrance. The superintendent was barely able to reach there before the remaining senators—Cameron, Stanfield, and Oddie—arrived; of the three, only Oddie was the least bit friendly. L.C. Speer, the *New York Times* correspondent assigned to travel with the group, warned Albright that the committee was out to get him. Indeed, its staff had already been busy, for when he arrived at his office the next morning Albright found his desk ransacked.[31]

Hearings were held at Gardiner on August 29. The subcommittee had not found it difficult to muster a crew of malcontents who were delighted to testify against Albright, the National Park Service, and the federal government in general. Most citizens of that dilapidated little community depended upon the reservation for their livelihood; among such people many a simmering grudge was awaiting just such an opportunity as this one to surface.

More than a dozen witnesses were heard, all of them with a complaint. The *Times* reporter suggested that if their charges against Albright were true, then a federal grand jury should be convened. "But," he added, "in justice to Colonel Albright...it must be said that on the surface at least the evidence so far is of a flimsy nature." (Why the reporter referred to Albright as "Colonel" is a mystery.)

Senator Oddie questioned Max Imo, a bootlegger who had been ordered out of the park. Had he ever been convicted of selling liquor? " 'No sir,' " Imo replied, " 'I pleaded guilty.' " Richard Mayer, "a picturesque character who had lived in the Yellowstone country for forty years," complained of being banned from the park because he had carried dynamite with which to test a mineral claim just outside the park—but reached only through Yellowstone. " 'They were afraid it would scare the dudes,' " he explained. " 'What do you mean by dudes?' " Senator Cameron asked. " 'City fellows,' " was the reply.[32]

The most controversial matter uncovered was Park Service cooperation with wealthy Easterners in the purchase of Silver Tip Lodge, located on Slough Creek just north of the park boundary. For years a poacher named "Frenchy" Duret had lived there. Park Service scouts had known for years that Frenchy enticed animals to the vicinity of Silver Tip and then trapped or shot them. In 1922 he was killed by a grizzly; Albright had done several acts of kindness for his widow. When unsavory characters took steps to purchase Silver Tip Lodge, the superintendent brought the matter to the attention of eastern interests. The upshot was that a man named Cochran, who was affiliated with J.P. Morgan and Company, purchased the lodge, retaining title but granting the Park Service jurisdiction over it. The senators seemed to see something sinister in the agreement. Other testimony embraced the buffalo stampede and Albright's policy toward the overpopulation of elk.[33]

The Duke of Yellowstone was the last man to take the stand. " 'I have been on trial', " he stated, " 'all morning with convicted bootleggers, a quack doctor, a disgruntled ex-road foreman, an ex-ranger with a bad record, and other men with personal grievances, testifying against me through the convenient method of leading questions from the man who assembled this group of malcontents. . . .' " So well did he defend himself that Senator Cameron's kangaroo committee adjourned immediately, packed up and headed for Helena, where hearings were to be held to embarrass the Forest Service. As the *Times* correspondent wrote, the committee had "caught a tartar" when it tried to humiliate Horace Albright.[34]

While some residents of nearby communities resented Albright for his strictness, others considered him a symbol of federal intrusion upon their rights and prerogatives. When speaking out for park extension into the Tetons or against proposals by irrigationists, the superintendent stepped on the toes of influential people. Nor did he let up after he stepped from the superintendency into the directorship of the service in 1929. They resented it—and him—and made their feelings known. "It would seem that right now is the time to exert some restraint upon the avaricious activities and designs of our Director of National Parks, Horace M. Albright," wrote C.E. Piersell, president of the Wyoming branch of the Izaak Walton League of America, "before he attains monarchical jurisdiction over the entire, remaining, public domain of the State of Wyoming." Albright left government service of his own volition in 1933, entering the borax business and doing very well in it.[35]

It is difficult to mention anything that happened in Yellowstone and its environs in the twenties decade without Albright's name being mentioned. He and Mather and the men they gathered around them worked as a winning team. The Duke of Yellowstone, as the man on the scene, was responsible for building an excellent, capable, courteous ranger force of about eighty men (and an occasional woman). They somehow held in control a visitation that increased year after year. He supervised construction of camps, interpretation facilities, and operations meant to keep the park clean and well policed. He successfully fought off the reclamationists and tried to cope with elk overpopulation. In the balance, and in spite of a few minuses, Horace Albright was the man for the Yellowstone superintendency at the time. He filled the position admirably.

With Horace Albright's departure from Yellowstone, a period of transition began in the park superintendency. This reflected changes that were apparent in the Park Service itself. As it grew it took on the aspects, good and bad, of a typical government bureau. Director Albright, with the cooperation of Congressman Louis C. Cramton, chairman of the subcommittee on Interior Department appropriations, brought about a 46 percent increase in Park Service funds within three years. As Professor Swain says, the new director "upgraded and professionalized" the service and in 1931 succeeded in placing park and monument superintendents under Civil Service. Although he was politically conservative and would later do well as a businessman, Albright did not hesitate to increase drastically the number of Park Service employees.[37]

The gradual change from a small service of dedicated men, many of whom had already been successful outside of government, to a major government bureau staffed with career employees concerned with their own futures, was discernible to close observers. They noticed the inevitable proliferation of paper work and the emergence within the larger bureau of cliques and empires. The service was changing from what had been a refreshing newcomer in Interior to just another stodgy, elephantesque bureau.

An indication of this transformation was the declining power of the field representatives—the superintendents—as more and more decision making was concentrated in Washington. Improvements in long distance telephone communication and the increasing use of fast commercial airliners accelerated the trend. Thus Albright's two immediate successors in Yellowstone, Roger W. Toll and Edmund G. Rogers in that order, are transition figures. Both were first generation Park Service people and as such retained the dedication and coveted the esprit of the original service. They were administrators who still made decisions without "clearing it with Washington." But even as they went about their duties they could see the changes happening. Above all they were aware of the new ranger, college educated and career minded, weighing every move in terms of how it would affect his future. As the old-timers fumed over them, the newcomers fidgeted away their time until their new breed could take over.

In 1929 Roger W. Toll was forty-six years old. Colorado born, he had been educated at Columbia University, had served briefly with the Coast and Geodetic Survey in Alaska, and had been chief engineer for the Denver Tramway Company. He had risen to the rank of major during the First World War and, afterwards, had turned his back upon private employment and joined the National Park Service. In 1919 and 1920 he was superintendent of Mount Rainier National Park; from 1921 until his promotion to Yellowstone, he was superintendent of Rocky Mountain National Park in Colorado.[38]

Superintendent Toll, whose superior (Albright) was also his immediate predecessor, assumed Yellowstone's management with minimal disruption. He maintained vigilance against reclamationists who remained active throughout the 1930s and continued Park Service policies which by now had assumed a status of permanence. During Toll's first three years Yellowstone's concessionaires were prosperous, although the country at large was sinking more deeply into depression. By 1932, however, visitation was down from the 1929 high of 260,697 to just 157,624. Some hotels and lodges were closed and the concessionaires were wailing, yet there was among them no panic. A nationwide depression that cut park visitation was, in fact, a godsend to the park. Nature gained a respite and service personnel could tend to long overdue repairs and improvements.[39]

Nationally an election brought a change in party and presidents. Franklin D. Roosevelt was concerned with the plight of unemployed youth, especially young men in the cities whom he thought would benefit from a job corps placing them in the country; he also believed in a program of reforestation. Such thoughts materialized into the Civilian Conservation Corps—the CCC. Suddenly the military, primarily the army, was charged with handling thousands of young unemployed men, feeding, clothing, and sheltering them, and putting them to work conserving and improving the nation's natural resources. At its peak in 1935 more than a half million unmarried men were housed in more than twenty-six hundred CCC camps.[40]

The CCC was authorized in the early spring of 1933 and by early summer young men had signed up, camps had been established, and the boys were at work; by New Year's 1934 most early mistakes had been identified and rectified and the corps was functioning with relative stability. Unfortunately several of the first camps where administrators had to learn lessons by trial and error were in Yellowstone National Park.[41]

In 1933 the park was host to four of the 1,331 camps that were operational by the end of June. One each was located at Mammoth, Canyon, Lake, and West Gallatin (on Bacon Rind Creek toward the northwest boundary). Most of these CCC boys (as they were usually called) were among the 55,000 eastern city dwellers who, after a "reconditioning" of one to three weeks at places like Fort Dix, New Jersey, were shipped to camps in the Far West. Because of changes in the program in the first few months, the precise number of enrollees in each of the Yellowstone camps is indefinite, but the number 190 appears in the records. In addition there was the camp superintendent, usually an army officer, and seven foremen or supervisors who were often unemployed local war veterans able to pass as experts in landscaping, forestry, or engineering. "The boys did a wonderful job," wrote Conrad Wirth, one of the CCC administrators. And indeed they did. As time went on, camps were sought by communities which recognized the good they could accomplish and the money they brought into town.[42]

However, *initially* many a western community was apprehensive of the arrival in its midst of two hundred healthy, street-wise young men from big cities. Generally the success of a camp, the harmony of its relations with the nearby community, and the quality and usefulness of the projects it completed depended upon the camp superintendent's competence, although certainly the presence of disruptive elements in the camp could have given it a bad name despite the best administration. Since newspapers took a consistently enthusiastic view of the CCC, the public at large formed a somewhat rosy but distorted image of the corps. When six hundred enrollees returned to New York from Glacier National Park, their superintendent spoke in glowing terms of their behavior. "Without strict military regulations the boys in camp were put on their own in the matter of self-government," he said. "Within a week . . . rowdyism had become both unfashionable and unpopular. As self-governing young Americans, these youths found their own way of eliminating or taming the bully and tough guy."[43]

Such praise was not heaped on the personnel of the Yellowstone camps. Misunderstanding and apprehension about the young men extended from Superintendent Toll to the president of Livingston's chamber of commerce.

Horace Albright, who was deeply involved in launching the corps, clarified to Toll the program's goals. The superintendent had suggested that the corps was more expensive for park jobs than were local laborers. But cost was not the point. Albright explained that for the young men, character building was the real aim. "The President is extremely anxious," he informed Toll, "that the welfare of these enrolled men shall be given every possible consideration in order to build up their faith and restore their courage where distressing conditions resulting from the depression have broken down their morale. . . ." He reiterated that the young men were guaranteed work-free weekends, a lunch hour and transit as part of their working day.[44]

People down the Yellowstone Valley were agitated over the presence or near-presence of the CCCs. The first trainload pulled into Livingston where it stayed overnight prior to chugging up to Gardiner. The enrollees got off, stretched their legs and took the measure of the town, shoplifting "a great many small articles." In a letter to Albright, whom he knew, the president of the Livingston Chamber of Commerce expressed fear of rapes in the park during the coming season. "Certainly the young men sent us from New York . . . are not the type we are used to having in Yellowstone," he commented. "In fact, they are very far from it. Personally I do not believe that I ever saw such an irresponsible and nondescript outfit in my life and I saw some pretty tough bucks during the World War at that." According to the best information he could gather, the "whole bunch is recruited from the lower east side, New York, and they certainly show it." He added that local CCC officials were worried over how to discipline them. "At present," he said, "these young men spend their evenings around Mammoth and even down around Gardiner and display a very irresponsible attitude." Everyone in Mammoth had taken to locking doors and keeping everything under lock and key. "Certainly," he added, "they are anything but the type that the newspapers have been picturing in such glowing terms."[45]

Yet the sense of fair play that is so much of the western psyche said, give them a chance. "I would not deprive these boys of their rights, neither would I attempt to judge them harshly," wrote the *Enterprise* editor. "It is my opinion that they are simply foreign to this nature of a location."[46]

All told, about six hundred young men, three companies, from New York appeared in Yellowstone (the fourth arrived later) and, with the entire CCC program not yet three months old, the situation was unstable and chaotic. Albright explained to the *Enterprise* editor that he (Albright) and the head of the Forest Service had pleaded for a larger employment of local men, "however, the President felt that it was absolutely necessary . . . to get the unemployed young men out of the big cities . . . I had hoped," Albright continued, "that there would be enough local men in the companies to hold the boys under control until they get settled down to their work and I still believe it will work out that way."[47]

Superintendent Toll attempted an impartial, careful appraisal of the situation. "Conditions are necessarily abnormal during the first two weeks after the establishment of these camps," he stated, and indeed there were many cases of misconduct: the Lake Camp boys removed the damboards at the intake of the fish hatchery supply line, thus threatening the loss of millions of eggs worth thousands of dollars; they fished at the hatchery pier ignoring NO FISHING signs and speared and stoned fish; members of the Mammoth Camp stoned a Park Service truck because the driver did not give them a ride; the boys deserted on the way to work and loitered through the day; some would sit down at the job site and do nothing.[48]

The situation constituted a race between chaos and discipline. Although the latter prevailed, in Yellowstone the race was close. Troubles reached a crisis stage at Lake Camp. On Monday, June 19, even though they had been free all weekend, the personnel refused to climb into trucks and be driven to work. When the camp commander informed the ringleaders that they would be discharged, Toll later wrote Albright, "they said they would refuse to go until the entire camp was discharged and asked that all men be sent home." They complained about—what else—food! At noon a number of men refused lunch, saying they would raid the kitchen later and take whatever they wanted. It was a tense situation, a strike and a rebellion.

About one o'clock, at the request of the camp commander, a number of Park Service rangers appeared along with some men from Canyon Camp armed with pick handles. "Most of the men had knives," Toll reported, not specifying whether he meant the men on strike, the reinforcements, or the whole lot of them, "and it was generally expected that a fight would result when the ringleaders were sent out but no trouble developed." Nine troublemakers were discharged, trucked out and placed on a train for New York. Three more were discharged from Canyon and two from Mammoth camps.

Toll pointed out that the discipline problem was created because the army's instructions specified that "disciplinary punishment as such is not applicable." Moreover, army authority only existed in camp; to and from their place of work the young men were subject to the rules and regulations of the Park Service. "We can arrest for specific violation of park regulations but in general the men have the rights of any civilian," said Toll. "If they do not report back to camp at night, the commander has no punishment he can give."

He estimated that 80 percent of the men at Lake Camp were "fairly well satisfied and about 95% at Mammoth and Canyon." About half were under twenty-one years of age, certainly younger than men the service would normally employ. "They represent a cross-section of the population of Brooklyn and lower New York," he wrote. "Many races are represented and there are large numbers of Italians, Jews, and Irish in the group. No generalizations will apply to all men," he added. "Probably 30% of the men are good men, 50% are about average and 20% of them are poor or worse." He felt that a good many would have to be discharged before the camps could work successfully. Toll also established some spike camps, temporary, small, isolated work camps, to "isolate some of the men and reduce the number of men in the main camp....We expect to treat these men not as outcasts but as ordinary civilians," he added. "Troublemakers will be arrested and discharged but it is believed that conditions will continue to improve during their stay here." And Toll was right: after the June 19 confrontation, conditions changed for the better at Lake, Mammoth, and Canyon camps.[49]

But a more serious crisis occurred about a month later at the remote camp on Bacon Rind Creek in the park's northwest quadrant. Again, discipline problems were the basic cause.

It involved an eighteen-year-old Bronx youth named Abraham Yancovitch. After breakfast on July 13 he and his buddies were expected, as usual, to wash their eating utensils below the Bacon Rind Creek dam. A sign so directed them, and since their drinking water was taken from the stream above, there was no question as to why. But young Yancovitch chose to ignore the sign and wash his utensils above the dam. The First Section Leader, regular army first sergeant George Satriano, ordered him to obey the sign. Yancovitch's reply, a refusal to obey, was sprinkled with obscenities. Satriano suggested that the two go over the ridge and settle the matter in a direct, physical way. According to the official report, in the ensuing fisticuffs Satriano landed a blow to Yancovitch "on the left side of his head with his right fist. Yancovitch fell, rolled around on the ground, holding both his hands over [his] left eye. Seemed to be in pain. Somebody else picked him up." Seven hours later he was dead of a fractured skull and a cerebral hemorrhage—died, wrote camp superintendent, J.W. Cunningham, "due to his own misconduct in the deliberate and direct disobedience of a lawful order given by a lawfully appointed superior." For a few hours the camp was tense. A campmate named Singer was stirring up trouble, and was arrested; an enrollee named Bressler said he was wiring New York City for an attorney. Both men were summarily discharged and sent home. Sergeant Satriano was cleared and "was acclaimed by all the men upon entering the camp and has continued to be popular."[50]

Following this unfortunate incident, the U.S. Attorney for the District of Wyoming wrote to the aging John Meldrum, U.S. commissioner in Yellowstone, that "It is necessary that strict discipline be observed in these E.C.W. Camps.* There is much insubordination and considerable com-

plaints are being made over the country because of the lack of discipline...."
This would seem to indicate that the problem was not just localized at Yellowstone but was a nationwide problem.[51]

What is remarkable is not the existence of a discipline problem, which was expected, but the rapidity with which it was solved. A policy enunciated toward the end of June stressing both incentives and discipline worked. Even in that first hectic summer the young men at the Yellowstone camps made impressive beginnings at roadside cleanup, bank erosion control, reforestation at auto camps, game range improvements, construction of fire protection trails, telephone lines, and fire tool cache buildings; construction of boat docks at Yellowstone Lake, and measures to control the depredations of the mountain pine beetle.[52]

And this was just the beginning. As Park Service supervisors became aware of the labor available from the program, they evolved general park beautification plans that would have been financially impossible prior to the New Deal. With as many as fifteen camps assigned to the park during some summer seasons and in some years even a camp stationed there during the winter, all kinds of useful work was accomplished. Philetus Norris's old Capitol Hill headquarters building was destroyed and the hill returned to its natural state. Roadcuts were sloped gracefully from roadbed back to timber, auto camps improved by planting shrubs and trees, and dead timber was removed. New barns and corrals were built where needed and abandoned buildings, many dating from stagecoach days, were destroyed and all signs of human habitation removed. Eyesores such as old trash dumps behind hotels were hauled away. Where roads had been abandoned, the CCC boys plowed them up in such a way as to encourage the return of natural flora. Barren slopes were reforested.[53]

After 1933 the CCC system was managed in such a way that, at least in Yellowstone, there was no repetition of the crises of 1933. Many of the young men in later years came from Ohio and Indiana and fitted more easily into the park's rustic setting. Some assignments in later years were above the day laborer's variety. A few of the enrollees were trained in wildlife and forestry and research involving taxidermist's skills. Museum cataloging and filing, mounting photographs, and classifying herbarium specimens were likewise useful tasks, and the corpsmen "were enthused over the project." With always a sprinkling of Montana, Idaho, and Wyoming natives in each camp, with weekly educational talks by rangers and naturalists, and, of some significance, with the cooperation between camp superintendents and the Park

*E.C.W. or Emergency Conservation Work Camps was simply another name applied to CCC installations.

Service, the Civilian Conservation Corps greatly improved Yellowstone's appearance. Let us hope that for the great majority of the young men involved, the six month's tour was a character-building experience also.[54]

By 1936 Yellowstone appeared to have weathered the worst of the Great Depression. Visitation was on the rise—it reached over 317,000 in 1935— and all evidence pointed to even more tourists in the forthcoming year. Extensive road building was planned, the CCC was doing good work, and the concessionaires were once again operating in the black. It was February 25, 1936: Superintendent Toll, fifty-two years old, popular, competent, his Park Service career doing well, was traveling on professional business with George W. Wright, chief of the service's Bureau of Wild Life, from Alpine, Texas, to Deming, New Mexico. About seven miles east of Deming a tire on an approaching car blew, hurtling the car out of control across the median and head-on into the Toll vehicle. Toll, Wright, and the driver of the other car were killed instantly. The whole Park Service was saddened by this tragedy.[55]

Toll's successor was Edmund B. Rogers, a tall, pipe-smoking, mountain-climbing Colorado outdoorsman. In his veins surged the blood of Captain Robert Rogers whose colonial rangers were immortalized in Kenneth Rogers's historical novel, *Northwest Passage*. A Yale B.A., class of 1915, Edmund Rogers returned to Denver where he became a trust officer with the Colorado National Bank. Again, as with Mather and Toll, a spirit of noblesse oblige appears to have led Rogers, already successful in the private sector, to abandon that career for one paying less monetarily but with more rewards in other ways. Rogers had succeeded Toll in the Rocky Mountain National Park and now he again stepped into Toll's position in Yellowstone.[56]

He was the last of the old-style superintendents, respected by Washington superiors who looked upon him more as colleague than subordinate. He made decisions unilaterally. Yet the changes wrought by time, retirements and deaths, an explosive, mobile society, a depression followed by a Second World War, were to affect Yellowstone and the superintendency in a myriad of ways.

Much of Rogers's administration, and the most controversial part, took place after the war.

NOTES TO CHAPTER TEN

1. Announcement of the orders appeared in the *Enterprise,* August 26, 1916.

2. 39 *U.S. Statutes at Large,* 535–36.
The story of the creation of the National Park Service is told in Donald C. Swain, "The Passage of the National Park Service Act of 1916," *Wisconsin Magazine of History,* Vol. 50, No. 1 (Autumn, 1966), 4–17; _____, *Wilderness Defender: Horace M. Albright and Conservation* (Chicago: University of Chicago Press, 1970); Robert Shankland, *Steve Mather;* and Alfred Runte, *National Parks: The American Experience.*

3. Runte, *National Parks,* 99.

4. Swain, *Wilderness Defender,* 36.

5. Ibid., 193.

6. Shankland, *Steve Mather,* 95. Chapter 8, "The Power of the Press," 83–89, gives names of many more people who helped popularize the national park idea. The railroads fostered a similar campaign since the early 1900s. See Pomeroy, *In Search of the Golden West,* 132.

7. R.G. 48, General Classified File, "Publications," Frank A. Miller, owner of the Mission Inn, Riverside, California, to Franklin K. Lane, May 17, 1919.

8. A brief biography of Lane is in the *National Cyclopaedia of American Biography* (New York: James T. White Co., 1926), Vol. 19, 101. See also Swain, *Horace Albright,* 28.

9. *Enterprise,* September 21,22, and 24, 1916.

10. Ibid., June 10, 1917. It was the 1st Squadron of the 7th Cavalry, consisting of 420 men, eight officers, 432 horses, nine wagons and some mules. They had pursued Villa in Mexico. Ibid., June 27, 1917. Lindsley's daughter became the service's first female ranger.

11. R.G. 48, Central Classified File, "General," Vogelsang to Secretary of War, July 3, 1918; Ibid., Vogelsang to Secretary of the Interior, December 13, 1918; Swain, *Horace Albright,* 88.

12. Ibid., and author's interview and correspondence with Mr. Albright.

13. *Enterprise,* August 19,1919; Swain, *Horace Albright,* 150–51.

14. Swain, *Horace Albright,* 110–42.

15. Ibid., 133.

16. R.G. 48, Central Classified File, "Privileges," Albright to Joseph J. Cotter, Administrative Assistant, Department of the Interior, August 30, 1919.

17. Ibid., Acting Director (name not given) to J.H. Waters, President of Gray Line Motor Tours, Salt Lake City, Utah, June 11, 1926. The statement about companies leaving when profits dry up is specious; never has it happened in Yellowstone.

18. Ibid., "Privileges," Albright to Secretary, February 6, 1933; Ibid., Charles L. Gable, Chief Auditor, Park Operators' Accounts, to Director, January 6, 1930; Ibid., Albright to Director, February 13, 1931; January 25, 1932.

19. R.G. 79, National Park Service, Central Classified File, 1933–1939, "National Park Yellowstone," 8805-01, Box No. 1771.

20. Ibid., Arno Cammerer to Albright, April 22, 1922, This memorandum states the flat rate fee: to $20,000 = 0 percent; $20,000 to $40,000 = 1 percent; $40,000 to $60,000 = 2 percent; $60,000 to $80,000 = 3 percent, and everything over $80,000 = 4 percent. See Ibid., "Administration," John H. Edwards, Assistant Secretary, to Senator John B. Kendrick, January 19, 1926, in which Edwards states, "It may interest you to know that the Yellowstone Park Hotel Company pays the United States 2½% of its gross receipts, while the Yellowstone Park Transportation Company pays 4%." He gives the amounts paid: for example, in 1925 the former paid $22,167 and the latter $47,620.

21. Ibid., "Investigations," E.C. Finney, Assistant Secretary, to Secretary, July 15, 1921; Ibid., "Privileges," Finney to Acting Director Cammerer, September 27, 1926.

22. Ibid., "Complaints," Wilbur to Albright, October 21, 1929.

23. For listings of such donations "for roadside cleanup" from the Committee for Outdoor Education (a Rockefeller cover) and "for museums," see R.G. 48, Central Classified File, "Donations."

24. New York Times, January 25, 1925, 7, 5; Ibid., March 3, 1925, 20. For more about early Westerns see Tim McCoy with Ronald McCoy, Tim McCoy Remembers the West (Garden City: Doubleday and Co., 1977); Kevin Brownlow, The War the West and the Wilderness (New York: Alfred Knopf, 1978).

25. New York Times, March 3, 1925, 20.

26. R.G. 48, Central Classified File, "Wild Animals," R. Lee Ste. Fleure to Interior Secretary Work, April 30, 1925. Enclosures include copies of a telegram to Jesse Lasky and a letter to Will Hays.

27. Ibid., Mather to Work, May 13, 1925; Ibid., Albright to Work, June 1, 1925.

28 New York Times, August 30, 1925, 1,3. I first heard stories of the buffalo imbroglio in a Gardiner restaurant in 1963.

29. Senator Cameron's vindictiveness stemmed from controversy over the Grand Canyon. See Douglas Hillman Strong, "The Man Who 'Owned' Grand Canyon," *The American West*, Vol. 6, No. 5 (September, 1969), 33–40.

30. Ise, *Our National Park Policy:* 302ff.

31. Author's interview with Horace Albright; Swain, *Horace Albright,* 166ff.

32. *New York Times,* August 30, 1925, 1,3.

33. Ibid., and August 31, 1925,5.

34. Ibid.

35.R.G. 48, Central Classified File, "Boundaries," Piersall to Kendrick, January 24, 1930.

36. Swain, *Horace Albright,* is an excellent biography.

37. Ibid., 188–91.

38. *Who Was Who in America,* Vol. 1, 1244; *New York Times,* February 26, 1936, 1

39. Haines, *The Yellowstone Story,* 2, 479.

40. William E. Leuchtenburg, *Franklin D. Roosevelt and the New Deal* (New York: Harper and Row, 1963), 53; 174.

41. For more information on the CCC, see John A. Salmond, *The Civilian Conservation Corps, 1933–1942; A New Deal Case Study* (Durham, North Carolina: University of North Carolina Press, 1967). Conrad L. Wirth, *Parks, Politics, and the People* (Norman: University of Oklahoma Press, 1980) is also a good overview, especially chapters 5 and 6, 94–157.

42. My essay on the CCC camps in Yellowstone is based primarily upon National Archives Record Group 79, National Park Service Central Classified File, 1933–1939, "Yellowstone," Boxes numbered 1770 and 1771, hereafter cited as R.G. 79, CCC.

43. *New York Times,* September 24, 1933, 2.

44. R.G. 79, CCC, Albright to Toll, June 5, 1933.

45. Ibid., D.C. Bates, Secretary, Livingston Chamber of Commerce, to Director Albright, June 13, 1933.

46. Ibid., L.E. Flint, Ed., *Enterprise,* to Albright, June 14, 1933.

47. Ibid., Albright to Flint, June 17, 1933.

48. Ibid., Toll to Director, June 21, 1933; Ibid., Fred J. Foster to Toll, June 11, 1933.

49. Ibid., Toll to Director, June 21, 1933.

50. Ibid., Report of J.W. Cunningham, Captain, U.S.M.C., Commanding, July 16, 1933. It is interesting that Captain Cunningham was a Marine, not an army officer. It is a commentary on the nationwide desire for New Deal programs to succeed that not a word of these incidents appeared in the eastern press. The first news story in the *New York Times* denoting trouble concerned a walkout at the Bear River, California, camp. *New York Times*, July 30, 1933, 13.

51. R.G. 79, CCC, Carl L. Sackett, U.S. Attorney for the District of Wyoming, to Meldrum, July 26, 1933.

52. Ibid., Assistant Director Demaray to Toll, June 29, 1933; Toll to Director Albright, June 28, 1933.

53. Ibid., Clipping from *Boston Evening Transcript*, August 11, 1934; "Yellowstone Getting Spruced Up, and the Sprucers Like the Job."

54. Ibid., "Final Narrative Report—Fourth Enrollment Period—April 1, 1935," signed by J.W. Emmett, Acting Superintendent. This report covers activities of Company 1349, E.C.W. Camp, Yellowstone Park No. 1, Mammoth Hot Springs.

55. *New York Times*, February 26, 1936, 3; *Washington Post*, February 26, 1936, 1.

56. Author's interview with Edmund G. Rogers, October, 1966; *Who's Who in America*, Vol. 29 (1956–1957), 2187.

RAIDERS & DEFENDERS

CHAPTER ELEVEN

The Railroaders and the Poachers

From 1884 until 1919 diverse promotional schemes involving railroad encroachment on the park were advocated by businessmen residing from Cooke City and Livingston, Montana, to New York City and Washington, D.C. Considering the impact the railroads had upon American life in the period 1865 to 1920, the prevalence of these plans should come as no surprise. A changing America has always had an impact upon Yellowstone and in this period the railroads posed the greatest threat to the park's integrity. It is something of a miracle that Yellowstone escaped the iron horses.

While people were wary of the economic power of railroad corporations, they nevertheless felt that the long, centipede-like railroad train speeding down the twin steel rails was the sure solution to many of the nation's problems. Its relatively inexpensive cost of construction, its remarkable cost-profit ratio, its speed when compared with animal-powered transportation, and belief in its profitability spawned thousands of schemes. Small wonder, then, that businessmen, miners, railroad promoters and speculators considered seriously a spate of railroad schemes involving Yellowstone National Park.

The plans received high-pressure promotion from powerful interests. In addition, often supporting the big schemers in hopes of enjoying some minor benefits should the big ones succeed, were certain residents of Yellowstone's environs who poached, cut timber, mined coal or committed other depredations in the park and who protested every attempt by the authorities to restrict their operations. The clear need for stronger protective legislation, and the campaign for a railroad, soon mingled in Congress—the one could not be had without the other—and the result was an impasse of nearly a decade's duration.[1]

Railroad and mining interests nearly succeeded on several occasions. Their friends advanced bills through the Senate and on occasion through both the House and the Senate, only to have them die in conference committee when time ran out. Each bill usually identified a railroad by name. Depending upon the year, it was called the Cinnabar and Clarks Fork, the

Cinnabar and Cooke City, the Bullion Railroad Company, or the Montana Mineral and Railroad Company. Regardless of name, all the bills provided for a railroad through the park, or what then constituted the park, from Cinnabar, just north of the boundary and railhead (at the time) of the Park Branch Line, south into the reservation to the Lamar River, east up that stream to Soda Butte Creek and northeast via that canyon to Cooke City and the New World Mining District. Most of the proposed legislation suggested that the northeast quadrant of the park (approximately), which would embrace the proposed railroad, be segregated from the park and placed back in the public domain.

Although the campaign for a railroad to Clarks Fork and Cooke City was to continue well into the twentieth century, the greatest threat of its becoming a reality was in the 1880s and 1890s. Incentive for the plan came from several sources. First perhaps was the Hobart-Douglas-Hatch crowd. They envisioned profits from the anticipated mining activity that such a railroad would engender at Cooke City and the New World Mining District. Another interested group comprised local miners and a number of wealthy mining investors who possessed properties or some monetary interest in some of the Clarks Fork claims. In 1884 a miners' union at Cooke City passed a resolution favoring a railroad, stating that 237 mineral claims were recorded in the district. Later it was pointed out that a railroad would bring down the per-ton costs of drayage, Cooke City to Cinnabar, from twenty-five dollars with horse-drawn wagons to five dollars a ton by rail.[2]

Livingston businessmen believed that a railroad to Cooke City would be to their benefit since that mining community would need their goods and services. All over the region north of the park boundary were elements that forecast profits if the northeast quadrant of the park was returned to the public domain. Coal veins, hotel sites, and hay meadows lay along the way.

Two arguments were put forth consistently to justify the land segregation or at least construction of a railroad through it. (It should be pointed out that some measures merely provided for a 100- or 160-foot right-of-way, others called for cutting off the Montana strip so that the boundary would be synonymous with the Wyoming state line, while still other proposals advocated cutting off everything north of the Lamar River and east of the Yellowstone below its confluence with the Lamar.)

The first contention was that the northwest section, save for Soda Butte, contained no thermal phenomena. Thus, it was argued, it was like thousands of other square miles of the Rocky Mountains. This nullified any justification for keeping it a part of the park. Secretary Teller so expressed this belief in an ambivalent, lengthy letter to Senator Vest.[3]

The second justification was simply that the miners and investors at the New World Mining District deserved relief in the form of a railroad. This argument became more dominant as mining and speculative activity increased in the region during the 1880s. By 1885 it was reported that "considerable population has gone into the region on the expectation that Congress would allow the road to be built this season."[4]

Fortunately, a dedicated group of men in strategic positions was aware of the threat and was willing to devote hundreds of hours fighting the schemes. Their ranks included such public and prestigious men as General Sheridan; Captains Kingman and Chittenden; geologist Arnold Hague; Interior Secretaries L.Q.C. Lamar and John W. Noble; the Washington, D.C., lawyer W. Hallett Phillips; George Bird Grinnell, editor of *Forest and Stream;* Senators Vest of Missouri, Logan of Illinois, Harrison and Voorhees of Indiana, Garland of Arkansas, Call of Florida, Allison of Iowa, Manderson of Nebraska, and others; among many in the House, Representatives Kiefer of Minnesota and Lacey of Iowa were prominent in the struggle for park integrity.[5]

These civic-minded men of foresight mustered potent arguments just as the conservation movement was beginning to gain momentum. At the highest level was the aesthetic argument. In defending the park from one of the railroad bills, Secretary Lamar wrote that the "dominant idea in Congress...has been the preservation of the wilderness forests, geysers, mountains, etc., so to speak, and the game...in as nearly the condition in which we found them as possible, with a view to holding for the benefit of those who shall come after us something of the original 'Wild West' that shall stand while the rest of the world moves...." Senator Call of Florida insisted that the park was "set aside to be preserved for future generations, for the naturalist and the philosopher."[6]

Arnold Hague pushed a new argument involving the forests in that rugged region. While he acknowledged that much could be said in favor of existence of the park "based upon sentimental grounds," the most important concern was preservation of timber, which was the watershed for the area. Hague even took the offensive, proposing a park extension twenty-five miles east and nine miles south. Although he was an idealist, the geologist was convinced that more than an aesthetic argument was necessary to bring victory. "It is all very well to use the arguments based upon sentiment but if the bill is going to go through it must be upon economic grounds," he wrote to Captain Harris at Mammoth Hot Springs.[7]

A third argument—that a railroad would destroy game—was heard from military men as well as from George Bird Grinnell through *Forest and Stream* and from members of the Boone and Crockett Club. They knew they could not hunt legally in Yellowstone, but in an embryonic way they saw the park as a place to preserve species in danger of extinction, such as the buffalo, and to keep such species preserved there as a sort of genetic bank. Prior to 1900 one of the favorite grazing ranges for the buffalo was along the well-watered meadows of the Lamar Valley. It was further pointed out that the present boundaries, which ran across impenetrable mountains, constituted greater protection than the proposed new boundaries could offer.[8]

Finally, the park was saved from the railroads and segregationists by the growing national awareness of the monopoly menace. When such an old spoilsman as Senator John A. Logan of Illinois spoke out against the Cinnabar and Clarks Fork Railroad bill, surely some change of heart had taken place. "This is but the entering wedge," cried the senator. He lambasted Rufus Hatch and lectured his colleagues, in a shocking statement implying a reversal of his public philosophy, "Sir, I think it is about time for us to stop in this career that we have been marching in for years. The Congress...seems to be a mere football to be used according to the desires of men who wish to use everything in this Government for their own personal gain." He added that he had been lobbied "more this winter in behalf of this railroad by an officer of this Government who is getting $5000 a year than I ever was in my life." That official, he indicated, was an employee of the Interior Department and a friend of his.[9]

It is therefore historically accurate to state that the national mood against monopoly and railroads and the growing recognition of the need for conservation, a mood strongly reflected in Congress, had much to do with the continued defeats of the various railroad bills affecting Yellowstone. It should be added that in one or two sessions sheer luck—lack of time—saved the park from emasculation.

Coexistent with or incorporated in the railroad right-of-way bills was legislation to strengthen law enforcement and protection of the park's game and its curiosities. Some proposals included clauses adding as many as two thousand square miles to the reservation. S. 221 in the 48th Congress, 1st Sess. (1884), introduced by Senator Vest, provided for an extension south between nine and ten miles and east nearly thirty, "so as to take in a large extent of country, which is the home of large game and covered with forest trees, the preservation of which is absolutely necessary to protect the sources of large rivers . . .," the senator explained, revealing Hague's influence upon his thinking.[10]

The bill called for additional changes. Both the Idaho and Montana strips were to be eliminated, thus placing Yellowstone solely within Wyoming. A jog ten miles southward at one point removed the Clarks Fork mines from the proposed eastward extension. The laws of Montana Territory were specified for Yellowstone's jurisdictional purposes, however, on the very practical grounds (at the time) that the main entrances to the reservation were from Montana. This bill, which was a good one, was passed by the Senate, but the session ended before final passage was possible. It was too bad: had the bill passed, a lot of troubles could have been avoided.[11]

In 1884 at least four bills were introduced involving railroads and the park; the next year still more legislation was introduced along with Senator Vest's own proposal for extending the boundaries, protecting the park, and satisfying the railroaders. None passed. Some Congressmen even junketed to the park to see the situation first hand. [12]

As would be expected, Montana residents reacted bitterly to the repeated failures. After the Cinnabar and Clarks Fork bill was defeated in 1884, Senators Logan and Vest felt the barbs of the frontier editor's pen. Vest was described as "a sort of chronic objector . . . the self-constituted guardian of the park . . . [who] conceives it to be his duty to resist the encroachments of civilization on his pet domain. We presume," the editor added, "that in his heart of hearts [he] . . . would fain have it remain a wilderness devoted to nothing more civilized than the trail of a cayuse." [13]

Thus was the clash joined between Westerners intent upon developing the region and Easterners determined to protect it. Nor were feelings sweetened in the Livingston-Gardiner region when certain parties received false information confirming passage of the railroad–park segregation bill and were informed cryptically by telegram "to secure that horse." That phrase was the signal to make haste into the supposedly segregated area and secure land claims to previously selected acreages. "In the stampede over the mountains that bitter Friday night [for it was February] almost every man at Gardiner and Mammoth Hot Springs 'secured his horse,'" chortled the *Enterprise*. [14]

Year after year the thrust continued for both a strong park protection bill and a railroad through the park to Cooke City, or through land cut off from the park for that purpose. Year after year Senator Vest continued his fight, determined to protect the reservation from the railroaders' raids and equally dedicated to passage of a strong protective bill. Fortunately because of his own insertion in an 1883 bill which provided for army policing of Yellowstone if Congress failed to act, the park was saved in 1886 when Wyoming withdrew its protection and Congress failed to appropriate funds. However, the railroaders continued their schemes and protective legislation was still not forthcoming. [15]

Reading those Congressional debates of nearly a century ago, one is struck by the similarity of arguments on both sides to those heard today. The campaign launched in December 1886 by the railroaders, and their opposition, is a good example of the continuing debate. The Cinnabar and Clarks Fork forces were led in the House by Judge Payson of Illinois, who had been humiliated in a fracas with a Wyoming justice of the peace in the park the previous summer. The Public Lands Committee reported unanimously in favor of the bill while Mr. Toole, Montana's delegate to Congress, added in the Committee of the Whole that the area involved was "wholly unattractive country." But Congressman Cox of New York countered by stating: "I believe this bill is wrongly titled. It should be denominated, 'A bill for the spoliation of this Yellowstone Park. . . .' This is a measure which is inspired by corporate greed and natural selfishness against national pride and natural beauty!"[16]

Congressman Payson replied that he could not "understand the sentiment which favors the retention of a few buffaloes to the development of mining interests amounting to millions of dollars." Congressman William McAdoo of New Jersey then assured his colleagues that they need not vote for the bill out of political considerations. "Every member of this House," he reminded them, "knows that in the recent canvass for the Fiftieth Congress there was no question so pertinent in which the people were so vitally interested as that of preserving the public domain from spoilage and from land robbery." Further, he hoped the bill would be defeated because the railroad would be a monopoly. "Let us prefer the beautiful and the sublime and the interests of millions to heartless mammon and the greed of capital," he urged. The bill was defeated. (Antimonopolists were indeed powerful at this time; in February 1887, just two months later, Congress passed the Interstate Commerce Act.)[17]

The 50th Congress (March 4, 1887–March 4, 1889) felt a tidal wave of public opinion protesting the rampant exploitation of America's natural resources. A flood of petitions poured into Congressional offices from thirty-one states calling for protection of Yellowstone National Park through passage of Senator Vest's bill, S. 283. Their common source of inspiration was the Boone and Crockett Club. In the Senate, 258 of these documents were laid on the table. Since most of them contained two score and more signatures and a few several hundred, they may have represented more than three thousand petitioners.[18]

In spite of the efforts of sportsmen's clubs coordinated by the Boone and Crockett Club membership, Vest's S. 283 failed in both sessions. Both times it passed in the Senate but ran into trouble in the House. There the railroaders tacked on the usual crippling amendment: Yes, they would support the park protection bill, provided that the Cinnabar and Cooke City Railroad was granted a right-of-way through the park. Thus in 1887 and 1888 did the park protection bill get railroaded to a dead end. Nor did similar legislation pass in the 51st Congress.[19]

But time was on the side of the park defenders. In 1890 the *New York Times* began assuming an interest, editorializing how the protection bill had failed in the House "through the selfishness of persons who care much for the success of their private schemes and very little for the public right and interest in Yellowstone."[20]

Harper's Weekly also entered the fray, insisting that the residents of Montana, Wyoming, and Idaho had no more right to mutilate Yellowstone than did the people of the District of Columbia "to set up cigar and candy stands on the landing of the Washington Monument." A year later the periodical was quoting Captain Anderson (at the time acting superintendent) about the fire danger that would exist along the line of the proposed railroad. "I think," he was quoted, "it would be burned off as black as your hat in six months."[21]

In that year (1892) railroad lobbying for the route to Cooke City probably crested. "There are no votes in the Yellowstone Park for the Republican or Democratic party or for the third party," Senator Vest lamented. "The result is that outside of those of us who are aesthetic and sentimental...there seem to be very few persons who care anything about it." He described the railroad lobbyists as being like "a compact military organization working for one object alone."[22]

These years of controversy brought out the cynicism of some Congressmen who favored abolishing Yellowstone Park completely. Such a solon was Senator James Zachariah George of Mississippi; his colleague, Senator James H. Berry of Arkansas, favored dividing Yellowstone into 160-acre tracts for sale. "I do not believe that the Government ought to engage in the raising of wild animals," he said. In this same session Representative Thomas R. Stockdale of Mississippi introduced H.R. 7693 to repeal the Enabling Act of 1872; that is, he proposed abolishing Yellowstone Park altogether.[23]

Of the several bills concerning the park and the railroad that were introduced in both houses of Congress in 1892, the most interesting, and in its failure the most unfortunate, was S. 2373 which passed the Senate by a vote of thirty-two to eighteen. Senator Vest this time cast his ballot affirmatively. He did this because S. 2373 contained a proviso that the park would be expanded by nearly a third across the rugged mountains to the east and by a smaller percentage to the south. In exchange the railroaders wanted as little as eleven miles square of park land for their right-of-way.* Only in 1892 was such a park extension politically possible. Even then sufficient ranching and mining development had entered those mountain fastnesses to constitute opposition. Rumors of such actions by the 51st Congress in 1890, had prompted some citizens of the little community of Red Lodge, northeast of the park on the other side of the Beartooth Plateau, to file a protest with Congress. It can be argued, therefore, that the protectionists' resistance to giving up a small parcel of land for a railroad right-of-way prevented passage of a bill that would have annexed to Yellowstone as much as two thousand square miles of magnificent mountain country, teeming with game and drained by superb fishing streams.[24]

This was the lost opportunity of 1892. Meanwhile the railroad age was changing as technology advanced. In that year were heard suggestions for an electric railway into the park—a sort of trolley free of smoke and sparks and

---

*The land (about 121 sections) would have been spread out along the railroad's right-of-way.

cinders. It appealed to some people who were dead set against the steam locomotive. Power would originate from generators hidden far off, or even hideously placed at Yellowstone Falls. All the while Union Pacific and Burlington interests, as well as mining investors, continued taking the lay of the land in and around the park. Probably wisely, the "esthete Easterners" remained adamant. If they had their way there would be no segregation of a part of the park, and no railroads, steam or electric, would ever roll inside its borders.

During the quarter century or so after 1892, while railroads were still dominant, many proposals continued to be heard for a railroad into Yellowstone. The momentum for a Lamar Valley route to Cooke City seemed to have collapsed, but interest in constructing a line into the park from Jackson Hole; Market Lake, Idaho; or up the Madison River from West Yellowstone remained strong. In the 65th Congress (1917–19) a bill was introduced granting the Union Pacific the privilege of building a Teton-Yellowstone line. Although the legislation failed to pass, Interior Secretary Lane felt the proposal had merit. He requested Walker D. Hines, director general of the United States Railroad Administration, "to consult with the opposing forces in an endeavor to explain the features of the plan that are troubling them." Nothing came of the scheme.[25]

Even as park defenders took satisfaction in frustrating the railroad builders, they grimaced at their failure to obtain legislation providing punishment for violations inside the reservation. In 1892 a Senate report had favored such a law. Passage was not forthcoming in that session, but clearly the slow, grinding wheels of the legislative process were creating a climate of awareness that is so often the vital prelude to Congressional action.[26]

Two years later in 1894, Congress enacted two bills vital to park welfare. The Hayes Act concerns leases, granting them for ten years with provisions for renewal and enunciating rights and restrictions of concessionaires. The other act, providing justice and punishment, advocated for years by Senator Vest, is formally known as the National Park Protective Act. However, since it was sponsored by Congressman John F. Lacey of Iowa, a Republican in a Republican-dominated Congress, it has since been known as the Lacey Act.[27]

Poaching increased in the late 1880s and 1890s. Near extinction of the buffalo raised the selling price of a mounted buffalo head to $500. The growing membership in the Benevolent and Protective Order of Elks cost many a Yellowstone (as well as Teton) elk its life. Poachers knocked out the animals' molars which were made into watch fobs for two-legged elks; the remainder of the carcass was left to the elements. Drifters abounded in the mountains in those days, constituting a small army of lonely and economically desperate men quite willing to risk capture for the money that poaching would bring them. Miners at Cooke City, Virginia City, or Electric (north of the park) were glad to purchase a side of venison or elk for a few shekels, no questions asked. Taxidermists welcomed a bear or buffalo hide and were equally prone to silence.

Every poacher in the region knew that the most a park official could do to him if caught was confiscate his gear and expel him from the reservation. Even that was not always final. Rifles, saddles, and horses were sometimes retrieved by the culprit after he had enlisted in his behalf a territorial delegate or some politician with influence in Washington, who brought pressure in his behalf via the Interior Department.

With a puzzling ambivalence, even the territories whose citizens were already protesting the conservation policies of Easterners had taken some measures to protect their disappearing game. Both Montana and Wyoming in the 1880s legislated against killing buffalo. Wyoming, it will be recalled, had passed protective legislation for Yellowstone in 1884; however, in late 1886 it repealed the statute. Thus from 1886 until 1894 no statutes existed, territorial, state, or federal, imposing penalties for the killing of game or spoliation of the thermal phenomena.[28]

Stories emanating from the park by the mid-eighties told of skin hunters killing as many as two hundred elk in a single herd, of one hunter who caught a herd of deer floundering in deep snow and killed forty at a single stand, and of the killing of twenty bison. Unfortunately, Secretary Teller's 1882 order forbidding hunting of many different kinds of birds and animals inadvertently left out others. It included blackbirds and other migratory birds, but omitted squirrels, rabbits, and bears. As W. Hallett Phillips pointed out in 1886, shooting was still permitted to a limited extent in the park. The consequence was "that under the excuse of hunting bear and other animals, not on the enumerated list, the large game in the park which the government is so much interested in protecting, have been slaughtered."[29]

The depredations were widespread. As early as 1882 it was reported that Montanans just above the northern boundary were chasing deer and elk out of the park with dogs, then slaughtering the graceful animals at leisure. A United States Geological Survey party was accused of killing an old buffalo in the park and packing out about a hundred pounds of the meat, the skin, head, and hooves. One man took the animal's penis, dried it, stretched it, and made a walking stick of it. An informer signing his name "Timothy Quill" told Superintendent Wear of two Gardiner men, Thomas Bush and Charles White, who, he said, had poached all the past winter on the Blacktail Plateau. Bush had boasted that he was " 'too cute for any park policeman to get him'" and, added the informer, "it really looks to an outsider as if all the park policemen were afraid of him."[30]

During his brief superintendency (May 1885–August 1886) Colonel Wear acted with promptness. He secured the arrest of two poachers named Reeder and Ferguson and their conviction from the Wyoming courts. Late in October 1885 assistant superintendents Edmund Wilson and J.W. Weimer captured Box Miller, J.M. Pearson, David Gard, R.W. White and John F. Hoskins, all of whom were convicted of hunting and killing one elk and five deer. Three paid fines of fifty dollars each and two of twenty-five dollars each and costs. Two Sharps, one Marlin, one Winchester and one Remington rifle were confiscated.[31]

Yet the superintendent knew the battle was far from won. Hunters, now on the alert, began using American wood powder, which was almost noiseless. At three hundred yards a 45-60 cartridge filled with it sounded no louder than a common firecracker. Then on March 10, 1886, Chapter 103 of the Wyoming Territorial Laws was repealed, leaving the park without a court or enforceable laws.[32]

Six months later the army arrived. Senator Vest believed turning over the park to the army was tantamount to destroying the reservation. But this time the senator was wrong. The peacetime army was singularly prepared to cope with the drifting men of the mountains. If poaching was rumored in some remote area—the southwest and northeast quadrants were always prime—it was the army that quietly sent armed patrols to investigate. The records of Fort Yellowstone reveal its efficiency. A secret telegraphic code prevented people at Livingston or up the Yellowstone Valley from knowing what the army was doing. Personnel were ordered "on the quiet" to remote places "to carry out verbal instructions received concerning poaching in the vicinity."[33]

The army's record against poachers was commendable. Making full use of the regulations and the one penalty provided, expulsion from the park, Acting Superintendents Harris, Boutelle, and Anderson sent their men in pursuit of the skin hunters, tooth hunters, head hunters, and fur trappers. When they did capture them, they resorted to delaying tactics, incarcerating the culprits in the guardhouse for weeks or even months while the slow process of justice, carried on between Washington, D.C. and Mammoth Hot Springs and between two secretaries (Interior and War), slowly brought about the inevitable release of the captured hunters. As an example, Cooke City poacher Van Dyke was kept by Anderson in the guardhouse from May 7 until June 8 before the authorities had to release him.[34]

Plans were well coordinated. Patrols stayed in remote, hidden shelters called snowshoe cabins where food and bedding were stored. Telephone lines were strung from every patrol station to headquarters. Poachers began to feel the pressure. Year by year the list of those caught and expelled increased: William James, captured while trapping beaver; Frank Chatfield, relieved of his gray pony, Bullard rifle, field glasses, saddle, bridle, pack, and cartridge belt; and Ira Dodge, E. Van Dyke, and Ed Howell. The army was aware, however, that many culprits were never caught. Captain Anderson received a letter from Henry's Lake in July 1893, in which a resident applied for a game warden's job. "I know all of the poachers who live at Henry's Lake and the Madison Basin," wrote the applicant. "Two of them are old ofenders [sic] they killed five bison last fall in the park to my certain knowledge and they or someone else killed eleven in the winter and shiped [sic] them to Chicago."[35]

A few farsighted local residents understood the necessity of strict game law enforcement and secretly gave aid. One rancher, after informing the superintendent of poacher activities, reminded the recipient that "this must be confidential if it were known my horse and stock would not be worth a cent, we have some hard citizens here." Others wrote poison-pen letters. A Livingston taxidermist informed Captain Anderson of a man who had contracted with a competitor for 100 elk heads, implying that they would be obtained from the park herds. John Dudley Sargent, a wealthy Easterner who established Merymere Ranch on Jackson Lake, was of considerable aid in helping control poaching in the southern part of the reservation.[36]

Even though the army men knew their enforcement policy was only partially successful, the results were significant, especially in the tourist-frequented areas of the reservation. Bears appear not to have been a marked feature of Yellowstone prior to 1890. Somehow their brute brains comprehended that they were safe in Yellowstone, and by 1889 a few black bears had begun frequenting the garbage dumps. At first they appeared only at night, fleeing at the appearance of man, but within a few years they came to accept, if not welcome, his presence. They continued scavenging as people watched. At first black bears were prevalent only in the upper park, but by 1910 they were common as far north as Mammoth. Grizzlies appeared three or four years after their smaller, friendlier relations, the black or brown (cinnamon) bears.[37]

The greatest concern was over the Yellowstone buffalo. With the high price on buffalo heads, the cumbersome creatures were rapidly threatened with extinction; the poachers' quest for them was matched only by the army's determination to protect them. Fortunately, at a crucial period during the debates over the Lacey Act in Congress in 1894, a poaching incident involving a man named Ed Howell occurred which received heavy press coverage and helped insure the law's passage.[38]

Captain Anderson's men were aware of poaching activities in the Pelican Valley district northeast of Yellowstone Lake. A scouting party on snowshoes had discovered along Astringent Creek the trail of a man with a sled. The tracks were such that Captain Anderson knew the man had not carried out any trophies, but the possibility existed that some dead animals were lying frozen awaiting his return. This prompted Anderson to send out a search party. On March 6, therefore, Captain G.L. Scott, Lieutenant Forsyth B. Burgess, two sergeants, and photographer F. Jay Haynes set out for the region hoping to capture the culprit. They headquartered at Lake Hotel.

On March 12, in a blizzard, scout Burgess and one of the sergeants started through the Pelican country, camping for the night about two miles northwest of Fern Lake. The next morning they found a cache of six buffalo scalps and skulls, three skins and three more with the hair partially scraped off, the usual process in preparing hides. The trail was clear; they followed it until about noon when they ran across tracks leading to a crude lodge near Astringent Creek. At this juncture they heard several shots and soon spotted the man responsible in the middle of Pelican Valley.

Near him were five, freshly killed buffaloes. Scout Burgess and his sergeant had one .38 army revolver between them, while the poacher, subsequently identified as Ed Howell, was certainly armed with a powerful repeating rifle. "Here," reported Captain Anderson, Burgess "performed an act of bravery that deserves special mention and recognition." He and the sergeant boldly strode across the four hundred yards of open valley that separated them from the poacher. But fortunately for them Howell, wearing a flapping, wide-brimmed old hat, was occupied with skinning one of the animals. With the wind in the wrong direction his dog failed to give an alarm and the plunderer did not see Burgess until the scout was within fifteen or twenty feet of him. Howell surrendered, for it was too late for him to reach his rifle.

He was subsequently brought to Mammoth where Captain Anderson incarcerated him in the guardhouse. There the man remained until the slow process of law came to his defense, for there were no statutes justifying his imprisonment, and Captain Anderson knew it. All the officer could do was destroy the man's property, which he did, and expel him from the park. However, while the wheels of justice ground slowly, Howell remained in the cold, uncomfortable guardhouse.

The man's outfit demonstrates the poverty of these drifting men who eked out an existence in the western mountains. Howell was ragged, dirty, and unkempt. He wore faded overalls and a jumper. His feet were covered by thin socks wrapped in burlap; when skiing, he placed his feet in meal sacks nailed to the skis; as for those implements, they were twelve feet long and made of pine and spruce, the curved tips wired on. The bottoms were anything but smooth and were coated with resin. Howell also pulled a cumbersome toboggan with which to carry out his trophies. He even had along a block and tackle to help him load the carcasses. He was short, with protruding teeth, a forward slouch of his head, blue eyes, and long hair.

The trophies were brought in, Haynes took photographs of the poacher and his kill, Emerson Hough wrote thrilling articles of the event, and Captain Anderson sent off long letters detailing the story. Along with two previously apprehended Cooke City poachers named Van Dyke and Pendleton, Howell's capture completed the roundup of a trio who knew the fate of many a Yellowstone buffalo, elk, and bear. "I believe," the captain said, "this can be made the occasion for a direct appeal to Congress for the passage of an act making it an offense triable before the United States court in Wyoming, for anyone to kill, capture or injure any wild animals in the park."[39]

The publicity certainly helped. In presenting its recommendation to the House favoring passage, the subcommittee noted that "a few days ago poachers entered the park and commenced the slaughter of these animals.... Prompt action is necessary or the last remaining herd of buffalo will be destroyed...." Thus was the Lacey Act brought before the House and guided through under the watchful eyes of Congressmen Lacey and Henderson; through the Senate the bill was shepherded by Senator Vest. Differences were ironed out in conference committee and the bill became law May 7, 1894.[40]

The Lacey Act placed the park "under the sole and exclusive jurisdiction of the United States," made it "a part of the United States Judicial District of Wyoming," provided punishment not only for federal offenses or violations of Interior Department regulations, but also offenses under the laws of Wyoming. The hunting, killing, wounding or capturing of any bird or wild animal "except dangerous animals when it is necessary to prevent them from destroying human life or inflicting an injury," was prohibited. Fishing was closely regulated. Anyone committing the enunciated violations, including vandalism of the natural wonders, was guilty of a misdemeanor and subject to a fine of $1,000, two years imprisonment, or both. Guns and other trappings were subject to forfeiture and confiscation.[41]

The first commissioner stayed a long time. Judge John W. Meldrum arrived at Mammoth in 1894. At the mouth of Clematis Gulch he occupied a building which served as his residence, office, and one-cell jail, never occupied. There he held high court until 1935; he died the next year. Most of his business, and that of his successors, was concerned with minor disruptions to the peace, some vandalism to the thermal phenomena, inebriation and, during prohibition, bootlegging, and automobile traffic violations. Most misdemeanors involved college students employed by the concessionaires. As for poaching, there were fewer violations after 1894. Not only had the army got the problem under control, but the "sense of the people" in the surrounding areas had switched from hostility to understanding and to at least a modicum of cooperation. Yellowstone, after 1894, was quite secure.[42]

NOTES TO CHAPTER ELEVEN

1. The story of the railroads and Yellowstone is adequately presented in H. Duane Hampton, *How the U.S. Cavalry Saved Our National Parks,* and in Reiger, *American Sportsmen.*

2. *Enterprise,* June 16, 1884; August 1, 1885.

3. PMLS, Teller to Vest, February 29, 1884.

4. *Enterprise,* March 14, 1885.

5. Cramton, *Early History of Yellowstone National Park and Its Relation to National Park Policies,* traces Yellowstone-oriented legislation during this era.

6. PMLS, Lamar to Senator Manderson, April 22, 1886; *Congressional Record,* 48th Cong., 1st Sess. (May 27, 1884), 4548.

7. Arnold Hague, "The Needs of the Yellowstone National Park," in U.S. Department of Agriculture, Forestry Division, Bulletin No. 2, Report of the Forestry Conditions of the Rocky Mountains and Other Papers (Washington: G.P.O., 1888) 206–11; PMLS, Lamar to Manderson, April 22, 1886, which includes Hague's letter to Lamar; Hague Papers, Hague to Captain Harris, January 6, 1888; Ibid., Hague to Professor J.A. Holmes, University of North Carolina, January 24, 1888, 206–11. Hague's part in the fight to save Yellowstone is well chronicled in Manning, *Government in Science:* 151–67. Finally, Hague's theories about water retention conflicted with Hiram Martin Chittenden's. See Gordon B. Dodds, *Hiram Martin Chittenden: His Public Career,* 155–85.

8. PMLS, W. Hallett Phillips to Lamar, April 22, 1886; Y.A., Item 937, Grinnell to Senator Charles J. Faulkner, Chairman, Committee on Territories, April 2, 1894.

9. *Congressional Record,* 48th Cong., 1st Sess. (May 27, 1884), 4549. Commenting on the lobbyist employed by Interior, the *Enterprise* said, "It is supposed he [Logan] referred to Assistant Secretary Joslyn. Mr. Joslyn has been a devoted friend of Mr. Logan's, and does not believe he referred to him." Then on May 31, 1884, the *Enterprise* added sarcastically, "Readers will understand without giving the name the identity of the 'prominent official' who used his influence for the bill and will understand the purity of his motives. He is a large owner of Clarks Fork mining property and for that reason desires to see the district reached by railroad. His interest in the park is as small as any person's can well be." The official was obviously the clerk of the P&M Division, later to be chief clerk of the Interior Department. His name was Edward M. Dawson. See U.S. Congress, House, Committee on Public Lands, *Inquiry Into the Management and Control of the Yellowstone National Park,* 53rd Cong., 1st Sess., 1892 (Serial No. 3051), 279–83.

10. *Congressional Record,* 48th Cong., 1st Sess. (March 4, 1884), 1580–82.

11. Ibid., (March 5, 1884), 1609–12.

12. Cramton, *Early History,* 42,43; U.S. Congress, House, Report 1076, 49th Cong., 1st Sess. (Serial No. 2438).

13. *Enterprise,* May 28, June 3, 1884.

14. Weekly *Enterprise,* February 21, 1885.

15. *Congressional Record,* 49th Cong., 1st Sess. (July 12, 1886), 6798; 22 *U.S. Statutes at Large,* 627.

16. *Congressional Record,* 49th Cong., 2d Sess. (December 14, 1886), 150.

17. Ibid.

18. Hague Papers, Hague to George Bird Grinnell, March 30, 1888, sent just as Vest's bill passed the Senate. "Now is the time," wrote Hague, "to fire away with your petitions from gun clubs and others to members of Congress." See also Hague's letter to Captain Harris of April 28, 1888: "During the winter there has been worked up a good deal of interest all over the country by game associations for the Park protection, and the 'Boone and Crockett' Club of New York, composed of many prominent men, are determined to see the thing put on a proper basis and they act as a sort of central organization in the matter." See also *Congressional Record,* 50th Cong. Index, 816; see also *Forest and Stream,* Vol. 28, No. 4 (February 17, 1887), for a listing of groups petitioning Congress.

19. *Congressional Record,* 51st Cong., 1st Sess. (September 29, 1890), 10; 696; Ibid., 51st Cong., 2d Sess. (February 12, 1891), 2538–39.

20. *New York Times,* April 21, 1890, p. 4.

21. *Harper's Weekly Magazine,* Vol. 36, No. 1838 (March 12, 1892), 158; Vol. 37, No. 1888 (February 25, 1893), 170–71; Ibid., No. 1881 (January 7, 1893), 2.

22. *Congressional Record,* 52d Cong., 1st Sess. (May 10, 1892), 4119–27.

23. Ibid., 2676; 4119–27.

24. Ibid.; for the protest see 51st Cong., 1st Sess. (March 10, 1890), 2106.

25. N.A., R.G. 48, Central Classified File, "Boundaries," Lane to Walker D. Hines, May 10, 1919.

26. Senate Report 322, 52d Cong., 1st Sess. (March 7, 1892), (Serial No. 2912).

27. The Hayes Act is entitled "An Act Concerning Leases in the Yellowstone National Park," 28 *U.S. Statutes at Large* 222. The Lacey Act is entitled "An Act to Protect the Birds and Animals in the Yellowstone National Park," 28 *U.S. Statutes at Large* 73; as amended June 28, 1916, 39 *U.S. Statutes at Large* 238; and August 25, 1916, 39 *U.S. Statutes at Large* 535; and as amended June 2, 1920, 41 *U.S. Statutes at Large* 732.

28. Y.A. Box No. 5, Governor Warren (Wyoming) to Acting Superintendent Boutelle, December 2, 1889. See T.S. Palmer, "Chronology and Index of the More Important Events in American Game Protection, 1776–1911," United States Department of Agriculture, Biological Survey Bulletin No. 41 (Washington: 1912).

29. *Congressional Record,* 49th Cong., 1st Sess. (August 2, 1886), 7864, and the *Enterprise,* December 2, 1885. Phillips's statement is in his "Report of W. Hallett Phillips, Special Agent on Yellowstone Park," Sen. Exec. Doc. No. 51, 49th Cong., 1st Sess. (1886), 2.

30. PMLR, Letter forwarded to the Secretary of Interior from William Clancy, May 12, 1882; Y.A. File No. 3, Item No. 103, Affidavit signed by W.B. Tolander, Mammoth Hot Springs, August 8, 1885; Ibid., File No. 4, Anonymous (or "Timothy Quill") to Superintendent Wear, August 14, 1885.

31. Y.A. File No. 1, Item 150, Interior Secretary to Superintendent Wear, October 29, 1885; PMLR, Wear to Lamar, October 9, November 2, and November 3, 1885; *Enterprise,* November 7, 1885.

32. *Enterprise,* November 28, 1885; PMLR, Wear to Muldrow, March 26, 1886.

33. *Congressional Record,* 49th Cong., 1st Sess. (August 2, 1886), 7844; N.A., R.G. 98, Records of the United States Army Commands, Acting Superintendent Pitcher to Military Secretary of the Department of Dakota, May 15, 1905; Ibid., Special Orders No. 2, January 20, 1906, Captain Anderson to Captain G.L. Scott and Second Lieutenant Elmer Lindsley, are examples.

34. Y.A. File No. 2, Noble to Anderson, June 16, 1891.

35. Ibid., File No. 1, Muldrow to Captain Harris, March 30, 1888; Ibid., File No. 4, Conger to Superintendent, October 13, 1889; Ibid., Frank Chatfield to Captain Boutelle, June 29, 1890; Ibid., File No. 2, Noble to Captain Anderson, June 16, 1891; quotation from File No. 4, M.P. Dunham, Madison County, Montana, to Captain Anderson, July 7, 1893.

36. Ibid., File No. 4, R.R. Cummings to Captain Anderson, May 18, 1892; Ibid., File No. 3, January 9, 1894; Ibid., John Dudley Sargent to Captain Anderson, July 30, 1892. Sargent is a tragic figure. See Robert B. Betts, *Along the Ramparts of the Tetons* (Boulder: Colorado Associated University Press, 1978), 150–53.

37. Milton Phil Skinner, *Bears in Yellowstone* (Chicago: A.C. McClurg and Co., 1925), 5–7.

38. Material on Howell's capture is abundant. I have used the article in the *St. Louis Globe Democrat,* March 28, 1894; Ralph Pierson, "The Czar of Wonderland," *Denver Westerners Brand Book,* Vol. 11 (1955), 376–86; Emerson Hough's article in *Forest and Stream,* Vol. 42, No. 18 (1894); Trefethen, *An American Crusade for Wildlife,* 85–90; and Hampton, *How the U.S. Cavalry Saved Our National Parks,* 121–24.

39. *St. Louis Globe-Democrat,* March 28, 1894; Pierson, "Czar of Wonderland," 376–86.

40. House of Representatives, 53rd Cong., 2d Sess., House Report No. 658, to Accompany H.R. 6442 Relating to "Protection of Game in the Yellowstone National Park."

41. 28 *U.S. Statutes at Large,* 73–75.

42. Joseph Joffe, "John W. Meldrum, The Grand Old Man of Yellowstone Park," *Annals of Wyoming,* Part 1, Vol. 13, No. 1 (January, 1941), 5–47; Part 2, Vol. 13, No. 2 (April, 1941), 105–40.

CHAPTER TWELVE

Beginnings of Wildlife Policy

*P*assage of the Lacey Act and the declining threat from railroad promoters meant that Yellowstone National Park was virtually secure and inviolate after 1894. The American people now were well aware of Yellowstone and proud of it. The conservation impulse, maturing in the nineties, cresting under Theodore Roosevelt, and running along a plateau for many years thereafter, added to the park's security. Forest reserves, soon virtually surrounding the park, increased the impression of permanence.

But the idea of a people's park far from a city and a thousand times larger that a city park was still new. Policies still had to be formulated; solutions to problems not yet faced by governments had to be found. Captain Dan Kingman's concept of a belt road system with a minimum of other arteries honeycombing the reservation was soon accepted as fixed policy. Yet the idea of maintaining the wilderness as natural as it was before the coming of the white man did not receive absolute support from the army, or from the Interior Department. Civilization crept in.

On the barren plain just south of the boundary at Gardiner the army maintained a substantial vegetable garden. A Chinese farmer was allowed to raise vegetables nearby, on park land, which he sold to concessionaires. Cattle for milk and beef grazed in the park, and a meat processing plant was maintained by the hotel company on Swan Lake Flats. Hundreds of horses belonging to concessionaires grazed on the Black Tail Deer Plateau. Concessionaires cut wildflowers, pressed them in books made for the purpose, and sold them.

The concept of keeping exotic plants and animals out of the park had not matured into hard policy until the National Park Service took over. The army acting superintendents, as with all men since the beginnings of civilization, tried to improve upon nature. To make the parade ground more attractive several inches of rich soil were spread and then planted in bluegrass. Just inside the north entrance an attractive flower garden was given tender loving care. Sequoia seedlings were planted in Yellowstone by a professional gardener. They all died, however, probably from the intense cold.[1]

Superintendents also expressed an interest in introducing animals not native to the area. In 1898 and 1899 Captain Anderson opened correspondence aimed at acquiring some War Department reindeer used for a relief expedition to the Klondike. The matter was dropped temporarily, partly because some wise zoologist suggested that "in view of the lack of moss in the park, the natural food of the reindeer...it was deemed inexpedient." In 1908 the idea was renewed when a United States official in Alaska wrote Acting Superintendent Allen that the beasts would be a great convenience "as they would travel with sleds on snow no horse could get through. Riding after reindeer," he added, "comfortably tucked up in fur robes in a Pulk [reindeer sled] is a very great improvement on skis. It would be the difference between a Pullman and a caboose car!" Fortunately the reindeer were never introduced.[2]

Apparently white goats from British Columbia and chamois (Swiss antelope) were introduced into Yellowstone in 1907 and 1908, but in neither case did they survive. These animals were imported at the incentive, or at least with the cooperation, of Dr. William T. Hornaday, director of the New York Zoological Park. That such an outstanding early twentieth-century zoologist would have encouraged introduction of exotic species into the park is a commentary upon the infancy of the science of ecology.[3]

It was probably Dr. Hornaday who suggested populating the new National Zoological Park in Washington, D.C., with animals from Yellowstone. As early as May 1890 he was thanking Captain Boutelle for the "fine lot of mountain birds your enterprising son had collected for the national zoo." By January 1891 the idea of Yellowstone animals in the zoo had received Secretary Noble's approval, Superintendent Boutelle had indicated his cooperation, and Elwood Hofer, the well-known Yellowstone guide, had been appointed "Smithsonian Hunter" (the zoo was and remains under Smithsonian management.)[4]

For the next several years Hofer was busy trapping moose, buffalo, antelope, black and grizzly bears, foxes, porcupines, hawks, mountain sheep, mountain lions, wolverines, wildcats, mink, marten, badgers, gophers, beaver, and otter, all for shipment to the National Zoological Park. He learned most of his trapping and shipping techniques by experience, mastered them quickly, and was getting most of the charges to Washington alive and well.[5]

In what is now recognized as a major policy error, the army made short shrift of the large predators, the coyotes, wolves, mountain lions, and wildcats (also known as bobcats or lynx). In retrospect the practice appears so incredibly stupid that we wonder at the policy makers' intelligence—that they failed to foresee the proliferation to the point of calamity of these animals' prey, especially of deer, elk, and rodents. Fortunately other beasts that could have been considered predators were not included. Bears on occasion will kill deer and elk and eat the flesh. Hawks, owls, skunks, weasels, and mink are certainly meat eaters, but were usually classed as vermin. In Yellowstone, of the coyotes, wolves, mountain lions, and bobcats that were considered fair game in all places and seasons, the mountain lions (also called pumas or painters) and wolves were the most hated and the most hunted.

The loathing for these carnivores was a spillover from the ranching frontier. Undeniably, they were destructive beasts. Mountain lions developed a particular appetite for horse flesh, but sheep and cattle appealed to them also. A puma has been known to leap a nine-foot fence carrying a grown sheep, quite an accomplishment for an animal weighing only 140 pounds. Theodore Roosevelt once described a treed cougar as "the big horse-killing cat, the destroyer of the deer, the Lord of stealthy murder, facing his doom with a heart both craven and cruel."[6]

An equally hated predator was the gray wolf. This skillful hunter had flourished in the American wilderness for millenia. When the buffalo were nearly exterminated, the wolf developed a taste for their replacement, "tame beef." Montana ranchers in the 1880s figured normal annual cattle loss to the carnivores at 10 percent. It became an unwritten rule in the cattle country that no cowboy would pass a carcass, regardless of how the beast had died, without inserting strychnine to make it lethal bait. Professional wolfers could receive $1.25 a pelt plus a cattlemen's association bounty of as much as five dollars per carcass. Hatred of the wolf in western American simply knew no bounds.[7]

The army allowed the killing of predators by its personnel on the reservation. Station commanders were "authorized and directed to kill mountain lions, coyotes, and timber wolves." They were to do it themselves, never delegate authority to others, report each month on the number of such animals killed, and "retain all skins or scalps in their personal possession until directed what to do with them."[8]

In 1903 a pack of hounds was purchased for lion and lynx hunting, and a keeper assigned to them. Don, the oldest at seven years, and Ring, three years old, were considered among the best-trained hunting dogs in the United States. In 1904 the game warden and scouts with dogs killed fifteen lions and lynxes. Although the pack was sold in 1908, the war against the predators continued. One hundred twenty-nine coyotes were killed in 1911, 154 in 1913, 155 in 1914. In that year packs of up to ten gray wolves were spotted in the park, but by the early 1920s these had been eliminated. Along with strychnine, steel traps were used in the campaign.[9]

The time came when park officials rued the day they ordered destruction of the predacious beasts. No mountain lion has been confirmed as inhabiting the park since 1930, and the presence of wolves there is a matter of conjecture. The living things they preyed upon, from rodents to stately elk, no longer die from the lethal pounce, powerful jaws, and incisive fangs of the carnivores. Nature's balance being thus upset, the prey have multiplied in the absence of natural enemies until they pose serious, continuing problems.

There is one category in which most people would probably approve of interference with nature, yet even here a modern icthyologist might hedge approval. Captain Boutelle instituted the idea of stocking Yellowstone's lakes and streams with game fish, exotic species not native to Yellowstone's waters; Captain Anderson continued his predecessor's cooperation with Marshall McDonald, the United States fish commissioner. Stocking the streams with game fish was first carried out in the fall and winter of 1888 and 1889. The dimensions of the project are indicated by the statistics of fish stocked the following winter (1890–91): 45,000 lake trout, 10,000 Von Behr, 7,000 Loch Leven, 8,000 brook, and 10,000 whitefish, the latter of which went into Yellowstone Lake.[10]

By the spring of 1891 McDonald could report that the park's river basins contained representatives from all the important species of Salmonidae except the salmon itself. Goose Lake, off from the Upper Geyser Basin, was even stocked with 500 black bass in 1893 and an additional 800 in 1894. For several years a fish hatchery was maintained near Yellowstone Lake.[11]

One of the icthyologists who helped in this work was David Starr Jordan, a leading scientist-educator of the time. Jordan relates how Spencer Baird, secretary of the Smithsonian Institution, hired a man recommended by Jordan to be a Smithsonian naturalist assigned to the park. However, Representative Courtland C. Matson of Indiana insisted upon his Congressional prerogative whereby Congressmen made such selections. Honorable Courtland Matson's first appointee could not accept, being at the time in jail on a larceny charge. The second heard of his appointment while trying to ride a horse through a saloon. He accepted but died soon thereafter at Mammoth Hot Springs.[12]

From destroying predators and introducing new species of fish and mammals, the authorities turned their attention to game preservation. This demanded a hurried formulation of policies and procedures concerning pronghorn (antelope) and bison. By the mid-1880s both of these creatures faced extermination, yet once as many as forty million antelope and thirty-two million bison grazed the plains of North America. As with the ill-fated passenger pigeon, the fate of the graceful antelope seemed to be sealed. By 1921 only an estimated 11,749 were left in the United States. Yet measures taken to protect these animals, and their rapid reproduction rate, ran up their number to well over 300,000. Today they are as safe as any wild animals can be in our rapidly changing, explosively populating world. [13]

To flourish, the Yellowstone antelope needed only protection. Their tendency to drift out of the park and down the Yellowstone Valley placed them in jeopardy. Local hunters were accused of using dogs to chase them out of the reservation so they could be killed legally. So park authorities ordered a fence built along the boundary near Gardiner. Unfortunately some of the pronghorn crawled under it, so three miles of poultry wire netting was erected to keep the animals in. This worked fairly well, and the park antelope thrived. [14]

It was the American bison, the buffalo, whose imminent extinction caused the greatest alarm. Destruction of this shaggy beast was noticeable even before the Civil War, but it was the increased tempo of American settlement coupled with the coming of the railroads that by the mid-1880s had brought the near demise of this great natural resource. So fast did it happen that authorities hardly had time to take protective measures. [15]

Few accurate statistics exist about the buffalo. It is a certainty, however, that the bovid *Bison bison americanus* was destroyed primarily in the 1870s, and remnants were killed off rapidly in the 1880s. The *Enterprise* noted that the winter of 1885 was the first in Montana's history in which nothing had been heard of buffalo hunting, "no large herds seen on the ranges, no Indian parties following their favorite game." Only the herd that had long inhabited Yellowstone Park was still in existence. Numbering two to three hundred, it was "the largest herd reported this winter south of the British line," according to the *Enterprise*. [16]

At the end of 1885 George Bird Grinnell returned from an extended western trip. He informed the *New York Sun* that to his positive knowledge there were not more than seven hundred bison or buffalo left on the American continent, and 180 of them lived in the park. He expressed righteous anger at the report that twenty of the park beasts had been killed by a party of English tourists. "The Government," he said, "should certainly do everything to protect the few survivors." [17]

And they were. All the Yellowstone superintendents arrived as at least nascent conservationists and bloomed into vigorous advocates. Most Interior secretaries encouraged them. When George W. Noble was informed that a herd of sixty or seventy buffalo had wandered out of the park and was being slaughtered, he wrote Captain Boutelle for verification and was pleased to hear that the report was false. As between a troublesome bear and the safety of buffalo calves, Noble took an emphatic stand: kill the bear. If there were any herds or stragglers outside the park boundaries, could they be brought into the park and "retained . . . until they feel greater security there than elsewhere and thus be induced to remain? It would be," Noble added, "an achievement that would long be remembered with approbation."[18]

Despite this official interest, the Yellowstone buffalo did not thrive. In 1891 two herds of about thirty each, plus many "single ones and small bunches," were reported on the reservation, with the total number estimated at two hundred to four hundred; in 1895 the secretary reported just 200 bison, most of them in the vicinity of the Idaho boundary. In 1896 the estimate was cut to fifty, in 1897 the number was fixed at twenty-four, in 1898 back up to fifty, no estimate was made in 1899, but twenty-nine were counted in 1900 and twenty-five in 1901.[19]

Because their skins and mounted heads were increasingly valuable as they became scarcer, bison were sought by poachers. In the winter of 1893–94 most of the beasts moved from the Pelican and Lamar valleys into the west and south sections of the park, especially onto the Madison Plateau. Heavy poaching was always believed to take place in these remote areas, with the lawbreakers coming in from the Jackson Lake or the Henry's Lake regions. They reportedly had a rendezvous on the park's west side. On fairly good authority it was said that poachers killed seventy-six head that winter plus another sixty which had moved northward into the Gallatin Valley, still in the park.[20]

By the mid-1890s, then, one could scarcely speak of a Yellowstone buffalo herd. Just a few animals survived, the exact number difficult to determine. There could have been half the numbers listed by the secretaries (which were based upon the superintendent's reports), or there could have been twice as many. From our vantage point today an "educated guess" would be that there were never fewer than fifty bison in the park and possibly the number was double that. However, due to inbreeding (which brings on infertility), poaching, and other undetermined reasons, it was clear by 1896 that the park bison were jeopardized. The herd, if it could be called any longer by that name, was probably declining.

Officials expressed concern over this but were not at all certain what could be done to reverse the trend. In 1895, with funds from the Smithsonian Institution, a corral was erected to hold bison, elk, and other beasts that gamekeepers might drive in or which could drift in during the winter. "Should this plan succeed it will be possible to retain at least a small herd of bison and keep them nearly in a state of nature," the Interior secretary reported. It did not work that way. Eight bison did wander into the corral but the gates were left open for others to enter; the eight consumed their fill of hay and departed.[21]

Into the buffalo story now comes one of Yellowstone's characters, a man of some fame, much of it misplaced. This was Charles Jesse "Buffalo" Jones. Born in Illinois in 1844, Jones attended Wesleyan University for two years. He contracted "western fever," and after his marriage in 1869 he headed for western Kansas, finally settling at Garden City. He worked as a buffalo hunter, townsite speculator, and sometime rancher before in the 1880s conceiving the idea of acquiring a herd of the disappearing buffalo. His reasons for doing this are not known, but his later actions lead us to believe that they were monetary and speculative rather than purely conservationist. Whatever his motives, he purchased bison in Texas, rounded up a few wild ones he discovered on the plains, and placed them on his Kansas ranch where he experimented with crossing them with cattle.[22]

Jones, on the lookout for opportunities, thought he saw a big one in the struggle to save the Yellowstone buffalo. In June 1896, he made the Interior secretary a proposition, heavily weighted in his favor, that he be appointed Yellowstone buffalo keeper; by his terms, even if he failed he would profit handsomely from the employment. This arrogant, one-sided proposition was nevertheless submitted to Captain Anderson for his opinion. That competent officer replied in part that he had "had some correspondence with Mr. Jones on this subject in 1891, and found him both unpractical and untruthful." At this time Jones was not hired.[23]

But the buffalo collector was persistent and kept in touch. He wrote letters. He became widely (and mistakenly) identified as the lone savior of the American bison. Meanwhile the Yellowstone herd continued to decline. By the winter of 1902, when Major Pitcher reported that his scouts had located just twenty-two running wild at the head of Pelican Creek, even the slow-moving American Congress viewed the situation with alarm. On January 30, 1902, the Senate passed a resolution requesting the secretaries of Interior and Agriculture to transmit facts about the preservation of bison in the United States and Canada, whether they were increasing or dying out, whether they were of pure or mixed blood, and finally, "whether or not steps might be taken by the United States for the prevention of extinction of such animals."[24]

The immediate result of this action was a survey conducted by Major Pitcher to determine who owned bison, where they were located, the purity of the herds, and the possibilities of their sale. Before the winter of 1902 was over, the major was able to report that in the park and surrounding areas there were 330 known head: twenty-two in the park herd; four on Dot Island, owned by Captain E.C. Waters; four at Henry's Lake in the possession of R.W. (Dick) Rock; and at or in the vicinity of the Flathead Indian Reservation in western Montana, 300, for a grand total of 330. Pitcher's survey letters also explained that the major contemplated starting a fresh park herd. "For this purpose," his letters read, "we may wish, in the future, to purchase a few head of pure blooded buffalo. Please let me know if you have any for sale and at what price you will be willing to dispose of them."[25]

A few days later the major described his plans for a new herd. He requested authority "to catch up all the young buffalo that were left"—two or three calves approaching yearling age plus those born more recently—and place them "under fence" in army care. "By doing this each year," he explained, "I believe that we can soon start a new herd and at very little cost." He also suggested purchasing a few animals to infuse new blood into this proposed herd. He hoped such a new grouping, being raised in confinement, would become sufficiently tame and so accustomed to seeing people that it would stay where it could be seen, rather than flee to the high mountains. "As far as I know," he reported, "not a buffalo has been seen by the tourists for a number of years."[26]

The upshot of this interest was a $15,000 appropriation for the purchase of buffalo, a good fence, feed, and $2,500 for additional expenses. Even before this Congressional action, the secretary had cleared the way by obtaining Treasury permission to use funds derived from park leases and concessions for the purchase of buffalo.[27]

Major Pitcher pushed his campaign even before funds were definitely available. He hankered after Dick Rock's young bull and planned to hire Rock to round up the park buffalo calves. These plans failed because one bison which Rock had "tamed" to be saddled and ridden, bucked him off, gored and killed him.[28]

Of much more significance was the reply received from the Pennsylvanian-turned-Westerner, Howard Eaton, of Medora, North Dakota, Expressing genuine interest in preserving the buffalo, he took an option on about sixty of the beasts which belonged to Charles Allard's heirs (Allard had maintained one of the larger herds still in existence), offering to sell them to the government for $250 a head. "Mr. Eaton is a personal friend of the President," Pitcher informed the secretary, "and is anxious to see his herd to the park." Yet even after Eaton had traveled to Washington to confer with Roosevelt the matter was not settled.[29]

The hesitation was almost certainly because of the $15,000 appropriation. News of it got out fast, and among those who scented green paper money was none other than Buffalo Jones. He informed Major Pitcher of his abilities at handling bison and also offered to sell to the park some of his own stock. A few weeks later Pitcher suggested that a game warden be employed to care for the herd and live in a cabin near the corral.[30]

When the $15,000 became available, Secretary Hitchcock appointed Buffalo Jones game warden as of July 8, 1902. There is no indication that Hitchcock consulted with Pitcher about Jones's qualifications. The buffalo keeper was instructed to confer with Pitcher, and then, while a corral and fence were being built, the acting superintendent was to correspond with owners of pure-blood buffalo, ascertaining at what price the beasts could be purchased and delivered in sound condition to the Yellowstone corral.[31]

Aware of the inbreeding problem, Pitcher specified that males and females would not be purchased from the same parties, that the animals were to be two to seven years old "with perfect bodies, limbs, and horns," and they must be "full blooded American bison." They were to be subject to inspection both at place of purchase and when delivered in the park. The eleven owners contacted ranged from millionaire W.C. Whitney, who had a few bison in Lenox, Massachusetts, to Texas ranchman Charles Goodnight; at least one other owner contacted Major Pitcher. Seven owners made offers ranging from $650 a head f.o.b. down to $250. All were leery of the responsibility of rounding up the beasts and getting them safely loaded and unloaded from railroad cars. Only Howard Eaton offered to deliver his bison, for an additional $1,500, but he refused to be responsible for any loss in transit. Even then he made the proposal only because, he said, "I am interested in the preservation of the buffalo."[32]

Meanwhile Buffalo Jones had arrived. He and Major Pitcher agreed on Pitcher's choice of a corral site about a mile from Mammoth with timber and grass and a stream of cold water running through; in addition, it was accessible throughout the year. Jones also constructed a modest corral on Pelican Creek with hopes of capturing the small herd grazing in that vicinity. The strong Page Woven Wire Fence was soon being erected, and by August 30 the major could report that the time had come to purchase the bison.[33]

Pitcher suggested that fifteen females be purchased from the Howard Eaton herd at $500 a head, and three males obtained by Jones from the Goodnight herd at $460 a head. (Actually eighteen cows were purchased from Eaton.) Jones was to accompany Eaton to the Flathead Reservation out of Selish, in western Montana, where the herd was grazing.[34]

There, under Jones's supervision, the buffalo were loaded on train cars for Cinnabar, there unloaded and driven into the new corral. "Fourteen fine buffalo cows have been delivered in corral and are in fine condition," Pitcher wired the secretary in October 1902. Jones was then sent to Goodnight, Texas, for the bulls and they too were subsequently delivered in good condition. Early in February he delivered four more cows from Selish for a total acquisition, bulls and cows, of twenty-one.[35]

With these animals safely enclosed in the Mammoth corral, attention turned to the "wild herd" along Pelican Creek. During the summer of 1902 a corral had been built in the vicinity about twelve miles from the Lake soldier station. Officials released one of the Goodnight bulls in the Pelican area in hopes that it would join the wild herd and lead it to the corral, but the experiment did not succeed. Jones did count the wild herd, however, which numbered twenty-nine critters with a few others believed to be nearby but out of sight. Including the beasts in the square-mile corral at Mammoth, about fifty bison were accounted for in the late winter of 1903.[36]

By early 1904 two bull calves and a young heifer had been captured from the wild herd and added to the new "tame herd," giving that group three distinct blood strains. In its first year in the park this herd produced only five calves; however, there was no question that the herd was thriving; in the spring it produced eleven fine calves with indications of three more, bringing the total, as of June 1904, to thirty-nine animals. The young heifer from the wild herd was being successfully suckled by a domestic cow brought in for the purpose. There was every reason for optimism, every reason to believe the danger of extermination had ended. The buffalo were safe and reproducing.[37]

The next step in development of the park herds took place in 1905. Major Pitcher moved some of the animals from the new herd to the Lamar Valley and turned them loose. The section from Soda Butte to Lamar Junction offered the best year-round grazing in the park, and in past times has been the home of the large herd of wild buffalo. However, to make the animals feel at home there, he wanted them kept for a time in a corral, gradually to be freed but probably never to wander far from a nearby haystack. Pitcher was allotted $1,500 to build the corral, which was at the mouth of Rose Creek; in the vicinity seventy-five to one hundred tons of hay could be harvested every year. Presumably the gamekeeper's cabin was also constructed nearby.[38]

From here on the story of the Yellowstone buffalo is essentially one of success. The "wild herd" did not take hold for a time, but by 1916 the superintendent reported seventy-two bison actually counted with some animals beginning to disperse from their Pelican Creek grounds. Real success came with the "tame herd" which numbered seventy-four in 1908, 147 in 1911, and 276 by 1916. (These were the animals moved to the buffalo pasture in the Lamar Valley.) Each summer ten to twenty bulls were transferred to the old pasture at Mammoth where tourists observed them. An outbreak of a contagious disease, hemorrhagic septicemia, struck the "tame herd," but the animals were vaccinated and the threat was eliminated.[39]

In these years other policies were formulated as park officials endeavored to protect not only the bison but also the antelope (which grew to number 1,000, most of them below Mammoth), mountain sheep (which lived on Mount Everts), moose (rarely observed), whitetailed deer (about one hundred), blacktailed deer (1,000 and increasing), and elk (over 32,000 by 1916). Feeding of the animals in winter became an established practice. Alfalfa was planted in the field south of Gardiner; for a few years it yielded between eighty and a hundred tons of hay. Foxtail and other weeds finally crowded it out, so it was plowed and, as an experiment, wheat was sown.

The weather was unusually favorable that year, and eighty tons of the grain were harvested in 1910 to serve as fodder. Timothy seed was planted in the Lamar Valley and up to two hundred tons of excellent hay were harvested for the hungry buffalo. Even irrigation of the hayfields was permitted, something that would throw a modern Park Service ranger into apoplexy.[40]

Protection from poachers as well as from legitimate hunters on the other side of the northern park boundary was greatly aided with completion of a boundary survey in 1904. The northern line was marked in such a way as to be easily followed. In addition, the Wyoming legislature in 1905 proclaimed a twenty-five-mile strip south of the park boundary into the Jackson Hole country as a game preserve, thus giving protection to deer, elk, antelope, and other valuable animals which might cross the line. In 1911 Montana set aside as a game preserve a seven-mile-wide stretch of land extending from the boundary crossing at the Yellowstone River westward to the northwest corner of the park, and then south along the line for seven miles.[41]

In addition, in 1903 and 1904 Page Wire Fence was erected across the field south of Gardiner. Even so, elk occasionally broke through the fence, prompting ten to thirty troopers to head down the valley to drive them back into the park. Each year new trails were cut through the wilderness to better aid the scouts and patrols. Telephone lines were extended even to the remote Bechler River station in the southwest corner.[42]

A final string needs tying in our narration of early policies towards fish and animals. This is the Yellowstone career of Charles J. "Buffalo" Jones. Major Pitcher had not wanted him but the man had been arbitrarily appointed gamekeeper over his head. It is possible that President Roosevelt was responsible for Jones's appointment, but proof is lacking.[43]

During his first year in Yellowstone, Jones appears to have carried out his tasks satisfactorily. He was sent to inspect and bring back the beasts from the Allard herd outside Selish, Montana, upon which Howard Eaton had taken an option, and he obtained three young bulls in Texas and returned with them to the park. For these two tasks he was paid five dollars a day subsistence for an illogical total of $142.55, indicating that he was traveling a total of twenty-eight days. No one could drive buffalo to the park from those distances (Selish and the Texas Panhandle) in so short a time, yet the ridiculous rumor persists that he did just that.[44]

In a short while Jones's erratic, cantankerous personality began to cause trouble. Major Pitcher, in carrying out orders which he obviously considered politically motivated, placed Jones in charge of all park scouts, giving him full authority over them and power to discharge any of them at any time if they failed to obey his instructions. Soon, however, Jones requested that he be relieved of his task since he did not get along with the scouts. He even found it difficult to coexist with his brother, N.C. Jones. As complaints came in from officials of the hotel and camp companies, Major Pitcher soon discovered that the buffalo keeper was indeed a confounded nuisance.[45]

Certainly "cantankerous" fits the man. One sensitive tourist related how he and his lady friends had been behind the Canyon Hotel conversing in normal tones while waiting to observe a bear when someone rudely ordered them to be silent. "I stated I thought we could talk, and was told to either keep still or he would call a soldier and place me in the guard house," the distressed visitor complained. "I learned he was Buffalo Jones."[46]

In 1904 complaints were registered against Jones for his methods in chastising bears. Now bruin was indeed causing trouble. The army was learning by trial and error of things to do and not to do in the handling of these wild animals. People patted them and received bad bites and scratches in return. Bears were fed at garbage dumps while tourists watched. It soon became clear that the bears' growing fearlessness towards man was more likely than not to increase conflicts between the two. At Lake Hotel bears had broken into outbuildings, they had broken a door and smashed a window at a Wylie Camp, and had so threatened a garbage wagon driver that on several occasions he had fled in terror, leaving the bears to feast on the garbage.

Buffalo Jones thought he had a solution. "I caught three of the worst of these bears in a rope snare and hauled them up with a block and tackle," he boasted. "I then gave them as big a scare as possible and switched them besides. I also prodded them in a humane manner with a pole and prod, but so short as not to reach through the fur and skin. These animals now believe everybody has a snare and a prod for them and they will not stand for a person to come within fifty feet of them."[47]

According to Major Pitcher, however, "within a few minutes after being turned loose, the bear returned to his usual feeding ground, the whipping having had no effect whatever except rendering the bear more fearless of man than before." Moreover, Jones enacted this chastisement while many tourists looked on, and had motion pictures made of it. Some tourists protested the brutality of the procedure and found it disgusting, so that Major Pitcher forbade its continuance and gave orders that troublesome bears be killed. In 1913 five of them were killed.[48]

Relations between the irascible and independent Jones and Major Pitcher deteriorated rapidly, but Jones had some elements of fate on his side. The nation was conservation conscious and Jones, who sought publicity and was literate and tenacious, wrote letters which gained him sympathy in high places. As a result, Interior Secretary Ethan Allen Hitchcock peremptorily ordered Major Pitcher to grant Jones full authority over all the game in Yellowstone. "I have to request that you will extend him every facility and assistance practicable to enable him to properly discharge his duties." So ended the secretary's letter.[49]

This was too much. Major Pitcher shot off a letter to Hitchcock, questioning the wisdom of granting such favored treatment to the buffalo man. Persuasively, the acting superintendent justified his orders in denying Jones the right to abuse bears and defended his own (Pitcher's) decision ordering destruction of the dangerous ones. Pitcher did, however, grant Jones credit for the successful care of the tame herd of buffalo in 1901 and 1903. But, he added, "for the past two years he has apparently become interested in other matters to such an extent that he has neglected his duty as buffalo keeper." The major cited statistics showing that the 1905 calf crop was six and two of them died, whereas the previous year there were twelve. "This fact alone," he emphasized, "in my opinion, shows neglect on the part of somebody concerning the management of the herd, and as Mr. Jones had absolute control over this herd, he alone can be held responsible for any failure to care for it."

Jones also demanded the right to sell horns, hides, claws, and the teeth of animals and was angered when the superintendent refused him permission. "Mr. Jones has never been honestly interested in the propagation of pure blood buffalo, or of any other game in the park. His sole idea in seeking the position . . . was to attain a little notoriety, and to use his position for the purpose of making a few friends who would stake him to the necessary funds for the purpose of establishing a ranch where he could carry out his pet hobby of raising 'cattalo,'" the major wrote, warming to his subject. Jones had so abused a team of mules assigned to him that the superintendent had taken them away from him; his own brother had left him; and at present Jones was in Arizona establishing a cattalo ranch. "I think it is evident," Pitcher concluded, ". . . that Mr. Jones's day of usefulness in the park has gone—in fact, his presence is now a positive detriment and a source of annoyance. . . ." He recommended Jones's transfer out of the park, or his forced resignation.[50]

Pitcher's letter had the desired effect: the position of gamekeeper was abolished as of September 15, 1905. Thus was the park rid of the eccentric, publicity-conscious Buffalo Jones. However, the army had not heard the last of him. A few months after his discharge Jones delivered a lecture in New Haven, Connecticut, in which he questioned the bravery of the soldiers and "classed them as being utterly useless in protecting game in Yellowstone Park." He told of a soldier retreating to safety while hunting mountain lions there. "These fellows are taught to shoot men," he said, "but when it comes to shooting mountain lions they apparently want no part at all."[51]

In replying to these "false and slurry remarks," Major Pitcher pointed out that when Jones "first arrived here he could not recognize a mountain lion track when he saw one." The superintendent had never heard of a soldier deserting Jones while hunting lions. "Any soldier who has been in the park for a short while quickly learns the cowardly habits of mountain lions, and has no more fear of them than . . . of domesticated cats," he said. Jones had kept a live mountain lion in captivity at the buffalo corral, and the story spread that he had his picture taken with the animal "illustrating himself in the act of capturing a wild mountain lion out in the forest" while the lion was in fact securely chained. "If he is using this picture in his lectures, without explaining how it was taken," suggested the major, "he is imposing on the public and is simply a fakir."[52]

Jones finally stayed in Arizona where he tried to raise cattalo. In a letter of November 25, 1907, to President Roosevelt he asked to borrow a buffalo bull and a bighorn ram from Yellowstone, but Colonel S.B.M. Young, then in charge, replied "that the character of C.J. Jones ("Buffalo" Jones), so far as it may be judged from the records of the Department, would scarcely justify the Department in entrusting the park animals to his keeping."[5]

The notoriety given to this man both angers and frustrates historians endeavoring to present accurate history. We come across the problem constantly—the shallow, superficial person of minor attainments who because of charisma, a flair for the dramatic, an instinct for public relations, the fortunate reality of being in the right place at the right time, a preoccupation with something that is exotic or that piques the public whim—receives an undeserved place in the historical record. Long after Major Pitcher and his scouts are forgotten the sensational, distorted accomplishments of Buffalo Jones will be gracing Sunday supplements, drugstore paperback bookshelves and, alas, an occasional "scholarly" nonfiction western history. Truth is, Jones did make a minor contribution to saving the buffalo. He was the only buffalo broker in America. It was to him that the dozen or so collectors of live buffalo turned when they wanted to trade, sell, or purchase stock. But this was his only accomplishment.[54]

As for the park buffalo, they thrived under the care of several more keepers, one of whom was Buffalo's brother, N.C. Jones, but he was fired for incompetence. In 1907 the herds were consolidated at Rose Creek in the Lamar Valley. In the 1920s they divided of their own volition into three herds totaling about eight hundred animals. They tend to stay away from tourists (although in June 1981 several were grazing on the plain in front of Old Faithful Inn), and are rarely seen in summer when they go to the higher areas to escape the flies. The beasts suffer from brucellosis (undulant fever) which causes cows to abort fetuses, and although the animals are considered in good condition, their numbers remain nearly stationary.[55]

And so the animals in Yellowstone Park were saved. In retrospect the officials, while formulating policy, committed many errors. Predator killing resulted not only in the proliferation of deer, and especially elk, until their numbers posed a feeding problem; it also resulted in explosive growth of the rodent population which in turn deteriorated the grass cover. Fortunately exotic animals did not "take" in the park and exotic plants have apparently done no harm; neither have exotic fishes been harmful to Yellowstone's waters. But this has been good luck. *No one knew.* Many of Yellowstone's problems have been solved, temporarily, by trial and error because no sure satisfactory solutions were known. Great advances in knowledge and a big bank of experience have taught much; even so, Yellowstone's naturalists are the first to admit that much, much more remains to be done.

NOTES TO CHAPTER TWELVE

1. Most of the material for this chapter was culled from the Yellowstone Archives. Since I used these records, they have been reorganized twice; however, a researcher should be able to correlate my references with those of the reorganized files.

Y.A. File No. 16, Secretary Ryan to Superintendent, August 30, 1900; Y.A. File No. 27, Ryan to Superintendent, September 21, 1905; Y.A., Letters Sent, Vol. 16, Superintendent to Captain Kirby Walker, Acting Superintendent, Sequoia National Park, 1906.

2. Y.A. File No. 14, Lovich Pierce, Acting Commissioner, Bureau of Education in the Department of the Interior, to Secretary, July 30, 1898, Ibid., File No. 29, Assistant Secretary Pierce, to Acting Superintendent Allen, May 25, 1908; Ibid., Sheldon Jackson to Major Allen, February 25, 1908

3. Ibid., File No. 29, Interior Secretary to Superintendent, December 6, 1907; Ibid., Secretary to Superintendent, February 14, 1908; *Dictionary of American Biography,* Vol. 22, Supplement 2, 216–17.

4. Y.A. File No. 3, Hornaday to Captain Boutelle, May 6, 1890; Ibid., File No. 5, Elwood Hofer to Captain Anderson, February 5, 1891. Prior to assuming his New York position, Hornaday had been involved in plans for the National Zoological Park.

5. Ibid., File No. 5, Hofer to Captain Anderson, October 26, 1894.

6. Stanley P. Young and Edward A. Goldman, *The Puma: Mysterious American Cat* (Washington, D.C.: The American Wildlife Institute, 1946), 140–42; Quotation

from Theodore Roosevelt, *A Book-Lover's Holidays in the Open* (New York: Charles Scribner's Sons, 1916), 22.

7. Stanley P. Young and Edward A. Goldman, *The Wolves of North America* (Washington, D.C.: The Wildlife Institute, 1944), 264ff.

8. N.A., R.G. 98, Park Orders No. 4, June 30, 1917.

9. Y.A., File No. 29, Superintendent to Miles Buford of Silver City, New Mexico, August 3, 1908; Ibid., Chief Clerk at Yellowstone to C.M. Knox of Logan, Montana, August 24, 1908; Ibid., Circular Letters, July 15, 1908; Ibid., File No. 21, Secretary Ryan to Superintendent, March 23, 1903. See also *Annual Report of the Secretary of the Interior for 1904,* 179.

Roosevelt had an interest in the use of dogs for hunting predators. See Morison, *Letters of Theodore Roosevelt,* Roosevelt to Interior Secretary Hitchcock, February 4, 1903, 425 (Item 2583); Roosevelt to Major Pitcher, February 18, 1903, 429–30 (Item 2591).

10. Y.A., File No. 4, McDonald, United States Fish Commissioner, to Boutelle, August 18, 1889; Ibid., July 8, 1890.

11. Ibid., McDonald to Anderson, March 16, 1891; July 10, 1893; August 8, 1894. See also John D. Varley and Paul Schullery, *Freshwater Wilderness — Yellowstone Fishes and Their World* (Yellowstone Park, Wyoming: Yellowstone Library and Museum Association, 1983). David Starr Jordan states that, pursuant to his report, eastern brook trout, European brown trout, and shasta rainbow of California were introduced into Yellowstone's streams. Jordan, *The Days of a Man* (New York: World Book Company, 1922) two vols.: Vol. 1, 341. The bass in Goose Lake did not survive. According to Ron Jones, project leader for the Fish and Wildlife Service, the lake is not suitable habitat and the fish probably died quickly. The fish hatchery closed in the mid-1950s. Correspondence with Timothy Manns, Yellowstone Park Naturalist-Historian, 1983.

12. Jordan, *The Days of a Man,* Vol. 1, 315. Jordan gives the year of the incident as 1882. I have been unable to confirm the story from official records; however, since Jordan gives the last name of his choice (a zoology student named Meek) and Congressman Matson was from Indiana, where Jordan was president of the state university, it may well be true, though perhaps delightfully embellished.

13. U.S. Department of the Interior, Fish and Wildlife Service, *The Pronghorn Antelope,* Conservation Note 11 (Washington, D.C.: G.P.O., 1961), 149. Tom McHugh, *The Time of the Buffalo* (New York: Alfred Knopf, 1972), 17, is the authority for the figure thirty-two million.

14. Y.A., File No. 29, Superintendent to Secretary, November 20, 1908.

15. The accepted authority on the buffalo is Frank Gilbert Roe, *The North American Buffalo* (Toronto: University of Toronto Press, 1951) although Tom McHugh's research is more timely by twenty years. See also Phillip D. Thomas, "The Near Extinction of the American Bison: A Case Study in Legislative Lethargy," in *Western*

American History in the Seventies, edited by Daniel Tyler (Fort Collins: Educational and Media Information Systems, 1973), 21–33.

16. Weekly *Enterprise,* March 7, 1885. Probably there were never less than one thousand buffalo in the United States as well as several thousand in Canada.

17. Quoted in *Enterprise,* December 12, 1885. The story involving the English tourists is not confirmed; I doubt that it happened.

18. Y.A., File No. 2, Secretary Noble to Captain Boutelle, September 20, November 20, 1890; Noble to Captain Anderson, June 13, 1893.

19. *Annual Reports of the Secretary of the Interior,* 1891, cxxxvi; 1895, lxv; 1896, cii; 1897, lxxiii; 1898, xcix; 1900, cxxvii; 1901, clv.

20. Martin S. Garretson, *The American Bison* (New York: New York Zoological Society, 1938), 199–206.

21. *Annual Reports of the Secretary of the Interior,* 1895, lxv; 1896, ciii.

22. While Jones's Yellowstone activities reveal him as a mercenary, egotistical, and eccentric person not deserving of adulation, two sources that present him favorably are Robert Easton and Mackenzie Brown, *Lord of Beasts, The Saga of Buffalo Jones* (Tucson: University of Arizona Press, 1961; Lincoln: University of Nebraska Press, 1970), and Buffalo Jones, *Buffalo Jones' Adventures on the Plains,* compiled by Colonel Henry Inman (Lincoln: University of Nebraska Press, 1970, comprising part of an 1899 edition). The citation is to Easton and Brown, 3–8.

23. Y.A., File No. 8, Jones to Secretary, June 9, 1896; Ibid., Letters Sent, Vol. 15, 313–21, Captain Anderson to Interior Department, June 27, 1896, cited in letter from Major Pitcher to the Secretary, July 20, 1905.

24. Ibid., Letters Sent, Vol. 11, Pitcher to Secretary, February 5, 1902; Ibid., Letters Received, Vol. 1, 315; "The American Bison in the United States and Canada," Sen. Doc. 145 (57th Cong., 1st Sess.).

25. Y.A., Letters Received, Vol. 2, 357 (included in this file although they are letterpress copies of letters sent, an apparent case of misfiling), Pitcher to Secretary, February 25, 1902; Y.A., Letters Sent, Vol. 11, Pitcher to J.M. Keith, Missoula, Montana; to Conrad Brothers, Great Falls, Montana; to Douglas Carlin, Cheyenne River Agency, South Dakota; to Mr. Dick Rock of Henry's Lake, Idaho, February 10, 1902.

26. Ibid., Pitcher to Secretary, February 14, 1902.

27. 31 (Part I) *U.S. Statutes at Large* 574; 1119; Y.A., Letters Received, Vol. 4, 387, endorsement dated March 3, 1902.

28. Y.A., Letters Sent, Vol. 11, 210, Pitcher to Rock, February 24, 1902. A photograph of Rock mounted on his pet bison and a notation of his death is in Garretson, *The American Bison,* 48.

29. The matter was much more detailed than presented here. See Y.A., Letters Sent, Vol. 11, 250, telegram, Pitcher to Secretary, March 14, 1902; Ibid., 259, 252, 274; File No. 21, Secretary to Pitcher, March 18, 1902; Letters Received, Vol. 4, 26, Eaton to Pitcher, May 17, 1902.

30. Ibid., Letters Sent, Vol. 11, Pitcher to Jones, April 21, 1902; Letters Received, Vol. 3, 500, Jones to Pitcher, April 26, 1902; Letters Sent, Vol. 4, 313–14, Pitcher to Secretary, July 6, 1905, in which Pitcher quotes his earlier letter.

31. Ibid., Letters Received, Vol. 4, 89–91, July 8, 1902, Secretary Hitchcock to Pitcher.

32. Ibid., Letters Sent, Vol. 12, 43 ff., Pitcher to W.C. Whitney, August 1, 1902; to W.C. Toomy, August 24, 1902; on p. 118 of this Letters Sent volume is a recapitulation of offers made. This includes Howard Eaton's offer.

33. Ibid., Letters Sent, Vol. 12, 119–21, Pitcher to Secretary, August 30, 1902.

34. Ibid., Pitcher to Eaton, September 6, 1902.

35. Ibid., Letters Sent, Vol. 12, 136, 222, 277, 294, Pitcher to Secretary; 331, December 24, 1902, Pitcher to Howard Eaton; 333, December 25, 1902 (but clearly incorrect), Pitcher to Secretary Hitchcock; 397, Lindsley, Interior clerk in Yellowstone, to Pitcher, February 10, 1903; File No. 21, telegram of January 3, 1903, instructing Jones to proceed to Selish.

36. Ibid., Letters Sent, Vol. 12, 327–28, Pitcher to Secretary, December 16, 1902; 461–62, Pitcher to Dr. Frank Baker, Superintendent, National Zoological Park, March 16, 1903; *Annual Report of the Secretary of the Interior,* 1905, 669. In addition, Eli Waters had two bulls and two cows in a corral on Dot Island in summer, and in a corral on the mainland in winter. Ibid., 495, March 25, 1903.

37. Ibid., Letters Sent, Vol. 14, 279–80, Pitcher to Secretary, June 24, 1904.

38. Ibid., Letters Sent, Vol. 15, 146–47, Pitcher to Secretary, May 25, 1905; Ibid., Letters Received, Vol. 6, 22, May 23, 1905, Jones to Pitcher.

39. *Annual Reports of the Secretary of the Interior,* 1916, 786; Ibid., 1911, 572; 1913, 702; 1916, 786.

40. Ibid., 1911, 702; 1905, 663; 1911, 571.

41. Ibid., 1904, 177; 1905, 669; 1911, 572.

42. Ibid., 1904, 177; 1911, 571; 1913, 700.

43. Y.A., Letters Sent, Vol. 3, 494, Pitcher to Howard Eaton, June 12, 1902; Ibid., Letters Received, Vol. 4, 89–91, Hitchcock to Pitcher, July 8, 1902; Easton and Brown, *Lord of Beasts,* 260–63, fn. 3.

44. Y.A., File No. 21, Pitcher to Secretary, November 19, 1902. The telegrams instructing Jones to go to Selish, Montana, and Goodnight, Texas, are dated October 7, 1902, and January 2, 1903.

Easton and Brown, *Lord of Beasts,* 120–21. The authors also have Jones purchasing the buffalo at Eaton's headquarters at Medora, North Dakota. Eaton had an option on the Allard herd that was out of Selish, on the Flathead Indian Reservation, in western Montana.

45. Y.A., Letters Sent, Vol 15, 313–21, Pitcher to Secretary, July 20, 1905.

46. Ibid., Letters Received, Vol. 5, 84, W.E. Priestly to Major Pitcher, August 9, 1903.

47. Ibid., Vol. 6, 60–64, Jones to Pitcher, August 7, 1904.

48. Ibid., Letters Sent, Vol. 15, 313–21, Pitcher to Secretary, July 20, 1905. *Annual Reports of the Secretary of Interior,* 1913, 702.

49. Ibid., Letters Received, Vol. 6, 58–59, Secretary to Pitcher, July 6, 1905.

50. Ibid., Letters Sent, Vol. 15, 313–21; Pitcher to Secretary, July 20, 1905.

51. Ibid , Letters Received, File No. 23, Judge Ryan to Superintendent with Jones's discharge letter attached, August 31, 1905; Ibid., copy of clipping from the *New Haven Register,* November 15, 1906, with the banner, BUFFALO JONES SAYS SOLDIERS LACK BACKBONE.

52. Ibid., enclosure of Pitcher's reply to Captain George E. Albee, U.S. Army (Retired), who had requested an explanation.

53. Ibid., Letters Sent, Vol. 18, 130–31, Young to Secretary, December 14, 1907.

54. Richard A. Bartlett, "How Many Were Left? An Appraisal of the Buffalo Situation in the 1890s," unpublished paper delivered at Western History Association meeting, October, 1970.

55. Y A., Letters Sent, File No. 23, July 22, 1905; Ibid., Ryan to Superintendent, January 17, 1906; Ibid., File No 26, Ryan to Superintendent, October 27, 1907; Letters Sent, Vol. 18, Young to Secretary, December 14, 1907; File No. 26, Assistant Secretary Ryan to Superintendent, October 27, 1907; Ibid., telegram, Acting Secretary Woodruff to Superintendent, September 20, 1907

CHAPTER THIRTEEN

The Great Reclamation Raids

A mong the Secretary of Interior's files in the National Archives is the following duplicate of a cryptic telegram. It is from an Interior Department official named Cotter to Superintendent Horace Albright in Yellowstone; it is dated July 31, 1919:

> UNVOUCHED SEAMASHIP TOPONYM TO PERRINE TO SUB-ACUTE PRELIMINARY VERGE IN FISTFUL

Fortunately the deciphered message is handwritten below:

> Secretary of the Interior has given permit to Perrine to make preliminary surveys in Yellowstone[1]

The explanation of this strange communication is complex. Its background involves the American view of the West in the late nineteeth and early twentieth centuries, of conservation and the most efficient way of using the public domain, and of reclamation.

Awareness of the possibilities inherent in the irrigation of arid lands dates at least from the Mormon migration when, in 1847, those diligent people brought water by means of dams and ditches to their first planted fields in the new Zion. The Saints' experiment with irrigation was a demonstrable success. By 1865 they had dug nearly a thousand miles of canals and ditches which watered 1.5 million acres. Western promoters were greatly impressed at the Saints' achievements in making the desert bloom.

In the 1870s irrigation plans were implemented successfully by non-Mormons in Colorado and California. Nevertheless, as the twentieth century loomed, western boosters realized that successful arid land development was expensive, challenging in its social and engineering complexities, and full of

347

imponderables. The director of the U.S. Geological Survey, John Wesley Powell, had tried to quash their grandiose plans with his *Report on the Lands of the Arid Region of the United States,* published in 1878. The hydrographic survey launched by his agency so offended western interests that it was abrogated. Congress listened to the arguments of western promoters rather than to the federal government's own experts.

Although several earlier acts touched upon irrigation and reclamation, the first real milestone in federal reclamation policy was the Carey Act of 1894 (named for its sponsor, Senator Joseph M. Carey of Wyoming). By this act the states were to receive up to one million acres which they could then reclaim—that is, irrigate—and settle with farmers. Moreover, states could enter into contracts with private interests. Idaho and Wyoming citizens, especially, made considerable use of the act.[2]

The Carey Act is usually considered as only partially successful because irrigation projects proved too expensive for state and/or private enterprise to finance. Meanwhile, by the turn of the century considerable information had been assembled concerning reclamation possibilities. In his first message to Congress President Theodore Roosevelt advocated both forest conservation and irrigation. Senator Francis G. Newlands of Nevada introduced a reclamation bill which passed in 1902 and became the basic legislation under which a myriad of projects was constructed in the West.[3]

Today conservationists rarely favor reclamation, in the sense of dams, artificial lakes, and irrigation, as a part of their crusade. In the Progressive Era, however, the two were certainly loosely joined. Samuel P. Hays has shown in his profound study, *Conservation and the Gospel of Efficiency,* that the Progressive Era was one in which leadership accepted a concept of conservation within a framework of usage and general benefits to society. Reclamation was closely related to Gifford Pinchot's ideas about forestry. Coming onto the scene a few years later, the conservation thoughts of John Muir and Steve Mather emphasized aesthetics and preservation over use. By their criteria some reclamation projects created ugly scars on the face of mother earth. Indeed, horrid examples were not long in coming.[4]

People of the strangely shaped state of Idaho were quick to grasp the potentials of the irrigation panacea. While the northern part of their state is forested and blessed with Lakes Pend Oreille and Coeur d'Alene, much of the state's lower half is volcanic badlands and sagebrush plains. Through the barren terrain, however, flows the Snake River after its rise in southern Yellowstone Park; just east of the Tetons it flows to the south and curves around their southern end onto Idaho's volcanic plain. Tributaries add to the Snake's waters as it flows across Idaho in a wide arc: Henrys Fork, Boise, Payette, Salmon, and Clearwater rivers.

Idaho's population grew from 88,000 in 1890 to 431,000 a generation later (1920). Many of its settlers were farmers, among whom were cooperative, cohesive, hard-working Mormons. They knew irrigation techniques through experience, and they soon discovered that the dusty Snake River plain needed only water to produce an abundance of fruits, grains, and vegetables; the soil was fertile. Passage of the Carey and Newlands acts provided the incentive for creating productivity out of sterility.

In 1904 Idahoans helped the new federal Bureau of Reclamation launch the Minidoka project with its American Falls Dam. While the village and the dam both lie in south-central Idaho, a second facet of the project called for damming the outlet of Jackson Lake, that body of water that so magnificently mirrors the spectacular Tetons. After completion, the water companies demanded still more water, resulting in the raising of the Jackson Lake Dam by seventeen feet and increasing the storage capacity of the lake from 380,000 to 789,000 acre-feet.[5]

As a result of the Jackson Lake operation, the unaesthetic results of dam building have been witnessed by millions of tourists for more than seventy years. Those who pass the Tetons in August or September and view what was once one of the world's most beautiful lakes, now gaze upon ugly mud flats, driftwood, and rotting fish lying between the high and low water marks. When the dam was built, reclamation was a no-fault proposition. Few people were bothered by the prospect of desecration of a beautiful natural scene. Within a decade of the dam's construction, however, interest groups dedicated to the value of natural beauty per se were being heard. Jackson Lake Dam came along too soon.[6]

The Minidoka project was just one of many schemes spawned by the Newlands Act. In 1910 the Shoshone Dam west of Cody was completed; it at least created a lake which in the geologic past had existed there before. In eastern Montana the Yellowstone River was dammed about eighteen miles below Glendive. Other schemes were planned by land speculators, farmers, town boosters, and occasionally by engineers who pinpointed practical locations for dams, canals, and prime land for irrigation usage.

Political philosophy and the climate of opinion led others in high positions to advocate reclamation schemes. During the two decades from 1900 to 1920 Progressive Era leaders supported projects calling for planned land settlement for the downtrodden. As time went on this blended with a concern for returning World War I veterans, for a good many Jeremiahs in high places predicted massive unemployment. It is at this juncture that President Wilson's Interior secretary, Franklin K. Lane, enters the story. He advocated a back-to-the-soil movement which envisioned placing veterans on farms in planned agricultural communities. The *planned* aspect of Lane's proposal was pure Progressivism, but the tradition of rewarding veterans with land was rooted in American history; hardly a war had been fought without its veterans being offered military land script. More than a hundred bills touching upon land for veterans failed to pass Congress, and Lane's dreams did not materialize. However, before he gave up he had given Yellowstone defenders a scare they would not soon forget.[7]

In the immediate post–World War I years reclamation boosters seemed as numerous as timber walkers, who for years had sought good forests for timber company exploitation. No stream, beaver pond, or lush meadow escaped irrigationists' notice. Yellowstone Park contained the streams, ponds, meadows, swamps, and canyons they coveted. With a well-financed lobby and a good public relations drive, part of the park might be segregated, placed back into the public domain, and thence delegated for reclamation uses. Or Congress might be persuaded to pass special legislation allowing a dam and an artificial lake here or there. In the background was someone who stood to make a lot of money. Until the early 1920s the promoters appear to have been relatively immune to opposition. Dams, reservoirs, ditches and canals continued to be built without a thought to aesthetics, ecology, or anything else save monetary gain. What mild protests did arise came from "effete Easterners," so the Westerners said, who did not understand Westerners' needs.

The first reclamationist threat to Yellowstone's integrity was particularly menacing because Secretary Lane, immersed in his soldier settlement plan, was amenable to the Idaho proposition which involved some veterans and in many ways duplicated his own ideas. Farmers, some of them veterans, would be living and working in an agricultural enclave in which they had to cooperate because of their common dependence upon irrigation.

The attack came quietly, the first inkling of it appearing in the winter of 1919. Some Idahoans found two small lakes in the southwest corner of Yellowstone Park which they suggested damming for irrigation purposes. Scouts searching for a soft spot in an army's lines could not have found a more vulnerable place to attack than did these water seekers. This was the Cascade Corner, or Falls River Basin, or the Bechler Basin—confusingly, quite well known by all three names—accessible only by trails or boats. Few people other than poachers ever went into it. It was one of the park's wilderness areas. Unlike the thermal grounds or Yellowstone's Grand Canyon, the southwest corner was vulnerable to the argument that there were dozens of other wilderness areas in the West just as pretty.[8]

Geographer Henry Gannett had been in the Cascade Corner with the Hayden Survey in 1878 and his description remains one of the best. In his report he described the Bechler River (named for Gustavus Bechler, one of Hayden's better topographers), as running at the base of a deep, rugged canyon which cut like a ribbon through the high Madison Plateau. It was, he wrote, "well timbered and with large coniferae." Then abruptly the plateau ended with a line of cliffs over which the stream spilled into the Falls River Basin. This Gannett described as "a large valley, part of which is open, while a part is covered with a dense growth of large coniferae, and the ground is cumbered with fallen timber to such an extent that, added to the swamps, springs, and nature of the soil, the Basin is wellnigh impassable." As for the Falls River (which flows into the Bechler, though Falls River is the larger stream), Gannett described how, when it emerges from Beulah Lake, it becomes turbulent. Half a dozen spectacular falls ranging in height from six to thirty feet bring it to the Great Falls, five of which register a total descent of about one hundred forty feet.[9]

In 1909 a construction engineer named F.T. Crowe spent several weeks with a pack outfit in the corner locating a possible road from Ashton, Idaho, to Jackson Lake. He described the area as follows:

> My recollection of the Falls River Basin and Bechler Meadows is one of great swarms of mosquitoes, plenty of beaver dams and bogs, innumerable moose, it being ideal country for all three species. However, if a nature lover wishes to go through that country looking for beauty spots, he can, of course find many as there are innumerable beautiful grassy meadows surrounded by pines with many creeks and small ponds. And the fishing at that time was especially good.[10]

A map of the region drawn in 1883–85 was found so faulty by Colonel C.H Birdseye of the U.S. Geological Survey, who was in the basin in 1921, that he recommended a new survey and map. He found little evidence of swampland. As with most parts of Yellowstone, what one finds in the Cascade Corner in the way of dry or wet land, and insect life, depends upon what time of year one is there. Until roughly mid-July swamps and insects can destroy much of the pleasure of a trip into Yellowstone's backcountry; after that time most of the snow will have melted, the bogs will have dried, and the insect life, much of it, will have died off. What was a marshy mosquito-infested swamp in June will have become a grassy swale full of colorful wildflowers.[11]

But the Idaho promoters insisted that the whole area was just useless swamp-land, that no one ever went there anyway, and that by rights the hard-working farmers of their state deserved the water. An additional part of their promotion was that this was to be a private enterprise. The dams they planned, one across Fall River and one across Mountain Ash Creek, were within the cost range of private funding. They enlisted in their behalf Idaho's Senator John Frost Nugent and Representative Addison T. Smith in whose district the recipients of the water would dwell. Since perhaps 20,000 voting farmers might enjoy a windfall if the project materialized, to say nothing of enriching a few powerful promoters, Nugent and Smith were willing to introduce bills in Congress to satisfy the water interests.[12]

It was at this point that the politically sophisticated irrigationists approached Secretary Lane and received his support. In 1919 he ordered Mather and Albright to allow a survey to be made of the Cascade Corner to be followed by a report *favoring* the Idaho project. Mather and Albright were his subordinates. By the rules of bureaucracy they should have carried out his mandate.

But the power of subordinate bureaucrats can negate the best-laid plans of a politically appointed short-term secretary. Mather and Albright had "their man" in the Interior Department in Washington. Thus the telegram: UNVOUCHED SEAMASHIP TOPONYM. . . . In a model case of bureaucratic foot dragging, the two men postponed writing the report and were prepared even to resign if Lane approved the proposal. Albright, given advance warning by the cryptic telegram from the insider at Interior, was thus prepared to checkmate the surveyors. When they arrived in Yellowstone, the horses they needed had just been removed from the park and put out to winter pasture. When the men requested boats, it developed that the boat company had already placed them in winter storage.[13]

Mather and Albright in 1919 successfully prevented passage of legislation providing reclamationists a foothold into Yellowstone, but soon discovered that this was but the opening salvo in a campaign that was to last a decade, then lapse for a few years, only to rise again in the late 1930s. Moreover, what had begun as the project of a few promoters out of Ashton, Idaho, expanded into several projects involving also the states of Wyoming and Montana, especially Montana.

Fortunately for park defenders, Secretary Lane resigned in February 1920 before another summer season arrived. The office was run briefly by an acting secretary, Alexander Vogelsang; he bided his time and made no decisions. Then John Barton Payne of Chicago was appointed; he was a staunch conservationist and refused to permit any survey that would look at Yellowstone's waters as sources for reclamation projects. In March 1921 President Harding appointed Albert B. Fall as interior secretary; he was followed in 1923 by Hubert Work. These men were at worst neutral and for the most part positive in their support of the park defenders.

Checking Secretary Lane's plans in 1919 was only a brief respite. In April 1920 Senator Nugent's bill passed the upper house without debate.

This was the signal for concerted opposition from the Interior Department and organizations devoted to conservation, and the opposition succeeded: The plan went down to defeat in the House of Representatives. The fury of the defeated western interests was not unlike that of a woman spurned. Their tirades remind us that the Sagebrush Rebellion of the 1980s is only the most recent manifestation of a sectional clash of interests that has strong historical roots.

YELLOWSTONE PLAN DEFEATED BY HIGHBROWS headlined the *Blackfoot* (Idaho) *News*. "This bill," protested the writer, "was fairly well on its way to passage when the American Civic Association [and] other Boston aesthetes bombarded their Congressmen against what they termed the desecration of the Yellowstone Park. The fact," the editorialist added, "that this bill would have permitted the creation of a lake where a swamp now exists did not appeal to these easterners at all for they maintain that nothing but nature shall be allowed sway in the sacred precincts of the Yellowstone." The *Enterprise* dubbed opponents of the plan "nature Fakers" and the *Pocatello Tribune* cried, PARLOR CONGRESSMEN OF EAST BLIND TO REAL DEVELOPMENT. [14]

The newspaper editors might have added, like a losing coach, "Wait Until Next Year!" Suddenly reclamation schemes proliferated all over the West and especially around Yellowstone National Park. The Falls River plan looked paltry compared with some of the ambitious schemes suggested in the next three or four years. [15]

All the while the push for the Cascade Corner continued. Eventually it was included in a bill that proposed a change in the park boundaries that would remove from the park the Falls River Basin. Their opposition, meanwhile, grew stronger and remained adamant to any change in boundaries or intrusion upon the park. Albright trekked into the basin and reported on its beauties—its trees, probably the biggest in the park, its lovely meadows, its abundance of wildflowers and berries, its native cutthroat trout, and moose, grazing on the grasses and mosses of the stream floor. [16]

William C. Gregg, representing the Audubon Society, explored the corner in the summer of 1921. His photographs, which appeared both in *The Outlook* and *The Saturday Evening Post,* had considerable influence in molding public opinion on the side of the conservationists. The guide Billy Hofer wrote a long letter about the proposed raid which appeared in *Forest and Stream*. "Why is it," he asked, "that so many people—money-making schemers—are unwilling to see a few spots in this land where nature is left alone?" [17]

The Falls River plan was a relatively simple proposal. At almost the same time that the plan surfaced in 1919, Idaho's commissioner of reclamation, Warren G. Sevendsen, examined Yellowstone's waters. He noted that 800,000 to 1,000,000 acre-feet of the precious fluid was going to waste in the Missouri River system. Much of it, he suggested, could be diverted and stored in upper Snake River reservoirs. It could then be used to irrigate thousands of acres of Idaho's parched volcanic plains.

The plan was a logical one since nature herself had once drained Yellowstone Lake via the Snake River. She had made some changes during the millenia, however, so Sevendsen proposed to rearrange things. He would dig a tunnel from the extreme south end of the Flat Top Mountain arm of Yellowstone Lake through the Continental Divide to Heart Lake which was part of the Snake River drainage. Stone removed from the tunnel, he suggested, could be used to surface park roads. Also, the Yellowstone Lake outlet would be dammed beneath a new, artistic Fishing Bridge. He claimed that the lake waters would never rise above the present high-water level, or be allowed to fall below the present low-water level. As Sevendsen's project developed, it included reclamation-type surgery at Heart, Shoshone, and Lewis lakes. This was just a start: the Snake River would have dams and reservoirs all down the stream, much as the Colorado River was to be compartmented. [18]

Somewhere a link formed in the chain of ideas of the Idaho interests and those of some residents of the upper Yellowstone Valley centered at Livingston. Their valley had suffered from dry years—1919 and 1920 were parched—and from wet years in which the flooding Yellowstone did considerable damage. Dozens of creeks flow into that mighty stream below Fishing Bridge, but all of a sudden the valley citizens decided that the solution to all their troubles was a dam at the outlet of Yellowstone Lake. Livingston's chamber of commerce asked for a fifteen-foot dam for flood control, so they said, and the chamber's president even insisted that such a dam would add to Yellowstone's beauty. [19]

Soon valley businessmen had formed the Yellowstone Valley Irrigation Association (at another time known as the Yellowstone River Water User's Association). They estimated the cost of the proposed Fishing Bridge Dam at a half million dollars. It was predicted that with the dam, which was soon growing tentacles of irrigation canals throughout the upper valley, Livingston could expect a population of 50,000! A request was made to the secretary of interior that the Reclamation Bureau be put to work on the project, but then-acting secretary Vogelsang refused saying he lacked authority and appropriations from Congress. [20]

Secretary John Barton Payne likewise refused to allow any irrigation surveys of park waters. Montanans sputtered and fumed. An irrigation association official and Senator Walsh called on the secretary in hopes of accomplishing what correspondence had failed to do. Secretary Payne was adamant. To this the *Butte Post* growled, "The people of the Yellowstone Valley are not going to be denied a right to protect themselves from floods . . . nor will they abandon the project that will conserve water sufficient to reclaim seven hundred thousand acres of land. . . ."[21]

A few months later Senator Walsh assured Livingston's Rotarians that "a permit to construct a dam in Yellowstone National Park is the one piece of legislation now uppermost in my mind." *His* dam (for by now there were several proposals involving the dam at Lake outlet) would have been just six feet high and serve as the fishing bridge. It would, the senator said, store 480,00 feet of floodwater, enough to irrigate about 250,000 acres.[22]

In November 1920 the irrigation association published a booklet, "The Lake Yellowstone Project: What Is it? Why Is It?" Its cover photo showed the town of Forsyth under water in the flood of 1918. The description stated that the flood did $700,000 damage to the little prairie town of 2,000 and implied that a dam in Yellowstone Park, several hundred miles away, could have prevented the deluge. Already the promoters were suggesting that a damsite two and a half miles downstream from Fishing Bridge would be better. Such a dam would be 300 feet long and thirty feet high.[23]

Conservationist reaction to these schemes rapidly strengthened. Albright, assuming the dam to be twenty-five feet high (a sensible average of the many proposals), came up with some alarming but almost certainly accurate statistics: "9,000 acres submerged, of which 4,350 acres are timberland, including 18,000,000 board feet; 3,600 acres are meadowland and feeding ground for wild game; three and a third miles of road and bridges would be destroyed . . . three beautiful islands will be submerged, the Hot Springs at Steamboat Point, the Thumb Paint Pots and Springs and the Butte Springs will be destroyed." He predicted that Idaho's ambitious scheme would end the beauties of Shoshone, Lewis, and Heart lakes. It would, he added, "turn upon a comparatively few farmers the water belonging to all of us. . . . Shall the Yellowstone National Park become an agricultural reservoir or is it to remain a National Park?"[24]

Year after year various plans were embodied in Congressional bills introduced by Idaho or Montana solons, yet just as consistently they failed to pass. Professor Ise elaborates upon the proliferation of the plans. Besides the Cascade Corner and Montana proposals there was the Bruneau project, which embraced within its scheme Yellowstone, Shoshone, Lewis, and Heart lakes plus the Bechler area; the DuBois project was similar, while the Carlisle project called for a twenty-nine-foot dam and diversion of Yellowstone Lake waters to the Snake River.[25]

The rage manifested by the irrigationists and their sympathizers was intense. In December 1920 the Western States Reclamation Association, meeting in Denver, demanded a probe of United States government officials suspected of preventing passage of such legislation and voted $93,000 for its own propaganda campaign.[26]

In the mid-1920s the Cascade Corner controversy merged with proposals for park boundary changes, especially in the southeast, south, and southwest (Cascade Corner) portions. In 1925 a Coordinating Committee on National

Parks and Forests, which included the head of the Forest Service and director of the National Park Service, had investigated Yellowstone's boundaries and made recommendations. Some involved the northern and eastern lines; these suggestions were enacted into law during the second session of the 70th Congress in 1929. The committee's proposals concerning the southeast, south, and southwest boundaries were not approved. Two subcommittees, one from the Senate in 1926 and one from the House in 1928, visited the Bechler region. The Senate group favored eliminating the area from the park while the House members had not in early 1929 submitted their report. The upshot of all this interest without a resolution was a Yellowstone National Park Boundary Commission created by Senate joint resolution and approved by President Coolidge on February 28, 1929. It was to submit its report to Congress on or before January 1, 1931.[27]

This group convened in Cody in July 1929 and held hearings there and at Jackson, Wyoming, and Ashton, Idaho, spent two weeks inspecting the controversial areas, and held final hearings in Washington, D.C., on February 3, 1930. It subsequently submitted its report.[28]

So bitter were the controversies involved that even the committee's operations were criticized. Publicist Robert Sterling Yard, writing in his capacity as secretary of the National Parks Associaton, protested that the committee had consulted the "political, business, and sporting sentiments of two individual states [Idaho and Wyoming] . . . without also investigating the sentiments of the immense national park public in other states."[29]

The committee recommended that the Bechler area be retained in the park. (It also recommended that the Thorofare region to the southeast be embraced within the reservation and that a rugged acreage along the southern boundary become a part of the Teton National Forest in order to straighten the boundary line.) "The Bechler River Meadows," the committee stated, "are of scenic charm and afford an engaging foreground to natural features of unusual interest. The foothills . . . include the beautiful falls of Dunanda, Silver Scarf, and Ouzel, which are embraced within the panorama of the Meadows. The region with its setting and surroundings forms a worthwhile part of Yellowstone Park." The Idaho irrigationists gave up—temporarily.[30]

But the Montanans refused to capitulate. In the early 1930s a new threat to Yellowstone's waters came from the army engineers, but the sure hand of Montana's politicians seems apparent. Under provisions of the Rivers and Harbors Act of January 21, 1927, and section 10 of the Flood Control Act of May 15, 1928, the engineers requested permission from the Interior Department to make a survey of Yellowstone Lake's shoreline and the proposed outlet damsite.[31]

By design, one suspects, Secretary Ray Lyman Wilbur waited six months, until March 10, 1931, to reply. Then he rejected the request. His initial paragraph is as succinct and exact a statement of policy toward Yellowstone's integrity as anyone has ever written:

> The Yellowstone National Park was the first national park of the great system of national parks to be created by the Congress. In the organic act of its establishment of March 1, 1872, it was specifically "dedicated and set apart as a public park or pleasuring ground for the benefit and enjoyment of the people." Since that time repeated attempts to utilize its wonderful streams and lakes and waterfalls for commercial uses have been made. Fortunately, all have been frustrated. The United States should be the last one to attempt to mar or destroy any portion of this magnificent wilderness area, perhaps the most important natural heritage we can preserve for posterity in this country.

Wilbur went on to cite statistics presented in the Senate hearings which proved that Yellowstone Lake, even if dammed, could not prevent floods or have much effect upon downstream flow. For these reasons, and the harm that would be done to the lake, Wilbur politely but firmly rejected the engineers' request.[32]

Still the Montana irrigationists would not give up. In June 1932 Congress passed "An Act Granting the Consent of Congress to the State of Montana and Wyoming to Negotiate and Enter into a Compact or Agreement for Division of Waters of the Yellowstone River." Interior Secretary Ickes was alerted to the legislation and let the proponents know that he was aware of their plans. "I will vigorously oppose any plans of the state to enter the Park for the purposes of raising or lowering the waters of Yellowstone Lake, and shall take the same position with reference to any compact or other agreement contemplating such action which may be submitted to the Congress for its approval," the old curmudgeon wrote Governor Frank Cooney of Montana.[33]

According to an interested layman, Frank B. Sheppard of Denver, who wrote Ickes, there was more to this ploy of Montana and Wyoming interests than met the eye. "The details of this scheme are shrouded in mystery, and [are] as yet unobtainable," he said. "Concealment is itself a portent of evil omen."[34]

In a later letter Sheppard elaborated on the scheme. He said that the state engineers of Wyoming and Montana, men named Lillis, James, and Whiting, with a presidentially appointed official nambed Lamb, had agreed tentatively that Montana would relinquish to Wyoming unrestricted use of the water resources of the Bighorn River, in return for which Wyoming would favor construction of a six-foot dam at the outlet of Yellowstone Lake for the storage of water to be carried by ditches at and above Billings.[35]

Whatever the scheme, Governor Miller of Wyoming beat a hasty retreat; Ickes complimented him for his "fine, statesmanlike view." Montana's Governor Cooney, however, insisted that Montana needed the dam at the outlet of Yellowstone Lake. Ickes, using the usual arguments, put him in his place.[36]

The new Roosevelt administration took steps to check the act granting Wyoming and Montana the right to form a water compact. On April 3, 1934, the Department of the Interior had introduced into Congress H.R. 8954 which provided that nothing in the act of June 14, 1932, "shall apply to the waters within Yellowstone National Park or establish any rights within its boundaries." It became law on June 19, 1934. "The Department, through the National Park Service," Ickes wrote a concerned citizen, "spared no effort to have this bill receive favorable consideration."[37]

From 1934 until 1937 the Yellowstone reclamation raiders were quiescent, but then a project elsewhere revived their hopes. In Colorado irrigationists succeeded in gaining passage of legislation for a Colorado–Big Thompson project, often called the Grand Lake Diversion. Water was to be diverted by tunnels from the western slope of the Rockies across Rocky Mountain National Park to the dry plains of northern Colorado. The integrity of Rocky Mountain National Park was violated. If it could happen for Coloradoans, then why not for Idahoans who coveted Yellowstone waters? Hardly did the Idahoans have the thought than they acted: In February 1937 their legislature petitioned Congress, requesting favorable consideration of an act allowing construction of the dam at Yellowstone Lake and the tunnels and other projects necessary to carry out their ambitious plan to place water into the Snake River drainage.[38]

The campaign pro and con began all over again—delegations calling on Park Service Director Cammerer, a Senate joint resolution to allow Wyoming and Idaho to enter into a compact respecting disposition and apportionment of Snake River water, and hard public relations work. By early 1938 Idaho's Senator James Pope and Representative Compton I. White had tried a joint resolution and, when it failed, a bill calling for construction of a weir at the lake outlet and a tunnel. This renewed interest in the Idaho scheme may have been President Franklin Roosevelt's incentive for visiting the park in the fall of 1937. It was while accompanying the president around the park that Superintendent Rogers extracted from him the comment that he would oppose all reclamation plans involving Yellowstone Lake.[39]

Again the reclamationists were defeated. Yet their thirst for Yellowstone's water continues. As the old frontiersman said when attacking Indians left the fort: "they'll be back."

NOTES TO CHAPTER THIRTEEN

1. R.G. 48, Secretary of the Interior Central Classified Files, "General," July 31, 1919.

2. 14 *U.S. Statutes at Large* 251; Alfred Rudolph Golze, *Reclamation in the United States* (Caldwell, Idaho: The Caxton Printers, 1952), 15, 28. The Carey Act is 28 *U.S. Statutes at Large* 422. A quick overview of the History of reclamation is Michael C. Robinson, *Water for the West: The Bureau of Reclamation 1902–1977* (Chicago: Public Works Historical Society, 1979). The U.S. Geological Survey's work on irrigation is well documented in Manning, *Government in Science*, 168–203.

3. The Newlands Act is 32 (Part I) *U.S. Statutes at Large* 388.

4. Samuel P. Hays, *Conservation and the Gospel of Efficiency* (Cambridge: Harvard University Press, 1959; New York: Atheneum, 1979).

5. George Wharton James, *Reclaiming the Arid West: The Story of the United States Reclamation Service* (New York: Dodd, Mead and Company, 1917), vii–xiii; 146–60; William E. Smythe, *The Conquest of Arid America* (New York: Harper and Brothers, 1899; Seattle: University of Washington Press, 1969), 3–50; 185–96.

6. The best summary of damage is in David J. Saylor, *Jackson Hole, Wyoming* (Norman: University of Oklahoma Press, 1970), 154–58. See also Robert W. Righter, *Crucible for Conservation: The Creation of Grand Teton National Park* (Boulder: Colorado Associated University Press, 1982), 9–11.

7. Bill G. Reid, "Franklin K. Lane's Idea for Veteran's Colonization, 1918–1921," *Pacific Historical Review*, Vol. 33, No. 4 (November, 1964), 447–61.

8. From *The Saturday Evening Post*, March 1, 1919, in Yellowstone Park Clipping Scrapbook, "Irrigation, 1919–1921." These scrapbooks are in the custody of the Yellowstone Park Library at Mammoth Hot Springs.

9. Hayden, *Annual Report for 1878*, Part 2, "Geographical Report of Yellowstone Park Division, By Henry Gannett," 469. Professor Frank Bradley of the survey had visited the region in 1872. Hayden, *Annual Report for 1872*, 258.

10. U.S. Geological Survey, Files of the Topographical Branch, "Yellowstone," F.T. Crowe to Morris Bien, Assistant Director, U.S. Reclamation Service.

11. Ibid., Birdseye to Arthur E. Morgan, Antioch College, June 11, 1929.

12. The bills were S. 3895 and H.R. 12466 in the 66th Cong., 2d Sess. (1920). The initial group was called the Fremont-Madison Reservoir Company.

13. Author's interview with Horace Albright, April, 1970; "The Fight for Yellowstone's Waters," *Literary Digest*, Vol. 57, No. 4 (October 23, 1920), 88–91.

14. Yellowstone Park Scrapbook, "Irrigation, 1919–1921," clipping dated April 27, 1920, See also Ibid., clippings from *Boise Statesman,* May 31, 1920; *Enterprise,* May 20, 1920; *Pocatello Tribune,* April 26, 1920.

15. Ise, *Our National Park Policy,* 307–17, gives a legislative outline of these plans.

16. Horace M. Albright, "Yellowstone's Chief Describes Bechler Basin," *National Parks Bulletin,* Vol. 8, No. 51 (December, 1926), 6–7.

17. *The Outlook,* Vol. 129, No. 121 (November 23, 1921), 469–76; *The Saturday Evening Post,* Vol. 193, No. 23 (November 20, 1920), 11; Elwood Hofer, "Letter," *Forest and Stream,* August, 1920 (in Yellowstone Clipping File).

18. Yellowstone Park Scrapbook, "Irrigation, 1919–1921," clipping from *Boise Statesman,* August 29, 1919. Sevendsen also advocated the Falls River project because, he insisted, the region's remoteness made it a liability due to fire danger! Warren G. Sevendsen, "Preserving the Heirloom," *New West Magazine,* Vol. 11, No. 1 (November, 1920), copy in Yellowstone Scrapbook.

19. *Enterprise,* November 14, 16, 1919.

20. Ibid., March 19, 1920. In 1980 Livingston's population was less than 7,000.

R.G. 48, Secretary of the Interior, Central Classified File, "Lake," Vogelsang to Senator Henry Lee Myers of Montana, December 4, 1919. Ibid., "Lands," contains a mimeographed copy of proposed legislation entitled "An Act Granting the Yellowstone River Water Users Association Certain Rights of Way In Over and Through Certain Lands in the Yellowstone National Park, for the Purpose of Creating a Storage Reservoir, and for Other Purposes." The document is undated and was probably never introduced in Congress. Such a bill, if passed, would have destroyed Yellowstone's beauty below the lake.

21. *Enterprise,* June 17, 1920; Yellowstone Park Clipping File, *Butte Post,* June 30, 1920.

22. *Enterprise,* August 30, 1920.

23. Copy in Yellowstone Clipping File, "Irrigation, 1919–1921."

24. Quoted in the *Philadelphia Public Ledger* in a letter from J. Horace McFarland, President of the American Civic Association, June 6, 1920. Others involved in fighting the plunderers were George Bird Grinnell, in *Literary Digest,* Vol. 65, No. 10 (June 5, 1920), 90–92; Frederick Law Olmsted, "Fundamental Objections to the Walsh Bill," *National Municipal Review,* Vol. 10, No. 5 (May, 1921). George Horace Lorimer, editor of *The Saturday Evening Post,* editorialized actively against the raids. All are in the Yellowstone Park Scrapbook, "Irrigation, 1919–1921."

25. Ise, *Our National Park Policy,* 310–11. Some of these plans were almost certainly linked with schemes of hydroelectric power interests. *Outlook,* Vol. 126, No. 2 (September 8, 1920), "Letter from Senator Walsh," and editor's reply, 68.

26. *Enterprise,* December 11, 1920.

27. R.G. 48, Central Classified File, "Boundaries," Interior Secretary Ray Lyman Wilbur to Dr. E.E. Brownell, April 1, 1929.
The act changing the northern and eastern boundaries is Public Law 888, 45 *U.S. Statutes at Large* 1435; the act creating the new Commission is Public Resolution 94, 45 *U.S. Statutes at Large* 1413; 1644. This activity is more or less related to and coexistent with the controversy involving the Grand Tetons and Jackson Lake. The Forest Service also had a vested interest in the affair.

28. R.G. 48, Central Classified File, "Boundaries," Vol. 1 of "Report of the Yellowstone National Park Boundary Commission to the President of the United States." This document was published as 71st Cong., 3d Sess., House Doc. 710 Serial No. 9360 (1931).

29. Ibid., Yard to President Hoover, February 5, 1930. The hearings exemplify the attitudes, prejudices, and interests of the local populations and offer excellent insight into what in the 1980s has been called the Sagebrush Rebellion.

30. Ibid.

31. R.G. 48, Central Classified File, "Lake," Acting Secretary John H. Edwards to the Acting Secretary of War (name not given), September 4, 1930.

32. Ibid. Wilbur referred to the hearings before the Senate Committee on Irrigation and Reclamation on Senate Bill 4529, introduced by Senator Walsh of Montana in the 66th Cong., 3d Sess., and Senate Bill 274 in the 67th Cong., 2d Sess.

33. R.G. 48, Central Classified File, Ickes to Cooney, May 12, 1933. An identical letter was sent to Governor Leslie Miller of Wyoming. The legislation is Public Law 178 of the 72d Cong., passed June 14, 1932.

34. Ibid., Sheppard's letter of March 3, 1933.

35. Ibid., Sheppard's letter of May 18, 1933.

36. Ibid., Ickes to Miller, May 20, 1933; Ickes to Cooney, June 14, 1933. I did not find Cooney's letter to Ickes, but internal evidence in Ickes's reply makes it clear what Cooney said.

37. Ibid., Ickes to Willard Van Name, March 28, 1943.

38. Ibid., "Yellowstone Lake: 1937–1953," letter of Acting Secretary Charles West to Ira H. Masters, Secretary of State, Boise, Idaho, April 12, 1937.

39. Correspondence and memos concerning the 1937–38 campaign for the Idaho plan is to be found in R.G. 48, Central Classified File, "Yellowstone Lake: 1937–1953."

PARK VS. PEOPLE

Yellowstone Since 1940

CHAPTER FOURTEEN

The Continuing Concessionaire Problem

At some point towards the present, history ceases and becomes instead a chronicle of current events. Without the all-important dimension of time, history, which implies interpretations of events and judgments about the actions of men and women, cannot exist. This is not to say that current events should not be chronicled—they should be. But the results and the wisdom of decisions and policies cannot be positively judged nor can criticisms or praise of actions be anything more than conjectural.

Tomorrow's historians will find an abundance of today's events to challenge their synthesizing and interpretive capabilities. Indeed, changes in America since 1940 have been so massive that they defy diagnosis. The nation's population has increased by nearly 100 million (from 131,660,000 in 1940 to more than 226,504,000 in 1980). Wyoming, Yellowstone's host state, nearly doubled in population, from 250,000 to 470,000 and even Montana gained more than 285,000 residents, for a population of 786,000 in 1980.

Accompanying population growth were advances in technology, rapid urbanization, rising affluence, and increasing mobility. In 1940, a good year, the nation's factories produced nearly four and a half million cars, trucks, and buses, in 1981 (a poor year) nearly eight million were manufactured. RVs (recreational vehicles), snowmobiles, trail bikes, and four-wheel-drive off-road vehicles now occupied the garages, carports, and driveways of affluent, energetic, mobile middle and upper class America. On weekends and vacations that strange genus *Homo Americanus,* accompanied by his mate and their progeny, converged in his motorized monster on America's recreational and beauty spots. Yellowstone National Park was one of the prime destinations.

Fortunately for the reservation the four World-War-II years (1942–45) were a period of rest and rehabilitation. In 1943 the park was visited by just 64,144 people, the fewest since 1919. In 1945, the last war year, visitation jumped to 178,196, still a modest number. The next year (1946) numbers took a quantum leap as 814,907 tourists strained all the park's facilities. Thereafter visitation increased steadily (with occasional one-year declines) until it crested in 1965 at 2,602,475. In the seventeen years from 1966 to 1982 registration topped two million fifteen times, falling below that number only in 1974 and 1979 when gasoline was hard to come by. In 1976, 1978, and 1981 visitation topped two and a half million; in 1982, the most recent year at this writing, 2,404,862 human beings entered Yellowstone.[1]

No longer did park officials have to worry over railroad encroachment or threats of reclamationists. Now they were confronted with new problems, and people—a sheer inundation of humanity—ranked as their number one dilemma. How could a wilderness be protected when humanity equal to or greater than that of metropolitan St. Louis or Pittsburgh passed along the park's roads every year, and primarily in a three-month period?

During those first postwar years the great questions had to be delegated to the administrators' subconscious psyche. Pragmatism had to dominate at first, meeting headlong each problem that was assuming crisis proportions, applying a temporary solution and then turning to the next difficulty. Roads, camping facilities, restrooms, bear jams, and vandalism all demanded more attention, but above all it was that old Yellowstone curse, the concessionaires, that supplied the biggest dilemma. The trouble had been brewing since the 1930s.

It is worth recalling that Yellowstone's visitation began rising in the depression year of 1934 when, at 260,775, registration exceeded, though just slightly, the record year of 1929. In 1940 it topped the half million mark for the first time. To serve such numbers the Park Service lobbied for increased appropriations, receiving some of the funds needed, but never enough. As for the concessionaires, try as Superintendent Rogers would, they would not budge. They stalled, complained, pleaded, whined, argued, procrastinated, and politicked to avoid spending money on renovation and new construction. In 1937 President Roosevelt, as he was leaving the park, commented upon the rising visitation, and, by implication, the park's needs: "Our chief problem in the future will be taking care of people, because people are going to come [to Yellowstone] whether we like it or not and it is up to us to look after them."[2]

Even in the late 1930s problems of more people than personnel or facilities could adequately handle plagued the park, and during the war, understandably, all construction, and nearly all planning, ceased. At war's end, however, between the Park Service and the concessionaires the service did the best job. The concessionaires, thanks to their reluctance to upgrade facilities in the late 1930s, were totally unprepared for the tide of humanity expecting service and facilities in the immediate post–World War II years. Protests streamed into Congressional offices, appeared in newspapers, were heard at chamber of commerce meetings in Wyoming and Montana, and appeared in such national media as the *Christian Science Monitor,* the *New York Times,* and, at a more local urban level, in the *Denver Post*. Soon the whole nation was aware of Yellowstone's poor food, wretched housing, surly clerks, and inadequate management.

What people did not know, unless they were participants in the regional rumor mill around the reservation, was that the owners of the principal park company had lost interest in the business, had no desire to sink more money into it, and in fact wanted to sell—but at what most potential buyers considered an absurdly inflated price. To best understand the situation it is necessary to go back to 1931.

After Harry Child's death in that year, control of park operations fell to his son-in-law, William M. "Billie" Nichols. A tall, affable, gentlemanly person, Nichols had been affiliated with the businesses since his marriage to Child's daughter in 1907. Now he was president of the Yellowstone Park Hotel Company, the Yellowstone Park Transportation Company, the Yellowstone Park Lodge and Camps Company, and the Yellowstone Park Boat Company, "and the control of these companies remained in the hands of the H.W. Child Corporation, a family holding company, and the H.W. Child Trust."[3]

In 1936, the year Edmund B. Rogers became Yellowstone superintendent, a new twenty-year contract was signed by the Child interests with the Park Service. At the urging of the Interior Department the four companies were consolidated into the single Yellowstone Park Company, but ownership and management continued in the hands of the Child's and Nichols's families. The new company had "no subsidiaries or affiliates," but it had a one-half interest in a partnership, Yellowstone Park Service Stations, which it operated jointly with Hamilton Stores, Inc.[4]

The company claimed to have experienced a cumulative net loss between 1940 and 1949 of $750,000, although the loss could have been the product of an accountant's legerdemain. In 1952, due to "certain business and family problems," the Trust took positive steps to dispose of the property. The decision was long overdue, for the years of lackluster, uninspired management had taken their toll. And while the Yellowstone Park Company deserved blame, those war years and the human tidal wave that followed did constitute extenuating circumstances.[5]

Nor were the Park Service and the Interior Department above criticism. Aware of the bad situation, the bureaucracy had lacked consistency in its approach to the concessions problem. At a time of rapid inflation it was reluctant to allow the company to raise prices. The report of a "Concessions Advisory Group" in 1948 simply increased Park Service-Interior Department indecision; the bureaucracy could not make up its collective mind what to do. Meanwhile the situation deteriorated.

Some improvements were made. Nichols claimed that between 1947 and 1953 the company had spent $4,644,470 on improvements, built cottages at Old Faithful and Mammoth, and enlarged kitchens and laundries. Plans were under way for Canyon Village, which opened in 1957.[6]

The season of 1948 was probably the worst of the entire post—World War II era. Horror tales, "of scalping [$9.50 for a cabin with no bath, triple the Park Service approved rental], high prices, 'firetrap hotels,' dirty cabins, woefully inadequate sanitary facilities, official indifference and vast over-crowding everywhere," led the *Denver Post* to send a reporter to the park to find the truth.[7]

The newsman chose as his first place of inspection possibly the worst facility, Fishing Bridge (or "Syphilis Junction" as the student employees called it). The charge for a room was $3.75. Extra blankets were twenty-five cents each and extra sheets twenty cents. Since the company furnished one sheet, the city dweller usually paid for a second one and, Yellowstone nights being cool, an extra blanket was often considered worth the quarter. The reporter's family obtained the last blanket available at Fishing Bridge but was less fortunate when it requested a second sheet—the company was fresh out. Having signed in at the office, a college boy directed them down "some 200 yards of dusty roadway between rows of tightly packed, dun-colored cab-ins . . . ." The reporter went on:

> Their home for the night was not exactly luxurious. The floor was still wet from water-hose treatment. The wall was chinked with ancient news-paper and Kilroy had been there. A small wood stove, not much more substantial than the converted gasoline tin variety, a metal washpan with pitcher in matching motif, two wooden benches and a built-in table of sorts completed the furnishings.
>
> The beds, lofty structures, were slathappy hybrids which might well have come into existence when a drunken carpenter stumbled over a pile of rough-hewed lumber while celebrating the end of the First World War. One mattress was fairly new; the other, atop ancient, bare coil springs, was about as thick and efficacious as a serving of yesterday's wheat-cakes.[8]

A good two city blocks away were the washrooms and toilets.

The journalist found Lake Hotel (known to the locals as "Bat Alley") still boarded up. Lake Lodge provided one washroom for 175 cabins. It consisted of four washbowls and two showers. Old Faithful Inn had no elevators, and only the previous winter had it received its first sprinkler system. Canyon Hotel was dilapidated and due to be replaced. "Tourist cabins in general are old, unattractive, drafty, of light construction, miserably furnished, and completely inadequate in numbers," the newsman commented. "Of 1,872 such cabins, none has modern toilet facilities and only 958 boast so much as inside running water." Overall, for every twenty-five to forty cabins was one toilet-washroom-shower. "Garbage," he noted, "is collected once a day by park employees, much oftener by bears." He did concede that bathhouses were kept remarkably clean. After July 15, 1948, visitors waited in line fifteen to forty-five minutes for such rentals; if, upon seeing them, they wanted their money back, only seventy-five cents was refundable.[9]

Park Service and concession officials had stock answers to complaints. "This is not New York City or Miami Beach; you cannot expect posh facilities in a rustic area. The Company has to make a profit during a very short season. We are not allowed to charge enough to make it worthwhile to build better cottages."

But the truth was, housing and service were inexcusably bad. To spread the criticism, it is true that the Park Service, despite postwar inflation, had held the rental at $3.75, just twenty-five cents higher than in the depression year of 1936. The hovels were not too different from those found at many a 1920s cottage camp. But 1948 was nearly three decades later and motorists were already accepting Holiday Inns as the norm; while comfortable new motels were being built all over the country, Yellowstone's facilities remained discouragingly unimproved.

With a Park Service and Interior Department that were clearly undecided over concession policy, a Park Company whose owners wanted to sell, a captive clientele flocking into the park in ever increasing numbers, and service and facilities deteriorating, authorities began to contemplate drastic changes. It was known that the twenty-year franchise was up for renewal in the mid-1950s, and that few prospective buyers had shown real interest (the price of eighteen million dollars asked by the company had something to do with that). The state of Wyoming took action. Its legislature asked Congress "to investigate conditions in Yellowstone Park and to implement action to improve them." It bluntly charged that park facilities for the public were "so inadequate, old and worn out that their condition verges on a national scandal."[10]

The legislature also appropriated $50,000 to hire specialists to study the feasibility of Yellowstone's concessions being purchased by Wyoming and run by a state commission. Such a memorial, and such an appropriation, did not come from the Wyoming legislature because of grass roots interest. Behind it were entrepreneurs who entertained the hope of big profits.

The Wyoming governor who requested passage of the appropriation was a large stockholder in the Husky Oil Company, headquartered at Cody. The investigating commission was headed by Glenn E. Nielson, head of the same company. These men knew that a fantastic quantity of gasoline was sold in the park at high prices. (Sales of 3.2 million gallons in 1981 convey some idea of the profits involved.) The Continental Oil Company (Conoco, now a DuPont subsidiary) had furnished the gasoline and oil.

Why, other gasoline wholesalers asked, should Conoco enjoy those huge profits year after year? In 1940 Pat Griffin, the Phillips Petroleum wholesaler in Fort Collins, Colorado, had attempted to obtain the franchise in Yellowstone, but had failed. During that learning experience he discovered that Congress had in a weak moment granted the Interior Department the privilege of continuing park monopolies without publicizing their availability. In 1954 the Carter Oil Company and Sinclair both tried to break Conoco's park monopoly, but to no avail. Now Glenn Nielson and his friends thought they saw a way to break it: have the state of Wyoming gain control of park concessions. Then Phillips, Carter, Sinclair, Husky, or other companies would compete for Yellowstone's petroleum business. Conoco would lose its franchise, or else the company would have to make a deal, sharing its profits with its competitors. [11]

Wyoming's plan proved a bit too complex. First a sale price for the Yellowstone Park Company had to be agreed upon, then approved by the Interior Department; federal enabling legislation had to be passed to allow a state commission to run facilities in a national park; this in turn would be followed by state legislation and finally by sale of bonds to finance the purchase and initial operations of the concessions. It was all a bit too much for the Wyoming people, and the plan fell through. [12]

In 1956, no purchaser appearing, the Yellowstone Park Company had its lease renewed for another twenty years. John Q. Nichols, Billie Nichols's son, was appointed president with his father becoming chairman of the board. The family interest in the concern is obvious from the list of officials: Huntley Child, Jr., first vice-president; E. D. C. Nichols, second vice-president, and Hugh Galusha, Jr., whose father before him had been Harry Child's close friend and the company accountant, one of the board members. John Nichols considered himself a native of Helena and had been the company's general manager since 1935. [13]

Meanwhile construction continued on Canyon Village, the facility that would replace Canyon Hotel, condemned in 1959 and later destroyed by fire. The reputable Los Angeles architectural firm of Welton Becket and Associates designed the complex. Four hundred workers labored on the structures through the fall and winter of 1956–57 until thirty-five-degree-below-zero temperatures forced them to cease operations. Well into May they battled snowdrifts ten feet high, but by Independence Day the lodge was open and 150 motel-type cottages were operational. Eventually 500 such cottages were constructed. With additional facilities for the Hamilton Stores, Haynes Picture Shops, and others, the cost of Canyon Village was said to have been eight million dollars. [14]

So the Yellowstone Park Company stumbled along while rumors continued about possible purchasers. Finally, on March 22, 1966, it was announced that the Goldfield Corporation had purchased the company. Six months later it was announced that the General Baking Company (Bond

Bread) had acquired, among other properties, Goldfield's outstanding stock in the Yellowstone Park Company. The cost to General Baking was $6,353,662 in cash and assumption of a mortgage debt of $96,634. On April 20, 1967, General Baking changed its name to General Host, Inc. The word in the 1960s for a company like General Host was "conglomerate." Yellowstone's principal concessions were now in the hands of one of those hydra-headed monsters. [15]

Let us take a closer look at the background of the Goldfield Corporation, the initial purchaser. When Goldfield purchased the company in 1966 it was operating under a charter issued by the state of Wyoming on November 13, 1906. At that time its title was the Goldfield Consolidated Mines Company; the present name (Goldfield Corporation) was adopted in 1963, and a new charter for a company of the same name was issued in Delaware in 1968. The original company had mining interests in the Goldfield District of Nevada. In 1961 a young financier named Richard Chadwick Pistell became chairman of the board of this corporation, which was listed as being concerned with gold, silver, lead, zinc, and chrome. Between 1920 and 1970 the corporation paid one dividend, five cents a share in 1933. [16]

Under the direction of Pistell, described around Yellowstone as another Harry Child, things began to happen to this long dormant company. After some preliminary merging of mining stocks, Goldfield came out of the closet in 1962 and away it flew with 65.8 percent of the outstanding stock in Frontier Airlines, Inc. Then it merged with the American Chrome Company, sold its Frontier Airlines stock, and finally in mid-1965 acquired 51 percent of the voting stock of the General Baking Company; however, it later sold much of this stock so that by 1969 or 1970 it owned only 16 or 17 percent. Such, as far as published reports tell us, was the early history of the speculative organization that purchased the Yellowstone Park Company. [17]

In 1965 Pistell became chairman of the board of General Baking, which was chartered in 1911 and had acquired twenty bakeries, mostly in the northeast. In 1956 it began to expand, acquiring, among others, Eddy Bakeries, Inc., headquartered in Helena. Possibly this is a link with the Yellowstone purchase. Then the list of General Baking acquisitions began to lengthen: the park companies (including the concession for Everglades National Park), Associated Distributors of Tampa, Pik-a-Pak Corporation, Royal Baking Company, and finally, in the late 1960s, an attempt to control Armour and Company. Now known as General Host, the company failed in this attempt but in selling its Armour stock to Greyhound apparently realized $5,036,000. Due to some strange peregrinations along the corporate trail, in 1970 the Goldfield Corporation was suing General Host for seventy-seven million dollars, crying that its stockholders were shut out of a General Host stockholders meeting. [18]

In the 1970s General Host acquired and sold, sold and acquired, at an astonishing rate. It dispensed with its Bond (Bread) Division, but purchased Cudahy Meats and the Solar Salt Company of Salt Lake City, dispensed with its Vernell Fine Candy Division, but acquired Hot Sam (soft pretzels); sold its Allied Leather Division, and in 1979 under pressure, sold the Yellowstone Park Company to the United States government for nineteen million dollars—not a bad price when it is remembered that the conglomerate in 1966 had paid slightly less than six and a half million dollars for the same property.[19]

Whatever may have been their rationale, Park Service officials allowed Goldfield/General Host to purchase the Yellowstone Park Company, and from the first season of its ownership authorities regretted the sale. So bad did the situation become that in 1976, the last year of the two-year Ford presidency, the Department of Interior/National Park Service allowed a "concessions study team" to investigate the deteriorating situation and submit its report to the park superintendent, the regional director of the Rocky Mountain Region, and the director of the National Park Service. Entitled "Yellowstone National Park Concessions Management Review of the Yellowstone Park Company," this lengthy study was described as "the most intense evaluation of an existing concession operation every undertaken by the National Park Service."[20]

The service made thorough preparations. The review team was divided into a core group led by Andrew C. Wolfe of the Denver Service Center and included John A. Townsley, who later became a popular superintendent of the park; John M. Spurgeon of the service's Rocky Mountain Regional Office, John B. Amerman, president of the Yellowstone Park Company, and Trevor S. Povah, president of Hamilton Stores. It included also a study team of Park Service personnel specializing in concessions; and finally, at least nine specialists hired as consultants. From February until October 1976, the study team applied its time and expertise to its charge.[21]

The 300-page report is one of the most unusual documents ever to emanate from the Park Service or its parent, the Interior Department. It is reasonably thorough, incredibly candid, and scathing in its denunciation of the Yellowstone Park Company as managed from 1966 to 1976 by General Host. It supplied the fuel by which the company was literally fired, its franchise canceled (a rarity indeed!), and the government placed in a position to purchase the facilities. Not since W. Hallett Phillips's report in 1886 denouncing the Yellowstone National Park Improvement Company had government officials been allowed to write their thoughts and vent their frustrations. Indeed, the report makes interesting reading.[22]

It states that the Park Service "welcomed the financial support and ownership of the Yellowstone Park Company by Goldfield Corporation and its dynamic president, Richard Pistell." In its background history of the Yellowstone Park Company the report fails to mention the Nichols's long-known desire to sell out. Instead it blames Nichols's problems on a professional management team hired in 1957 to show the company how to earn maximum profits; the earnings came at the price of deteriorating facilities and services.[23]

An initial sore point between General Host and the Park Service concerned the former's written agreement to upgrade facilities at a cost of ten million dollars in ten years. As of 1976 General Host had done nothing, and facilities, in bad condition in 1966, were deteriorating at an intolerable rate. The company was granted a two-year extension—until September 30, 1977—to get renovations under way.[24]

Part 3 of the report, which dealt with the conditions of visitor services, stated that tourists were not receiving respectable, consistent service as good as in other parks or outside in the free enterprise system. Principal problem areas were listed as "management structure, policy emphasis, personnel policy, food services, lodging, facility deterioration, decor, and maintenance." What was left? "The problems of the Yellowstone Park Company are major in nature, and it will require a major overhaul of Company attitudes and policies to solve them," the report went on, adding that "The management cannot respond to visitor needs because the Company is not oriented to service to the public, but only to the generation of profit dollars."[25]

Outrage surfaces again and again throughout the report. Note the preliminary statement about facilities that were by contract supposed to be improved to the extent of ten million dollars over ten years:

> Most facilities throughout the park show extensive signs of advanced age and improper maintenance. Roofs are given little attention until severe leaking occurs; painting is not done often enough; windows and screens are left cracked, broken, and torn, draperies, shades, and blinds are frayed and broken; floor coverings are characterized by warped and broken tiles and worn, stained, and frayed rugs; and hand-lettered signs are the rule rather than the exception. Maintenance is not planned, but exists as a crisis-by-crisis effort of fixing and patching.[26]

Company management was accused of lacking "broad professional hospitality experience." The team suggested that executive bonuses should be eliminated, that the company should maintain a year-round chief operating officer in the park, and hosts at Old Faithful, Lake, Canyon, and Mammoth should be hired on a year-round basis.[27]

General Host, as the parent company, was faulted severely for its employee supervision. Both Hamilton Stores and the company hired seasonal supervisors who were often transients, unqualified for the work. No orientation of any kind was provided. Employees became disenchanted. "The Company attitude [this does not apply to the Hamilton Stores] toward most employees is that they are necessary evils to accomplish an end." Employee attitude reacted accordingly: "As a rule, the Yellowstone Park Company employees are unhappy with their situation," the report stated, and their reaction is "If the company is going to rip us off, we are going to rip them off."[28]

The employee turnover rate, always bad, steadily worsened in the 1970s as it became increasingly clear that absolute profit was the only criterion by which the company operated. The rate went from 50 percent in 1973 to 57 percent and 65 percent in 1974 and 1975 to an incredible 80 percent in 1976; the average for the four years was 63 percent. By contrast, Hamilton Stores' average for the same four-year period was just 30 percent with as little as 19 percent turnover in 1975 and 43 percent in 1976. The Yellowstone Park Service Stations had the least turnover of all, averaging just 6 percent overall.[29]

Only the company's employee turnover was unacceptable. Hamilton Stores could have been better, but Trevor Povah, who managed the facilities, was well liked by the young people, and the firm's record was tolerable. As for the service stations, they were administered independently, subject to Hamilton and the company only insofar as profits were involved. Service station personnel was carefully screened before being offered jobs, working conditions and room and board were the best of all the concessionaires, and pay was somewhat better.

Since the company in the 1970s was serving 1.3 million meals in sixteen separate facilities at five locations, the study group took a careful look at that branch of operations. "The service," the team concluded, "varies from adequate to unbearable, often at the same time in the same facility." Problems with food preparation led to a suggestion that the company bring in consultants from fast food chains.[30]

Next the team turned its attention to lodging, taking some pride in stating that at least one member had inspected every room. Since the number of guests that can be accommodated in a single night was at that time 8,628, inspecting each unit was indeed quite a task. They found that 59 percent of that number had private baths. In 1975 these lodgings were rented to 666,448 visitors.[31]

That the structures, save for Canyon Village, were all very old was no surprise. The group did not find them dangerous (to visitors) in the "imminent future," but it was clear that routine maintenance was lacking. The committee members "found rotting base sills and roofs, much roof leakage on the larger buildings, and many door and screen and window mullions past repair. . . .In all too many rooms they found damaged tables, insufficient chairs and lamps, and warped, cracked doors and windows with nearly ineffective locks." It was noted that from mid-July through August large blocks of rooms were out of service because of lack of maids to serve them, resulting in a huge revenue loss to the Company as well as inconveniencing thousands of potential guests daily.[32]

It is not necessary to go on. The extensive report seems to catch about every sin of which Yellowstone concessionaires have been guilty since the days of the old Park Improvement Company in 1883. What does surprise the reader is the study team's conclusion that because of its poor management policies the company was losing an estimated one and a half million dollars a year in gross revenues. "In 1975, since the company had a net income before taxes of 15.5% of gross income, this would result in a net income of $232,000," the team suggested. It categorically stated that the company could achieve the modest National Park Service standard of visitor services and still "return a reasonable profit to the Company. . . ."[33]

Results of the concessions review team's report were ultimately far reaching. For the first time a major concessionaire had its franchise canceled. True, General Host bowed out with a $19.9-million sale price, after having used the facilities since 1966 with an absolute minimum of maintenance, after having defaulted on its agreement to invest ten million dollars in restaurants and hostelries, and with a profit of nearly fourteen million dollars over the price paid for the company in 1966. Yet so profitable had been Yellowstone's hotel, transportation, and food business that the conglomerate's executives were reportedly unhappy about losing the franchise. General Host's Yellowstone managers were described as being surprised and flabbergasted at the service's action. This sort of thing simply did not happen!

Into the vacuum stepped another conglomerate: Trans World Corporation, which at the time included Trans World Airlines, TWA Tours, Century 21 Real Estate, Hilton International Hotels, Canteen and Spartan Food Services; since then it has shed the unprofitable airline. This group ran the facilities as TWA Services for a two-year trial period; then service proved so satisfactory that in 1982 they were granted a thirty-year contract.

There is more, much more, to TWA's contract than the granting of a generation-long license. Even Harry Child could only wrest twenty years out of the Interior Department! What had happened in recent years to make the Park Service so much more permissive?

The Park Service had little to do with it. Behind the liberalizing of concessionaire contracts lay a little-known national concessionaires association representing franchised businesses in all national parks and monuments.

The Park Service today administers more than three hundred separate units, ranging from Yellowstone Park to seashores, parkways, cemeteries, and historical sites. If any kind of retail or service business exists in the reservation and is not run by the service, then it is operated with a franchise issued by the service. And provided these concessions are run according to sound business principles, they are extremely lucrative. It should come as no surprise, therefore, that they have formed their own association and lobbying group.

The thirty-five or so concessionaires possess one overriding fear: that the Park Service will eliminate them, purchase their facilities, and, after public bidding, lease the facilities on a short-term basis—five years is a commonly mentioned period. Thus the hotel host would bring in his staff, the storekeeper his staff and inventory, the restaurateur his managerial and service help. The facilities would all be owned and maintained by the Park Service. At the end of the season the service groups would add up their profits and losses and, with their personnel and inventories, leave until another year. Similar leasing is done very satisfactorily in a large number of federal food establishments (cafeterias in large government office buildings, for example), and in a number of state parks.

This is clearly the answer to the concession question. Certainly the history of Yellowstone concessions indicates that there is simply no way of keeping politics out of a system whereby franchisers own property within the reservation that is worth millions and that can earn for them annual profits in six and sometimes seven figures. Concession problems, some serious and some relatively moderate, have existed at most Park Service–administered areas. As in any business, concessionaires range from respectable people who provide excellent service to persons whose handling makes their facilities a public nuisance. True, politics would still be present, but with that strange ownership arrangement eliminated, the money involved would not be so great, and neither would be politics.

In 1965 that fear—that the service would succeed in acquiring their facilities—led to passage of an act "relating to the establishment of concession policies in the areas administered by the National Park Services, and for other purposes." It is called the Concessions Policies Act. This legislation, which reads like it was written by counsel for the national concessionaires association (any may well have been) states in part that "a concessioner shall have a possessory interest therein, which shall consist of all incidents of ownership except legal title, . . . The said possessory interest shall not be extinguished by the expiration or other termination of the contract and may not be taken for public use without just compensation. The said possessory interest may be assigned, transferred, encumbered, or relinquished."[34]

Whatever its background the Concessions Policies Act clearly tied the hands of any Park Service/Interior administration that might decide to eliminate concession-owned facilities and replace them with government-owned ones (for although the government had the title, the possessory clause gave the concessionaires a proprietary right).

If this terminology seems opaque and obfuscated, then the aim of the act's authors has been achieved. Shrewd lawyers know that with the phrase "possessory rights" they have created a legal broth to warm a Philadelphia lawyer's heart. Precisely what does "possessory right" mean? *Precisely*, no one knows, but its object is clear: to guarantee a monetary claim under any and all circumstances to concessionaires' facilities—or concessionaires who *run* government-owned facilities—in the national parks and monuments.

Thus when General Host was deprived of its Yellowstone franchise in 1979 it received 19.9 million dollars; it hardly suffered when the Yellowstone Park Company was sold to the federal government. But when TWA was granted the franchise, it entered into business under that same protective umbrella; it automatically assumed a "possessory right." Instead of the National Park Service maintaining the facilities, the task fell to TWA, and in so doing, TWA in a sense insured itself of, or earned, that "possessory right." Prior to the Concessions Policies Act, concessionaires paid a small percentage of their revenues to the government; in essence, this was their lease rental. Now that system was eliminated. When TWA was granted a thirty-year contract in 1982, it agreed instead to commit "22% of the gross revenue, along with all pretax profits in excess of 5%. . . in repair and maintenance and capital improvements to government-owned, concession operated facilities and equipment." To demonstrate the kind of profits that can be made in Yellowstone, the sum of $748,914 was available for the above purposes in 1981 from TWA Services. This change, from paying a small percentage of gross revenues to the government as rental or franchise charge, to contributing a percentage of gross revenue and pretax profits over 5 percent to maintenance, was an obvious ploy by those in the private sector to claim a "possessory interest" in the concession facilities. This in turn would guarantee, along with the Concessions Policies Act, the continuance of private concessions in the national parks.[35]

The Park Service had not planned it this way, but the concessionaires and their political lackeys forced the change. As the *New York Times* reported, "The Yellowstone dispute is being watched closely by the more than thirty-five concessionaires in other national parks, who jointly gross over $200 million annually according to government figures." It pointed out that in 1977, the year after the concessions review team made its report, the Yellowstone Park Company earned a 14.9 percent profit on gross receipts of "$12.8 million, while the parent company, General Host, posted losses for the year."[36]

The Yellowstone dispute was but one of several disagreements involving concessionaires—especially those of Yosemite Park—and the Park Service. Superintendent John Townsley made no attempt to deny his preference for the federal ownership/short-term lease method. Neither did President Carter's first Park Service director, a young career man named William J. Whalen, who wanted Congress to cancel the "possessory interest" of concessionaires in park facilities. Townsley survived the political fire fight, only to die tragically of cancer while still in his fifties, but Whalen was a casualty. He was removed from office. "My firing," he said, "is a clear signal that you don't mess around with those powerful concessioners. Park Directors that stand up and do the job won't last long."[37]

Whalen was removed in the spring of 1980; in 1981 the Reagan administration came to power. Its first secretary of interior was James Watt. "We [meaning the Reaganites] have tremendous biases," he told a convention of concessionaires. "We have a bias for private enterprise. We believe concessioners can do the job." While he gained the businessmen's support, he sent shudders down the spines of Park Service personnel. He said he wanted to give private investors a greater role in running the parks, even to the extent of allowing concessions personnel the privilege of orienting visitors at the gates. He wanted more entrepreneurs to invest and manage park resources. He informed the concessionaires that if any member of the Park Service gave them a problem, "we're going to get rid of the problem or the personality, whichever is fastest."[38]

Of course, concessionaires are a most favored kind of private enterprise; had Mr. Watt said "private monopoly" he would have been more accurate. The private enterprise is the gasoline retailer at Gardiner or West Yellowstone or Cody who has to compete with another retailer across the street and one down at the crossroads; the motel owner in competition with several other inns along main street; and the restaurateur who vies for tourist dollars with fast food chains, franchised steak houses, and locally owned competitors.

It was Secretary Watt who reacted to concessionaires' fears and suggested that a model contract should be drawn up that waived the old franchise fee in return for concessionaires investing part of their earnings in improving their park facilities; it was this kind of contract that TWA Services won in Yellowstone. The former secretary also spoke out for even larger concession contracts involving larger investments, and he suggested that campgrounds should also be run by private interests.[39]

Many of Watt's ideas are being given the opportunity to prove themselves in Yellowstone. TWA Services is investing in the facilities, and so far seems to be giving satisfactory service. The company has had considerable experience in the hosting business, it wanted the franchise, and to date appears to have fulfilled its obligations well. The young people who wait on the public are cheerful and helpful. Food is good. A hundred new overnight units have been opened at Grant Village (as of 1983) and plans are under way for 200 more plus an employee dormitory. It is unusual to read in a Yellowstone superintendent's report the following:

> TWA Services operated the visitor facilities at a satisfactory level and we feel park visitors were well serviced.
>
> TWA Services has assisted the National Park Service in providing a quality visitor experience in Yellowstone. They have added string music and historic readings in both the Old Faithful Inn and Lake Hotel this summer. They have also conducted historic chambermaid tours of various rooms with period furnishings.

The superintendent's report is also encouraging with regard to the Hamilton Stores (which purchased the Haynes Picture Shops in 1968) and the service stations. As of 1983 the concessions situation in Yellowstone was the best it has been in many years—a happy note upon which to end this phase of the history.[40]

NOTES TO CHAPTER FOURTEEN

1. Robert D. Barbee, Superintendent, "Annual Report of the Superintendent of Yellowstone National Park for 1982," duplicate manuscript, courtesy of Timothy R. Manns, North District Naturalist/ Historian, Yellowstone National Park, 1983, 87.

2. *New York Times*, September 26, 1937, 1, 39.

3. Duff, Anderson, and Clark, Industrial Investment and Financial Analysts, "Report: Yellowstone Park Company Proposed Transfer of Ownership to Wyoming Park Commission, August, 1955," Report in custody of the American Heritage Center, University of Wyoming, Laramie.

4. Ibid.

5. Ibid.

6. *Denver Post*, September 6, 8, 1955, in "Yellowstone Clipping File," Denver Public Library, Western History Room.

7. Elvin R. Howe, "Yellowstone Waltz," *Denver Post*, "Empire" Section, September 12, 1948.

8. Ibid.

9. Ibid

10. Lawrence Martin, "State Socialism vs. Free Enterprise," *Denver Post,* September 4, 1955.

11. Ibid., September 4, 9, and 11, 1955.
In Continental Oil's defense, it must be stated that (1) the company carries out its obligations in a satisfactory manner, and problems of supply in so remote a region are enormous; (2) prices are fixed by the Park Service; (3) the stations accept just about any company's credit card.

12. Ibid., December 7, 1956.

13. Ibid.

14. *New York Times,* July 21, 1957, B-27.

15. Ibid., March 22, 1966, 63; Ibid., October 6, 1966, 71. See also *Moody's Industrial Manual,* 1970 Edition, 2148.

16. *Moody's Industrial Manual,* 1969 Edition, 2448.

17. Ibid.

18. Ibid., 1970 Edition, 2148; *Value Line Investment Survey,* 1970, 1151; *New York Times,* August 25, 1970, 55.

19. *Moody's Industrial Manual,* 1982 Edition, Vol I, 1438–42.

20. U.S. Department of the Interior, National Park Service, "Yellowstone National Park Concessions Management Review of the Yellowstone Park Company," prepared by the Yellowstone Concessions Study Team for the Superintendent, Yellowstone National Park, Regional Director, Rocky Mountain Region, Director, National Park Service. February–October, 1976.
The review is not published but is available at the Interior Department Library, Old Interior Building, Washington, D.C.

21. Ibid., 3.

22. In a conversation on May 19, 1981, with John Burchell, of the National Park Service, at that time chief of the division of concessions in Yellowstone, I received a much different estimate of the report. Mr. Burchell was extremely defensive of General Host. "Where," he asked, "was the government when conditions were going down hill?"

23. Report, 7.

24. Ibid., 7–8.

25. Ibid., 12.

26. Ibid., 11–12.

27. Ibid., 15–17. Mr. Burchell's reaction to this suggestion was that hosts are gregarious people who do not like Yellowstone's isolation in the off-season.

28. Ibid., 26–27.

29. Ibid., 26–28.

30. Ibid., 33–35.

31. Ibid., 40.

32. Ibid., 41–42.

33. Ibid., 129–130.

34. 79 *U.S. Statues at Large,* 969.

35. Superintendent's Report for 1982, 7.

36. *New York Times,* August 20, 1978, 126. (The *Times* was on strike at this time and the page reference is to a duplicated letter-size news sheet put out by the paper.)

37. *New York Times,* May 15, 1980, A-24.

38. Ibid., March 28, 1981, A-1.

39. Ibid., June 19, 1981, A-15.

40. Superintendent's Report for 1982.

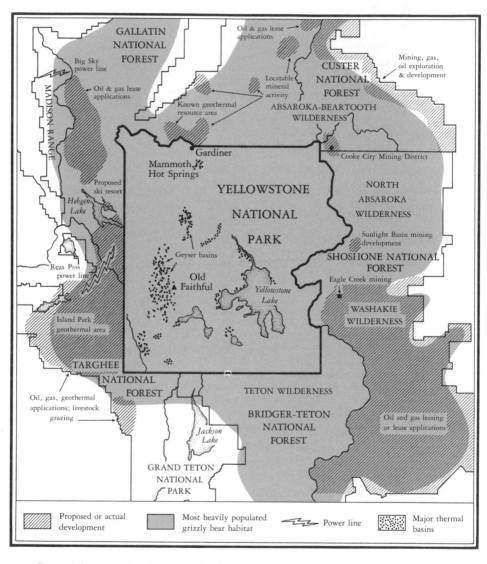

Potential energy developments in the greater Yellowstone ecosystem as of 1982.
Adapted from map by James F. O'Brien, National Parks, *January-February 1982.*

CHAPTER FIFTEEN

Problems of the Present:
Elk, Bears, Boats, and P.R.

*E*ven if we are too close to the post–World War II years to evaluate events since 1945 with historical perspective, certainly a number of developments, changes, and trends have appeared in Yellowstone which deserve mention today and will command the attention of future historians. Some of these are ongoing problems, or conditions, whose main aspects can only be chronicled up to 1984.

For example, a few words should be said about the superintendents since 1945. As retired Superintendent Edmund B. Rogers said in an interview at his Denver home in 1971, "The old guard comes through here and they cry on my shoulder. They can't believe what is happening to the Service."[1]

He was speaking of the maturation of the National Park Service. Rogers, who retired in 1956, represented the last of the originals. Now the old guard was dying off or retiring. The National Park Service was rapidly adding personnel as well as widening the dimensions of its charge. Bright young men from all branches of learning were being added to the service's personnel rolls. They were—and had a right to be—full of new ideas. The change was inevitable and, following a period of adjustment, not necessarily bad. Park Service personnel standards have always been high. But for the old-timers, the changes came hard.

Certainly future historians will note the increasing instability of tenure in the office of superintendent. Three superintendents served during the service's first forty years in Yellowstone; six served in the next twenty-seven. Perhaps, and perhaps not, historians will note something else: a change from the strong-willed, proud, confident, independent executives in the Albright, Toll, and Rogers tradition, to indecisive subordinates obeying a fidgity Park Service director in turn responsible to a politically attuned Interior secretary who was a yes-man to an insecure president.

The records of Lemuel Garrison, John McLaughlin, Jack Anderson, and John Townsley, the most recent superintendents, are simply too current to be fairly appraised. There is no reason to discredit these fine men. All made good and bad decisions; all have had troubles with concessionaires, politicians, environmentalists, and sportsmen. They have participated in national programs and done their share towards trying to ensure their success. For example, Rogers, Garrison, and Anderson participated in Director Conrad Wirth's Mission 66, a crash program of the 1950s-60s to modernize Park Service facilities. Although the program nationwide was far from a great success, it at least staved off the deterioration that was bringing the parks and monuments to the brink of disaster; through publicity it alerted the nation to a realization of their poor condition.[2]

Historians will probably show interest in at least two major problems confronting Yellowstone superintendents since the Second World War. Speaking generally, the first is the continuing wildlife problem; the second one concerns boats. The first problem is further cut into segments of which the two most important are the elk problem and the bear problem.

The American wapiti, stateliest member of the deer family, commonly known in the United States as the elk, has long inhabited Yellowstone Park. The animals have grazed along the Gallatin, in the meadows of the southern reaches of the park and down into Jackson Hole (where resides the largest elk herd in the world), and in the meadows along the Lamar River, on the Black Tail Deer Plateau, and into the meadows of the upper Yellowstone Valley north of the reservation.

In the 1890s superintendents estimated that roughly 25,000 of the herbivorous beasts were within the reservation. "It is useless to try to convey to the eastern mind the number of elk in the park," wrote Captain Anderson in February 1891. "One can simple say there are thousands of them. The country at times looks like an overstocked cattle range at roundup time."[3]

What is certain is that by 1914 their number had increased to a probable 35,300. Not only did many starve to death, which was bad enough, but the herd was also destroying the grass cover and browse. In 1928 a Forest Service biologist, W. M. Rush, announced that the winter range in Yellowstone had deteriorated a full 50 percent since 1914, and "that on more than one-half of the available range, sheet erosion had removed one to two inches of topsoil." Therein lay the serious problem. Cheat grass and rabbitbrush, plants of lesser value, were spreading across the lower ranges due to overgrazing.[4]

Drought on the winter range in 1919 made necessary the feeding of the beasts: in 1920 conditions worsened. It was estimated that 14,000 elk in the northern herd died of starvation in Yellowstone while 25,000 perished in the southern herd concentrated south of the park in Jackson Hole. Thereafter the northern herd numbered from a high of 14,500 to a low of 9,200 in 1952. But it was determined in 1934 that for the sake of the grass and browse, and for the vigor of the animals themselves, the herd should be reduced to 5,000 animals.[5]

Reduction and subsequent control of the herd was to be by three methods: First by harvesting the elk (as the hunter kill was designated) outside the park. (The elk migrate down the Yellowstone and Gallatin valleys, and into Jackson Hole); second, by live-trapping the Yellowstone elk and shipping them to any state that applied for them; and finally, if the first two methods failed, by hunting inside the reservation. Over a period of twenty-seven years (1934–61) the National Park Service killed 8,825 animals by shooting, dispensed with 5,765 by live-trapping, while hunters harvested an estimated 40,745 from the northern herd which had grazed beyond park boundaries.[6]

But an investigation carried out in 1961–62 showed continued, serious deterioration of Yellowstone's winter range. Ten thousand elk still constituted the northern herd, yet the authorities of the time insisted that the range could support only half that many. The Park Service took strong measures, killing 4,283 of the beasts, which were then processed and distributed as food to Indian communities, while 850 more were eliminated by hunting outside the park or by live-trapping or normal winter kill. A subsequent census conducted by helicopter revealed a manageable herd of 3,725 elk. It had been unpleasant work carried out after the hunting season was ended, often at forty degrees below zero. Many of the slaughtered beasts were cows with fetuses; their meat was not very palatable but possibly the hungry Indians consumed it anyway.[7]

By the mid-1960s the public believed the elk situation in the park was under control. Unbeknownst to them, but very obvious to park authorities, were the rapidly multiplying elk. When the herd was cut, survivors thrived with more forage and their calf crop jumped as high as 25 percent. Without consulting the proud hunters and sportsmen of Montana, Wyoming, and Idaho, the service announced plans on February 4, 1967, to eliminate by direct reduction 600 elk.

At this juncture Park Service relations with sportsmen in the surrounding states reached a new low. Somehow elimination of 600 more elk by "direct reduction" without advance information of the necessity, without consultation with local sportsmen's clubs or even state game commissions, struck a nerve. The citizenry rose up in wrath. The upshot was hearings at Casper, Wyoming, March 11, 1967, with that state's Senator Gale McGee presiding.

Why should residents of Wyoming and Montana, where the game harvest is in excess of 100,000 animals a year, be angered over a Park Service announcement of an impending reduction of just 600 elk? It had something to do with the people, and something to do with hunting, and it involved regional resentment against some individuals in the service. Bureaucratic arrogance, "tin-godism," the attitude that the service, as part of the federal government, will do whatever it wishes and the natives be damned all entered into their hostility. And in those parts, hunting elk is almost a rite of passage into manhood.[8]

Possibly Senator Clifford P. Hansen of Wyoming best epitomized the feelings of the Montana and Wyoming people when he testified at the elk population hearings:

> In Wyoming, hunting licenses can be issued to our young citizens at the age of 14. How many of us remember each little mountain meadow, patch of timber, high and windy divide, and rocky draw, where we have seen the little bands of cow and calf elk, sleek with green summer grass, or a big six-point bull stepping from behind a cover of trees in the fall of the year to issue his challenge to the world? How many of us have felt the hair crawl on the back of our necks as a bull bugles close by and then is answered again and again until the mountain valleys are filled with a symphony of brassy sound?[9]

Senator Hansen was speaking for the real hunter, who may live on Fifth Avenue in New York City or in Dubois, Wyoming. It is not where he resides that is important, but his view of the sport and the degree of his dedication to the highest sportsman's ethics. For the real hunter, the hunt includes crisp autumn air, lonely wilderness, search for game, tracking across trailless terrain, killing as humanely as possible, and carefully dressing the carcass. At its best, such hunting is truly a sport of kings; such a hunter was Theodore Roosevelt. There are still many such hunters.

The others are frauds, the kind who, in years past, kept the Gardiner bars open twenty-four hours a day, gambled, belted down too much whiskey, and at dawn or a little later drove down a road to what locals called "the firing line" where they took aim at Yellowstone elk that had crossed the boundary into Montana. If a man could hit the broadside of a barn he got his elk. He hired a local butcher to process the carcass and, if the antlers were good, had a taxidermist mount the head. The great hunter then headed back to Gardiner's bars to boast of his prowess.

But whether real hunters or not, there are a lot of concerned citizens in the nation who resent arbitrary decisions by a federal agency. Park officials had proceeded with "Operation Elk Kill," and the Columbia Broadcasting System had televised some of the action. The service received the hunters' wrath. Park Service Director George B. Hartzog accepted full blame, admitted that someone had "goofed," and assured the committee that the situation would be rectified.[10]

The apology was hardly sufficient. At the hearings Chuck Morrison of the *Casper Star-Tribune* expressed the undercurrent of antagonism that had been brewing in the park's environs for some time. "It has become increasingly difficult for the past ten years to maintain adequate and proper public relations with park personnel at all levels," he charged. "Unless you people take it upon yourself to change your public image," he warned, "and work more closely with we [sic] who are dedicated to the greatest good for the greatest number, you will be the losers. . . . If you people do not remove some of your empire building, politically-oriented personnel and clean house from top to bottom, you will lose my friendship and my respect for what was, at one time, a fine service."[11]

The elk story does not end with the bad publicity over Operation Elk Kill in 1967. In the late 1960s the service assigned one of its biologists, Douglas B. Houston, to study effects of the elk upon the Yellowstone land, its grass cover and browse. After ten years he made his report, concluding that the elk were *not* denuding the land and suggesting that the normal number in the park should fluctuate between 16,000 and 25,000. The service has accepted those numbers and at present is not cutting the herd. (Dr. Houston found that suppression of forest fires, which had allowed big pines to encroach upon meadows and aspen groves where elk grazed, was at least one of the principal causes of decreased browse.)[12]

Such a turnabout after nearly sixty years of belief that there were too many animals for the ground cover points out that lessons are still being learned in the relatively new discipline of ecology. Meanwhile a new problem has arisen: ranchers in the upper Yellowstone Valley are protesting that park elk are crossing the frigid waters of the Yellowstone and are grazing unchecked on both public and private lands, destroying the cattle range. The animals are following their custom of hundreds of years, drifting far down the valley as winter closes their meadows in the park. More troubles loom for the Park Service.[13]

Indeed, animals constitute a substantial percentage of park administrators' problems today. In attempting to maintain Yellowstone as a wilderness not too unlike the pristine land observed by John Colter, the service has allowed animals to exist in their primitive state at their natural level of numbers. When the park's northern herd of bighorn sheep contracted chlamydia, a type of pinkeye occurring from a naturally existing bacteria, the service allowed the disease to run its course. Officials have also let brucellosis exist in the park buffalo herd, but ranchers outside the park protest that the disease may be transmitted to their cattle.[14]

Above all, the service is under fire for its policy towards bears, those lovable, dangerous, wild creatures that have been a problem in Yellowstone ever since people began visiting the park. Bearjams and confrontations with people led park zoologists to remove all members of family Ursidae from roads, campgrounds, and concession facilities. Protests were raised, but the superintendendent could report that "there were no bear-caused injuries reported in the 1982 season."

This is a plus for the Park Service, but in clearing the bears from populated areas and garbage dumps the beasts have, in effect, been forced to live off the land as they did two hundred years ago. Some insist that the service has sentenced the bruins—black, cinnamon, and grizzlies—to extinction in Yellowstone Park. The controversy still raged as of 1984.

Underlying the moves to make the park safer for humanity, and a little less hospitable to bears, lies a philosophical struggle that iself is the subject of strong controversy: to make Yellowstone as pristine and natural as it was in the days of John Colter. To a degree that concept has been around since 1872, but not until the report of a committee formed after an elk imbroglio in 1961–62 did the Park Service crystallize these ideas. The committee, headed by Dr. A. Starker Leopold, in essence advocated restoring everything to its condition prior to white man's arrival. This was philosophical idealism rather than sound scientific sense. Elk formerly migrated as far down the Yellowstone Valley as Livingston, sixty miles north of the park boundary; grizzlies loped around a territory three hundred to six hundred miles in circumference, large even for Yellowstone; given that 2.5 million people now pass through the park every year, the ideal pristine wilderness of the frontier can only be an impossible goal, its attainment restricted by common sense. [15]

Injuries from wild animals, and resultant lawsuits, combined with the concept of restoration of Yellowstone to pure wilderness led the service, based upon recommendations in the Leopold report and the advice of its own scientists, to close the garbage dumps and move the bears to the park's remote areas, there to forage as in prehumanity days. Environmentalists charge that the bears, far from flourishing, are suffering diet deficiencies and are disappearing rapidly. The charge applies to blacks and cinnamons as well as to grizzlies. [16]

If this is true (for the Park Service denies it and the truth may not be known for some time), the real animal in danger of extinction is not the milder, smaller species, but the grizzlies. Of the eighteen reported confrontations between people and bears in the park in 1982, ten involved grizzlies. These magnificent beasts constitute a clear, present, and horrible danger. Backpackers wear bear bells that tinkle as they walk along. Hikers sing and whistle and speak in high voices, all to warn bears that humans are around and to prevent chance encounters in which a grizzly might instinctively attack. [17]

But the grizzly, an animal whose numbers may have reached 100,000 as late as the 1880s (mostly on the Great Plains, not in the mountains) is today an endangered species. Indeed the beast is dangerous, but as an animal possessing fierce, imposing majesty, it is too much a product of God's work to allow it to disappear from the face of the earth. It is endangered not only in

Yellowstone but also in the park's vicinity where oil, gas, and mining development, and encroaching ranch operations on Forest Service or privately owned wilderness lands, are cutting into its wide-ranging habitat. Its habitat is similarly in jeopardy in the five or six other regions in the United States where it is known to roam. The animals do not procreate rapidly. And a grizzly, foraging around sheep or cattle is, in the mind of herders, fair target for a Winchester rifle.[18]

One frustrated writer ended his essay with an epilogue in which he stated that an unfaced danger threatens: "Simply put, it is the inability of many of the bear's partisans . . . to get along, to cooperate. . . . Time after time it was clear to me that personal resentments, ego-tripping, empire-building, professional jealousy, turf obsession, and plain old nasty machismo have played prominent roles in what ought to be objective discussions of a very important and significant threatened animal." Park Service personnel was included in this reproach.[19]

Current events: Since the Second World War air pollution by too many automobiles, the grating buzz of trailbikes and snowmobiles, and the pollution of lake waters by ever more powerful motorboats have all troubled the Park Service in Yellowstone. While trailbikes and four-wheel-drive automobiles are somewhat restricted, Yellowstone now has substantial visitation from snowmobile-type vehicles in winter, which warms the wallets of the concessionaires but does nothing for the environment; likewise problems of pollution and motorboating on Yellowstone Lake in the summer have ended in a draw. The motorboating fiasco of 1959–60 is a good case study of how complex are the issues confronting park officials, and of how powerful outside elements can be in determining the extent and nature of park regulations.

Anyone who has experienced sore shoulders after a day of rowing a boat will acknowledge that the motorboat was a great innovation. But the little five-horsepower Johnson Sea Horses gave way to sophisticated outboards of up to 135 horsepower; soon enthusiasts were placing two such motors on their crafts. Along with motor improvements came more sophisticated boats and boat trailers. Nowadays the boating enthusiast may appear at Yellowstone Lake in his $25,000 RV, pulling a $1,500 trailer carrying a $20,000 boat. This lover of the wilderness with his portable generator, television, and refrigerator is incensed at regulations limiting his boat speed to thirty-five miles an hour; he is even more distressed at occasional speed restrictions down to five miles and hour and launches into an anarchistic tirade at the authority that dares to declare certain parts of the south end of Yellowstone Lake off limits. He must also steer clear of certain islands. Finally, his boat has to meet certain rather stringent specifications.

Soon after Captain Waters had his passenger steamer plying the waters between the Thumb, Lake Hotel, and Dot Island, motorboats appeared in the park. Almost before they were aware of what happened, park officials had five to ten thousand of those buzzing nuisances making waves in Yellowstone's lakes. One of the most beautiful high-altitude bodies of water in the world was now dotted with motorboats like fly specks on a slice of apple pie.

Something had to be done. In 1959 the service, aware of the destruction to shorelines by waves caused by speedboats, and of the chaos among the bird rookeries on the lake's islands, restricted the Flat Mountain of Yellowstone Lake to "hand propelled boats." In 1960 it further proposed to ban all powerboats from the south end of the lake, including the south and southeast arms. In addition to shoreline damage and interruption of bird nesting, the service cited a growing sanitation and security problem, both on the lake and along its shores.[20]

Powerboat fanciers protested. Through numerous boating associations, certain chambers of commerce, and civic clubs they gave vent to their feelings. The upshot was four hours of hearings at Cody, Wyoming, on February 3, 1960.[21]

Testimony was weighted heavily for the motorboaters, as pointed out by *National Parks* magazine. Of twenty-eight oral arguments, twenty-two were against the proposed regulations; the published statements (often in greater detail than the oral ones) were likewise heavily weighted on the boaters' side. Their testimony was permeated by arrogance, rudeness, and ridicule of Park Service arguments. Senator McGee also seemed biased in their favor. In his interrogation of Superintendent Lem Garrison the senator rather narrowed the Park Service argument down to birds, finally suggesting that perhaps only a few miles of the south and southeast arms needed protection.[22]

These hearings were followed by similar ones in Wyoming and Idaho in August 1960. Clearly the service was confronted with a politically powerful boating lobby. But as we have observed with regard to policies toward elk and bears, the service can, and often does, exacerbate the situation by acting unilaterally in the face of opposition. On December 19, 1960, the Department of Interior made public the proposed regulations, and the ban on powerboats on the lower (southern) 20 percent of Yellowstone Lake was retained.[23]

And then, in ways unspecified in the written record, the boaters' lobby applied pressure. On June 9, 1961, about six months after Interior's announcement, the department issued new regulations carefully couched in legalese. Motorboats could now go anywhere they pleased on Yellowstone

Lake, only at certain places being required to slow to five miles per hour.[24]

This was total capitulation. "We find it hard to credit reports that Senator McGee of Wyoming considers his political future to hang on motorboating on Yellowstone Lake," editorialized *National Parks*. "Perhaps he should try firmness in the right as the political method." The editorial suggested that the pressure had been so great that President Kennedy had taken the decision out of the hands of Interior Secretary Udall and his department solicitor.[25]

The Park Service was at least pragmatic about the situation. It did what it could (and never underestimate the power of a bureaucracy). Today landing areas are restricted; motorboats are banned on the extreme south portions of the southeast arm and south arm of Yellowstone Lake, as well as on the extreme end of Flat Mountain arm; and the remainder of the southeast and south arms is designated as a five-mile-per-hour zone. Vessels sixteen feet or longer are prohibited from proceeding closer than a quarter mile from the shoreline of the arms of the lake islands.[26]

More than just the technology of movement—railroads, automobiles, snowmobiles, trail bikes, four-wheel-drive vehicles, and motorboats has encroached upon Yellowstone. The technology of electric power has caused park officials more than a few headaches. For years the Park Service supplied energy by diesel plants situated strategically throughout the reservation. After the Second World War studies determined the feasibility of contracting for electric power from outside sources. Montana Power Company received the principal contract, at least partly because it could string wires from the northern boundary along the telephone line route, thus preventing additional scarring of the wilderness. (This policy, said Congressman John E. Moss, was "more favored in the breach than in the observance.") Fall River Electric Cooperative of Ashton, Idaho, received a lesser contract to supply the park's West Entrance facilities. Then when NPS asked for bids to extend service to the inner park, accusations were made that the Park Service favored Montana Power and discriminated against the R.E.A. cooperatives, Fall River Electric and Shoshone River Power. It was a brouhaha involving policy, politics, and some incompetence.[27]

Yellowstone and the fine people who are charged with its custody have no choice: threats to the reservation will change as America changes; as custodians Park Service personnel must adjust to the shifts intelligently and with reasonable acceptance. A hundred years ago the park was exploited by concessionaires, poachers, and tourists who pilfered the thermal phenomena, shot animals and birds, and overfished the cold waters. Forest fires raged because fire prevention, involving such simple expedients as flooding out the breakfast fire or clearing dry grass from the campfire site, were not a part of America's habits.

Pioneer conservationists such as geologist Arnold Hague, Senator George Vest, lawyer W. Hallett Phillips, sports magazine editor George Bird Grinnell, and Theodore Roosevelt and the Boone and Crockett Club, were but leaders in a steadily enlarging coterie of defenders who were determined that Yellowstone should be protected. They fought the concessionaires and at least restricted their destructive activities; they fought railroad interests that were determined to run tracks up the Lamar Valley and harbored expanded plans for running railroads throughout the park. When the army arrived it developed public campgrounds to keep track of visitors, and it penalized those who defiled the hot springs and geyser basins with their graffiti and who failed to control their fires. Rules and regulations began to be posted in Philetus Norris's time and a federal marshal was stationed in the park after 1894. Gradually legislation was passed backing up the authorities. By the 1890s Yellowstone was secure, well under control, and thriving.

Then the army left (1916–18) and the new National Park Service assumed control. Its personnel, young career men and middle-aged conservationists who had already established their competence in the business world, were now in charge. Dedicated and energetic, they advertised the parks and, in retrospect, answered the needs of a nation that was optimistic and newly mobile. If the concessionaires failed to serve this very middling of the middle class, the class itself did not seem to mind. As Emerson Hough said, this was the era of Maw's first vacation, and she, along with husband and children and family dog, made the most of it.

Coexistent with the Progressive Movement had come the reclamation impulse. The new Park Service may not have had to fight railroaders, but it found an equally formidable menace in the irrigationists who in the 1920s proliferated on the perimeters of Yellowstone. Again the American people, as represented by some Congressmen and many journalists, including publicist Robert Sterling Yard and editor George Horace Lorimer of the powerful *Saturday Evening Post,* came to the park's defense. Presidents Harding and Franklin D. Roosevelt spoke out against the plans: the proposals never materialized.

Just as the rest of the nation was affected by the Great Depression of the 1930s, so was Yellowstone. It gained a very short respite (from 1932 through 1934), but then visitation began to climb. The service kept up fairly well with the increased traffic, but concessionaires lagged behind. Then came the Second World War and another breather for the park.

Even though they suspected that a deluge of people was coming, neither Park Service officials nor concessionaires could do much in preparation while the war was on. When hostilities ended, the service and concessionaires held on because they had no choice. Everything—roads, restrooms, campgrounds, hotels, restaurants, and tourist cabins—were hard pressed. The service rose to the problem best, the dedication of its personnel contributing to whatever successes it had; but the concessionaires did not fare so well. Mission 66 eventually helped the service adequately meet the swarms, but concessions worsened. Yet even that problem was met, at least partially, and in 1984 visitors could obtain respectable services in acceptable facilities. As for the Park Service, it is used to functioning with less money by far than it needs. It will prevail.

In 1982 Representative John F. Seiberling's Subcommittee on Public Lands and National Parks asked then-Superintendent John Townsley what Yellowstone's three greatest problems were. He cited potential threats from a proposal to develop geothermal power at Island Park west of the reservation; proliferation of oil and gas leases—and the implications thereof—on the peripheries, especially outside the east boundary; and problems of maintaining a beautiful wilderness through which passed 2.5 million visitors a year. A fourth problem has also been discussed here: that is, bears, most especially Yellowstone grizzlies.

The geothermal menace is much more threatening than common sense might indicate (namely, the obvious belief that so much superheated magma lies under the region that some geothermal exploitation could not possibly affect Yellowstone). Unfortunately, experiences with other thermally active parts of the world do not grant this assurance. The Beowawe Geysers in Nevada were thus exploited in the 1940s, and the field dried up; the geysers of Steamboat Springs near Reno likewise succumbed to geothermal use. An entire area, the SPA in New Zealand, is now dormant due to geothermal energy development.[28]

If oil and gas prospecting takes place, and a field is brought in, probably the howl from conservationists will be so loud that the companies, if they do develop the find, will have to spend millions to hide their industrial christmas trees, pumping jacks, and pipelines.[28]

Already, in its 112-year history, a historian can detect the influence of the pulsation of national attitudes, the swinging of the pendulum, as it is sometimes called, upon park destiny. In 1984 a move was underway, initiated by a lawsuit filed by the National Rifle Association, to force national parks and monuments to allow trapping and hunting within the reservations. A century ago poachers killed elk for their molars, which were sold to members of the Benevolent and Protective Order of Elks for use as watch fobs. Today poachers kill the elk for their antlers, which, ground into powder, are sold in Korea as an expensive aphrodisiac. Pilferers no longer pursue buffalo; now they capture falcons (hawks) which are sold to Near East oil moguls to be used in the ancient sport of falconry.

As for the 2.5 million visitors: again, the service will handle the problems. It is a bit premature for someone to write articles such as "Will the National Parks Survive?" No one has yet suggested filling in Yellowstone's Grand Canyon or jamming the thermal wonders, or firing the forests, draining the lakes, or, since the 1930s, damming them or tunneling under the park mountains. More timely is the question of the quality of the wilderness with all those visitors passing through. The answer is that the park will still be worth seeing. It will not be as John Colter saw it in 1807 and 1808. It will be a semipristine land of forests and streams and lakes and geysers. Save for concessions at specified locations, it will lack commercial exploitation. In a nation of 235 million people, who can ask for more?

NOTES TO CHAPTER FIFTEEN

1. Author's interview with retired Superintendent Edmund G. Rogers, Denver, Colorado, October 21, 1971.

2. For more about Mission 66, see Conrad Wirth, *Parks, Politics, and People,* (Norman: University of Oklahoma Press, 1980), 237–84.

3. 90th Congress, Senate, 1st Sess., "Control of Elk Population, Yellowstone National Park: Hearings Before a Subcommittee of the Committee on Appropriations United States Senate," March 11, 1967, 81. Herafter referred to as Hearings.

4. Ibid., 13–14.

5. Ibid., 102–7.

6. Ibid., 100.

7. Ibid., 100; 78; 82.

8. For a recent study showing western attitudes see Richard D. Lamm and Michael McCarthy, *The Angry West,* (Boston: Houghton Mifflin Co., 1982).

9. Hearings, 10.

10. Ibid., 2–3; 35.

11. Ibid., 69.

12. *New York Times*, January 28, 1982, A-14.

13. Ibid.

14. See also Superintendent's Report, 1982, 33–39, and *New York Times*, January 28, 1982, A-14. See also Mary Meagher, *The Bison of Yellowstone Park* (Washington: National Park Service, 1973). Detailed, accurate, scholarly, and dull.

15. Hearings, 17.

16. Alston Chase, "The Last Bears of Yellowstone," *The Atlantic*, Vol. 251, No. 2 (February, 1983), 63–73; for the Park Service reply see Paul Schullery's letter and Mr. Chase's reply in Letters to the Editor, *The Atlantic*, Vol. 251, No. 5 (May, 1983), 4–5. See also Gary Blonston, "Where Nature Takes Its Course," *Science 83* (November, 1983), 43–33.
Much of the knowledge we have of the Yellowstone grizzlies is based upon the research of Frank and John Craighead. See John and Frank Craighead, "Knocking Out Grizzly Bears for Their Own Good," *National Geographic*, Vol. 118, No. ? (August, 1960), 276–91; John Craighead, "Studying Grizzly Habitat by Satellite," *National Geographic*, Vol. 150, No. 1 (July, 1976), 148–58; Frank Craighead, Jr. , and John Craighead, "Trailing Yellowstone's Grizzlies by Radio," *National Geographic*, Vol. 130, No. 2 (August, 1966), 252–57.

17. Superintendent's Report for 1982; Jim Jubak, "Only Teamwork Can Save the Yellowstone Grizzly," *National Parks*, Vol. 55, No. 9–10 (September-October, 1981), 28–30; Tom McNamee, "Breath-Holding in Grizzly Country," *Audubon*, Vol. 48, No. 6 (November, 1982), 69–83.

18. Chase, "Last Bears of Yellowstone."

19. McNamee, "Breath Holding," 83.

20. 86th Congress, 2d Sess., Senate, "Hearings Before a Subcommittee of the Committee on Appropriations . . . on Proposed Boating Regulations on Yellowstone Lake," (1960). Hereafter referred to as "Boat Hearings."

21. Ibid.

22. *National Parks*, Vo. 34, No. 149 (February, 1960), 16; "Boat Hearings," 33–34.

23. *National Parks*, Vol. 34, No. 154 (July, 1960), 14; Ibid., Vol. 35, No. 161 (February, 1961), 14; Ibid., No. 167 (August, 1961), 2; 9.

24. Ibid., (August, 1961), 19.

25. Ibid.

26. *Code of Federal Regulations,* Title 36, "Parks, Forests, and Public Property," (1981), Chapter 7:13.

27. U.S. Congress, House, Committee on Government Operations, *Electric Power Contract for Yellowstone National Park,* 86th Cong., 1st Sess. House Report 1932 (1960), 20 pp.; Moss quotation from page 20.

28. "ENERGY: Geothermal Lease Plans Threaten Yellowstone's Geysers," *Audubon,* Vol. 84, No. 3 (May, 1982), pp. 104–105.
The dangers of encroachment on Yellowstone's borders are nevertheless frightening. See Bill Schneider, "The Incredible Shrinking Wilderness," *National Parks,* Vol. 56 (January-February, 1982), 20–26. The map on page 382 brings chills to the spine of anyone interested in the preservation of Yellowstone.

Epilogue

*O*ccasionally Yellowstone visitors gazing upon Old Faithful's rising plumes of water and steam sight the contrails of Air Force bombers as they fly in the turquoise sky 30,000 feet over the park. Possibly the aircraft are from Mahlstrom Air Force Base at Great Falls, Montana. Perhaps they are on a practice run in which atomic destruction is theoretically lodged in the bomb bays.

The contrast between happy people observing a nature-made geyser in a national park administered by the federal government "for all the people," and a bomber manned by intelligent, highly trained personnel capable of using their equipment and expertise to destroy hundreds of thousands of human beings considered enemies of America, is striking.

Despite the expensive, sophisticated, almost incredible technology invested by the government in the bomber, it still represents nothing more than a manifestation of war, "common defense," one of the original reasons why governments came to be.

But Yellowstone National Park represents what an enlightened government can accomplish for its citizenry. It is a vast reservation for independent leisure. It is nature maintained as much as possible for everyone, not for a nobility, a military elite, the super rich, or any privileged class. Anyone can go there who has the money and the time, and in America a substantial portion of citizens possess those prerequisites.

It has not been an easy task maintaining Yellowstone; humanity has proliferated, increased technologies have made it easier to get there, mercenary entrepreneurs have allowed greed to exceed respect for the wilderness, and government has seemed always too busy with other tasks to devote time to Yellowstone's problems.

And yet the park, a wilderness besieged in myriad ways, has remained. There it is, still wilderness, still beautiful, still friendly and inviting, a testament to what governments or, if we wish, strong-minded men of good will can accomplish when they operate at their best.

And this will happen: Some day a recreational vehicle will pass through one of Yellowstone's entrances, a vehicle with a very special passenger. He is a lad of tender age, eight, ten, possibly twelve years old. He is sprawled on the mattress in that tiny bunk area over the truck cab while mother and teenage sister sit inside it beside dad, who is driving. Propped on his elbows, hands on his ruddy cheeks, the boy gazes at the pines, the mountains, the geysers, thrills at the sight of an elk or a moose, and observes Old Glory waving in the breeze at a ranger station. The lad's heart is filled with pride and love of country. Sometimes, his mother tells him, he dreams too much. But there is something about the lad. He wants to do great things, *good* things.

He is impressionable now, and he leaves Yellowstone National Park with warm, happy memories of so much that is good about America—and so much more good can be achieved, his parents tell him, if Americans will try.

Some day that lad (or lass)—one of hundreds of thousands who have observed Yellowstone from the little window over the cab—will be President of the United States.

And he will be one of the great ones.

Select Bibliography

The long research journey that led to the writing of this book precludes an exhaustive bibliography, while limiting it only to "sources cited" distorts the true extent of research conducted. Moreover, as the reader should be well aware, notes throughout this book are numerous, comprehensive, and in many cases annotated. At today's publishing costs, excessive repetition of sources seems unwarranted. Yet the desire remains to provide the interested reader and researcher with a helpful, succinct source of additional information. Within these bounds the following essay and listing of selected sources have been prepared.

ARCHIVAL SOURCES

Park headquarters and the post office address of Yellowstone National Park, Wyoming, are actually Mammoth Hot Springs at the extreme northern edge of the reservation. The Yellowstone Archives are housed at the museum there. Filed in boxes or in huge, old volumes is Correspondence Received and Sent, generally from 1882 until 1918; the U.S. Commissioner's court records; and station reports and records of the park's army era. Much of the correspondence is letterpress or otherwise duplicated; the originals are likely to crop up among pertinent records in the National Archives in Washington. Nevertheless, for research into the army period in Yellowstone, the Yellowstone Archives are absolutely essential.

The Yellowstone Park Archives have been reorganized twice since I used them. Strictly speaking, they should be housed at the Federal Records Center in Denver, where they would be much more accessible to researchers than in faraway Yellowstone Park, and be serviced by professional archivists. (Note: The manuscripts, pamphlets, and rare books in the Yellowstone Library are mentioned elsewhere in this essay.)

The National Archives houses several Record Groups that are indispensable for study of the Yellowstone Park. The most obvious one is R.G. 79, Records of the National Park Service. The researcher should obtain National Archives Publication No. 62-2, "Preliminary Inventories No. 66, Records of the National Park Service," compiled by Edward E. Hill, (Washington: National Archives, General Services Administration, 1966). A scholar, even if investigating a single national park or monument, must be selective, for the quantity of materials in this massive collection is overwhelming.

For the early period (1872 to 1907) I have used from R.G. 79, Letters Received and Letters Sent by the Office Of Secretary of the Interior Relating to National Parks: Yellowstone. Categories in R.G. 79 for the more recent period, sometimes rewarding and often disappointing, are records pertaining to the Civilian Conservation Corps (usually disappointing) and small collections of official correspondence of Horace Albright, Roger W. Toll, and other superintendents and Park Service directors.

I used more extensively papers in R.G. 48, Records of the Office of the Secretary of the Interior. A part of this Record Group, useful for the earlier period (1872 to 1907) are "Records of the Office of the Secretary of the Interior Regarding Yellowstone National Park, in the Patents and Miscellaneous Division." They are especially rewarding for information about superintendents and assistant superintendents. From R.G. 48 I also used records of the Appointments Division, Letters Received and Letters Sent, 1872–1886.

Of greatest significance for the period 1907 to 1936 was R.G. 48: Department of the Interior, Office of the Secretary of the Interior, Central Classified File: Yellowstone Park. This voluminous category is further subclassified by subject: Roads, Rules and Regulations, Timber, Wild Animals, [Yellowstone] Lake, Administration, Boundaries, Privileges [which includes concessionaire relations], Lands, etc. Because only the important or controversial matters make their way from superintendent through Park Service director to the secretary, these records are filled with good material.

R.G. 57: Records of the United States Geological Survey, contain the Arnold Hague papers. Hague's assignment was to study Yellowstone's geology. He came to both know and love the park as few did and, with powerful contacts in Washington, he made park protection almost his avocation. His papers are enlightening for the period 1883 until about 1900.

R.G. 98: Records of the United States Army Commands: Fort Yellowstone, Letters Sent, 1902–1906; Post General and Special Orders, Memorandums and Circulars, 1891–1913, was a valuable source for understanding "the army way" of making Yellowstone National Park secure.

I also consulted R.G. 115, Records of the U.S. Bureau of Reclamation, for pertinent material on the Falls River Project and the proposed Yellowstone Lake Dam.

Northern Pacific Company Records in custody of the Minnesota Historical Society, St. Paul; I was allowed to delve into these records prior to their being prepared for public use. Most useful is the President's Subject File: Yellowstone. Park matters crop up in a number of other places in these records.

MANUSCRIPTS
(Including Dissertations and Unpublished Reports)

The greatest source of manuscripts—letters, journals, diaries, reminiscences, and typescripts given by their owners or from other collections—is the Yellowstone Library in the museum building at Mammoth Hot Springs. Those manuscripts I list have been cited in the text. Many, many more are on deposit at the library.

Although tourist memorabilia are to be found just about anywhere, manuscripts of key individuals in Yellowstone history, be they businessmen or government officials, are much more difficult to come by. The listing below shows the geographical range of these collections, from Washington, D.C., to Los Angeles, California.

Barbee, Robert D. "Annual Report of the Superintendent of Yellowstone National Park for 1982." Courtesy of Timothy R. Manns, North District Naturalist/Historian, Yellowstone National Park.

Boutelle, F. A. Papers, Special Collections, University of Oregon Library, University of Oregon, Eugene, Oregon

Brackett, Julia S. "Information Received from Mrs. Julia S. Brackett." Yellowstone Library.

Bullock, Seth. "Diary of a Trip to the Yellowstone in 1872." Montana Historical Society, Helena, Montana.

Child, Harry W. "Miscellaneous Files." K. Ross Toole Collection, Missoula, Montana.

Doane, Lieutenant Gustavus C. "Exploration of Snake River from Yellowstone Lake to Columbia." Typescript, Yellowstone Library.

Grinnell, George Bird. "Through Two-Ocean Pass." Grinnell Papers, Southwest Museum, Los Angeles.

Hagan, Olaf T. "Interview with G. W. Marshall." Bancroft Library; also in the Information Files of the National Park Service in offices (as of 1980) at 1100 "L" Street, N. W., Washington, D.C.

Haynes, F. Jay. "Diary." In custody of Mrs. Bessie Haynes Arnold, Tucson, Arizona.

Hays, Howard H. Collection. American Heritage Center, University of Wyoming, Laramie.

Lacey, Michael James. "The Mysteries of Earth-Making Dissolve: A Study of Washington's Intellectual Community and the Origins of American Intellectualism in the Late Nineteenth Century." Ph. D. Dissertation, George Washington University, Washington, D.C., 1979.

LeHardy, Paul. "Expedition into Yellowstone Plateau under Captain W. A. Jones in 1873." Typescript in Yellowstone Library.

Norris, Philetus. Papers. Henry E. Huntington Library, San Marino, California. These papers are a collection of disorganized material, primarily clippings of Norris's long letters home when he was traveling in the West. Some Yellowstone material is included.

Northern Pacific Papers. Robert Lewis Peterson Collection, Missoula, Montana.

O'Brien, Robert R. "The Yellowstone National Park Road System: Past, Present, and Future." Ph. D. Dissertation, University of Washington, Seattle, 1964.

Osmund, Mabel Cross. "Memoirs of a Trip Through the Yellowstone National Park in 1874." Yellowstone Library.

Phillips-Myers Papers. Southern History Collection, University of North Carolina, Chapel Hill.

Sherman, W. T. Papers, Manuscripts Division, Library of Congress. Box No. 55.

Switzer, M. A. "1876 Trip to the Geysers Written as a Diary in a Book Dated 1874." Library, Montana State University, Bozeman.

INTERVIEWS

Although I have acquired important Yellowstone information from scores of individuals, the following persons are mentioned because they granted me somewhat formal, scheduled interviews or their information was of such significance that they deserve mention.

Horace Marden Albright and I spent a long autumn afternoon in 1970 in Los Angeles discussing his experiences as a Yellowstone superintendent. He in turn gave me Mrs. Bessie Haynes Arnold's address in Tucson, Arizona. The following year Mrs. Arnold granted me three days of in-depth questioning. She was a spry ninety-two years old at the time, but her memory was incredible. Each morning she informed me of what she had not recalled the day before—during the night her memory had returned. With her collection of over five thousand microscopic seashells, she was the most extraordinary person I have ever met.

My intereview with former Superintendent Edmund B. Rogers at his Denver home was valuable, but Mr. Rogers was not in good health and out of consideration for him I left after about two hours with many questions never asked.

One of my most pleasant interviews was with Mrs. Jane Reamer White in her Tryon, North Carolina, home. She supplied me then, and with correspondence both before and after, with much of my information on her architect father, Robert Reamer.

To mention a few of the many others who have given of their time, Professors K. Ross Toole and Robert L. Peterson of the University of Montana gave not only of their time but made available manuscripts in their possession. Briefly, John Burchell, at the time Chief of the Division of Concessions at Yellowstone, gave me a succinct lecture on his views of N.P.S. concession policies. One autumn while working in the park archives I stopped at the Ragsdale Ranch in Paradise Valley and spent a late afternoon and evening learning about the country north of the park and the view those people had of Yellowstone.

At my own Florida State University I interviewed Mr. Ashby Stiff of the School of Restaurant and Hotel Management who in the late 1960s managed Canyon Village for the Yellowstone Park Company.

Finally, the long hours I spent one summer with Aubrey Haines, "Mr. Yellowstone," the official park historian, cannot be overlooked. No one alive knows more of the history of Yellowstone National Park than does Mr. Haines. Beyond giving me all kinds of factual information, he instilled in me the "flavor" of *The Yellowstone Story* (as he named his own Yellowstone history). His kindness that summer exceeded his official obligations, and for his thoughtfulness I thank him.

PUBLIC DOCUMENTS

These citations include Congressional hearings, publications of government bureaus, annual reports of the secretaries of executive departments, and diverse other publications produced by the United States Government Printing Office which, to save space is abbreviated G.P.O.

"The American Bison in the United States and Canada." Sen. Doc. 147, 57th Cong., lst Sess. (1902).

Annual Reports of the Chief of Engineers

Annual Reports of the Secretary of the Interior

Annual Reports of the Secretary of War

Baldwin, Kenneth H. *Enchanted Enclosure: The Army Engineers and Yellowstone Park.* Washington: G.P.O., 1976.

Battle, David C., and Thompson, Erwin N. *Fort Yellowstone: Historical Structure Report.* Denver Service Center: National Park Service, 1972.

Compendium of the Tenth Census, 1880.

Cramton, Louis C. *Early History of Yellowstone National Park and Its Relation to National Park Policies.* Washington: G.P.O., 1932.

Gibbon, General John. "Report of the Commanding General of the Department of Dakota, General Gibbon Commanding." *Annual Report of the Secretary of War.* House Exec. Doc. No. 1, 45th Cong., 3rd Sess. (1878).

Gregory, Lieutenant-Colonel James F. "Report of Lieutenant General P. H. Sheridan . . . of his Expedition Through the Big Horn Mountains." Washington: G.P.O., 1882.

Hague, Arnold. *Geology of the Yellowstone Park.* U.S. Geological Survey, Monograph No. 32, Part 2. Washington: G.P.O., 1899.

Hayden, Ferdinand Vandiveer. *Sixth Annual Report of the United States Geological and Geographical Survey of the Territories.* Washington: G.P.O., 1872.

———. *Twelfth Annual Report of the United States Geological and Geographical Survey of the Territories.* 2 Vols. Washington: G.P.O., 1883.

Jones, Captain William A. *Report Upon the Reconnaissance of Northwestern Wyoming Including Yellowstone National Park Made in the Summer of 1873.* U.S. Congress, House Exec. Doc. 285, 43rd Cong., 1st Sess., 1875. Serial No. 1615.

Journey Through the Yellowstone National Park and Northwestern Wyoming, 1883. Photographs of Party and Scenery Along the Route Traveled, and Copies of the Associated Press Dispatches Sent Whilst En Route. Washington: G.P.O., 1883. (This is President Arthur's trip).

Kappler, Charles J. *Indian Affairs: Laws and Treaties.* 4 Vols. Washington: G.P.O., 1903–1929.

Keefer, William R. "The Geologic Story of Yellowstone National Park." U.S. Geological Survey Bulletin No. 1347. Washington: G.P.O., 1972.

Langford, Nathaniel J. "Report of the Superintendent of the Yellowstone National Park for the Year 1872." In *Annual Report of the Secretary of the Interior for 1872.* Washington: G.P.O., 1873.

Ludlow, Captain William. *Report of a Reconnaissance from Carroll, Montana Territory, on the Upper Missouri to the Yellowstone National Park and Return Made in the Summer of 1875.* Washington: G.P.O., 1876.

Meagher, Mary, *The Bison of Yellowstone Park.* Washington: National Park Service, 1973.

Norris, Philetus. "Annual Report of the Superintendent of Yellowstone National Park for 1877." In *Annual Report of the Secretary of the Interior for 1877.* Washington: G.P.O., 1878.

Phillips, W. Hallett. "Special Report to the Secretary [of the Interior] Dated September 12, 1885." Later published as "Letter of W. H. Phillips on the Yellowstone Park." Senate Exec. Doc. No. 51, 49th Cong., 1st Sess., 1885. Serial No. 2333.

Sheridan, General P. H., and Sherman, General W. T. *Reports of Inspection Made in the Summer of 1877 by General P. H. Sheridan and W. T. Sherman of Country North of the Union Pacific Railroad.* Washington: G.P.O., 1878.

Statistical Abstract of the United States, 1974. Washington: G.P.O., 1974.

United States Department of the Interior. *General Information Regarding the Yellowstone National Park for the Season of 1912.* Washington: G.P.O., 1912.

———. National Park Service. "Yellowstone National Park Concessions Management Review of the Yellowstone Park Company." Washington: National Park Service, 1977.

U.S., Congress. *Congressional Record,* Washington, D.C.

———. House, Committee on Government Operations, *Electric Power Contract for Yellowstone National Park,* 86th Cong., 1st Sess. House Report 1932 (1960), 20 pp.

———. House. "Inquiry Into the Management and Control of the Yellowstone National Park." 52d Cong., 1st Sess., 1892. Serial 3051.

———. Senate. "Control of Elk Population, Yellowstone National Park: Hearings Before a Subcommittee of the Committee on Appropriations United States Senate, March 11, 1967." 90th Cong., 1st Sess., 1967.

———. Senate. "Hearings Before a Subcommittee of the Committee on Appropriations . . . on Proposed Boating Regulations for Yellowstone Lake." 86th Cong.,
2d Sess., 1960.
United States Statutes at Large.
Wilson, A. D. "Report of A. D. Wilson, Chief Topographer." In Ferdinand V.
Hayden. *Eleventh Annual Report of the United States Geological and Geographical Survey.* Washington: G.P.O., 1878.

NEWSPAPERS

The one newspaper that is a gold mine of information on Yellowstone National Park
is the *Livingston Enterprise,* both the daily and weekly editions. Whoever edited this
newspaper in the era 1883 to 1920 was far above the general run of country editor. It
is small-town journalism at its best, and a delight to use. I covered many entire years
and spot checked many other periods when matters of concern demanded it.

Other newspapers received study during several periods that I was researching.
Among them were the *Bozeman Avant Courier, Chicago Tribune, Christian Science
Monitor, Denver Post, London Times, Minneapolis Pioneer Press, Montana Standard*
(Butte); *The New Northwest* (Deer Lodge, Montana); *New York Graphic, New York
Times, St. Louis Post-Dispatch,* and *Washington Post.*

In addition, a number of newspapers are quoted in the text with the additional
information that the stories are included in the Yellowstone Scrapbooks in the Yellowstone Museum. This is especially true of the scrapbook labeled "Irrigation 1919–
1921." Because of isolated references, the above listing does not necessarily represent
every newspaper quoted in the text.

PERIODICALS

Albatross (White Motor Car Company
    house organ)
American Journal of Science and Arts

American Naturalist
American West
Annals of Wyoming

Atlantic Monthly
Audubon
Auk
Century Magazine
California History
Forest and Stream
Frank Leslie's Weekly
Harper's Magazine
Harper's New Monthly Magazine
Idaho Yesterdays
Independent
Inside Husky (Husky Oil Company house
    organ)
Literary Digest
Montana: The Magazine of Western History
Nation

National Geographic
National Municipal Review
National Parks
Nature
Old Cars
Outing
Outing and the Wheelman
Outlook
Pacific Northwest Quarterly
Railway Age
Saturday Evening Post
Science 83
Scientific American
Wisconsin Magazine of History
World's Work
Youth Companion

LIBRARIES AND
HISTORICAL SOCIETIES

American Heritage Center, University of Wyoming, Laramie, Wyoming
Buffalo Bill Historical Center, Cody, Wyoming
Colorado State Historical Society, Denver, Colorado
DeGolyer Foundation Library, Dallas, Texas
Denver Public Library, Western History Room, Denver, Colorado
Department of the Interior Natural Resources Library, Washington, D.C.
Huntington Library, San Marino, California
Idaho State Historical Society, Boise, Idaho
Library of Congress, Washington, D.C.
Minnesota Historical Society, St. Paul, Minnesota
Montana Historical Society, Helena, Montana
Montana State University Library, Bozeman, Montana
Newberry Library, Chicago, Illinois
Norlin Library, University of Colorado, Boulder, Colorado
Robert Manning Strozier Library, Florida State University, Tallahassee, Florida
Southwest Museum, Los Angeles, California
State Historical Society of North Dakota, Bismarck, North Dakota

University of Texas Library, Austin, Texas
Wyoming State Archives and History Department, Cheyenne, Wyoming
Yellowstone National Park Library, Mammoth Hot Springs, Wyoming

SECONDARY SOURCES:
BOOKS, ARTICLES, PAMPHLETS

Because of the thoroughness of the notes, many of which are annotated, secondary sources are listed without annotation. The listing is broken down into "Books" and "Articles and Pamphlets." Many books and articles, some very significant, were consulted but not cited.

BOOKS

Adams, Henry. *The Education of Henry Adams*. New York: The Modern Library, 1931.
_____. *Henry Adams and His Friends*. Edited by Harold Dean Cater. Boston: Houghton Mifflin Co., 1938.
_____. *Letters of Henry Adams*. Edited by Worthington Chauncey Ford. Boston: Houghton Mifflin Co., 1938.
Albright, Horace Marden, and Taylor, Frank J. *"Oh, Ranger!" A Book About the National Parks*. Rev. ed., New York: Dodd, Mead & Co., 1934.
Allen, E. T., and Day, Arthur L. *Hot Springs of the Yellowstone National Park*. Washington: Carnegie Institution of Washington, 1935.
Athearn, Robert G. *William Tecumseh Sherman and the Settlement of the West*. Norman: University of Oklahoma Press, 1956.
Augspurger, Marie M. *Yellowstone National Park: Historical and Descriptive*. Middletown, Ohio: The Naegele-Auer Printing Co., 1948.
Badger, Joseph E., Jr. *Diamond Dirk, or, The Mystery of the Yellowstone*. New York: Beadle's Pocket Library No. 13, 1876(?).
Baldwin, Mrs. Alice Blackwell. *Memoirs of the Late Frank D. Baldwin, Major General, U.S.A.* Edited by Brigadier General W. C. Brown, Colonel C. C. Smith, and E. A. Brininstool. Los Angeles: Press of the Wetzel Publishing Co., 1929.
Bartlett, Richard A. *Great Surveys of the American West*. Norman: University of Oklahoma Press, 1962; 1981.
_____. *Nature's Yellowstone*. Albuquerque: University of New Mexico Press, 1974.
Beal, Merrill D. *"I Will Fight No More Forever": Chief Joseph and the Nez Perce War*. Seattle: University of Washington Press, 1963.

Belasco, Warren James. *Americans on the Road: From Autocamp to Motel, 1910-1945*. Cambridge: Massachusetts Institute of Technology, 1979.

Betts, Robert B. *Along the Ramparts of the Tetons: The Saga of Jackson Hole, Wyoming*. Boulder: Colorado Associated University Press, 1979.

Bonney, Orrin H., and Bonney, Lorraine. *Guide to the Wyoming Mountains and Wilderness Areas*. Denver: Sage Books, 1960.

————. *Battle Drums and Geysers: Lieutenant Doane*. Chicago: The Swallow Press, 1970.

————. *Bonney's Guide: Grand Teton National Park and Jackson Hole*. Houston: Published by the Authors, 1972.

Brimlow, George F. *The Bannock Indian Wars of 1878*. Caldwell, Idaho: The Caxton Printers, 1958.

Brower, J. V. *The Missouri River and Its Ultimate Source*. Minneapolis: Harrison and Smith, 1893.

Brown, Mark H. *The Flight of the Nez Perce*. New York: G. P. Putnam's Sons, 1967.

————. *The Plainsmen of the Yellowstone*. Lincoln: University of Nebraska Press, 1969.

Brownlow, Kevin. *The War the West and the Wilderness*. New York: Alfred Knopf, 1978.

Burroughs, John. *Tramping and Camping with Roosevelt*. Boston: Houghton Mifflin Co., 1907.

Carpenter, Frank D. *Adventures in Geyserland*. Edited by Heister Dean Guie and Lucullus Virgil McWhorter. Caldwell, Idaho: Caxton Printers, 1935.

Carpenter, John A. *Sword and Olive Branch: Oliver Otis Howard*. Pittsburgh: University of Pittsburgh Press, 1964.

Chittenden, Hiram Martin. *The Yellowstone National Park*. First Edition. Cincinnati: R. Clark & Co., 1895.

Craighead, Frank C., Jr. *Track of the Grizzly*. 1979. San Francisco: Sierra Club Paperback Library, 1982.

Crook, General George. *General George Crook, His Autobiography*. Norman: University of Oklahoma Press, 1946; 1960.

Cutright, Paul Russell. *Theodore Roosevelt the Naturalist*. New York: Harper & Brothers, 1956.

Dale, Edward Everett. *The Range Cattle Industry*. Norman: University of Oklahoma Press, 1930.

Dallas, Sandra. *No More than Five in a Bed*. Norman: University of Oklahoma Press, 1967.

Dodds, Gordon B. *Hiram Martin Chittenden: His Public Career*. Lexington: University of Kentucky Press, 1973.

Dudley, William Henry. *The National Park from the Hurricane Deck of a Cayuse, or, The Liederkrantz Expedition to Geyserland*. Butte City, Montana: F. Loeber, 1886.

Dunraven, Windham Thomas Wyndham-Quin, 4th Earl of. *The Great Divide*. London: Chatto and Windus, 1876.

Durkin, Joseph T. *General Sherman's Son*. New York: Farrar, Strauss, and Cudahy, 1959.

Easton, Robert, and Brown, Mackenzie. *Lord of Beasts, The Saga of Buffalo Jones.* 1961. Lincoln: University of Nebraska Press, 1970.

Elliott, L. Louise. *Six Weeks on Horseback Through Yellowstone Park.* Rapid City, South Dakota: *The Rapids City Journal,* 1913.

Ellis, Elmer. *Henry Moore Teller: Defender of the West.* Caldwell, Idaho: The Caxton Printers, 1941.

Everhart, William G. *The National Park Service.* New York: Praeger, 1972.

Foresta, Ronald A. *America's National Parks and Their Keepers.* Washington, D.C.: Resources for the Future, 1984.

Garretson, Martin S. *The American Bison.* New York: New York Zoological Society, 1938.

Glasscock, C. B. *The Gasoline Age: The Story of the Men Who Made It.* New York: The Bobbs-Merrill Co., 1937.

Golze, Alfred Rudolph. *Reclamation in the United States.* Caldwell, Idaho: The Caxton Printers, 1952.

Grinnell, George Bird. *The Passing of the Great West: Selected Papers of George Bird Grinnell.* Edited by John F. Reiger. New York: Winchester Press, 1972.

———. *Hunting at High Altitudes: The Book of the Boone and Crockett Club.* Edited by George Bird Grinnell. New York: Harper and Brothers, 1913.

Guptill, A. B. *Practical Guide to Yellowstone National Park.* St. Paul, F. Jay Haynes and Bro., 1890.

Haines, Aubrey L. *The Yellowstone Story.* Two vols. Boulder: Yellowstone Library and Museum Association with Colorado Associated University Press, 1977.

———. *The Valley of the Upper Yellowstone.* Norman: University of Oklahoma Press, 1965.

Haines, Francis. *The Nez Perces.* Norman: University of Oklahoma Press, 1955.

Hampton, H. Duane. *How The U.S. Cavalry Saved Our National Parks.* Bloomington: Indiana University Press, 1971.

Hardman, William. *A Trip to America.* London: T. V. Wood, 1884.

Harrison, Jim. *Legends of the Fall.* New York: Dalacorte Press/ Seymour Lawrence, 1979.

Hay, John. *Letters and Diaries of John Hay.* Edited by Clara S. Hay. Three vols. Washington: Printed but not Published, 1908.

Hays, Samuel P. *Conservation and the Gospel of Efficiency.* 1959. New York: Atheneum, 1979.

Houston, Douglas B. *Northern Yellowstone Elk.* New York. Macmillan, 1982.

Howe, George Frederick. *Chester A. Arthur: A Quarter Century of Machine Politics.* New York: Dodd, Mead and Company, 1934.

Huntley, Chet. *The Generous Years.* New York: Random House, 1968.

Huth, Hans. *Nature and the American: Three Centuries of Changing Attitudes.* 1957. Lincoln: University of Nebraska Press, 1972.

Ise, John. *Our National Park Policy.* Baltimore: Johns Hopkins University Press, 1960.

James, George Wharton. *Reclaiming the Arid West: The Story of the United States Reclamation Service.* New York: Dodd, Mead, & Co., 1917.

Johannsen, Albert. *The House of Beadle and Adams*. Three vols. Norman: University of Oklahoma Press, 1950.

Jones, Billie M. *Health-Seekers of the Southwest, 1817–1900,* Norman: University of Oklahoma Press, 1967.

Jones, Buffalo (Charles Jesse). *Buffalo Jones' Adventures on the Plains*. Compiled by Colonel Henry Inman. Lincoln: University of Nebraska Press, 1970.

Jordan, David Starr. *The Days of Man*. Two vols. New York: World Book Co., 1922.

Journey Through the Yellowstone Park and Northwest Wyoming. 1883. No place: no publisher, no date. Copy in custody of the DeGolyer Foundation Library.

Kipling, Rudyard. *From Sea to Sea, and Other Sketches; Letters of Travel*. Two vols. London: Macmillan Co., 1904.

———. *American Notes: Rudyard Kipling's West*. Edited by Arrell Morgan Gibson. Norman: University of Oklahoma Press, 1981.

Kirk, Ruth. *Exploring Yellowstone*. Seattle: Yellowstone Library and Museum Association in cooperation with University of Washington Press, 1972.

Lamm, Richard D., and McCarthy, Michael. *The Angry West*. Boston: Houghton Mifflin Co., 1982.

Langford, Nathaniel Pitt. *The Discovery of Yellowstone Park*. Edited by Aubrey L. Haines. Lincoln: University of Nebraska Press, 1972.

———. *Vigilante Days and Ways*. Chicago: A. C. McClurg and Co., 1912.

Leeson, Michael A., Editor. *History of Montana, 1739–1885*. Chicago: Warner, Beers & Co., 1885.

Leopold, Aldo. *Sand County Almanac*. New York: Oxford University Press, 1949.

LeRoy, Bruce. *Hiram Martin Chittenden, A Western Epic*. Tacoma, Washington: Washington State Historical Society, 1961.

Leuchtenburg, William E. *Franklin D. Roosevelt and the New Deal*. New York: Harper & Row, 1963.

McCoy, Tim, and McCoy, Ronald. *Tim McCoy Remembers the West*. Garden City, New York: Doubleday & Co., 1977.

McDougall, W. B., and Baggley, Herma A. *Plants of Yellowstone National Park*. Yellowstone Park: Yellowstone Library and Museum Association, 1956.

McHugh, Tom. *The Time of the Buffalo*. New York: Alfred Knopf, 1972.

Madsen, Betty M., and Madsden, Brigham D. *North to Montana!* Salt Lake City: University of Utah Press, 1980.

Madsen, Brigham D. *The Bannock of Idaho*. Caldwell, Idaho: The Caxton Printers, 1958.

Malone, Michael P., and Roeder, Richard B. *Montana: A History of Two Centuries*. Seattle: University of Washington Press, 1976.

Manning, Thomas C. *Government in Science: The U.S. Geological Survey, 1867–1894*. Lexington: University of Kentucky Press, 1967.

Miller, Joaquin. *An Illustrated History of Montana*. Two vols. Chicago: The Lewis Publishing Co., 1894.

Nash, Roderick. *Wilderness and the American Mind*. Revised Edition. New Haven: Yale University Press, 1978.

Newhall, Nancy. *The Conservationist Activities of John D. Rockefeller*. New York: Alfred A. Knopf, 1957.

Norris, Philetus. *The Calumet of the Coteau*. Philadelphia: J. B. Lippincott & Co., 1883.

Norton, Henry J. *Wonder-Land Illustrated: or, Horseback Rides Through the Yellowstone National Park*. Virginia City: No publisher, 1873.

Overton, Richard C. *Burlington Route: A History of the Burlington Lines*. New York: Alfred Knopf, 1965.

Pammel, L. H., Editor, *Major John F. Lacey Memorial Volume*. Cedar Rapids, Iowa: The Torch Press for the Iowa Park and Forestry Association of Ames, Iowa, 1915.

Pinchot, Gifford. *Breaking New Ground*. New York: Harcourt, Brace and Co. 1947.

Pomeroy, Earl. *In Search of the Golden West*. New York: Alfred Knopf, 1956.

Raftery, John H. *The Story of Yellowstone*. Butte: McKee Publishing Co., 1912.

Randall, Leslie W. (Gay). *Footprints Along the Yellowstone*. San Antonio: The Naylor Co., 1961.

Rand McNally and Co. *Auto Road Atlas of the United States*. Facsimile Edition, 1926. Chicago: Rand McNally and Co., 1974.

Reeves, Thomas C. *Gentleman Boss: The Life of Chester Alan Arthur*. New York: Alfred A. Knopf, 1975.

Reiger, John F. *American Sportsmen and the Origins of Conservation*. New York: Winchester Publishing Co., 1975.

Richards, Mrs. Mary B. *Camping Out in the Yellowstone*. Salem, Massachusetts: Newcomb and Gauss, 1910.

Richardson, James. *Wonders of the Yellowstone*. New York: Charles Scribner's Sons, 1889.

Righter, Robert W. *Crucible for Conservation: The Creation of Grand Teton National Park*. Boulder: Colorado Associated University Press, 1982.

Robinson, Michael C. *Water for the West: The Bureau of Reclamation 1902–1977*. Chicago: Public Works Historical Society, 1979.

Roe, Frank Gilbert. *The North American Buffalo*. Toronto: University of Toronto Press, 1951.

Roosevelt, Theodore. *The Wilderness Hunter*. 1900. Upper Saddle River, New Jersey: Literature House, 1970.

_____. *Letters of Theodore Roosevelt*. Edited by Elting E. Morison et. al. Eight vols. Cambridge: Harvard University Press, 1951–1954.

Runte, Alfred. *National Parks: The American Experience*. Lincoln: University of Nebraska Press, 1980.

_____. *Trains of Discovery: Western Railroads and the National Parks*. Flagstaff, Arizona: Northland Press, 1984.

Russell, Don. *The Lives and Legends of Buffalo Bill*. Norman: University of Oklahoma Press, 1960.

Salmond, John A. *The Civilian Conservation Corps, 1933–1942: A New Deal Case Study*. Durham: University of North Carolina Press, 1967.

Sax, Joseph. *Mountains Without Handrails: Reflections on the National Parks*. Ann Arbor: University of Michigan Press, 1980.

Saylor, David J. *Jackson Hole, Wyoming: In the Shadow of the Tetons*. Norman: University of Oklahoma Press, 1970.

Schafer, Joseph. *Carl Schurz, Militant Liberal.* Evansmith, Wisconsin: Antes Press, 1930.

Schullery, Paul, Editor. *Old Yellowstone Days.* Boulder: Colorado Associated University Press, 1979.

Shankland, Robert. *Steve Mather of the National Parks.* Third Edition. New York: Alfred A. Knopf, 1970.

Skinner, Milton Phil. *Bears in Yellowstone.* Chicago: A. C. McClurg & Co., 1925.

Smalley, Eugene V. *History of the Northern Pacific Railroad.* New York: G. P. Putnam's Sons, 1883.

Smythe, William E. *The Conquest of Arid America.* 1899. Seattle: University of Washington Press, 1969.

Spence, Clark C. *Montana: A Bicentennial History.* The States of the Nation Series. New York: Norton, 1978.

Stanley, Edwin J. *Rambles in Wonderland, or, A Trip Through the Great Yellowstone National Park.* Fifth Edition. Nashville: Publishing House of the Methodist Episcopal Church, South, 1898.

Starling, Edmund W. (as told to Thomas Sugrue): *Starling of the White House.* New York: Simon and Schuster, 1946.

Stevenson, Elizabeth. *Henry Adams: A Biography.* New York: The Macmillan Co., 1955.

Stone, Mrs. E. A. *Uinta County, Wyoming: Its Place in History.* Laramie: Laramie Printing Co., 1924.

Strahorn, Carrie Adelle. *Fifteen Thousand Miles by Stage.* New York: G. P. Putnam's Sons, 1911.

Strong, General William Emerson. *A Trip to Yellowstone National Park in July, August, and September 1877.* Introduction by Richard A. Bartlett. Norman: University of Oklahoma Press, 1968.

Swain, Donald C. *Wilderness Defender: Horace M. Albright and Conservation.* Chicago: University of Chicago Press, 1970.

Thayer, William Roscoe. *The Life and Letters of John Hay.* Two vols. Boston: Houghton Mifflin Co., 1920.

Tilden, Freeman. *Following the Frontier with F. Jay Haynes, Pioneer Photographer of the Old West.* New York: Alfred A. Knopf, 1946.

Toole, K. Ross. *Montana: An Uncommon Land.* Norman: University of Oklahoma Press, 1959.

Topping, E. S. *The Chronicles of the Yellowstone.* St. Paul: The Pioneer Press, 1883.

Trefethan, James B. *An American Crusade for Wildlife.* New York: The Winchester Press for the Boone and Crockett Club, 1975.

Turrill, Gardner Stilson. *A Tale of Yellowstone or, In a Wagon Through Western Wyoming and Wonderland.* Jefferson, Iowa: G. S. Turrill Publishing Co., 1901.

Twitchell, Colonel Heath. *Allen: The Biography of an Army Officer, 1859–1930.* New Brunswick, New Jersey: Rutgers University Press, 1974.

Van Merie, Isaiah, Editor. *History of Black Hawk County, Iowa, and Representative Citizens.* Chicago: Biographical Publishing Co., 1904.

Van Orman, Richard. *A Room for the Night: Hotels of the Old West.* Bloomington: University of Indiana Press, 1966.

Varley, John D., and Schullery, Paul. *Freshwater Wilderness—Yellowstone Fishes and*

Their World. Yellowstone Park, Wyoming: Yellowstone Library and Museum Association, 1983.

Wecter, Dixon. *The Saga of American Society.* New York: Charles Scribner's Sons, 1937.

White, Leonard D. *The Republican Era.* 1958. New York: Free Press, 1965.

Williams, Walter, and Shoemaker, Floyd Calvin. *Missouri: Mother of the West.* New York: American Historical Society, 1930.

Wingate, George W. *Through the Yellowstone Park on Horseback.* New York: O. Judd Co., 1886.

Winser, Henry J. *The Yellowstone National Park: A Manual for Tourists.* New York: G. P. Putnam's Sons, 1883.

Wirth, Conrad. *Parks, Politics, and the People.* Norman: University of Oklahoma Press, 1980.

Wister, Owen. *Owen Wister Out West.* Edited by Fanny Kemble Wister. Chicago: University of Chicago Press, 1958.

_____. *The Virginian.* New York: The Macmillan Co., 1902.

_____. *The Writings of Owen Wister.* Eleven vols. New York: The Macmillan Co., 1928.

Young, Stanley P., and Goldman, Edward A. *The Puma: Mysterious American Cat.* Washington, D.C.: The American Wildlife Institute, 1944.

_____. *The Wolves of North America.* Washington, D.C.: The American Wildlife Institute, 1944.

ARTICLES AND PAMPHLETS

Adams, Charles Francis. *Jim Bridger and I Discover Yellowstone Park.* No place, No publisher, No date. Custody of the Newberry Library, Chicago.

Albright, Horace Marden. "Harding, Coolidge, and the Lady Who Lost Her Dress." *The American West* September, 1969, pp. 25–32.

_____. "Yellowstone's Chief Describes Bechler Basin." *National Parks Bulletin* December, 1926, 6–7.

"An American Tour." *London Times* September 5, 10, 1883.

Anderson, Captain George S. "Work of the Cavalry in Protecting the Yellowstone National Park." *Journal of the United States Cavalry Association* March, 1897

_____. "A Buffalo Story." In *American Big Game Hunting. The Book of the Boone and Crockett Club.* Edited by Theodore Roosevelt and George Bird Grinnell. Edinburgh: David Douglas, 1893, 9–18.

_____. "Protection of the Yellowstone National Park." In *Hunting in Many Lands: The Book of the Boone and Crockett Club.* Edited by Theodore Roosevelt and George Bird Grinnell. New York: Forest and Stream Publishing Co., 1895, 380–402.

"Are We a Happy People?" *Harper's New Monthly Magazine* January, 1857, 207.

"Arnold Hague." *Dictionary of American Biography* 3, 85–86.

Atwater, Edward C. "The Lifelong Sickness of Francis Parkman." *Bulletin of the History of Medicine* 41, 413–39.

Baker, Ray Stannard. "A Place of Marvels: Yellowstone National Park as It Now Is." *Century Magazine* August, 1903, p. 484.

Bartlett, Richard A. "The Senator Who Saved Yellowstone Park." *The Westerners New York Posse Brand Book* 16 (1969): 42.

———. "Those Infernal Machines in Yellowstone." *Montana: The Magazine of Western History* 20 (1970): 16–19.

———. "How Many Were Left? An Appraisal of the Buffalo Situation in the 1890s." Unpublished paper delivered at Western Historical Association Conference, Reno, Nevada, October, 1970.

———. Review of Gordon Dodds. *Hiram Martin Chittenden*. In *Pacific Historical Review* 43 (1974): 423–24.

———. "The Army, Conservation, and Ecology: The National Park Assignment." In *The United States Army in Peacetime*. Edited by Robin Higham and Carol Brandt. Manhattan, Kansas: Military Affairs/ Aerospace Historian Publishing Co., 1975, pp. 41–59.

———. "The Concessionaires of Yellowstone National Park: Genesis of a Policy, 1882–1892." *Pacific Northwest Quarterly* 74 (1983): 2–20.

"Bicycling in Montana." *Outing and the Wheelman* December, 1884, p. 6.

Blonston, Gary. "Where Nature Takes Its Course." *Science 83* (1983): 45–55.

Bulow, W. J. "When Cal Coolidge Came to Visit Us." *Saturday Evening Post* January 4, 1957, p. 65.

Chase, Alston. "The Last Bears of Yellowstone." *The Atlantic* February, 1983, pp. 63–73.

Christiansen, Robert L. and Smith, R. B. "Yellowstone Park as a Window on the Earth's Interior." *Scientific American* February, 1980, pp. 104–17.

Clawson, C. C. "Notes on the Way to Wonderland, or, A Ride to the Infernal Regions." *The New Northwest* 3 (No. 10): 1871; 3 (No. 48): 1872.

Clements, Kendrick A. "Engineers and Conservationists in the Progressive Era." *California History* 58 (1980): 282–303.

Colburn, Edward F. *To Geyserland*. No place: Oregon Short Line Railroad, 1913.

Cowan, Mrs. George D. "Reminiscences of a Pioneer Life." *Wonderland*. Gardiner, Montana: No Publisher, March 12, 1904. Copy in Yellowstone Library.

Davis, Chester C. "Motoring Through Wonderland: A Tour With the Montana A.A." *American Motoring* October 1, 1915, pp. 593–96.

Ditti, Barbara H., and Joanne Mallman. "Plain and Fancy: The Lake Hotel, 1889–1919." *Montana: The Magazine of Western History*, Spring, 1984, pp. 32–45.

Dix, William Frederick. "American Summer Resorts in the Seventies." *The Independent* June 1, 1911, pp. 1211–15.

"Dowager Queen's Demise." *Inside Husky* (House organ of the Husky Oil Co., Cody, Wyoming) March-April, 1981.

Drake, C. S. T. "A Lady's Trip to the Yellowstone." *Every Girl's Annual* (London: Hatchard's, 1887): 346–49. Copy in Yellowstone Library.

Editorial (Subject, Irrigation). *The Outlook* November 23, 1921, pp. 469–76.

———. *The Saturday Evening Post* November 20, 1920, p. 11.

———. (Subject, Yellowstone). *The Nation* 35 (1882): 343–44.

"Energy: Geothermal Lease Plans Threaten Yellowstone's Geysers." *Audubon*, May, 1982, pp. 104–5.

"Fight for Yellowstone's Waters." *The Literary Digest* October 23, 1920, pp. 88–91.

"First Car to Venture in Yellowstone Park." *Montana Motorist* September, 1962, p. 5.

Fisher, Albert Kennick. "George Bird Grinnell." *The Auk* January, 1939, pp. 1–12.

Fisher, S. G. "Journal of S. G. Fisher, Chief of Scouts of General O. O. Howard During the Campaign Against the Nez Perces Indians, 1877." *Contributions of the Historical Society of Montana* 2:1896.

"Geology of Western Wyoming." *American Journal of Science and Arts* 6 (1873): 426–32.

Gibson, Dan W. "Souvenir of Construction of the New Canyon Hotel, Yellowstone National Park, 1910–1911." No place: No publisher, 1911?

Gray, John S. "Last Rites for Lonesome Charley Renolds." *Montana: The Magazine of Western History* 13 (1963): 40–51.

Grinnell, George Bird. Comments against irrigation plans. *Literary Digest* June 5, 1920, pp. 90-92.

Hague, Arnold. "The Yellowstone Park As a Game Reservation." In *American Big Game Hunting: The Book of the Boone and Crockett Club.* Edited by Theodore Roosevelt and George Bird Grinnell. Edinbugh: David Douglas, 1983, pp. 240–70.

Hamp, Sidford. "Exploring the Yellowstone with Hayden, 1872: The Diary of Sidford Hamp." Edited by Herbert O. Brayer. *Annals of Wyoming* 14 (1942): pp. 252–90.

_____. "With Hayden in the Yellowstone." Edited by Herbert O. Brayer. Denver Posse of the Westerners. *1948 Brand Book: Twelve Original Papers Pertaining to the History of the West.* Edited by Dabney Otis Collins. Denver: Artcraft Printers, 1949.

Haynes, Jack Ellis. "The Expedition of President Chester A. Arthur to Yellowstone National Park in 1883." *Annals of Wyoming* 14 (1942): 31–38.

_____. "The First Winter Trip Through the Yellowstone National Park." *Annals of Wyoming* 14 (1942): 89–97.

_____. "Yellowstone Stage Holdups." In *Denver Westerners Brand Book.* Denver: Denver Corral of the Westerners, 1952, pp. 85–98.

Henderson, C. Hanford. "Through the Yellowstone on Foot." *Outing* May, 1899, pp. 161–67.

Hofer, Elwood. "Letter." *Forest and Stream* August, 1920. In Yellowstone Clipping File, Yellowstone Park Library.

Hough, Emerson. Untitled article on capture of buffalo poacher. *Forest and Stream* 41 (1894).

_____. "Maw's Vacation: The Story of a Human Being." *Saturday Evening Post* (October 16, 1920, pp. 14–15. Also published as a pamphlet. St. Paul: F. Jay Haynes, 1921.

Howe, Elvin R. "Yellowstone Waltz." *The Denver Post,* Empire Section, September 12, 1948.

Iddings, Joseph P. "Memorial To Arnold Hague." *Bulletin Geological Society of America* 29 (1918): 35–48.

Jackson, W. Turrentine. "British Interests in the Range Cattle Industry." In Frink, Maurice, Jackson, W. T., and Spring, Agnes Wright. *When Grass Was King: Contributions to the Western Range Cattle Industry Study.* Boulder: University of Colorado Press, 1965.

Joffe, Joseph. "John W. Meldrum, The Grand Old Man of Yellowstone Park." *Annals of Wyoming* January, 1941, pp. 5–47.

Jubak, Jim. "Only Teamwork Can Save the Yellowstone Grizzly." *National Parks* September-October, 1981, pp. 28–30.

Kipling, Rudyard. "Kipling Among the Geysers." Introduction by Pamela Herr. *The American West* 15 (1978): 59–61.

Kirk, Ruth. "Five Days in the Other Yellowstone." *Westways* August, 1967, pp. 40–43.

Kuhr, Manuel Irwin. "How George Vest Came to Missouri." *Missouri Historical Review* 59 (1965): 424–27.

Land of the Geysers. Northern Pacific promotional pamphlet in custody of Western History Collection, Denver Public Library.

Lang, William L. "At the Greatest Personal Peril to the Photographer." *Montana: The Magazine of Western History* 33 (1983): 14–29.

Lashbrook, Lawrence G. "The Utah Northern Railroad, 1871–1878." In *The Golden Spike*. Edited by David E. Miller. Salt Lake City: University of Utah Press, 1973.

Lenz, Frank. "Lenz's World Tour Awheel: Yellowstone Park." *Outing* February, 1893, pp. 378–83.

Lindsey, Lieutenant Elmer. "Winter Trip Through the Yellowstone." *Harper's Weekly* January 19, 1898, pp. 106–10; January, 1897.

McFarland, J. Horace. Statements against irrigation. *Philadelphia Ledger* June 6, 1920. In Yellowstone Clipping File, "Irrigation."

McNamee, Tom. "Breath-Holding in Grizzly Country." *Audubon* November, 1982, pp. 69–83.

Martin, Lawrence. "State Socialism vs. Free Enterprise." *Denver Post* September 4, 1955.

Mattison, Ray. "Report on Historical Structures of Yellowstone Park." Mimeographed. Washington: National Park Service, 1960.

Miller, Joaquin. "In the Yellowstone Park." *The Youth's Companion* November, 1910.

Mitchell, S. Weir, M. D. "Through the Yellowstone Park to Fort Custer." *Lippincott's Magazine* June, 1880, pp. 688–704; July, 1880, pp. 29–41.

"Nathaniel Pitt Langford." *Dictionary of American Biography* 10: pp. 592–93.

Olmsted, Frederick Law. "Fundamental Objections to the Walsh Bill." *National Municipal Review* May, 1921. In Yellowstone Scrapbook, "Irrigation."

Owen, W. E. "The First Bicycle Tour of the Yellowstone National Park." *Outing* June, 1891, pp. 191–95.

Parry, Dr. C. C. "Botanical Observations in Western Wyoming." *American Naturalist* 8 (1874): 175–80.

Pierson, Ralph. "The Czar of Wonderland." Denver Posse of the Westerners, *Brand Book* 11 (1955): 376–86.

Pronghorn Antelope. U.S. Department of the Interior, Fish and Wildlife Service, Conservation Note 11. Washington: G.P.O., 1961.

Raftery, John H. *A Miracle of Hotel Building; Being the Story of the Building of the New Canyon Hotel in Yellowstone Park*. No place: No publisher, 1911?

Reid, Bill G. "Franklin K. Lane's Idea for Veteran's Colonization, 1918–1921." *Pacific Historical Review* 33 (1964): 447–61.

Remington, Frederick. "Policing the Yellowstone." *Harper's Weekly* January, 12, 1895, p. 36.

Replogle, Wayne, F. *Yellowstone's Bannock Indian Trails*. Yellowstone Park, Wyoming: Yellowstone Library and Museum Association, 1956.

"Report of Duff, Anderson, and Clark, Industrial Investment and Financial Analysts." (1956). American Heritage Center, University of Wyoming, Laramie.

Rush, N. Orwin. "Fifty Years of the Virginian, 1902–1952." *The Papers of the Bibliographical Society of America* 43 (1952): pp. 99–120.

Schneider, Bill. "The Incredible Shrinking Wilderness," *National Parks* January-February, 1982, pp. 20–26.

Sedgewick, Henry D., Jr. "On Horseback Through Yellowstone Park." *World's Work* 6 (1903): 3572.

Sevendsen, Warren G. "Preserving the Heirloom." *New West Magazine,* November, 1920. Copy in Yellowstone Scrapbook, "Irrigation."

Sherman, Tom. "The National Park." *The Woodstock Letters* 2 (1892), 25–42.

Shivley, John. "Shivley, Guide for the Nez Perces." Appendix 2 in Frank D. Carpenter. *Adventures in Geyserland*. Edited by Heister Dean Guie and Lucullus Virgil McWhorter. Caldwell, Idaho: Caxton Printers, 1935.

Stewart, John. "Stewart's Story." *Bozeman Avant Courier* September 27, 1877.

Stone, Ben. "Ben Stone's Account." *Bozeman Avant Courier* September 6, 1877.

Strong, Douglas Hillman. "The Man Who 'Owned' Grand Canyon." *The American West* September, 1969, pp. 33–40.

Swain, Donald C. "The Passage of the National Park Service Act of 1916." *Wisconsin Magazine of History* 50 (1966): 4–17.

Switzer, M. A. "1876 Trip to the Geysers Written as a Diary in a Book Dated 1874." Original in custody of Montana State College Library at Bozeman, transcript used in custody of Montana Historical Society.

Sydenham, Lieutenant Alvin H., U.S.A. "Tommy Atkins in the American Army." *Harper's Weekly* August 13, 1892, pp. 780–81.

Thomas, Diane. "White Bus is Veteran of Yellowstone Scene." *Old Cars* (1973): 20–23.

Thomas, Phillip D. "The Near Extinction of the American Bison: A Case Study in Legislative Lethargy." In *Western American History in the Seventies*. Edited by Daniel Tyler. Fort Collins: Colorado Educational and Media Information Systems, 1973.

Van Tassel, C. *Truthful Lies of Yellowstone Park*. Bozeman: Published by the Author, 1932.

Vest, George Graham. "Eulogy to the Dog." *The World's Great Speeches*. Edited by Lewis Copeland and Lawrence Lamm. New York: Dover Books, 1958.

Walsh, Senator Thomas. "Letter from Senator Walsh" and "Editor's Reply." *The Outlook* September 8, 1920, p. 68.

Weikert, Andrew J. "Journal of the Tour Through the Yellowstone National Park in August and September, 1877." *Contributions of the Historical Society of Montana* 3 (1900).

Wheeler, Edward J. "A Trip Through Yellowstone Park." *The Literary Digest* March 12, 1904.

Whittlesey, Lee H. "Marshall's Hotel in Yellowstone Park." *Montana: The Magazine of History* October, 1980, pp. 42–51.

Wister, Owen. "Old Yellowstone Days." *Harper's Magazine,* March, 1936 pp. 471–76.

"Yellowstone National Park." *Laws of Wyoming* Chapter 103: 177–83.

MISCELLANEOUS

Reference books include *American Biographical History of Eminent Men . . . Michigan Volume.* Western Biographical Publishing Co., 1878; *Biographical Directory of the American Congress: 1774–1971; Dictionary of American Biography; An Illustrated History of the Yellowstone Valley Montana.* No author or editor specified. Spokane: Western Historical Publishing Co., 1908; *Moody's Industrial Progressive Men of Montana.* No author or editor specified. Chicago: A. W. Bowen and Co., 1902; Rand McNally & Co., *Auto Road Atlas of the United States.* Facsimile Edition, 1926. Chicago: Rand McNally & Co., 1974; *Value Line Investment Survey,* 1970; *Who's Who in America; Who Was Who in America.*

Correspondence was conducted with people from coast to coast; where such individuals have added to the narration, they have been cited in notes.

Index